LECTURES

ON THE

HISTORY AND PRACTICE

OF THE

LAW OF SCOTLAND,

RELATIVE TO

CONVEYANCING AND LEGAL DILIGENCE.

By WALTER ROSS, Esq.

WRITER TO THE SIGNET.

THE SECOND EDITION.
TO WHICH IS ADDED

A DISCOURSE ON THE REMOVING OF TENANTS,

AND

A GENERAL INDEX.

IN TWO VOLUMES.

VOL. I.

EDINBURGH:
PRINTED FOR BELL & BRADFUTE.

1822.

TO THE RIGHT HONOURABLE

ILAY CAMPBELL,

OF SUCCOTH,

LORD PRESIDENT OF THE COURT OF SESSION,

THE FOLLOWING SHEETS ARE,

WITH THE GREATEST RESPECT,

INSCRIBED,

BY

HIS LORDSHIP's MUCH OBLIGED,

AND MOST OBEDIENT,

HUMBLE SERVANT,

THE EDITOR.

ADVERTISEMENT.

THESE prelections were delivered by Mr Rofs, to a numerous body of the Gentlemen of the law, who attended the private clafs which he taught in Edinburgh during the years 1783 and 1784. The ' *Addrefs to the Members of the College of Juftice*,' publifhed by the Author previous to opening the clafs, and now prefixed to this volume, will explain the nature of the plan, the reafons of the particular arrangement of the fubjects, and the mode of inveftigation adopted in the profecution of the undertaking.

It is much to be regretted, that a new line of bufinefs, in which Mr Rofs found himfelf unexpectedly engaged, and which required almoft conftant attendance in another country, withdrew his attention from his favourite ftudy, and prevented him from completing the plan he had in view. Had he been allowed to put a finifhing hand to the work, it would no doubt have appeared in a different fhape, and have been productive of more honour to himfelf, and of greater benefit to fociety.

The following Lectures, however, being complete in themfelves, in confequence of the Author's method of treating each fubject feparately, without any connection with, or relation to another, led the Editor to entertain the idea, that the publication of them would be of confiderable public utility. But, being unwilling to hazard the reputation of the Author, he judged it proper, before putting the work to the prefs,

to

to fubmit it to the perufal of two Gentlemen of the Law, of diftinguifhed knowledge and abilities ; and with their approbation he now offers it to the Public.—In doing fo, he wifhes that thefe volumes fhould be confidered rather as confifting of fo many *practical effays*, or *law tracts*, than as being a complete courfe of Lectures, of which, indeed, they were intended to be only a part.

The Editor returns his grateful thanks to the Gentlemen who fo kindly took the trouble of revifing the manufcript. Without their affiftance, he never fhould have ventured to give the prefent work to the world.

It is hoped, that the Reader will excufe any fmall inaccuracies in the work, which are unavoidable, efpecially in a pofthumous publication.

EDINBURGH,
1ft *January* 1792.

CONTENTS

CONTENTS OF VOLUME I.

TO

TO THE

MEMBERS

OF THE

COLLEGE OF JUSTICE.

———

THE Education which the Youth of this country, deftined to the profeffion of the Law, ufually receive, is infufficient to qualify them for the immediate practice of it, either at the Bar, or even in the inferior departments of the fcience. The young Lawyer is aftonifhed at difcovering how little his abftract ftudies have fitted him for practice. He comes, perhaps, to argue upon *Deeds*, the parts of which he has never eonfidered with attention; and to conduct himfelf by *Forms of Court*, till then almoft unheard of: Confequently, in the moment of debate, of expanfion of mind, he hefitates, and feels himfelf the echo of the Agent *. The Writer is

fenfible

———

* Sir George M'Kenzie's characters of the Lawyers, his cotemporaries, are drawn with a Mafter's hand.—The effect of the difadvantage here pointed out is finely marked in one of thefe portraits:—' *Cunninghamus* natura difertus, et lucubrationibus doc-
' tus; dotes fuas continuata per multos annos cum his difputatione mire auxerat. *Ab*
' *initio chartulas etiam neglectiffimas omniaque facti ramenta perfcrutando, clientibus potius*
' *quam famae fe accommodaverat*, nec in arguendo ea quae juris erant fibi in fuis orationi-

fenfible of an embarraffment no lefs difcouraging, upon quitting the Office of his Mafter. The time of an apprenticefhip is not always employed as it fhould be; nor are the opportunities of inftruction which that period affords fufficient to fit him for the exercife of his profeffion. He trembles at the thoughts of trufting to his own ftrength; and goes on, like a man in the dark, doubtful, timid, and groping every inch of his way. Knowledge is then to be picked up by experience, by accident; and the practitioner's hairs often begin to change colour before he acquires that confidence in himfelf, that eafe in the execution of bufinefs, which is indifpenfibly neceffary to the happinefs of his life.

There are many, however, whofe opportunities of information have been great, and who have properly improved them. There are men of natural ability, who quickly furmount all difadvantages, and reach the fummit of their profeffion againft every defect of education: At the fame time, there is *no man* of bufinefs who is not more or lefs affected by the circumftances I have mentioned: If Forms have not been ftudied by a young Lawyer in a comprehenfive manner, he muft, in the courfe of his practice, meet with new ones, which will, for a little, ftop his progrefs. However varied and extenfive the bufinefs of fome Writers may be, there are branches of Practice which never (or at great intervals) appear in their Offices. The employment of *one*, is chiefly *conveyancing*—that of another, *agenting*—money-matters, and the management of eftates, of a *third*; fo that the apprentice has not an opportunity of learning a great part of what he ought to know.

The bad confequences of this want appear from the methods which have been attempted to fupply it. In the beginning of the present

' bus indulfit, donec hos per plures annos difputantes audiverat, invidiamque ita pru-
' denter vitavit, donec eam fuperaverat.—*Tandem tamen vere maturus fuaviter doctique*
' *oravit*, et exiftimationem, quam alii audacia rapiunt, ille modeftia fua fibi conciliavit.'

present century, an apprenticeſhip in a Writing-chamber was deemed an indiſpenſible part of the education of a young Lawyer; and, even in later times, ſeveral of theſe Gentlemen have dedicated a part of their time to attendance at the Offices of well employed Writers. But the ſlowneſs, the want of variety, the partial manner in which buſineſs there ſhewed itſelf, ſoon diſguſted them. They perceived, that ſufficient time could not be ſpared for imbibing knowledge in that broken manner. ‘ The evident want (ſays Sir William Black-
‘ ſtone) of ſome aſſiſtance in the rudiments of legal knowledge, has
‘ given birth to a practice, which, if ever it had grown general, muſt
‘ have proved of extremely pernicious conſequences: I mean the
‘ cuſtom to drop all liberal education, as of no uſe to the Students
‘ of Law; but to place them, in its ſtead, at the deſk of ſome ſkilful
‘ Attorney, in order to initiate them early in all the depths of Prac-
‘ tice.’ He is here ſucceſsfully pleading the cauſe of univerſity edu-
cation, of the then novel Vinerian eſtabliſhment at Oxford: But, with the moſt profound deference to that learned Profeſſor, it may be averred, that if a Lawyer could be initiated in Practice, without dropping his liberal ſtudies, it would be the moſt compleat education he could receive.

So far from baniſhing liberality of accompliſhments, even from the ſecond branch of the profeſſion, the Writers to the Signet have been careful to enſure a claſſical and genteel education for their Members; and, by late regulations, none are admitted to ſerve ap-
prenticeſhips who have not received it.

Conſcious of the defects of chamber-education, and how little pains their more advanced clerks take in inſtructing apprentices, ſeveral of theſe Gentlemen, of diſtinguiſhed abilities, have, at different periods, determined to dedicate ſome time to lecturing upon the ſeveral branches of their buſineſs, which they wiſhed to impart to the Youth under their care, in a regular method. I have no doubt that
b 2   theſe

these good endeavours have been attended with the beſt conſequences; but the interruption of real buſineſs could not fail to diſtract the attention, and break in upon the plan. Having often, in the midſt of practice, amuſed myſelf, by tracing the origin, the principles, and the progreſs of particular parts of our Forms, I inſenſibly contracted an inclination to the ſtudy, and felt a wiſh for leiſure to proſecute it. This inclination came at laſt to be gratified, in a manner little enviable. Reſidence in the town became incompatible with health. In this ſituation, the thought of the preſent undertaking preſented itſelf: And though the ſmall diſtance to which I had retired proved unſuitable to practice, it appeared to be no obſtacle to an employment which required a regular attendance. I reflected, that other profeſſions, Medicine in particular, were furniſhed with ſeparate inſtructors in all their branches, which rendered the education of Students ſcientifically compleat; that the Practice of the Law was communicable by the ſame method as the Theory of that ſcience; that, in Medicine, the Profeſſor muſt wait till Nature produce the diſeaſe, or Accident the fracture, upon which his Clinical Lecture is to be given; and, conſequently, the order of inſtruction muſt wait upon Nature and Accident;—whereas, in the Practice of Law, all the Forms are at hand, ready to be exhibited, arranged, and combined at pleaſure. Thus, by degrees, I was led to think, that I could not employ my time with more advantage to my profeſſion, or more pleaſure to myſelf, than by dedicating it to the ſtudy of the Practical Part of the Law of Scotland, and to the inſtruction of young Gentlemen, deſtined either to the Bar, the Writing chamber, or other branches of the profeſſion *.

There

---

* In the Seminary of Juriſprudence at Paris, there are a certain number of Teachers conjoined (or aggregated as the French term it) to the Faculty of Advocates, whoſe province it is to give public and domeſtic lectures upon the laws—to ſmooth the entry of the ſtudy of them to beginners—to prepare the ſtudents for the examinations they are to undergo—to certify their abilities previous to their admiſſion to trial; and to aſſiſt at the examinations. Le Grand Encyclop. v. Aggregé.

There was a time, it is faid, when Conveyancers and Formalifts in Scotland poffeffed a degree of learning and information, in which they acknowledged no fuperiors—when Styles were confidered as the foundation of the fabric of our Law.

In the days of Sir John Fortefcue, the Students of the Law of England fet out in their progrefs from this goal.—' The Students in ' the Inns of Court (fays he) are for the moft part young men: ' Here they ftudy the nature of original and judicial Writs, which ' are the firft Principles of the Law.'—Without a thorough under-ftanding of the Forms of Writs, it was Lord Coke's opinion, that a knowledge of the Law is not to be attained.

Styles, as the unerring records of our jurifprudence, were of the greateft authority with our forefathers.—' Arguments brought from ' Style (fays Sir George M'Kenzie *) are a great part of our funda-' mental law.—They, to Lawyers, are, what the *Chart* is to Geogra-' phers, or the *Compafs* to Seamen.'—And, in another place, fpeak-ing of the Forms of Gifts, he afferts, that Styles were, by our prac-tice, obferved as *Statutes.*—' It is well known (fays the Hon. D. ' Barrington †; that there is no legal argument which hath fuch force ' in our Courts of Law, as thofe which are drawn from the *words* ' *of Antient Deeds* ; and that the *Regiftrum Brevium* is therefore ' looked upon to be the very foundation of the Common Law.'

It is a trite, but juft remark, that the value and rank of every art and fcience, is in proportion to the mental powers employed, or the mental pleafure created by it. The Conveyancer, the Formalift, the Writer, are inferior to the Barrifter.—His employment is wholly li-beral—their's is partly mechanical ; and the more they deviate from

the

* Obfervations on the 42d Act of James VI.
† Obfervations on Antient Statutes, p. 111.

the employment of the mind, the lower they fink in efteem.—Hence
that gradation from the intelligent refpectable man of bufinefs, to the
practitioner in thofe inferior parts, in the execution of which *all are
upon a level.*

There are many of my Brethren in ftation, whofe knowledge and
abilities would infure a very different fuccefs to an undertaking of
this kind; but they are too deeply engaged in the duties of their
profeffion.—Were any of thefe Gentlemen propofing to employ their
time in this manner, it is needlefs to declare that I would not attempt
it. I can fay nothing for myfelf, but that I am fond of the ftudy.
My fituation enables me to dedicate my time entirely to the undertaking. Inclination and induftry, therefore, muft be offered, in place
of all other qualities.

'The Styles, in former times, (fays Mr Dallas of St Martin *) were
'good and formal; yet, not being digefted in method, required a
'long time, and great experience and employment, before Youth at-
'tained to perfection in the art of writing to the Signet, and diving
'into the knowledge of Securities.' To fhorten the road, he collected and publifhed a *Syftem,* for which his profeffion has been infinite-
ly indebted to him; but the oldeft Members may recollect, how their
hearts *failed within them;* with what difguft they turned away, when
prefented, in the Writing-office, with fuch a frightful volume of arid,
naked, unintelligible Forms. A confiderable time paffed before they
could be brought to think of Styles or Forms of any kind, but as
maffes of impenetrable dulnefs.—What adds to this early averfion is,
that our Writs have not always followed the changes of the Law:
They are often replete with cuftoms, rules, and terms, the veftiges
of which are no-where elfe to be feen. Before a perfon can underftand what *now is,* he muft go back to what *has been.*—Styles and
Forms

* Preface.

Forms cannot, therefore, be comprehended, without some acquaintance with antient customs, manners, and history both civil and ecclesiastical. How can a competent knowledge of the Civil Law be attained, without the aid of Roman history and antiquities?—By a liberal distribution of national facts, events, and remains of former times—by a judicious application of general principles, and a familiar exposition of technical terms—Professors Blackstone and Sullivan have drawn aside the sable curtain which covered the mysteries of the Law of England, and given a lasting value to their own works.—' Nondum satis statuere potui (says a Civilian) plusne juris ' historia ex jurisprudentiae libris, an jurisprudentia ex historicis mo- ' numentis accipiat.'

The study of the Law is often said to be hedged' round with the brambles and thorns of writs, precedents, and authorities. Discouraged and dejected, the young mind, therefore, needs every allurement to fix its attention, and every assistance to encourage its perseverance in a path so little suited to its wishes. What then shall be said of the thorns and brambles themselves?—Even these rough plants bear not unpleasing flowers.—' Law (says Lord Kaims) be- ' comes only a rational study, when it is traced historically. And ' yet Law is seldom conducted in this manner: It is taught as a col- ' lection of facts; the memory is employed, seldom the judgment. ' Were it otherwise treated, in place of a dry, intricate, and crabbed ' science, it becomes an entertaining study.'—I shall take the liberty of applying his Lordship's idea to the inferior department,—to the practice of the Law. Let this branch likewise be treated historically. Let every part of it be traced from its origin. Let illustration be borrowed from Law—from history—from antiquity—from manners. No science will refuse its aid to embellish the rugged path.—If a youth has received a liberal education, why should the business of his life be taught him in a manner adverse to every thing he has read or heard? Why should imagination be darkened, and every

agreeable

agreeable idea banifhed from his ftudy? Would it not be better to
give him fome employment for his acquirements, to excite his recol-
lection by hiftorical allufions, to awaken his attention by pictures of
ancient manners, and to furprife him now and then with a flower of
the Belles Lettres, amidft the brambles of his profeffion? Thus reafon may be induced to take a fhare, where memory only would have
been employed; and memory may become, not an *index* of fteril
facts, but, as it always ought to be, a ftorehoufe to the judgment. Is
it not a fhame to fee people, during the whole courfe of their lives,
writing words, nay whole claufes of Deeds, they do not underftand;
and going gravely, like horfes in a mill, the round of Forms, without knowing one iota of their origin, their progrefs, or even their
prefent importance? The only reafon they have to give for doing
any thing is, that it has been done before. The leaft deviation, then,
from practice, confounds and diftracts them.

To the ignorant in their profeffion, bufinefs is a game at chance,
where the odds are againft the player. To the knowing, it is a
fcience where fuccefs will be due to conduct; not to fortunate hits, or
unexpected advantages.—I might fay a great deal upon this fubject;
but it is unneceffary: The defect of the education I have pointed
out, is univerfally felt and acknowledged. I can mark out the dif-
eafe much better than prefcribe the cure, which fhall notwithftanding be attempted.

If the origin and progrefs of our Law and Forms ftood any-where
difcovered; if every word to be found in them were explained, reduced to its legal import, and its proper etymon; if every branch of
Practice had been illuftrated by particular treatifes, as in England;
then I fhould have had little to do, but to arrange, methodife, and
collect materials fcattered in volumes, and to render them palatable
to the minds of beginners:—But I have no fuch affiftance. Our
Antiquaries, though not behind their Brethren in acutenefs or diligence,

gence, have expanded their refearches upon points of mere curiofity, or of national difpute. We have no hiftory proper to our Law, but fome loofe unconnected hints, thrown out by Sir Thomas Craig, and Lord Stair. We have no gloffary, but Skene's little Tract; no explanation of our Statutes, but the hurried, fuperficial Remarks of Sir George M'Kenzie *; and not a word relating to our Forms or Practice, but what is owing to the learning and ingenuity of Lord Kaims. ' As to our Law-books, or Syftems, what are they (fays his Lord- ' fhip) but a mafs of naked propofitions, drawn chiefly from the de- ' cifions of our Supreme Courts, rarely connected either with pre- ' miffes or confequences?'

Sir George M'Kenzie difplayed high abilities, heightened by a wonderful induftry, confidering the buftle of his public life. He, it appears, became fenfible of the very defect which is the object of this addrefs, and had actually begun to fupply it.—In the Prefaee to his Treatife of Heraldry, the following paragraph is to be found:— ' Having defigned to learn from our old rights and evidents, the ori- ' gin and progrefs of our Styles, and by what fteps they arrived at ' their prefent perfection, (in which work I have made confiderable ' progrefs); but becaufe I want time to fit it to the Prefs, I refolve to ' leave the MS. as a new teftimony of my kindnefs to my native ' country.'—This, in all probability, would have been a performance replete with information; but it feems the fubject did not appear important enough to thofe who had the care of that Gentleman's papers. The Treatife is not printed, and the MS. not to be found. In Mr Spottifwood's † Notes upon Hope's Minor Practicks, mention is

* I was at firft informed, that the public were to be favoured with a learned illuftration of the Scottifh Statutes, from the acceffion of James I. to the acceffion of James VI. by Lord Hailes; but I have fince learned with regret, that various obftacles have prevented his Lordfhip's defign from being put in execution.
† Profeffor of Scots Law, in the 1715.

VOL. I.   c

is made of a *Scots Law Lexicon*, and a *Special History* of the Law of Scotland, as both written by that Author: And, in the preface to his Styles, he promises an *analitical*, and what he is pleased to term a *nomological* method of illustrating Writs, for the use of Youth. But none of these books have ever appeared in public: So that I have all my materials, as well as the arrangement of them, to think of, and prepare.

The plan I have laid down, has for its principal object *the education of a Man of Business*; and, in point of method, I have been directed by no other rule than that of *practice*.—I have endeavoured to render my Prelections subservient to the education of the Writing-Chamber, and to the line of daily business. I wish to accompany the young Writer, during the time of his apprenticeship, to analise the Deeds he sees passing under his eye; and to give an account of their origin, their progress, their principles, and their effects; to explain the different terms he meets with; and to trace actual business, in all its steps, from the beginning to the end of every branch.—I have revolved many methods of executing this undertaking; and, after all, I am obliged to determine upon treating each deed, and each branch of business, *separately*; taking it up as it occurs or grows out of preceding transactions, and pursuing it as far as it will go.

It has been suggested by several respectable Gentlemen of the Bar, that the best plan would be, to follow the order of Mr Erskine's Large Institute, *i. e.* to give the several Styles and Forms as they there arise; by which my work would become a Practical Supplement to that received System, and at the same time prove subservient to the Prelections of the Professor of Municipal Law.

The idea was extremely natural to Lawyers, who, from the Institutes of Justinian downwards, have constantly studied in the imperial

order

order of perfons, things, and actions. But I will hazard the affertion, that, however the Inftitutional Order may beft comprehend the *Theory* of the Law, it is by no means fuited to the *Practice*, or the purpofes of Practitioners; and it is a chief part of my propofal to break through this Roman wall, and to range at large in the direction of our own cuftoms, rules, and bufinefs.

Dallas of St Martin experienced the fubftantial ufe of a different arrangement; and, accordingly, the firft part of his Styles, intituled, *Real and Perfonal Diligence*, begins with a Moveable bond, and purfues it in the actual tract of bufinefs (in the Author's time) till it becomes an heritable fecurity upon the debtor's land, by apprifing and adjudication.—I appeal to all my Brethren of practical knowledge, if this firft part of St Martin has not proved of more real fervice, than all that has been written or faid upon the fubject. Men of bufinefs, then, will underftand me, when I declare that I am to treat every branch of my fubject *in this order*. When the fubject changes its nature, I will follow that change, and fpeak to every article as it muft occur in the courfe of bufinefs. Subjects that will not enter into this arrangement, fuch as the Hiftories of Courts, Offices, and Particular Cuftoms, I will treat by themfelves: Others may be capable of being introduced in an epifodical manner.

The impropriety of the other method muft forcibly ftrike any perfon who will take the trouble of confulting *a lift of Styles*, faid to have been made up in the order of M'Kenzie's Inftitutions, by Mr Hay of Carribber; and publifhed by Spottifwood, to remedy, as he tells us, the *want of order obfervable in Chamber Style-books* *.—If his own Book of Forms is looked into, the arrangement appears a great deal worfe. Deeds belonging to branches of bufinefs diftinct and irreconcileable, are there claffed together, for no other reafon

c 2   than

* Spottifwood's Styles, 2d edit.

than that they happen to go under a common or general title, such
as *Bonds*; and to rank under some Roman division, such as *Obligations*.—These writs are never found to be confecutive in practice;
nor have they any connection or dependence upon each other;
whereas, in the method propofed, each Deed grows, as it were, out
of the preceding one—a circumftance fufficient to decide in its favour.

Theorifts, with great propriety, clafs all the fubjects of Law under general titles, in order to regulate them by the broad principles
and maxims of the fcience. With them, Marriage, Decreets of
Forthcoming, Confirmations, &c. are all *Affignations*. Practitioners
muft confider thefe matters as quite diftinct from each other; and,
in place of referring particulars to general rules, they muft be content with the humbler province of breaking thefe general rules into
particular cafes *.

As the arrangement of the fubject is to follow the order of practice, fo the method of information is to wait upon the fimple order
of time.—For example, I am to begin at the earlieft Law or Cuftom
relating to any one fubject. This is to be traced to the firft Statute
made in that behalf: The Statute is to be annalifed, and the variations and improvements introduced by it explained.—Next follows
the practice upon that Statute, i. e. the extention, reftriction, or literal application of it, to be found in the Decifions of our Supreme
Court. The defects or evils yet remaining or arifing from change
of manners, or civil alterations, lead to the next Act of Parliament,
or of Sederunt; and fo downwards to the prefent times. This done,

the

---

* In the Linnean fyftem, the moft diminutive plants are arranged with thofe of the
largeft fize, becaufe they agree in the number of the ftamina of their flowers.—Knowledge in this mode of clafling makes the Modern Botanift; but, of itfelf, it would never
make a *Gardener*. The cultivation, progrefs, and ufeful diftinctions of individuals in
the vegetable tribe, muft be the fubject of his attention and labour.

the oldeft Form of the Deed which is the fubject of examination is to be analifed, and the relation of its parts to thefe progreffive Laws pointed out, till the comparifon terminates in the Writs now under the eye. During this hiftorical courfe, every antiquated term or cuftom alluded to, is propofed to be explained. And thus, I flatter myfelf, knowledge neceffary to bufinefs may be communicated by an agreeable fpeculation, where the mind is kept in a conftant progrefs from truth to truth, and from difcovery to difcovery, almoft in the clofe relation of caufe and effect.

My principal care muft be, to imprefs upon the mind, with the greateft precifion poffible, the *prefent rule and practice in every cafe*. Sometimes to encourage the free exercife of thought, I propofe to indulge that fceptical inclination upon legal topics, fo much applauded by Lord Kaims. The frequent miftakes, defects, and weakneffes of our authorities, difcovered in the courfe of examination, fufficiently prepare the mind for an amufement fo conducive to the enlargement of its faculties. Opinions have been often compared to *light gold* taken without weighing—fometimes to *counters* taken in a hurry; but it is by the ufe of the fcales, and the practifed eye, we are to difcover the want, or the adulteration. If Students could be induced to think, and to reafon with freedom upon thefe fubjects, the young Lawyer would imbibe the very foul of his profeffion, and the Writer attain to a fovereignty over thofe rules of practice, which for a long time embarrafs and reftrain him.

I mean to quote authorities for whatever I advance, or reafon from : I am fenfible it becomes my knowledge, my experience, and fituation in life ; none of which entitle me to fpeak upon my own credit. I wifh young gentlemen to examine, and to think for themfelves. In place, likewife, of making the ideas or reafonings of authors appear to be my own, I intend to give their own thoughts always in their own words, except when they have written in another language ;

guage; and in that cafe I fhall, to accommodate every perfon, tranf-
late as clofe to the original as I am able.

One branch of my undertaking remains to be fpoken of; that is,
an endeavour to accompany our own Forms, with an idea of thofe
of England, in the fame cafes. To fay the truth, I found the inquiry indifpenfibly requifite to the underftanding of our own Styles
and Forms. What Lord Kaims affirms of the Law, may, with equal
truth, be applied to a very great part of the Practice.—' In both na-
' tions it has fuch a refemblance, as to bear a comparifon almoft in
' every branch; and it only fo far differs, as to illuftrate by oppofi-
' tion *.'

And now it is but juftice to confefs, that the plan I have imagined
will not be completed to my own fatisfaction for fome years. If my
firft attempt is approved, I can promife no more than to work upon
the defign with unwearied diligence.—In regard to the language,
nothing correct or elegant is to be expected from a man who has
laboured more than twenty years in the exercife of his profeffion,
and admitted all the corruptions of it into his ftyle. If I fin not in
being obfcure, the impropriety of expreffion, or the barbarifms, will
only recoil upon myfelf.

* Lord Coke obferved a wonderful conformity, not only between the great lines of
the conftitutions of both kingdoms, but alfo in their *writs*, their *cuftoms*, and even the
language of their jurifprudence; and thence concludes, that the common law and practice of each has been originally the fame. 4. *Inft. p.* 345.

' I have (fays the Hon. D. Barrington, p. 111.) compared the Writs of Nouvelle
' Diffeifin with that ancient book in the Scots Law, intituled, *Quoniam Attachiamenta.*
' The comparifon of thefe Writs feems fully to prove, that the Law of Scotland agreed
' anciently, not only with the principles of the Law of England, but with *its Practice*,
' though there might be fome variances of no great importance.'

ERRATA.

Page 74. line 20. for *bond* read *benefit*
—— 125. —— 21. *for* fili *read* filii
—— 169. —— 5. *for* debtor *read* creditor
—— 184. —— 29. *for* intimation *read* affignation
—— 246. —— 7. for *confiftata* read *confiftat*
—— 283. —— 31. *for* James VI. *read* James I.
—— 390. —— 24. *dele* charter
—— 446. —— 4. *for* 1649 *read* 1469

LECTURES

ON THE

PRACTICE

OF THE

LAW OF SCOTLAND.

The Perſonal or Moveable Bond.

IN an advertiſement formerly publiſhed, upon the ſubject of the Lectures which you are now to do me the honour of attending, I mentioned, that the arrangement of the matter was to be directed according to the line of practice; and the method of information to wait upon the ſimple order of time.

Without attending, therefore, to the rules, which a ſyſtematic theory might dictate, I am to endeavour to render my prelections ſubſervient to the education of the writing office; and to the line of the buſineſs in which you are to be employed, during the remain-

der of the day. For this reason I have (after the example of Mr
Dallas of St Martin) chosen to begin with the history, and the ana-
lysis of a simple moveable bond for borrowed money; and, in this
first part of the course, to follow it in the tract of our present business, through the variety of its effects, first in personal and then in
real diligence. At the same time, I must notice, that though the
common bond be always first presented to young gentlemen upon
their entry to business, and although for these one hundred and
fifty years, the custom has been to place it in the front of every
private collection of forms; yet, were the history of our stiles to be
given in the order of time, the moveable bond, however simple and
brief it now seems to be, would appear in the last rank of our deeds.

According, therefore, to the order of history, I should lay before
you the whole body of real or heritable securities, before speaking
of the moveable bond, because the first and most ancient securities
for money were taken by mortgage,—by wadset,—by reserved
rents,—by annualrent rights, and other real devices; in comparison
with which, both our heritable and moveable bonds are but
the productions of yesterday. Though this would be found to
be the order of time, the order of practice is entirely different. By
practice we every day learn, that the personal bond, for the most part,
forms the basis of our securities, and of our executions real and
personal.

It is natural, therefore, that the bond should be the first deed
which is explained to a young conveyancer; and, accordingly, it is
the first writing which he is generally entrusted to put upon paper;
a circumstance which determined my choice, as it did that of Mr
Dallas of St Martin, who in one sense may be called the Father of
our Scottish forms.

In treating of my subject, I pretend not to teach law; I am to
make use of that science, so far as may be necessary to establish the
principles, to deduce the history, and explain the tenor of the writings, judicial and extra-judicial, which are the subjects of our employment.

ployment. No information, therefore, which I am able to promise you, will encourage any individual to flacken his ftudies of the Roman or Scottifh law, as fcientifically taught by their learned Profeffors. My province is to teach you, what my brethren the Writers would teach the gentlemen committed to their care, if the other duties of their profeffion could poffibly admit of it. In order that you may be able to profit by practice under them, the ftudy of the law as a fyftem, has long been recommended, and even enforced by regulations. In place of teaching the law, I borrow it only at times for the illuftration of particular points of practice. Lawyers have long ufed writs and forms to illuftrate the law. This is indifpenfibly neceffary. I am now to make a humble effort to illuftrate the writs and forms by the law. The firft method has folely in view the gentlemen deftined to the bar.—The other is directed to the ftudents of our national jurifprudence in general, and to Writers and practitioners in particular. From me you are to have only the information proper to your employment, culled from every fource where I have been able to find it. Upon the Profeffors, and your own private ftudies, you are to depend for that fcientific knowledge, and comprehenfive view, of the laws, which form the accomplifhment of members of the College of Juftice.

There is one inconvenience attending the broken method which I am under the neceffity of adopting. The principles, and fometimes the hiftory, of one deed or part, of practice, will apply to, and account for feveral others. I am alfo often cafually to touch upon matters intended to be treated of in another place; hence I fhall fometimes be involved in repetition and prolixity. Thefe, however, are but a fmall part of the faults, for which I will have occafion to pray your indulgence.—If I am not able to fhew you the road to truth, I flatter myfelf with the profpect of preventing your induftry from being mifapplied. When I reflect upon the labour I have beftowed, I cannot help entertaining fome hopes of fuccefs; but when, on the other hand, I look to the

A 2   extent

extent of the undertaking, and to myfelf, the refult of my application fhrinks almoft to nothing.

When our fyftematic writers on the law touch upon any of the fingularities in the form of deeds, they have a fhort account of the matter at hand ; they tell us, that this or that was done, or fo conceived, in order to avoid the prohibition of ufury, or taking a profit for the loan of money, which was contrary to the laws of the church. The general pofition is fo true, that to the devices fallen upon to defeat thofe laws, the greateft part of the deeds now in ufe, both in England and Scotland, owe their original forms. The notice thus taken of a caufe which lafted through ages,—which had effects fo ftrange,—fo lafting ; is a great deal too flight and unfatisfactory to the inquifitive mind. We wifh to examine this prominent feature in the hiftory of the law ; to know fomething of the origin and nature of thefe prejudices ; and to trace them in their progrefs and effects upon the practice of our forefathers. For thefe reafons, gentlemen, I have chofen to introduce my account even of perfonal deeds, and of the bond in particular, with a circumftantial detail upon the fubject of ancient ufury. When we arrive at our own country, and within the ken, if I may ufe the word, of our own laws and ftatutes, we fhall find, that the hiftory and principle of the common bond is nothing but a fmall branch of this great tree, which could not with propriety be detached from it.

Money is by its nature a barren commodity ; it does not, like land or cattle, afford any increafe to the poffeffor. When one man hires out properties of the laft kind to another, they produce an evident gain, which is more or lefs according to his own care and induftry ; the lender, therefore, at all times, thought himfelf entitled to a certain fhare of this profit, in confideration of the loan.

It is by commerce alone, that the holder of money can procure increafe to the ftock ; and, therefore, it is only in commercial countries that people borrow money of one another, with a view to advantage. In countries that are not commercial, the only motive for

borrowing

borrowing muft be the fupply of fome immediate neceffity ; and, therefore, feveral nations among the ancients looked upon the tax-ing of that neceffity as a moral evil, a demand dictated by cruelty and oppreffion ; for which reafon they reprobated the practice, and held in abhorrence the perfons who followed it.

The Egyptians were a commercial nation ; ufury of confequence was known and permitted among them. The Ifraelites, by their re-fidence in Egypt, became alfo well acquainted with it ; and, perhaps, had fuffered from the confequences. Whether from this reafon, or that their Legiflator judged the practice unfuitable to the fituation of his people, upon their departure from that country, is not known ; but we certainly know, that there is no evil more directly profcribed in the Judaical law.—' Thou fhalt not (fays Mofes) lend ' upon ufury to thy brother, ufury of money, ufury of victuals, ' ufury of any thing that is lent upon ufury : Unto a ftranger thou ' mayeft lend upon ufury ; but unto thy brother thou fhalt not *.'

Whatever refpect has been paid by the Chofen People to the firft part of this law, certain it is, that no precept given by the infpired Legiflator has had fuch perfect obedience paid to it, as this laft. Upon ftrangers, the Jews had never any mercy in their exactions, which entailed upon them the hatred of ancient nations ; and, in modern times, the injury came to be dreadfully retaliated almoft in every country in Europe.

Many writers have taken much ingenious pains to juftify this ex-ception in the law of Mofes, but their arguments do not concern the prefent fubject ; in general, they are drawn from the horror in which this people were taught to look upon the nations around them. With regard to their own people, the Jews continued, if not in the obfervance, at leaft in veneration of the precept. Nay, ufury appears to have been ranked among crimes of the deepeft dye. ' He hath oppreffed the poor and the needy, hath fpoiled by ' violence, hath not reftored the pledge, hath lifted up his eyes to ' the

---

* Deut. chap. xxiii. ver. 19. 20.

' the idols, hath committed abomination, hath given furth upon
' ufury; and fhall he then live ? he fhall not live; he hath done all
' thofe abominations, he fhall furely die; his blood fhall be upon
' him *.'

In the New Teftament, the idea of a loan is carried to perfection,
and ufury is prohibited without any national diftinction. ' There is
' no difference (fays St. Paul) between the Jew and the Greek, for
' the fame is Lord over all †. If you lend to them, of whom you
' hope to receive, what thank have you ? for finners alfo lend to
' finners, to receive as much again; but lend ye, hoping for nothing
' again, and your reward fhall be great ‡.'

. In the firft ages of the Roman Commonwealth, ufury was difcharged; it fuited not the manners of a plain and warlike people.
When thefe manners changed, it came to be allowed; and, when
allowed, produced many evils and feditions in the commonwealth : ' Sed vetus urbi foenebre malum et feditionum difcordia-
' rumque creberrima caufa.' Many laws were made to obviate
the fraud committed by ufurers, which were as often defeated; and ufury arofe again by wonderful arts. ' Multifque plebifcitis
' (fays Tacitus) obvium itum fraudibus, quae toties repreffae miras
' per artes rurfum oriebantur §.'

. Although ufury came at laft to be authorifed by the Roman law,
under reftrictions, it was ftill looked upon as a pernicious crime :
' Cicero mentions, that Cato being afked, what he thought of
' ufury ? made no other anfwer to the queftion, than by afking the
' perfon who fpoke to him, what he thought of murder ‖ ?' As the
Romans increafed in power, riches, and luxury, the neceffities of
part of the people increafed; and experience demonftrated the propriety of allowing a profit to be taken, in order to encourage the
money holders to throw their cafh into the circle; and, on the other
hand,

---

* Ezek. chap. xviii. ver. 12. 13.   † Rom. chap. x. ver. 12.
. ‡ Luke chap. vi. ver. 34. 35.   § Tacitus annal. 6. Ann. Urb. 786.
‖ Cicero lib. ii. de officiis in fine.

hand, to prevent the oppreffion of the people, by too fevere a tax upon their neceffities: A variety of laws, therefore, were made to limit the profit, or fruit, as it may be termed, of money, and to defeat the rapacity of lenders. The ingenuity, however, of the latter clafs appears to have been always fuperior to the laws; and hence the gain, fqueezed from the neceffitous above the legal rate, came to be termed ufury, and the receivers of it ufurers.

The word *ufura* fignifies originally nothing more than the ufe or enjoyment of any thing; Cicero thus expreffes himfelf: ' Natura ' dedit ufuram vitae tanquam pecuniae.' Since it has been applied to illegal exactions, the term has continued in an odious acceptation.

From the writers of the Auguftan age, we learn that this matter had not at that time been brought under fufficient regulations. If the defcription which Horace gives of his ufurer in the Satires, is to be credited, the practices of the money lenders were execrable beyond belief *.

The principal fum is expreffed by the word *caput*, from whence we have our *principal* or *capital* fum; *merces* is the intereft, or the reward which Fufidius draws from it; and the deduction of the intereft *per* advance, is happily conveyed by the verb *exfecare* to cut out; becaufe it was taken out of the principal before lending. Among the Romans, intereft was always counted by the month. Horace's ufurer then lent one hundred pounds for a month, at the expiration of which he became entitled to one hundred and five; but to make fure work, he advanced only ninety five, and took from the debitor an obligation for one hundred, which turns out to 60 *per cent per annum*, in round numbers; befides the retention

and

---

* Fufidius vappae famam timet: ac nebulonis,.
   Dives agris, dives pofitis in foenere nummis.
   Quinas hic capiti mercedes exfecat; atque
   Quanto perditior quifque eft, tanto acrius urget.

                    HOR. lib: i, Sect. 2.

and its intermediate profits. We need not wonder then that ufury was held in abhorrence among this great people. The law, however, continued to authorife a legal intereft, which varied at different periods, according to the plenty or want of money, and the demands of the people.

Upon the converfion of the Empire to Chriftianity, the religious doubts arifing from the texts of Scripture, which you have heard, began to revive, and to exercife the minds of men, at that time prepared to receive and to convert every circumftance of life into a fubject of difquifition. The Emperor Conftantine allowed the exaction of intereft at the rate of *1 per cent. per* month, termed *ufura centefima*, and Juftinian made feveral regulations concerning it; prefcribing different rates to different ranks of the fubject, allowing it upon contracts of certain denominations, and refufing it upon others. The difpute again arofe among the Fathers of the Church, who agreed in condemnation of the practice, holding it up to the deteftation of the Chriftian world, in ftronger terms than Mofes had done to the Ifraelites, and making little or no diftinction between moderate intereft and exceffive ufury.

A meafure fo impolitic, threw the commerce of money almoft entirely into the hands of the Jews, who enriched themfelves, and every where diftreffed the people. This effect, in place of pointing out the true and natural remedy to the evil, called down upon the practice of ufury or intereft in general, the condemnation of councils, the prohibition of the Popes, and the execrations of the churchmen all over Europe.

Impelled by reafons of this kind, the Emperor Bafil, in the 9th century, without diftinguifhing between legal intereft, and abfolute extortion, abolifhed the practice, *in totum,* by Imperial authority. His fon Leo foon found himfelf neceffitated to recal this order: ' Matters (fays he) have fince the date of the late regulation turned ' a great deal worfe, thofe who formerly lent with a view to gain, ' will lend no more.—Every thing is at a ftand. Et in eos qui pe-
                                                            ' cunias

' cunias indigent, difficiles atque immites funt.' The Emperor, therefore, fixed the legal intereſt at a moderate rate, but the rule did not long continue in obſervance *. The allowance made, it ſeems, did not prove adequate to the wants of the people, or the demands of the money lenders ; the old evils revived,—the Jews ſtill held the beſt part of the commerce in their own hands,—the churchmen continued to rail ; and the practice of taking profit for money, without diſtinction, was at laſt ſolemnly condemned by the Canon law : ' Dare pecuniam mutuo (ſay the Canoniſts after St Thomas) non ' ideo eſt peccatum, quia eſt prohibitum ; ſed potius ideo eſt prohi-' bitum, quia eſt ſecundum ſe peccatum ; eſt enim contra juſtitiam ' naturalem.'

From the miſtaken doctrine thus canonically eſtabliſhed, and promulgated over all Europe, and the impolitic meaſures which they dictated, we ſhall find the true reaſons and principles which gave birth to the forms of the generality of private deeds and conveyances.

The effects of theſe univerſal prejudices entirely influenced, for a long period, the whole ſyſtem of ſecurities upon heritable property. The Church, after cloſing the door herſelf, ſoon found it neceſſary to point out a variety of methods, of handſomely evading the rigour of her own doctrines, by mortgages, annualrents, truſts, annuities, &c. With reſpect to perſonal deeds for money lent, the common evaſions did not ſo well apply to them ; and, therefore, the churchmen themſelves dealt in realities ; when they ventured to give a perſonal loan, it was always upon a pledge.

The lending then of money upon perſonal obligations, appeared to be an object not worth attention ; it was very little practiſed among the body of the people, either in France or in England, in the firſt ages of their Monarchy ; the few neceſſaries of life were procured by barter, and loans of money were only given according to the original principles, *i. e.* to relieve the neceſſity of friends.

Vol. I. B While

* Nov. Leon. 83.

While the clergy themselves were taking, and teaching others to take, the highest advantages in the management of land rights, they confined the ideas of usury entirely to the loan of money upon personal obligements, for the declared purpose of taking a profit: Upon this subject, the consciences of the people were kept in perpetual alarm, and their eyes in some measure shut to the very opposite system practised in the management of heritable property.

The personal debt is the only subject of the present discourse; and, therefore, I am now to connect the history of its form, with that of usury, as it appeared in this island.

In the Roman law, the writing similar to our bond went under the name of *obligatio, i. e.* a binding for some cause assigned; because every obligation contained a cause or reason for coming under it, which we term the cause of granting. ' Obligatio' (say the Civilians) is so called, ' ab obligando seu vinciendo;' and Justinian defines it to be ' juris vinculum quo necessitate adstringimur alicujus ' rei solvendae, secundum nostrae civitatis jura *.'

The Roman lawyers distinguished obligations into a number of kinds, assigning to all of them different effects, and different actions. These distinctions serve rather to display the subtlety than the wisdom of the profession. Against each of these actions they furnished a set of established defences and exceptions, imagined with an equal degree of laborious refinement. The Roman law had been preserved in Italy, in Spain, and the southern provinces of France, notwithstanding all the revolutions of manners, and of people; but the study of it did not become universal, till after the accidental discovery of the Pandects, or the great body of the Roman law, about the middle of the 12th century, when schools for teaching it were established in Italy.

In

* Inst. lib. iii. tit. 14.

In thefe fchools a revolution was preparing in the bufinefs of conveyancing, which it is neceffary to defcribe, before entering upon the particular effects of ufury in England.

Towards the beginning of the 13th century, the language and ideas of the Roman jurifprudence became vifible in the ftyle, and in the manner of all deeds upon the Continent, and even in this Ifland. Before that time, the ftyle in general appears to have been laconic and fimple, the clerks were equally frugal in their expreffions, and in the materials they made ufe of; but, in going downwards, the ftyle lengthens, a thoufand precautions ftart out formerly unheard of, a thoufand frauds which our forefathers had not a fingle idea of, feem all at once to have burft forth; and, if the manners of the times were to be taken from the works of the notaries and public conveyancers, any perfon would have good right to conclude, that one half of mankind had, in lefs than fifty years, learned more wickednefs, than their fathers had done in the courfe of ages: At the fame time, that the other half had as fuddenly acquired wifdom, addrefs, forefight, and ingenuity, to guard againft and defeat the frauds of their neighbours. The Hiftorian, who fhould make fuch a reflection, would commit a great miftake. No fuch revolution had happened, either in the affairs or minds of men. The churchmen, the lawyers, the notaries, and clerks, in moft countries, had got hold of the Roman law, which prefented them at once with the experience of ages, and with the wifdom and refinements of the lawyers of the governours of the world. Proud of this new acquifition, and fond of difplaying it, thefe men filled their deeds with precautions againft evils which were never intended,— with refervations, declarations, prohibitions, &c. the want of which never had been felt among their forefathers. So far from beftowing fecurity, this new ftyle only ferved to drown the meaning of parties in an endlefs redundancy of words. In place of preventing, it ferved for a long time to eternize difputes, by affording a

world

world of new materials for the inexhauftible lucubrations of the
doctors of the laws.

In England, as in other places, the canon law prohibited the
taking of intereft, and was ftrictly obeyed. When people lent money it was only upon pledge, and no vifible profit was got in return. The common law admitted the prohibition of the canons;
and the clergy carried it fo far, that abfolution could not be given to
the breakers of it, without fpecial powers from Rome. The ufurer
was not only punifhed by the civil magiftrate, but if, after the
death of any perfon, it came to be difcovered, that he had been
guilty of ufury, we have the authority of Lord Coke, and of the ancient hiftorians to mention, that his goods and chattels were forfeited to the King; fo fays our Regiam Majeftatem, ' all the goods and
' gear pertaining to an ocherer, whether he dies tefted or untefted,
' pertains to the King.

' Among the reft of the King's dittays, it ufes to be enquired and
' proven be threttie tua liellmen, lawfully fworn of neighbours, that
' any man until the time of his deceafe ufed and exercifed ufury and
' ocher.

' Whilk being proven in judgement, all the moveable gudes and
' cattle, quhilks pertained to the ufurer, quha deceafed, fhall be in-
' brought to the Kingis ufe, in quhais poffeffion ever they be
' found *.'

It is impoffible that a people can have made any advance in the
arts of life, without feeling the want of the commerce of money;
and the only method by which that commerce can be eftablifhed, is
by the public toleration of taking a profit for it. Volumes have
notwithftanding been written, and continue ftill to be written, a-
gainft this practice. Thefe writers totally evade the queftion, which
is certainly a fimple one; for if profit can be made of money, either
by commerce, or in any other fhape, it is evident, that the proprietor of the money is entitled to a reafonable fhare of it. He who
buys.

* Reg. Maj. lib. ii. c. 54.

buys land and lets it out to rent,—he who buys cattle and fells their produce,—what is he doing but making profit of his money? Yet in Spain, at this moment, the taking profit for the loan of money is highly punifhable; and even in France, the avowed bargain for intereft is not legal among private individuals, though tolerated in the cafe of fome trading companies; as the Farmers General, and the Eaft India Company, &c. It is long fince the fpirit of commerce in Great Britain triumphed over it; but that was not till after an obftinate and various ftruggle, the detail of which will be a matter equally curious and inftructive.

The canonical prohibition againft the taking of intereft threw, as I have faid, the valuable commerce of money all over Europe into the hands of the Jews; that people made it a point of their religion to improve this opportunity to the utmoft. Their legiflator having allowed them to take ufury from ftrangers, they bent their whole attention to the bufinefs; and monopolized both the trade and the materials of it. They poffeffed a great part of the ready cafh, and became verfant in all the arts of turning it to account. This traffic in England, it feems, profpered exceedingly, and attracted a number of the Jews from the Continent, who fettled in the feveral towns during the reigns of William the Conqueror, and his fons. Towards the beginning of the thirteenth century, and in the reign of Henry III. the hiftorians aftonifh us at the height to which the Jews carried their ufurious extortions; the opulence to which they had arifen; and the horrid oppreffions committed againft them by the crown. At that time, they were, it feems, admitted to receive mortgages upon real property, as is evident from many of the deeds relating to thefe tranfactions, which are yet preferved. Their principal branch, however, confifted in taking pawns; and, being free of all reftraints either from law, or from confcience, they did not fcruple to exact 50 *per cent.*; nay, in the cafe of the Oxford Scholars, it required even

a

a royal mandate to limit them to that ufury. This curious mandate was iffued in the 9th year of Henry III.

‘ Judei Oxon. non recipient a Scholaribus pro libra in feptimana ‘ nifi duos denarios, et fimiliter fiat in minore fumma, fecundum ‘ fuam quantitatem, alioquin praedicti Judei puniantur, juxta confti- ‘ tutionem regni.’ It appears, that, by thefe means, the Jews at laft got hold of all the books belonging to the Scholars, who were obliged to apply to Edward I. for relief.

On the other hand, the whole Jews, their families, and their pro- perty, were confidered to be at the pleafure of the King ; and Henry III. certainly made them feel the utmoft extent of tyranny. He mortgaged the whole nation to his brother Richard for payment of thirty thoufand merks, and empowered him to diftrain their bo- dies and eftates for that money. A particular exchequer was ap- pointd to receive the monies fqueezed from the Hebrew race ; and upon occafions the tyrant added infult to oppreffion.

Hiftorians report feveral inftances of cruelty committed upon the perfons of thefe people by torture, particularly that, at one time, the King demanded ten thoufand merks from a certain Jew at Exeter, and commanded one of his teeth to be pulled out every day till he paid that fum. The Jew held out feven days, but fubmitted on the eighth, and parted with his money to preferve the reft of his teeth.

Regulations were often promulgated againft this ufury, and dif- penfed with as often for the convenience of the crown. In fhort, the tyrants of thefe times made ufe of the Jews as leeches to fuck the blood of their fubjects, and then forced the fuckers to regorge into the royal exchequer. Thefe glaring inftances of bad govern- ment brought on the famous ftatute, *de Judaifmo,* in the beginning of the fucceeding reign, *anno tertio Edwardi primi* ; which having cut off the favourite branch of their bufinefs by the abfolute prohi- bition of ufury, the Jews began to clip and corrupt the coin, for which the whole of them were banifhed England, in the eighteenth year of the fame prince, and were not properly re-admitted until the reign of Charles II.

The

The Ifraelites, however, were not the only people who fhared the fpoils, which the folly and prejudices of the canonical interdict in this ifland held out to ftrangers. The States of Italy, fituated upon the coafts of the Mediterranean, were the firft people of modern Europe who ferioufly engaged in trade; and for a confiderable time they engroffed the commerce of the Weftern World. In order to manage their bufinefs with fuccefs, they fent companies of their countrymen to the feveral kingdoms with whom they were concerned; and experience foon demonftrated that England deferved their particular attention. 'Hiftory informs us, that, about the twelfth century, a number of Italian merchants had eftablifhed themfelves at London. Thofe from Lombardy were termed Lombards; and others from Pifa, Milan, &c. the Caurcini. Whether thefe laft took their name from a particular family of negociators, is not known; but it is certain, that both they and the Lombards, envying the profits of the money-trade in the hands of the Jews, dropped their mercantile character, and rendered it entirely fubfervient to the arts of money-broking, ufury, and extortion. According to Matthew Paris, the hiftorian of the times, the Lombards carried the matter fully as far as the Jews, and found means to draw 60 *per cent. per ann.* for their money, which at laft defervedly drew upon them the utmoft feverities of the law. The conduct of the Caurcini was not lefs blameable; but thefe gentlemen fecretly put themfelves under the protection of the Pope, who fatisfied their confciences, and protected their perfons. They termed themfelves *Scambiatores Domini Papae,* the exchangers or bankers of our Lord the Pope. If his Holinefs did not fhare the booty, which was ftrongly fufpected, he converted thefe brokers into miffionaries, for the purpofe of facilitating the perpetual exactions of the Holy See from the kingdom of England. When the clergy or the people wanted money, thefe brokers were ready to lend it them. Upon what conditions you will immediately be informed.

The Roman law had eftablifhed a diftinction between ftipulated ufury and damages and intereft. Even the modern civilians, who

have

have written againſt the practice of taking profit for money, gravely
tell us, that none of theſe prohibitions take place in the caſes where
the borrower failing in payment at the time appointed, the creditor
demands payment of his money judicially ; for then the lender not
being longer obliged to grant a new delay, it is but juſt that he
ſhould have intereſt to indemnify him for the loſs he ſuſtains by the
injuſtice of his debtor ; but this intereſt (ſay they) hath nothing in
it like to that which the creditor takes before the demand *.   Here
then we have the diſtinction between the words intereſt and uſury ;
the firſt is underſtood, not to be a profit for the uſe of money, but the
legal damages a creditor is entitled to, by delay of payment upon the
part of his debtor.   All the theologians are agreed, that intereſt of
this kind is not prohibited, but may be exacted according to equity
and juſtice ; and they term it *legitimae uſurae*.   This diſtinction, rather frivolous than ſubtile, is ſupported by a text of the civil law.
' Uſurae non propter lucrum petentium, ſed propter moram ſolven-
' tium, infliguntur †.'   All this is a mere parade of words, ſignifying
nothing ; for what conſolation is it to the debtor to pay, under the
name of damages or intereſt, what he would have paid under the
title of uſury.   The Roman law further pointed out many inſtances where damages and intereſt became due, in ſome caſes, upon demand ; and others without demand, particularly diſtinguiſhing
between a loan and a tranſaction.   In the laſt, damages were allowed to be ſtipulated ; becauſe people might make what conditions
they pleaſed, and the party contractor was ſuppoſed to give value
for it.

Again, it was allowed to fix the damages, upon a failure, to a
certain ſum of money ; and, in doing ſo, another diſtinction was
made between the ſums which were of a penal nature, in order to
force performance, and ſums determinately ſtipulated, beyond which
the creditor could not raiſe his demand, but was obliged to accept of
that

---

* Domat. de mutuo.   † Dig. lib. 22. tit. 17.

that sum in full satisfaction of his loss. ' Quia non facit quod pro-
' misit in pecuniam numeratam condemnatur, sicut evenit in omni-
' bus faciendi obligationibus *.'

The Italian brokers settled in England, were perfectly instructed
in all these evasions, subtilities, and distinctions ; they also brought
the forms of obligations with them, drawn in all the cautions of the
civil law. This clearly appears from a curious bond granted by the
Prior and the Convent of Barnwell to the Caurcini, in the month of
April 1235, and in the reign of Henry III. †. This bond, like all
other deeds of that age, and of ages after it, is written in Latin, to-
lerably

---

* Cod. l. 42. tit 1. De re judicata.

† ' To all men that see this present writing, Thomas the Prior and the Convent of
' Barnwell, with health in the Lord : Know ye, that we have borrowed and received at
' London, for ourselves, profitably to be expended for the affairs of our church, from
' Francisco and Gregoris, for them, and their partners, citizens and merchants of Mi-
' lan, a hundred and four merks of lawful money, thirteen shillings fourpence Ster-
' ling being counted to every merk. Which said one hundred and four merks we pro-
' mise to pay back on the Feast of St Peter *ad vincula*, being the first day of August, at
' the New Temple in London, in the year 1235. And, if the said money be not all
' paid at the time and place aforesaid, we bind ourselves to pay to the said merchants,
' or any one of them, or their certain attorney, for every two merks, forborn two
' months, one merk of money, for recompence of damages which the foresaid mer-
' chants may incur by the non-payment of it, so that they may lawfully demand both
' principal, damages, and expences, as above expressed, together with the expences of
' one merchant, for himself, horse, and servant, until such time as the aforesaid money
' be fully satisfied. And, for payment of such principal, damages, and expences, we
' oblige ourselves, our church, and successors, and all the goods of our church, move-
' able or immoveable, ecclesiastical and temporal, which we have, or shall have, where-
' soever they shall be found, to the foresaid merchants and their heirs. And we fur-
' ther recognise and acknowledge, that we possess and hold the said goods from the
' said merchants, by way of courtesy, until the premisses be fully satisfied ; renouncing
' for ourselves and successors all help of canon or civil law, all privileges of clerkship,
' all customs, lectures, statutes, indulgences, and privileges obtained for the King of
' England from the See Apostolic ; as also the benefit of all appeal, or inhibition, from
' the King of England, with all exceptions, whether real or personal, that may be ob-
' jected against the validity of this instrument. All which things we promise faithful-
' ly to observe ; and in witness thereof, have affixed hereto the seal of our convent.'

lerably correct, and is the oldest deed of that kind to be met with in
the records of England. Although dated seven hundred and fifty
years ago, it may challenge any one drawn in the present century,
in point of form, security, caution, and accuracy.

It contains the names and designations of the granters and receivers; the receipt of the money; and, as the borrowers were a fociety, a declaration of its being applied for the use of the community. It has a specific term for repayment, and a most rapacious penalty in cafe of failure. Upon this penalty two obfervations occur.
The two merks *per* month, to be paid after the term, is not said to
be for the use of the money: It is for recompenfe of the damages
fuffered by the creditor, according to the exact diftinction of the
Roman law. Not fatisfied with that, the greedy Italian boarded
himfelf, his fervant, and horfe, upon the poor convent. The
word intereft is not mentioned, and nothing is ftated from the
date of the bond to the day of payment; but, after that time,
they indemnify themfelves by the monftrous exaction of 60 *per
cent. per annum,* ftating the damages by months, according to the
ancient Roman practice, in the cafe of intereft. This bond is more
than perfonal. The convent is made to hypothecate their church
goods, moveable and immoveable, both prefent and to come, for
payment of the money; and, as the Roman hypothec was a real
right, which entitled the creditors to take poffeffion of the property,
the granters of the bond are made to declare, that they hold every
thing by courtefy from the brokers until the debt be paid. Confcious of grofs iniquity, the framers of this extraordinary bond concluded it with a renunciation of every law and every defence in equity, by which that injuftice might be redreffed.

Hence, it appears, that the Roman obligation, or bond, which
was the model of ours, found its way to Britain as early as the
beginning of the thirteenth century.

The canonical prohibition ftill remained, which prevented a rate
of moderate intereft from being fettled by law, and at the fame time
corrupted

corrupted the manners of the people, by forcing them upon a variety of mean shifts in order to evade it. Dr Burnet, in the History
of the Reformation, tells us, ' That, for avoiding the severity of the
' law, the invention of mortgages had been fallen upon ; and those
' who had no land to sell, fell upon another way : The borrowers
' bought their goods, to be paid within a year; for instance L. 110,
' and sold them back for a sum to be presently laid down, as they
' should agree, it may be L. 100. By this measure, the one had a
' hundred pound in hand, and the other was to have ten pounds,
' or more, at the year's end *.' But this being in the way of sale,
continues the Dr, was not called usury. These were miserable devices ; at last people tired of these evasions, and went roundly to
work. Any bargain might be made, which did not specify interest,
and any damages might be stipulated for delay of payment ; and,
therefore, when a man lent a sum of money, he took a bond or obligation not only for the sum actually lent, but for a third or fourth
part more, equivalent to the premium, or interest, agreed upon between the date of the bond, and the term of payment. This was
called a simple obligation, or single bond, and sometimes a bill.

The later regulations of the civil law allowed damages and interest
to the extent of double value in the cases of sale, location, and certain
other contracts. From this a hint was taken. People lent a sum, and took
a bond for the double ; which bond was sometimes qualified by a separate
memorandum, bearing, that if the debtor paid a sum certain at such a
time, he should be discharged ; if not, the whole became due as damages. This was a sharp abuse of the civil idea of damages and
interest ; but it answered the purpose. The bond thus taken came
to be called double, because they were taken for double the sum. If
the condition happened to be performed, there was an end ; if not,
it was provided that the bond should stand firm and good.

Thus the prohibition of interest was evaded by the grossest of all
devices ; and the debtor stood obliged to pay the rate of interest ex-

C 2   acted,

acted, or forfeit the bond. All obligations, by the common law of England, received an interpretation according to the strictness of the words; and, therefore, when an action was brought in a court upon these bonds, the judges, although they knew the real intention of parties, thought themselves obliged to give decree for the whole sum. Sir William Blackstone apologizes for this. ' The penalty of a bond, originally contrived to evade the ' absurdity of these monkish constitutions, which prohibited taking ' interest for money, was very pardonably considered as the real ' debt in the courts of law, when the debtor neglected to perform ' his agreement for the return of the loan with interest; for the ' judges could not, as the law then stood, give judgment, that the ' interest should be specifically paid *.' Imagination itself is incapable of conceiving a higher degree of inconsistency in the affairs of men. The judges could not award interest for the money; that would have been contrary to law, a moral evil, and an oppression of the debtor; but upon the idea of damages, and the failure of the debtor in performance, they unmercifully decreed for double the sum borrowed. Thus the ideas of forfeiture, of obligation, and damages, imbibed from the Roman law, joined to the prohibitions of the church, concurred, in direct opposition to their original principles, to produce that monster in practice—an English double bond. The injustice was too glaring to be suffered; and therefore debtors applied for relief to the courts of equity, who did not think themselves bound by the same rules, which at that time constrained the courts of law. In these courts, the double bond was constructed according to the true intendment, and reasonable damages given for the loan, at the pleasure of the judge. At last, the eyes of the nation began to open upon this matter. They began to discover, as Sir William Blackstone well expresses it, ' That the absolute prohi- ' bition of lending upon any, even moderate interest, introduces the ' very inconvenience, which, it seems, meant to remedy; the necessity

* Vol. 3. p. 434.

' ty of individuals, will make borrowing unavoidable. Without fome
' profit allowed by law, there will be but few lenders ; and thofe
' principally bad men, who will break through the law, and take a
' profit, and then will endeavour to indemnify themfelves from the
' danger of the penalty by making that profit exorbitant. In the
' dark ages of monkifh fuperftition, and civil tyranny, commerce,
' when intereft was put under an interdict, was alfo at its loweft
' ebb ; and fell entirely into the hands of the Jews and Lombards ;
' but when men's minds began to be more enlarged, when true re-
' ligion and real liberty revived, commerce grew again into credit,
' and again introduced with itfelf, its infeparable companion, the
' doctrine of loans upon intereft *.'

By the act 37. of Henry VIII. this intereft was fixed at ten *per
cent*. In the days of his fon Edward, the old prejudices revived.
Henry's act was repealed, and all gain for money once more difcharged. Elizabeth was too wife a princefs to allow this prohibition to remain. In the thirteenth year of her reign, her father's act
was reftored. The rate of intereft has always varied according to
the quantity of cafh in the nation ; for, if a man can get money to
borrow at fo much *per cent*. his damages for want of payment muft
be limited to the fame rate. In the reign of James I. the trade of England increafed from the advantage of a long peace. Individuals grew
more opulent, and ready cafh more plenty. Lenders of money may be
faid to underfell one another, like dealers in other commodities; and
therefore by the 17. act of the 21ft parliament of James I. the legal intereft was reduced to 8 *per cent*. In the time of Charles II. it fell to
fix. What was intereft in the days of Henry and James, turned ufury
in thofe of Charles. When intereft came thus to be publicly allowed,
it might have been expected, that the form of the common Englifh
bond would have altered. This, however, did not happen. Hear
Judge Blackftone's reflections upon the fubject : ' But when after-
' wards the taking of intereft became legal, as the neceffary compa-
' nion

* Blackftone, vol. ii. p. 456.

' nion of commerce ; nay, after the 37th of Henry VIII. c. 9. had
' declared the debt or loan itfelf to be the juft and true intent, for
' which the obligation was given, their narrow minded fucceffors,
' *i. e.* the judges at common law, ftill adhered willfully and techni-
' cally to the letter of the ancient precedents, and refufed to confider
' the payment of principal, intereft, and cofts, as a full fatisfaction
' for the bond.   At the fame time, more liberal men, who fat in the
' courts of equity, conftrued the inftrument according to its juft and
' true intent, as merely a fecurity for the loan, in which light it was
' certainly underftood by the parties; (at leaft after thefe determina-
' tions) and therefore, this conftruction fhould have been univer-
' fally received *.'

The inconveniences which followed this oppofition of the courts
of the kingdom, in the conftruction of a bond, the deed moft frequent of any other in the bufinefs of life, obliged the Legiflature to
interpofe. This was done by the 4th and 5th of Queen Anne,
c. 16. which provided, that, ' in debt upon bond, if the defender be-
' fore action brought, had paid the principal and intereft due by the
' condition or defeafance, he may plead payment in bar; and pend-
' ing an action on fuch bond, the defendant may bring in principal,
' intereft, and cofts in law and equity, and the court fhall give judg-
' ment to difcharge the defendant.' And by 7th of George II. c. 20.
the matter was brought to perfection ; and the courts of law fpecially empowered to act in the fame manner as a court of e-
quity.

After all this, it was certainly to have been expected, that the
Englifh bond would no more have been taken double, but put in a
form fimply expreffive of the purpofe of the deed : Conveyancers
were now no longer under the reftraints which forced them to continue a fiction in their practice ; yet fo it is, that little or nothing
has been altered. The deed remains at this moment, in words and

in

---

* Blackftone, vol. iii. p. 434. 435.

in ftyle, the fame that it was in the days of ignorance and error.
The reafon is, that however the Englifh change the underftanding
or legal conftruction of a writ, they almoft never change its form ;
nay, they feldom alter even the terms of an ancient law. They rather choofe to preferve its original appearance, and effentially to
new model it by the aid of fictions. This renders the Englifh jurifprudence myfterious, and almoft incomprehenfible to ftrangers or fuperficial inquirers. On the other hand, by preferving in the form,
all the gradations of the progrefs, it offers a fure path to the ftudent,
and forces him to purfue the knowledge of it in a fcientific and hiftorical method. The law of Scotland, on the contrary, after de-
parting from its ancient and original fource, which was the very
fame with that of England, has affumed almoft an oppofite character. The revolutions it has admitted have in many parts been fo
fudden, fo abrupt, and often fo complete, as not to leave a veftige
behind it, by which the change can be marked ; or the ftudent informed of what it formerly had been.

After having endeavoured to develope the principles and the
hiftory of the Englifh bond ; I fhall now give the form, and offer a
few obfervations upon it ; for, as Lord Coke obferves, it is forms
and examples which do effectually teach *.

The

---

* ' Know all men by thefe prefents, That I David Edwards of Lincoln's Inn in the
' county of Middlefex, Efq; am held and firmly bound to Abraham Barker of Dalchall
' in the county of Norfolk, Efq; in ten thoufand pounds of lawful money of Great Britain,
' to be paid to the faid Abraham Barker, or his certain attorney, executors, adminiftra-
' tors, or affigns : For which payment well and truly to be made, I bind myfelf, my
' heirs, executors, and adminiftrators, firmly by thefe prefents, fealed with my feal.
' Dated the fourth day of September, in the twenty-firft year of the reign of our fove-
' reign Lord George the fecond, by the Grace of God King of Great Britain, France,
' and Ireland, Defender of the Faith, and fo forth, and in the year of our Lord one
' thoufand feven hundred and forty-feven

' The condition of this obligation is fuch, that if the above bounden David Edwards,
' his heirs, executors, or adminiftrators, do and fhall well and truly pay, or caufe to be
' paid,

The recognifances authorifed by ftatutes, in the cafe of merchants, are the firft proper and legal bonds or obligations to be met with in the forms of England; and feveral of thefe ftatutes prefcribe the exact form to be ufed upon every occafion; beginning with '*noverint univerfi* '*per prefentes me*,' ' know all men by thefe prefents, that I;' for all deeds were at that time written in Latin. As the forms of thefe obligations, which were termed bonds of record, were approved of by act of Parliament to be perfect affurances, it was natural to adopt the fame form in the cafe of private deeds. The modern Englifh bond is not after the Roman model, but exactly that of the judicial recognifance; though the difference between thefe confifts in this, that the former creates a new debt, while the latter acknowledges a debt already contracted, the one fpeaking in the prefent, and the other in the preterite tenfe. There is no term of payment mentioned in the writing itfelf, becaufe the old common law confidered it only as the evidence of a debt, or as a fimple obligement, which the creditor might demand when he pleafed, by action in a court of juftice. The condition then is the only circumftance which difcovers the nature of the tranfaction : ' The principal thing (fays Wood in his ' Inftitute of the laws of England) contained in an obligation, are ' the parties, and the fum of money ; and when both are properly ' expreffed, it will be fufficient. The fum of money intended, may ' be often found out by comparing the obligation and the condi- ' tion ; becaufe the obligation is ufually in a double fum to the fum ' mentioned in the condition *.' It is the condition then which alone qualifies the bond ; fometimes it was made by a feparate writing, or

as

' paid, unto the above named Abraham Barker; his executors, adminiftrators, or affigns, ' the full fum of five thoufand pounds of lawful Brkifh money, with lawful intereft for ' the fame, on the fourth day of March next enfuing the date of the above written ob- ' ligation, then this obligation fhall be void and of none effect; or elfe fhall be and re- ' main in full force and virtue.

' Sealed and delivered, being firft duly ftamped in the prefence of ————.'

* Inft. Law of Eng. p. 289.

as we would say, by a back bond.; at other times it was written on the back of the bond itfelf, and then by univerfal practice, came to be annexed at the foot, where it now always makes its appearance.

Before intereft came to be publicly allowed, a certain fum was mentioned in the condition, equal to the intereft or damages during that time ; and if the debtor did not continue to pay according to the fame rate, he was inftantly attached for the whole, and could not be relieved, but by a court of equity, upon payment of the principal, cofts, and damages, in proportion to what the Civilians term the injuftice of the delay : For the judges in equity being always churchmen, their decifions were often modelled upon the rules of the Roman law. I fhall difmifs the Englifh bond with a fingle obfervation, viz. that if it was to lie over for twenty years, without any payment of intereft, the intereft would then equal the capital, and the effect of the writing change fides : The creditor would lofe all the intereft becoming due after that time, becaufe the utmoft extent of his demand could go no further, than the forfeiture of the debtor's condition. In this light Lord Stair confidered it ; he looks upon the intereft due upon this deed in the true primitive light, *i. e.* not as due by ftipulation, but as a penalty for non performance ; and as penalties can or ought to go no further than the principal, ' therefore, (fays he) we extend not annuals in the Eng-'lifh double bonds beyond the ftock, becaufe they are penal, and 'fhould do the like in any penal annuals, but not in conventional ' annuals *.'

I now come to the Scottifh *band*, for fo in our language this writ was termed. A *band* is the Gothic or Swedifh word for it at this moment. In our ancient laws, by which I mean the Regiam Majeftatem, and the ftatutes and treatifes publifhed by Skene, no fuch technical term is to be found, it is always denominated by the Ro-

* Stair, p. 153.

man term *obligatio*. ' An debt (fays the *Quoniam attachiamenta*)
' may not be otherways proven, but by ane letter obligator, or by
' confeffion of the debtor in court*.' Neither does it appear that
any form, fimilar to the Englifh judicial recognifances, was eftablifhed in Scotland ; for though our Robert I. made an act for payment
of merchants debts, in imitation of the ftatute merchant of Edward I. his act refpects the execution againft the debtors, rather
than the eftablifhment of the debt. Edward's ftatute chalks out the
mode of the recognifance for that purpofe, but that of Robert fuppofes it to be done : The preamble of the Scottifh ftatute is, ' gif an
' merchant has proven his debt owing to him be an affize, or by
' any other manner, the mayor of the town fhall take and appre-
' hend the debtor,' &c.

Towards the end of the fourteenth, and beginning of the fifteenth
century, the Roman law had become the prevailing jurifprudence in
Scotland ; and, as I formerly obferved, the notaries-public, and clerical conveyancers, had exhaufted their learning and their knowledge, by introducing into the fubftance of private writs and fecurities, all the niceties, the technical terms, the fubtleties, and exceptions of the Roman jurifprudence, though it neither correfponded to
the manners of the people, nor to the ftate of fociety at the time. It
is to the introduction of the Roman law, and the vanity of the
ecclefiaftical conveyancers of the fourteenth century, that the tautology, redundancy, and repetitions, fo much complained of in our
ftyles, are wholly to be imputed. All the tranfactions between
England, France, and Scotland, were executed by deeds formed in
this oftentatious manner ; entirely founded upon the Roman law.
This ftyle had the benefit of being univerfal, like the Latin language
itfelf, all over Europe ; and it was the pride of the notaries-public,
who were then appointed and inftructed by the Pope, to vie with each
other in the number of their claufes, in the excefs of precautions,
and endlefs verbofity of expreffion.

After

---

* Reg. Majeft. c. 81.

After detaining our James I. eighteen years in England, the governors for Henry VI. refused to allow him to return to his kingdom, but upon condition of paying the enormous sum of L. 40,000 Sterling. The miseries of the Scottish government at the time, and the ardour of the people to recover their lawful Sovereign, forced the men in power to comply with a demand so much exceeding the abilities of the nation. The securities demanded by the English governours, were separate bonds from the towns of Edinburgh, Aberdeen, Perth, and Dundee, the delivery of a great number of the young nobility as hostages, bonds from each of their fathers, obliging themselves that their sons should remain in that character, till payment of the money, and last of all a bond from the King himself. All these deeds are to be found verbatim in the noble collection of ancient records, published by Mr Rymer, from which I beg leave to give as a specimen of the style of the times, the bond granted by James, which is dated the 8th March 1424 *.

D 2   This

. * ' James by the Grace of God King of Scots, to all to whose knowledge these letters
' shall come, greeting:—Know ye that we James King of Scots, aforesaid, are held and
' firmly bound to the Serene Prince Henry King of England, in forty thousand pounds
' lawful money of England, to be paid to the said Henry, his heirs, and successors, or
' to their certain attorney or depute, in the church of St Paul of London, in England,
' viz. ten thousand merks within six months, computing from the first day of our entry
' into our kingdom of Scotland, or from the first day that we might have entered into
' our said kingdom : And also ten thousand merks each following year, beginning one
' after another, computing from the first day of our said entry or power of entering,
' within six months from the beginning of each year, in the church of St Paul, afore-
' said, until the said forty thousand pounds be fully and entirely paid : For the which
' payment, well and faithfully to be made, at the days, terms, and place aforesaid, we
' oblige us, our heirs, and successors, whatsoever, Kings of Scotland, and all our
' goods, moveable and immoveable, present and to come, wherever the same are si-
' tuated or can be found.—And we hereby submit ourselves, our heirs, and successors,
' aforesaid, and our goods abovementioned, to the laws, coercions, rites, compulsitors,
' statutes, confuetudes, and plain jurisdiction of our Lord the Pope, his auditors, vice-
' auditors, and other courts, as well ecclesiastical as secular, wherever the same are
         ' constituted,

This bond, though sufficiently diffuse and redundant, is less exceptionable in that respect, than any other deed of the same period I have met with.—To explain all the parts of it, would, at present, take up too much time: I shall only make a few observations; which may throw light upon the remainder of our subject.

'*To all to whose knowledge these present letters shall come.*' Before the use of writing became common in Europe, all deeds public and private, judicial and extra-judicial, were termed by way of distinction *letters*; afterwards they came to be distinguished by the different purposes to which they were applied: The bulls of the Pope were anciently termed *literae apostolicae*; the King's letters were termed *literae regales*; and private deeds were termed *literae obligatoriae*; letters of discharge, *literae acquietantiae*, &c. Charters were distinguished into *literae patentes*, and *literae clausae*. In short, letters were a general title, sometimes even applied to contracts and indentures, which no doubt had its origin from the Roman distinction, in the execution of contracts, *re, verbis, et literis*. From these, letters between private persons were distinguished, as they are yet, by *literae missivae*; but, in fact, all deeds whatever, were, and still are, conceived

' constituted; in which either these present obligatory letters, or true or authentic tran-
' sumpts thereof, happen to be presented or produced. Renouncing hereby publicly
' and expressly, all and whatsoever laws, as well canon, as civil, divine and humane,
' written or not written, new and old, general and special, promulgated or to be pro-
' mulgated, with all other statutes or confuetudes whatsoever: As also, the exceptions
' of fraud and fear, not numerate money, action upon the case, *conditio indebiti*, with-
' out a cause, or from an unjust cause, the privilege of the forum, the feriae and the
' holidays of harvest and vintage, the Papal letters or rescripts, either granted or to be
' granted, impetrated or to be impetrated, and generally all and whatever laws, privi-
' leges, and defences, of whatever denomination, by which, or through which, we
' could come against these present obligatory letters, or whereby we might be bene-
' fited in any shape: And in testimony of all and singular the premises, we have made
' our seal be appended to these presents.

' Given under our privy seal, this eight day of March 1424, in the eighteenth year
' of our reign *.'

* Rhymer, vol. x. p. 326.

conceived in the form of a letter of correspondence. The Greeks observed a formula in their letters, both public and private; they began with the name of the writer, and the person to whom they were written, then followed a salutation; and in the conclusion a wish for health and happiness to the party. The Romans copied this formula, and modern Europe has followed them; only, in place of the ancient simplicity, we have adopted the unmeaning terms of French compliment. A charter from a Prince, or an order of Government, is a letter directed to his officers, or to his subjects in general; and therefore, began with the broad address of ' omni- '.bus tam futuris quam presentibus;' or, ' universis praesentes li- ' teras inspecturis;' or some equivalent expression. The clerical notaries, in taking deeds in favour of the church, began by an invocation in the name of the Father, Son, and Holy Ghost; and, as the Christian donors thought that the world were concerned in a good example from them, their deeds were directed: ' Universis Christi- ' fidelibus presentibus et futuris;' and hence the old style of deeds in this island; ' Be it known to all men that this present writing ' shall see or hear.'

When we come to treat of the charter, I propose to give a more succinct account of all these phrases of common style, according to the order of their introduction. So far was necessary at present, to account for the accustomed style of common bonds, and other personal deeds, which were all with us formerly termed letters; although, that term, both in France and in Scotland, is now confined to royal letters alone, or such as are issued in the King's name, for the purpose of execution. But to return to the bond of James I.

' Know that we the foresaid James King of Scots, are held ' and firmly bound to the Serene Prince Henry King of England, ' in L. 40,000 lawful English money.' This is not the style of the Roman obligation, but of the English recognisance; the writer of the bond did not mean it should be so, for in every other respect the deed is taken according to the dictates and ideas of the Roman law;

law; and confequently, fuited to the underftanding of the lawyers of all countries, and capable of execution every where. There is no mention of intereft for the money; that would have been entirely incompatible with a public deed of this kind; but the King is made not only to bind himfelf, his heirs, and fucceffors, for the payment, but likewife his whole moveables, and immoveables, prefent and to come, fimilar to the Italian bond formerly taken notice of. The Roman law allowed a man to grant a right upon his lands, and even his moveables, without quitting the poffeffion of them; and this from the Greek term is called a *bypothec.* This right gave the creditor a preference to others over the goods hypothecated. The right which King James is here obliged to give, is, what the Civilians term an univerfal hypothec, which was to affect his whole property. There is no penalty or damages in the bond; that matter was to be determined by the Judge named to enforce the execution. This Judge could be no other than the Pope or the dignified clergy, who were at that time the arbiters of princes; and therefore, James fubmits himfelf and his property, to the laws, coercions, rights, and compulfion, of his Holinefs the Pope, and his fub-auditors, before whom his obligatory letter might be produced. This was the claufe of regiftration in thefe days; and we fhall afterwards learn, that the execution iffuing in confequence of it, was fufficiently effectual. Next follows a renunciation of all the exceptions and fubtleties, which by that time had diffufed themfelves from the Roman law, over all the Courts of Europe. Here we find the ' exception of not ' numerate money,' the *condictio indebiti*, or action for recovery of a fum wrongfully paid, and other exceptions, which our forefathers never thought of, until the Roman law put them into their heads; and what fhews the abfurd rage of the notaries for every thing that was Roman, the King of Scotland is made to renounce the benefit of the *feriae* or holidays of harveft and vintage, a cuftom peculiar to old Rome, and the countries of the vine.

I have

I have annalized this ancient bond, in order to give an idea of the ftyle which followed the introduction of the Roman law, and to fhew that our forefathers, the Scots conveyancers and writers to the figner, are not to be blamed for the redundancy, tautology, or other faults of our forms; they found them all made to their hands, and have, upon the whole, rather abridged than extended them.

There are none of our acts of Parliament, prefcribing any particular form of the bond, or of the recognifance, like thofe in England. After the acceffion of James, every thing to which our old cuftoms did not apply, came to be regulated by the Roman law, and among others, the form of the bond, which was entirely Roman. The act of James III. 1469, introducing the negative prefcription of obligations, mentions, ' That it was advifed that the ' party to whom the obligation is made, fhall follow the faid obli- ' gation.' No mention is made of the term bond.

Accordingly, our oldeft lawyer Balfour extracts from the Roman title *de Obligationibus*, almoft every word he has left us upon the fub- ject: ' An obligation (fays he) is ane band of the law, be the whilk a ' man is bound by reffoun of ony band or contract; ane obligation ' fhould contain fax principal parts and punctis, quhairof gif only ' ane failzies, the reft is of nane avail, force, nor effect; firft, His ' name and firname wha makes the obligation,—2d, His name and ' firname to whom it is made,—3d, The thing wherefore it is ' made, and quhat it is, and how meikle it extend to,—4th, The ' caufe quhairfoir the obligation is made, viz for buying, felling, ' lending, borrowing, or any other reafonable caufes,—5th, The ' place and term of payment,—6th, Securitie for fulfilling of the ' premifes, and alfo for payment to be made als well of the princi- ' pal thing or foume contenit in the faid obligation, as of the in- ' tereft, coftis, and fkaithis, that fall happen to be made throw non- ' payment thereof. *Item,* Sum ar of opinion that an oblig. on

' fould

" fould contene ane pane to be upliftit fra him, that is oblift in cafe
" of his failzie, be the judge under quhais jurifdiction he dwells *."

The obliging, or hypothecating a man's property, according to
the Roman law, as James was obliged to do in his bond, continued
long to be the law of Scotland.: ' It is liefom (continues Balfour)
' to any man to bind or oblis his gudis and gear, prefent or to
" come, or the fruits of the ground purtenand to him, and it beand
' thereupon.; gudis or gear corporal, as horfe, or incorporal, as obli-
' gations of debts, weddis, or liferents.' The very fame method of
forfeiting double the fum borrowed, under pretence of failure,
feems to have been attempted in Scotland ; and to have fucceeded
during the prohibition of intereft, and that, though done in a more
direct and open manner than in England. Balfour cites two decifions upon the fubject, which fhew, that bonds were taken for
the real fum lent, under the condition of forfeiting the double in
cafe of non-payment upon a fixed day ; whereas the Englifh more
cunningly took their bonds for double the fum lent, and made the
reftriction of it conditional : ' gif ony man obliffes him to content and
' pay to an uther, ony certain foume of filver, or uther money, at
' an certain term or diet, convenient betwixt them, and contenit in
' the obligation, under the pain of double payment of the faid
' fum.; or if he failzies to make payment of the famin, after the
' tenor of the faid obligation, and at the day or termis to the whilk
' he oblift himfelf ; he may be callit be his creditour to hear him
' difcernit be an judge, to content and pay the faid principal foume,
' togidder with the double thereof ; viz. als meikle again as the
' fame foume extendis to, becaufe he falziet, as faid is, to mak pay-
' ment at the day appointit. 5th Julii 1501, The Laird of Cock-
' puil againft Simon Carutheris of Maufwall ; 26th Februarii 1506,
' The King's Thefaurer againft the Earl of Caithnefs †.' Thus the
prohibition produced the very fame effect in Scotland, as it did in
England.

* Balfour, p. 149. 150.   † Ib. p. 150.

England. Inftead of preventing oppreffion in the commerce of money, it brought on the inevitable ruin of the debtor; and the courts of law, actuated by the ideas of the civilians, which directed a ftrict interpretation of the engagements and ftipulations of parties, thought themfelves bound to give legal force to thefe acts of rapacity.

The ancient laws of both kingdoms, with refpect to ufury, exactly coincided, not only in the mode of prohibition, but in the punifhment of the ufurer; and it is almoft certain that they continued to be fo for a very long time, and yet there is no mention of it in any of the ftatutes of the five James's, excepting the twenty-third act of James II. which provides that the keepers of victual to a dearth, fhall be punifhed as ockerers, i. e. ufurers; confequently ufury was a crime commonly punifhed, and the punifhment familiar to the people; and, rather than admit any kind of direct profit, by the laft decifion quoted from Balfour, the judges chofe to award double the fum againft the debtor, under the title of conventional damages. This feverity no doubt taught people to beware of granting bonds of this kind. They made the penalty, therefore, no higher than they laid their account with paying. Upon another rule, however, of the doctrine of penalties, all drawn from the Roman law, the debtor attempted to turn the tables upon the ereditor. When a penalty, fay they, comes in place of the principal obligement, it is optional to the party bound, either to perform or to pay the penalty. The debtor gives, therefore, a bond for a hundred pounds payable upon a day certain, under a penalty of thirty, in cafe of failure. Now, fays he, I choofe to incur the penalty, and pay the thirty. This was as unjuft upon the part of the debtor, as the demand of double the fum had been on the ereditor. The court, however, decerned both for the penalty and the principal fum; 19th July 1502, Bruce againft Lindfay *. At laft, about fifty years afterwards, the judges feem to have put the matter of penalty upon the proper and folid footing;

E   and

* Balfour, p. 157.

and thereby cut off the oppreffion which took place between man and man, upon account of the miftaken notions about thefe ftipulations. In March 1548, in a cafe Home againft Hepburn, the Lords found, ' That, by the law of this realm, *poena conventionalis*, fic as
' an foume of money adjectit, with confent of parties, in ony con-
' tract or obligation in name of pane, may not be afked by any per-
' fon, but in fo far as he is intereftit, hurt, or fkaithit ; becaufe all
' fic panis are in ane manner ufury, and unhoneft, made for lucre
' or gane *.' The penalties being thus reduced to their proper and equitable intention, it may be prefumed that the judges continued to allow a reafonable part of it in confideration of the intereft, fkaith, or damages ; however, from the following decifion, it is evident, that the prohibition continued againft bargaining for, or taking any direct fum upon loans in name of profit. ' Gif ony man borrows
' fra anuther an certaine foume of money, and obliffis him to pay
' zierly a certain quantity of filver thereof, fafine following there-
' upon ; or zit ane certain quantity of victual, ay and quhile he re-
' ftoir and deliver the principal foume, he may not be compellit to
' content and pay the faid zierly foume or quantitie: Albeit the ob-
' ligation be regiftrat and infert in the books of an ordinar judge ;
' becaufe, gif he that lent the money feik execution upon the obli-
' gation, the borrowers thereof may alledge the famin to be foundit
' upon an obligation, or act of mere ocker ; the quhilk he prievand
' fufficientlie, aught and fauld be decernit to reftoir the principal
' borrowed foume allenarlie ; 26. January 1561, Dick againft Lo-
' gan †.'

There is a decifion in Haddington, which, if the date be right, though I fufpect it is not, goes to prove, that the court returned again to their ancient error. Thus it ftands in the Dictionary : A fum being contained in an obligation, with a back-bond written on the back thereof, declaring that the creditor, in cafe of payment of the half of the fum at a day certain, fhould difcharge the whole,

the

* Balfour, p. 151. † Ibid. p. 533.

the debtor having failed, the Lords found that he might be charged for the whole, and that it was not ufury; July 1595, Craven againſt Wilſon *.

By the decifion, Dick againſt Logan, no penalty feems to have attended the demand of intereſt; for the creditor was entitled to get back his principal fum. This decifion was given in Scotland only about five years after the act of Henry VIII. allowing 10 *per cent.* to be taken upon money lent in England. The next year, it was found, that a debtor might pay intereſt, or maintain a minor during his minority, without diminution of the principal fum, ‘ and that the ‘ fame was na ways ufury;’ 15. December 1562, Gourlay againſt Thomſon †.

. Notwithſtanding the general prohibition of the law, the commerce of money in Scotland went on by means of bargains of victual, pledges, and other covered methods; fo that, before any direct alteration, the taking of a profit for money feems to have been eſtabliſhed in practice, which was no doubt encouraged and fupported by the public introduction of intereſt into England. This ſtands completely proved by the firſt ſtatute to be found upon the fubject, c. 52. of the 11. parliament of James VI. *anno* 1587, about thirty-five years after the date of the Engliſh act ‡.

It is plain, that this act was not meant to authorife or introduce, but to reſtrain the practice of taking profit upon money to the fixed rate of 10 *per cent. per ann.* as eſtabliſhed in England. Here we have the methods pointed out, in which the money tranfactions had been executed; and by the exception made of all bonds, contracts, &c. dated prior to the ſtatute, it is plain, that thefe muſt have carried more profit to the creditor than the intereſt allowed by the act, and yet they are therein termed lawful bonds, contracts, &c. From all which we are entitled to conclude, that we owe the abolition of the ancient monkiſh prejudices in this country, not to the wifdom of the legiſla-

E 2   ture,.

* Dict. of Dec. vol. 2 p. 498.   † Balfour, p. 533.
‡ Scots Acts, vol. 1. p. 559.

ture, but to the common fenfe and invincible neceffities of the peaple. This ftatute then eftablifhed with us the folid diftinction between the words *ufury* and *intereft*. Legal intereft is what the law allows to be taken; and ufury is confined to the excefs or furplus profit for the loan of money more than the law allows. The ufurer is, by the act, to receive punifhment, conform to the laws of the realm, already made and eftablifhed thereupon. None of thefe laws, however, can be found, except thofe mentioned in the Regiam Majeftatem.

The reference to the old law feems to have been a carelefs expreffion. It left the crime of ufury without any determinate punifhment, which the legiflature very foon found neceffary to fupply. This was done by the 226. act of the 14. parliament of James VI. *ann.* 1594, which declares, ' That the ufurer taking more than ' 10 *per cent.* fhall forfeit the principal fum to the debtor; and if ' he concealed it, any other perfon informing, was to have had the ' fame title.' Sir George M'Kenzie fays, that taking annualrent before hand, is by this act determined to be ufury *. This is a miftake. The act fays, that whoever fhall take more than 10 *per cent.* before hand, or after the year or time, fhall be counted ufurers. Thefe words fhow, on the contrary, that taking intereft before hand was at this time allowable.

The difpofition of the money-lenders to ufury feems to have been almoft invincible. The old methods went on, and new ones were contrived chiefly by the means of bargains of victual, wadds, or pledges; as alfo by retaining the ufury out of the capital at the time of lending. Thefe evils grew to fuch a height, that a very particular act was made to fupprefs them in the 15. parliament of James VI. c. 251. when the bonds, contracts, &c. were declared null, and the principal fums forfeited to the King. From this ftatute we learn, that the paffion of avarice fuggefted the fame devices to ufurers of all ages and countries. Horace's money-brokers, in

old

---

* Mackenzie, vol. 2. p. 144.

old Rome, practifed the fame ftratagems with the Scottifh ufurer in the 1597. The purpofes of the act were defeated from the difficulty of proof; and therefore, by the 7th act of the next parliament, 1600, it was explained, and the fact rendered probable, either by writ, or oath of party, or witneffes. The money-lenders, by this ftatute, had their ingenuity very much confined ; and, at laft, they reftricted themfelves to the very ancient method of taking the intereft beforehand. An act was therefore made to check this evil, in the 23. parliament of James VI. 1621, c. 28.

James VI. as you have heard, reduced the intereft in England to 8 *per cent.* In Scotland, it remained at ten till the 21. act of the firft parliament of Charles I. which reduced it to eight. The preamble of the act is, that his Majefty's fubjects ' have been heavily ' oppreffed and burdened with exorbitant annualrents and intereft, ' taken for the ufe of money, far exceeding the rate and proportion ' taken in England, France, and other neighbouring countries *.'

In the 1649, the intereft fell to 6 *per cent.* and was fixed at that rate by an act of the then parliament, c. 29. This being one of the ftatutes of the rebellious parliament, the act was firft refcinded, and then reftored by the 49th of Charles II. 1661 ; fo that, in the reign of Charles, the intereft of both England and Scotland ftood at 6 *per cent.* No alteration was made either in the reign of Charles, James VII. or William, only as often as extraordinary fupplies were raifed by the landed intereft to the King, retention was allowed to be made by debtors, out of all annualrents, by a train of acts of parliament, fometimes of one, and fometimes of a half *per cent.* in order to relieve the lands, and lay a proportion of the burden upon the monied intereft.

This eafe given to debtors was termed the retention ; and, as the allowance was temporary, our ftatute books, our deeds, and our diligences, from the reign of Charles II. to the union of the kingdoms, are full of regulations regarding that circumftance.

Having

* Vol. 2. p. 62.

Having thus given a detail of the laws and practice of Scotland, respecting the interest of money, and the different regulations on the same subject in England, which led to the explanation of their double bond, I come now to give the history and principles of the common Scottish obligation, termed a moveable bond. As I begin with the old form, which is the very first deed in Dallas of St Martin's collection, I stop the progressive account of interest at the laws which were in force when Mr Dallas published his system.

The Romans termed a bond, or other evidence for money, *nomina debitorum*; because the names of the debtors were usually inscribed upon the top of the deeds. They divided things themselves into moveable and immoveable, according to the nature of the subject. Lands, houses, and all their parts were immoveable; and cash, furniture, pictures, animals, and statues, were moveable. Debts, and other things which are not in the occupation of the party, but which he is entitled to be possessed of, such as debts due to him, &c. were called personal rights. Of these, the chief was the obligation, which is so termed, as it regarded the debtor, and obliged him to do and perform; but, as it stood in the creditor, had no proper name, but that of the right to demand the possession or delivery of the debt, or whatever else the debtor stood bound to pay or perform. The natural distinction of moveable and immoveable among the Romans had little or no relation to succession; the heir or the heirs took the whole property of the deceased, moveable and immoveable, in equal divisions. The northern barbarians, who established themselves upon the ruin of the Roman Empire, and founded the several kingdoms of modern Europe, paid little or no attention to any thing but to the land, and its appurtenances. The feudal system, which arose out of the customs and manners of these people, had the land alone for its object. The rude and simple manners of these savage conquerors, and their posterity, taught them to pay little regard to what we term moveables; which, for the most part, are intended to supply wants they did not feel. ‘ Immoveables, as lands, houses, and

‘ profits

' profits iffuing from them,' fays Judge Blackftone, ' were the prin-
' cipal favourites of our firft legiflators, who entertained a low and
' contemptuous opinion of all perfonal eftates, which they regarded
' only as a tranfient commodity *.' It was a confiderable time,
therefore, before the firft lawgivers, or the firft writers, paid any refpect to it; and even in England, as Judge Blackftone obferves, the
oldeft books of the law contain not a fingle chapter upon the head.;
and the little that is to be found in their immediate fucceffors, feems
principally borrowed from the civilians. When, with the progrefs
of fociety, perfonal eftates increafed, they drew more attention; and
the Roman law, by that time become univerfal, afforded maxims
ready formed for their regulation. Things then, in imitation of the
Romans, came to be diftinguifhed in this ifland into real and perfonal. The real anfwered to the Roman divifion of immoveables;
and the perfonal included both the moveables and the rights. To
anfwer that fubdivifion, the perfonal eftate alfo divided into chattels,
and what they term *chofes in action, i. e.* every thing not in a man's
own occupation, but of which he is entitled to be poffeffed by a fuit
or action at law; and thus money due on a bond is a *chofe in action*;
becaufe the actual poffeffion of it cannot be had, if the debtor refufes, otherwife than by judgment and execution of the law. The diftinction of moveable and immoveable, perfonal and real, became of
much more importance among the feudal nations, than it had been
among the Romans. The right of primo-geniture, eftablifhed by
the feudal fyftem, and which came at laft to affect the fubfiftence
and aggrandifement of families, beftowed the whole eftate, or immoveable property, upon the firft born male defcendant, and the
moveables, or perfonal eftate, upon the other children.

In Normandy, and in England, the feudal pride tended to
make every poffible diftinction, between the tranfcendent qualities
of a fief, heritage, or freehold, and rights or properties of any other
kind. Thefe laft were to be held in no degree of eftimation, when

compared

* Vol. 2. p. 384.

compared to the other. A fief was immoveable in its nature, and appeared eternal in its duration ; therefore all fubaltern rights, falling fhort of thefe high qualities, were held unworthy to ftand in the fame rank : It behoved them to fall into an inferior clafs of their own. Such properties were termed in Normandy *catalla*, and in England chattels. This feodal pride proved a happy circumftance for younger children : A leafe for years, though it concerns the poffeffion of heritage, yet becaufe it has only a duration, is a chattel ; a mortgage, though a right upon land, is only a right determinable at the will of another, *i. e,* may be redeemed by the proprietor of the lands mortgaged, and is there alfo a chattel ; and fo is every other debt upon land. To diftinguifh thefe from common moveables, they are only called chattels real, hence money due by a common bond or *chofe in aftion,* has always in England been a mere moveable, falling to executors.

With us in Scotland, matters took a very oppofite courfe.—To trace it in its changes, would at prefent lead us much too far ; but, being a fubject of great curiofity, will be refumed on another occafion. There are feveral caufes which contributed to the fame effect. The chief of them was, that our annualrents purchafed upon land in Scotland, were not redeemable ; and therefore, were confidered in the fame light as the lands themfelves. Our ancient apprifing of land for debt, carried the property immediately to the creditor, as effectually as a decreet of fale does at prefent, fo that no reverfion remained in the perfon of the debtor ; and by our adherence to the feudal forms in our wadfets and fecurities, all rights upon land carried the appearance of feparate feus. Every thing was done by charter and feifin, fuperior and vaffal ; all our fuperiors and vaffals were governed by the fame fyftem of laws ; fo that the rules which applied to a great Lord in quality of a fuperior, alfo applied to the fuperior of an annualrent, and a wadfetter ; and it behoved the fame forms to be gone through in either cafe. Thefe circumftances excluded the diftinction of the chattles real in Scotland.

land. Inftead of contemplating the defects of temporary rights, when compared with the complete and perfect fief, our anceftors looked only upon the points of refemblance between thefe things. They faw where they coincided, and refufed to pay attention to any other circumftance ; hence all rights which regarded, or ftood connected with a feu, were claffed along with it ; and hence the law of Scotland came to acknowledge no other diftinction, but that of heritable and moveable. The firft comprehends all immoveables, or things connected with, or dependent upon them, which the law has deftined without exception to the heir ; and fo fond have we been of the rights of primogeniture, that the very words real or immoveable, ufed by other nations, have been by us changed to *heritable*, a word which has no relation to the nature of the thing, but only to the legal deftination. For the other divifion, we have retained the term proper to its nature, *i. e. moveable*, a word relative to the thing, and not to the perfon who fucceeds to it : And hence has arifen the grand diftinction of property in the law of Scotland, into heritable and moveable.

Money lent upon the fecurity of land, is confequently heritable like the land itfelf. The common fecurity taken for it, is upon that account called an heritable bond, and money lent upon the fecurity of the perfon, being moveable, the obligation taken for it is called a moveable bond, which, in the courfe of fucceffion, goes to the executors of the defunct. In England, the latter would be fimply a chattle, and the other a chattle real, and both would belong to the younger brother, or neareft relations of the poffeffor, or, according to the language of our law, to the neareft of kin.

From the univerfal prohibition of taking a profit for money, the internal commerce of Scotland was for a very lo ngperiod reftricted, like that of the neighbouring nations. The ftatutes have informed us of the numerous contrivances, which the people were forced into, in order to elude the effect of thefe irrational and impolitic prejudices. The moft fuccefsful and unexceptionable of thefe methods,

proved to be the purchafe of annualrents out of land, and the taking of wadfets, both of which were deemed to be heritable rights,
defcending, like the land itfelf, to the heir. The lending money upon
perfonal fecurity, was a practice little known or heard of; for, as I
lately mentioned, land and its produce alone were the only objects
of confideration with our forefathers. Perfonal debts, therefore,
were contracted of neceffity and not of choice. In the progrefs of
things, the temptation of profit above what could be got by land,
proved to be the only inducement to the trufting of money upon
perfonal credit; and when the ftatutes reftricted that profit, and defeated the devices of money lenders, the commerce of money was
ftill more and more confined to the real fecurity of land. At laft
commerce increafed, and money became more plenty, the lenders
refted fatisfied with the intereft allowed by law, and then, and not
till then, the moveable bond became a deed common in practice;
fince that time, it has proved the mother of diligence real and perfonal, and confequently of the rights of property.

Sir Thomas Craig's celebrated treatife turns entirely upon feus or
real property: Like the old Englifh writers, feldom does he deign to
mention moveables, and then no farther than as they relate to heritage. Sir Thomas Hope of Craigiehall, is the firft of our lawyers
who has left us any thing upon the prefent fubject. His obfervations, which are commonly entitled Minor Practics, were compofed
about the year 1632, fome time after the period when moveable
bonds became common, and before our judges had fettled the legal
idea of their nature and effect. ' The diftinction (fays Sir Thomas)
' between heritable and moveable bonds, was of old thus: viz. A
' moveable bond was that which was made to the creditor by fim-
' ple bond, for payment of money, at any term, with a penalty, and
' did not contain an obligement to infeft in annualrent, nor to pay
' annualrent to the creditor, as well infeft as not infeft: And an
' heritable bond was, where the debtor fold lands, or annualrents
' out of his lands, under reverfion of the principal fum which was
                                                    ' lent

' lent to him by the creditor ; and alfo containing requifition of the
' debtor for payment of the principal fum, upon forty days warn-
' ing, or more or fewer as the party pleafed *.' The firft moveable
bond then, made no mention of intereft ; the creditor depended entirely upon drawing his profit from the penalty, and more commonly from a pledge. Such was the practice of France at the very
fame period. Sir Robert Spottifwood has preferved a decifion which
marks this : ' A French bond bearing no annualrent, but only da-
' mage, if the fum be not paid at the day, refolveth even into the or-
' dinary profits and annualrent, as being the cuftom of France.
' 6th March 1627, Roger Laurieton againft Kenedy †.' Kings did
not think it below them fometimes to pawn their jewels, and great
men their plate, when they wanted ready cafh. By a deed extant
in Rymer's Foedera, it appears, that Henry VI. of England pawned
his jewels to the Cardinal Bifhop of Winton, for L. 4095, in the
year 1434 ; and, for further fecurity, granted him a bond for the
money. In a fmall collection which goes under the name of Carruther's Styles, there is one of thofe old bonds mentioned by Sir
Thomas Hope, which contains a depofite of gold coin by way of
pledge ‡.

The bond is totally filent as to annualrent,—the hopes of the
lender lay upon the pledge. Even in the days of James VI. after
the exaction of intereft had been authorifed by act of Parliament, few
or no loans were made upon bonds ; for, if an annualrent happened to be exprefsly ftipulated to be taken for the money, that circumftance of itfelf made the bond heritable. So much bigotted had the
nation become to every thing that was feudal, that they would not
allow that clafs of rights to fuffer the leaft diminution. Annualrent had from the earlieft times been purchafed out of lands ; thefe
rights they had raifed up to the title of feus ; though Craig ob-

F 2   ferves,

---

* Minor Pract. p. 35.   † Spottif. Pract. p. 63.
‡ Carruther's Styles, p. 1.

ferves, that they ought only to have been termed heritable fervi-
tudes: ' Potius haec fervitutes haereditariae dici debeant, obtinue-
' rint tamen ut haec etiam feuda dici poffunt *.' The reafon why
annualrents were always connected with lands, was evident; they
could not legally be purchafed in any other fhape. The Legiflature now allowed annualrent to be taken for a loan of money upon
perfonal bond, independent of land. The judges oppofed themfelves to this national improvement, and would not fuffer the leaft
diminution of this fpecies of feudal property; and therefore, they
agreed to hold all money given out avowedly to return annualrent
to the lender, to be heritable, and to defcend to the heir in the fame
manner as if it had been fecured upon land by infeftment. A
ftronger inftance of the power of legal prejudice fcarcely occurs in
the hiftory of the law; nor is there any cafe in which our jurifprudence took a courfe more directly oppofite to that of England.
Both nations meant to pay honours to the idol of feudalifm. The
Englifh allowed nothing to approach it but what was completely of
its own nature. They therefore funk the chattles real into an inferior order. The Scots, on the contrary, exalted every thing into
a feu; however defective, they appeared the fame in effential requifites. Their annualrents payable out of land, turned *feoda pecuniae*,
and the holder of it was dignified with no lefs than feudal honours;
he was held to be a Baron, and died vefted and feized as of fee.:
And, laftly, the bare intereft of money, though not arifing from
land, was alfo forced upwards into the clafs of feudal property.
They invented terms and reafons which had no real meaning; intereft, they faid, had a *tractum futuri temporis;* whatever a man
gave out for time, could be intended only for his heir, &c. Lord
Stair does not make a good excufe for this peculiarity; , The diftinc-
' tion of heritable and moveable (fays his Lordfhip) is divided into
' rights and obligations, as the matter thereof is heritable or move-
                                                        ' able,

* Jus Feud. p. 82. §. 37.

' able, and fo all difpofitions or obligations for conftituting any
' right of the ground in property, commonty or fervitude are
' heritable, although they have not yet attained their effect, and be-
' come real rights complete ; as difpofitions of lands, annualrents,
' pafturages, thirlage, &c. which is fo far extended, that all which
' is by deftination to have its accomplifhment, by a real right of the
' ground, is heritable ; as bonds bearing a claufe of annualrent,
' which becaufe annualrents were ufually by infeftment, therefore,
' the very provifion of annualrent, though but a perfonal oblige-
' ment to pay it yearly or termly without mention of infeftment,
' made the provifion or bond heritable, and not to defcend to exe-
' cutors, children, or wives, but to heirs only *.'

The judges in this matter are not without apology, nor was the
point fettled without a confiderable ftruggle. We have feen
that the firft moveable bond confifted of no more than a fimple obligement, for payment of a principal fum under a penalty. In fact,
the people had no idea of giving a permanent loan upon that fecurity. Thefe obligements were not even termed bonds. In England they went under the name of *bills,* and in Scotland of *tickets.*
This technical term in the law is now out of practice, and out of
memory ; but our ftatute-book, and the decifions of the laft century,
are full of regulations and queftions about tickets. They were a
kind of recognifances payable to the bearer. The Scottifh ticket
differs very little from the form of the old Englifh bill : ' I
' A. B. grant me to be juftly addebted to C. D. in the fum of
' three hundred pounds Scots, which I bind and oblige me, my
' heirs, fucceffors, and executors, to pay to the faid C. D. his heirs,
' or affignees, or any having his order, and that againft the
' day of   next, under the penalty of fifty pounds Scots,
' in cafe of failure. In witnefs whereof,' &c.

                                    This

* Stair, p. 167.

This obligement was the forerunner both of our common bond, and of our inland bill, as we shall afterwards find.

The first effect of the legal toleration of annualrent was observable, not upon the bond or ticket, but upon the annualrent right. The creditors in these securities had formerly no title to call for the principal sum; but now, when annualrents were become legal, the writers first ventured to annex a proviso: ' That the creditor might ' demand back the principal upon notice given, under form of in- ' strument, forty days before;' and this was called the clause of re- quisition. The next improvement was to add a personal oblige- ment for payment of the money; though this obligement, by force of the clause of the registration, produced a charge against the debtor, upon ten or fifteen days, yet were the clauses of the requi- sition still retained, and the use of it was this. If the creditor meant to recover his money upon the personal obligement, he went on by registration and common diligence; but, if he meant to at- tack the land of the debtor, by apprising or real diligence, then it behoved him, in the first place, to make requisition.

' An heritable bond (says Sir Thomas Hope) was when the ' debtor sold lands, or annualrent out of his lands, under reversion ' of the principal sum which was lent to him by the creditor; and ' also containing requisition of the debtor, for payment of the prin- ' cipal sum, upon forty days warning, or more or fewer as the ' party pleased*.' In an action (says Sir Robert Spottiswood) pur- sued by the Laird of Clackmannan against Barrowney, the Lords found, ' That upon a bond bearing payment of a sum at a term, ' and in case of failzie of a penalty, together with an annualrent, ' the creditor might comprise at any time thereafter without requi- ' sition. July 1629.'

After this, the charge came in place of the requisition, and in all cases that ceremony fell into disuse. The next improvement was the

* Minor Pract. p. 35.

the alteration of the fimple moveable bond, or ticket, to an exprefs obligement for payment of annualrent; a circumftance which ex-actly marks the period, when perfonal credit, and perfonal eftate, arofe into eftimation; but. in doing this, our predeceffors, the writers, were fo rivetted to the idea of annualrent being fomething real, and *a quafi feudum*, that though they had detached it from lands, and tranfplanted it from the heritable to the moveable bond; yet did their ideas of its nature remain unaltered; they carried along with it the heavy provifo of requifition, and feveral other claufes proper only to annualrents fecured upon land; nay, even after the claufe of requifition had been folemnly found to be of no ufe, yet did they perfift in fuppofing it to be neceffary, and in continuing to provide againft it. Such a bond appears in St Martin, the words are *:
' But prejudice always to them, to fuit execution hereupon for pay-
' ment of the faid fums at the faid term of payment, or at any
' other term after, without any premonition or requifition to be
' made for that effect.' There is another in Carruther's Styles.
' But prejudice to fuit all manner of execution hereupon, notwith-
' ftanding of the claufe of annualrent, and that without any premo-
' nition or requifition, except the charge underwritten †.' It was no wonder that the judges were perplexed by this mixture of ftyle, and confufion of idea. Sir Thomas Hope has left a precife defcrip-tion of the effect it had upon the court: ' But now, (fays he) the
' forms of bonds are fo conceived, and the Lords decide fo uncer-
' tainly, that it is exceeding hard to difcern the diftinction between
' heritable and moveable bonds; for firft, the bonds are now con-
' ceived, bearing a claufe of annualrent, and after that, a provifion,
' that the creditor fhall have power to crave his principal fum at
' any time without requifition, which confounds the nature of heri-
' table and moveable bonds; for in the beginning of the bonds,
' they are conceived heritable, and by a pofterior claufe, the fame
                                             ' are

---

* Dallas's Styles, p. 708.   † Carruther's Styles, p. 5.

' are made moveable at the pleafure of the creditor, without ex-
' preffing any external act to diftinguifh whether it be heritable or
' moveable.'

' The Lords, in the decifion of thefe points, have been very un-
' certain ; for fometimes they judged no bonds to be heritable, ex-
' cept they bear a claufe to infeft : Otherways they found a bond
' heritable, without a claufe of infeftment, if it bore an obligement
' to pay annualrent to the creditor, as well infeft, as not infeft ;
' and, laftly, they have found it heritable, albeit it want both claufes,
' if it bears an obligement to pay annualrent *.'

To this laft opinion, though erroneous in the extreme, the court
firmly adhered, as appears by repeated decifions in Durie, which it
is unneceffary to point out.　At this period then, the mark
of a moveable bond or ticket, was, that it obliged the debtor to pay
the penalty, without mention of intereft ; and the characteriftic of an
heritable bond was a ftipulation for annualrent.　I ufe the word
heritable bond here, in its ftrict fenfe, *i. e.* as properly defcendible
to the heir without any relation to fecurity upon land.　But all
heritable bonds had fpecific terms of payment.　The law prefumes,
that it was the intention of the creditor to demand his money at
that term ; and therefore, where fuch creditor died before the term
of payment, the bond was deemed to be moveable, and fell to executors.　On the other hand, where the term of payment was allowed to pafs without fuch a demand, the prefumption took place, that
the money was meant to lie upon annualrent for behoof of the heir,
the bond then became, properly fpeaking, heritable.　When the creditor ferioufly chofe to raife his money, he ufed a requifition or a
charge, either of which pofitively declared his intention to recover
his money ; and therefore, fuch a requifition or a charge, by the
rules adopted in this matter, evidently made the contents of the
bond moveable.　The notions entertained by our judges, refpecting
the

---

* Minor Pract. p. 36.

the intention of the parties in lending the money, were not imaginary, they fuited the wifhes of many people at the time, and they continue to do fo at the prefent moment. Such as choofe, then, that their heirs fhould abfolutely fucceed to lent money, in preference to their executors, contrived to take the bonds payable to their heirs, and exprefsly to feclude their executors. This feclufion cut off the chances, both of the creditor dying before the term of payment, and of the effect of the requifition and charge.

Thus ftood the law refpecting bonds for borrowed money, when the parliament 1641, with a fpirit of real reformation, took up this fubject. Whatever the nation may have fuffered, by changes and convulfions in government, it has, in every cafe, received fome indemnification by the introduction of good laws, both civil and political. The acts of what came afterwards to be termed the rebellious parliaments, are the beft inftances that can be given in fupport of the general obfervation. The 57. act of the parliament 1641, concerns heritable and moveable bonds. The preamble is, ‘ That the provi- ‘ fions of law for younger children are fcanty ; that the generality ‘ of people, in lending their money, had no intention to difappoint ‘ their younger children ; that the heir profits by their ignorance ; ‘ and that a number of orphans and fatherlefs children are difap- ‘ pointed of their natural portion, are brought to poverty and mi- ‘ fery, and forced to become beggars, which is often found by piti- ‘ ful experience ; and therefore it enacts, that all contracts and ‘ bonds for fums of money, though with the condition of payment ‘ of annualrent and profit, fhall pertain to the bairns and neareft of ‘ kin.’

The whole acts from the 1640 downwards, were refcinded without diftinction at the reftoration ; but, as the good effects of an act fo juft and reafonable as that refpecting bonds had been long felt, the law was immediately revived by the 32d act of the firft parliament of Charles, 1661.

Vol. I.   G   This

This ſtatute takes no notice of the former act. That would have been doing too much honour to a rebellious aſſembly. However, it does this in effect; becauſe it has a retroſpect to the 1641, and confirms the intermediate effects of the firſt ſtatute. From theſe acts we learn, that the former interpretation of the law reſpecting bonds with annualrent, had been practically introduced, previous to any of theſe regulations, by an expreſs excluſion of the executor; and the ſame power is very properly reſerved to thoſe who chooſe to do ſo, as it was not the intention of the ſtatute to reſtrict or confine the ſubjects, in the ſettlements of their private affairs.

It is only, then, ſince the 1641, that the writing now ſo common with us could have been termed, a moveable bond.

We are now arrived at the period when Mr Dallas of St Martin collected his ſyſtem, *i. e.* about the year 1666. The firſt form he has given us is that of the *moveable bond,* which I ſhall now endeavour to analyſe and explain.

' *I A. B. by thir preſents, grant me to have borrowed and received* ' *from G. D. all and haill the ſum of* ——— *uſual Scots money.*'—— The Engliſh recogniſances, being public acts, begin with ' Know ' all men ;' becauſe they are addreſſed to every body, and all men were concerned in their effects upon the land of the debtor. The Engliſh bond is copied from the recogniſance; but the ſimple obligement, bill, or *obligatio ſimplex,* without a penalty, not being intended to remain as a ſecurity longer than the term of payment, began, like our ticket, with the name of the granter, none but the parties being preſumed to have any concern.

The Scottiſh moveable bond, or ticket, for the ſame reaſons, began with the name of the granter, whereof there are ſeveral early inſtances. The Earl of Murray, Regent of Scotland, borrowed five thouſand pounds from Elizabeth, to be applied towards the political purpoſes of the times. For this ſum he granted a ſimple bond, which is dated the 18th day of January 1568. It mentions neither

annualrent

annualrent nor penalty. It begins: 'We James Earl of Murray,
' Regent of the realm of Scotland, do grant and confefs, by thefe
' prefents, to have received, &c. ;' and he binds himfelf by the
faith and truth of his body amply to content and repay the money.

' *All and haill the fum of.*'—The words *all and haill, totas et*
integras, were invented when lands firft came to be defcribed in
charters. I fhall, in the proper place, mark out the particular
period. Our writers, accuftomed to thefe words in heritage, applied them to fums of money bearing annualrent, which were heritable,—*foeda pecuniae;* and therefore we find, All and Haill the fum
of ——, or, All and Haill the lands of ——; but thefe words never
were ufed in tickets, or moveable obligements. They are now mere
tautological expletives, and have therefore been for a long time omitted in perfonal deeds, but continue to be ufed when the money is to
be fecured upon land.

' *Whereof I hold me well content, fatisfied, and paid ; and, for me,*
' *my heirs, and executors, exoner and difcharge the faid W. D. and all*
' *others whom it effeirs of the famen.*'—This, in the analyfis of the
bond, is termed the receipt of the money borrowed. But why fhould
the borrower grant fuch a formal difcharge to the lender, and declare
himfelf fatisfied and paid thereof? This form, fingular in appearance,
arifes from a fubtlety of the Roman law. A loan of any thing, for
the purpofe of being confumed and changed, was called a contract of
mutuum ; mutui datio was that, where money, grain, or any other fun-
gible was lent by one man to another, on condition that the fame quantity fhould be returned at a time certain. The borrower then became
mafter of the thing given to him; he could ufe it in the fame manner
as the lender could have done. ' Inde etiam mutuum appellatum eft,'
fay the Inftitutes, ' quia ita a me tibi datur, ut ex meo tuum fiat *.'
Hence our common word *mutual,* and *mutual* contract. This is diftinguifhed from *commodatum,* where the thing lent muft be preferved, and the *ipfum corpus* returned. *Mutuum* then being a contract,

G 2

the

* Inft. §. 3. tit. 15.

the lender performs his part by delivering the money. The borrower acknowledges the receipt of it, and discharges the lender and his heirs of their part of the contract. It is a general rule, that the greatest number of the clauses in our deeds respecting moveables, are borrowed from the principles and practice of the civil Code; and those which regard our land rights, from the principles and practice of the feudal law. This form of receipt, or discharge, in our bonds, is still kept up for the sole purpose of expressing what we call the cause of granting, which, indeed, is not absolutely necessary; because it is presumed by the obligement to pay. No man would come under such an obligation, without a sufficient inductive cause for doing so. In separate bonds, however, the cause of granting should always be expressed. It stamps a character of plainness and integrity upon the transaction; and, in future questions, either with the party or his creditors, proves highly beneficial to the lender.

' *Whom it effeirs of the samen.*'—The word *effeirs* is a common term in the law of Scotland, and continually occurring in our styles. In this place of the bond, it means, all whom it may concern. This word is said to be derived from an old French word, *affurer, to tax* or *estimate*; and thence came the old English word, *affeirers*, who, in the ancient courts, were persons appointed to fine jurymen, or others who refused or neglected to do their duty. ' The amercia- ' ment or fine of every juror,' says the term *De la Ley*, ' shall be ' *affeired* according to his offence; and where a town was fined, ' the *effeirance* was said to be general.' The word came, therefore, to be used in two senses; the first to affirm, or confirm, because the jury fixed, or affirmed the fine, and in this sense it continued in England. As it related to proportion in the fine, we have retained it. In talking of interest, we say, ' such ' annualrent as shall *effeir* to such a sum.' Others derive it from the French word *affaire*, which means a process, a piece of business, a concern of any kind. *Affairé* is a person full of business. In the old Scotch language we called it *affeir*,

and

and in the law language, *effeir,* to be concerned with, to corre-
spond, or relate to ; and, therefore, *in form as effeirs,* means in such
form as in law belongs to the thing. Both these etymologies may
be just.

' *Renouncing the exception of not numerat money, and all other ex-*
' *ceptions and objections of the law whatsoever, that may be proponed*
' *or alledged on the contrary, by thir presents for now and ever.'*—
In the old bond, brought by the Italian merchants to England near
five hundred years before the date of the deed we are talking of,
there is an express renunciation of the exceptions that might be
drawn from the civil and canon laws, and all other exceptions that
could be made against the debt. The bond by James I. in the
1424, contains a renunciation of all the Roman exceptions then
known ; and among the rest, the exception of not numerat money.
At that time, the renunciation was by much the longest clause in the
deed. All these vanished by degrees, leaving the single exception,
non numeratae pecuniae, which remained for a long time in every
country where the Roman law was received. It relates to the case
where an acknowledgment is taken from a man without delivering
him the sum mentioned, by number or count, which the contract of
mutuum obliged the lender to do. The writing (say the civilians)
produces an action at law ; but natural equity furnished the defender with the exception, *non numeratae pecuniae,* in order to defeat the
action. When this exception was made, it behoved the lender to
prove the delivery of the sum. This power of excepting, was, by
the Roman law, restricted to two years ; but, when a man granted
a discharge for a sum of money, the circumstance was more favourable, and the granter was allowed no more than thirty days to complain of the not having received numerated money. I assigned one
reason already for the solemnity of discharging the creditor ; but
here we find another, and a stronger one. The exception of not
numerate money operated but a very short time against a discharge ;
for which reason, the borrower is made to discharge the lender. To
convert

convert a lender into a debtor, and a borrower into a creditor, merely, by a form, was (with deference to the learned civilians) unquestionably *fraudem facere legi*; yet our bonds at this moment retain, in their form, an evident vestige of this evasion. Since the law furnished such an exception, the renunciation of it seems to have been but a very poor device. If the law supposed that the creditor in the bond had got hold of the deed, without paying the money, the same supposition must have also applied to the renunciation; and therefore the defence militated as strongly as ever.

This exception of the civil law was antiently received all over France, and it must have also been received in Scotland; but now the French have rejected it. An authentic deed with them is evidence complete, upon condition that it mentions the receipt of the specific sum; but if it does not mention it, then the exception of not numerat money is still received in the southern provinces, where the Roman Code is acknowledged as the proper law of the country. With us, these things are now of little consequence; the exception, *non numeratae pecuniae*, has no force. The acknowledgment of the debt, as in England, is sufficient; though the cause of granting should seldom or never be omitted.

The receipt for the money being given with a discharge to the lender, and the civil law exceptions renounced, the lender's part of the contract of *mutuum* is complete. The borrower now proceeds to his own part of the business, *i. e.* to oblige himself for the repayment.

'	Which sum of —— money foresaid, as principal, with the annual-
'	rent thereof to the term of payment underwritten, I, as principal,
'	and C. D. as cautioner, suretie, and full debtor, for and with me,
'	by thir presents, bind and oblige us conjunctly and severally, our
'	heirs, executors, and successors, and intromitters, &c. whatsoever,
'	thankfully to refund, content, pay, and deliver again to the said
'	G. D. his heirs, executors, or assignees.'—Here the debtor engages to pay back the money, with the annualrent from the date of the

bond

bond to the term of payment. We have heard the reason why moveable bonds were generally made payable at short terms; the money was intended to be recovered at that time, or the interest depended upon the penalty being soon incurred, and the debtor rendered tractable by having a demand for the whole sum pendent over him. He obliges himself, his heirs, executors, and successors, and intromitters, &c.; under the, *&c.* are to be understood, his lands, goods, and gear whatsoever. By successors, are meant those who may succeed in virtue of a disposition. Successors relate to the lands, and intromitters relate to moveables, and those who meddle with them without a title. The order of the words should be heirs and successors, executors and intromitters. This anxious specification was of old not without a meaning. Obligations by the civil law received a strict literal interpretation; and the distinction of heritable and moveable affected the creditor as well as the debtor. The succession of the latter divided into heritage and moveables. The moveables were liable for the moveable debts, and the heritage for the heritable debts; and, consequently, the executor stood answerable for the former. Afterwards the whole debts seem to have been thrown upon the executor; and the heir was not obliged to answer till the moveables were discussed. This defence was removed by the 76. act of the 6. parliament of James IV. 1503, which will come to be fully examined in another place. I shall only point out the following authority from Sir Thomas Hope, which relates to the present subject. ' The executor is liable to the payment of ' moveable debts, and of old could not be pursued for heritable ' bonds; but now the Lords promiscuously sustain process against ' the executors and intromitters, as well for heritable as moveable ' bonds; and that without discussing of the heir; whereas the heir ' is not conveenable for moveable sums, *nisi post annum* after the de- ' funct's decease, albeit he be already entered heir [*].' To avoid these distinctions, and render the recovery of the debt plain and

easy,

* Page 37.

eafy, it was natural for the writers to make fure work by binding all the different fucceffors known in the law. In the 1708, a bond appeared in court, where a man bound only his heirs and executors, but not himfelf. It was objeĉted, that the bond was null ; becaufe, by an exprefs title of the Roman law, all obligations behoved to begin at the perfon of the granter, otherwife ' *nec profunt nec obfunt* ' *haeredibus.*' This fubtlety was rejeĉted, and the bond fuftained. Indeed it had been fo by the later conftitutions of the Roman law itfelf ; 21. January 1708, Lord Grange againft John Hamilton *.

I fhall referve what I have to fay upon cautioners or co-obligants, until the fimple bond be difcuffed.

' *Thankfully to refund, content, pay, and deliver again.*'—Here is a ftring of fynonymous terms. The immoderate ufe of words to the fame purpofe, in the claufes of deeds, is not imputable to our predeceffors, the lay clerks ; but, as I obferved before, it is entirely owing to the clerical notaries of the fourteenth century. The practice, however, is not entirely deftitute of ufe. One word of ftronger fignification affifts another of weaker import ; or, if one fhould happen to be blotted, or erafed by accident, the other ftands good of itfelf. At the fame time, 1 fhall never contend for fuch a clutter of words as are found in this old bond ; modern practice has reduced them to two, and fo it is right they fhould remain.

' *To the faid G. D. his heirs, executors, and affignees.*'—The deftination to the heirs of the creditor is a moft material part of the bond. Even here, the bond was anciently fuppofed to require a literal interpretation, and that the obligement went no farther than the exprefs words. It is an eftablifhed point, that, where an obligation or other deed is granted to a man himfelf, though his heirs be not mentioned, it is underftood to be granted to his heirs alfo, unlefs they fhall be exprefsly excluded ; and it is this declaration or exclufion, which it is our bufinefs to attend to in cafes of that kind :

' Heirs

* Fount. Dec.

" Heirs (fays Lord Stair) have right not only to obligements con-
' ceived in favours of the defunct, and his heirs, but though there
' be no mention of heirs, unless by the nature of the obligement
' there be a specialty appropriating the same to the person of the
' defunct, only as in commissions, trusts,' &c *. The word, *heir*, in
a moveable bond, is not to be taken in the usual acceptation; it is
nothing more than a different term for executor : ' Executor haeres
' in mobilibus dicitur (fays Craig) is enim ex testamento vel ab in-
'·testato succedit.' Hence though a bond be taken to heirs alone,
without mention of executors, it would go *haeredi in mobilibus;* and
consequently, when taken to heirs, executors, and assignees, as in
the case before us, the money goes to the executor. It was the act
in the year 1661, which ultimately fixed that point, by declaring
that all bonds shall be moveable, where executors are not expressly
excluded. The word *heir* therefore was proper, before the date of
that act, when bonds bearing annualrent were heritable; and, when
the executor had only a small chance of the succession; but since
the date of that act, it is no better than an expletive, which writers
have kept in from mere custom, without any meaning. Where executors are excluded, then the word *heir* assumes its proper meaning.

' *Betwixt the date hereof, and the feast and term of*
' *next to come, but longer delay, fraud, or guile, with the sum of*
' *money foresaid, of liquidate expences, in case of failzie or registra-*
' *tion of thir presents in our default; together with the ordinar an-*
' *nualrent and profit of the said principal sum, conform to act of Par-*
' *liament, and that yearly, termly, and continually, during the not pay-*
' *ment thereof after the said term.'*—The purpose of making short
terms of payment, was of old to insure the interest in the name of damages out of the penalty. The law of this country soon suggested another reason for doing so. The moveables of debtors were carried by

VOL. I.   H   priority

* Stair, p. 474. § 5.

priority of diligence; and therefore, long terms of payment were,
and ftill continue to be, dangerous and inconvenient. According to
our prefent practice, bonds for borrowed money are always made
payable at the next term after the loan, which is generally about
three months. Six months is the longeft term I have obferved, excepting in fpecial tranfactions, and by particular agreement. According to the interpretation of the law, the words ' betwixt and a
' certain term' include the term day; and therefore, in this, and all
other cafes of the kind, the term day muft elapfe before any penalty
be incurred, or diligence proceed.

' But longer delay, fraud, or guile, with the fum of L.
' money, forefaid, of liquidate expences in cafe of faillie.'—The words
fraud or *guile* ufed here, are not in our ftyles fynonymous, or relative to the delay. They relate to the duty of the borrower in the
contract of *mutuum* prefcribed by the civil law. The penalty is not
only to be incurred by delay of payment, but by the borrower attempting any deceit or evafion in the performance of his obligement; and, though we have now omitted thefe words, the law retains the conftruction, and applies the penalty to the indemnification of the other party, againft whom any injuftice has been done,
or attempted to be done. ' If any party has difadvantage (fays Lord
' Stair) by fraud or guile, it ought to be repaired, not by virtue of
' the contract, but by the obligation arifing from that delinquence;
' and fo unjuft balances are an abomination to the Lord becaufe of
' the deceit thence arifing *.' Our old writers chofe to provide
againft the fraud and guile in the obligement itfelf.

' With the fum of   of liquidate penalty, in cafe of
' faillie.'—It was mentioned before, that the Romans, in order to
avoid the trouble of a judicial liquidation of damages, were accuftomed to fix upon a certain fum to be paid in cafe of non-performance; and to do this they were encouraged by the law: ' In ejuf-
                                                                ' modi

* Stair, p. 104. § 15.

' modi ftipulationibus (fays the text) commodius eft ceitam fummam
' comprehendere, quoniam plerumque difficilis probatio eft quanti
' cujufque interfit.' Money being in place of all things capable of
being eftimated, the fum fixed is termed liquid penalty. When the
annualrents depended on the damages afforded by thefe penalties, the
quantum, like the Englifh bonds, was fometimes taken at double
the principal fum, and always large ; but, after the legal toleration of
annualrents, the penalty could only relate to the expence of enforcing the payment ; and, therefore, the court confidered them not as a
real eftimate of damage, but as a precaution to enfure performance
of the obligement: Therefore they reftricted the damages to the
real expences, except in the cafes of apprifing and adjudication,
where the creditor was obliged to take his payment in a manner
quite contrary to his intention, and, perhaps, to his conveniency.
It alfo behoved him to be at confiderable expence in obtaining his
real diligence ; and therefore, to fhorten the matter, the Lords allowed him the fum agreed upon in his bond of liquidate expences.

In St Martin's bond, no mention is made of a fifth part, the fum
is blank, and were we to examine the bonds and contracts of the
feventeenth century, we would find the quantum of the penalty
differ in almoft every one of them ; fometimes it is lefs than a fifth
part, and fometimes it is more ; many inftances occur in the decifions of that period. In the bond, No. 2. of Carruther's Styles, the
penalty of five hundred merks is no more than fixty; and, in the
cafe Halkerfton againft Cadie, 1ft February 1628, the Lords fuftained a bond, having forty merks of penalty, for L. 80 of principal *.
In the 1672, the old diligence of apprifing gave way to the form of
adjudication, in confequence of the 19th act of the 3d feffion of the
fecond Parliament of Charles II. One of the complaints againft the
old apprifing was, the heaping up of penalties and fheriff's fees. It
was therefore ordained, that the Lords fhould adjudge to the credi-

* Durie, p. 335.

tor, such a part of the debtor's estate, as should be worth the principal and annualrents then resting; and a fifth part more, in respect the creditor wanted the use of his money, and was obliged to take land for it. This fifth part appeared to Parliament to be evidently an average of the former penalties, and was given in lieu of expences and sheriff's fees. The writers naturally adopted this proportion; and, in the present century, the fifth part of the principal sum came to be the practical penalty in all obligations for payment of money, and continues to be so at this moment, though it is not fixed by any law or stated rule. These conventional penalties being evidently of that class, which the Roman Magistrates were accustomed to reduce to the real damages of the party, the Courts of Equity in England followed their example in the case of the double bonds; and our Court of Session, exercising the mixed power of law and equity, have made penalties the subject of what is termed the *nobile officium* of the Court. Lord Stair expresses himself upon this subject, in a plain perspicuous manner: ' The Lords of Session
" (says he) modify exorbitant penalties in bonds and contracts, even
" though they bear the name of liquidate expences, with consent of
" parties, which necessitous debtors yield to. These the Lords re-
" trench to the real expences and damages of parties. Yet these
" clauses have this effect, that the Lords take slender probation of
" the true expences, and do not consider whether they were unne-
" cessary or not. So that they exceeded not the sum agreed upon.;
" whereas, in other cases, they allow no expences but what is necef-
' sary or profitable *.'

But, though the Court interpose in modifying penalties, they positively refuse to adject one where it is omitted: The following decision will properly illustrate this point: An assignee to a bond of six thousand merks adjudged the estate of his debtor; but, when he came to extract his decreet, he found no penalty liquidated in his
bond.

* Stair, p. 571.

Bond. It contained only the general words, with annualrent and penalty, without specifying what the penalty should be. ' Whereupon ' (says Lord Fountainhall) he supplicates the Lords, representing ' that this has been but an omission of the writer; and that the ' Lords commonly sustain the fifth or sixth part of the principal ' sum to be the conventional penalty and liquidate expences; and ' therefore craved the Lords would allow the extractor to insert ' that sum in his adjudication; otherways he would be a consider- ' able loser, being in all probability to lie long out of his money. ' The Lords thought the writer of the bond culpable and censur- ' able, for so gross an omission; but did not find they had power to ' supply this defect; and therefore, refused the bill.—Leslie against ' Ogilvie, January 6. 1705 *.'

The intention of the party in this case was plain; but even Lord Kaimes, the great advocate for the Pretorian power of our Supreme Court, and for the prevalence of equity over law, admits, that the supplying a defect in words is above the power of any court what- ever. ' However clear (says he) a will may be, a Court of Equity ' hath not authority to sustain action upon it, independent of the ' words where these are made essential, for this in effect would be ' to overturn †.' In all obligements, whether it consists in pay- ment of money, or performance of facts, the deeds should be guard- ed with proper penalties. And though these penalties in all cases of personal diligence are restricted to the real expence of recovery, it is convenient to have ready execution for the expences, and to get caution for them, in the event of a suspension. In small debts, which are disputed in Court, the real expences often rise far above the penalty, and sometimes above the principal sum. When the expences are given, the Court pay no attention to the quantum of the penalty, but award the costs of suit. In large debts, where the costs are within the penalty, there (as Lord Stair says) the cre- ditor.

---

* Vol. ii. p. 256.   † Principles of Equity, p. 42.

improperly tranfplanted by the conveyancers out of the annualrent
right into the perfonal bond ; and contributed to fix the judgment
of the Court, deftinating thefe laft to the heir. It was thought that
a ftipulation for annualrent after the term of payment, rendered this
bond alfo a pure annualrent-right, or more properly converted it
into a perpetual annuity ; and therefore, the money is declared payable at any other term or time, notwithftanding of the claufe anent
payment of annualrents ; by which is meant the annualrents after
the term of payment, not before it ; when the perfonal obligement
was firft added to the old heritable bond, then, if the term of payment had been allowed to pafs, and annualrent happened to be received thereafter, that receipt of annualrent prevented the perfonal
charge. Requifition muft have been ufed, in order to raife the
money, and therefore, the words ' without any premonition or re-
' quifition to be made by them to that effect', are underftood as an
addition to the claufe, and were generally added at that time *.

Having endeavoured to give the hiftory of the common bond,
down to the old form given us by St Martin, and having explained
the parts of that form, I now proceed to the few pofterior laws
which were made relative to the prefent fubject, fince the days of
Mr Dallas to the prefent times. The Englifh bills, the foreign obligations, and the Scottifh tickets, had frequently of old been made
payable to the bearer *latori praefentium.* The words of the Scottifh
tickets were : ' To pay to the faid C. D. his heirs or affignees, or
any having his order, on demand.' For a long period, difcharges
in feparate deeds were little known or practifed. The terms of the
ground of debt rendered it unneceffary, being payable to the bearer.
The poffeffion of the writ itfelf prefumed the payment in the literal
meaning of that axiom of the civil law : ' *Chirographum apud de-*
' *bitorem repertum praefumitur folutum.*' Accordingly we find, that,
in order to prevent difputes, debtors were often taken bound to pay
                                                        the

---

* Vide Dallas's Styles, p. 708.

the money upon no evidence or no pretence, but the delivery of the principal obligement itſelf. The clauſe uſed upon theſe occaſions was generally conceived in the following words : ' Promittentes nos ' non probare ſolutionem aut liberationem hujuſmodi debiti, niſi per ' praeſentes literas, inciſas vel cancellatas.'

The eſcheats or forfeitures of the moveable goods of indivi-duals, ſo frequent and ſo diſtreſſing among our forefathers, together with the embarraſſments occaſioned by the private prohibitory dili-gences of inhibitions, arreſtments, &c. put the ingenuity of the peo-ple to work to diſcover means of defeating the effeČts of theſe legal evils. The moſt effeČtual method, deviſed for the purpoſe, proved to be the execution and delivery of bonds blank in the creditor's name ; which, like the old tickets to the bearer, went from hand to hand, without bearing a trace of their tranſmiſſion ; and conſequently, eluded the effeČts of diligence of all kinds. This praČtice, it ſeems, increaſed with the internal commerce of the country, and grew up to a dangerous length towards the end of the ſeventeenth century. In England, the attornies, for a very long period, have kept bonds printed or engraved. They contain all the words of ſtyle, except-ing the names of the parties, ſums, and dates, which are filled up at the time of execution ; and, even then, the perſon who fills them up is not with them deſigned. I have not been able to learn that any cuſtom took place of delivering blank bonds ; for they neither had the inhibition nor arreſtment to fear ; and, with reſpeČt to the for-feiture of moveables, it had been for ages confined to the criminal law alone.

So ſoon as this praČtice came to be abuſed, the Court bent their attention to prevent it. Lord Stair tells us, ' That the firſt inſtance. ' which occurred to the Lords, was upon the 11th November 1665, ' when they found, That the delivery of a blank bond was in faČt ' an aſſignation of it ; and, as it did not appear at what time the ' name of the creditor had been filled up, they preferred the ar-' reſter.—Telford againſt Veitch.'

A practice of this kind, aided by the ingenuity of the people, proved an over match for the accidental checks given to it by the judges. The abuses multiplied; and the Courts were filled with intricate questions, created by blank writs. Parliament therefore interposed by the act, dated the 9th of October 1696 *.

The names of the parties ought, in every case, to be fully inserted by the same hand that writes the deed. If it is subscribed blank in the name of the creditor, the error is incapable of being supplied, and the bond is null. The allowance that the act gives, is, That if a party do happen to sign a deed before the name of the creditor is filled up, the name must be inserted before delivery, in presence of the same persons who had witnessed his subscription.

This act banished blank bonds and other writs of that kind out of our practice. It has been literally and properly executed by the Courts of law; and is seldom or never disobeyed in practice. A bond or other deed may be justly suspected upon this account: When the name of the creditor appears to have been filled up with a different hand, and different ink from the body of the deed; but this may happen in consequence of the words of the act of Parliament, which permits the name to be inserted at the time of the subscription and delivery; and therefore, that circumstance does not bring the deed under the act, unless it can be also proved that it had been omitted at the time of the execution, and supplied either after delivery, or in the absence of the witnesses †.

The next law which concerns our subject, is the 12th of Queen Anne, c. 15. which reduces the rate of interest to *5 per cent.* and discharges any greater profit to be taken, under the pain of nullity of the deed, and forfeiture of treble the value of the sum lent.

By a clause of the same act, ' all scriveners, brokers, and soli-
' citors in money affairs, are discharged from taking any reward or
                                                    ' brokerage

---

* 3d Sess. 1st Parl. Will. vol. iii. c. 25.   † Erskine's Inst. p. 428.

' brokerage for procuring the loans of money, or forbearing the
' fame, over and above the rate of five fhillings for the loan or *for-*
' *bearing* of L. 100 for a year, and fo rateably, or for 12 pence
' over and above the ftamp duties for making any bond or bill re-
' garding the premifes.'

To this laft part of the aƈ, we, in Scotland, have never paid any
regard, judging the provifo to be entirely levelled againft the innu-
merable corruptions of money broking in England. We know
little of them in this part of the ifland, and I hope we never fhall.

This is the laft law or ftatute which regards the prefent fubjeƈ;
and by it I am naturally led to fay a few words upon our own method in the management of the money bufinefs, which has always
been a branch of the profeffion of a Writer. There is no country in
Europe, where money can be fo conftantly and conveniently difpofed of as in Scotland. If it is meant to remain unapplied, or invefted only for a fhort time, the banker's houfe is open to receive
it, and to pay, formerly 4 *per cent.* and now 3 *per cent.* of intereft.
The bankers in England never do this; they will receive and fafely
keep money, but they give nothing for it in the mean time. When
money is to be lent upon bond or fecurity in London, the broker
muft be paid for finding out the fecurity; and if money is wanted
to borrow, the broker muft be doubly paid for difcovering the lender;
for, as this commerce has become the province of a particular fet of
men, their abilities have proved an overmatch for the ftatute of
Queen Anne. In this country, the agents of the lenders and the
borrowers fettle the bufinefs together. It is the privilege of the
doer for the lender to write the bond, becaufe it is the lender who is
to be fatisfied, with regard to its fufficiency. The borrower pays for
it, becaufe the tranfaƈion takes its rife from his neceffity. The
Englifh ftatute allows only a fhilling to be taken above the ftamp-
duties, but it allows five fhillings *per* hundred, or, as the merchants
fay, a quart *per cent.* for the brokerage or agency. This appears to
be little; but then it will be obferved, that it allows it to be taken

each

each year for forbearance ; and thereby tolerates a conftant oppreffion. I am informed many people are glad to pay the five fhillings
yearly, as regularly as they do the L. 5. We acknowledge no fuch
practice ; our payment is made at once, under the name of writing
the bond. Thefe payments are not limited by any regulation, but
bear a proportion to the quantum of the fum lent.

The circumftance of printing the bonds brought down the fees
of them in England to the petty rate of a fhilling. Trading people
keep them in the fame manner as they now do ftamps for bills.

It is proper to notice in this place, that the fecond claufe of the
act of Queen Anne extends to us in Scotland : Were any difpute
then to occur about the payment of a bond, the quart *per cent.* and
the fhilling are the legal ftandards. I hope it will not happen, and
that we fhall never know any thing of demands for forbearance of
money : They would be attended with a total corruption of our
manner in this bufinefs.

The generality of Writers make no demand upon their employers
for lending their money, though I have met with it ftated and paid
upon feveral occafions. Their profits then depend upon writing
the bond ; and it would be reckoned mean and difgraceful in any
man, to ufe ways and means to bring about the changing of money
from one hand to another, without good reafons. If it be no more
than to get the writing of a new bond, he finks into a broker, as
mean and contemptible as any in Change Alley.

The form of the bond remained with very little variation or abridgment, till within thefe twenty or thirty years paft. By degrees,
however, a number of the redundant words fell, and at laft fettled
in the following ftyle :.

‘ I A. B. writer in Edinburgh, grant me to have inftantly bor-
‘ rowed and actually received from C. D. writer there, the fum
‘ of one hundred pounds Sterling ; which fum of one hundred
‘ pounds, with the legal annualrent thereof, from the date of
‘ thefe prefents to the term of payment after fpecified, I bind and
‘ oblige

' oblige me, my heirs, executors, and fucceffors whatever, to repay
' and deliver again to the faid C. D his heirs, executors, or affig-
' nees whatever ; and that at the term of Martinmas next ; with a
' fifth part more of liquidated penalty in cafe of failure ; and the due
' and ordinary annualrent of the faid principal fum, from and after
' the faid term, fo long as the faid fum fhall remain unpaid. Con-
' fenting,' &c.

This is a plain form from which little or nothing can be taken,
when the bond is feparately written. Young men are often taught
to make divifions and fubdivifions of its fubftance, which is
of no manner of ufe. The fartheft I would carry it is, divide
the bond into two, firft the receipt of the money, and fecondly,
the obligation to repay it with intereft at the term fixed, under a
penalty.

The receipt of the money is a remainder of the old Roman form,
founded upon the contract of *mutuum*, which, though not abfolutely
neceffary, is, as I faid before, convenient, and often proves advan-
tageous. Some people ftill ufe the words, ' renouncing all excep-
' tions on the contrary ;' which is a very curious relict of the ancient ftyle. For into this fhort phrafe, the long renunciations of
the civil law exceptions, introduced many hundreds of years ago, is
now entirely fhrunk : We found it in the bonds in the beginning
of the thirteenth century ; and the ghoft of it ftill remains in this
phrafe.

Mr Spottifwood the Profeffor of Scots law, at the beginning
of this century, is the only perfon who has, fince the days of
Dallas, publifhed any fyftem of our perfonal forms. After giving
the ftyle of a bond differing little from that of Dallas, he adds,
' but, becaufe this form may be thought to contain claufes unnecef-
' fary and fuperfluous, though in daily practice, I give a bond in a
' more compendious ftyle.'

' I A. oblige me and my fucceffors to pay at Whitfunday next to
' B. his heirs or affignees, the fum of L. 1000 Scots, of borrowed.
                                                        ' money,

' money, under the penalty of L. 100 pounds, with the ordinary
' annualrent of the faid principal fum, from the date hereof, during
' the not payment.'

In this form the fubftance is facrificed to brevity, which very feldom happens.in legal writings. It is highly exceptionable, in fo far as the debtor is not obliged to pay intereft from the date to the term of payment, as ufual, he is only bound to pay it as a penalty; fo that, were he to pay the money at the precife term, he might difpute the intermediate intereft upon the fame principle, as he might refufe the penalty itfelf ; *ex contractu*, no intereft is due, but in the event of incurring the failure. This faulty model has been pretty much followed; at leaft, I have of late years feen many fuch bonds, efpecially in mixed deeds. I do not fay that they would, *de facto*, be attended with the effect mentioned. Equity and the plain intention of parties might perhaps get the better of the conftruction. The trial of the point would be dangerous to the lender, and would bring into hazard the character of the Writer, as a man of bufinefs.

From the commentary I have given, upon the fimpleft of all our fecurities, the moveable bond, we may perceive with what care and nice attention to the principles of the law and ftate of fociety, every word and claufe of this eftablifhed ftyle has been originally compofed. We will have the fame obfervations to make upon many others, and therefore, cannot be too careful in preferving and adhering to them in the courfe of our profeffion. So material did this matter appear to the Court, that one of the firft things done at the meeting of every Seffion, was to recommend this to the body of the Writers, who were obliged to attend for the purpofe; and I am told that this practice continued down to the 1745. Of late years, it is not uncommon to hear gentlemen avow a fixed difrefpect for the forms and manners of our anceftors, both in conveyances and
                                                                judicial

---

* Spottifwood, p. 9.

judicial proceedings, they talk of substituting their own good sense for style, and for doing business in forms of their own. If there is no information, no science peculiar to practitioners, if we are to destroy the system of practical jurisprudence, which the learning and long experience of our ancestors have transmitted to us, our title to a separate profession ought to accompany its fall. Every man may draw deeds as he pleases, and do business according to his own fancy; our manners then will corrupt the law by continued relaxation in favour of error, and the law must consequently corrupt the manners of practitioners, by repeated indulgences of their mistakes. Our approved styles are daily vanishing, and those clauses and terms to which the experience of ages have affixed a certain interpretation, are giving place to affected, equivocal, and too often to ungrammatical modes of expression. From these, among other causes, many of our profession of late years have sunk into an absolute dependence upon the gentlemen of the bar, and are obliged to have recourse to them for their assistance in matters of business, which the bar ought to learn from them, and which it is a shame for Writers not to know. By this means they depress their own importance, and multiply the expence of their employers. In the course of this undertaking, I shall have many striking and melancholy instances to give of professional errors and absurdities in business, which have been occasioned by the absolute ignorance of some, and the presumption of others, in venturing to substitute their own sense, and lame mode of expression, for the wisdom of ages. The more a man knows, his confidence in what I may term his innate powers, will lessen in proportion; in place of venturing upon novelties, and disregarding experience, he will learn to trust to nothing but a solid knowledge of the principles and established forms of business; and he will find, that to acquire these with certainty and pleasure, it is indispensibly necessary to trace the subjects of our profession through the different periods and changes they have undergone;

dergone, and to be able to compare our present with our former practice.

Before dismissing the subject of the bond, I have judged it necessary to take notice of some peculiarities, which most commonly occur in that article of business. It often happens, that the money is advanced some time before the date of the bond; and therefore, to keep the words to the real fact, the bond mentions this circumstance in these terms: ' I A. B. writer in Edinburgh, grant me to ' have borrowed and actually received, at the term of Candlemas ' last, notwithstanding of the date of these presents, from C. D. ' writer there, the sum of one hundred pounds Sterling; which ' sum of one hundred pounds, with the legal annualrent thereof, ' from the said term of Candlemas last,' &c.

This article of practice is of considerable standing. From a decision reported by Forbes *, 7th November 1711, Scott against Baillie, it appears, that a declaration of this kind had at that time been long in use. It is now become absolutely necessary.

Where the bond is granted for a debt already contracted, if there is more than a year's interest, it may be added to the principal, or, what is better, paid up to the date of the bond, because it is at that time exigible; but, if there be less than a year's interest, it ought not to be added, because it is properly not due, interest being only annually paid; the best and plainest method is to declare the fact in the bond, and to take the debtor bound from the term of the real advance or date of the debt.

A bond granted for debt already contracted, is evidently of the nature of a recognisance; and, in place of using the English words, ' am held and firmly bound,' we use the equivalent expression ' grant me to be justly addebted and owing,' &c.

When bonds are granted by men of landed property, who are necessarily parties to family settlements, it is usual to take their successors

* Forbes, p. 537.

ceffors bound, according to the fpecific enumeration of the law : ‘ I
‘ bind and oblige me and my heirs, as well male as of line, tailzie,
‘ conqueft, provifion, and all others my fucceffors, executors, and
‘ intromitters with my goods and gear whatfoever, conjunctly and
‘ feverally, renouncing the benefit of the order of difcuffing them.'
The complete explanation of this claufe would open a very wide
field, and carry us too far from our prefent fubject : I fhall at prefent fimply define thefe feveral heirs, account for the neceffity of
binding them, and fpeak to the privilege of difcuffion which is renounced.

An heir of line is a direct defcendent from the party, fuch as
fons, daughters, grandchildren, &c. Thefe are alfo called heirs-
general, becaufe they not only generally and neceffarily reprefent
the party in the common courfe of things ; but every property in
general, belonging to the predeceffor, goes to them, which is not
otherwife fpecially difpofed of. The heir male is fo termed, becaufe a female is fuppofed to exift in a nearer degree of propinquity, to whom he is preferred in confequence of a deftination exclufive of females. This was the firft and moft antient ftep to our
prefent entails, and hence it is, that the bond takes in the heirs as well
male as of line. This phrafe though twifted, as it were, in appearance, is exceedingly proper ; the heir-male, as fucceeding to the capital property, is put firft in order, and at the fame time the natural
and more clofe relation of the other duly marked.

The heir of tailzie fucceeds not by law, but in virtue of a fpecial
deed ; under that denomination, he is generally at a greater diftance than the heir-male ; and, as the line of propinquity is cut in
his favour, he is therefore called the heir of tailzie, from the French
verb *tailler* to cut.

The heir of conqueft can only fucceed to a middle brother, or the
fon of the middle brother, who ftood between two uncles. He is
the elder brother, and fucceeds to every thing conqueft, *i. e.* acquired or purchafed by his immediate younger brother, becaufe by

rthe law such conqueft afcends ; and the immediate younger brother is the heir of line to whatever property defcended to the defunct from the common predeceffor, for by law heritage defcends. The heir of conqueft then neceffarily fuppofes an heir of line to exift ; and it alfo fuppofes two feveral eftates to have belonged to the defunct, one afcending and the other defcending.

An heir of provifion is generally a fon or daughter of a fecond marriage, who ftands provided to certain fums or properties, in virtue of the contracts or fettlements made by their parents ; but whatever relations fucceed in confequence of any fpecial deed made in their favour, are termed heirs of provifion, though they be not children of the marriage.

Of thefe heirs none fucceed by law, but the heirs of line and of conqueft. The heirs-male, tailzie, and provifion, as before obferved, fucceed only to fpecial properties by virtue of particular deeds ; and even of thefe laft, fome are nearer in point of propinquity ; for the heir-male, or the heir of marriage, muft be nearer in blood than the heir of tailzie, who is often a remote kinfman, and fometimes no relation at all ; and hence thefe heirs became entitled, in our law, to what is termed, the *bond of difcuffion,* which they were allowed to propone by way of exception, againft the fuit of the predeceffor's creditors. Though the Roman law knew no fuch fucceffors, yet this exception or benefit is directly borrowed from the analogy of other difcuffions eftablifhed by that law. The civil law, in favour of cautioners, obliged the creditor to difcufs the principal debtor as a preliminary to an action againft his furety ; and it alfo forced the creditor to fue each of the fecurities for their fhare in proportion, which was called the *beneficium divifionis.* From the analogy of thefe rules, a like exception or benefit of difcuffion was admitted into Scotland, in favour of heirs. Our law, once the fame with that of England, fubjected the heir to the heritable debts alone, and the executor to the moveable debts. We have heard in what manner that came to be altered, and all heirs fubjected to the

debts

debts of their predeceffor; the only remainder of their privileges, is that of the difcuffion, to which they were entitled in the following order, which is concifely fet down in Mr Erfkine's fmall Inftitute.

' The heir of line is primarily liable for the debts of his pre-
' deceffor; for he is the moft proper heir, and fo muft be difcuffed
' by creditors, before any other can be purfued. Next to him the
' heir of conqueft, becaufe he alfo fucceeds to the *univerfitas* of the
' whole heritable rights which his predeceffor had acquired by fin-
' gular titles. Then the heir-male or of a marriage, for their pro-
' pinquity of blood fubjects them more directly than any other heir
' of tailzie, who is a ftranger, and who for that reafon is not liable
' till all the reft be difcuffed, unlefs for fuch of the predeceffor's
' debts or deeds, as relate fpecially to the lands tailzied, as to which
' he is liable even before the heir of line *.'

To avoid all inconveniency in the recovery of the money, the claufe binds all thofe different fucceffors without diftinction, and makes the granter renounce the benefit of difcuffing them in order. When the municipal jurifprudence of modern Europe found itfelf over-run with exceptions and defences furnifhed from that quarter, the remedy univerfally applied, was that of renounciation. The re-nouncing claufe was the longeft in the old deeds, examples of which we had in the antient bonds formerly noticed. The fame method was followed by the Writers, to get quit of this Scottifh de-fence, for fo I may term it, of the benefit of difcuffion.

The general definition of difcuffion, as applied by the law of Scotland to the cafe of heirs, is underftood to be execution by horning and caption againft their perfonal effects, and adjudication againft their heritage.—Durie, 22d March 1627, Edgar.

So much for the heirs of the granter of the bond. With refpect to the heirs of the creditor, I have formerly fhewn the import of that deftination, the claufe by which executors are excluded, and

K 2. the

* Erfkine's Inft. p. 371.

the money deſtined to the heir. Some people carry this·ſo far, that they not only exclude executors from the principal ſum, but alſo from the whole annualrents falling due thereon, and penalty incurred through failure. By this means, the bond for borrowed money is rendered more determinately heritable, than either land ‧ ͨ ‧ ‧ ‧ties upon land. For the rents of land and bygone annualrents upon heritable bonds, always go to executors. Common heritable bonds go to executors, if the creditor ſhall die before the term of payment, but bonds ſecluding executors do not; they are heritable *a principio.*—Fountainhall, 5th November 1587, Muir againſt Muir. They continue heritable through ſucceſſions of heirs, till the deſtination be altered by a ſpecial deed, but this cannot be done upon deathbed.—12th January 1725, Kames's remarkable deciſions, p. 141.

Bonds are but ſeldom taken from one perſon, two or more generally join in them, either as principals equally concerned in the loan, or as ſureties for a principal. I am to ſpeak of theſe caſes in their order. When people borrow money together, the loan is divided equally between them. The law preſumes that it is ſo ; and therefore, each party is only liable for their proportion of the debt. The rules for the regulation of this matter, have been entirely borrowed from the Roman law. Co·obligants in that juriſprudence were termed *correi debendi ſeu promittendi.* Antiently, I mean among the Romans, it was held that all co-obligants in a debt were liable *in ſolidum,* although they engaged by ſeparate obligations: Nay, although they were bound to pay at different times, yet the delay competent to the one afforded no defence to the other, who ſtood ſimply bound; if the one happened to be abſent or bankrupt, it followed that the other muſt have paid for him.

The Emperor Adrian introduced the benefit of diviſion, in order to mitigate this unreaſonable law. The creditor was thereby obliged to ſue each debtor for his ſhare or proportion. To get the better of this, the debtors were all taken bound *in ſolidum* ; but Juſtinian extended the law of his predeceſſors even to that caſe, ſo that thereafter

after it required an exprefs declaration or ftipulation to make co-obligants bound. Thefe rules were adopted every where with the civil law and the phrafe chofen for the purpofe was, *conjunctim et divifim*, and in France *conjointement et feparément* ; in England, *joint* and *feveral*, and with us, *conjunctly* and *feverally*. The word *conjunctly* imports, that all the debtors may be profecuted together ; and the other, that each of them may be fued fingly for the whole. If then they are only *conjunctly* bound, all of them behoved, *de facto*, to be purfued, the omiffion of one would afford an objection, and each is only liable for his own fhare ; or, according to the Roman idea, he would be entitled to the *beneficium divifionis*; but, if they were bound *feverally*, then each is fingly bound, and may be purfued for the whole ; fo that, of the two words, *feverally* is the moft important. Both of them are ufed together, and always reach the effect intended. We are fo habituated to thefe words *conjunctly and feverally*, as almoft never to disjoin them in idea. Indeed, when two perfons are bound together to do any thing, they are in fact *conjunctly*, bound, without the addition of the word : Thus, where two people obliged themfelves to a third party to deliver a powder mill or pay 500 merks, the Lords found, that the obligation divided, in refpect the price was divifible, becaufe the obligants were not bound conjunctly and feverally.—Urie againft Skene, January 20. 1630.

The obligants in bonds are oftener cautioners or fureties for the principal party, than concerned in the loan ; and the benefit of difcuffion was firft introduced in favour of the cautioner. The antient Roman law made no diftinction between the co-obligant and the cautioner ; the creditor might either attack him or the principal, as he pleafed. The law of the Emperor Adrian gave them the fame privilege, as the co-obligants, *i. e.* the *beneficium divifionis*, by which each of them could be purfued *pro rata portione*. Juftinian next beftowed upon them *beneficium ordinis*, *i. e.* the benefit of *difcuffion*, which rendered them only fubfidiarily liable, after
the

the property of the debtor had been difcuffed. The generality of the privileges, benefits, and exceptions of the Roman law, might have been renounced by the perfons entitled to them ; and it was not long before the cautioners were not only regularly obliged by the notaries to renounce thefe privileges, but alfo to declare them-felves to be principals or full debtors, and to be bound conjunctly and feverally.

So foon as money came to-be lent upon perfonal fecurity, both in England and Scotland, cautioners were demanded in lieu of the former land fecurity. In St Martin's time, the method was not only to take the cautioner avowedly bound in that character, but alfo to make him a principal in the matter of obligation. The words of our old bond are,

' *I as principal, and C. D. as cautioner, fouertie, and full debtor,* ' *for and with me, by thir prefents, bind us conjunctly and feverally.*' —And the fame deed frugally contains a bond of relief by the debtor, to indemnify his cautioner, fo that St Martin's moveable bond contains two diftinct obligations.

' *Full debtor with and for me.*'—Thefe words added to *cautioner* and *furety*, made a very complete obligement, exclufive both of the Roman benefits, and of divifion, and difcuffion. As cautioner and furety, it bound the party for the whole fum ; he could not therefore be a co-obligant ; as full debtor, he ftood alfo in place of a co-obligant *in folidum ;* and therefore, was not entitled to the benefit of difcuffion. The bond therefore contains no renounciation of it. I fhall fupport this conftruction by decifions. An heir being pur-fued upon a bond in which his father was bound as cautioner and full debtor, to pay the fum, alledged that he could only be liable for the half, beeaufe the bond wanted conjunctly and feverally :

' The Lords repelled the alledgeance ; and found him alfo liable to ' pay the whole fum without divifion, feeing the principal was ' bound in the whole, and he was his cautioner ; and the tenor of ' the bond bore, that they were bound as full debtors, which the ' Lords

' Lords found to oblige each one of them, and their heirs, *in foli-*
' *dum*, for the whole.—L. Cloverhill againſt Ladiland, 26th Janu-
' ary 1631 *.'

The ſame words, as I have ſaid, import a renounciation of the benefit of diſcuſſion, ſo the Court found in July 1665. A cautioner
bound as full debtor, claimed in a ſuſpenſion the *beneficium diſcuſ-
ſionis*, becauſe he had not obliged himſelf conjunctly and ſeverally.
The Lords found, that the words, ' full debtor,' imported and implied a renounciation of the cautioner's privilege.—Dunbar againſt
the Earl of Dundee †. Theſe deciſions precede the date of the
bond we are talking of, and demonſtrate the attention which the
men of buſineſs of that period paid to the progreſs of the law, and
the determinations of the Supreme Court.

To theſe authorities I beg leave to add the argument of a later
deciſion, becauſe it goes into a proper and perſpicuous examination
of the words of ſtyle under diſcuſſion. Five perſons joined in a
bond for a ſum of money, as co-principals and full debtors,—two of
them died inſolvent,—other two paid the money,—and ſued the re-
preſentatives of the third for three-fifths of the ſum, in reſpect of
the failure of the other two co-obligants. The defender, a female
repreſentative, objected, ' That ſhe could only be liable *pro rata* for
' a fifth-ſhare of the debt, her huſband being but one of five *correi*
' *debendi*, who were not bound conjunctly and ſeverally, but as co-
' principals and full debtors.—Replied, Full debtors are debtors *in*
' *ſolidum*, or *in totum*, in contradiſtinction to partial debtors, or
' debtors in part, and *qui totum dicit, nihil excepit*. Therefore the
' *correi*, being bound as full debtors, were all liable to the credi-
' tor *in ſolidum*, as if they had been bound conjunctly and ſeverally,
' and as if they had expreſsly renounced the benefit of diviſion.—
' Duplied for the defender, The ordinary clauſes of ſtyle, whereof
' the due obſervance is ſeſſionly recommended to the writers by the
                                                        ' Lords,

* Durie.   † Gilmer's Deciſions, p. 114.

' Lords, are not to be fupplied by equivalents ; and our law knows
' no other claufe, importing debtors to be liable *in folidum,* than
' when they are bound *conjunctly* and *feverally* ; nor can the words
' *full debtors* import any more, than that all are jointly debtors for the
' fum ; as if they had granted a receipt of all and haill a certain
' fum, and bound themfelves to repay the faid haill or full fum.
' The Lords found that the debtors in the bond were all liable to
' the creditor *in folidum;* but that the defender would have been
' liable in a fifth only for the purfuers relief, had all the *correi* been
' folvent. But two of them being bankrupt, the defender was
' found liable in a third fhare of the debt, December 26th 1707,.
' John Cleghorn, &c. againft Yeton *.'

   A cautioner by our common law, is not entitled to relief, until he
is diftreffed for the debt, *i. e.* charged for payment ; but, when the
cautioner ftood bound in this manner, the regiftration of the bond
was found to be fufficient. This regiftration againft himfelf as a
eo-obligant, gave the cautioner an opportunity of taking out another extract, in order to do diligence upon the bond of relief ; but
in this matter, an alteration foon took place, which it is now proper
to take notice of, becaufe a confiderable variation, both in the writs
and mode of the bufinefs, was thereby created.

   The miferies which individuals have, in all ages, brought upon
themfelves and their families, by entering into cautionary engagements for others, and the reluctance which is felt by the Judges in
awarding the execution of the law againft people in that unhappy
fituation, has at all times, and in all countries, inclined the Legiflature to try preventative remedies againft the practice ; and to promulgate laws for alleviating the fituation of the cautioner. In this
fpirit, the Roman privileges of divifion, difcuffion, &c. were introduced by the Emperors, but without effect. The cautioner was
' either reduced to renounce the privilege, or to bind himfelf as a
                                        ' principal,

* Forbes's Decifions, p. 212.

principal, which rendered his fituation, *de facto*, worfe than before.

The ftrict manner in which cautioners were taken bound in our bonds for borrowed money, and the mifchiefs which it brought upon them, called the attention of Parliament, and produced the act of the 1ft Parliament of William, c. 5*. which very much refembles the novel of Juftinian upon the fame fubject. It declares, that though a man be bound *for* and *with* another, *conjunctly* and *feverally*, he fhall notwithftanding remain bound only for feven years ; introducing thereby a prefcription of the cautionary obligement. The benefit, however, was to fall to thofe only who either had an obligation of relief in the principal bond, or a feparate bond intimated to the creditor. Now, let us attend to the confequences of this act, gracious in its intendment, and plaufible in its means. From that time forward, no lender would accept of any perfon in the quality of a cautioner ; nor would he allow a claufe of relief to enter into his bond. Writers infifted, that every perfon concerned fhould be taken bound in the fame terms as the principal, *i. e.* by the fame words, and without the leaft diftinction. Far lefs would they admit of the claufe of relief, whereby the fituation of the parties might be difcovered, and the prefcription of the act become current for the cautioner. From this time forward, then, all bonds for borrowed money were taken from the granters, *conjunctly* and *feverally*. The lender choofes to be kept in a convenient ignorance of the fituation of his parties, and to leave them to fettle that matter among themfelves. For the fame reafon, the old words, *full debtor for* and *with*, have been omitted out of all common bonds ; becaufe they have the appearance of pointing out a diftinction between the parties. Separate bords of relief, therefore, are always taken from the principal, or the perfon for whofe behoof the money is borrowed. The Legiflature forefaw that cautioners would be thus con-

verted

* Vol. iii. p. 396.

verted into principals, and that feparate bonds would be taken ; and
it was imagined, that the effect of this would be checked, by directing the feparate bonds to be intimated, but this idea failed upon
trial.   A co-obligant who fhould intimate his bond of relief at the
date of the loan, would do little or no favour to his friend. It would
prove no other than a notice to the creditor, to recal the money, as
foon as it could be done with decency ; and he would give this very
act of intimation, as his reafon for doing fo. The intimation of the
bond at any more diftant period, is juft to call a demand of the money
upon a man's felf ; and therefore, if he is uneafy about the circumftances of the principal debtor, he choofes to infift for his relief in
quietnefs, without alarming the creditor in the debt.

Thus, like the laws of the Emperors, the act of King William has
afforded no relief in the matter of cautionry by the common bond,
nay, it has fuffered a prejudice by it. In the old bonds, such as
have been the fubject of this commentary, the cautioners appear
avowedly in that character ; and, therefore, the favour of it every
where attended them ; whereas the diftinction of principal and cautioner is not now attended to. The bond is filent upon that circumftance ; and diligence often proceeds without the leaft refpect of
perfons.

Mr Spottifwood, in his firft chapter upon bonds, has touched
upon a great variety, which go under that common denomination,
though in themfelves totally unconnected ; fuch as bonds of provifion to children, bonds by minors, tutors, married perfons, bonds of
penfion, &c. ; thefe belong to feparate branches of bufinefs, which
are diftinct and irreconcileable to each other. This is the effect of
the order in our ftyle-books, which I have ufed the freedom to find
fault with, viz. the method of claffing our deeds under general
titles, in contradiction to the order of actual practice, and to the line
of bufinefs we every day fee paffing under our eye. I fhall now
conclude my obfervations on the moveable bond, with the only remaining cafes, viz. ' the lending money, and taking bonds from
' focieties

' focieties public and private.' In the hands of the former, fome
people choofe to place their money in preference to all others; and,
in the prefent ftate of commerce, the ftock of private companies is
often partly raifed upon the credit of their partners. A corporation
or body politic was by the Romans ftyled *collegium* or *univerfitas.*
' It is compofed (fays Mr Erfkine) of a number of men united or
' erected by proper authority, into a body politic, to endure in con-
' tinual fucceffion; as appears moft fuitable to the nature of that
' fpecial community, and moft neceffary for anfwering the purpofes
' intended by it. Cities, boroughs, and hofpitals, &c. may be thus
' incorporated; and we have frequent inftances of leffer corpora-
' tions within greater. Thus, in moft of the cities and boroughs of
' the kingdom, we fee wrights, weavers, merchants, &c. incor-
' porated with certain rights and franchifes granted to each of
' them *.'

The effential characteriftics of thefe political bodies, are, that they
are held to be perfons capable of fuing or being fued, purchafing or
felling, and confequently of holding property in the fame manner as
any individual could do. Another effential is, that being created for
the benefit of the kingdom, they are perpetual. This kind of per-
petuity can only be attained by fucceffion; and that fucceffion muft
neceffarily arife from admiffion of new members. The principal
matter of the conftitution of thefe focieties, is the appointment of
particular officers, for the adminiftration of their affairs, who act in
a body, and whofe deeds bind the corporation or community in the
fame manner as the deeds of a private perfon bind the individual.
Every corporation or body politic, then, has a particular conftitution, with a fet of rules and formalities peculiar to itfelf. It is
the magiftrates for the time, and the eftablifhed officers for the
trade, who act for, and bind their refpective communities. In particular, they are entitled to borrow money, and to grant bonds,

which

* Erfkine's Inft. p. 148.

which affect the funds of the society, in the same manner as the obligements of a private person affect his estate.

The acts and deeds of administrators of corporations are always presumed to be done for the benefit of the body politic. In order to insure this, they pass under certain previous formalities. The most antient and curious obligation I have met with, was granted by the town of Dundee for the ransom of James I. *

. This

* This bond contains a distinct recital of the treaty for the ransom, and the securities to be given therefor by the towns of Edinburgh, Dundee, Perth, and Aberdeen, after which it proceeds in these words :

‘ We therefore, the Provost and Baillies of the said Burgh of Dundee, and Community of the same, being assembled, as use is, at the sound of the bell, within our common court-house, for the special purposes after expressed : Considering that the liberation of our Lord the King is not only most desireable to ourselves, but would be most joyful to the whole Kingdom of Scotland, who have been in the highest expectation of his arrival and good government, these many days.—Therefore, in order that the said treaty and appointment may be effectually performed and fulfilled, we, by the consent and pleasure of our Lord the King, of our own accord, and in truth, in our own name, and in the name of all and singular our community, acknowledge and declare, that if the said Lord James our King, shall not at the time and place pay and perform in the precise terms of the said appointment and treaty ; then, and in that case, we bind and oblige us, and our successors to the said King of England, his heirs and successors, in the sum of fifty thousand merks, good and lawful money of England ; which sum of fifty thousand merks, we and each of us, for ourselves, and our several heirs and successors, *in solidum*, and likeways in name and place of all and singular our community, in case of the non-payment and performance aforesaid ; bind and oblige us well and truly to pay to the said Henry King of England, and his heirs and successors, or to their certain attorney, bearer of these letters, or of transumpts thereof, within the church of St Paul of London, in England, within a month to be computed from the term or time in which our said James shall fail in payment or performance of the treaty before recited ; and that without any farther delay.—Moreover, we will and grant by these presents, for us and our successors, that the said Henry King of England, his heir, or any successor to him whatsoever, shall have power to call and convene us and our successors, and every one of us, *in solidum* ; and which ever of us he may choose in vice and place of our community, and our said community itself, before any court, or judge, ecclesiastical, or secular, for payment of the aforesaid sum,
‘ either

This bond is written in Latin, as grammatical and as pure as the subject could possibly admit of, and the translation now given is almost literal; it fully justifies what I have observed, respecting the revolution of the style of personal writs, which took place in the fourteenth century, upon the prevalence of the Roman law. It is a bond of cautionry,—it is a bond by a community; and I may venture to affirm, that there is not a clause used in any one of our similar obligations, which is not to be found here, expressed in a manner which seems to exclude the possibility of equivocation; and that all the bonds of cautionry, and all the bonds by communities, or private persons, which are now known, or have been known for centuries past, seem to be no other than skeletons, carved out of this gigantic form.

For

' either in whole or in part; also that the receipt of a part of the said debt, from any
' one or more of us, either in judgment or without the same, shall in no shape prejudice
' the said King of England, or prevent him from demanding, or recovering from us,
' or the remainder of us, at his own pleasure, both principal and interest, *in solidum ;*
' promising at the same time, that we shall not prove payment or liberation from the
' same debt, in any other manner, than by production of these present letters cut or
' cancelled, or by discharge past under the Great Seal of England: And for the pay-
' ment aforesaid, and the faithful and perfect performance of the premises, we oblige
' us and each one of us, principally and *in solidum,* in name and vice of our foresaid com-
' munity ; our said community itself, and all our own proper goods, and the goods of
' the community aforesaid, present and to come, in whatever places or countries the
' same are situated or are to be found ; renouncing the exception of *rei non sic gestae,*
' (*i. e.* of a false or erroneous recital,; the benefits of laesion, restitution, and circum-
' vention, the aid of the laws canon and civil, and of all statutes, consuetudes, privi-
' leges, or pretences, whereby this general renunciation may be hurt or invalidated,
' together with all other exceptions, allegations, or defences, which can be objected,
' or opposed against these present letters, or the contents thereof.—In faith and testi-
' mony of all which, we have caused the Seal of the Community to be appended to
' these presents ; at the Burgh of Dundee aforesaid, upon the 20th day of February
' 1423'

* Rymer's Foedera, vol. x. p. 324.

For example, the English were not satisfied with taking the community or town of Dundee bound for the debt, but they take each one of the magistrates, and their heirs, as private persons, conjunctly and severally, *principaliter* and *in solidum.* They take the goods of the community, real and personal, future and to come, hypothecated for the security ; and lest, a payment of a part by any of the individuals, should entitle them to the benefit of division given by the civil law, the solidity of the obligation is anxiously preserved by a particular clause for the purpose, so that each person stands bound until the last merk be paid. The execution of this bond is a formal act of the corporation assembled in the town-house at the sound of the bell ; and such is the case at this moment, in almost all the boroughs of Scotland.

As these formalities were necessary, and as the obligants were intrusted with the performance of them, they are made to renounce the power of denying the *res gestae,* and all other exceptions of the law, canon and civil. Our predecessors the Writers misplaced this clause in the bond. After renouncing the exception of not-numerated money, they added the general words, ' and all other objec-
' tions or exceptions that can be proponed on the contrary ;' but this applied only to the receipt of the money, whereas by the old method of concluding with the renouncing clause, it was made to apply to all the parts of the obligement preceding. In other deeds, we have preserved this renounciation in its proper place, as I shall have occasion afterwards to notice. This bond was executed by appending the seal of the town, which is the hand of the artificial body politic ; and though seals have in all other cases given way to subscription, they still remain with the borough, and in many cases are applied to their antient use.

This old corporation bond will make the modern one easy of conception. It had long been the established custom of corporations of all kinds, either to declare the purpose for which money was borrowed in the deed itself, or to get an act of the body passed
and

and recorded, to authorise the ordinary officers to procure the loan. This arose from the prescription of the Roman law, from which we have our ideas of the *universitas* or corporation. They considered the political body as a kind of minor under curators, whose administrators must shew every thing to be applied to the real advantage of the minor, or the society. This caution was observable in the very antient bond brought by the Italians to England in the twelfth century. The loan was made to a convent, and the members declare, ' That it was applied to the real utility and advantage of their ' society.' Now, we have the same declaration in the form of a corporation bond, given us by St Martin *; the words are : ' Fore- ' asmeikle as A. C. his majesties master slater has at our earnest re- ' quest paid and delivered to us, towards the furnishing and provid- ' ing of our new mercat place in the Canongate, in timber and ' slate, visibly tending to the perpetual being and subsistence of our ' calling ; all and haill, the sum of,' &c. This striking resemblance between two deeds executed at the distance of more than five hundred years, demonstrates that both have been dictated by the same law, and the same principles.

The expression of the purposes of application was often long, and appeared not pertinent to the deeds of third parties ; and, therefore, as I mentioned before, separate acts were extracted and delivered to the lender, in order to prove his *bona fides*, *i. e.* that he considered himself as lending for the good of the society ; and also to authorise the ordinary officers to grant the bond. The managers of corporations very often omitted the usual formalities, especially when they had any private or sinister plan to carry on. The bad effects of this became general and visible, especially in the royal boroughs, in so much that an act was made in that behalf, in the 1st Parliament of William and Mary, 1693, c. 28. The penalties of this act are entirely pointed against the magistrates, who shall neglect the formalities

* Dallas, p. 707.

lities thereby prefcribed to them. The private party is kept entirely clear, and it is juft and right that it fhould be fo.   X

Since the date of this ftatute, however, it has been the conftant
practice for people who lend money, not only to royal boroughs,
but to corporations of all kinds, to demand an act of the fociety, declaring the purpofe or intended application of the loan,
and authorifing their officers to grant bond for it.   Independent of the act of Parliament, this formality never fhould be
receded from ; it has a diftinct and important ufe.   As each borough or fociety has its own conftitution, a ftranger may be uncertain of the number or quality of the officers who are entitled to
bind it.   Now, a previous act by the whole members of the fociety,
removes all difficulties upon this head, and renders the execution of
the bond by the perfons authorifed equivalent to an execution by
the whole members of the fociety.

The next queftion goes to the effect of this fpecies of obligation.
In general, then, it may be obferved, that bonds by magiftrates or
other officers of bodies politic, bind only the bodies politic themfelves, and the proper eftate and effects belonging to it.   They bind
alfo the prefent adminiftrators perfonally, during the fubfiftence of
their office, and their fucceffors in that office ; nay, the diligence againft the one fet of magiftrates or officers, may be
executed againft their fucceffors without renovation ; fo the
Lords found in the cafe of the Laird of Drumlanrig againft
the Baillies of Hawick, 15th January 1624*.   It is eligible in all cafes of this kind, to take the magiftrates or adminiftrators bound, not only as reprefenting their community,
but perfonally as private individuals.   The cities and confiderable
towns of the country, who have a large and fufficient common
good, never fubmit to this, excepting in particular exigencies, or
when they borrow from the public banks.   The leffer boroughs
often

* Durie, p. 97.

X *In loans to Societies, it is material to enquire
if their Grants of conftitution empower them
to Borrow money — Nº 24 of Rum Du —*

often do it, and no doubt where double fecurity of this kind can be had, it is a defireable circumftance for the lender ; particular attention, however, muft be paid to the conception of the bond to bring about this effect. In a cafe of the town of Culrofs, the queftion was, if the creditor in the bond followed the public faith of the town in accepting this fecurity ; or, if it was the meaning of the parties to bind the fubfcribers perfonally, or their heirs, feeing it obliged them to pay it conjunctly and feverally. The Lords having read the bond, found, ‘ That it bore to be for the town's ufe, and ‘ that they were defigned as magiftrates, and obliged themfelves ‘ and fucceffors in office, and they being now *functi* and exaucto- ‘ rated, they found it only obliged the town, and not them.—Feb- ‘ ruary 1695, Bowie againft Wilfon *.’

In a late cafe, however, of the magiftrates of Pittenweem, more attention was paid upon the part of the creditor; the money was lent by Mr George Innes of the Royal Bank, but not (fays the reporter of the cafe) till after ‘ the proper acts of council were ‘ made to fubject the community for the money borrowed.’ The granters of the bond as individuals, and their fucceffors in office were both charged. The former contended, that they ought not to be bound as private parties; and the latter configned a difpofition of the common good, and contended, that the effect of the charge againft them could go no farther, than to compel them to make payment out of the funds of the corporation, as to which they were already difcharged by confignment of the difpofition. But to this reafoning the Lords paid no regard ; they found the letters orderly proceeded.—July 20. 1752, Cleland againft Magiftrates of Pittenweem †.

About the beginning of this century, the citizens of Edinburgh were very fond of lending their money to fubaltern corporations of tradefmen, in preference to private people. Several of them abufed

---

* Fountainhall, vol. i. p. 667.   † Kilkerran, p. 132.

their credit ; failed for large fums of money ; and ruined their creditors. Since that time, few of the corporations have been trufted,
unlefs the officers and members bound themfelves as individuals.

In Royal boroughs, bonds for borrowed money are generally
granted by the provoft, where there is fuch an officer, baillies, dean
of guild, &c. treafurer, and town-council, or fuch a number of the
latter as are authorifed by an act of the whole. The bond recites
the previous act of council, and then the feveral obligants under
their refpective defignations, as reprefenting the whole body and
community of the borough, bind and oblige themfelves and their
fucceffors in office to repay the money. In corporations, the ordinary officers are the deacons, the box-mafter, and quarter-mafters ;
and bonds are granted by them, and as many of the members as are
agreed upon. The bond by thefe petty bodies, in analogy to the
act 1693, recites a previous act of the fociety. The receipt is
granted for the ufe and behoof of it ; and the obligants bind themfelves, and their fucceffors in office, and the remanent members of
the corporation, for the payment.

When the individuals of thefe focieties are taken feparately
bound, it muft be done in diftinct and unequivocal words, fuch as
thefe : ' As alfo, we the faid A, B, C, D, &c. bind and oblige our-
' felves as individuals, in our private capacities, conjunctly and fe-
' verally, and our refpective heirs, executors, and fucceffors, to
' make payment,' &c.

When corporations lend money, the bonds are taken payable to
' the treafurer of the town, or to the box-mafter of the fociety, and
' to their fucceffors in office, for the ufe and behoof of the commu-
' nity.' If, in either cafe, it is neceffary to know the number and
power of the officers of thefe bodies, the beft method is to procure
from the clerk, an extract of their laft election, from which every
article of information can be got. In lending money to public
trading companies, we muft be ruled by the patents or acts of Parliament by which they were conftituted, and in private copartner-
ſhips,

fhips by their contracts. I have lately feen inftances of partners fubfcribing obligements by the firm of their company. This is a novel, and not a commendable practice. A number of difficulties might be fuggefted, which would attend a deed of that kind, when made the foundation of legal diligence. The practice is purely mercantile, and ought to be confined to bills. In bonds, and folemn deeds, it is the bufinefs of the writer to defign each one of the partners as an individual. To declare that they are partners in company, under the firm and title in which they go, to bind them for that company, and for themfelves, conjunctly and feverally; and to make each of them fubfcribe in his ufual manner.

Claufe

Claufe of Regiftration.

NO circumftance diftinguifhes the jurifprudence of Scotland from the other European nations more, than their early invention of public regifters, and the perfection to which the ufe of them has at laft been carried; all our writers on the law have plumed themfelves upon this circumftance, and recommended the improvement to their neighbours : ' Sòme inventions (fays Sir George M'Kenzie) ' flourifh more in one country than another, nature allowing no ' univerfal excellency ; and God defigning to gratify every country ' he hath created ; fo Scotland hath above all other nations, by a ' ferious and long experience, obviated all fraud by their public re- ' gifters.' I quote this from a paper written by Sir George, in anfwer to a difcourfe publifhed in England againft the introduction of regifters into that country *. The author of this pamphlet, contemptuoufly derives the regiftration of our moveable bonds from the Italian brokers of the twelfth century. Thefe ufurers, it feems, kept a kind of regifter of their loans, and the circumftances of the people with whom they dealt, as a directory to their brethren and fucceffors in the art of impofition. Other Englifh writers imagined, that the idea was derived to us from a fimilar practice in the Apoftolic Chamber, in the reign of Henry III. ; and others from a general regifter actually eftablifhed by Richard I. appointing entries to be made of all mortgages given to Jews. Here the invention appears to have been put in actual practice ; and it is matter of great furprife,

* Philips on Regifters.

furprife, that regifters were not thenceforth eftablifhed in England. Sir George M'Kenzie is very much offended, that the inftitution, which he thinks has been beftowed by a favourable Providence upon Scotland, fhould be made to flow from fuch corrupt fources. He is willing to derive his favourite cuftom from any origin but thofe pointed at by his antagonifts, and the moft honourable he could find was that of the Roman law. With refpect to the regiftration of perfonal deeds in Scotland, our worthy countryman and his opponents are equally in the wrong. From a fuperficial view of the fubject, they agree in confounding two things entirely different in their origin,—in their intendment,—and in their nature; for no other reafon than becaufe time and practice brought thefe things at laft to a refemblance, and applied the common term of *regiftration* to both. There never was a regifter of moveable bonds, or other perfonal obligatory deeds, deliberately contrived or eftablifhed in Scotland, either for prefervation or publication to the world. The deeds went to the record of our courts, as the foundation of regular decrees, in the fame manner as they do in England, and all other countries in Europe. Thefe decrees, by means of the mandates of confent, or regiftration, turned at laft into a mere form or fiction of the law. And, in proportion as the decree turned fictitious, the bufinefs affumed the new form of a regifter, an effect never intended or forefeen by our remote anceftors. This matter, of confequence, is totally diftinct from the regifters, which are peculiar to our country, contrived for the purpofe, and eftablifhed by acts of Parliament; fuch as thofe of reverfions, feifins, inhibitions, &c. All thefe took effect at once, and were directly intended for the purpofes of prefervation and publication. The other kind changed by very flow degrees; and did not affume its prefent fhape, but by force of progreffive laws, made in the courfe of ages. Sir George M'Kenzie, therefore, had he confidered the fubject, would have had a fhort and decifive anfwer to make to his Englifh opponents; who, in attacking him upon the fubject of our regiftration of perfonal bonds,

only

only betrayed their ignorance of the laws and forms of their own
country.

It was a part of the Saxon polity, to have their civil bufinefs executed in the county courts. Thefe courts had the advantage of
being both civil and fpiritual; the fheriff and the bifhop acted as
judges, and the inferior clergy as clerks. When any tranfaction
was to be done between private parties, they repaired to the court,
where it was executed in prefence of the judge; and a memorial or
account of the particulars was entered in the cartulary of the mo-
naftery next adjacent. Matters of confequence between great men
were fometimes written in the blank leaves of church Bibles; and
held to be the moft authentic and unexceptionable of records.
This mode of executing private bufinefs, before unexceptionable
witneffes, was admirable both for its fimplicity and effect. It excluded all difputes between the parties concerned, by eftablifhing
the matter of fact to a degree incapable of contradiction. In doing
this, the civil and ecclefiaftical powers aided one another. In matters of religion, the bifhop, or his commiffary, was judge, and the
fheriff his affiftant. If the delinquent difregarded the cenfures of
the church, the fheriff enforced the fentence by imprifonment.
In temporal offences, the fheriff was the judge, and the bifhop
gave him advice, and enforced the fentence by ecclefiaftical cenfures.

The Norman conqueft ruined in a great meafure the Saxon conftitution, and forced the feudal law upon the nation. William and
his fons, though fworn to obferve the Saxon laws, did all in their
power to extirpate every trace of them. They introduced the Norman language, and Norman forms of procedure, into the courts,—
they deftroyed the union of the fecular and ecclefiaftical jurifdictions, which had preferved the peace of the country, and the inde-
pendence of individuals. A number of the Saxon forms and folemnities, however, either furvived the Norman violence, or were
afterwards

afterwards reſtored; ſuch as fines, recoveries, &c. which were no
other than the agreements of private parties, executed in the face of
a coµrt, and entered upon the record. The general maxim too, reſpecting the effect of ſuch tranſactions by record remained, and remains to this day. It is a ſettled rule, ſays Judge Blackſtone, ' That nothing ſhall be averred againſt a record, nor
' ſhall any plea, or even proof, be admitted to the contrary;
' and, if the exiſtence of a record be denied, it ſhall be tried
' by nothing but itſelf, *i. e.* upon the bare inſpection, whether
' there be any ſuch record or not; elſe there would be no end of
' diſputes *.'

In the ſpirit of theſe maxims, lineally derived from the Saxon
conſtitution, Edward I. the Juſtinian of England, obtained the Statute Merchant, which provides: ' That in every city, or great town,
' there ſhould be kept a recogniſance of debts due to merchants;
' and that, in caſe payment was not made, upon complaint of the
' merchant, and inſpection of the record, his body might be im-
' priſoned, and his eſtate delivered into the poſſeſſion of the mer-
' chant, according to a reaſonable extent or valuation.' After this,
ſeveral other acts paſſed, eſtabliſhing recogniſances in favour of
different ranks of creditors, who were all, in virtue of this ſtatute,
entitled to certain privileges and benefits.

As it behoved the parties in every caſe to appear perſonally, in
order to make the acknowledgement; and, as the force of the deed
lay upon its being made a matter of record, the advantages of the
ſtatutory recogniſance were, by an obvious and eaſy device, extended to common bonds. The original and real ſolemnities of court
are, in this buſineſs, kept up. An action muſt be brought by the
plaintiff; and, left that ſhould go for default, there muſt be an appearance of an attorney for the other party, who is not only to ſtate no
defence, but to confeſs the debt, in order that judgment may go out
againſt

* Vol. iii. p. 241

againft the defender. By this means, however, the direction of the bufinefs is entirely committed to the creditor, who enters up the bond, as it is termed, for the fame reafons as we regifter ours; but the effect is very different : ' Lands (fays the new abridgement of ' the Englifh law) are bound from the time of the judgment ; fo ' that execution may be of thefe, though the party aliens *bona fide* ' before execution is fued out. So of ftatutes, merchant, ftaple, and ' recognifances, which alfo bind the lands, from the time of enter- ' ing into them.' From thefe forms of the law of England, it is Lord Kames's opinion, that our mode of regiftration arofe. ' A ' deed (fays his Lordfhip) has fprung from the recognifance which ' requires peculiar attention.' In England, it is termed a bond in judgment, and with us a bond regifterable. ' With refpect to ' the evidence of Englifh bonds in judgment, (continues his ' Lordfhip) and Scottifh bonds having a claufe of regiftration, ' there appears no difference ; they bear full faith, and, without ' any extraneous evidence, are a fufficient foundation for execu- ' tion *.'

Although our claufe of regiftration bears a ftriking analogy to the warrant for confeffing judgment in England, and though there are words in St Martin's bond, which feem to fupport Lord Kames's idea of the one being borrowed from the other ; I mean the claufe which mentions the penalty being incurred upon regiftration on the debtor's default ; yet, from a clofe comparifon of the progrefs of the law of both countries, I remain perfectly fatisfied, that our man- dates for regiftration are of higher antiquity than their warrants to confefs judgment, as fome of our regifters, properly fo termed, are much older than any of the kind in England ; and it is not at all improbable, that the practice in both countries arofe from the fame fource.

I beg

---

* Law Tracts, p. 77.

I beg leave here to obferve a circumftance, which, upon inquiry, will be found to be literally true.—It is, That however
the ftyles and forms of the Englifh common law writs may be
found to vary from ours, after the middle of the fifteenth century
downwards, yet the public deeds of their notaries, their forms in
chancery, and their ecclefiaftical writings, without exception, differ
almoft in nothing from thofe either of Scotland, or of France. The
reafon was, that after the feparation of the ecclefiaftical and laic
jurifdictions, each of thefe adopted different laws, and different
forms. The former adopted the Roman law, and the ecclefiaftical
forms, which had fpread from Rome, all over Europe, while the
courts of common law, jealous of their rights, adhered to the antient maxims of the nation, and to the literal forms of their municipal jurifprudence. The civilians ftruggled to eftablifh their fyftem,
and the others held them off with determined firmnefs. In all ftate
affairs and public deeds, however, the forms of the civilians prevailed, and that from a reafon of neceffity. None other would
have been intelligible; and hence it was, that the antient bonds
relative to the ranfom of James I. are compofed in the language and the forms of the civil law, without a perceptible relation to the common law of England. This Roman ftyle in the
matters of treaties, contracts, inftruments, &c. became, after the
thirteenth century, fo univerfal over all Europe, and the ftyles and
forms of all churchmen became fo uniform, that there is no mark
in the order, or folemnities, by which we can diftinguifh a Spanifh
public inftrument from a French one, or a French one from a Scottifh or Englifh. The very atteft or docquet of the notaries, the ' Et
' ego vero,' &c. was ufed in the identical words in every kingdom
of Europe, juft as exact as it is now among ourfelves. At the arrival of James I. in Scotland, a great part of our antient laws and
forms remained; but, by the influence and prejudices of the ecclefiaftics, who ruled both church and ftate, they gave way by degrees
to the civil law,—to foreign feudalifm,—and the forms of the conti-

nent. The inſtitution of the College of Juſtice by James V. completed the revolution. This general obſervation kept in remembrance, will explain a number of circumſtances in our progreſs
through the unexplored periods of the hiſtory of our law.

It was mentioned, that, according to the antient Saxon conſtitution,
the biſhop and the ſheriff aided one another in the adminiſtration of
juſtice ; but, after the ſeparation of the eccleſiaſtical and ſecular juriſdictions, a competition took place between them, for the buſineſs of
the nation ; in which the churchmen prevailed almoſt every where,
excepting in England, where the courts of common law ſtood out
againſt them. In caſes where the clergy could not directly claim
the cognifance of a point, they prevailed with the parties to ſubmit
the matter to their determination ; and we are informed by the
learned Benedictines, the authors of the late admirable work upon
antient diplomas, that theſe references were almoſt the only methods of terminating diſputes in France, before the ſtudy of the Roman law became univerſal. Lord Kames's conjecture, therefore, is
hiſtorically true : ' That in difficult or intricate caſes, it was an early
' practice for judges to interpoſe, by preſſing a tranſaction between
' the parties : Of which (continues his Lordſhip) we have ſome in-
' ſtances in the Court of Seffion, not far back. This practice
' brought about many agreements between litigants, which were al-
' ways recorded in the court where the proceſs depended. The re-
' cord was complete evidence of the fact, and, if either party broke
' the concord or agreement, a decree went out againſt him
' without other proof *.' But there was another and ſtill more effectual method, by which the eccleſiaſtical courts monopoliſed the
national buſineſs ; notaries, in all their obligations and contracts, either inſerted a ſolemn oath of performance by the party, or made
them ſwear to do ſo, and took a ſeparate inſtrument upon the oath.
This brought the matter directly under the eccleſiaſtical juriſdic-
                                                    tion ;

* Law Tracts, p. 65.

tion; for, upon breach of the contract, the party applied to the church courts, who excommunicated the debtor, and held him so, until he paid or performed. At last the debtors were made to consent to their own excommunication, in the same manner as they do at this moment, that letters of horning may pass against them. Private people submitted themselves in this manner to the bishops of the diocese, or any others agreed upon; princes and great men to the Pope. The forms of these deeds of consent are exceedingly curious, and have, without a doubt, led the way to our clauses of registration. There is one of them published by the ingenious Monsieur Le Moin, among the other formulas in his Diplomatique Pratique: It is a tack granted by the Officiality of Toul, of a farm in July 1439; the tenants swear to pay the rent, and grant a hypothec upon their whole property in security. They renounce the exceptions of the civil law, and the deed concludes with the following clause: ' Insuper dicti debitores, quod nos ipsos per defectum
' dictae solutionis, per excommunicationis sententiam, compellere
' faciamus, si necesse fuerit, se et sua, quoniam ad hoc jurisdictioni
' et compulsioni curiae nostrae supponentes, ubicumque se duxerunt,
' transferendum; et hoc medio tempore per canonicam monitio-
' nem contra excurrenti; qui quidem debitores de eorum consensu
' moniti fuerunt vivae vocis oraculo per dictum notarium de dicto
' debito, prout in terminis est divisum persolvendum, quod nisi fa-
' cerent, voluerunt, quod pro quolibet termino sententiam excom-
' municationis incurrere absque alia monitione sibi in posterum ab
' hoc facienda. Quare vobis, qui super hoc a latore praesentium
' fueritis requisiti, praecipiendo mandamus, quatenus auctoritate
' nostra dictis terminis praelibatis aut uno eorum, ipsos quos
' nos ex tunc in his scriptis excommunicamus excommunicatos,
' publice nuncietis, usque ad satisfactionem praemissorum condig-
' nam *.'

The

---

* Diplomatique Pratique, vol. i. p. 228.

The ſame preciſe and terrible mode of procedure was univerſal in Scotland.   The clauſe and precept were the warrants
of the letters of excommunication; we term them letters of
curſing, which, in Scotland, were almoſt the only compulſitors for
ages.

  Princes, as I juſt mentioned, ſubmitted themſelves to the Pope.
We may remember the clauſe in James L.'s bond, which I remarked might be termed the clauſe of regiſtration of the times: ' And
' we hereby ſubmit and ſubject ourſelves, our heirs, and ſucceſſors,
' to the coercions, forms, ſtatutes, compulſions, and conſuetudes of
' the chamber of our Lord the Pope, his auditors, vice-auditors, or
' other courts, eccleſiaſtical or ſecular, in which theſe preſent obliga-
' tory letters, or true or authentic tranſumpts thereof, may be produ-
' ced,' &c. Lewis XII. of France, became indebted to that royal money
broker Henry VII. of England, in the large ſum of 74,000 crowns.
Lewis not only granted a complete and formal bond, upon the 4th
of July 1498, binding himſelf by every tie divine and human,
but Henry further obliged him to procure, at his own expence, a
bull of excommunication from the Pope, in order to inſure and inforce the payment.   The bull of excommunication was accordingly
procured and delivered ; it is publiſhed in Mr Rymer's invaluable
collection.

  Theſe were the clauſes of regiſtration, known among our anceſ-
tors, and ſuch were the executorials which iſſued upon them. Our
letters of horning are innocent weapons in compariſon with bulls of
excommunication, or letters of curſing ; and yet we ſhould deem it
an unpardonable act of oppreſſion, to oblige a debtor to raiſe and deliver diligence againſt himſelf ; but there was a reaſon for this ; letters of curſing could be iſſued before the term of payment, becauſe
they were conditional, and directed againſt the ſoul and conſcience.
Unleſs, therefore, a real failure or breach of oath took place, the
parties could not be curſed by the letters.

Of

Of old, there was no execution againſt the perſon for payment of debt; the only method of obtaining that advantage againſt the debtor, was to make him conform to the ſolemnities I have mentioned, *i. e.* to ſubmit to the direct juriſdiction of the church courts, and to conſent to his own excommunication. If the letters of curſing were accordingly iſſued againſt him, and he continued forty days without giving obedience; or, as the churchmen ſaid, obſtinate and unrepentant, then letters of caption were iſſued againſt him at the King's inſtance, not upon account of his failure in payment or performance of his contract, but for his wicked and horrible contempt of the cenſures of the Church.

We have an early act of Parliament in behalf of this matter, viz. c. 12. of the 6th Parliament of James II. Sir George M'Kenzie has taken no notice of this act, though extremely intereſting to the hiſtory of our law. The letters of curſing, and the caption, are by the act called the *old law;* and the improvement thereby introduced, is, that, in caſe the unhappy debtor withdraws his perſon, his lands are to be ſubject to execution.

Whatever was produced in an action to found a démand againſt any party, was with us, as among the Romans, and our neighbours the Engliſh, entered upon the record, there to remain *in futuram rei memoriam.* The ſentence ſigned by the judge remained, and a copy or extract was atteſted by the clerk, and delivered to the party in whoſe favour the judgment happened to be given. Upon this head Balfour has preſerved a very ſpecial authority : ' All ſentences and rollments of court, given by only ſheriff, ſtewart, baillie, provoſt, ' or any other judge within this realm, aucht and ſould be inſert in ' the court buik, extracted furth thereof, and ſubſcribed be the ' clerk of court; utherways, albeit the ſame be ſubſcribed be the ' judge, it is of nane avail, and makes na faith in judgment, or ' outwith the ſame. Aprile 1535, Thomas Spottiſwood againſt David Spottiſwood.'

When

When parties, in their contracts, confented to execution againſt
themſelves, by letters of curfing, the ſentence of the biſhop or his
official contained a preamble reciting the procedure and production;
then followed an exact copy of the deed; and, laſt of all, the ſentence of curſing, and warrant for the letters. The Pope's bulls of
excommunication did the ſame. The notaries in the civil inferior
courts, and the judges in our ſupreme one, were almoſt all eccle-
ſiaſtics. They knew no other form, and they conſtantly adhered to
it; of this we ſhall afterwards meet with many inſtances.

At this period (I mean during the reign of the five Jameſes) our
law regarding the effects of decreets, was quite different from what
it is now. Debts did not rank upon the property of the debtors,
according to priority of diligence, as came afterwards to be the caſe;
the antient maxim, which, as you have heard, continued to be the
law of England at this moment, then remained. The eſtate of the
debtor ſtood bound by the judgment of court, and not by the execution following upon it. Here is direct evidence upon a point,
one of the moſt material in the progreſs of our juriſprudence, which
now ſeems to be totally forgotten: ' Divers and ſundrie decreets
' (ſays Balfour) beand obtenit by divers and ſundry perſounes a-
' gainſt ony man, gif the obtainaris thairof cauſe arreſt his maillis,
' fermis, and duties in his tenants hands, for payment to be made
' to them thairof, the tenants aucht and ſould pay firſt to him quha
' obtenit the firſt decreet, and he beand fully and completely payit,
' they ſould make payment to him quha obtenit the ſecund decrete;
' and he beand completely payit, they ſould conſequentlie pay the
' reſt of the creditors quha obtained decreets, and cauſed arreſt-
' mentis to be maid, after the ordour and priority of time in ob-
' taining of their decreets. 5th Junii 1538, Earl of Crawfurd's
' tenants *contra* James Rolloch *.'

                                                              The

* Balfour, p. 391.

The form of the mandate, which in England produced the warrant to confess, and, in Scotland, the clause of registration, *i. e.* the procuratory to consent that a decree may immediately be given against the party, is evidently borrowed from the practice in the Apostolic Chamber. Our clergy were perpetually soliciting benefices, and transacting business at the Court of Rome. When any change, resignation, or other act was to be done by one man in favour of another, the former granted a procuration to resign to an agent at Rome. This agent appeared in the chancery, and performed the business for which he was appointed; as it was generally to consent to something in name of his constituent, the principal procuratory, and the act remained in the chancery, and the consent was noted on the back of the new letters, or other grant, in these terms: ' *Dictus A.* ' *per illustrem virum D. procuratorem suum literarum expeditioni con-* ' *sensit.*' This is not only the exact form, but the language of our registrations,—*consenting to the expeding of the letters* ; and it is certain, that, during the period when this form was common at Rome, the mandate or procuratory of consent, was equally common in all the courts of Scotland, both ecclesiastical and secular.

The scandalous abuse of the process of excommunication, and the trifling purposes to which it had been applied, contributed not a little to throw an odium upon the old religion, at the dawn of the Reformation. In place of curing the radical evil, and giving dignity to the censures of the church, by reserving them for the proper objects, the prelates thought only of increasing the severity of the process of excommunication, and giving it a double effect upon the civil business of the nation, with which it had not the least natural connection. This mistaken policy produced the act of Parliament 6th James V. c. 9. the violence of which was totally unsuited to the times, and hastened the downfal of the system it was intended to support.

This

This monster of a statute holds out to creditors all the terrors, divine and human, against their miserable debtors, upon condition that they will apply to the church, in preference to the secular judge. They are to have the old caption against the person; they are to have letters for poinding their moveables, and apprising their heritage; and, lastly, they are to have letters of four forms, to make the debtor a rebel to the King, as well as to God, in case the obligation was to perform any thing; for, at that period, letters of horning could not be issued for liquid debts. Another act in the same spirit passed in the 4th Parliament of Queen Mary, c. 7. which forfeited the moveables of the party, who presumed to remain under the sentence of cursing, for the space of a year.

The Reformers did not fail to make a proper use of this folly of their adversaries. John Knox, in his account of the Reformation, paints in lively colours the ridicule which the people began to throw upon this once awful process, which had for ages been the terror of their ancestors.

The Lords of the Congregation were no sooner in power, than they issued a proclamation, for suppressing the church judicatories, and, in particular, the practice of excommunication for civil debts. However plausible and beneficial this might at first appear, great complaints arrived from all quarters, of the inconvenience which the people suffered from the want of the church courts, and the violent stop in the business of the kingdom, which their suppression had created. Notwithstanding the Reformation taking place, and the complete revolution of the antient religion and government of the church, yet did the Reformers find themselves under the necessity of reviving the consistorial jurisdiction, which had appeared the most exceptionable of any part of the old fabric. About four years after the date of the last proclamation, an act of council was passed for erecting commissariot jurisdictions in the kingdom, and

empowering

empowering a number of noblemen to draw up articles and inftructions, for the direction and government of the new courts. Thefe inftructions are to be found annexed to Balfour's Practics. The thirteenth and fourteenth articles afford a full, diftinct, and fatisfactory proof, of the account given of the proceedings of the church courts in Scotland, of the methods they took to engrofs the civil bufinefs of the nation, and particularly the decreets of regiftration.

It is here proper to ftop, in order to confider for a little the nature of the act. The Englifh, in their warrant to confefs judgement, have preferved the effential characters of the bufinefs, which is a regular judicial decreet.; and the only difference between that, and an ordinary one, is, that the procurator for the debtor, in place of defending the action, confeffes that the demand is juft, and confents that the judge may award the fum againft his party. For this reafon, an action muft ftill be brought, the purfuer, or an attorney for him, muft appear, and produce the bond or other deed ; a feparate procurator for the defendant muft alfo appear, with the warrant to confefs, which is the reafon that thefe warrants are at this moment granted on a feparate paper from the bonds.

In Scotland, the difference originally was not great ; when a deed contained a fubmiffion to a particular jurifdiction, the firft ftep of the procedure was the production of the deed in prefence of the judge to whom the fubmiffion was made. If the deed went no further than a fubmiffion, it only founded the jurifdiction of that judge, whofe bufinefs it was to iffue a fummons againft the party ; but, if the writing contained a procuratory, confenting to a decreet, and to its execution, then another procurator, of whom the purfuer had the nomination, appeared and confented in terms of the mandate. It behoved the decree then to be regulated by the terms of the deed ; and as the deed was the only warrant of the decree, there being no debate about the matter, it was of confequence copied into the roll of court, kept by the clerk as the warrant, and an extract of the whole procedure given out under the hands of the clerk, for the purpoſe of execution.

The form of this buſineſs was ſettled at a very early period. In Balfour's Practics, we have the general revocation executed by Queen Mary, according to the cuſtom of the Scottiſh Princes, at their acceſſion to the throne. It is dated 20th June 1555, and bears a conſent : ' That this our declaration be intimated, inſinuated, and ' declared, in the next Parliament to be had in our burgh of Edin- ' burgh.' It bears no mandate to a procurator, becauſe the King's Advocate is the eſtabliſhed procurator for the Crown. The regi- ſtration which follows, is the preciſe form ſtill retained in all our decrees of regiſtration. It conſiſts of three parts, firſt the preſent- ment of the deed, and the requeſt of the Advocate ; ſecond- ly, the conſent of the Queen Dowager and Parliament, the judges in this affair ; and, thirdly, the execution of the re- queſt, *i. e.* the interpoſition of their authority in terms there- of.

In this place, I beg leave to repeat the propoſition, with which I prefaced this diſcourſe, that properly ſpeaking there is no ſuch thing as a regiſter eſtabliſhed for perſonal deeds. They were originally, and ſtill continue to be recorded, mere- ly as the warrants of the decreets following upon them. All our other regiſters, for the purpoſes of preſervation or publi- cation, were eſtabliſhed by particular acts of Parliament ; where- as the regiſtration of perſonal deeds aroſe from the natural forms of ordinary judicial procedure in our courts ; and are of much higher antiquity than any ſtatutory regiſtrations known either in England or Scotland. It is true, that the evident advantages ariſing from this mode of procedure, led people to adopt the very ſame method in the regiſtration of deeds, for the purpoſes of ſimple preſervation, a purpoſe for which they ſaw, at an early period, a particular regiſter erected. I mean the regiſter of reverſions eſta- bliſhed by James III.

It

It is neceffary to take this diftinct branch of the bufinefs of regi-ftration along with us, becaufe the pofterior laws and regulations, which I am foon to notice in their order, relate indifcriminately both to the regiftration for execution, and for prefervation, two things evidently different in their purpofes. This laft it was, which gave to our decreets of confent, upon claufes of regiftration, the title of *regifters*, and has occafioned the confounding of thefe decrees with our regifters, properly fo called, eftablifhed by act of Parliament.

As far back as can be traced, it was the practice on the continent to execute deeds, contracts, and tranfactions of every kind, in pre-fence of notaries. The parties themfelves could not write; and, therefore, they appeared before a notary and witneffes, and verbally made their agreements. The notary took notes or minutes of what had been agreed upon in his Protocol, and then delivered an ex-tract figned by himfelf, extended in due form, with all the claufes of common ftyle. This extract anfwered the purpofes of a principal deed. When the parties at any time found it neceffary to have au-thentic copies of the whole, or any part of thefe deeds, in order to be delivered to perfons concerned, or tranfmitted to diftant places, they appeared with a notary and witneffes in prefence of the judge, in the jurifdiction where they refided, but in general before the official or church court, produced the principal writing, and requeft-ed that it might be examined; and, if found to be valid and fuffi-cient, that the whole or certain parts of it might be copied and ex-tracted from the principal deed, and declared to be equally good and probative as the principal. At that period, there was no fuch practice known as the depofiting thefe deeds in the courts by way of regifter. Every thing was done by thefe kind of copies, attefted by a number of notaries, or certified by judges.

All deeds, private and public, were then written in Latin. The moft antient name given to a copy of this kind, was that of *exem-plum*; but afterwards a number of new epithets were found out for

this,

this, as well as every thing elfe relating to law or form, viz. *tranflatum, tranfcriptum, tranfumptum, vidimus,* &c. Of thefe, the word *tranfumpt* and *vidimus* came afterwards to be particularly diftinguifhed. When princes or great men gave copies from their archives of charters, or other deeds of confequence, they attefted them with their own authority, beginning with the word *vidimus.* When the charter, or other grant, was meant to be confirmed or renewed, the writing began with the word *infpeximus,* and took its title from that word. All private deeds, attefted, or, as the French fay, legalifed, by public courts, got the univerfal name of *tranfumpts.* Of all thefe forts of copies, nothing now remains but the notorial copy.

Thefe were the only methods of preferving or extracting writings among our anceftors in the thirteenth and fourteenth centuries. About this laft period, when decrees of regiftration upon confent came to be known, and the practice had turned common and familiar of fubmitting to the jurifdiction of the church-courts by fpecial claufes, the conveniency and advantage of having the principal deed depofited in the record of the public courts came to be perceived; and therefore, at firft for the direct purpofe, and afterwards, under the pretence of fubmitting or prorogating the jurifdiction of particular judges, mandates were inferted for the appointment of procurators to confent to the regiftration of deeds, for the fole purpofe of their prefervation *in publica cuftodia,* or, as the claufe then bore, *in futuram rei memoriam.* In this manner the feveral courts of law in Scotland came to hold regifters, and were made the cuftodiaries of perfonal deeds, without any fpecial eftablifhment, act of parliament, or grant from the crown, as is the cafe of all the other regifters in the kingdom.

In France, they adhered for a long period to the ftrict ideas of the civil law *infinuations.* The edicts, as in Rome, made them only neceffary in the cafe of donations, and the tranfmiffion of ecclefiaftical benefices. At laft, about the 1553, a regifter, properly fpeaking, of perfonal deeds, was eftablifhed in that kingdom. Sir George M'Kenzie

zie is certain, that they borrowed the practice from the Scots, which is not improbable, as their connection with us, at this particular period, was close and constant.

The laws, and the alterations I am now to speak to, will indiscriminately regard the matter of registration both for execution and preservation. When they respect one of these things only, I shall take proper notice of it. We left the history of this business as it stood at the Reformation; and, from the instructions to the new commissariote, at that time erected, it appeared, that, notwithstanding of the clauses of confent or mandates, the act of registration still retained its original and judicial formalities; that it behoved the judge to be present, and to know the parties contractors; and that it also behoved him to interpose his authority, and award the registration in judgment, in the same manner as he pronounced any other decreet, excepting in cases of ten pounds Scots, or under. These essential forms continued, to the great benefit of the lieges; of which we have the clearest evidence from the 4th act of the 9th parliament of James VI. All writings were at that time sealed by the parties, in the same manner as they always have been, and still are, in England. The purpose of the seal, as of the subscription, was to prevent forgery; but forgery could not happen in writs that were registered in the presence of a judge, who had knowledge of the parties. The act of parliament therefore declares, ' That the former ' statute appointing the sealing of writs of importance, is not to be ' understood of fik writs, contracts, and obligations, as are by the ' parties agreed upon to be registered in the books of our sovereign ' Lord's council, or other ordinary judges, seeing the parties consent ' to register the same, quhilk is *ane greater folemn act* nor the sealing ' thereof.'

At the date of this statute, then, viz. in the 1554, registration continued to be a folemn act; and this solemnity was universal in all the courts of the kingdom, as well as in that of the commissaries. As the solemnities of registration thus lessened the formalities of subscription,.

fcription, fo, when the folemnities of the former became totally fictitious, additional fecurities were required to the latter, and were accordingly introduced by the act 1681, as we fhall afterwards have
occafion more particularly to notice.   Even regiftration, for the fole
purpofe of preferving deeds, as I formerly obferved, could only,
even at this late period, be obtained *in forma judicii.* Of this we
have the moft complete evidence from the act 269. of the 15th parliament of James VI. *anno* 1597. It ordains, ' That all regiftrations
' of letters of horning, relaxations, inhibitions, &c. before what-
' fomever fheriff, fteward, or baillies, as well of royalty or regality,
' be either regiftered in time coming, judicially, or before ane notar,
' and four famous witneffes, by and attour the ordinar clerk.' This
act is complete evidence of the doctrine, that all forts of regiftrations
were for ages confidered in another light than that of formal decrees
of court. Even though the regiftration of the diligences here mentioned were ordained by act of parliament, yet it behoved this to be
done judicially, or at leaft before a notary, and four famous witneffes,
befides the ordinary clerk. If the party appeared when the judge
was fitting, and produced his letters in judgment for regiftration, he
was entitled to an act of court upon the fact, and to an extract of
that act for the probation of it. But letters of inhibition having formerly been ordained by parliament to be recorded within forty days
from the date of the publication, it fometimes happened that the inferior courts did not fit within that period ; and therefore a notary
public is raifed to be a judge *pro hac vice,* under the check of four
witneffes, in order that the ftatute refpecting inhibitions might be
literally obeyed, and the judicial folemnities of regiftration preferved.
Without attending to the original principles of regiftration, and to
the hiftory I have given, this act of parliament would be utterly
unintelligible ; and accordingly, Sir George M'Kenzie, and our
other fyftematic writers, have been obliged to pafs it over in filence.

In

·In the days of Sir Thomas Craig, the folemnities of regiftration began to fall off, and the act itfelf to vanifh into a mere fiction. ' Regiftrationes,' fays he, ' quae tantum in judicio fieri debebant, ' ubicunque vel ipfe regiftrarius, vel ejus deputatus adeft, licite fiunt*.'

As judgment in England could not be confeffed without the appearance of a procurator to authorife him, fo in Scotland, even at this period, it behoved the blank in the mandate of regiftration to be filled up before a decreet of regiftration could be granted. The creditor in the obligement was poffeffed of this mandate in the fame manner as the Englifh creditor was in poffeffion of the mandate to confefs. He therefore filled up the name of an advocate in the blank, and got him *de facto* to fign a confent at the foot of the deed to the pronouncing of a decreet in the terms thereof. This formality was found to be troublefome and inconvenient when regiftration came to be looked upon as a matter of courfe. It was therefore difpenfed with by an act of federunt of date the 9th of December 1670.

The prefence of the judge had been, it feems, practically difpenfed with for a confiderable time before. The regifter, or his depute, were fufficient; confequently decreets of regiftration came to be given at all hours of the day, upon the requeft of the creditor, or obligee in deeds. A defender, however, was ftill requifite. The act of federunt difpenfed with the very fhadow of him. The whole, then, was thus made to confift in handing the writing to the keeper of the record, juft as at prefent; and the keeper, by the act, had authority to fill up the blank in the mandate with the name of any advocate he pleafes. From this time forward, it was no wonder that the bufinefs got the name of regiftering, and the place in which the deed was depofited, the title of regifter.

Before taking leave of this period, it is proper to remark, that, when the folemnity of regiftration exifted, in place of the fhort claufe,

* Page 240.

claufe, which took place after the date of this act of federunt, deeds of importance contained a complete procuratory with all the claufes of ftyle, equal in length to the Englifh warrant, and containing all the phrafes commonly ufed in our folemn procuratories in heritable deeds *.

We are arrived at the period of St Martin's own claufe of regiftration, with a commentary upon which l propofe to clofe this fubject.

    ' And for the more fecurity, we are content, and confent thir pre-
' fents be infert and regiftrate in the books of council and feffion,
' or others competent, to have the ftrength of a decreet of the Lords,
' or judges thereof, interponed thereto, that letters of horning on
' fix days, and others neceffar, in form as effeirs, may be direct here-
' upon ; and to that effect conftitute

our procurators,' &c.

And for the more fecurity.—Thefe words are as old as the practice of regiftration itfelf. They allude to that period of the antient law, when decreets or judgments took place, not according to the dili-gence or execution of them, as they do now, but to the date of the decreet, as is the cafe in England at this moment ; and therefore the Englifh, when they want further fecurity for their bonds or oblige-ments, infift upon having a warrant to confefs judgment, in the fame manner as we would do an affignation to a debt, or an heritable bond upon land.

In the books of council and feffion.—l formerly obferved, that of old the churchmen made ufe of the claufe of regiftration to draw ci-vil bufinefs to their courts. When parties confented to the regiftra-tion in the books of a particular court, it imported a voluntary pro-rogation of the jurifdiction of the judge to be chofen. Thence it is, that, in the inftructions to the commiffaries, they are difcharged from judging upon contracts, or other deeds, regiftrated in the books of any other judges. As the churchmen had introduced the practice

of

* Vide Carruther's Styles, p. 6.

of condefcending upon particular judges, it appears, that it continued to be done for a confiderable time. Inconveniencies, however, occurred. The granters of the deeds fometimes retired out of the jurifdiction, and confequently gave defiance to the judges warrant. To remedy this, two or three different courts in the neighbourhood were mentioned, and often all the different courts in the kingdom. This was evidently troublefome and prolix. At laft about the 1670, it fettled in the ftyle of our text: ' In the books of Council and ' Seffion, or any other judges books competent.'

The word *books* relates to the circumftance of copying the writs given in to be regiftered in books kept for the purpofe, feparated from the ordinary record of court, which gives this bufinefs ftill more the appearance and character of a proper regifter. The clerks of inferior courts, without the leaft attention to their own jurifdictions, endeavoured to increafe their bufinefs of regiftration, by taking in writs granted by any perfons whatfoever, in confequence of the general terms of the claufes of regiftration above-mentioned, The Lord Clerk Regifter, however, obtained an act of Parliament c. 38. of James VII. 1ft Parliament 1685, for regulating the public offices, in which he took care to have a check given to this practice of the inferior courts. This ftatute is now little attended to by the clerks of the inferior courts, who take in every deed offered them, providing the claufe of regiftration admits of it; but, in cafes where parties are defigned in the deed, as locally refiding without the jurifdiction, I fhould think a good objection would lie upon the ftatute, becaufe the execution fhould proceed in virtue of letters of horning obtained in the ufual manner upon a bill, or petition, to the Lords; yet the decreet of regiftration of the inferior court is the true warrant of thefe letters; and the bill to the Lords fuppofes that warrant to be regular and valid.

' *To have the ftrength of a decreet of the Lords interponed thereto.*' —Thefe words are among the oldeft ufed in this mandate They relate to the period I have already mentioned, when decreets took

VOL. I.   P   effect

effect from their own dates, as the judgments do in England ; and, therefore, the English writers always term the effect of their warrant to confefs judgment, by faying that it ftrengthens other fecurities. Thus Judge Blackftone : ' And, therefore, it is very ufual, ' in order to ftrengthen a creditor's fecurity, for the debtor to exe- ' cute a warrant of attorney to any one, empowering him to confefs ' a judgment *.' Thefe remaining words of our claufe of regiftration clearly prove, that, as Lord Kames has averred, the Englifh bond in judgment, and the Scottifh regiftrable bond, have been originally the fame. Our decreet of regiftration, properly fpeaking, adds neither additional fecurity nor ftrength to our bond, it only gives expediency and difpatch ; but, though decreet be obtained, the creditor is neither fecured nor ftrengthened, unlefs he proceeds to execution by diligence, whereas the ftrength and fecurity in England lie, and formerly did lie with us, in the decreet itfelf.

' *That letters of horning upon fix days and others neceffar may be* ' *direct.*'—After the effect of decreets came to depend upon the diligence which followed upon them, the practice of mentioning that circumftance in the claufe naturally took place. Of old, as I formerly noticed, there was no diligence againft the perfon of a debtor, but by the ftrange circuit of excommunication ; letters of poinding and arreftment were executed againft his moveables, and apprifing againft his land, unlefs the demand confifted in *facta praeftanda*, and then letters of horning iffued againft him upon four charges, commonly called letters of four forms. The claufes of regiftration in this ftate of things did not fpecify the particular diligence, but left that matter to the direction of the law. But by the antient eftablifhed law of Scotland, no letters or executorials of any kind in civil matters could be iffued, but upon fifteen days from the date of the decreet, which were then termed,

and

and are fo ftill, *the days of law*; and this it feems had even been
the cafe in criminal matters. The firft inftance of this rule being
difpenfed with in Scotland, was in the cafe of the Earl of Huntly in
the year 1562. Queen Mary, in an expedition to the north, required admiffion to the caftle of Finlater. It was refufed by thofe
who held it for the Earl of Huntly; and a party fent by the Queen
to demand the furrender, were furprifed and defeated by the Earl's
fon. Upon this both the Earl and his fon were charged to prefent
themfelves perfonally before the Queen and council, within fix
days, under the pain of rebellion, and being denounced rebels.
' Whether this was law or not (fays John Knox) we difpute little
' thereuntil; but it was a preparative to others that were afterwards
' ferved with the fame meafures.' The charge was indeed difobeyed. Huntly prefented himfelf with an army, and was defeated and
killed at Correchy Burn near Aberdeen. The perfons whom Knox
alludes to, as afterwards ferved with the fame meafure, were the
ruffian confpirators who murdered David Rizzio. The Queen
charged them to appear before her and council, within fix days, under the pain of rebellion, and putting them to her Majefty's horn.
Complaint was made, ' That this had never been ufed in Scotland
' before; and that the fame was invented by her Majefty's coun-
' fellors, who underftood not law *.'

One of the moft frightful and abfurd fingularities in the law of
Scotland, was, that little difference exifted in punifhment, between
the non-performance of a civil contract, and an act of treafon by
real difobedience to the prince. People were equally denounced rebels for the one as for the other; the days of charge were the fame;
and, therefore, it was, that the abridging them from fifteen to fix,
was deemed by the multitude to be an illegal act. The practice
once eftablifhed, came foon to be introduced into the civil effect of
the diligence, and no fooner were letters of horning awarded by

P 2   law

---

* Append. Keith, p. 29.

law upon liquid debts, than creditors, taking advantage of the
clause of registration, forced their debtors to abridge the days of,
law by confent, from fifteen to fix, and hence the necessity of the
words : ' That letters of horning on fix days may be directed.'
Where no days are mentioned, the fifteen days of law are under-
flood under the words *in form as effeirs* ; and the letters of horning
muft bear that charge accordingly. Whether thefe fix days could
be again fhortened by confent, is a queftion undetermined. In my
own opinion, I think they could not ; becaufe denounciation cannot
in the nature of the thing take place, without a previous charge,
which is likewife neceffary by particular act of Parliament, before-
poinding can be executed. Six days has been held to be the *mini-
ma* of thefe purpofes, for near 200 years ; and I apprehend, that no
further alteration would now be tolerated.

' *Letters of horning and others neceffar as effeirs.*'—By the words.
others neceffar, are meant letters of arreftment, poinding, inhibition,.
and apprifing, which were fometimes feparately taken out ; though,
in St Martin's time, horning, poinding, arreftment, and apprifing,
were given in the fame warrant or letters.

Having thus explained or annalifed the mandate for regiftration
itfelf, I proceed to take notice of the changes it has undergone in-
the eye of law, from the beginning of the fixteenth century, to the
prefent time.

As one of the original purpofes of claufes of regiftration, had been
to confer a jurifdiction upon a particular judge the effect of this came
to be doubted and tried ; but by repeated decifions it was found, that
the confent did not prorogate ; and that it went no further than to fupport the diligence following upon the decreet of regiftration, without
conferring any judicial power. If parties mean that this fhould be done
in any particular cafe, they muft return to the antient method of
inferting a fpecial claufe for that purpofe. The difficulty, however,
would remain in what manner the party was to be cited out of the
jurifdiction

jurifdiction of the judge; this could only be done by means of letters of diligence from the Court of Seffion; and whether they would fupport fuch a claufe, by granting the letters, is a mute point.

A claufe of regiftration being merely a perfonal mandate, they fell, like all other mandates, under the rule of the Roman law: ' Morte mandatoris perimitur mandatum.' Hence they became ufelefs after the death of either the debtor or creditor, the granter or receiver. The fame confequence attended, and ftill attends the Englifh warrant to confefs judgment. No decreet can proceed at the inftance of a dead man againft a living, or at the inftance of a living againft a dead perfon. The heirs of the creditor, therefore, could not have a decreet of regiftration, without making up a title to their predeceffors, and exhibiting that title before a judge. In general, it was an eftablifhed rule during the fixteenth century, that though third parties had a direct intereft in any deed or contract, they could not regifter it after the death of one of the parties contractors againft the other. An ordinary action was the only remedy.— Shanks againft Eifton, January 15. 1635 *. And in the cafe Channel againft Sir Walter Seton, 16th February 1693†, the Lords found the regiftration by an affignee after the cedent's death was informal, becaufe regiftration was a decreet of confent, requiring an actor and a *reus, i. e.* a purfuer and defender, and the actor being dead, there could be no regiftration at his inftance.

With regard to the heirs of the debtor, a perfon at firft would imagine, that a common decree to conftitute the debt in the ordinary method, would have proved equally expeditious and effectual; but upon inquiry, we fhall immediately difcover, that confiderable advantages attended the action of regiftration. The principal of thefe was the prefervation of the deed itfelf; and, accordingly, this was one of the principal conclufions of the

summons,

* Durie, p. 742.　　　† Stair.

ſummons, *viz.* that the deed may remain in *publica cuſtodia,* which could not be demanded in any other caſe.

Another effect was, that execution proceeded in the ſame manner, and upon the ſame ſhort charge or *induciae,* as it would have done in virtue of the clauſe of regiſtration. Thus in a caſe, the ſeuers of Chappleton againſt Ernock, 1ſt December 1630, the Lords refuſed to ſuſtain the action of regiſtration, at the ſingular ſucceſſor's inſtance, for ſummary execution upon ſix days, but ordained him to purſue by an ordinary action.

By the act of the 4th ſeſſion of William and Mary's 1ſt Parliament, c. 15. this inconvenience was remedied, and the mandate for regiſtration was taken out of the rule of the Roman law. The act provides, that the holder of the deed requiring regiſtration, ſhall produce a right to it in his own perſon; and, in that caſe, he became entitled to the extract or decreet in his own name. This neceſſity went ſoon into diſuſe. The fees of the regiſtration, and the competition of the clerks offices, inclined them to diſpenſe with every ceremony or obſtruction, and now for a long time, any perſon offering a deed, gets it regiſtered without any queſtions aſked.

This practical alteration, though deſtructive of every idea of regiſtration as a decreet, has added to the convenience of the thing, while at the ſame time, the conſequence intended to be guarded againſt, by the proviſo in the act 1693, is more effectually done by another method alſo introduced by practice. The extract always bears the deed to be regiſtered at the requeſt of the granter or debtor, whether dead or alive; but, before any ſtep of diligence can be taken upon it by the heir of the creditor, or other perſon having right, he muſt produce the title (which by the act ought to have been produced at the regiſter) to a Writer to the ſignet, who gives in a common bill or petition, narrating the title, and praying for a horning or diligence, in name of the heir or executor, which title is examined by the clerk to the bills, and ſuppoſed to be examined by the Lord Ordinary, whoſe deliverance becomes then the warrant of

the

the diligence. The analogy of the act 1693, is the alledged foundation for this practice; but the ftatute goes upon the juft principles of regiftration, which the practice has entirely deferted. It was no great ftretch to continue a mandate in force, after the death of the granter, where the benefit of fuch mandate was intended for another party. In many cafes, the law does this without the interpofition of the Legiflature; but the act never authorifed any thing fo anomalous, fo inconfiftent, as an action and decree at the inftance of a dead man. It provides that the heir or perfon having right to procuratory, fhould produce it before regiftration, and that the extract fhould go out in that perfon's name. And, accordingly, his title was fpecified in the preamble of the extract; whereas, in practice, as I have faid, decrees of regiftration are every day taken in the names of perfons who are no more.

The act 1693 difpenfed with the procefs of regiftration only in the cafe of the death of the creditor; but, to render the convenience of regiftration complete, another act paffed about three years after the former, which beftowed the fame privilege after the death of the granter or debtor.

Both thefe ftatutes are in direct oppofition to the principle of mandates and decreets, for here a decreet was awarded againft parties deceafed, without any falvo or condition. The falvo, however, arofe from the nature of the thing,—the decreet of regiftration can have no effect againft the heirs of the granter, until a paffive title is proved, and the character of heir eftablifhed by a fecond formal decreet of conftitution founded upon legal evidence. The prefervation of the deed is the only advantage attained by it, and it was a very fmall ftretch to preferve the effect of a mandate for fuch a beneficial purpofe, after the death of the mandator. Accordingly, a writ regiftered after the deceafe of the granter, was allowed to have the effect of a decreet of tranfumpt.

This

This laft act naturally occafioned the conditions and principles of the former one to be totally neglected. After the death of the granter or receiver, the actual appearance of a procurator and the perfonal appearance of a judge became quite unneceffary, and thefe laft turned fo frequent that every diftinction was dropped, fo that the matter of regiftration has ever fince funk into an abfolute fiction.

A regiftered writing, however, notwithftanding it was gradually divefted of its formalities, continues in effect and execution, the fame as a decreet in abfence, taken upon or in terms of an unregiftered deed; as both paffed in abfence, objections are receiveable againft them, but not by exception. Actions of fufpenfion and *reduction* are neceffary to fet them afide, which lays the debtor under the neceffity of finding caution, and affords feveral other advantages to the creditor; nor is the grand objection of falfehood receiveable in any other fhape, than a folemn action of improbation.

The claufe of regiftration now in practice, differs in nothing material from thofe of St Martin: ' And we confent to the regiftration ' of thefe prefents (or hereof) in the books of council and feffion, or ' other judges books competent, that letters of horning on fix days ' charge, and all other execution requifite, may be directed upon a ' decree to be interponed hereto in form as effeirs, and for that ' effect we conftitute   our procurators.' This is the form inferted in all cafes where the deed contains obligements upon the granter to do, pay, or perform. Where that is not the cafe, the words are, ' therein to remain for prefervation.' Sometimes, though the purpofe of the deed be only for conveying, *it* contains certain claufes of warrandice, or conditional preftations, in which cafe the ftyle is: ' Therein to remain for prefervation; ' and, if neceffary, that all execution requifite may pafs upon a de- ' cree to be interponed hereto.'

The Testing Clause.

THE same formalities are by the law of Scotland requisite to the testing clause, as we term it, of every probative writing, whether the subject of it be heritable or moveable. It is of the utmost importance; for, upon the accuracy of its execution, the strength and effect of the deed totally depend. The origin and progress of the formalities of which it consists, reach the earliest periods of our law, and involve several questions, equally curious and useful. I have, therefore, bestowed a distinct commentary upon this clause of our deeds, similar to that upon the clause of registration.

Forms and ceremonies were at first introduced, not as parts of, or essential to a bargain, but to make certain evidence of its having been concluded. These forms being principally objects of sight, could exist only in the memory of witnesses, and hence every thing depended upon oral evidence. The lubricity of witnesses, and the doubts in which matters were often left, induced a rude and superstitious people to seek truth by different methods, sometimes by an appeal to heaven, *viz.* by the ordeal or trial by treading over red hot iron, or plunging the arm into boiling water; at other times, by single combat; and often by the person who was accused of a crime or breach of contract, swearing to his innocence, and producing a number of his friends, who joined him in his oath.

To remedy such difficulties in evidence, the practice mentioned on a former occasion was introduced, of parties appearing before a magistrate, and their finishing their agreement in the face of the

VOL. I. Q court

court. The particular fituation, and the inattention of the parties, occafioned this method to be often neglected; in all fuch queftions, therefore, witneffes were of neceffity admitted. By their evidence, every thing was determined, except in cafes of great magnitude and importance, where the extraordinary methods already noticed were reforted to. The art of writing, however, being introduced, experience proved that the evidence thereby afforded was much fuperior to the partial and uncertain declarations of witneffes. The courts of law, therefore, in all cafes, inclined to that evidence, and bent their attention to limit the effect of verbal teftimony.

The firft inftance of this alteration we find in the Quon. Attach. chap. 81. ' All men may prove their debt to the value of 40 fhil- ' lings, be two witneffes who heard and faw the fame, and fwa by ' diverfe witneffes, according to the quantity of the debt.'

Writing is a deliberate ceremony, a lafting fenfual object, and a living picture of the mind and intention of parties. It is not, however, properly fpeaking, the obligation, but only the evidence of the agreement; we ought, therefore, never to confound in our ideas the material or written paper, with the actual preceeding agreement of the parties, which had exiftence from their confent alone.

The art of penmanfhip gradually advanced, but was altogether confined to the clergy. A military people would not fubmit to the acquifition of fuch an inactive employment; and, therefore, though agreements might then be formed into writing, that writing could not be connected with the parties, fo as to authenticate its being their proper act and deed. The antients, I mean the Greeks, and Romans, and the nations connected with them, authenticated their deeds by fubfcriptions, by fuperfcriptions, and fometimes by particular fentences conftantly ufed. The greater part of our anceftors could make no fuch fubfcriptions; but they fupplied it by making the writer annex the names of the witneffes who were prefent at the bufinefs, and prefixing a particular mark, generally the fign of the crofs. The fubfcription by the crofs was an act of religion.

gion as well as neceffity. Sir Henry Spelman, the Englifh antiqua-
ry, fpeaking of the Saxons, tells us, that ' feals they ufed none at all,
' other than (the common feal of Chriftianity) the fign of the crofs,
' which they, and all nations, accounted the moft folemn inviolable
' manner of confirming. So fuperftitioufly did thefe times think of
' the crofs, that they held all things fanctified that bore the fign of
' it ; and, therefore, ufed it religioufly in their charters, as an
' amulet or prefervative againft injuries *.' To thefe barbarous
marks fucceeded the ufe of feals, which, in the form of rings, were
from the earlieft times ufed in the eaft. Princes ufed them as
badges of authority, and power was delegated by delivery of the
royal fignet or feal ring. From the eaft it is fuppofed the cuftom
was introduced among the Greeks and Romans. The former (as
they did every other art) carried the engraving of feals to the greateft perfection ; and next to the ftatues, the moft beautiful and pre-
cious remains of antiquity now in the world, are the engraved gems
ufed by them for private feals. By feals, both public and private,
writs in Rome were in ufe to be authenticated ; and, in the cafe of
teftaments, the witneffes were exprefsly required to affix them.
' Si teftes fuo vel alieno annulo non fignaverint, juri defecit tefta-
' mentum†.' By antiquaries, it is with great probability conjectured, that the ufe of feals defcended from the Romans to the kings
of the Franks, and from the kings to the nobility. The Normans
borrowed this cuftom from the other nations on the continent, and
brought it into England at the conqueft. After that period, the
evidence of a deed depended upon the feal alone, without any fubfcription ; but this practice was liable to many inconveniences ; the
feal, and confequently the writ, might be denied. That the validity
of deeds in England fhould have depended only upon the authen-

Q 2

ticity

---

* Per crucis hoc fignum, fugit hinc procul omne malignum.

Spelman's Remains.

† L. 12. C. de Teft.

ticity of the seal is not to be wondered at, while the nation continued in dark ignorance, and while none but clergymen could read or write ; but that the law should have so remained, when no such necessity existed, and when writing had become common, is certainly surprising. The tenacity of their customs has been supported by an equal integrity of manners, or there must have existed some separate and more effectual cheque, against a fraud in appearance so easily perpetrated.

Our countryman Mr Thomas Ruddiman, is clearly of opinion, that the Scots followed the practice of their neighbours the Anglo-Saxons in the method of authenticating their deeds. Of this (says he) the charter of King Duncan I. in Mr Anderson's collection, affords reasonable evidence. This antient deed is tested by the cross of the king, and crosses made by his brother, who consented to the deed, and the witnesses present.

The sealing by Duncan (continues Mr Ruddiman) was done in imitation of William the Norman, who first introduced the use of seals among the English, and often for the more perfect authenticity, joined both customs together, of writing the names of witnesses below, and likewise of appending the seal. In affairs of great moment, witnesses were inserted at the end of the instrument. This practice we borrowed also from the English, and all our kings, from Duncan, have observed it.

The principal method then of discovering the truth, was by a comparison of seals, as we since compare hand writing. Thus matters continued, so far as can be learned, till the 1429, when an excellent precaution was introduced by the 130th act of James I. 9th Parliament, ordaining all freeholders to compear at the sheriff's head court with their seals, and, if they could not attend, to send their attornies with the seals of their arms, under a fine. Sir George M'Kenzie says, that this act was complied with, and
every

every gentleman sent his seal to the clerks, many of which remained in their hands in his time.

When the antient manner of executing deeds by the crosses and seals
of the granters and the witnesses, went out of practice after the conquest, then every thing was made to depend upon the seal of the
granter alone. Deeds were considered to be nothing more, than
memorandums to keep the circumstances of the agreement or grant
in remembrance ; and, therefore, after being read over in presence
of the witnesses, their names were simply added by the scribe, with
no other preface than *hiis testibus.* Thus *magna charta* is witnessed,
and all the deeds and charters of the Anglo-Norman Princes, down
to Richard I. who altered the style to *teste meipso,* witness ourself,
which is the present form. In private deeds, the attest in general of
hiis testibus, continued down to the reign of Henry VIII. when
writing having become common, the witnesses signed the deeds, either at the foot or on the back, in order to testify their having been
present. In Scotland, the witnesses accidentally present, or standing
by, as Spelman says, continued to be inserted, whether men or women. Thus, a charter by David Earl of Huntingdon, afterwards
David I., is tested in this manner, ' Testimonio Mathildis Reginae
' et Willielmi fili sui.' This method was continued to the reign of
Malcolm IV., where a charter to Walter, Steward of Scotland, bears
hiis testibus, and another of the same Prince has about fifty witnesses, men and women of the first note*. This style came soon
afterwards to be altered to, ' In cujus rei testimonium sigillum nos-
' trum apponi precipimus, testibus,' &c. Deeds by subjects bore,
that the granter had set his seal to them, or caused the same to be
appended ; but it appears, that witnesses were of no consequence ;
only Craig informs us, that, where a party used the seal of another,
mention was made of it, and the person to whom it belonged, and
this, he says, in antient deeds frequently occurred†. Forgeries of
　　　　　　　　　　　　　　　　　　　　　　　　seals,

* Anderson's Col. No. 25.　　　　† P. 259. § 15.

feals, however, became common; and Heineccius, who has treated the fubject with learning and induftry, fpecifies no lefs than fix different methods of falfifying them. About eighty years ago, fays Sir Thomas Craig, full faith was given to charters, although fupported by the feal of the granter alone; but, in regard many inconveniencies happened, after the death of proprietors, either by the fraud of their widows, or of thofe into whofe cuftody the feals happened to come, and that deeds made after the death of the granter, were often found to be fealed with his proper feal; therefore, an act of Parliament was made, in the 1540, to remedy evils of fuch magnitude.

By this act, then, fubfcriptions were firft required; but writing had become a branch of education, and fubfcriptions commonly ufed, long before the act. People had become proud of being able to fign their names, and, unlefs this had been the cafe, the act would have required impoffibilities. Subfcription, however, did not get into fafhion all at once.

Every thing at thefe early periods was preferred, which carried an air of myftery and concealment; fo in place of the full fubfcription, people of confequence figned deeds, by the letters of their own name, and of Chrift or fome tutelar Saint, fancifully and barbaroufly combined. Thefe fubfcriptions, termed *monograms*, were originally ufed in feal rings, and were continued in authenticating writings, for ages after the days of Charlemagne, who is faid to have been the firft Prince who fubfcribed by them.

Malcolm Canmore is faid to have given furnames to his nobility; and others, not named by the King, took their furnames from their lands, and fitted their armorial bearings to thefe names. Buchanan thinks that furnames were introduced at a later period, firft among the French, and then with us; he obferves, that the fecond or diftinguifhing names of the antient Scots, were all taken from fome particular mark or quality of the perfon; or patronimicks from his

father

father or other predecessor ; and the same may be said of the French
and other nations. Accordingly, Father Mabillon remarks, that
surnames began about the commencement of the eleventh century,
being only *nicknames* before that period. Thus, Malcolm had
Canmore, from a large head,—Charles the *Gross,*—William the *Conqueror,*—Richard *Cœur de Lion,* &c.

As no law prevented people from assuming such names as they
pleased, so a latitude in the matter of subscription was also assumed.
The natural vanity of our ancestors was nourished by intercourse
with the French ; from them some signed by their surname without
the Christian name, and many by the name of their lands, altering
the title with their property. This bad practice was not corrected
till the 1669, by the 21st act of the 3d session of the 2d Parliament
of Charles II., which declares, ' That it is only allowable for noble-
' men and bishops to subscribe by their titles ; and that all others
' shall subscribe their christened names, or the initial letter thereof,
' with their surnames ; and may, if they please, adject the designa-
' tion of their lands, prefixing the word *of* to these designations,
' under the pain of being amerced by the Privy Council *.' I now
return to the other requisite of the act 1540, which regards the witnesses to subscription of parties.

Lord Kames notices a great impropriety in our old statutes,
which require the presence of witnesses, without enjoining them
to subscribe, in token that they did witness the obligor's subscription. The observation is just, but it does not apply to the act
1540, though the oldest on this subject. That act expressly requires the subscription, both of the party and of the witnesses. In
his Lordship's statute law, it is, indeed, thus abridged : ' That no
' faith be given to writs, unless the party subscribe *before* wit-
' nesses ;' but, in the act, the word *before* is not to be found ; it requires the ' subscription of him that awe the same (*i. e.* the oblige-
' ment);

* Vol. ii. p. 506. Act concerning the privilege of the Lyon.

' ment) and witness.' The words are doubtless, too loose and general, so was the practice following it, which I shall give in the
words of Mr Erskine : ' As this statute prescribed no plain rule,
' about inserting the names and designations of the witnesses in the
' deed, or about their subscribing as witnesses, the subsequent prac-
' tice was far from uniform. In a few instances, the witnesses sub-
' joined their subscriptions to the deed, without having their names
' inserted in the body of it ; and more frequently, their names were
' inserted without their subscribing. But this last practice afford-
' ing no degree of evidence, that the witnesses inserted were duly
' present at the granter's subscription, since it was in the power
' of the writer, even where the deed was truly signed, *remotis*
' *testibus,* to name any persons whom he pleased as witnesses *.' A
remedy was intended by the 80th act of the 6th Parliament of
James VI. 1579, which statutes, ' That all writs of great import-
' ance should be subscribed and sealed by the principal parties,
' otherways by two famous notars, before four famous witnesses, de-
' nominated by their special dwelling-places, or some other evident
' tokens, that the witnesses may be known, being present at the time,
' other ways to mak na faith.' Sir George M'Kenzie says, that
such writs by this act are to be subscribed and sealed before two famous witnesses. There is not in the act one word of witnesses required to a party's subscription who can write ; but four witnesses
are appointed to be present, and to be designed in the writ, in case
the party cannot write, and when the deed is executed by notaries.
The blunder then noticed by Lord Kames, is not to be found in
this last act ; for, though intended to supply the defects of the preceding statutes, it requires neither witnesses nor their subscriptions ;
the subscription and seal of the party who can write are held to be
sufficient as to his deeds. The error then lay not in our statutes,
but in the practice which deviated from the express appointment of

                                                              the

---

* Large Inst. p. 428.

the act 1540, and supplied what was not required in the 1579, by adhibiting two witnesses to the signing and sealing of parties, and by inserting the names and dwelling-places of these witnesses, in deeds, and thus introduced the imperfect cause mentioned by Lord Kames; for, as he well observes, the testing clause being necessarily inserted before the subscription of the party, cannot otherwise than prophetically be evidence, that the witnesses saw the obligor subscribe.

A mistake so egregious proved in fact almost fatal to the evidence of writings. To require witnesses to the subscription and seal, without any certain evidence of their having been present at the execution of the deed itself, was an evident returning to parole testimony by reducing deeds to dependence upon witnesses; and, consequently, opened a constant source of litigation. The designations of witnesses were allowed to be supplied, or more particularly condescended on; in short, every thing turned upon verbal evidence, and threw part of the property of the subject upon the disposal of the judges, who followed no fixed rule, and determined every case by its own circumstances.

No law or remedy appears till 1593[*]; but this act in place of supplying the imperfections regarding the evidence of witnesses, introduced an additional requisite in the tests of writs, by ordering the writers names and designations to be inserted at the end of all deeds. Though the act was special, pointed, and express, the Court of Session used the greatest freedom with it; upon presumption that the Legislature only meant to make certain of the writer, they allowed him to be condescended on. Though the act appointed the writer to be inserted before the witnesses, they admitted the insertion any where; and, what weakened it still more, they admitted general and uncertain designations, by which means this law was

Vol. I.   R   attended

[*] 13th Parliament James VI. c. 179.

attended with very little effect. Another act, which was made some
years prior to this statute, helped greatly to weaken the atteftation
of writs, viz. c. 4 of the 9th Parliament of James VI. whereby
the fealing of all writs agreed to be regiftrated was difpenfed with.
By this act, it is clear, that fealing remained neceffary in all writs
not agreed to be regiftered, or not containing claufes of regiftration;
but the omiffion in the one cafe induced the omiffion in the other,
and fealing foon thereafter went entirely into difufe, except in public
and private charters.

Matters were allowed to remain on this doubtful footing for upwards of eighty years. Rectification became indifpenfibly neceffary, which was at laft effected by the important act of Charles II.
1681*. This ftatute enacts, That only fubfcribing witneffes, in writs
to be fubfcribed by any party hereafter, fhall be probative, and not
the witneffes inferted not fubfcribing: And that all fuch writs to be
fubfcribed hereafter, wherein the writer and witneffes are not defigned, fhall be null, and are not fuppliable by condefcending upon
the writer, or the defignation of the writer and witneffes: And further, that no perfon fhall fubfcribe as witnefs, unlefs he then know
that party, and faw him fubfcribe. Sir George M'Kenzie tells us,
that this laft part of the act was occafioned by the following remarkable cafe. A gentlewoman pretended that fhe could not write
before company, and defired to fign the paper in her own chamber,
and at her return brought it back fubfcribed, after which fhe raifed
a reduction of the paper as not truly figned by her. The act, laftly,
provides: ' That the witneffes be defigned in the body of the writ
' otherways to be void and null.' This is the laft ftatute in behalf
of the matter of atteftation.

Hitherto, during the long period from the Norman conqueft, to
the reign of Charles II. deeds in England had depended upon the
feal alone; and the atteft was, ' fealed and delivered.' By an act
of

* c. 5. 3d Parl. Char. II.

of the 29th Charles II. a statute was made, requiring all grants of lands, and a number of other deeds there pointed out, to be signed as well as sealed by the party; so the English attest now is, ' sign- ' ed, sealed, and delivered.' The bond itself is evidence of the signing and sealing, and possession is legal evidence of the deli- very.

The present formalities of deeds in both nations came thus to be finally established in the reign of the same Prince; and, in that mat- ter, it is plain that the superiority has fallen to the law of Scotland.

It was formerly mentioned as a matter of surprise, that deeds in England from the Norman conquest to the reign of Charles II. should have entirely depended upon the *authenticity of a seal*, and a hint was given of a separate check, that must have subsisted against frauds so easily brought about. Such a check, then, certainly did exist, with regard to transmissions of land property, in the feudal method of entering the vassal, or giving him investiture before his brethren, named by the feudalists, *pares curiae*, and by delivering afterwards the *breve testatum*, which was not essential to the trans- mission, but a simple memorandum to preserve the circumstances of it in remembrance. The *breve testatum* came only to be frequent, ' cum *fides hominum labescere coeperat*,' says Craig, ' nam antea neque ' brevi hoc testato neque scriptura utebantur, tanta in paribus curiae ' fides et auctoritas erat.' This was the reason that formalities were so little attended to, and that witnesses were only mentioned as such, without subscribing their names. What gave security to the matter was, that, as judges, whenever disputes arose, the *pares curiae*, had the exclusive right of determination. At other times, such sales of lands were executed in the baron, county, or hundred court, in which case the *breve testatum* was verified in these words, *teste comitatu, teste hundredo* &c. This, together with legal re- straints upon alienations, the necessity of the superior's consent in- tervening at a sale, and the possession which behoved necessarily to follow, excluded frauds in a great measure from disturbing the

R 2   rights

. rights of lands, infomuch that conveyance by delivery, without
any writing, remained in England till the reign of Charles II. and
Craig affures us, that, in the highlands of Scotland, lands were
tranfmitted, in his time, by feizin *propriis manibus* of the fuperior.
With regard to moveables, the old Saxon cuftom was continued by
the Normans, of tranfacting bufinefs in prefence of their courts;
and, afterwards, by the various recognizances introduced by ftatute formerly explained, which rendered tranfactions of importance almoft independent of private formalities.

From caufes of the fame kind, the inconveniencies arifing from
the imperfections of the acts 1540, and 1579, were avoided in Scotland, which, at firft fight, would feem to have been intolerable.
Our forms in real rights were much better calculated than thofe in
England, to exclude impofition and forgery, not only in their own
nature, but from the fyftem of regifters, the greateft part of which
were introduced in that period; and in moveables, the fafe-guard lay
in the act of regiftration, which was not a. fiction, but a judicial
procefs, that put the attefts of the deeds of thefe times out of the
power of the granter to quarrel.

The infertion of a date in deeds, is not required by any exprefs.
- law; Lord Stair, however, holds it to be *de fubftantialibus*, when the
queftion regards the truth or authenticity of the writing. Mr Erfkine differs from his Lordfhip's opinion; ' as folemnities (fays he).
' are not to be multiplied without a warrant either from ftatute or.
' univerfal cuftom, deeds have been adjudged valid, without mention.
' either of the place or the time of figning;' and for this he cites two
decifions,—February 15. 1706, Duncan; and July 21. 1711,
Ogilvie *.

In very antient deeds no dates are to be found. There is no date
in the charter of Duncan, nor in many of the older deeds in Mr An-
derfo 's collection. The clergy firft began to infert dates in their.
writings;

* Erfkine, p. 433. § 18.

writings; but these being generally taken from their church feasts, were very uncertain, and often created great confusion : ' In. anti-
' quis monumentis (says Craig) data, ut ab hominibus priscae sim-
' plicitatis, solebant omitti *.'

Though writings of great antiquity be often found without dates, it has been the universal usage of writers, for centuries past, carefully to insert both the true date and place in the testing clause of all their deeds. If either of these are omitted, or indistinctly expressed, it is a slovenly omission ; at the same time, if any surmise of suspicion arises, or any reason can be assigned for supposing a designed neglect, every presumption will be admitted against the deed itself ; at least, it will be presumed to be of the date most unfavourable to its own validity.

Writings were anciently executed on the broadside of the sheets, and afterwards rolled up ; hence the word *volume* from the Latin *volumina, quia involvuntur et quasi in se retorquentur*. The record, minutes, or transactions of the whole courts of the nation, were written in rolls, and termed the *rollments of Court*. The keeper of the county records in England is named *Custos Rotulorum*, and our Lord Register, Clerk of his Majesty's Council and Rolls ; and in all the inferior courts, at this moment, the minutes are called the rolls of court. This form was evidently inconvenient. The practice was to paste one sheet to another ; and, in order to authenticate the whole, the party wrote his name at the joining of each sheet, the Christian name upon one sheet, and the surname upon the other. Practice had introduced this method, to supply the defect of evidence, which a deed behoved otherwise to be liable to ; but no law had inforced it. Neglects and errors in this article were consequently not uncommon, and, where they happened, the import fell to the determination of the Court of Session. In such a case, it was natural to determine every case by its own circumstances ; they

considered

---

* Craig, p. 211.

considered in what sheet the principal obligements lay; how the holder was affected by the objection; whether any thing suspicious appeared in the business; and sustained the deed or rejected it accordingly.

To introduce a certain rule in this particular, and obviate the other inconveniences of sheet writing, an act of Parliament passed in the 1696 * : ' Ordaining that every person should thenceforth be ' at liberty to write them upon sheets battered together as formerly, ' or by way of book, in leaves of paper, either in folio or quarto, ' providing that each page be marked by the number, first, second, ' third, &c. and signed as the margins were before; and that the ' end of the last page makes mention how many pages are therein ' contained, in which page only witnesses are to sign where wit- ' nesses are necessary, which writs so executed are declared to be as ' valid as if written on several sheets, battered and signed on the ' margin, according to the present custom.'

This act is the rule of our practice in these matters; and subscribing has thereby been made a statutory solemnity, which is therefore to be carefully attended to, wherever the old form of writing on sheets may happen to be preferred. The last requisite to our deeds is, that they should be written upon stamped paper, a requisite happily unknown to Mr Dallas, and our other predecessors of the seventeenth century; none of our writers on the law have ever looked farther for the origin of this business, than to the acts of Parliament of William and Anne; but, in fact, the marking or stamping of the paper for writing deeds is as old as the reign of Justinian. All notaries were discharged to write their deeds upon any other paper, but what should be furnished them by the public, marked with the name of the comptroller of the finances for the time. The papers so marked they distinguished by the title protocol.

From

---

* c. 15. 3d seff. 1st Parl. Will. III.

From the ftamp paper difcovered in the ftudy of the Roman law, feveral of the ftates of Europe, and particularly the French, taxed
the bufinefs of writing deeds, by obliging the notaries to write
upon protocols ftamped and marked on the top by an officer of the
crown. At laft, in April 1674, the tax was extended to all deeds,
and the paper upon which they were written was called *papier
timbré*. Though our King William mortally hated Lewis XIV.
he was glad to follow his example in this bufinefs ; no fooner was
the French revenue of the ftamps known in the Court of England,
than a fimilar tax was determined on. Accordingly, paper and ·
parchments were firft taxed and ftamped by Parl. in the 5th of
William and Mary 1693, and by various acts fince that time have
been extended and increafed, according to the demands of government, and the neceffity of the times.

Thefe acts declare, that no deeds written on any paper not
ftamped, fhall be available in law or equity, until payment of a penalty over and above the duties. In England, payment of the
duties and penalty is always received in the courts, becaufe the law
only meant to fecure the revenue, not to deſtroy the evidence of
parties. With us, the action ftops till the duties are paid at the
office, and the deed ftamped ; becaufe there is no perfon in the court
entitled to receive it.

Since the introduction of ftamps, we, in imitation of the Englifh,
never fail to mention in the tefting claufe of our deeds, that they
are written on ftamped paper, or paper duly ftamped. This is not
neceffary, the ftamp fpeaks for itfelf better than the writer ; but, as
our principal deeds are, for the moft part, lodged in the record, this
circumftance could not otherwife appear upon the extract.

We have now gone through the whole of our laws, regulating
the folemnities in executing of deeds deduced in the order of time ;.
the application of thefe laws muft be followed, as it occurs in the
decifions of our courts ; and thence we arrive, by the fureft road, to
a perfect knowledge, not only of the general import of the tefting
claufe,

claufe, as now underftood, but of all the exceptions and variations which have hitherto occurred in practice.

The atteft of a deed is its principal defence ; if this fort is not ftrong, all is in danger ; upon that fide it is fure to be attacked. No reduction is brought without alledging roundly, by way of random fhot, that the writings called for want the folemnities effential in law. That we may defend ourfelves then, and attack others with fuccefs, let us examine how this bufinefs has hitherto been carried on, obferving the order already laid down.

The firft thing then is the fubfcription of the party, required by the acts 1540, and 1579, regulated in method by the act 1672.

Thefe acts, in the matter of fubfcription at leaft, are fimple and exprefs ; the name of the parties is required if they can write, and, if they cannot, a method is prefcribed of fupplying the defect by notaries. A perfon who, by imitation of a couple of letters learns to make the initials of his name, cannot be faid to write, nor can fuch an aukward, fhapelefs letter be termed a fubfcription. It is the habit of writing that gives character to the hand, and affords that variety, and, at the fame time, that diftinction of writing to each individual, which has by fome been confidered as Providential. A perfon who writes no more than two letters, does it feldom ; what he puts upon paper has little or no character ; it is eafily forged, and cannot well be detected *comparatione literarum.* The ftatutory provifion of notaries excludes all thefe evils ; and, therefore, the Court of Seffion ought to have rejected *in totum* fubfcription by intitials, to deeds of importance Led, however, by the hardfhip of particular cafes, thefe falutary ftatutes have been weakened, nay, contradicted, both in the words, and in the fpirit, by the practice of the Court. They admitted fubfcription by initials, upon a proof brought, that parties were accuftomed fo to fubfcribe ; and they held the production of a fingle feparate writing, fo executed, as a proof of the fact.

When

Where the custom of the party was proved, and the instrumentary witnesses divided upon the actual subscription, the Lords called *ex officio* for the pursuer's oath, and allowed him to throw the balance in his own favour [*]. Afterwards, the objections to this practice being strongly urged, the Court retracted, and found, that a proof of the actual subscription of the deed quarreled is necessary, and that by the instrumentary witnesses, and none others [†]. The principle of this decision is presumed to be our present rule in this matter. If the initials are denied, and the witnesses alive, a proof of the actual subscription must be brought. The witnesses being dead, the Lords afterwards found a proof of the parties custom so to sign sufficient.

No device to make a party subscribe suddenly, who could not do it before, is admissible,—such as leading the hand,—writing with a pencil, and making the parties trace it. No such subscription can be said to be that of the party; and, therefore, in terms of the statutes, writs with names so adhibited are simply null. Such was the fate of a disposition, which the party had subscribed, by tracing the shapes of letters made with the mark of a pin [‡].

Contrary to the act 1672, an assignation was subscribed thus, *Fullarton of that ilk;* the want of the Christian name was objected to it, and repelled, because the act does not annull subscriptions, but subjects the party to punishment by the Privy Council [§].

The first words of the testing clause are, ' *in witness whereof I* ' *have subscribed these presents.* The want of the words, ' *I have* ' *subscribed these presents,*' was objected to a bond; but they were not necessary, because the law trusts not to the assertion of the party, or the writer of the deed, but to the subscriptions themselves [‖].

If

---

[*] November 16. 1667, Laird of Cultraes.   [†] June 1681, Coutts.
[‡] November 18. 1750, Crosby.   [§] June 21. 1765, Sir Thomas Gordon.
[‖] June 21. 1765, Gordon.

If the deed consists of more pages than one, the clause proceeds, ' *I have subscribed these presents, consisting of this and the ten pre-* ' *ceding pages.*'—The only case (except in seisines) where the objection of not having mentioned the number of the pages, happened to be pled. was against a testament of four pages written on one sheet. The testament upon that account was sustained*; so that it seems we are only to understand the act as applying to deeds consisting of more sheets than one; however, practice makes no such distinction, and the act is in every case literally complied with. The next requisite is, ' *written upon stamped paper.*' It has been adjudged, that two deeds cannot be written on the same sheet of stamped paper; but a discharge of a bond or other obligement on the same sheet is certainly good; neither is it a nullity, that the paper was not stamped at the date of the deed; it is sufficient to have it done before production in judgement.

The next thing is the name and designation of the writer, first introduced by the act 1593, and ultimately established by the act 1681. We have heard how the first of these acts, which was also special and express, was deprived of a great part of its authority and effect, by the subsequent practice of Court, which came at last to be corrected by the statute 1681, declaring that the want of the writer's name and designation should thenceforth be a defect, not suppliable by any condescendence.

Printed bonds have been sustained, where the names of the parties, the principal sum, annualrents, terms of payment, and penalty were inserted, and the insertor designed. The testing clause likewise has been disjoined from the deed, and sustained, though written with a different hand, without naming the adjector †. The first of these decisions is a dangerous deviation against the words and principle of the statute; it is dangerous, because it encourages irregularity.

* January 7. 1742, Robertson.   † June 9. 1710, White.

irregularity in the engrossing of deeds, and brings all such under the power of the Court. The essential clauses differ in every security, and the judges of consequence can only determine what are essential, and what are not; it is against the words and principle, because the act intended that the writer of every word of the deed should be mentioned; if, therefore, there was any part, the writer of which did not appear, that part ought to have been held *pro non adjecto.*

The writer of a deed is not always at hand, at the time of its being subscribed. It is, therefore, extremely commodious, that the testing clauses of deeds may be inserted by any person employed. Sometimes the deed is first subscribed by the party and witnesses, and the testing clause afterwards filled up. In these cases, a sufficient blank space is always left between the writing and subscription. Errors in this have often occasioned disputes. When the space is insufficient, the superfluous words have sometimes been razed to procure room, and at other times part of the testing clause has reached below the subscription. The Court have no doubt sustained such deeds, where they appeared to be otherwise unsuspicious; but those decisions are no precedents. By a series of decisions, the Court found that the act 1681 extended only to the writer of the body of the deed; so that the omission of the name and designation of the writer of the testing clause is not fatal. The letter of the act 1681 will no doubt bear this construction; but it could not be the meaning of the Legislature, if it was of importance, that the writer of the body of the deed should be known, it was certainly necessary that the writer of the testing clause should also be ascertained. When the name or designation of the writer happened to be totally omitted, the judgements of Court were for a considerable time regulated by the statute; they refused to admit the nullity to be supplied in any case; at last, they began to relax, and an opportunity soon offered, in which the obvious innocence and ridicule of the case carried them against the judgment of law:

S 2 'A

A scroll of a discharge was sent by a Writer in Edinburgh, to be executed in the country. The scroll contained his own name as the writer. It was copied by a country procurator verbatim, retaining the name of the writer of the scroll. The objection of this plain nullity was made to the discharge. The Court allowed the writ to be supported by a proof of the verity [*]. Ridiculous as this accident was, it occurred again three years afterwards. The Court saw the danger of their last judgment in its proper light, and, in terms of the act 1593, found the writing null, the real writer being neither named nor designed. At a later period, they again relaxed, and, at last, two cases occurred, in which the Court in a manner repealed this part of the act altogether. They sustained the objection to the want of the writer's designation in the docquet of accounts; but they found the omission suppliable by proof, and upon a proof sustained the docquet [†].

The necessity of the date, as before observed, not being established by statute or universal practice, bonds without a date were sustained, in regard they contained a specific term of payment [‡]. Though, in a case reported by Lord Stair, 7th June 1666, the date seems to have been considered to be an essential solemnity; in all cases, where the validity or the preference of a deed depends upon its date, that date, as remarked, is essential by the nature of the thing. Thus a disposition in prejudice of the heir at law, having no date, would be presumed to have been granted within the sixty days of death-bed; and, in a competition with other deeds or diligence, the most unfavourable date would be annexed to the one deficient in that article. An innocent error in date would not infer a nullity; but where a bond was antedated, to preserve it from an inhibition, the Court, in resentment of falsehood, annulled the bond *in totum*. According to the same principles, an assignment with a

false

---

[*] 23d December 1707, Irving.   [†] 23d November 1743, Duke of Douglas.
[‡] Durie, 11th December 1621, Hamilton, &c.

false date was totally set aside, and presumed to be done in order to obtain a preference in a competition *. An objection of a false date, in order to avoid the plea of death-bed, was moved against a disposition. The defender answered, ' That a false date by law is not ' fatal to the deed, unless designedly done to prejudge a party : ' That the present error was imputable allenarly to the stupidity of ' the writer, who, in copying from a former disposition, transcribed ' the date of it in the new one.' The Lords allowed a proof of this defence by the instrumentary witnesses.

The omission of the place of subscribing has been uniformly found not to be a nullity †. By custom, however, the place is seldom or never omitted to be inserted, and the omission of it in a doubtful or suspicious case would have considerable weight. As the true place aids the memory of all concerned in the transaction, so a wrong or false place would mislead, and in some cases might prove fatal to the deed.

The Testing Clause concludes with the names and designations of the witnesses. For a considerable time, the Court adhered strictly to the letter of the statutes, and refused action to all deeds in which an omission in these particulars appeared ; nay, an error in the Christian name being inserted, different from that of the witness subscribing, annulled a bond ‡. At last, as in the former matters, the Judges began to relax ; they sustained the very general designation, indweller in Edinburgh, upon the person interested condescending upon circumstances sufficient to distinguish him §. Where the designation of the last witness, might in language be applied to both, they applied it accordingly, thus, ' A. B. writer hereof, and ' C. B. at Leckie ;' the last words *at Leckie*, were held to be the designation of both witnesses ‖. Afterwards they refused to do this,

in

---

* 29th March 1626, Keith.
† 14th July 1709, Vallay. 21st July 1711, Ogilvy.
‡ Forbes, 15th July 1707, Abercromby.   § 29th November 1698, Grant.
‖ Forbes, 14th December 1708, Sheriffs.

in a similar and more favourable case *. A bond, in which one of the witnesses wanted a designation, was sustained, because the obligor had paid a part of it. This was to find the nullity, not a total one, but resolvable into an exception which the party might renounce or homologate †. Having thus reduced the act 1681 to an exception, in place of a simple denial of action, which the words clearly import, a distinction was introduced between deeds defective in the matter of witnesses, and those which wanted them altogether. Homologation, or an implied acknowledgement of the verity of the deed, was admitted to exclude the exception, consequently the direct acknowledgment by oath behoved to be also admitted. Thus, a contract having only one witness, and consequently null by the act, was allowed to be supported by a reference of the verity of the subscription to the granter's oath ‡. In the other case, where there were no witnesses, action was totally denied §. Such uncertain anamolous judgments must always follow a deviation from the solid ground of express statute law, and time, in place of rectifying, multiplies the contradiction, and broadens the error. Thus, so late as the 1738, the Court refused to supply a defective obligation, upon offer of the most pregnant proof ‖; and they had, in the 1710, acted upon the same principle, in refusing to admit a reference of the verity of the subscription, or even of the debt itself, to the granter's representative ¶. Yet, in the very same year, they allowed the omission of a writer's name and witnesses to be supplied by a condescendence and proof **.

These decisions, however, it is to be hoped, will be no precedent, and that the Court will return to the rules of the statutes. Their decision, 26th December 1752, seems to promise as much. A bond

was

* 9th November 1714, Halden.   † 17th February 1715, Sinclair.
‡ 26th December 1695, Beattie.   § 22d December 1710, Gordon.
‖ 25th January 1738, Low.   ¶ 4th January 1710, Leopi.
** 2d February 1710, Maxwell.

was then annulled, becaufe one of the witneffes happened to be defigned brother-german, in place of brother-in-law, to a third
party *.

These varying opinions of the Supreme Court have had little or
no effect upon the practice of our conveyancers. Thefe gentlemen
have ftrictly and circumftantially adhered to the folemnities required by the legiflature, which is the only method to avoid the uncertainty of legal decifions. Experience has taught, that objections
upon informality are often fuftained or rejected, not according to the merits of the error or omiffion itfelf, but according to the favourable or unfavourable circumftances of the cafe,
or the ideas of equity or expedience thereby impreffed upon the
judges.

There is no exprefs law for regulating the additions on the margins of our writings, except they are confidered as diftinct deeds,
and confequently included in the general rule of the act 1681 ; but
the natural prefumption is, that they are added after execution, unlefs the contrary appears. Being parts of the deed, they require fubfcribing. The practice therefore is, to comprehend them within the
fubfcription ; *i. e.* writing the Chriftian name upon the left fide, and
the furname upon the other, which muft be done before the fubfcribing witneffes. Thefe additions are attended with all the requifites
in the body of the deed, feparately expreffed, or rather repeated ;
and, if they are made at a different time, or before different witneffes, all this, as already mentioned, muft be diftinctly expreffed. The
common term, *marginal note*, is an improper one. A *note* is an obfervation, criticifm, or explanation of fome part of the text ; whereas, the matters we are talking of are additions to, or amendments of
the text, and fhould be fo named. The fubfcription at the bottom
of the page does not apply to the interlineations, and therefore they
ought to be totally excluded from practice, even where it may be
thought

* 26th December 1752, Crediters of Graham.

thought to be obviously innocent. An assignment, in the narrative, bore 4000 merks to be due by the cedent, and that the assignee had advanced to him an equivalent sum. In the assigning words, however, the writer mentioned only 3000 merks, and, upon discovering the error, he amended it by an interlineation. The Lords sustained the assignment, but they condemned the interlining as unwarrantable *. The security of deeds, in the case of amendments, so excellently provided for by practice, has also been weakened by posterior decisions of the Court of Session. An amendment upon a backbond, signed by the granter, was found good against the user of the deed, though no mention was made of it in the testing clause †. The reason, in this case, was the presumed impossibility of adding any thing to a writ in the possession of a creditor. It was objected, in another instance, that marginal notes were thus attested, ' and witnesses to ' the marginal notes also.' Answered, that these words did not bear the marginal notes to be signed before witnesses. The Lords, however, repelled the objection ‡. Where there are many parties to a deed, they subscribe at different places, upon different dates, and before different witnesses. A writer must be particularly attentive to have all these separately and distinctly expressed.

As these long attests can more conveniently be filled up by the writer of the deed, or at least by one writer, the method is, to keep notes of the several dates, places, and designations of the witnesses, until the subscription be complete. A bond by a son as principal, and a father as cautioner, happened to be thus tested, ' I have ' written and subscribed these presents.' It was objected that the cautioner's subscription was not attested : The bond, however, was sustained, in respect of the cautioner's being an accessory obligor §. This decision, it is apprehended, would not be a precedent; it is clearly against the statutes, and against the nature of cautionary o-
bligements,

---

* Forbes, 21st December 1709, Lyon.   † Kilkerran, June 17. 1741, Spottiswood.
‡ Dec. 7. 1752. Broomfield.   § Feb. 11. 1748. Taylor.

bligements, which require every point of solemnity to be strictly adhered to. In the case of a mutual contract, the testing clause was thus expressed, ' In witness whereof, these are subscribed with ' *my* hand at Edinburgh.' It was objected, that the pronoun *my*, could apply only to one of the subscriptions, and particularly to neither. This was justly repelled, as a grammatical mistake, the bond being signed by both parties *.

By a due observance of the legal solemnities, a presumption is introduced in favour of the deed, it is then held to be genuine, and gives evidence, *per se*. This evidence is, therefore, weakened by scores, super-inductions, or other vitiations, all which are presumed to have been done posterior to the execution. The Court sometimes set aside deeds upon the simple inspection of such errors. Slighter, though dangerous objections, arise from a diversity of writing, or writing by different hands appearing upon the paper; also, from interlineations, or cancellations; and, lastly, if contractions or figures are used to express any thing which should have been written at length. Every word of these observations are applicable to our daily practice; and, as the matter so nearly concerns every practitioner, it will be useful to call back to remembrance the several cases which have hitherto occurred, and to profit by the experience they afford. As soon as instruments or writs were in practice, alterations by razure were attempted and objected to. So early as the 1511, it was established by a solemn decision, ' That writings being razit in ony substantial part should ' make no faith; although a proof was offered of its being done by ' the party or nottar.—Balfour, King against Boyd.' A bond being vitiated *in substantialibus*, and suspected of being intentionally done, the Lords again refused a proof by the instrumentary witnesses, that the vitiation was done at the time of subscribing †.

Vol. I.   T   A

---

* February 9. 1759. Dunbar.
† Stair, 22d November 1671, Pattullo.

A difposition quarrelled upon the head of death-bed, appeared to be vitiated in date and place. The purfuer contended, that, in that cafe, the date and place were *inter subfantialia*, the prefumption of law being, that the real date had been erazed, and another fuperinduced, more than fixty days prior to the death of the granter, in order to avoid the challenge of death-bed. The Lords allowed the verity of the date and place to be inftructed by the inftrumentary witneffes. Here the circumftance feemed to exclude the poffibility of antedating*. A difposition under the fame objection, appeared to be written with different inks fome old and fome new. It was figued by a woman, but had been originally intended for a man, the word *his* being altered into *her*. The Lords fubjected the holder to prove, that this deed had been read over to the granter, and fubfcribed of a date feclufive of death-bed †.

Obliterations or illegibility, have often been attended with effects equally fatal ; half a line in a material part of a bond being plainly obliterated and unintelligible, the Lords annulled the bond, upon the prefumption of a bad defign, as the words might have been material ‡. The condition of a bond being partly fcored, and partly illegible, the bond was found not to be probative §.

In fhort, every error, even of the flighteft kind, in this very material claufe, is attended with danger ; and thefe errors are not only taken hold of by the Court, in cafes where unfavourable circumftances are prefumed, but alfo in competitions, where the debt happens to bear hard upon other creditors : fo that in the writing and execution, we cannot be too careful ; for, like an open countenance, or a plain fimple fpeech, integrity is prefumed upon the fight of a fair, diftinct, clean written deed, regularly attefted, as the law directs.

The

* February 1730, Errot.   † Fountainhall, 19th February 1702, Livingfton.
‡ Stair, 22d November 1671, Pattillo.
§ Forbes, 18th July 1712, Earl of Bute.

The omiffion to fign any of the pages is attended with the worft confequences. Cautioners have infifted to be liberated; and confenters, that their confent fhould be limited to the part of the deed by them fubfcribed. To omit the fubfcription of pages, would be juft equal to the omiffion of fubfcribing fheets. A deed was found null upon this head*. A difpofition againft which the fame quarrel lay was fuftained, in regard the fheet fubfcribed contained every thing material in the deed†. In the cafe 13th February 1728, Earl Dalkeith, it was argued, that the atteft of the fubfcription of confenters was not within the act 1681. The act, however, was found to be general. The fubfcription of a party as confenter to a contract of marriage, confifting of fixteen pages, happened only to be adhibited on the laft. The Lords found that this fingle fubfcription did not affect the confenter as to any thing contained in the fifteen pages unfigned.

All the neceffary blanks fhould be carefully filled up, and no void fpaces be left in which any fraud may be perpetrated, or fuper additions made; and it is to be taken for a facred rule, that, after fubfcription, no blank is to be filled up, by which the intereft of the parties can in any fhape be affected. To leave dates, and fometimes defignations, blank in the narrative, is common; but this is done, only *narrativé:* the deeds, or other matters alluded to, fully fupplying thefe words. In general, the prefumption of law is, that all blanks were filled up at the date of the fubfcription; but, if any other matter of importance turns upon this circumftance, and any thing appears, to be done, *ex poft facto*, it leads to an inquiry by parole evidence, and places the deed in danger.

This is the place to confider the proper perfons to be chofen as inftrumentary witneffes, at the execution of deeds. The firft thing to be attended to, is the age of fuch witneffes. A minor is habile,

T 2   becaufe

* Bruce, 18th December 1714, M'Donald.
† Forbes, 23d November 1708, Sym.

because his judgment is presumed to be sufficient for the purpose; but a pupil is not. A contract was set aside upon the objection, that one of the witnesses had been at the time a few days short of fourteen years of age [*]. Witnesses to deeds are in law presumed to be chosen or required; and, therefore, the nearest relations may be chosen. Sir George M'Kenzie doubts if women may be witnesses, although no law expresly excludes them. The exclusion of the female sex arising from antient customs and manners, was kept up by other concomitant circumstances, and by the nature of the thing. Men who could write their names, were long very scarce in both kingdoms, but women much scarcer, writing to them is a very modern piece of education. In general, they are opener to imposition than men in matters of civil busines, and as instrumentary witnesses are always presumed to be chosen or required by the parties, the choice of women was avoided as suspicious. In criminal matters they came to be admitted, because accident or necessity made them witnesses without any choice, they were therefore necessary, and often no other are to be had. Inveterate practice has now made it a rule, that women are totally shut out from being instrumentary witnesses. Whether in the want of men, a deed witnessed by women would be sustained or not, has never yet come to trial.

A creditor cannot be witness to an obligement in his own favour; and it is a general rule, that no person is a proper witness, where he has a direct interest to support the deed; though the favour of testaments once prevailed with the Court, to allow the subscription of a legatee as a witness [†].

Famous witnesses, as the law terms them, or witnesses of the best character, should always be called upon; but if a person lying under objections in point of character, happen to be made a witness, one of the parties cannot afterwards object to him, the choice being presumed to be made by mutual consent [‡].

The

---

[*] 12th December 1738, Davidsons.   [†] Harcus, March 1685, Graeme.
[‡] Fountainhall, 1st February 1710, Baillie.

The act 1781, requires that the witnesses should know the party who is to sign the deed and see him actually subscribe, or at least hear him acknowledge his subscription. That the witness should know the person of the party, is the most material requisite of the statute; for, unless this be the case, any one man may personate another; which is the very imposture intended to be prevented by the act; and yet this most essential circumstance is daily neglected, and deeds of all kinds are attested by witnesses, who never till that moment saw the parties. Nothing is more common than to call strangers off the street,—the waiters of taverns,—and what is indeed universally practised, the waiters of coffee-houses, who are ready witnesses in every case, and constantly at hand. They are not always asked, if they know the person who is to sign; and it is not to be expected they are to put the question. The want of this most necessary knowledge has been fatal to a number of deeds. A witness to a bond deponed, that being then a boy of fourteen years of age, he was called off the street to be witness to the subscription of a party whom he did not know. Here there was no suspicion of a fraud, and yet the Court, in terms of the act 1681, annulled the bond *. In a late case, the Lords found a bond not probative, in regard the instrumentary witnesses made oath, that, at the time of their subscribing as witnesses, one of the obligors was not present, nor his subscription then adhibited †. These instances are sufficient to teach us, that we ought to be at some pains, in procuring proper witnesses to the execution of deeds, especially where they are important; and not to trust them to the attest of any persons whom accident may offer; for the statute 1681 itself, exposes the deed to the parole evidence of instrumentary witnesses, who may deny their subscription, either from corruption or extreme stupidity. For the same reason, though near relations may be competent, yet it is more prudent to choose such persons as are quite uninterested;

---

* Fountainhall, November 1698, Campbell.   † February 2. 1761, Young.

uninterested; for instances there have been, where such relations have denied their subscriptions, and set aside deeds to
their own prejudice. This objection is at present not much
in practice. It remains, however, in full force, and would be
fatal to many of our late writings, should the experiment be
tried.

It is now proper to observe, that instrumentary witnesses have
no concern with the subject matter of the deed, to the attestation of
which they are called; and, therefore, though the paper must either be read over to, or read by the party, before his subscription,
there is no necessity for this being done in presence of the witnesses,
—it is the subscription alone that they are called upon to attest.
It is, however, expedient to allow the witnesses to be present at
reading of the deed; and it is plain, that if witnesses had not been
made more acquainted with the contents of deeds formerly, than they
generally are now, it is impossible they could have so often supplied
the want of solemnities, as from our decisions it is evident they
have done. As a witness is considered to be a simple attester of the
subscription, he is consequently bound by nothing to his own prejudice in the deed. To bind him he must be taken as a consenter,
but if it could be proved, that the deed was read over, and he notwithstanding remained silent, though he might not be bound, strong
presumptions would arise against him in an after dispute; nay, if he
was present at the agreement, or concerned in it as a relation, it
will go far to exclude any quarrel afterwards made by him, especially in contracts of marriage, where a father or a brother signs
witness to his daughter or sister's deeds.

It happened that a person signed a deed as a witness; *i. e.* he added
the word witness to his subscription, and it was pled, that he was
not bound; luckily the party interested was able to prove, by the
real witnesses, that the deed was read over in their presence; the
adjection, therefore, was justly held to be an error of no bad consequence. In one case, it is absolutely necessary, that the witnesses

be

be made acquainted with every particular of the transaction; and that is in deeds granted by Roman Catholics, which are all by a special act 1695, c. 26. deemed gratuitous and void, so far as regards their succession, unless the granter, writer, and witnesses, declare upon oath, and give satisfactory evidence before the Judge Ordinary, that such deeds were granted for ' true, onerous, and ade-
' quate causes.'

There are cases, in which the writer of the deed, or other person, happens to be witness to several subscriptions made at different times. The practice then is, to subscribe as often as he happens to be witness, for unless he does so, the writ cannot be said to be tested in terms of the act. The Court, indeed, sustained a deed, where the writer had neglected this rule. He had witnessed the subscription of two consenters to a contract of marriage, and then signed himself. He was afterwards witness to the signing of two other consenters, but did not repeat his own subscription. The Lords were pleased to sustain this deed, upon the old idea of favouring simple errors; but the quarrel is certainly founded in the statute, and is to be avoided by every attentive conveyancer *.

An exception from all the statutes has been introduced by repeated decisions of the Court. In cases where members of a community, or any considerable number of people, subscribe a deed at the same time and place. These subscribers have been considered as sufficiently attesting one another; and, therefore, separate witnesses were adjudged not to be necessary †. Neither does the act 1681 apply to foreign writings. The law of Scotland justly admits action upon all such deeds, as appear to be executed according to the forms of the country where they were granted.

Notwithstanding the anxiety of the Legislature to secure the execution of our deeds, certain it is, that a practice took place of subscribing deeds blank in the name of the creditor and receiver. These

* Falconer, December 6. 1749, Edmonstone.   † 19th July 1676, Forest.

These passed from hand to hand, and, if filled up by the last holder, were held to be sufficient ; it is impossible to conceive a practice in more direct opposition to the letter, the spirit, and the genius of all our statutes, and even our common law. It arose from the weak-ness of these statutes, as explained and supported by the decisions of the Court. It being once determined, that the parts of a deed might be filled up by a person different from him who wrote the body of it, then it came to be of little importance how much of it was left blank at subscription. The name and designation of the cre-ditor, or receiver, was, no doubt, one of the most essential parts of the deed. It behoved the name of the writer of the essential part, at least, to be inserted ; but that rule was in this case dispensed with. It was next objected, that these blanks were plainly filled up, after subscription, different from the intention of the granter ; but this was easily ob-viated by a presumption borrowed from the civil law : ' Omnia ' presumuntur, solemniter acta ; et interpretatio sumenda est, ut actus ' valeat.' In general, the insertions quarrelled, were presumed to have been made at the time of subscription. Writings without a creditor or receiver, were in reality no deeds at all ; they invited the commission of fraud in all its shapes, and ridiculed all our laws upon these subjects ; yet did our Courts support this bad practice, until it became an unsufferable nuisance, and as such, was rooted out by the act 1696, c. 25. By this act, a writ may still be subscribed blank, but then, if it is afterwards filled up, the same witnesses must be called to see it done, and, if filled up with a different hand from the body, the docquet must bear the *res gesta.*

Having gone through the history of the solemnities necessary to the execution of deeds by parties who *can* write ; it is now requi-site to consider the provision made by law for the convenience and security of these people who *cannot :* Formerly this class was much more numerous than it is at present. From the barbarous pride of the feudal superiors, and the depressed state of the common people, writing was for a long time confined to the clergy. However

unnatural

unnatural and impolitic the inftitution of monafteries now appears, it is certain that to them we owe the prefervation of that learning which has taught the world to defpife them. The painful copying of a book was the only poffible method of multiplying it.—Unlefs there had been men feparated from the world, freed from its cares, and fhut up in cells, who could have fubmitted to the tedious, weary, fplenetic labour of copying volumes? Habit to the monks made this an entertainment; and fancy exercifed itfelf in illuminations, paintings, gildings, and ornament. Books muft have been the rareft, and moft valuable property; and education, of confequence, limited to few. What was to repay the trouble of learning to read, when nothing was to be had to be read? And, without being a clergyman, little opportunity could occur of exercifing the art of writing, fuppofing it to be allowed. However much the Roman clergy encouraged the art of writing in their own order, they were not at any trouble to extend it among the laity. Every day's experience pointed out the value of the diftinction. It fecured them in the exclufive office of notaries,—in that of clerks to the courts of juftice,—to the power of making teftaments,—and the profit of all civil bufinefs. They were the only clerks, and, on that account, obtained in moft places, for their order, the *benefit of clergy*. Originally, the privilege lay in the exemption of the perfons of clergymen from trial by a civil judge; and it was competent only to actual clerks wearing the habit, and properly tonfured; but, as none (clergymen excepted) could read or write, therefore the faculty of doing either came to be held by courts of juftice to be an immediate proof of that perfon being in orders. A perfon who could read or write might plead his clergy, either upon the indictment being preferred, or in arreft of judgment. The Pope, we are told, infifted for a total exemption of his order from the civil jurifdiction. The civil courts refufed this, unlefs the perfon was actually claimed by the bifhop as his clerk. For this purpofe the bifhop, or his deputy, attended in court to determine the fact. The accufed was made to read ; and if the bishop, upon hearing him, said, *legit ut clericus*, he was delivered to the ecclesiastical judge, who, after a mock trial, by brethren clerks, most assuredly acquitted the learned culprit. This was a very great encouragement to the acquisition of these arts. In a statute of Edward III. *anno* 1344, ordaining an investigation into many national abuses, we find the following curious article of inquiry : ' Also into the con-' duct of keepers of prisons, who teach lay persons who are in their ' custody the use of letters, in order to save their lives, in distur-' bance of the common law, and the prevention of justice being ' done against lay persons, in deceit of the King *.' Thus the jailors turned schoolmasters to thieves and murderers; a strange academy sure enough ! It was, after all, the discovery of printing, and the reformation of religion, which accelerated the knowledge of letters, at least amongst the reformed. To read the scriptures, was for a long time the most desirable faculty imaginable, and, next to that, writing came naturally to be established as the common and general education. The Reformation, however, did not in England banish the old benefit of clergy ; it continued above a century, and in full force ; but, in the mean time, reading and writing continued to gain ground, consequently clergymen grew extremely numerous, and, therfore, felonies came to be distinguished into clergyable, and not ; and every statute establishing a crime, to this moment, prescribes the punishment, and excludes the benefit of clergy.

In Scotland, no such absurdity gained ground ; because, having little municipal law, and few established customs, we never were strongly attached to any. Before the reformation, the laity of Scotland were extremely ignorant, and the unsettled state of the country, and the extreme poverty of a great part of our people, prevented their progress in the arts of life, and particularly in reading and writing. In every act of Parliament, therefore, regulating the

execution

* Barroyl. p. 235.

execution of deeds, provision is made for the convenience of thofe who cannot write. Our firſt reformers were ignorant, and the people in general more fo. In the reign of the Epiſcopal clergy, common education made fome progreſs among us ; but the Preſbyterian revolution threw every thing back again. Their firſt clergy were not choſen from the knowing claſs of the nation, they aroſe from among the people they prepared to teach.

I now proceed to the deduction of our ſtatute law, regulating the mode of executing deeds for thoſe who could not, or who cannot yet write. The 117th act of James V. 7th Parliament, firſt required both the ſubſcription and ſeal of the party, ' or elſe gif the ' party cannot write, with the ſubſcription of an notar thereto.' Long before this act, ſubſcriptions had been uſed ; notaries themſelves authenticated all their inſtruments by their ſign and ſubſcription ; and, in caſes where ſubſcriptions were deemed neceſſary, they led the hand of the party. One notary was ſufficient by this ſtatute, a circumſtance which argues the greateſt confidence in theſe officers. It will be remembered that the ſubſcription was only a novel requiſite, adhibited in *majorem cautelam.* The law truſted principally to the ſeal. This method of ſupplying the want of a ſubſcription, by leading the hand, was certainly an improper device. The ſubſcriptions were not done by the parties, and, in leading the hands of others, the writing behoved to be aukward and devoid of character. The only objection, therefore, for ſome time, moved againſt deeds ſo executed, turned upon the authenticity of the notaries ; for the deeds *ex facie* proved nothing. At laſt, the ſolemnity of ſubſcription of parties who could write, acquiring more and more confidence, the ſeal came proportionably to be leſs relied on ; and experience taught, that the truſt to a ſingle notary, of ſubſcribing for another perſon, was too great ; and, therefore, by the act of James VI. 1579, c. 80. all deeds of importance were ordained to be ſubſcribed and ſealed by the principal parties, if they could ſub-

U 2 ſcribe :

scribe: ' Utherways by two famous nottars, before four famous
' witnesses, denominated be their special dwelling-places, or some
' other evident tokens, that the witnesses be known; otherways to
' mak na faith.' It was by this act plainly left to the Court to determine what is, or is not, a deed of importance, so as to fall within the meaning of it. Accordingly, the Court reduced an obligement for more than a L. 100 Scots, because it was signed only in
presence of three witnesses. At the same time, they declared, that any
thing exceeding that sum in value, without regard to the quality of
the parties, was to be reputed a matter of great importance *.
These decisions have, accordingly, been observed as a rule ever
since; and, consequently, deeds for or within L. 100 Scots, are
not held to be within the statutes, and may be supported by witnesses, if the evidence they afford be suspicious. And, upon the
same principle, defective writs for more than L. 100 Scots, are often
restricted to that sum; and, in general, it may be held, that witnesses
are competent in every case to that extent.

It is here necessary to remark, that, unless the value is precise in
money, we are never to trust to this exception.—We are never to
apply it to annual prestations, however small, to tacks, or any part of
heritable rights; for, in the case of a disposition of heritage, where
the lands were within a L. 100 Scots in value, the deed was reduced †. The value of lands may alter considerably; and, therefore, all deeds respecting them are within the statute. It is the value
or interest with regard to the debtor, not to the creditor, that is to
be considered : Thus, a bond of provision to three daughters, for
L. 100 Scots each, was reduced; because, although it formed three
separate bonds to the creditor, it made a bond of L. 300 to the
debtor ‡. So far as regarded the number of the notaries and witnesses, the decisions of Court have been strictly regulated by this
act.

---

* Durie's, *ult.* January 1623, and 18th November 1613, Marshall.
† Edgar, 29th June 1725.   ‡ 16th January 1668, Anderson.

2d. They uniformly reduced, where any of these were wanting, or restricted the deeds quarrelled, to L. 100 Scots. In some cases, where the deeds were granted in implement, or satisfaction of former ones, they went the length of supporting them. Such as a bond granted in implement of the sum due by a contract of marriage, and a disposition of moveables in security of bygone tack-duties. The principle was, that such deeds, being strictly in terms of their relatives, were not, *per se*, of importance.

The act requires that both notaries and witnesses should be present, and that the notaries subscribe at the same time, or *unico contextu*; for it is the number, and the joint act and evidence of that number, to which the law trusts. They are termed *co-notaries, i. e.* joint attestors of the same fact; so, in all cases where notaries or witnesses subscribed at different times or places, the Court have uniformly set aside deeds so attested.

At this time, the evidence of writings lay entirely upon the subscription of the notaries, and the memory of the witnesses, if alive; for the last act did not require the subscription of the witnesses, in testimony of their presence. This was supplied by the important statute 1681, which, so far as relates to deeds signed by the granters themselves, has been fully explained. To find four persons who could write, would, in the times alluded to, have been extremely difficult; and, therefore, the solemnities of deeds, it is evident, kept pace with the improvement of the people. In the 1681, writing was observed to have been ordinary; and, therefore, the old defect was supplied, and the subscription of witnesses required. The act likewise gives the reason of this requisite, viz. that the subscription might assist the memories of honest witnesses, and afford a check against the intentional denial of dishonest ones. Six persons, therefore, must now concur, two public officers, and four witnesses, in one act, before a deed can be signed for another person, and the deed fortified with all their subscriptions. By the same act the witnesses must know the party; ' and see or hear him give warrant to a not-

' tar

' tar or nottars to fubfcribe for him; and, in evidence thereof, touch
' the nottars pen, otherways the witneffes to be punifhed as accef-
' fory to forgery.' Accordingly, in practice, notaries always fign
their attefts. Sir George M'Kenzie puts a queftion, whether a witnefs fubfcribing contrary to the direction of this act, would not be
liable to an affignee for damages upon reduction ? but he does not
refolve it. The witneffes muft fee or hear the command given.
M Kenzie again afks, How a witnefs can *fee* a command given ?
and whether a nod from the party, upon the notary afking the
queftion, would be fufficient ? that being the only way of hearing a
command, and *nutus* by the civil law being fufficient to conftitute a
mandate. I apprehend the word *fee*, in this place, to be an inaccuracy of expreffion; it can only apply to the evidence of the command, the feeing the party immediately thereafter touch the notary's
pen, or deliver him one for that purpofe.

This command muft be given in practice to both the notaries, one
after the other, and the atteftation or docquet of the notaries muft
bear the command to have been fo exprefsly given, otherwife the
omiffion is fatal to the deed; nor is it fuppliable by witneffes, being
an effential folemnity, and the very conftitution of the deed. To
allow it to be fupplied by parole evidence, would be to allow a deed
to be made by that evidence. The fubfcription of twenty notaries
would not make a deed to be mine. The command then being the
effence of the deed, the act of Parliament, with great propriety, required a repetition of it by a vifible ceremony; it required that
the eye fhould judge of it as well as the ear, two fenfes being neceffary in a matter of fuch importance. The Court, however, were
pleafed to difpenfe with this form, becaufe a mandate may be effectually given, and fubfift independent of it. Notaries generally and
properly mention this folemnity *of touching the pen*; the want of
it was objected, but, as the ftatutes are filent upon that circumftance,
the objection was repelled; but practice has carefully preferved this
circumftance. Additions on the margin muft alfo be figned by notaries,

taries, and the atteſt muſt alſo bear their being commanded to ſub-ſcribe them. The want of this annulled ſuch an addition *; the reaſon is plain, notaries muſt do every thing the granter ought to have done, could he have written ; and the notaries might other-wiſe adject or amend at their own hand, *ex intervallo.* But the at-teſt muſt be true, as well as regular, otherwiſe it is of no effect. Therefore, in a late caſe, where three of the witneſſes denied upon oath, that they heard the command given, or the pen touched, the deed, though a teſtament was ſet aſide †. This is a proper and ſen-ſible regulation, it makes theſe deeds carry *in gremio* the exact de-grees of evidence which ought to be given to them, and, if fraud is committed, fixes that fraud.

Notaries can only thus act for parties who cannot write. This inability is often occaſioned by ſickneſs, blindneſs, and other acci-dents. The atteſt, therefore, muſt mention ſuch reaſons diſtinctly ; but the alledgeance of the notary is not probative, and, if quarrelled, muſt be ſupported by proof.

By the act 1681, the identity of the perſon executing deeds in this manner, lies entirely upon the witneſſes ; it was not made requiſite for the notaries to know him, or even to be informed of that cir-cumſtance ; they were accordingly careleſs in this particular, which gave root to impoſitions. The Court of Seſſion, therefore, made an act of federunt, 21ſt July 1688, diſcharging theſe officers to ſubſcribe writs for perſons, unleſs they perſonally knew the parties deſigned as granters of the deed, or that the ſame be atteſted to them, by the inſtrumentary witneſſes, or other credible perſons, and that they ſpe-cify their cauſe of knowledge in their docquet. This was a proper and ſenſible extenſion of the act 1681.

It was before obſerved, that clergymen acted antiently as no-taries; and, therefore, ſubſcribed for people who could not write. Our Miniſters of the Goſpel are now diſcharged from the exerciſe

* Fountainhall, 6th December 1695, Elliot.
† June 25. 1760, Farmer.

' tar or nottars to fubfcribe for him; an⸺ ⸺rom the offices of
' the nottars pen, otherways the ⸺ ⸺ as the prohibition is
' fory to forgery.'   Accordin⸺ ⸺ty of the deeds, fo it is
their attefts.   Sir Georg⸺ ⸺hey yet might act as com-
nefs fubfcribing ⸺ ⸺this is extremely doubtful, and, by
liable to a⸺ ⸺ for others in any cafe, is limited to
refolve it
M‘Ken⸺
and ⸺
qu⸺
c⸺

Bond

Bond of Relief.

FROM the hiſtory of the laws made in favour of cautioners, from the days of Juſtinian down to the act of Parliament 1695, which was given upon a former occaſion, it appeared, that the interpoſitions of the Legiſlature to prevent the practice of one man engaging for another, or to relieve the ſituation of cautioners when engaged, had either been totally ineffectual, or were attended with oppoſite effects. The money lenders not only eluded theſe laws, but, by the form and nature of their ſecurities, rendered the ſituation of cautioners a great deal worſe than it had been before the act. Thus, prior to the 1695, cautioners were taken bound expreſsly in that character, and the bond contained a ſeparate obligement by the principal debtor to relieve his cautioner of the debt. The concern of the granters of the bond being thus *ex facie* apparent, the natural favour due to the cautioner was preſerved, and when the creditor put the bond into the regiſter, in order to recover payment, the cautioner took out another extract, and raiſed diligence in his own name for relief: But, when the act 1695 had introduced a kind of ſeptennial preſcription in favour of cautioners, alterations in the form gradually took place, by which the purpoſes of the act of Parliament have been completely eluded. I am now to ſtate the progreſs of theſe alterations in their real order, from the days of St Martin to the preſent time.

Separate bonds of relief were in uſe to be taken, a conſiderable time before the act 1695. Very great inconveniences had been found to attend the other method, whereby the cautioner was made to depend entirely upon the claufe of relief contained in the principal bond, which was not at his command ; and, although he might have juft reafon to apprehend danger from his debtor's fituation, yet he could take no ftep for his own fecurity ; in fhort, he muft have been actually diftreffed, and forced to make payment, before he could be in a capacity to act for himfelf. By our old law, though a cautioner had not made payment, yet, if decreet was taken againft him, he had an immediate right to adopt the fame meafure againft the debtor for his relief, without paying the debt. When bond debts became more common, a charge of horning was found to be the act of diftrefs, which gave a cautioner title to relief. The reafon of this, was, that the bond might go to the regifter without an intention of recovering the money ; and, therefore, a charge of horning was neceffary, to mark the intention of the creditors ; the regiftration of the bond was afterwards found to be a diftrefs fufficient to entitle the cautioner to feek his relief. The regiftration was no doubt equal to a decreet ; in order, therefore, to avoid thefe inconveniences, feparate bonds were taken by cautioners. As the old ftyle of thefe deeds differs confiderably from the modern form, it will be here neceffary to give a fhort illuftration of it.—The bond begins with, ' Know all men by thefe prefents, me A. B. Foraf- ' meikleas,' &c. After a recital of the principal bond, and the claufe of relief, it proceeds in the following terms : ' And I being ' defirous that the faid P. D. fhould fuftain no damage, through his ' being cautioner in manner forefaid ; therefore wit ye me to be ' bound and obliged, likeas by the tenor hereof, I bind and oblige ' me, my heirs, executors, and fucceffors, to warrant, free, and re- ' lieve, harmlefs, and fkaithlefs keep the faid P. D. my faid cau- ' tioner, of his faid cautionry above-mentioned ; and of all coft, ' fkaith, or damages he may happen to fuftain and incur there- ' thorough, any manner of way ; providing always that thir pre- ' fents, with the claufes of relief above-mentioned, in the forefaid

' bond

' bond of cautionry, fhall no ways infer double warrandice upon
' me.'

' *Me A. B. Forafmeikleas,*' &c.—This is very ftrange language,
or rather, it is neither language nor fenfe.   The reafon of this
childifh inaccuracy evidently has arifen from a wrong tranflation of
the Latin idiom, ' *Sciatis me A. B. dediffe ;*' or ' *Sciatis me teneri*
' *et obligari ;*' fo that this Latin conftruction of the accufative before
the infinitive has been literally tranflated.   In fome cafes it was
grammatical or a Latinifm ; at leaft fuch as ' Know me A. B. to
' have given and granted.'   The preface, ' *Be it known to all men,*'
is daily going out of fafhion ; but where it is ufed, and that is generally in deeds of importance, the old error is ftill frequently to be
obferved.   The recitals of relative deeds in the prefent manner
came only into practice about the 14th century.   Before that period,
the tranfactions of civil life do not appear to have afforded many
occafions for a feries or progreffion of deeds.   The treaties of the
Princes of Europe, like other writings, grew to an enormous length.
We find them proceeding upon narratives of former treaties of the
fame kind : Thefe, together with all private deeds, were drawn by
the church notaries, to whom the Roman law furnifhed a fuper-
abundance of language, and of claufes ; we then find numbers of
deeds become neceffary about one and the fame piece of bufinefs,
even regarding moveable or perfonal fubjects ; and to that period
may juftly be afcribed the proper commencement of progreffive
writings, where the firft are recited in the laft ; and each appears
founded on the other.   Thefe recitals are ufeful upon feveral accounts, they render each deed of the progrefs intelligible by itfelf ;
and, therefore, if the progreffive writings relate more particularly to
any fpecial claufe or matter of the obligement, that claufe or matter
ought to be verbatim, or at leaft circumftantially related.   This gives
the writer an opportunity of referring to it, as often as he pleafes ;
and faves him the introduction of aukward allufions, and explana-
tions, by which the fixed claufes or form of his writing are inter-

X 2   rupted

rupted or broken. Thefe narratives are alfo the moft unexceptionable materials, or adminicles as they are termed, for fupplying writings that are loft, by proving the tenor. Thefe are great advantages;
but in a feries of papers it muft be acknowledged, that long recitals
increafe in arithmetical proportion, and become tirefome, and even
fometimes naufcous. Brevity and concifenefs fhould always be ftudied, fo far as is confiftent with accuracy and perfpicuity.

' *Therefore wit ye me to be bound and obliged.*'—To *wit*, is a
Saxon derivative for to *know*. It is ufed by Spenfer, Shakefpear,
and by the old Scottifh poets. *Witting* was *knowing*; and hence the
original fignification of the word *Wit*, denoting the intellectual faculties of imagination, and quicknefs of fancy; nothing remains of
the old ufe of the word, except the phrafe *to wit*, ufed in explana-
tions, for ' *that is to fay*,' ' *Therefore, wit ye me*,' i. e. ' *Know all
men again*,' which clearly points out the blunder of language which
has been explained before. The firft addrefs to all men has told
them nothing at all; and, therefore, to make common fenfe, the
writer is here obliged abfurdly to repeat it. The old Latin addrefs
of the notaries was both fenfe and grammar: ' *Omnibus ad quos prae-
' fentes literae pervenerint, falutem, fciatis quod ego A. B.*' &c.
The deed then is fenfibly directed to thofe whom it may concern,
and not to all men. The granter falutes them, or greets them well,
and then fays, ' know ye that I am fo and fo bound.' Our old
writers by omitting the polite part, which is the falutation, have
made nonfenfe of the firft addrefs, and forced themfelves to the
aukward repetition of *wit ye me*. The writers during the beginning of this century copied thefe blunders; and we are now but flow-
ly throwing them off.

' *To be bound and obliged, likeas I bind and oblige me, my heirs*,'
&c. This repetition in the prefent tenfe is a literal tranflation of
the old Latin of the notaries. ' *To be bound and obliged*,' relates to
the agreement and obligation fubfifting antecedently upon the party,
independent of the writing; the granter, therefore, acknowledges
the

the exiſtence of the obligation or agreement in the firſt place, and then *de praeſenti* repeats it, by the evidence of the writing itſelf. The phraſe continues in a number of our deeds at this moment; and, as the words are the moſt eſſential of the whole form, there can be no harm in repeating them in different tenſes.

' *Warrant, free, relieve, harmleſs, and ſkaithleſs keep the ſaid C. D.*
' *of his ſaid cautionry; and of all coſt, ſkaith, and damages he may*
' *happen to ſuſtain or incur there-through, any manner of way.'*—
Theſe words were not originally applicable to bonds of relief for borrowed money; they were taken from the old engagements which people were obliged to give for one another in courts; either a pledge or cautioner were to be found in every caſe, before the action proceeded; and theſe were the terms in which the principals engaged themſelves to relieve their cautioners. When bonds for borrowed money became common, and perſonal ſureties were accepted in place of rights upon land, the ſame terms were made uſe of, though not properly applicable to the caſe. Taken altogether, however, they import no more than what by the law itſelf is incumbent upon the principal debtor, to indemnify his cautioner of all conſequences ariſing from the engagement. The word which we call *ſkaith*, is directly from the Saxon *ſcath*, for damages or miſchief. This clauſe of the bond of relief is a very old one. As the ſtyle of Engliſh writs, particularly recogniſances, are fixed by acts of Parliament, ſo various clauſes of our ſtyle have a meaning and import beſtowed upon them by our acts of Parliament and ſederunt. This clauſe was abſolutely rendered neceſſary, in all bonds of relief, ſo early as the 1610. At that time, intereſt of money was not properly fixed by ſtatute, and only became due by ſpecial paction; cautioners, therefore, after being diſtreſſed for the debt, were often not entitled to intereſt; and, therefore, the Lords ordained: ' That upon all contracts, bonds, and
' obligations made between principal parties, and their cautioners,
' bearing the clauſe following, viz. That the ſaid principal party
' bind and oblige him, his heirs, executors, and aſſignees, to warrant
' and

‘ and relieve the said cautioner of the whole contents of the fore-
‘ said contracts ; and of all cost, skaith, damage, expences, and in-
‘ terest that they or either of them, their heirs or assignees, may
‘ any way sustain or incur there-through : They will grant in time
‘ coming, against the said principal parties, their heirs and execu-
‘ tors, action at the said creditors instance, their heirs and executors,
‘ and in their favours, immediately after they be distressed and
‘ compelled to fulfil the contents of the said contracts, by payment
‘ of sums therein contained, or by poinding of their goods or com-
‘ prising of their lands for payments thereof ; not only for recovery
‘ of the principal sums contained in the said contracts, but also to
‘ compel them to repay, with the said principal sums, the whole an-
‘ nualrents extended to ten for the hundred of all years and terms
‘ bygone, that the said cautioners have been compelled to satisfy the
‘ said sums, or their lands or goods have been comprised and poind-
‘ ed therefore ; and also, to content and pay to the said cautioners,
‘ their heirs, and executors, yearly and termly, in time coming, ten
‘ for the hundred ; aye and while the said principal sum be repaid
‘ to them and their forefaids.’ The want of this clause was objected to a cautioner in the 1629, because the obligation bore only
that the principal should relieve his cautioner from the premises in
the bond, which was only principal sum and penalty, and that it did
not relieve him of all *costs, skaith, damages,* and *expences*, which the
cautioner might have incurred. The Lords, however, found the
principal obliged to pay the distressed cautioner both the principal
sum and the annualrents *. Although bonds of relief carry all cost,
skaith, damage, &c. yet the Lords interpreted the same only to extend to the principal and annualrents ; so that, although a cautioner
be denounced, and his escheat fall, his lands be comprised, &c. yet
the principal will be only obliged as above. In a case, however,
where the cautioner’s lands were comprised for the principal sum,
                                                  annualrent;

* 4th December 1629, Laird of Cockpule against Johnston.

annualrent, and penalty, in a purfuit for relief, the Lords obliged the principal to refund to the cautioner all that he had deburfed; and that upon the cautioner's own oath *.

This cafe was attended with particular circumftances, which take it out of the general rule. Dirleton doubts, ' If a cautioner be de-' nounced for his cautionry, will the principal be liable to relieve ' him of the lofs of his efcheat?'—Stewart anfwers, ' A cautioner ' may crave all coft, fkaith, and damage, that happens to. him ' directly by his cautionry; but, if he be denounced and efcheated ' for not paying, it is his own fault who performed not the obliga-' tion of his cautionry †.' The principle of the opinion is the pre-fent rule; and, therefore, the obligation of relief, of all cofts, fkaith, and damage, reaches not fuch as are incurred by the cau-tioner's own fault.

' *Providing always that thir prefents, with the claufe of relief* ' *above-mentioned, in the forefaid bond of cautionry, fhall noways in-* ' *fer double warrandice upon me.*' — This cautious provifo was thought to be neceffary at this time, becaufe all bonds had claufes of relief; and fometimes the cautioner, as in this cafe, chofe likewife to have a feparate bond. Thefe words feem to have been borrowed from the warrandice in heritable fecurities, merely from the refem-blance of the words; for it is impoffible that double warrandice could be incurred by different obligements of relief; the claufe, therefore, was changed for the following one : ' Therefore, in cor-' roboration of the claufe of relief before recited, and without de-' rogation therefrom, or prejudice thereto, or to any diligence com-' petent to follow thereon.' This claufe had more meaning than the former one, and is expreffive of the fact. Though cautioners ftood poffeffed of bonds of relief in the foregoing terms, yet they could not take any effectual ftep in confequence of them, againft the debtor,

* 19th March 1630, Lord Lundie againft Earl of Argyle.
† Dirleton's Doubts, p. 24.

debtor, who ftood only bound *ad factum praeftandum*, i. e. the relive-
ing of the cautioner; but, as formerly obferved, this could not be
done till diftrefs or actual payment of the debt. Thus an apprifing
was found null, becaufe it had been led, not by the creditor, but by
the cautioner upon his bond of relief, before he was either diftreffed or had made payment *. This opinion was afterwards altered;
a Writer to the Signet gave in a bill, craving an adjudication upon
a bond of relief, though there was no diftrefs. The clerk to the
bills hefitated, and moved the matter to the Lords. The Lords allowed the extract of the adjudication to go out, with this quality,
that it fhould not take effect till diftrefs †.

Thefe inconveniences plainly fhewed the bond of relief, as then
taken, to be defective in form, and infufficient to effectuate the indemnification propofed by it. The firft improvement devifed for
this purpofe, was a claufe in the following terms, which immediately followed the general obligation : ' And for that effect to obtain
' and report to the faid D. and his forefaids, the above-mentioned
' bond unregiftered ; or elfe a full and fufficient difcharge, duly
' fubfcribed ; the fums principal, annualrents, and expences therein
' contained ; and of the famen bond itfelf, bail heads, claufes, and
' contents thereof ; with all claufes requifite and needful ; and that
' betwixt and the term of ————— next, with the fum of
' ————— money forefaid, of liquidate expences, by and attour
' performance of the obligation of relief, report, or difcharge above
' fpecified ; and together with,' &c. We find an inftance of this
in a decifion of a pretty early date. It is thus marked in the Dictionary, p. 127. ' A bond of relief was found to be the ground of
' a charge, though no diftrefs was produced, it bearing an oblige-
' ment to pay at a certain time ‡.' The hint given in this decifion

                                                          feems

---

* November 1686, Dickfon againft Govan.
† November 20th 1685, Burnet againft Veitch.
‡ Gosford, 7th July 1668, Paton againft Paton.

feems to have been pretty long of being followed, at laft it was attended to, and the above claufe devifed for that purpofe. In place
of taking the principal party bound to report the bond difcharged
or cancelled, the next ftep in the progrefs was to bind him to make
payment of the money to the principal debtor. Accordingly, a
claufe was devifed in the following terms : ' And for that effect, at
' Whitfunday next, to make payment to the faid A. B. (the credi-
' tor in the bond) of the forefaid principal fum, with what annual-
' rents thereof fhall be refting for the time ; and to retire from him
' the bond above mentioned ; and to deliver to them, and each of
' them, their fubfcriptions torn therefrom, or otherways a fuffi-
' cient difcharge thereof ; and that under the pain and penalty of
' L. 600, Scots money, to be paid by me to them, in cafe of failzie,
' by and attour fulfilling of the premifes.' This is the form of the
bond given by Spottifwood * in his time, i. e. in the beginning of
the prefent century. What was underftood to be the then import
of it, we learn from Sir James Stewart. It is one of Dirleton's
queftions, ' Whether a perfon obliged conjunctly with another, up-
' on a bond to be relieved, may not, after regiftration of the princi-
' pal bond, charge for relief ; and, for that effect, to pay the fum,
' and poind for the fame ?' Stewart anfwers : ' A perfon bound
' for another, and having a bond for relief, may, after regiftration
' of the principal bond, charge for relief, in terms of his bond ; but,
' if he hath not paid the debt, and be only charged, it is thought
' the perfon for whom he ftands bound, finding him good fecurity
' for affurance of his relief, fhould be no further liable ; for it would
' be hard that a cautioner only charged, but not paying, fhould, on
' pretext of his relief, have accefs to poind or diftrefs the perfon of
' the principal †.' The form ftill remained materially defective ;
though a term was fixed for retiring the principal bond, by making
payment to the creditor ; yet ftill the obligation refolved into the

Y

per-

* Page 20.   † Dirleton, p. 120.

performance of a fact; which could with propriety afford nothing but diligence against the person of the granter. A poinding could not yet proceed upon the bond of relief; nor could arrested goods be made forthcoming; because, by the nature of these executions, they can only take place for liquid debts in the person of the creditor. A very obvious alteration in the bond of relief was sufficient to give them this material advantage; and yet no deeds of that kind, containing such an improvement, are to be met with anterior to the year 1730. Before that period, cautioners were often cut out by other creditors; because it behoved them to recover a decree in consequence of their distress, or, *de facto*, to pay the debt, before they could secure themselves upon the estate of their principals. About this time, some man of business fell upon the very natural thought of binding the principal to make payment to the cautioner himself of the debt in the relative bond, and that at the very same term of payment therein mentioned, in order that it might be in his power, if he pleased, to retire the bond himself. This gave perfection to the bond of relief; it put it in the power of the cautioner to secure himself at any time when he thought proper, without being distressed, or paying up the debt himself.

In a modern form, published in Spottiswood's Styles, we may observe all the progressive steps and improvements of the bond of relief, standing as it were in the order of their introduction; and it is by tracing the improvements made in our deeds from time to time that we can alone arrive at the true reasons and principles of our forms, and at a perfect understanding of their legal import. This bond being published, as the editors of Spottiswood declare, by a gentleman of eminent knowledge and practice in business, it may be observed from the Register, that several people, trusting the word of the bookseller, have condescended to follow the same style in their practice. Though it does contain the modern improvement in the matter of relief, it is a confused form, exceptionable both in grammar and sense, and, what is worse, it is materially wrong. The

principal

principal error is, that the cautioner's demand of payment to himfelf is only made conditional upon the debtor's failure in retiring the
bond, and performing other circumftances there mentioned ; whereas
it ought to have been unconnected with the preftation of the facts,
and entirely optional to the cautioner himfelf. This form would
require two feparate charges ; one *ad facta praeftanda*, to eftablifh the
failure, and found the fecond and liquid charge for the debt, fo as
diligence of all kinds might freely proceed. For, if it be not the
failure, no term is mentioned for payment to the cautioner ; and
confequently no precife day for the penalty's taking place, which
therefore appears moft aukwardly introduced *.

Many individuals have fuffered by blunders in bonds of relief, particularly by the omiffion of the obligement to pay to the cautioner
himfelf, which is the moft effential claufe of the deed. It behoved
to be more effential, no doubt, before the laft bankrupt act, when
the preference upon moveables was entirely determined, by poinding,

Y 2   and

---

* It may be here proper to give the modern form of the bond of relief. After narrating the principal bond, it proceeds : ' And feeing that the faid principal fum of
' L. 400 was entirely applied to my ufe, and no part thereof to the ufe of the faid D.
' who became bound with me in the faid bond at my requeft, and confequently is en-
'titled to be relieved of his engagement. Therefore I, by thefe prefents, bind and
' oblige me, my heirs, executors, and fucceffors whatever, to free and relieve the faid
' D. his heirs and fucceffors, from payment of the faid principal fum of L. 400, of the
' annualrent and penalty contained in the bond above mentioned ; as alfo of all cofts,
' damages, or expences, which the faid D. may fuftain or incur by his having become
' bound with me in manner before mentioned : And, for that purpofe, I bind and oblige
' myfelf, and my forefaids, to make payment to the faid C. or any other perfon in right
' of the faid bond at the time, of the whole forefaid principal fum of L. 400 Sterling, and
' that at the term of Candlemas next, with the bygone intereft due thereon, and penalty
' if incurred ; fo as the principal bond, granted in manner forefaid, may be retired and
' cancelled ; or otherways, and in the option of the faid D. or his forefaids, to make
' payment to him or them, at the forefaid term of Candlemas, of the faid principal fum,
' intereft, and penalty, fo as he or they may operate their own relief, by procuring the
' faid bond to be retired or properly difcharged, and that under the penalty of L. 100,
' in the event of my failure, befides full performance. Confenting,' &c.

and arreftment. Of this a particular inftance may be given. James
Beveridge had become bound for Jamiefon in one thoufand pounds
Sterling, and had taken a bond of relief. Beveridge had early notice of Jamiefon's bad circumftances, and had given him the firft
charge of horning. Several other charges of horning followed ; upon which a meeting of the creditors was called. Upon production
of the grounds of debt, it appeared that, from the erroneous conception of Beveridge's bond, he could not poind ; in confequence of
which his debt was poftponed. The fact came out to be, that Beveridge and Jamiefon had fome how or other got hold of an old fa-
fhioned bond of relief ; and, in order to fave writers fees, Jamiefon
cunningly copied a bond in the fame form for his friend ; which
taught him a leffon at a very high price. Were the example of thefe
people to be copied by others, more law-pleas would arife in one
year than are at prefent produced in twenty.

Where there are feveral cautioners in a bond, if the fum be large,
each of them takes feparate bonds of relief ; but, in fmaller debts,
the bond is lodged with one of them, who grants an obligement,
generally in the form of a miffive-letter, to produce it on demand :
for the debt may be required from any one of the conjunct obligants ;
and therefore each of them is entitled to act for his own fafety, independent of the reft. In cafe the debt is paid by any one perfon,
the law eftablifhes for each of them relief *pro rata* againft his neigh-
bour; without any fpecial provifo or agreement to that purpofe.

If the cautioner is averfe to diftrefs the principal debtor himfelf,
and at the fame time wants to get clear of the engagement, he has
the direct method of bringing the matter to a point. He intimates
his bond of relief, under form of inftrument, to the principal creditor, which gives a commencement to the feptennial prefcription introduced by the act 1695. Intimations of this kind, as obferved
before, have the effect to bring on the immediate demand of the
debt ; and it is the duty of the agent for the principal creditor not to
let it lie over   for a variety of accidents may concur to put thefe
                                                    intimations,

intimations out of remembrance, such as the death of the agent or the party. If no diligence be done within seven years thereafter, the cautioner is free; and, though diligence be done, it will carry no more than the principal sum, and the interest fallen due within the seven years.

There are cases, however, in which intimations of this kind are prudent and adviseable. For example, a cautioner dies, leaving a personal and real estate subject to debts which require management upon the part of his representatives. If the principal debtor remains alive, and in circumstances, such an intimation of the relief brings the demand of the debt immediately upon him, and his estate, to which the principal creditor has immediate access. He will therefore, in all probability, choose to discuss them before meddling with the estate of the deceased cautioner, which cannot be so readily affected.

Our writers are agreed, and decisions of the Court have established, that the space of seven years, mentioned in the act 1695, though commonly termed the *septennial prescription*, is not of the nature of prescription. Prescription is always founded on a presumed dereliction of the right or debt; but this is a benefit introduced by the public law in favour of cautioners, which must take place according to the letter. Other prescriptions are cut off by interruption, which destroys their principle; I mean the presumed dereliction upon which they are founded. The act 1695 declares that no cautioner shall continue bound for a longer term than seven years. ‘ This emphatical expression,’ Mr Erskine justly observes, ‘ seems to be made use ‘ of on purpose to distinguish the limitation of the act from prescrip- ‘ tion, and to make the elapsing of the seven years a virtual avoid- ‘ ing or discharge of the obligation; with this only reservation, that ‘ the special diligence used against the cautioner before the running ‘ out of that term, by horning, arrestment, inhibition, and adjudica- ‘ tion, for the sums then fallen due, shall have its course after that ‘ period.”

' period *.' No renewal of the cautionry obligement is to be trusted
to ; nay, not even an exprefs renunciation of the benefit. All other
advantages introduced, either by the Roman law or ours, have been
defeated by renunciations ; but that is not the cafe with the feptennial limitation. A creditor imagined that he fhould retain his fecurity, by making the cautioner annex a docquet at the foot of the
bond, ' difpenfing with any benefit he may have by the act of par-
' liament 1695, anent the prefcription of cautionry obligements,
' and declaring himfelf bound notwithftanding thereof.' It was
pled for the charger, that a man might renounce any benefit introduced by law in his own favour ; but the Lords found that the cautioner could not difpenfe with the act of parliament †.

A decree taken againft the cautioner within the feven years will
not preferve the debt ; the debtor is as much bound by the bond as
he can be by the decree ; it is diligence alone that, by the act, is
fufficient for the purpofe ; and even that diligence will only fecure
the fpecial fubjects thereby affected. Suppofing, therefore, you had
adjudged a particular part of the cautioner's eftate, or attached a fpecial fum or moveable by arreftment, without doing diligence by
horning againft his perfon ; all that you could do, after the elapfe
of the term, would be to recover the particular fubjects adjudged or
arrefted ; and, if you failed in that, the debt was gone. The effential diligence, therefore, is by horning denounced and regiftered,
which preferves the debt itfelf againft the cautioner's reprefentatives,
that is, the principal fum and intereft due within the feven years.

Several difputes have occurred refpecting the mode of intimation, i. e. whether equipollents, or the private knowledge of
the debtor in the principal bond were fufficient ; but it is an
eftablifhed point that private knowledge will not do. However, it is advifeable for the principal creditor who lends the money
to keep himfelf in a convenient ignorance of the fituation of the
                                                        obligants ;

* Page 531.   † Edgar, Feb. 19. 1724, Norie againft Porterfield.

obligants; and, particularly, not to be present at, or concerned in, any settlements between them about the matter of their relief. We shall state a case which puts this in a strong light. A writer took a bond for his wife's portion from her brother, and another gentleman, in which they were bound as joint obligants. The writer, fond of business, made out the bond of relief by his brother to the other gentleman, and signed as a witness to the execution of it. The seven years in the act 1695 were allowed to expire. The cautioner being charged, suspended, and pled, That, although private knowledge was not sufficient in a case of this kind, yet the writing and being witness to a bond of relief ought to afford the benefit of the act, because it is really an intimation, the suspender being but a cautioner; for the law does not provide that the intimation should be by a notary before witnesses. ' The Lords found private know-
' ledge not relevant; but that the charger's writing the bond of re-
' lief, and signing as witness to it, on the date of the bond charged
' on, was a sufficient intimation *.' Since it is so dangerous for the principal party to meddle in this business, it cannot be altogether convenient for his agent to interfere. It is therefore prudent that the bond of relief should be written by the cautioner's man of business, and not by the person who wrote the principal bond. Neither he nor his employer should have any concern in that affair. This, however, is a point of prudence, not of necessity.

* June 22. 1714, Ranken against Shaw.

Assignation.

Affignation.

THE next deed in the practical order is an Affignation of the Bond. This happens moft frequently when the credit of the granter is unexceptionable. Then, the bond paffes from han to hand like a fum of money. It happens alfo in a hundred other ca-fes daily occurring. Our lawyers have often been furprifed at the fingularity in which the ftyle of the Affignation is conceived. In place of words importing a *fimple conveyance* of the debt by the granter to the receiver, the latter is conftituted *a ceffioner and affignee in* and *to* the money; he is fubftituted in the place of the former, and vefted with fpecial powers for recovery of the debt: And it is this particular ftyle which, in our practice, characterifes an affigna-tion. The prefervation of original forms, as obferved upon ano-ther occafion, however uncouth they may appear in modern times, has, in our neighbouring kingdom, preferved the hiftory of their law almoft entire. When the original progrefs and principles of a deed are known, there can be little difficulty in fixing the prefent import of it. The affignation is one of the few writings relating to perfonal deeds which has come down to us in its primitive form, and therefore we are enabled to give a diftinct account of its pro-grefs. The hiftory of this deed affords an irrefiftible proof that the law of the whole ifland was originally the fame.

In place of the *nomina debitorum*, by which title the Romans diftin-guifhed all debts or claims conftituted by obligement, contract, or other

writings,

writings, our anceflors chofe, it feems, to found their diflinction upon the nature of the thing. Property, with them, was either in poffeffion or in action ; and, under the latter clafs, were ranged all thofe
things which we have a right or title to recover by action at law.
When the language of the law came to be Norman, thefe were termed *chofes in action ;* comprehending all the Roman *Nomina;* and,
confequently, all debts due by bond, contract, or other writings ; for
poffeffion of the debt cannot be attained till it is recovered by a
courfe of law. This right, then, it behoved him to exercife in perfon ; he could not make it over to another ; for a notion had taken
place that fuch a right of conveying would be hurtful to the public,
by promoting an univerfal difpofition to law-pleas ; and therefore
no fuch affignments from one man to another were admitted in the
courts, or allowed to take effect.

Sir William Blackflon, however, informs us, that this ancient
principle of the common law was made to yield to the more polifh-
ed and commercial manners of after times *. Without altering the
law itfelf, the Englifh always choofe to reach their purpofes by fiction. The perfon in whom the debt was meant to be completely
vefted is made an attorney for the granter ; and, as any man may
fue by an attorney, the law was not contradicted. Still the original
creditor appeared as the purfuer ; and, upon recovery of the money,
the declaration of truft cut off any action for account. The word
affignment is an Englifh term; derived from the Latin *affignare*, to
appoint, diftribute, or affign. ' It has', fays Dr Cowel, ' two figni-
' fications ; one general, as to appoint a deputy, or affign a right to
' another. In which fenfe, Britton (one of the oldeft Englifh wri-
' ters) mentions that this word was firft brought into ufe for the fa-
' vour of baftards, becaufe they cannot pafs under the name of heirs,
' and therefore were and are provided under the name of affignees.
' The affignment of any thing, is the fetting over of a man's intereft .

* Vol. ii p. 442.

' to another ; in which manner is ufed alfo the words *affignee, affig-*
' *natus,* for one that is deputed or appointed by another, to do any
' act, or perform any bufinefs, or enjoy any commodity.'

 Practice has taught us, in Scotland, to confider the word *affignee*
as applicable only to perfonal rights. This, however, is a miftake ;
it was introduced originally in heritage, and only afterwards applied
to denote that particular kind of attorneyfhip which the common
law rendered neceffary for the tranfmiffion of *chofes in action* from
one man to another. In heritage, we have retained the words in its
original fenfe—' Ex ufu noftro (fays Craig) affignatus idem eft cum
' fingulari fucceffore.' By our practice, an affignee is the fame as a
fingular fucceffor.

 The civil law drew a different confequence from that which we
have heard as to their *nomina debitorum.* ' Rem in bonis noftris ha-
' bere intelligimur quoties ad recuperandam eam actionem habe-
' amus.' This kind of poffeffion, then, might be given up to another, as well as any thing elfe, *in bonis* of the party ; and this, in
the civil law, was called *ceffio.* ' Affignations (fays Lord Stair) are
' more frequent with us than anywhere elfe. There is fcarce men-
' tion thereof in the civil law.' ' Perfonal rights (he obferves) are
' fometimes uncommunicable, yea generally all obligations are in-
' tranfmiffible, upon either part, directly, without the confent of the
' other party; which is clear upon the part of the debtor; who
' cannot, without the confent of the creditor, liberate himfelf, and
' tranfmit his obligation upon another, though, with the creditor's
' confent, he may by delegation. Neither can a creditor force his
' debtor to become debtor to another without his own confent, as
' when he takes him obliged to pay to him or his affignees ; yet,
' that obligations may become the more ufeful and effectual, cuftom
' has introduced an indirect manner of tranfmiffion thereof without
' the debtor's confent, whereby the affignee is conftituted procura-
' tor ; and fo, as mandator for the creditor, he hath power to ex-
' act and difcharge ; but it is to his own behoof ; and fo he is alfo
         ' denominated

' denominated donator ; and this is the ordinary conception of af-
' fignations *.'

Since thefe intranfmiffible qualities of obligations fubfifted among
the Romans, how comes it, that, as Lord Stair acknowledges, there
is fcarce any mention of affignations in the civil law ? It imported
the Roman lawyers to make their obligations ufeful ; and they were
acquainted with *procuratories in rem fuam.* i. e. powers given by one
man to another to do fomething in his name, the effect or produce
of which was to belong to the procurator himfelf ; and yet thefe
were never made ufe of in the tranfmiffion of debts. Befides, it is
certain that obligations were granted to affigns before the civil law
was acknowledged as the law of this country. But it was not the
terms of the bond or other ground of debt which rendered them
intranfmiffible ; it was the law itfelf ; and therefore all the old bonds
uniformly bore to be payable to the creditor, or his certain attorney.

The form and the title of our affignation, I apprehend, belong
entirely to the law of England, or, in other words, to our ancient
law ; whereby no debts or rights were capable of tranfmiffion ; and
therefore it behoved the party to act as an attorney, and to take his
right in the form of a power of attorney. When the Roman law
came to be in a manner the fole ftudy in Scotland, and all our old
forms and cuftoms were fuppofed or pretended to be derived from
it, without dreaming of the ancient law of the ifland, or taking the
trouble to reflect whether our anceftors had a law or not, our old
lawyers fuppofe the form of our affignation to have been introduced
by our own cuftoms, in order to avoid the accidental inconveniences
arifing from the Roman law ; and the analogy between the ftyle
and the Roman idea of *procuratories in rem fuam* ferved to convince
them of the fact. Thus, in another place, fpeaking of procuratories
of refignation, and precepts of feifine, Stair fays, ' They are no.

Z 2   ' more

---

* Stair, p. 380.

' more recoverable than affignations, which, by their nature and
' ftyle, are procuratories by the cedent to the affignee *in rem fuam ;*
' for debtors are not obliged to pày to any other but the perfons
' mentioned in the obligations, or their heirs, which, *fictione juris,*
' are efteemed the fame perfons with the creditors ; and therefore,
' unlefs the obligement bears exprefsly to affignees, the debtor is not
' the affignee's debtor ; and fo the affignee obtains payment, as
' being the procurator or mandator of the creditor ; yet the man-
' date is not revocable by the death of either cedent or affignee, e-
' ven by our own former cuftom *.' This former cuftom had its
rife from a fource which has not been mentioned by any of our writers, and which, notwithftanding, can with certainty be difclofed.
The French, who are governed almoft by the letter of the Roman
law in every thing refpecting moveables, found nothing in that jurifprudence of Lord Stair's objections, raifed upon the prefumed
form of ancient obligements, which difcharged the direct tranfmiffion of *nomina debitorum* of rights and claims of all kinds to be *in
bonis ;* which is another word for being in poffeffion. And they alfo
found that the Roman creditors very often fubftituted others in their
place, by delegation. The French admitted the practice of delegation, upon condition that it was done by writing ; and, at the fame
time, in order to avoid the neceffity of procuring the debtor's confent, they alfo introduced a direct conveyance of the debt or right by
one man to another, which was termed *un tranfport.* He who made
the *tranfport* was called *cedant,* and he who received it *ceffionaire.*
This French deed was a direct conveyance, without the fiction of an
attorney, or any other fiction ; and the terms adopted are evidently
expreffive of its nature. In the reign of the James's, particularly in
the reigns of James IV. and V. our anceftors in Scotland grew im-
moderately fond of every thing that was French. Our writers, our
lawyers, and our churchmen, had their education at Paris, and vied
with each other in importing the Gallic manners and cuftoms, particularly

* Page 788.

cularly in judicial matters. This inclination appeared eafy and natural, from the Roman law being the acknowledged public jurifprudence of both nations. In this fituation, the real effects of the French
act of tranfport were brought to Scotland, and ingrafted upon our affignation. We dropped the old Englifh terms of *affignor* or *affignee*,
or whatever they were, for the French ones of *cedent* and *ceffionary ;* and retaining the ancient form and title of affignation, we
adopted the French conftruction and execution of the tranfport.

Let us now attend to our ancient laws upon this fubject. The
oldeft trace of this deed is to be found in Balfour, who has preferved a decifion as far back as 22d June 1492. It is in the following
terms : ' Gif ony creditor makes and conftitutes ony perfon his cef-
' fioner and affignee to ony debt auchtand to him, the faid affignee
' aught and fould mak lawful intimation of the faid affignation to
' the debitor ; utherways, gif the faid debitor happenis to pay the
' creditor, or any others in his name havand his power and right,
' befoir ony intimation made to him, he on na ways fould be com-
' pellit to mak ony payment to the faid affignee be reafon of his af-
' fignation ;' Drummond againft Mufhet *. The queftion lay here
only between the debitor and the affignee ; but, by another decifion
about forty years thereafter, we find the intimation rendered effential to the completion of the right, and eftablifhed as the rule of
preference between third parties precifely according to the law of
France: ' Gif ony perfon makes divers and fundry affignies to ony
' reverfions, for redemption of ony lands, the affignee wha makes
' firft intimation and warning, has juft titill to redeem the famin, and
' fould be preferrit thereintill to all other affignies; 21ft Feb. 1533,
' Erle of Murray againft Lord Ruthven.'

The points eftablifhed by thefe decifions Sir Thomas Craig has a-
dopted as the principles of the law in his time. ' Alias affignationes
' apud nos licitae funt; fed nifi affignatus jus fuum infinuaverit,
' (quod nos intimari dicimus), tuto cedenti folutio fieri poteft †.'

Talking

---

* Page 169.   † Page 131. § 31.

Talking of reverfions, he tells us, in terms of Balfour's laft decifion, ' Si duobus feparatim jus redimendi conceffum fuerit, aut af-
' fignatum, qui prius jus fuum infinuaverit, praeferetur: Nam prae-
' ter jus, civilis quaedam poffeffio per intimationem concurrit. Ita-
' que qui prius infinuaverit, five ut nos loquimur intimaverit, pof-
' fefforis loco eft, et proinde potior.' Lord Stair tells us, ' That the
' affignation is not a complete right till it be orderly intimated to
' the debtor, which, though at firft, it is like, hath been only ufed
' to put the debtor in *mala fide* to pay the cedent, or any other af-
' fignee, yet now it is a folemnity requifite to affignations ; fo that,
' though the debt remain due, if there be divers affignations, the
' firft intimation is preferable, though of the laft affignation ; and
' that not as a legal diligence, which can be prevented and excluded
' by another diligence, but as a full accomplifhment of the affigna-
' tion *.' There is no evidence that the intimation of an affignment had no other original meaning than to put the debtor in
mala fide. The effect in France is as old as the ceremony ; and the
Scotch adopted both ready made for the purpofe. We muft either
hold that the naked conveyance was fufficient *per fe* to carry the
right, or that the intimation was an effential part of the conveyance.
We cannot affent to the firft propofition, without expofing an innocent debtor to the unjuft hazard of making double payment ; and,
if we agree that he is at liberty to make payment to the cedent,
then it is an undeniable confequence that the fubject remains where
it was, that is, in the poffeffion of the firft owner. Now, it was an
old principle in the law, and it ftill remains to be fo, that an affignment of any moveable is good for nothing while it remains in the
cedent's poffeffion, or, as the lawyers term it, *retenta poffeffione.* A
debt, or *chofe in action,* is incapable of delivery ; and therefore the
application of an affignment by intimation is the only kind of poffeffion which the matter is capable of. The reafoning, then, of Sir
Thomas Craig, and our old lawyers, is ftriking and conclufive.

The

* June 13. 1629. Finlayfon.

The effect given to the deed by intimation is diametrically oppofite to the nature and principles of the English affignment, which was a device to avoid the common law, by recovering, in the the quality of an attorney, and in the name of the affignor, what he could not recover in virtue of a direct conveyance, and in his own name. A deed of this nature did not abfolutely tranfmit the right from the affignor to the affignee ; it only gave the latter a power to get the debt into his own poffeffion, and cut off the claim of the conftituent to call his attorney to account. Accordingly, we are affured by Judge Blackftone, and we fee from the ftyle of the English affignment, that, to this day, the profecution of the action muft be brought in the name of the affignor ; who therefore binds himfelf, in the firft place, to allow his name to be made ufe of, and not to receive any payment from his original debtor. During the dependence of the fuit, therefore, the common law of England ftill confiders the property of the debt, or *chofe in action*, to be remaining in the perfon of the original creditor. Intimation, as we underftand it, is quite incompatible with thefe ideas ; and accordingly the English practice does not, and never did, know any thing of it ; neither would it have been of any ufe ; the poffeffion of the bond or other ground of debt renders the affignee fecure, and the debtor will pay to no body but the holder of the bond ; and, if he pays any thing to account, a receipt muft be written upon it, in the fame manner as upon a bill. They have no regifters for principal deeds, and no arreftments to cut out the affignee. Befides, an action, for moft part, inftantly follows an affignment. The creditor, therefore, is in poffeffion of all the right which the law can give him ; and a fecond affignee, without poffeffion of the grounds of debt, would not be heard in an attempt to defeat the firft one. Our affignation, on the other hand, notwithftanding its ftyle, has been, fince the days of Craig and Balfour, a direct conveyance of the whole clafs of debts, rights, and claims, by one man in favour of another. It is completed by intimation ; and the cedent, from that moment, is entirely denuded. This change, however, did not fuddenly take place.

place. Though our lawyers adopted the principles of the French tranfport, they could not, for fome time, get quit of the ancient principles which remained in our practice, and were fupported by the ftyle of the deed. It is thefe changes in our law, thefe mixtures of principles, which render the practice and decifions of our Court, in the days of James V. Mary, and James VI. fo contradictory, and to us almoft inexplicable. Some of thefe confequences reached down to our own times.

Notwithftanding the effect given to an affignment by intimation, it was a long time before the Scots affignee could execute any decreet in his own name, which had been obtained in the name of the cedent. The firft remedy applied to this was to confider the affignee as a fingular fucceffor, and to allow him the benefit of a decreet of transference active, for transferring into his own perfon the right and title of the decreet pronounced in favour of the affignee ; an effect which his deed and intimation did not beftow. This was evidently to confider the affignation as a mandate, according to the original idea of the national cuftoms, and to admit it to be a procuratory alfo *in rem fuam*, in terms of the civil law. As fuch they held it to be fufficient to convey the right ; but ftill it was but a procuratory ; and therefore it behoved the party to act in name of his conftituent. Although this form was altered in the time of Sir Thomas Craig, the point appears not to have been well eftablifhed ; for we find it brought under trial a little after his death. ' It was ' objected to an affignee, that he could not do diligence in his own ' name upon a decreet obtained by his cedent ; but the Lords found, " That the affignation being intimate in the cedent's lifetime, the " affignee was under no neceffity to transfer the fentence, but might " lawfully proceed by letters of horning upon the faid intimation fo " intimated, without any transferring, or other action *." If, however, no information happened to be made during the life of the cedent, the affignee could do nothing in his own name. This is

fo

* Durie, Feb. 3. 1624, Stevenfon againft Craigmillar.

fo clearly ftated by Sir Robert Spottifwood, as not to require the
fupport of any decifions. ' An affignee to a bond, regiftrating the
' fame, may charge upon it. If the affignation be to a fentence, and
' the cedent alive, the like may be done ; but, if the cedent be de-
' ceafed, it muft be transferred at the affignee's inftance. Not only
' a fentence muft be transferred, but likewife an action, the cedent
' or defender being dead *.'

A transference was not only neceffary, but, before the affignee
ftood entitled to transfer, he was obliged to confirm, i. e. to obtain
a fecond legal affignation from the ecclefiaftical court. This went
upon a curious mixture of principle and intereftednefs. We are fpeaking of the cafe where the cedent died without the tranfmiffion being
completed by intimation, as the completion of the transfer lay upon
the act of intimation in the lifetime of the parties ; fo, upon the
death of the cedent, the fubject was held to remain *in bonis* of him.
Here the Bifhops ftruck in to claim the quot of the teftament. Your
affignation (faid they) is only a procuratory, which has fallen upon
the death of the conftituent. You cannot act in name of a dead
man, and therefore a confirmation is neceffary for that purpofe.
This fubtility the Bifhops maintained, not only after the Reformation, but fo late as the 1690. By the 26th act of that parliament,
it was declared : ' That, where fpecial affignations and difpofitions
' are lawfully made by the defunct, though neither intimated nor
' made public in his lifetime; they fhall be yet good and valid rights
' and titles to poffefs, bruik and enjoy, purfue or defend, albeit the
' fums of money or goods therein contained be not confirmed.' By
this time, people had got into a method of fettling their moveable
effects in the form of affignations, in place of teftaments, which
proceeded entirely upon the idea of the former deed being a direct
tranfmiffion of the debt, or other fubject, and not a procuratory or
mandate ; and no doubt they expected, by this means, to elude the
expences of confirmation. But this was prevented by the Bifhops,

Vol. I.   A a   under

* Tit. Affignation.

under the idea of affignments being merely procuratories. The act
1690, however, gave them relief, in fo far as refpected fpecial affignations. Thus matters continued until the act 15th of the 3d
feffion of William and Mary's firft parliament, 1693. This ftatute
keeps the mandate for regiftration in force, and empowers the
parties interefted to regiftrate them, i. e. to obtain a decree of regiftration after the death of the granter or mandator, contrary to the
nature of mandates, which by law fall upon the death of the granter. The act provides : ' That this regiftration fhall only take place
' upon production of a fervice or retour, in cafe of bonds or other
' writs heritable, or a confirmed teftament, containing the bond or
' other writs, in cafe they be moveable, or of a fpecial affignation,
' though not intimated in the cafe of either.' The act then proceeds : ' And, further, it is ftatuted, that, if it fhall happen the pur-
' fuer to deceafe, at any time during the dependence of any procefs
' raifed at his inftance, there fhall be no need hereafter for his heir,
' executor, or affignee, to raife and obtain a transferring active : But
' the faid heir, executor, or affignee, is hereby allowed, upon pro-
' duction of his fervice or retour, confirmed teftament, or fpecial af-
' fignation, though not intimate, to infift in the principal caufe.'

Upon this ftatute, feveral obfervations occur. Practice, it will be
obferved, has very much varied from it. The act confidered the regiftration of a deed in a very folemn light, in the light of a regular
decreet ; and therefore, before we could put the obligement of a
dead man upon record, in terms of this act, we ought to produce to
the keeper of it the fervice, the retour, the confirmed teftament, or
the fpecial affignation. The profits of regiftration induced the keepers of the records to afk no queftions, but to regifter, without ceremony, any deed put into their hands. In place, therefore, of fhew-
ing thefe titles to them, we produce them at the Bill Chamber when
we come to raife diligence in the name of the heir, the executor, or
affignee. This act confiders a fpecial affignation in the fame light
as it confiders a fervice or retour, i. e. as vefting the full right of the
fubject, or, according to the civil law term, the *jus crediti*, in the
                                                          perfon

perfon of the affignee, which is precifely according to the idea adopted by Sir Thomas Craig, of holding the affignee to be a fingular fucceffor of the defunct. A fervice or a confirmation operates as a complete tranfmiffion in favour of the heir or executor ; and all of them, anterior to this act, needed judicial decreets of transference to veft them in the perfon of the heir or the executor. The ftatute only concerns fpecial affignations ; fo that general affignments ftand upon the fame footing as they did before the act, and confequently, ftrictly fpeaking, need an action of transference to veft any particular right or action in the perfon of the general affignee. Practice, however, has difpenfed with it *.

Upon

* The 39th Article of the Flucidations of the late learned and very ingenious Lord Kames is intituled, ' Commentary upon the act 35th Parl. 1693, concerning Procuratories of Refignation, and Precepts of Safine.' His Lordfhip, in explaining this ftatute, has confounded it with the former one in the 1690, ' Anent the Confirmation of Teftaments.' After giving an account of what he fuppofes to have been the former practice, in the matter of affignations, he proceeds in thefe words : ' Thus ftood the law down to the year 1693, when the act of parliament under confideration was made, authorifing procuratories of refignation, and precepts of fafine, to be executed, after the granter's death, and alfo authorifing fpecial affignations .a is intimated after the cedent's death. The privilege was not extended to general affignations, which, as obferved above, require confirmation. To make this ftatute accord with principles, has not been attempted by any writer ; nor does it feem to be an eafy tafk ; for furely the Legiflature could not mean to empower one to act *procuratorio nomine*, without a conftituent. I underftand the ftatute as empowering thefe feveral acts to be done not *procuratorio nomine*, but by exprefs authority of the ftatute itfelf†.' Now, there is not one word about affignations, either general or fpecial, in the ftatute, as referred to by his Lordfhip ; it folely refpects procuratories of refignation and precepts of feifine, which, till that time, were confidered as *perfonal mandates*, and fell upon the death of the granters. The principles of this ftatute are entirely inapplicable to the former one about affignations. Though Lord Kalmes, by blending the ftatute together, imputes a miftake of principle to the legiflature, of which it ftands entirely clear. ' There feems (fays his Lordfhip) to have been no occafion for a ftatute with refpect to the cafe laft mentioned. The fimple addition of the word *affignees*, in a money-obligation, removes all difficulties. Were our forefathers fo defective in invention, as to overlook an improvement fo obvious ? If I bind myfelf to pay a fum to John, I am not bound

A a 2

' to

† Eluc. p. 320.

Upon looking into Spottifwood's Introduction *, we find the following definition : ' An affignation is a writ of conveyance, and ' applied only to fuch as relate to moveable fums, rents, or duties ; ' for, when other moveable goods, as plenifhing, merchandife, or the ' like, are conveyed, the writ is called a *difpofition to moveables*.' This definition is practically juft, and it is exceedingly curious. Spottif-wood does not fo much as give a hint at the reafon of the diftinction he makes, but prefents it without a difference. We here fee the ancient

law

' to pay it to James ; but, if I bind myfelf to pay it to John, or his affignee, the bond ' has a free circulation. The affignee can affift againft me in his own name, without ' needing a procuratory ; he can intimate his own name, whether the cedent be dead ' or alive ; and his difcharge to me in his own name extinguifhes the debt (p. 321.).' In a preceding paragraph, his Lordfhip had informed us, ' That an obligation for a ' fum of money, without mentioning affignees, is not affignable. To fupply that want, ' a method was invented to affign it indirectly, by giving a procuratory to the affignee ' to ufe the cedent's name in demanding payment. But this was an imperfect method. ' If the cedent died before intimation, the procuratory died with him ; and the affig-' nee's only refource was a procefs againft the cedent's reprefentatives to make up a ' title to the fubject affigned, and to grant a new affignment. Intimation during the ' cedent's life was indeed held fufficient to transfer the *jus crediti* to the affignee, enti-' tling him to drop his character of procurator, and to act in his own name (p. 319.).' His Lordfhip is here certainly miftaken, both in law and in fact. It was not the want of the word *affignees* which, in our law, gave birth to the invention of conveying by a procuratory. The word *affigns* is to be found in heritable rights at the earlieft periods ; nor were our forefathers defective in invention upon this article ; but it was the law it-felf, that, upon a principle of public utility, difcharged the conveyance of debts, or rights in action, from one man to another. The addition of the word *affigns*, therefore, though it might have met the objection deducible from the Roman law, to which Lord Kames alludes, would not have had any effect upon the law of this ifland ; for, though bonds have all along been taken payable to affigns in England, yet the affignee cannot, at this moment, infift in his own name, he muft ftill recover under the title and quality of an attorney. As the fpecification of affignees did not remedy this affair in England ; fo, after the affignation in Scotland came to be confidered as a direct conveyance, the want of that word did not hurt the deed ; and fo, in the laft century, it has feveral times been decided. Befides, the very word *affignation*, in its original import, does not mean a conveyance, as Lord Kaimes fuppofes, but an appointment or conftitution for a particular purpofe.

* Page 72.

lawof the ifland furviving only in form and words; and we fee our
practitioners obliged to ufe differences in ftiles, and in titles, where
they acknowledge none in reality. The true caufes of the diftinction are only to be found in the hiftory of the deed. All rights and
debts, or, as the Englifh fay, *chofes in action*, are ftill with us, as
they were of old, conveyed by a writ under the form of a procuratory or attorney, and under the ancient title of affignment, which
denotes the nature of the writ; while all other goods, or moveable
property, which are not *chofes in action*, but in the poffeffion of the
party, are tranfmitted by a deed of direct conveyance, under the
title of a *difpofition of moveables*. The ftyle of the firft is, to conftitute an affignee; but, by the other, the granter at once fells and
difpones *. It is proper, therefore, to keep up a diftinction in terms
between

* Mr Erfkine expreffes himfelf upon this fubject with a remarkable degree of doubt
and timidity, and takes up the common, and (if I may ufe the expreffion) erroneous notions of the matter : ' Though the terms *difpofition* and *affignation* (fays he) may
' be either of them apt enough to exprefs the alienation of any right whatever, yet, in
' their common ufe, conveyances of debt, or of particular moveable fubjects, go by
' the name of *affignations*. The property, indeed, of a number of moveable fubjects,
' confidered as an *univerfitas*, ex. gr. houfehold ftuff, is fometimes faid to be tranfmitted
' by difpofition; but that word, in its proper fenfe, is applied only to the grant of heri-
' table fubjects, and is a deed containing procuratory of refignation, and precept of fa-
' fine (Page 281.).' The conveyance of a particular moveable fubject does not go by
the name of *affignation*, but is called a *difpofition*. Suppofe the fale of a carriage and
horfes, and a deed neceffary to explain the tranfaction, the feller would not conftitute and appoint the purchafer his lawful affignee in and to this carriage, with full power to drive it where he pleafes, &c. he would fell and difpone it to him, and the
writing would with propriety be called a *difpofition*. A man may act as a procurator,
or in name of another, in recovering a debt, or claiming a right; but, in the purchafe
of moveables, which are inftantly delivered to him, he certainly acts for himfelf, and
takes direct poffeffion, which puts an end to the bufinefs. Mr Erfkine, indeed, fays,
that, where a number of moveables, fuch as houfehold ftuff, are to be tranfmitted, it
muft be a difpofition, becaufe they are confidered as an *univerfitas*. It is not eafy to
conceive what is here meant by an *univerfitas*; but certain it is that our forefathers did
not make the diftinction between the difpofition and the affignation upon that account.
The

between deeds which have a feparate mode of execution. Where moveables are tranfmitted, and require poffeffion and delivery, let us term the deed *a difpofition of moueables* ; and, where debts, rights, or actions, are to be made over, and which can only be completed by intimation, let us continue to term them *affignations*.

We now come to the ftyle itfelf, as given us by St Martin. He fuppofes the bond to have been regiftered, and therefore he begins with a recital of the deed, and the decreet of regiftration. Next follows the caufe of granting, which is always in the form of a fub-fumption or inference.

' *Made payment to me of a certain fums of money.*'—This, in general, continues to be the common expreffion in affignments of debt at this moment. Few people purchafe the debts of o-thers, but, upon getting a deduction of the amount of the debt ; and this was the method taken to exprefs the diminifhed value given. The law therefore prefumes, in every cafe where thefe words occur, that the full value has not been paid ; a circumftance, however, by which the tranfaction is not materially hurt. Some writers, wifhing to intimate that their clients took no advantage, ex-prefs it in this manner : ' For a certain fum of money, equivalent to ' the fums after affigned.' This is affuming an air of myftery, with-out any reafon, and concealing that part of the tranfaction which it is the intereft of the purchafer to make known. Bonds, in the prefent practice, go often from hand to hand by affignment ; and, when full value is paid, the beft way is to exprefs it in one fum, which commenfurates of itfelf with the debt affigned, better than a-ny writer can make it do by words. It fometimes, indeed, happens, that the debt is affigned by a kind of barter, for an illiquid con-fideration ; then it is certainly right to mention that fuch confidera-tion is held to be fully equivalent in value to the debt affigned.

' *Made*

The word difpofition, in its proper fenfe, is not applicable only to heritable fubjects ; we fhall prove, in the proper place, that it was originally ufed in our law for tranf- if-fion of moveables, and was only applied to its prefent practical ufe after the feudal charter grew lefs frequent, and heritage became an object of daily commerce.

' *Made, conftituted, and ordained, and by thir prefents make, confti-*
' *tute, and ordain, the faid W. G. his heirs and affignees, my very*
' *lawful, undoubted, and irrevocable ceffioners and affignees, in and to*
' *the faid fum of ———— of principal,*' &c.—Here is the pure old
Englifh ftyle of an attorney. They faid, and ftill fay, *have made,
conftituted and appointed, and by thefe prefents do make, conftitute,
and appoint, J. B. of, &c. my true and lawful attorney, &c. irrevocable for me, and in my name, to afk, require, &c.* So far the
ftyle of the Englifh and Scotch is the fame, word for word. When
our forfathers came to confider an affignment, not as a mandate,
but as a real conveyance, they added the word *irrevocable* to *ceffioners* and *affigns ;* fo that we fee *ceffioners* and *affigns,* at a former
period, had been revocable at the pleafure of the conftituent.

' *In and to the faid fum of ——— as principal.*'—The Englifh affignment has no fuch expreffion ; the ceffioners and affignees are
there conftituted, not in and to the debt, but to afk, require, and
demand the fame. The phrafe, *in and to,* is abfolutely inconfiftent
with the appointment of an attorney ; they are a part of the French
tranfport or direct conveyance introduced into the old form, when
it came to be confidered as a direct conveyance.

' *And in and to the forefaid bond, decreet interponed thereto,*' &c.
—The fame may be faid of this part of the deed. *Nomina debitorum,*
or grounds of debts themfelves, could be ceded by one man to another by the Roman law, and were confidered in feveral views diftinct from the right which they created to the debt. Hence, in
France, and in Scotland, we continue to make a diftinction between
the right of the debt itfelf, and the inftruction of it ; and that is the
reafon why, in all cafes, we find firft the bonds, bills, and other inftructions of the debt, as a feparate kind of property, and then the
money contained in or due by them.

The Englifh never admitted thefe diftinctions of the Roman law,
and therefore know nothing of this form. The grounds of debt,
with them, are confidered in no other light than as evidences of the
claim.

claim or action and to go along with it, without any fpeciality in the deed.

'*And I have furrogated, and by thefe prefents furrogate and fubfti-* '*tute, the faid W. G. and his forefaids, in my full right, vice, and* '*place of the premifes.*'—Our affignation is a ftrange compound. This claufe was taken by the French from the Roman formula of delegation, and has been by us *verbatim* copied from them. It is perfectly oppofite to the language and principles of a procuratory, becaufe a procurator or attorney only acts for and in the name of another. Delegation, in general, fay the French lawyers, is the act by which one man fubftitutes another, either in his place, or in a debt. Except in the matter of bills, we know nothing of delega- tion in Scotland ; but our forefathers were pleafed to enrich the form of the affignation with the language and the ftyle of it.

'*With full power to the faid W. G. and his forefaids, to intromit* '*with, afk, crave,*' &c.—Here, again, is the original ftyle of the power of attorney almoft *verbatim* from the old Englifh affignment, and quite inconfiftent with the immediate preceding claufe of furro- gation ; for, if the right itfelf be conveyed, the former owner has no title to grant further powers ; all thefe are included in the con- veyance itfelf ; and therefore, in a cafe obferved by Lord Stair, where a bond was affigned, both againft principal and cautioners, but the cautioners were omitted in the claufe ' with full power,' no fpecial power feemed to be given againft them. The Court repelled the objection, becaufe they thought the claufe itfelf of very little confequence *. In this claufe, however, we find the old powers ab- folutely neceffary in an Englifh affignment, I mean that of purfuing in the name of the affignee, which, in fome cafes, is ftill conveni- ent to be done. By an old decifion, we find that a cedent difclaim- ed the procefs brought by the affignee in his name ; becaufe the claufe we are talking of did not contain a fpecial liberty for that purpofe. The Court, however, with great propriety, found that the affignee might ufe his name whether he would or would not †.

'*Which*

---

* Page 381.   † Hope, 20th Nov. 1621, Grierfon againft Maxwell.

' *Which affignation, I bind me, my heirs, and executors, to war-*
' *rant*.'—We fhall not here enter into the etymology of warrandice, which more properly belongs to heritable rights. We fhall
only obferve, that fo foon as deeds come to be executed in writing,
the feller of the land, or the feller of the moveables, were taken
bound in warrandice to the purchafer or the buyer. Only, in the
fale of goods, cattle, or perfonal effects, the warrandice was underftood to extend no further than to the title of the feller; and not to
the quality of the goods, of which it behoved the purchafer to
judge for himfelf.

The import of warrandice in the conveyance of debts, does not
feem to have been fixed even at a very late period of the law, as is
clear from the following queftion put by Sir Robert Spottifwood.
' How far one is obliged to warrant the affignation of a bond, &c.
' made by himfelf to another? Whether that it is truly owing by
' the debtor fimply, or that it is both owing, and that the debtor is
' refponfal? This was drawn in queftion by Alexander M'Nag-
' when and Giles Carfon; but the parties agreed between them-
' felves, 4th February 1632 *.' This indetermination of the law
upon fo material a point, is the reafon why the import of the warrandice in St Martin's affignment is explained by the claufe beginning with ' that is to fay.' This doubt in the author's time came
to be cleared up; but not fooner than the 1671. At that period
there were three different kinds of warrandice ufed in affignations,
the firft was fimply from the fact and deed of the granter, fuch as
we find in St Martin's affignment, where the bond is directly granted to the affignee. And, therefore, there could be no other facts
or deeds to guard againft but his own. The fecond was, where the
bond had gone through feveral tranfmiffions; and might be affected
by the facts or deeds of the intermediate holders. Here the writers
properly and juftly took the cedent bound in warrandice, not only

Vol. I.   B b   againft

* Spottifwood Pract. p. 21.

againſt his own ; but his author's facts and deeds. At other times, whether from the ignorance or inattention of the conveyancer, the aſſignment was warranted like a charter or diſpoſition in heritage, to be good, valid, and effectual, at all hands, and againſt all mortals, which is termed abſolute warrandice. Sometimes, it appears, that this clauſe was inſerted in conſequence of an agreement between the parties ; and was expected to take place *in terminis.* In a caſe mentioned by Stair, Sir Robert Barclay accepted of an aſſigment to bond from Robert Liddel. The deed contained abſolute warrandice ; and the debtor having failed, Sir Robert charged the cedent. The Lords found, ' That ſuch clauſes of abſolute warrandice do not im- ' port that the debtor was ſolvent at the time of aſſignation, but ' only that there was no exception that could defend him either ' from the cedent's deed or otherwiſe *.' The deciſion has eſtabliſh- ed our rule of practice in this point. It was in entire conformity to the maxims of the Roman law. The granter of a conveyance of a debt is bound in no higher warrandice, than that the debt is legally due ; he is not to anſwer for the ſolvency of the debtor, unleſs it be ſo ſpecially agreed. Now it has alſo been determined by the Court, that an agreement of this kind will have the proper effect. An aſſignee did not attempt the recovery of a debt for ſix years after acquiring right to it, the debtor then failed, and an action was brought upon this ſpecial warrandice. The cedent did not diſpute that he was bound to anſwer for the ſolvency ; but he contended, that his ob- ligement related to the debtor's condition, at the date of the aſſign- ment. The charger inſiſted, that the warrandice inferred the actual recovery of the debt at any time when demanded. The Court found, ' That this clauſe imported the ſolvency of the debtor ; but ' that the ſame was preſumed, unleſs it were proven that he was a ' notour bankrupt, or that the aſſignee uſing diligence did not ' recover ; and if reſponſality be alledged, allows the cedent
                                                    ' to

* Nov 24. 1671, Barclay againſt Liddel.—Stair.

' to condefcend upon any vifible eftate he had to effect the
' fame *.'

From thefe premifes, we fee that there are four different kinds of
warrandice proper to affignations : Firft, From the fact and deed
of the cedent ; Secondly, From the facts and deeds, not only of the
cedent, but of his authors ; Thirdly, From facts and deeds, and
from legal exceptions againft the debt ; and, Fourthly, The folvency
of the debtor, or the abfolute affurance of the affignee's recovery
thereof. Thefe form a kind of fcale, rifing above each other in
importance, and therefore it is our proper bufinefs to ftipulate the
one or the other, according to the nature of the tranfaction, and the
agreement of our employers.

We have now only to mention the cafe where the claufe of warrandice has been entirely omitted. This was tried upon the 4th
March 1707, Riddle againft White. The Lords found, ' That
' Whyte's affignation to Creighton, though it bore for onerous
' caufes, yet, having no warrandice, could not be interpreted to
' imply abfolute warrandice, but only from fact and deed, which is
' the common natural warrandice inferted in affignations to debts or
' decreets. For the brocard, that no warrandice muft be underftood
' to be abfolute warrandice, muft be applied according to the nature
' of the right. If it be a fale of lands, for onerous adequate cau-
' fes, then it holds ; but not in affignations to perfonal rights,
' though it fhould at leaft import *debitum fubeffe*. And here there
' was no debt at all, he having, on his being reponed to his oath,
' deponed negative ; yet, at the time of White's affignation, there
' was a decreet ftanding, though afterwards annulled, *quod fen-
' tentia judicis pro veritate habetur*, till it be reduced and taken
' away †.' When no warrandice is expreffed in a deed, and the
warrandice is faid to be implied, the implied warrandice in an affignment, where the claufe is omitted, is, by this decifion, limited to
fimple fact and deed.

B b 2

' *Likeas,*

* Feb. 7. 1678, Stewart againft Melville.   † Fount. Vol. ii. p. 354.

' *Likeas, I have inftantly delivered to the faid W. G. the forefaid*
' *regiftered bond, to be kept and ufed by him and his forefaids in time*
' *coming.*'—A declaration of this kind is extremely ufeful, and in practice never omitted. This claufe fixes upon the affignee, or other
receiver, the particulars of the grounds of debt conveyed, and entirely
cuts off the pretence of their not being delivered. Before this
claufe was devifed, the principal difputes, in matters of warrandice, turned upon the delivery of the papers, which were affirmed or denied by the parties, as their intereft directed. A writer, therefore, muft take care to allow no paper to be fixed upon
him but what he actually receives, to fpecify thofe received in this
claufe, and to take a particular obligation for the production of o-
thers neceffary, within a fixed time, under a penalty, and a declaration, that, if the want of them fhall be objected, in the recovery
of the debt, the cedent fhall be liable in the confequences.

. Having thus analifed the old ftyle given by St Martin, it only remains to be obferved, that the modern affignation differs from it only in the abridgment of the feveral claufes; and that, in place of reciting the bond, the deed is fometimes fhortened, by affiguing it directly, and thereby faving the repetition.

INTIMATION.

The moment we receive an affignation, it is our bufinefs to have
it intimated to the debtor with all defpatch; for, till then, nothing
is done. It was formerly obferved, that the intimation, and its effect, were borrowed from the French, and that it put an end to the
ancient conftruction of our affignment; for, from the moment of the
intimation, the right to the debt paffed to the perfon of the affignee,
who thenceforth did not act as a procurator, but in the fame manner as a French ceffionary in confequence of his tranfport. Thefe
rules were eftablifhed with us in the fifteenth century, as appears
from

from Balfour *. By a decifion, alfo there mentioned, in July 1558, we have the exact form prefcribed. It is as under : ‘ Gif ony per- ‘ fon havand, be gift of the fuperior, the marriage of ony air, he ‘ fould lauchfullie intimate the famin to him, viz. he or his procu- ‘ rator fould come to the perfonal prefence of the heir, and uther ‘ read his gift, or give and deliver him ane copie thereof, and tak an ‘ inftrument in the hands of an nottar thereof ; for, gif he or his ‘ procurator pafs to the perfonal prefence of the heritor, and expone ‘ to him be word that he has the gift of the marriage difponit to ‘ him be the fuperior, or that he is ceffioner and affignee lauchfully ‘ conftitute be the donator thereof, and makes intimation to him of ‘ the famin ; the famin verbal intimation maid, *nuda voce*, is not ‘ fufficient ; and therefoir, albeit the heir marrie without confent of ‘ the faid donator, or his affigney, he fould not be compellit to pay ‘ to him the double avail of the marriage, but the fingle avail alle- ‘ narlie, 1558 ; the Abbot of Coupar donatour, againft the Laird of ‘ Duffus. And the like to be obfervit in all intimations of any uther ‘ richts, evidentis, or titles.’ There is a circumftance in the form thus prefcribed, which of itfelf directly proves from what quarter it came to us, I mean the alternative of reading or giving a copy to the party ; which was, at this period, and ftill is, precifely the rule in France. In Craig’s time, the effect of intimation feems to have been perfectly fettled. The form he prefcribes is the fame with that of Balfour ; only, by that time, the giving of the copy feems to have given place to the reading. The legal effect alfo ap- pears to have been fettled. Intimation, even then, was not merely a notice to the cedent, but an effential folemnity in the tranfmiffion.

We muft here remark a very great omiffion in the work of our formalift, Mr Dallas of St Martin. Though he gives the affigna- tion, and fubjoins practical remarks, he has totally neglected to give the form of the intimation, or even to mention the neceffity of it, for completing the deed, which is certainly one of the greateft

faults

* Page 169.

faults to be met with in his book. Lord Stair's conjecture, it may
be alfo remarked, about an intimation being only neceffary at firft to
put the original creditor in *mala fide*, has no foundation in the hiftory of our law. It might have been fo originally in France; but
certain it is that the act was adopted by us as an effential requifite.
In this he has been followed by all our after writers; and, fo far
has our Court been fwayed by the fame idea, that they admitted notice by equipollents, and have thereby occafioned a prodigious number of queftions, which might have been totally excluded, by adherence to the form and to the law of the country from whence we
had the form improved to our hand. In France, nothing will do
but a folemn act of intimation; as no equipollent with us will fupply
an inftrument of feifine. Even an action brought upon the affignment will not be fufficient to tranfmit the right, until the party appear
in that action, and actually fees the affignment. Each cafe, therefore, falls with us to be determined by its own circumftances; but,
as that is a matter of pure law, it is not within our province, or
within any rule of practice. Our bufinefs is to adhere to and underftand the eftablifhed forms, and not to truft to what the Court
may receive as equivalents in their place. So far it is eftablifhed,
that the private knowledge of a debtor, of an affignation being
granted, will have no effect; nor is it expedient that it fhould; for,
otherwife, a general defence would be afforded to all debtors. They
might, in every cafe, pretend that the debt ftood affigned to third
parties, and obtain delays upon that head. It is neceffary, therefore, that debtors fhould be furnifhed with fome immediate evidence of the fact, in order that they may inftantly produce or condefcend upon it.

The form of the intimation we are to analife, is taken from the Office of a Notary Public, a book of confiderable merit of its kind.

   ' At, &c. compeared *A.* as procurator for the within defigned *B.*
' whofe power is fufficiently known to me notary public.'—The intimation is made, not in the name of the cedent, but in the name of
the affignee. Had Lord Kaimes deigned to confult this humble
                                    performance,

...formance, he would not have fallen into the error which he has ...ne in his Elucidations. ' The intimation (fays his Lordfhip) muft ...e in the cedent's name, as the affigney has nothing to fay to the ...ebtor but *qua procurator ;* and his procefs againft the debtor for ...ayment ought to be carried on in the fame character *.' His Lord-...has, in this place, drawn the fact from his principles, in place of ...drawing his principles from the fact. We borrowed the intima-tio...from France, where a conveyance of debts or rights was never co...fidered as a procuratory ; and therefore the act is done, not in the...name of the cedent, but in the name of the affignee. We find it...efcribed in the ancient form given by Balfour ; and fo it has e-...fince been practifed.

Whofe power of procuratory was fufficiently known to me, N. P.'—...circumftance, of old, was material to the form ; becaufe, unlefs ...e intimation had been made by order of the affignee, it was at-tended with no effect. A fpecial feparate power, therefore, was re-quifite ; or, at leaft, that the notary fhould hear the order given, and mention his knowledge of it in the inftrument ; for a ftranger might be poffeffed of the affignation by accident. Hence we find, by an old decifion, that an inftrument of this kind was on that ac-count fet afide. Upon fimilar principles, the Court afterwards redu-ced another intimation, becaufe the fame perfon was both notary and procurator ; for the Lords found, ' That the bufinefs ought to have ' been perfected by two diftinct perfons ; and that one and the fame ' perfon could not be both procurator to intimate in the affignee's ' name, and alfo notar to take inftruments on the doing thereof †.'

' *Paffed with us, refpective et fucceffivé, to the perfonal prefence of* ' *the within defigned C. and D.'*—This fuppofes the bond to be granted by two co-obligants ; and therefore the intimation is, with propriety, made to both of them, according to Lord Stair's direc-tions : ' Where there are many *correi debendi* principal or cautioners, ' intimation made to any will be fufficient as to all ; yet this will ' not

---

* Page 319.　　　† July 3. 1628, Scott againft Drumlendrig.

' not exclude payment made by another of the debtors *bona fide*, to
' whom no intimation was made. Had. Feb. 23. 1610, Lyon againſt
' Law ; to ſecure which, it is ſafeſt for aſſignees to intimate to all
' the *correi debendi* *.'

' *To the perſonal preſence.*'—Intimation, if poſſible, ſhould always
be made perſonally, becauſe it puts an end to all ſubſequent queſtions about *bona fide* payment by the debtor.   When the party cannot be found, the form is, to intimate at his dwelling-houſe, and to
leave a ſchedule for him, i. e. a brief note, containing the eſſential
parts of the inſtrument, and the witneſſes preſent at the delivery.
This form is taken from the analogy of common executions ; for,
ſince arreſtments are competent at dwelling-houſes, intimations
muſt be ſo alſo ; otherwiſe the former would have an unreaſonable
advantage.   It is a general rule in all caſes, where parties are not
found perſonally, to leave a written notification for them. Indeed, too
much care cannot be taken to give complete notice ; for, in the event
of the debtor making a *bona fide* payment, his caſe is very favourable.   If, by our ancient law, creditors could not impoſe another in
place of themſelves upon the debtors, the change is rather too great,
not only to be able to do this, but to ſubject the debtor to the riſk
of double payment.   From the analogy of executions, intimations
were ſometimes made at the market-croſſes of the head-borough of
the ſheriffdom where the party dwelt ; but the Lords found theſe
intimations ineffectual ; and they even doubted how far intimations
at dwelling-houſes ought to be ſuſtained †.

' *Having and holding in his hands the principal bond within nar-*
' *rated, made and granted by them to the within deſigned E. with*
' *the principal affignation thereto.*'—The cuſtody of theſe writings
by the procurator is juſtly held to be a ſufficient power to him ; and,
in all caſes, he ought to be poſſeſſed of the principal bond, as well
as the affignation ; for the debtor is then deprived of every pretence of tranſacting with his original creditor ; he knows with
whom

<hr />

* Stair's Inſtit. p. 384.   † July 21. 1632, Hume againſt Hume.

whom his principal bond is. And, in England, this is the proper
security of the affignee ; though, with us, the affignation would no
doubt be fufficient ; and, in cafe the bond be not at hand, we ought
not to wait for it, for expedition in this bufinefs is of the laft importance.

' *Which bond and affignment the faid A. delivered to me, no-*
' *tary public, to be publicly read over and intimated ; and which being*
' *accordingly done to the faid C. and D. perfonally prefent.*'—The reading is the effential intimation ; the bare exhibiting of the affignment will not do ; it muft be *verbatim* read, and what is not read
is not intimated ; for, as is obferved in an old decifion on this
point, a party may intimate his right *pro parte*, and keep it uninti-
mated *pro reliquo* *. There are conveyances, parts of which only
need intimation. The beft way, in all cafes, is to read over the
whole ; but, if that be not convenient, an excerpt of a particular
part of the writ fhould be delivered, and the inftrument of the intimation fhould diftinctly fpecify the fact.

' *The faid A. procurator forefaid, protefted, that the faid affigna-*
' *tion was duly and legally intimated, and that they might be both*
' *liable in payment of the fums of money above affigned, and not pre-*
' *tend ignorance of the faid affignment and intimation.*'—The reading,
it will be obferved, is trufted to the notary public, not to the procurator ; becaufe the notary is prefumed to be a public and impartial
officer, who will read fairly, and conceal no part neceffary to be
known to the party. The procurator's bufinefs is to have the fact
afcertained ; and therefore he declares the purpofe and effect of
what the notary has done, by protefting.

Since arreftments came to be allowed in the hands of perfons out
of the kingdom, there is an abfolute neceffity for putting affignations on a level with them, otherwife arreftees would have a great
advantage, which voluntary affignees had not ; but no private
party, nor his procurator, has a right to do any thing againft a per-

Vol. I.   C c   fon

* Nov. 30. 1622. Murray againft Durham.

fon out of the country at the time. The market-crofs of Edinburgh, pier and fhore of Leith, have for a long time been fuppofed, by a fiction of the law, to be the *communis patria* of Scotchmen, and they are bound to take notice of every thing done at thefe places in the fame way as they muft have done had the citation or notice been given them at their own houfes, when within the king-dom. But it is only the voice of their Sovereign that people who are abfent are obliged to hear ; and therefore, whoever means to act or do any thing at the market-crofs, pier and fhore, muft have a fpecial authority for that purpofe, and muft act, not by him-felf, but by a King's meffenger, to whom alone warrants of that kind are directed. The form, upon this occafion, is to prefent a bill or petition to the Supreme Court, reciting the bond and affign-ment, ftating that the debtor in the bond is out of the kingdom ; and therefore praying for letters of fupplement for intimating the affignation at the market-crofs of Edinburgh, pier and fhore of Leith, which are granted of courfe.

Thefe fupplements are now more neceffary in our practice than they ufed to be, from the frequent abfence of the people. The pro-curator for the party fometimes makes the intimation by reading the letters, which is certainly wrong, as the meffenger (the perfon to whom the letters are directed, and whofe voice the lieges are on-ly bound to attend to,) is thus rendered a cypher in the bufinefs. The following expreffion is alfo fometimes to be found in thefe Sup-plements : ' And proteft, that the faid complainer having done the ' utmoft in his power to intimate the faid affignation, the faid A. B. ' fhould not pretend ignorance thereof.' This is an improper claufe in the King's letters. The form itfelf is entirely fictitious. The law alone has prefcribed, and given it a determined effect. This ex-preffion, therefore, weakens that effect, by acknowledging the abfo-lute infufficiency of the form. This, indeed, gives us a hint that it ought to be fupplied ; and, in a number of cafes, it has been the practice, when affignations of confequence are intimated upon fupplements,

plements, to give feparate notice to their factors, relations, or con-
nections, in Scotland; and, even in the cafe before noticed, of Lau-
rie againft Hay, where the inftrument of intimation was fet afide,
as being too general, notice had been given to the curators and factor of the debtor, and fchedules of intimation affixed at the market-
crofs. It is alfo advifeable, in thefe cafes, to write a letter to the
debtor, informing him of what has been done; and, in general, to
take every ftep which may render the edictal citation a real one, by
conveying the knowledge of the tranfaction to the debtor. It is
difficult, and fometimes almoft impracticable, to intimate an affignment to all the members of a corporation, or of a trading company;
and therefore, in the cafe of an Hofpital, it was found, that an intimation to the treafurer was fufficient *. Such a narrow intimation
is not to be trufted to; and therefore it is our bufinefs to intimate,
not only to the treafurer, but to the other officers of the corporation,
becaufe they may be eafily known, and feldom exceed three or four
in number. Where trading companies are concerned, we cannot
difcover all the members, but the prefent managers or acting part-
ers may eafily be known. Intimation, therefore, may be made to
them, or the principal clerks, who have very often procurations
fro m their mafters. In a cafe reported by Lord Tinwald, whofe
collection is not yet printed, an intimation was fuftained made to
two clerks of a company, but they were managers by procuration,
and a minute had been inferted in the books, which may not always
happen to be done †.

A ffignments are alfo effectually intimated, by ufing diligences in
virtue of the affignment, fuch as charges of horning and arreftments, and alfo by fummonfes in the name of the affignee, or by
production of the affignation in a procefs, if depending at the death
of the cedent; but, upon the 14th of March 1626, Laird of Wef-
terhall againft Williamfon, the Lords found, ' That the execution

C c 2

of

---

* Kilkerran.—Jan. 10. 1739, Keir againft creditors of Lethem.
† Nov. 19. 1755, Watfon of Muirhoufe againft Murdoch.

' of an inhibition was not a legal intimation, not being fpecified,
' executed, and intimated, to the debtors ; efpecially that inhibitions
' had only force againft immoveables, and did not ftrike againft the
' fubject contraverted.' This was a very juft and proper determination ; for the publication and regiftration of inhibitions can reach
no further than the law has ftrictly given them. An affignee, as
before obferved, may, if he pleafes, do diligence or profecute in the
name of the cedent ; but, as the oath of the debtor will be received
againft an affignee, at any time before intimation ; fo, if the cedent's
name continue to be ufed, every defence will alfo continue to be
probative by the oath of the cedent. Therefore, if it can be avoided, neither procefs nor diligence fhould be ufed in the cedent's name.
If the procefs depended at the date of the affignation, the production or intimation of it by the affignee makes no difference, becaufe
the matter had already become litigious, and therefore the cedent's
oath will continue to be probative *.

It is not meant here to treat of the equipollents admitted in place
of intimation, as that branch is not within our province. It may in
general be obferved, that regular intimation is chiefly neceffary to
complete the conveyance, and preferve it from third parties, creditors of the cedent. Therefore affignments are often good againft
the debtors themfelves, though infufficient in queftions with third
parties.

The practice of England at prefent differs from ours only in
words and form, the remains of the ancient laws from which we
have explained the ftyle of this deed. If a debtor fhall, after notice
of an affignment, pay to his original creditor the affignor, the Court
will oblige him to pay the money again to the affignee, notwithftanding of the action being brought in the affignor's name. If the
affignor dies during the action, the mandate falls exactly as it did
with us before the act of parliament ; the executor or adminiftrator
muft lend his name to the affignee ; and, if no perfon take up the
fucceffion,

* Feb. 12. 1678, Frafer.

fucceffion, the Doctor's Commons allow the affignee a limited adminiftration, which is exactly the fame as our fpecial confirmation
on a general affignment at this moment. The foundation for
is the ftyle of the Englifh affignment, where the affignor con-
ts and appoints the affignee for him, and in his name, and alfo
name of his executors and adminiftrators, &c. ; fo that, in
ect we have been treating of, the laws and practice of Eng-
nce, and Scotland, have at laft coincided in every fubftan-
· for, as there is no arreftments in England, there is no
nations.

o~ Blackftone moft ingenioufly attributes the change in the
law of England, with refpect to the conveyance of debts and rights,
to the principles of commerce, and juftly confiders it as a capital
improvement in the national jurifprudence. ' The introduction
' and eftablifhment of paper credit, (fays he), by indorfement upon
' bills and notes, has at laft fhewn the poffibility, fo long doubted,
+ of affigning a *chofe in action* *.' Thus we fee, that what is fo familiar to us, was for ages thought to be impoffible by our neighbours.

TRANSLATION.

WHEN an Englifh affignee means to again convey the fame right
or debt to another perfon, he makes another deed in form of a fecond power of attorney, which is alfo provided for by the ftyle of
the affignment. Among the other powers there given, the affignee
is authorifed to appoint one or more attornies under him. This is
keeping clofe to the principles and form of the ancient affignment ;
whereas in Scotland, after adopting the French practice, and
confidering an affignment as a *ceffio in jure*, carrying the debt directly from the cedent to the affignee, we dropped entirely the old
form of the procuratory, and introduced the precife words and form
of the French *tranfport*, which we term *tranflation*, from the Latin
tranflatio,

* Vol. IV. p. 441.

tranflatio, which is alfo the Latin term for *tranfport.* The word *tranflation* feems to have been preferred by us, becaufe it was the common term for the removal of a churchman from one charge to another, and had become familiar to our forefathers before they heard of the tranfport. The ftyle of the tranflation is an additional and complete proof, that the change in our law with refpect to affignments of rights and debts, took place by imitation, and not from any gradual change of manners arifing among ourfelves. Hence it is that the Englifh appoint another attorney, where we transfer at once. This is the true caufe of the difference, which is moft remarkable, between the ftyle of our affignation, and our tranf- lation. The firft is a remainder of the ancient law of our remoter anceftors ; and the other marks the revolution introduced into this branch of that law by our connection with France. The Englifh made the fame change in effect, but they have done it by degrees, and preferved a confiftency in the form ; whereas we feem to have taken it up at once, without the leaft attention either to our prin- ciples or forms. The confequences of this rafhnefs remain recorded in the ftyle of the writings. An affignee, with us, is ftill made by a deed in the ftyle and language of a procurator or attorney ; and yet, when the fame man comes to tranfmit the fame debt to ano- ther, he fpeaks the language of a full proprietor, and makes a con- veyance in plain language, divefting himfelf of the right, and veft- ing it in his party. This inconfiftency in ftyle, the Englifh have a- voided by the conftitution of attornies under the firft affignee. Our fyftematic lawyers could not avoid noticing the difference between the form of the affignation and the tranflation, but do not feem to be able to account for it ; they content themfelves with the dry in- formation, that the legal effect is the fame. Thus Lord Stair : ' An ' affignation doth neceffarily require the clear expreffing of the ce- ' dent, affignee, and thing affigned ; and, though the ordinary ftyle ' of it be known, yet any terms that may exprefs the tranfmiffion ' of the right affigned, from the cedent to the affignee, will be fuf- ' ficient ;

' ficient; as if the cedent affign, transfer, and difpone, make over,
' fet over, gift or grant, the thing affigned to the affignee, or nomi-
' nate or conftitute him his ceffioner, affignee, donator, or procu-
' rator, to his own behoof *.'

This inaccuracy of expreffion, and declared indifference about legal language, muft have tended to involve the hiftory of our law in
darknefs. But his Lordfhip, a learned theorift and philofopher,
feems to have paid little attention to the principles and progrefs of
our ftyles. His fubject obliges him to talk of them, and he does it
in this general and uninftructive manner ; not fo the great lawyers
in England ; Littleton, Coke, Bacon, in fhort all of them, have
built upon the foundation of writs ; the beft part of their works
are truly commentaries upon deeds. The etymology, the value
and legal import of every word, are carefully weighed and determined. The proper application of thefe forms, and the practical
knowledge of the conveyancer, furnifh the lawyer with principles
and argument. Our lawyers have unhappily taken an oppofite
courfe, and have in a great meafure neglected the common writs,
the forms, and even the records of their native country. In place
of the law terms thus given by Lord Stair, and which he fays
are all to the fame effect ; Lord Coke informs us, that part of them
are proper to an affignment of *chofe in action;* which becaufe of the
common law, muft be affigned by the fiction of a procuratory.
That others of them are the language of an *affignment of property,*
whereof poffeffion may be immediately given, and the tranfmiffion
of which is allowable by the law. Lord Stair, on the contrary,
hold's out at once, the whole language of tranfmiffion, as no other
than a ftring of redundant fynonymous words. His Lordfhip
has in fact, put together the ftyle of our affignment of debts, of
our difpofitions of moveables, and of our old gifts, as indifcrimi-
nate and equivalent terms : But we may reft affured, that our law,

* Page 381.

as well as that of England, had a choice in the determination of its language ; and that there is very little of it, which had not an original and fpecific ufe.

This leads us to fay fomething of the words *donatory*, *give*, and *grant*, which we fometimes find in our old writs of tranfmiffion. Heirs and donators are juft in effect heirs and affigns ; but the word *donator* belonged to a peculiar part of our practice. In the reign of the Stuart family, the property of individuals was fo often forfeited to the Crown, by reafon of civil rebellion, fines, feudal delinquencies, &c. that had the Crown infifted on its rights, the whole property of the fubject would have, by fucceffion, gone through the hands of government. The eftablifhed practice was, to return thefe forfeitures in the way of gifts to favourites of the Court, but generally to the relations and creditors of the forfeited perfons, or to truftees for their behoof. The fecond part of Mr Dallas's ftyles confifts of the forms of thefe gifts, according to the practice of the Scots Exchequer. And the general ftyle is, ' Likeas his Majefty *gives*, ' *grants*, and *difpones* to his lovite.' Our feudal fuperiors, fond of adopting the practice of the Crown, compounded or fold the efcheats and forfeitures of their vaffals which fell into their hands, and thefe deeds of tranfmiffion they proudly termed *gifts*, although they bore, *in gremio*, a price paid for them. The pretence was, that he the fuperior had, notwithftanding, acted mercifully, in taking lefs than the law entitled him to. From this circumftance, he commonly ufed a mixed ftyle, viz. ' Therefore I *fell*, *give*, *grant*, ' and *difpone**.' The receivers were termed *donatories* ; and from our decifions, it appears, that one half of the bufinefs of the Court in the two laft centuries, was, that of determining the rights and preferences of thefe donatories, with the creditors and voluntary affignees of the forfeited perfons ; fo that, without knowing fomething of the
nature

---

* The forms of thefe private gifts may be feen in Carruthers's Styles. St Martin has omitted all private grants out of his fyftem, for what reafon cannot be conceived.

nature and confequences of thefe gifts, we cannot read the records of our Supreme Court with profit or fatisfaction. What has been faid leaves very little to be obferved upon the ftyle of the tranfla- tion, which runs thus :

' *To have affigned and transferred, and by thir prefents affigns* ' *and transfers.*'—Here the procurator or attorney is doing what his conftituent by the ftyle of his right cannot do. The latter is only *conftituted* and *appointed* ceffioner and affignee; and yet he, as fuch, directly *transfers* and *makes over.* Without knowing the hif- tory of thefe deeds, it was no wonder that this appeared unintelli- gible.

' *Together with letters of horning, caption,*' *&c.*—It was former- ly obferved, that our practice directs not only the affignment of the debt itfelf; but alfo of the grounds of it, which we, in imitation of the Romans, confider in a diftinct view, as *nomina debitorum ;* and to thefe we confequently add all the diligences or progreffive writs taken out for recovery of the debt itfelf. Mr Dallas here fuppofes, that a variety of diligences followed ; and fpecifically con- veys them, which ought always to be done. The law, indeed, holds, that an affignment to a principal deed, carries every thing acceffory to it, fuch as diligences, additional fecurities, &c. though not exprefsly affigned. To comprehend thefe, the general words are extended, and are never forgot : ' With all that has followed, ' or may be competent to follow thereupon.' Lord Stair takes no- tice of a cafe, ' where an affignation of a bond was found to carry ' a bond of corroboration of the original bond, though not men- ' tioned therein ; albeit the affignation did not bear, with all that ' has followed, or is competent to follow thereon ; which is but an ' explicatory claufe of ftyle of that which *ineft de jure* *.' In this cafe, however, the bond of corroboration was produced by the affignee. Our bufinefs is not to truft to thefe opinions, but to con-

Vol. I.   D d   vey

* Stair.—February 3. 1676, Cully.

vey fpecifically the whole progreffive writs of the debt, and to retain our explicatory claufe.

'*With full power to uplift, afk, crave, and receive the fums of*
'*money above transferred.*'—This claufe is borrowed from the old
ftyle of the procuratorial affignment, and has only been added to
lengthen the tranflation. The powers of a procurator acting for a-
nother, may be enlarged, limited, or fpecified, becaufe the radical
right remains in the conftituent ; but a man who *transfers* and *con-
veys*, and who confequently is divefted of the fubject, has no right
to give any further powers or directions about the management of
the matter. Among other things, this fecond affignee is empowered
to ufe the letters of diligence already raifed, either in his own, or
in the name of the granter. This is a remainder of the old procu-
torial power; by which a perfon might act either in his own name,
or the name of his conftituent. Properly fpeaking, it is inconfiftent
with the nature of a total *ceffio in jure* ; and confequently, with the
nature of a tranflation. However, practice has continued it, as a
wreck of the ancient form ; but it is to be obferved, that diligence
already raifed, can only be executed in the name of the perfon obtainer of the letters ; becaufe a meffenger is a minifterial officer of
the Crown, who can do nothing but in conformity to the will of
the warrant directed to him,—what he ventures to do beyond it, is,
ipfo facto, void and illegal. If, therefore, the affignee choofes to act
in his own name, and, it is advifeable that he always fhould do fo, he
muft obtain new letters upon production of his affignment ; for the
Supreme Court, and not the meffenger, is the fole Judge of the propriety of the tranfmiffion. This matter came to be particularly
confidered by the Court, upon the 11th of June 1745, Stewart a-
gainft Hay * ; when upon a report relative to the practice, from the
Society of Writers to the Signet, it was determined, that new diligence muft always be raifed.

Let us now attend to Mr Spottifwood's definition of the deed we
are talking of, which is, indeed, naked and verbal. ' A tranfla-
' tion

* Falconer's Decifions.

" tion (fays he) is a continuation of the conveyance of a moveable
" fubject, by the affignee to another perfon ; and generally, the fol-
" lowing conveyances are called tranflations, though in a fourth or
" fifth degree of diftance from the affignee : others again call fuch,
" difpofitions ; but there is no fettled denomination for fuch writs ;
" albeit the ftyle of them be fixed.' It is curious, that there fhould
be no certain denomination for writs that have ftyles differently
fixed ; but this is not furprifing, when our lawyers never attended
to the reafons and differences of the ftyles themfelves. However,
as Spottifwood obferves, we have no certain name for any fecond
or third tranfmiffion of the right. By our prefent practice, indeed,
every deed after the tranflation is called a *conveyance* ; which is not
an improper change of the term. Spottifwood goes on, ' in the
' beginning, to the ordinary defignation, you put an additional one,
' thus : affignee after fpecified, or, as having right by affignation, or
' tranflation, or difpofition, in manner after mentioned.' There is
no neceffity for this addition to the defignation of the granters of
affignments, or other prefonal rights. It is borrowed from charters
and difpofitions of heritage, where the relation of difponer to the
lands is properly pointed out, by terming him heritable proprietor ;
but in perfonal deeds, where the right of the granter is immediately
to be recited, the anticipation of that title is quite unneceffary.

It now only remains to mention, that all tranflations and pofterior conveyances, require intimation in the fame manner, and for
the fame reafons, as the original affignment ; nor is there any difference in the form, except the addition to be made in the narrative.

It muft be here repeated, that Mr Dallas paffes over all thefe
writs, without noticing in the leaft that point of practice, ufed
by many people in affignments and tranflations, viz. ' turning
' and transferring the fame, and whole right thereto, from me and
' my forefaids, to and in favours of the faid B. and his forefaids.'
This is a round flourifh of old ftyle, borrowed *verbatim* from the
French *tranfport*, and is of no importance to the deed.

Difcharge.

Discharge.

WHEN a bond is paid to the original creditor, a short discharge is written upon the back of it; and no person chooses, or can be obliged to pay upon other terms; for, although the possession of the bond itself might appear to be sufficient, yet it is proper that the debtor should be able to shew that he got it back by fair and honest payment. As consent, proved by a written deed, constitutes a written obligation by the debtor, so it is extinguished by the consent of the creditor, which ought also to be proved by another deed. The one being of equal importance to the other, must be executed with equal solemnity. A maxim in the Roman law came to be universally received: ' *Quod chyrographum apud debitorem repertum, praesumitur solutum;*' and therefore the method of the church notaries was to cut or cancel the deed after payment of it: Nay, to avoid the ordinary civil law evasions which at that time had become prevalent, debtors were often expressly bound not to prove the payment of their obligations in any other manner but by production thereof cut and cancelled; and hence we frequently meet with the following clause in the obligements of these times.' ' *Promittentes nos, non probare solutionem aut liberationem, hujusmodi* ' *debiti, nisi per praesentes literas incisas vel cancellatas.*' Separate discharges, however, were absolutely necessary in partial payments, and in many other cases. Discharges are coeval with obligations. The form and the language of them were almost the same over all Europe.

rope. This deed in France was, and ftill is, termed *quitance*, of which the notaries made *acquietantia*. Excepting the folemnities in the execution, the ancient difcharges would anfwer every purpofe at this moment. Many old Latin difcharges are to be met with, proceeding upon exact recitals of the deeds difcharged; and, in abundance and variety of expreffion, far exceeding any ftyle of that kind in our modern practice. Indeed, we may take it for granted that the art of conveyancing was brought to perfection by the churchmen and notaries; and that our more immediate predeceffors, the laic writers, into whofe hands the whole of the bufinefs fell after the Reformation, have only been tranflating, and too often fpoiling, the works of the more able mafters, which they found in their hands. When the fums in any obligation were totally paid, then the difcharge or *acquietantia* proceeded upon an exact recital of the original writing, juft as ours do now; but, when partial payments were made, feparate difcharges were granted, with abridged recitals, and in a form which does honour to the art *.

The

* The following partial difcharge, granted by our King James III. to Edward IV. of England, for a part of the dower ftipulated with his intended daughter-in-law, may be given as a fpecimen. The fame, or a fimilar ftyle, was ufed in all money tranfactions between Scotland and England, during the 14th and 15th centuries. ' Jacobus, Dei ' gratia, Rex Scotorum, univerfis et fingulis, ad quorum notitias prefentes literae vene- ' rint, falutem: Sciatis nos, recepiffe ab excellentiffimo Principe Edwardo, Rege An- ' gliae, noftro confanguineo cariffimo, per manus difcreti ac magnae prudentiae clerici ' Magiftri Alexandri de Lye, dicti confanguinei cariffimi noftri Elimofinarii, in Ecclefia ' Beati Egidii de Edinburgh, tertio die menfis Februarii; anno Domini millefimo qua- ' dringentefimo feptuagefimo quinto; fummam duorum millium marcarum, bonae et ' legalis monetae Angliae, in partem folutionis, fummae viginti millium marcarum ' ejufdem monetae, nobis per prefatum noftrum confanguineum cariffimum, cum ' illuftri Principeffa Cicilia, fua juniore filia, nomine dotis, et caufa matrimonii, cum ' illuftri Principe Jacobo, noftro primogenito haerede et filio unico cariffimo debita- ' rum, prout in indenturis inter nos et dictum confanguineum cariffimum inde confect's ' latius continetur.

' De ·

The old difcharge will prepare us for the ftyle given by St Martin two hundred years thereafter. Mr Dallas fuppofes that the payment of the bond has been obtained by the laft holder without compulfion. Where the original bond, or any of its tranfmiffions, has been put into the Regifter, a feparate and formal difcharge is evidently requifite, becaufe the debt might at any time be revived upon taking out a fecond extract. And this is a general rule in our bufinefs ; for, by this means, the Regifter becomes an account of debit and credit between individuals. In putting the difcharge into the regifter, it is a convenient and commendable practice to mark the date of the regiftration of the difcharge on the margin of the record of the bond. When bonds have been tranfmitted by affignments and tranflations, moft people infift to have a feparate and regular difcharge, in the fame manner as if it had been put upon record. The reafon given is, that, having paffed through feveral hands, entries may afterwards be found in books ; and fchedules of intimation, and letters of the parties, may remain in the poffeffion of the affignees, which their heirs might choofe to have explained, and perhaps attempt to reftore, by a procefs of proving of the tenor of the original bond ; and therefore the fafeft way is to have a difcharge upon record. There is no doubt but this may be infifted for ; but then the creditor, unlefs he pleafes, is not obliged to pay for it. Difcharges of debts are always drawn by the doer for the debtor. His employer is to pay the money ; and therefore his intereft is principally concerned in the propriety of the deed. The term *difcharge* is from the French *charger, decharger,* to *load* or *unload, charge* or *difcharge.* The Englifh ufe it principally in fines and criminal matters. ' Difcharge (fays Jacob) is, where a man, con-
' fined

' De qua quidem fumma duarum millium marcarum, monetae predictae, fatemur
' nos bene pacatos, contentos et plenarii in pecunia numerata perfolutos, et dictum
' excellentiffimum Principem, Edwardum Regem Angliae, fuofque haeredes et fuccef-
' fores, ac regnum ejufdem, pro nobis, haeredibus et fuccefforibus noftris, ac regno
' noftro, de eadem fumma duarum millium marcarum, quietos clamamus, et in per-
' petuum exoneramus, per prefentes.'—Vide Rymer, Vol. 5. Part 3. p. 58.

' fined by fome writ or authority, doth that which by law he is re-
' quired to do, whereupon he is releafed or difcharged from the
' matter for which he was confined.' In civil matters, they retain
the term *acquittance*, which is the fame as our difcharge.

We now come to the ftyle given by Mr Dallas.

' *Be it kend, &c. P. G. to whom, and in whofe favour, the bond*
' *after fpecified, and fums of money therein contained, are affigned and*
' *transferred, in manner after mentioned.'*—This introductory explanation of the party's title is here quite unneceffary. We formerly
hinted at the rule in this cafe, and fhall now once for all repeat it.
Where the titles of a granter of a deed are fpecially recited, additions of this kind are evidently ufelefs and redundant; but, where
that is not the cafe, then it is right to add the title to the defignation, fuch as, *heritable proprietor, executor confirmed, apparent*
heir, &c.

' *And now feeing A. B. has inftantly made payment, &c. whereof I*
' *hold me well content, fatisfied, and paid.'*—Thefe words, it will be
remarked, are the exact tranflation of the ancient Latin deed, ' *Nos*
' *bene pacatos, contentos et plenarie perfolutos.'* Though this phrafe-
ology feems rather fuperabundant to us, it was compofed for a purpofe now entirely forgot. The Roman lawyers appear to have been
wonderfully fond of new and fubtile diftinctions, which they multiplied as much as words could exprefs. Thus, they diftinguifhed
between actual payment, or the direct performance of an obligation,
and the cafe where the creditor accepts of fomething elfe in lieu of
it. The form of this laft was by an acknowledgment of value received, when in fact it had not been received. This laft kind of
difcharge was termed *acceptilatio.* ' We (fays Lord Stair) make
' more ufe of the term *fatisfaction* than *acceptation*; which fatisfac-
' tion, if it be upon the grounds equivalent to payment or direct
' performance, it is equiparate thereto in all points, and has the pri-
' vilege to liberate, though the obligation be not performed *.' The
church-

* Page 160.

church conveyancers, who were often doctors in both the laws civil
and canon, in order to guard their discharge against all chances, used
the language both of payment and acceptation ; and hence the *bene
placatos, contentos, et plenarie solutos*, the *well content, satisfied, and
fully paid*, of our style. If the granter afterwards denied the payment, the debtor was free by acceptation.

The narrative and cause of granting being past, we now come to
the characteristic words of the deed.

'*Therefore, wit ye me to have exonered, quit claimed, and* simpli-
'citer *discharged*,'—This is exactly the *Quietus clamamus, et in perpetuum exoneramus* used by James III. The word *discharge* is the
only modern addition.

'*Quit claim*.'—This is the ancient *quietè clamare*, a feudal term
common between lords and their vassals, and between people dispu-
ting titles to lands. When a lord had received every thing he could
demand from his tenant, he declared or proclaimed him *quit ;* and,
when one private party gave up his right to another, he gave him a
renunciation, or a *quieta clamatio*. '*Clamare* (says Skene, in his
'treatise De Verborum Significatione) idem est, quod *dicere, affir-
'mare ;* as *clamare* aliquod tenementum, aut aliquam terram esse
'suam *.' The word *quietus* is yet used in the Exchequer for the
discharges given to those who receive the King's money. The
church-conveyancers had many other terms of discharge, which they
suited to various occasions, and used for the purpose of diversifying
their style. They did not always repeat the same verbs in different
tenses as we do, but enriched their deeds with a different set. Thus,
in the discharge granted by Henry VI. of England to our James I.
in the 1424, we find the clause varied in the following manner :
'Preafato Jacobo Rege, et ipsius haeredibus et successoribus, occasi-
'one praemissa, et de avisamento consilii nostri, pardonaverimus,
'remiserimus, et relaxaverimus, ac ipsum, suosque haeredes et suc-
'cessores,

---

* Vide Disclamation.

' ceffores, pro nobis, haeredibus et fuccefforibus noftris, regibus An-
' gliae futuris in perpetuum, decem millibus marcarum, praedictis
' acquietaverimus, et exoneraverimus *.'

' *Forefaid bond, decreet interponed thereto, fums of money,'* &c.—
It will be obferved that the bond itfelf is here firft difcharged, then
the money, and next the diligence proceeding upon it. This is extremely proper, and perfectly agreeable to the principles of the matter. An affignment, as obferved before, is exactly *venditio nominis,*
not of the money itfelf, but of the right to recover the poffeffion of
it. A difcharge is therefore *liberatio nominis;* for it is not the loan
of the money that is recited in it, but the obligation for repayment ;
and, unlefs fuch an obligation or bond had exifted in writing, there
would be no neceffity for a written difcharge : And therefore this
order fhould be preferved in all difcharges of this kind, i. e. firft the
bond or written obligement, then the money, and laftly the diligence, which is prefumed to have operated the recovery.

' *All action, purfuit, inftance, and execution.'*—Thefe words diftinguifh the effect of the diligence from the letters themfelves ;
which was always done by the old notaries, and ferves very well to
round this period or claufe of the deed ; for which reafon it continues ftill to be ufed. In our Decifions, we find a number of blunders, arifing from the carelefs or negligent ufe of the general words
in difcharges of debts. They have given birth to a great number
of law-pleas, each of which was, and, as often as they happen a-
gain, muft be determined by the particular circumftances of the cafe.
The receivers of thefe difcharges always endeavour to extend the
general words, and the granter to reftrict them ; fo that an excellent
fubject of difpute muft, in every inftance, be afforded. It is not here
intended to go into the rules of interpretation of general difcharges,
either when annexed to deeds, or written feparately ; we fhall only
juft take notice, that general claufes, and general difcharges, are ex-

VOL. I.   E e   ceedingly

* Rym. Vol. IV. Part 4. p. 107.

ceedingly dangerous, between people who have a continued inter-
courfe of tranfactions. If they do not give ground to difputes during the lives of the parties, the confequence is unavoidable upon
their death. In this fituation, it is the bufinefs of individuals themfelves, or their doers, to make every receipt, and every difcharge,
relate with anxious fpeciality to the matter to which it belongs.
Such is the deed we are now analyfing ; the general words are all
made relative to the particular debt recited in the difcharge,

   ' *And I bind and oblige me, &c. to warrant, acquit, and defend*
   ' *this prefent difcharge to be good, valid, and fufficient, againft all*
   ' *hands, and againft all deadly, as law will.*'—In moft cafes, warrandice is a natural confequence of the tranfaction itfelf, independent of any particular claufe ; but, as the degrees of fecurity given
differ with the nature of the bufinefs, the claufes of warrandice determine the extent, either of the recourfe upon the granter, or of his
obligation to the party. When the warrandice is implied, or left to
the law, it requires an action upon the fact to bring the party
into the field ; but, when bound by a fpecial claufe, he can be immediately charged to perform, and obliged to take the bufinefs upon
himfelf. The warrandice, both expreffed and implied in difcharges,
always was, and ever muft be abfolute ; for the perfon who fairly
pays his debt ought certainly to be kept free of all future diftur-
bance. We are not at prefent to go deeper into the matter of warrandice, becaufe the hiftory and the terms of it fall to be explained
when we come to heritable rights. The word *acquit* is from the
French *acquiter.* It has two fenfes in the law ; one, as before noticed, fignifieth a difcharge in writing of a fum of money, or other
duty, which ought to be paid and done. The next, is a clearing
from any offence or crime. A man is then faid to be acquitted ;
and the act of his difmiffion is termed *an acquittal.* Lord Coke derives it from the law Latin verb *acquietare,* which imports that the
tenant be fafely kept ' from any entries or moleftation from any o-
' ther lord but his own.' Hence it is ufed in warrandice for freeing
the fubject from any claim or pretentions at the inftance of third
                                                          parties.

parties. Accordingly, we fay, in common language, to quit a claim
or right, to get quit of any danger or trouble.

This deed may be refolved into the following parts; the
narrative,—the caufe of granting,—the difcharge,—and the warrandice. Spottifwood divides difcharges, as he does all other perfonal deeds, into two claffes, fimple and compound. There
is no difference, but that the laft is granted to an affignee,
and proceeds upon a recital of the affignment; a few words of difference would make the laft compound and the firft fingle; they
are both relative deeds. The diftinction he makes is altogether
groundlefs.

There is very little difference in the form of the modern difcharge, from the old one already confidered. In thefe given by
Spottifwood, he erroneoufly and improperly alters the order, by
firft difcharging the money, and then the bond; whereas in the fucceeding form, which he calls a compound difcharge, he, after St
Martin's method, firft difcharges the bond, and then the money.
This irregularity arifes from inattention to the principles of the
deed. Both of them in law may be equally effectual; but an intelligent writer, from thefe marks, will always know, whether a man
is directed by a folid knowledge in his profeffion; or whether he is
the fervile copiator of any ftyle which accident throws into his
hands. In the difcharges, Spottifwood fuppofes horning to have
been raifed and executed, and he obferves, that, upon producing the difcharge at the regifter, the bond may be got up. This is
certainly true; but after raifing and executing a horning, it is by
no means advifeable, efpecially if the bond happened to be regiftered in the books of an inferior court; for, in this cafe, the horning
muft have been paffed upon a bill, and that bill being given into the
fignet, puts the debt upon a kind of record. Several other reafons
might be given, why bonds fhould not be taken out of the regifter,
after diligence being done upon them. The proper method, is, to
record the difcharge, and to have the date and regiftration of it
marked upon the regifter, oppofite to the bond itfelf. It is ufually

done,

done, not in the record, but in the minute-book; becaufe writs are
extracted from the principals, which are put up in the order of the
minute-book, the record itfelf being very feldom confulted. The
form of a modern difcharge of a bond, by an affignee, in Spottifwood's appendix, may be found p. 506. As it is in common
practice at prefent, it is unneceffary to give any other; and
wherever there is any thing publifhed of this kind, I apprehend
it to be the propereft text to comment upon. Where none fuch
are to be found, then we muft fupply them. In fact, there is
no difference between this difcharge, and that of St Martin's, already
confidered. Only in place of narrating the laft tranfmiffion, the
granter of this modern acquittance, introduces his own title in this
manner. ' To which bond and whole diligence above recited, I
' have right by affignation, of date,' &c. This is the general practice at prefent. It gives fome little variety to the uniform narrative
of grounds of debt and tranfmiffions. We have fimplified the receipt of the money, and generally ufe the words *exoner* and *difcharge*, in place of all the reft. We alfo feldom or never omit a
claufe of delivery of the fpecial grounds of debt; and are careful,
upon payment, to leave no veftige with the creditor, of diligence,
or any fteps taken upon the bond, becaufe it has feveral times happened, that thefe being found by the reprefentatives of creditors after their deceafe, occafioned a great deal of trouble to people
who had honeftly paid their debts. In cafe, therefore, any of them
happen to be fallen by, they fhould be excepted in the claufe of delivery, and an obligation added to produce them when found. The
natural and proper claufe of regiftration in a difcharge is for prefervation; but as there is an obligement of warrandice, it generally bears for prefervation, and, if requifite, for execution. As
the debtor pays the money, and is folely concerned in the validity
of the difcharge, it is always written by the doer upon his part, and
paid by the creditor-receiver of the money. This is a kind of tax
upon the perfon who does diligence; and, indeed, often prevents
it from being rafhly and injurioufly done.

Difcharge

Difcharge and Affignation.

OUR Formalift next fuppofes, what in practice we find too frequently occurring, that the cautioner has been diftreffed, and obliged to pay the debt himfelf. The next deed, then, with which he prefents us, is a *difcharge and affignation;* which is always demanded by the cautioner upon an occafion of this kind. We have already explained the principles, and the forms of thefe two deeds, feparately; which, in appearance, leaves very little to be faid upon them when put together. The fubject, however, of relief, to which cautioners are entitled, and the management neceffary in making it effectual, form an important branch of our practice. We have already difcuffed the methods and the deeds, whereby cautioners fecure to themfelves the power of acting againft the debtors for whom they are engaged, and for preventing the demand by the principal creditor upon themfelves, by forcing the debtor to make payment in due time. We are now to confider the cafe, where thefe methods either have been omitted, or have failed in their effect. The cautioner muft now be fuppofed to have paid the debt himfelf. In this cafe, in place of acting upon his bond of relief, he takes a difcharge, fo far as refpects himfelf, and an affignment to the debt and diligence done upon it, in order to put himfelf in the place of the creditor, and to entitle him to recover the debt, either in the affignee's name, or his own, in virtue of the diligence already done. It is the benefit of this diligence, which renders the measure often neceffary;

necefary ; for by being generally prior in time, it has many advantages above fuch execution as has already followed upon the bond
of relief; and confequently, muft be greatly preferable in point of
fecurity and effect, to any new fteps that can be taken. In the hiftory of this bufinefs, the firft difficulty occurring, is, the objection
which creditors make to grant affignations.

By the Roman law, the cautioner had direct recourfe againft the
debtor, either upon being diftreffed himfelf for the debt, or making
payment of it. The fame recourfe was afforded by our law; and
hence our lawyers tell us, that the creditor, upon payment, could
not be obliged to grant an affignment, becaufe the law had already
provided for the cafe. A difcharge was as good a foundation for an
action of relief as a conveyance. And accordingly we find, by the
decifions of the Court in the laft century, that creditors could not be
forced to affign their debts. In a queftion where compenfation was
propofed againft a debtor who had paid a debt upon a fimple difcharge, the defender *objected*, ‘ That he produced no affignation to
‘ the debt, but only a fimple difcharge, which could do no more
‘ than extinguifh the debt, but never could produce an action, or
‘ ground of compenfation. *Anfwered :* Some creditors are fo fcru-
‘ pulous, they will not grant an affignation, unto which they can-
‘ not be forced by law ; but a difcharge to a cautioner operates the
‘ fame effect *quoad* his relief as an affignation would do, except as
‘ to the fummar difcharge and prefent execution. The Lords re-
‘ pelled the objection in refpect of the anfwer *.’ In another cafe,
where the cautioner judicially demanded an affignation from the
principal creditor, ‘ The Lords found the creditor rigid in refufing
‘ an affignation, yet that they could not compel him ; but the cau-
‘ tioner behoved to purfue as accords upon his claufe of relief †.’
Thefe decifions only refpected the cafe where the cautioner could

　　　　　　　　　　　　　　　　　　　　　　　　　qualify

---

* Decem. 12. 1695, Wood againft Gordon.
† Decem. 31. 1697, Watt's children againft Ponton.

qualify no other intereft in the affignment than that of fummary diligence, or a more direct and expeditious accefs againft the debtor ;
but, if he was able to fay that the creditor ftood poffeffed of any feparate fecurity for the debt, or that by diligence he had affected any
eftate, real or perfonal, of the debtor, he had a direct title to
demand a conveyance, upon payment of the debt. The reafon was
plain : Without it thefe fecurities would be entirely loft ; becaufe,
unlefs an affignment be given, they could not be pled upon or ufed
by the cautioner. The Court therefore, at a pretty early period,
refufed to decern againft a cautioner until the creditor affigned the
debt, and all the fecurity he had for it from the principal. Thus,
in a cafe reported by Lord Stair, a cautioner fufpended, ' in refpect
' the principal creditor ftood poffeffed of an affignment to a bond in
' fecurity of the debt, which he refufed to make over. The char-
' ger anfwered, That he was only obliged to give a difcharge to the
' cautioner, and not an affignation of the bond itfelf, much lefs any
' fecurity he had got *ex poft facto* therefor. The Lords declared
' they would not give the charger procefs till he affigned the bond,
' and all fecurity he had therefor, to the cautioner *.' And to this
decifion the practice of the Court has ever fince uniformly adhered.

If, indeed, the principal has a feparate intereft to retain the fecurity, which might be hurt by conveying it, then the law forms an
exception in his favour ; ' he cannot be obliged to affign to his
' own prejudice.' So far as to the cafe where there is but one debt-
or and one cautioner ; but, where there are two, three, or more cautioners, there, a feparate reafon arifes for infifting on an affignment.
Without that, the particular perfon diftreffed will be forced into the
delay and circuit of a procefs, before he can reach the other cautioners concerned. Co-cautioners, by the Roman form, were not
bound in one deed, as with us, but each of them granted feparate
obligé—

* Jan. 10. 1665, Lefley againft Grey.

obligements, and stood thus unconnected one with the other ; or, as the civil law expresses it, ' Nullum negotium gestum est,' between them ; so, though one cautioner should be obliged to pay the whole, he had by law no immediate right to recover the proportions from the rest, or, in the law phrase, to obtain relief *pro ratis proportionibus.* Since, then, the law did not afford an immediate action for this purpose, the distressed cautioner applied to the creditor to be put in his place by a cession of the debt, which it was unnecessary to refuse, because he could be obliged to do it by the cautioner's claiming the *beneficium cedendarum actionum.* The cautioner paying the debt was thereby put in the right of the principal creditor, and entitled to act against the other co-cautioners for his indemnification or proportionable relief. Indeed, this in general seems to have been particularly stipulated. If it was not, the text of the civil law hardly authorises the demand in point of right. Cautioners with us are bound together in one deed. The law, of itself, gives them relief against one another, and, as in the former case, denies them the ' *beneficium cedendarum actionum,*' or the right of obliging the principal creditor to assign his debt. Accordingly, we find, that a Lady, who had several cautioners for her liferent, refused to assign. One of the cautioners alledged, ' That she ought to
' assign to him, seeing the bond wanted a clause of relief, whereby
' he will have difficulty to have relief of the other cautioner's
' bound. The Lords found that he could not compel the charger
' to assign, but, in so far as of her own own consent *.' But, by a long train of decisions marked in the Dictionary †, it is established, that either co-debtors or co-cautioners have, from the nature of the thing, relief against all others concerned, without an assignation, upon receiving a simple discharge of the debt.

The obligation, then, of a creditor to assign his debt to a distressed cautioner, arises not from the law, but from the equity and propriety

10th July 1666, Hume against Crawfurd.   † Vide Debtor and Creditor.

priety of the tranfaction itfelf. This point afforded an excellent fubject for the reafonings of Lord Kaimes. He confiders this to be in the creditor an act of benevolence, which the nature of the connection raifes into a duty.

According to his Lordfhip's doctrine alfo, there is no difference in the legal effect between the real and implied affignation, *i. e.* whether an affignation be actually granted or not, excepting the convenience of ready execution *. But the practice of the Court informs us, that there is a very material difference ; and, therefore, it is our concern thoroughly to underftand it. A cautioner paying the debt, can only demand from each of the other cautioners, his proportional fhare of the debt, after deducing that of the payer. Thus far the Court have gone without an affignation, or upon the implied affignation fuppofed by Lord Kaimes. The following cafe from Harcarfe is in point : ' By a claufe of relief in a bond, my
Lord Annandale, Lamberton, and four more, bound therein as
' co-principals to Craigiehall, being obliged to relieve each other
' for their own part, without the taxative word *allenarly ;* and Lam-
' berton having upon diftrefs paid the debt, purfued my Lord An-
' nandale, to relieve him of half of the debt ; alledged for the de-
' fender, that he could only be liable for a fixth part, they being
' obliged to relieve *pro rata.*—Anfwered, The other four *correi de-*
' *bendi* being abfolutely bankrupt, the purfuer who paid the whole
' debt, ought to be relieved of the half by the defender.—The
' Lords, in refpect of the notour infolvency of the other four co-
' principals, decerned the defender to pay the half of the whole
' debt †.'

Now let us fee what difference the taking of the affignation makes : ' Lord Bankton tells us, that he who is affigned to the
' principal debt, may feek payment from any one, as the principal
VOL. I.   F f   ' creditor

* Vide Principles of Equity, p. 14, 15, &c.
† February 1683, Lamberton againft Earl of Annandale.—Harc. p. 57.

' creditor might do. Yet ftill he muft allow his own proportion,
' for this he gives as authority, a decifion obferved by Prefident
' Gilmour, No. 124. Kincaid againft Lecky *.' This is a very plain
and confiderable advantage ; the cautioner by getting the affignation, is confidered in the light of the original creditor, exactly as if
he had lent the money ; now by attaching the moft refponfible of
the remaining cautioners, he avoids the danger of the others infolvency, which perhaps might have happened in confequence of his
own diligence. Hence we may practically infer : That co-obligants in a bond fhould not, if poffible, allow any one to obtain an
affignation to the whole ; they ought upon notice of diftrefs to pay
their fhares, and take an affignment in the name of a truftee, in order to operate their relief againft the principal debtor, or the other
co-cautioners who have not paid. Thefe advantages arife entirely
from the circumftance of the affignation, and feem to be allowed by
the Court to indemnify the diftreffed cautioner, for fuffering in the
firft inftance. But if, before the diftrefs, any of the cautioners have
already become infolvent, the taking of the affignation will not entitle the creditor to demand the full debt of the co-cautioners, without deducing his own fhare of the lofs arifing from the deficients.
Thus one of four cautioners being bankrupt, another paid the debt,
took an affignment from the creditor, and purfued a co-cautioner
for the three parts, deducing his own fourth. The defender craved
allowance for a fourth part of the bankrupt's proportion, and pled,
that ' the cautioners were to bear equal burden with one another;
' and if the purfuer did not bear as great a part of the lofs by the
' infolvency of the *correus* as the defender, there would be an in-
' equality †.' And in a cafe of the fame kind, about two years afterwards, one co-cautioner fued by another, anfwered, that he could
be only liable for his own fhare, or *pro rata.* ' The Lords found,
                                                        ' That

* Vol. i. p. 163.
† February 2. 1682, Muir againft Chalmers, obferved by Harcarfe, p. 57.

' That the purfuer having an affignation, might purfue the de-
' fender for the whole, with the deduction of the purfuer's own
' fhare, and of the fhares of the nottourly infolvent copartners *.'

Lord Kaimes declares this effect of the affignation to be unequita-
able, and he lays down a different plan for our future practice.
' To preferve (fays his Lordfhip) a real equality among the cau-
' tioners, every one of them, againft whom relief is claimed, ought
' to bear an equal proportion with the affignee. For the fake of
' perfpicuity, let us fuppofe fix cautioners bound in a bond for fix
' hundred pounds ; the firft paying the debt, is entitled to claim the
' half from the fecond, for a plain reafon, that the fecond ought to
' bear equal burden with the firft. When the firft and fecond again
' attack the third, they have a claim againft him, each for a hun-
' dred pounds, which refolves in laying the burden of two hundred
' pounds upon each, and fo on, till the whole cautioners be difcuffed.
' This method not only preferves equality, but avoids after reckon-
' ings in cafe of infolvency †.' Lord Kaimes's method may be very
equitable, and very plaufible, but it would be found next to impoffible in practice, where the cautioners themfelves were not willing to
contribute in this manner. We are to fuppofe, that the diftreffed
cautioner gets an affignment, and we have heard that the law allows
him, in right of the principal creditor, to attack all or any one of
the co-cautioners for payment of the debt, deducing his own fhare,
for with refpect to the principal, there is no queftion. If he attack
the whole of them, he runs the rifk of haftening an infolvency,
which otherwife might not have happened at the time, and a part
of the lofs would in that fituation fall upon himfelf. On the other
hand, there is a chance of fome of the parties fufpending and giving
judicial fecurity. If he attacks only one for the whole, and that
one pays upon a difcharge and affignation, he gets out of the fcrape

F f 2

altogether,

---

* March 1684, Smiton againft Kinimond.—Harcarfe, p. 58.
† Principles of Equity, p. 14.

altogether, though it is fuppofed, that in the cafe of an after infolvency, of any other of the cautioners, an action would lie for repetition of his fhare, which is one of the inconveniencies intended
to be avoided by Lord Kaimes's method. No inftance of this has
occurred, and confequently the point remains undetermined. One
thing is plain, *i. e.* that the cautioner in this cafe touches his money; as to the action of repetition, it will depend much upon the
diligence of the party who demands it in difcuffing the other *correi
debendi.* A man's conduct in this bufinefs, therefore, is to be directed by prudence, and the particular circumftances of every cafe.
We fhall now confider St Martin's form of the difcharge and affignation.

' *And now feeing the faid C. D. as diftreffed cautioner has made*
' *payment,*' &c.—The diftrefs appears from the narrative of the diligence againft him, which is fuppofed to be againft the cautioner in
this deed. The purpofe of this expreffion is to intimate, that it is
only in confequence of diligence, that the cautioner has paid ; for a
cautioner who pays upon diftrefs, has a variety of privileges, which
thofe who pay without diftrefs have not. In the firft place, by the
act of federunt 1ft February 1610, the Lords declared, ' That after
' the cautioner is diftreffed and compelled to pay, they will in time
' coming grant action to the cautioner, not only for recovery of the
' fums contained in the contract, but alfo to oblige the principal
' debtor to pay annualrent of all the fums exacted from the cau-
' tioner, in confequence of the diftrefs.' This is now an eftablifhed rule, and has been adhered to in every cafe, where the demand
happened to be made. Where this accumulation of annualrents is
an object, it muft be noticed, that it cannot be recovered in confequence of the affignation, becaufe the cautioner there acts in right
of the principal creditor. Where the cautioner has paid up any
confiderable fum in annualrents and expences, and has been kept
long in advance, it is his intereft to feek relief, rather by way of
action than by diligence upon the affignment. The fecond advantage

tage to a diftreffed cautioner, is, that if he has given due notice of
the diftrefs, there can no objection lie againft his relief, whereas, if
he pays without diftrefs, and without intimation, it is on his own
peril ; for if the principal had a good defence againft the debt, he
is not bound to relieve the cautioner, who thus rafhly advances it *.
The next thing is, that a cautioner paying upon diftrefs, retains his
relief againft his co-cautioners for forty years, notwithftanding of
the act 1695, which declares them to be free in feven. In the Dictionary †, there is a decifion marked in thefe words : ' It was
' found, That action againft the cautioner for relief, is not cut off
' by the feptennial prefcription ; but runs the courfe of 40 years,
' February 1726,—Forbes againft Dunbar.' Where the cautioner
pays upon diftrefs, there can be little doubt that the principle of
this decifion is right ; but when he pays without diftrefs, it is apprehended, the cafe would be reverfed, the cautioner would be held
in the fame light as a ftranger, choofing to lay out his money upon
that fecurity ; and of confequence the co-cautioner would be free.
For all thefe reafons, therefore, it may be inferred, that cautioners
ought never in general cafes to pay, but, upon diftrefs ; and that the
difcharge and affignation ought always to mention that circumftance.

' *Has made payment to me of the faid fum, annualrents, and ex-*
' *pences*, &c.—In deeds of this kind, it is always proper to fpecify
the precife fum paid, in place of fuch a general receipt. The ufe of
it is twofold ; firft, becaufe it prefents at once an accumulate fum,
which is to bear intereft againft the debtor and other cautioners
proportionally from that date ; and, fecondly, it removes all queftions about the quantum of the fum paid ; otherwife it may be alledged, that the cautioner has tranfacted the debt, and that he has
got an eafe or deduction at the payment. Now it has feveral times
been found, that fuch eafes muft be communicated to all concerned,
excepting it appears, that the principal creditor intended a perfonal
compliment

* Durie, 19th December 1632.—Maxwell.   † Vol. ii. p. 116.

compliment or donation to the cautioner. Two things are fuppofed to point out thefe kind of tranfactions. The receipt in the deed is ufually in general terms, and the debt itfelf is fometimes not affigned to the cautioner, but to a truftee for his behoof. This matter is argued by Lord Kaimes, who concludes thus: ' Upon the ' whole, my notion is, that if a cautioner in the view of objections ' againft the debt, or in the view of any circumftance which re-' gards the principal debtor, obtain an eafe, he is bound to commu-' nicate that cafe to his fellow cautioner, upon the following ratio-' nal conftruction, that he acted for the common behoof. This ' clearly enough appears to be the *ratio decidendi* in the cafe report-' ed by Stair, July 27. Brodie againft Keith. But if upon prompt ' payment by one cautioner, after the failure of others, or upon ' any confideration perfonal to the cautioner, an eafe be given, ' equity, I think, obliges not the cautioner to communicate the be-' nefite to his fellow cautioners. And this was decreed, Stair, July ' 8. 1664, Nifbet againft Leflie *.' Where the deduction is perfonal to the cautioner, the beft method is, to mention the fact truly and diftinctly in the affignment. If it arifes from the nature of the tranfaction, the fame thing fhould be done, with the direct view of communicating it to all concerned.

The deed under our view is complex, confifting of a difcharge and an affignation; and the difcharge which is in the ufual ftyle, with great propriety comes firft in order. A difcharge was neceffary upon this occafion, in order that the diftreffed cautioner might be relaxed from the horn; which otherwife might have proved exceedingly inconvenient. Accordingly, it will be obferved, there is an exprefs confent for the purpofe. The cautioner prefented a fufpenfion, together with the difcharge, which paffed of courfe, and had the effect to remove the procefs of horning, in confequence of a warrant for relaxation, contained in the letters of fufpenfion, which will

* Principles of Equity, p. 25.

will afterwards come to be confidered. A difcharge was alfo at that time, and ftill is, equally neceffary to extinguith the debt, in the perfon of the principal creditor. It takes effect from the moment of delivery, and, therefore, cannot be hurt by any pofterior deed; and, efpecially, when proceeding upon diftrefs. This fhould be done, even in the cafe where a difcharge only has been granted, without an affignation. The reafon is, that a difcharge in this cafe is held in law to be an affignation, fo far as refpects the indemnification of the party difcharged againft all concerned. To avoid all miftakes, however, real or pretended, between the principal creditor, and others concerned, it is the cautioners bufinefs immediately to notify his affignment, either by inftrument or diligence.

‘ *Difcharges the faid C. forefaid, his heirs, &c. of his faid caution-*
‘ *ry, and of all action competent againft him.*’—This difcharge it will be remarked, is limited to the individual and his heirs; for, if a creditor pleafes, he may difcharge any one or more of the cautioners, upon allowance of their fhare to the reft. In the fame manner he may difcharge any diligence or fecurity belonging to any one of the cautioners; but if he does fo he muft give allowance to the amount; becaufe the other-cautioners concerned have right to an affignation to that fecurity. Thus a principal creditor having confented to the relaxation of a joint obligant in a bond, and having thereby loft the gift of his efcheat, the other obligant contended for allowance of half of the debt. ‘ The Lords found the char-
‘ ger liable to make up the damage fuftained by the fufpender, by
‘ confenting to relax the cautioner*.’ The cautioner then being difcharged of his perfonal obligation, the debt is immediately vefted in him by affignment for recovery.

‘ *But alfo for the faid C. D. his better relief,*’ &c.—This is a fecond induction or caufe of granting, applicable to the affignment, and is extremely proper. In St Martin's time, there could be no doubt

---

* January 25. 1717 —Wallace againft Lord Elfbank.

doubt about the character of the cautioner, becaufe the bond itfelf always expreffed it; but fince bonds of relief have been taken a part, it is neceffary for the creditor to fee that bond of relief before he grants affignation, and to recite it in the deed, which is accordingly now always done; nay, it is not uncommon for the principal creditors to take the word of the perfon that pays them, in which cafe the fact is mentioned, and the difcharge reftricted to the legal right or title, which the obligant paying, may have to relief.

' But any prejudice or derogation to the claufe of relief contained in ' the faid bond, or any relief apart,' &c.—It is a general rule in our bufinefs, that wherever any new obligation is granted, fecurity added, or deed executed in favour of a creditor, care is always taken to exprefs, that thefe new or additional acts are not to prejudice or innovate the former fecurities. Thefe claufes are intended to avoid the Roman doctrine of novation, whereby a creditor accepting of a new obligement for a debt, the former fecurity was underftood to be difcharged.

' Affign, transfer and difpone in favours of the faid C. D. the fore- ' faid bond.'—It will here be obferved, that the proper ftyle of the affignation is dropt. In place of making and conftituting, the affignee directly affigns and transfers the bond; and this is now the univerfal ufage in drawing complex deeds, the old ftyle being confined to the fimple affignment. It is not, however, the money which is firft in order, it is the bond and decreet and then the money contained in them; and this ought to be their conftant order in tranflations or conveyance of debts.

' In fo far allenarly, as concerns and may be extended to, and as ' the fame may militate againft the faid A. B. principal party, and ' his reprefentatives; and as execution may be had and ufed againft ' them therefore, and no further.'—This reftriction is intended to avoid the poffibility of any after queftion upon the nature of the

warrandice

* Feb. 12. 1678, Frafer.

warrandice in the affignment, to throw the difpute about the extent of the relief competent to the cautioner, entirely between him and his principal; alfo to prevent any ufe being made of the affignation againft the party difcharged, and his heirs. The difcharge is war-ranted from all hands; and the affignment from fact and deed. St Martin makes the one follow the difcharge, and the other the affignment, which is a very proper and diftinct method. They are generally, by the prefent forms, put together. About the beginning of this century, fome writers, befides the reftriction above-mention-ed, inferted, from an exceffive degree of verbal caution, a *falvo* a-gainft the double warrandice deducible from the difcharge and affignment. In this, they were flaves to the phrafe *double war-randic*, which could never be incurred by two deeds quite rational, and compatible with each other. Such declarations are now totally out of ufe.

We difmifs the difcharge and affignation, with this fingle remark, that though the affignation can in few or no cafes be now refufed, yet fome people take advantage of the law in the matter of pay-ments: They will grant a difcharge and pay for it, but if you want an affignation, you muft pay it yourfelf. The difference in the ex-pence is fmall; and, therefore, when bufinefs is done in an amica-ble manner, this fubtlety is never made ufe of. When perfonal dif-ferences fubfift, parties are too apt to take the advantage.

WE are now to suppose with our text-book, That, in place of
paying the debt contained in the bond and decree of regiftration, the debtor either from inability, or want of inclination,
refuses or delays to make payment; and that the creditor is obliged
to have recourse to those methods which the law provides for enforcing compliance with its decrees.

The writs fued out in England to compel obedience to the law,
are termed *writs of execution*; in Scotland they go under the name
of *diligences*. ' They are called diligences (fays Lord Stair) be-
' cause they excuse the users thereof from negligence; whereby
' posterior diligences being exactly followed, are preferable to prior
' diligences being neglected, *vigilantibus non dormientibus jura fub-*
' *veniant*; they are also called diligences, because, though the effect
' do not follow, yet the user thereof hath endeavoured what he
' could; and fo is held as in the fame cafe, as if he had obtained
' the command of the precepts or decreets. Thefe precepts or de-
' creets are called executorials before execution be thereupon; but
' they are only called diligences when they are executed in due-
' time. The diligence in executorials, after decreet (continues he)
' are horning, caption, poinding, &c*.' This etymology is no o-
ther than an ingenious conjecture of Lord Stair, founded upon the
common

* Stair, p. 705.

common acceptation of the word *diligence*. That word is purely
French, and is the ordinary practical term ſynonymous to the word
purſuit. Sometimes it means the proceſs itſelf, and at other times
the execution. In the other ſenſe, they ſay that a cautioner is not
liable till diligence be done againſt the principal, which is our own
precife practical language. Lord Stair's diſtinction between diligence and executorials is purely from the French practice, and coincides exactly with our own. When letters are iſſued by the King,
or the Sovereign Courts, for compelling obedience in civil buſineſs,
they were, and ſtill are termed, *lettres executoires ;* when executed,
the become *diligences.* Thus, by the 86th article of the Cuſtoms of
Normandy, it is provided, that adjudgers ſhall remain poſſeſſed of
the original diligences of their decreet, which is alſo our practice,
even in that very branch of buſineſs. Our letters and precepts before execution, are alſo termed executorials ; hence the language of
our clauſes of regiſtration : ' That letters of horning, or other exe-
' cutorials neceſſary, may paſs hereon.' It is only after execution,
that, properly ſpeaking, they become diligences; in which term is
included the execution or indorſations themſelves. In general,
however, the King's letters are termed diligences even before execution. The practical phraſe is to *raiſe* ſuch and ſuch letters, or, according to our older ſtyle, *to purchaſe them.* Theſe laſt modes of
expreſſion are alſo directly from the French practice ; they ſay *lever
lettres,* i. e. to relieve them by payment of the fees at the office.
In this ſenſe, the Engliſh underſtand the matter at this moment.
' When a perſon (ſays Judge Blackſtone) wants redreſs from the
' law, he is to make application or ſuit to the Crown, the fountain
' of all juſtice, for that particular remedy he is determined to pur-
' ſue ; he is to ſue out or purchaſe, by paying the ſtated fees,' an
' original writ from the Court of Chancery, which is the *officina
' juſtitiae,* the ſhop or mint of juſtice, wherein all the King's writs
' are framed.'

Another

Another term ufed in this branch of practice, is that of *expeding* letters. There is no fuch Englifh word. We had it from the French verb *expedier*, which fignifies the making out the principal copies of letters, judgments, and other juridical writs. It is alfo a term in the Roman Chancery, where bulls and other writs prepared by the writers, are called *efpediziones*. Accordingly, by expeding letters, we mean writing out the principals, procuring them to be figneted, fealed, and completed. When a charter has to pafs through the feals, we call it paffing the charter, formerly, the term was to expede it.

The common terms of the bufinefs being thus explained we go on to our text book.

The next thing to be confidered, is, ' What if the debtors will ' not pay without legal compulfitors ; in which cafe the creditor ' may ufe perfonal or real execution, or both, in his option ; and, ' becaufe perfonal execution is for the moft part ufed, I fhall difcufs ' it firft ; and fo concluding both debtor and creditor to be in life, ' (if otherwife, the cafe would alter, as afterwards appe rs) the ' bond would be regiftrat, and if not affigned, horning may be ' raifed thereon *.'

If the ground of the decree confifted in the performance of any fact, then the effence of the horning is a warrant commanding the party to perform his obligation under the pain of being denounced rebel to the King ; and this denunciation becomes the warrant for iffuing a writ of caption to compel obedience by imprifonment of the perfon, for no other kind of diligence is competent *ad facta praeftanda*, or forcing performance of illiquid obligations. But if, as in the prefent cafe, the decree be given for a precife and liquid fum of money, then the letters iffued, befides the warrant of denuncia-tion, which is, properly fpeaking, the horning, contains a feparate warrant for poinding fuch moveable effects as are in the debtor's

                                                              poffeffion,

* Dallas's Styles, p. 8.

poffeffion ; and arrefting thofe belonging to him, which are in the poffeffion of other people. It is then called *horning and poinding* ; and is the warrant or firft ftep of complete perfonal execution, by which we are always to underftand, execution againft the perfon and moveables of the debtor.

If the bond has been regiftered in the books of Seffion, the decree of regiftration contained in the extract is, properly fpeaking, a decree of the fupreme court ; the extract therefore is *per fe* a warrant for iffuing the horning. The letters of horning bear to be given of the fame date with the date of regiftration or extract. It is the bufinefs of the officer who attends the fignet under the deputy-keeper to examine the validity of the extract, and alfo whether it agrees with the date of the horning. If, on the other hand, the bond has been recorded in the books of any inferior judicature, fuch as a fheriff, commiffary, or magiftrates of a royal borough, then the precept of the judge muft either be previoufly executed, by charging the debtor to make payment within the days mentioned in the decree of regiftration ; or, if no days be mentioned, within fifteen after the date thereof. After elapfing of the charge, or at leaft after elapfing of the fame number of days from the date of the regiftration, in cafe no charge has been given upon the precept of the inferior judge, which is now very often omitted, a bill muft be prefented to the Lords of Seffion, praying their Lordfhips to grant warrant for letters of horning in terms of the decree of the inferior judge. The reafon of this is, that fheriffs and other inferior judges (the magiftrates of royal boroughs excepted) have no power to grant diligence againft the perfon of the debtor ; they can only authorife the poinding and arrefting of his moveables within their own particular jurifdictions. The fupreme court neither will nor can extend the powers of other judges beyond their determined limits ; but, having the direction of the King's letters, they iffue them in his name, agreeable to the decree of the inferior judge, the execution of which is thereby rendered univerfal over the kingdom. The letters of the Supreme Court are

are in aid of the inferior judicatures; and the precepts of the latter were anciently termed *letters conform.* They were granted by the Court of Seſſion, upon a ſecond ſummons, requiring the parties to hear and ſee them granted, or to ſhow a reaſonable cauſe on the contrary, the ſentence pronounced upon that occaſion was called a decreet conform. Theſe decreets conform gave place in courſe of time to the preſent ſhorter mode of bills or petitions; for, in the old law language of the whole iſland, all petitions were termed bills. This bill or petition is given in to the clerk of the bills, who is one of the clerks of court entruſted with this department. It is his province to examine the validity of the warrant, and to conſider whether it be a legal foundation entitling the complainer (for ſo the party who makes the application is termed) to have letters of horning, or other letters which he craves. The expiration of the charge, and diſobedience of the command of the ſheriff, is the eſſential circumſtance which founds the letters of horning; and if this is neglected, which ſometimes happens, it would formerly have been an eſſential nullity in the new letters. What the court might at preſent determine, it is not my province to conjecture. If the clerk to the bills finds the warrant ſufficient to authoriſe the prayer of the bill, he writes the date of preſentment upon the back of it, and then ſays, ' *Fiat ut petitur ;* becauſe the Lords have ſeen the precept within ' mentioned.' He alſo writes his name towards the foot of the bill, as an atteſtation that it is examined; for, without this, the Lord Ordinary upon the bills, to whom it is immediately thereafter preſented, will not, or at leaſt ought not, to ſign it. This atteſtation makes the clerk anſwerable for its propriety. It is the warrant upon which the Lord Ordinary upon the bills ſigns the interlocutor. The regiſtered bonds, or, as we term them, the proper warrants of the bills, are not produced to the Lord Ordinary.

Till within theſe very few years, the year and month upon the back of the bills were not marked with common Arabic figures, but with the ancient numeral letters uſed by the Roman chancery in the dates

.of

of bulls, and other ecclefiaftical writs iffued by the Court of
Rome. The month was alfo marked in Latin. As to us mo-
derns, the hand-writing of the clerk to the bills rendered
thefe dates complete fecrets; at any diftance of time they could
not be decyphered by themfelves, or the keepers of the fignet.
The prefent clerks to the bills have very fenfibly parted with
this hieroglyphic, by writing their dates in the common and intelligible manner. The former method was a curious relict of antiquity.
The terms of granting the petition are no lefs fo; *fiat ut petitur.*
Our Lords of Seffion, upon no other occafion, affume a ftile of fuch
fuperlative grandeur. This exalted phrafe in fact belonged originally to his Holinefs the Pope. It is a circumftance of no fmall curiofity, that every *item* of this very common form of ours has been taken from the practice of the Roman chancery by the firft judges of
our courts, who were originally ecclefiaftics, and who were no doubt
proud to copy their procedure from the firft model in the world.
When a requeft was prefented to the Pope, praying him for fome be-
nefice, favour, or indulgence, it was put into the hands of an officer
called the *dattary,* who, like our clerk to the bills, inftantly marked
upon it his name and the day of prefentment in majufculine letters,
fo termed from their fuperior fize. If the requeft regarded an inferior piece of bufinefs, it was granted by the prefenter of the fignatures in thefe words: ' Conceffum eft ut petitur, in praefentia Domi-
' ni noftri Papae;' but if the matter was of high importance, his
Holinefs granted it in perfon by, *fiat ut petitur.* This was written
with his own hand; with the addition of the initial letter of the name
under which he went before he was raifed to the chair, and the writing
was termed the *fignature.* Thence the petition itfelf fo granted came
univerfally to be called a fignature, a title well known in another
branch of our practice. The date of the prefentment alfo continues
to be the date of the fignature, and not the real date of the fubfcription; which is precifely the cafe at this moment with many of our

common bills *. The Englifh ecclefiaftics, in fome degree, borrowed the fame ftile. *Fiàt execut. iftius breve* is an ancient phrafe in
granting the defire of writs.

If there is any thing particular in the bill, or out of the ufual form,
it is the duty of the writer to the fignet, prefenter of it, to point out
the fpeciality to the clerk, who ftates it to the Lord Ordinary ; and,
if he finds any difficulty, he reports to the court. If they get over
the difficulty, the bill paffes upon report ; and the interlocutor bears :
' The Lord Ordinary having advifed with the Lords, paffes this bill.'
When this is done, the letters are made out, and the date of the bill,
like the Roman fignature, muft be the date of the letters.

It was mentioned, that, when a bond is regiftered in the books of
Seffion, or a decree given by that court, there is no occafion for a
bill ; but, as the date of the decree muft be the date of the letters,
it is evident, that, if the decree is allowed to lie over above a year,
then the date of the figneting varies too far from the date of the
letters, and from the year of the King's reign. The officers at the
fignet, however, make no fcruple about this ; they fignet a horning
of a date ten or twenty years back, though in the reign of another
King. This is a very flovenly practice ; and, as little care is taken
to mark the real year of the reign, egregious blunders are frequent
in that circumftance, and would go far to annul the diligence, if obferved and objected to. Before the jurifdiction act, at leaft when
efcheats fell upon hornings, writers were more attentive in this particular. When a decree of the Court of Seffion lay over more than
one year, they paffed bills upon them ; and then the date of the bill
gave a proper date to the letters. It is, at any rate, an advantage in
every cafe to pafs hornings upon bills. The bills became a record,
from which the letters can at any after period be extracted ; whereas diligences upon decreets of the Court of Seffion cannot be fupplied
when loft ; and there are feveral inftances where debts have been
loft upon that account.

When

* Vide Caftillo upon the forms and ufages of the Court of Rome, vol. 1. p. 10.

When the letters are figneted, they are put into the hands of a, meffenger, who charges the debtor to make payment in the precife terms of the will of the letters. The fpace of charge being expired, the debtors goods are poinded or arrefted; but, if his perfon is meant to be taken in execution, he is denounced rebel by the meffenger, under a proclamation faid to be made by three blafts of a horn. Of old, this ceremony was literally performed at the market crofs of the boroughs or fheriffdoms where the debtor dwelt. It is now a mere form, paffed over in filence. The meffengers, however, return executions, bearing all the ceremonies to have been diftinctly performed. Within fifteen days after denounciation, the horning and execution thereof muft be regiftered in a particular regifter for hornings and inhibitions kept for each county, or in the general regifter kept at Edinburgh for the whole kingdom. The keepers of thefe regifters give certificates of the regiftration upon the horning itfelf. The debtor is by thefe forms made guilty of rebellion; and the horning fo prepared becomes a warrant for iffuing letters of caption for apprehending and imprifoning him as a rebel to the king.

Every ftep of this procefs muft be to a ftudent of the law matter of alternate wonder and difguft: We find debtors for civil debts imprifoned, not properly for failure in payment; but for rebellion to their fovereign. If magiftrates and judges do not enforce this unreafonable punifhment, they too are very foon involved in the fame rebellion, and thrown into prifon. In fhort, to whatever part of the law of Scotland we turn, ftill we find the procefs and the penalty the fame; without the leaft refpect to the poffibility of the thing, or any inquiry whether the failure of the party was occafioned from obftinacy or want of ability. We find rebellion and its dreadful confequences to be the capital execution of the laws of this country. Looking backwards, we are amazed to fee actual treafon againft the ftate, and the innocent refufal to pay a debt, put almoft upon an equal footing; the fame writs, the fame procefs, the fame forms, and the fame punifhment, being common to both. The account given by our lawyers of this aftonifhing peculiarity in the laws or practice of their country, gives little or no fatisfaction. Lord Kaimes alone, ftruck upon the proper method of explaining this myftery. What his Lordfhip fupplied by conjecture, we have endeavoured to fill up from authority; and by our carrying our inquiries nearer to the real fource, we fhall attempt to develope this curious and interefting branch of our perfonal diligence; and to deduce the circumftances of the modern practice, from the primitive manners, and pofitive inftitutions of our anceftors. The former is certainly perfectly unintelligible, without an acquaintance with the latter. In endeavouring to do this, we fhall be obliged to fpeak of a variety of laws and of forms, which are now little known or attended to. As they are clofely connected with the progrefs of manners and of fociety, they will not prove altogether uninterntaining.; nothing, however, is to be introduced, but what is thought neceffary for conveying a proper knowledge of the forms we are daily putting upon paper, with the reafons and fundamental grounds of the feveral modes of execution, which at this moment continue to follow upon them.

However ftrict the prohibition of the Scripture might be againft the oppreffion of debtors, by ufurious devices and demands; certain it is, that, among the Jews, creditors had not only the power of imprifoning their debtors, but of making flaves of their perfons, and felling their wives and children. By the ancient Roman law, the condition of the debtor was ftill more terrible, and, like the people themfelves, inhuman and barbarous. The laws of the Twelve Tables allowed creditors the fhocking power of tearing their debtor to pieces, and dividing among themfelves the members of his body. The fame law put it in the option of the creditors, to fell their debtors as flaves to foreigners, and apply the price received for them in payment of the debt. Barbarity itfelf hefitated to make ufe of the detestible privilege firft mentioned; yet was the condition of the

debtor,

debtor, for a long period of years, rendered extremely miferable; and thence arofe the dangerous infurrections which fo often threatened the exiftence of the ftate, in the firft ages of the re-public. Though there had been but a fingle creditor, he might have fold his debtor, or employed him in labour, or treated him in any manner he pleafed. A citizen reduced to the condition of a flave, for payment of his debt, was termed *nexus*.—So Varro fays, ‘ Liber qui fua opera in fervitute pro pecunia quam debet, dum fol- ‘ veret, dat, nexus vocatur.’ At other times, they were termed *ho- mines addicti*. Their condition was fo much the more deplorable, that they got no credit for their labours or their fufferings,—their debts were not thereby diminifhed. This feverity of the law, and unhuman ufage, continued down to the year of Rome 429, during which period, it occafioned a number of dangerous infurrections.— The law even went the length of obliging children to furrender their liberty, and become flaves for payment of their father's debts. At laft, a law was paffed, importing that the effects of debtors fhould thenceforth alone be anfwerable or faleable for their debts; and that their perfons fhould not be enflaved, ‘ Pecuniae creditae ‘ (fays Livy) bona debitoris non corpus obnoxia effent, ita nexi ‘ foluti, cautumque in pofterum ne necterentur.’ Creditors, how- ever, were ftill allowed to confine the bodies of their debtors in prifons belonging to the public; until Julius Caefar, commiferating the condition of unhappy men in this fituation, procured them the benefit of *ceffio bonorum, i. e.* the benefit of furrendering their whole effects in favours of the creditors, which was upon that account termed the *lamentabile remedium.*

The Gauls and Germans, when unable to pay their debts, and even thofe incurred by gaming, fold themfelves as flaves to their creditors and great men, who had the fame right over them, that the Romans had to the *addicti homines.* The learned Seldon, fays, that among our anceftors, ‘ vinculis coercere rarum erat,’ but from the remains of the Saxon laws, it is certain, that creditors had the power of feizing the properties of their debtors,—of imprifoning their perfons,—and of holding them in flavery till fatisfaction was received. The feudal ideas and laws of the continent, eftablifhed themfelves in Britain, after the Norman Conqueft. The connection and duties owing by the vaffal to the fuperior, and the fafety of the kingdom at large, depending upon the prefervation of that connection, produced a confiderable alteration. Imprifonment of one man at the inftance of another, merely for payment of a debt, was looked upon as inconfiftent with juftice to the fuperior, who had a higher intereft in the perfon of the vaffal, than could arife upon a debt or claim to any third perfon. The King was the univerfal Lord of the whole nation, to whom all o-ther fubjects owed obedience. So foon, therefore, as the courts and judges inftituted by him, drew to themfelves the bufinefs of the nation, all were bound to pay obedience to their orders and to obey their decrees. The jurifdictions which they exercifed, were beftow-ed upon them by immediate warrants from the King; and thus acting by royal commiffion, difobedience to them was held to be difobedience to the Prince, and punifhed accordingly. Actions be-fore the courts were brought by original writs, called *brieves;* whereby the defendant was commanded to do what was required, or to give a reafon why it ought not to be done. The purfuer ftood bound to give fecurity that he would profecute the action, and the defendant was obliged to give fecurity for his appearance, and for defending himfelf. If he did not appear, an order was iffued to the fheriff to diftrefs him, by feizing fo much of his effects from time to time. If he had no effects, a writ was iffued for feizing his body, and committing it to prifon, called a *capias ad re-fpondendum.* If the debtor difobeyed, and abfconded from the purfuit of the fheriff, then, in the cafe of crimes, the court, in fupport of their own dignity, proceeded to declare him an outlaw, and to for-feit his property as a rebel. In procefs of time, the fame mode of compulfion, partly by cuftom, and partly by ftatute, began to be

extended

extended to a great number of common actions, and particularly to actions for common debts *.

This fevere mode of legal compulfion is in daily ufe in England at this moment ; fuch an outlawry, as Judge Blackftone tells us, is putting a man out of the protection of the law, fo that he is incapable to bring any action for redrefs of injuries ; and all his goods and chattles are forfeited to the King. A reverfal may be had, by the defendant appearing perfonally in Court, and pleading any objection, it being confidered only as a procefs to compel appearance. The defendant, however, has to pay the cofts, and put the plaintiff in the fame condition as if he had appeared before the writ was awarded. ' If the defendant did not appear, then (fays Judge ' Blackftone) he was gradually ftript of all his fubftance by ' repeated diftreffes, till he rendered obedience to the King's ' writ. In cafes of injury, however, accompanied with force, ' the law to punifh fuch breach of peace, and prevent fuch dif- ' turbance for the future, provided alfo a procefs againft the ' defender's perfon, in cafe he neglected to appear upon the ' former procefs of attachment, or had no fubftance whereby to ' be attached, fubjecting his body to imprifonment by the writ of ' *capias ad refpondendum.*' This writ made fure of the refpondent's bodily appearance ; and, therefore, in order to obtain it for civil debts, a fiction of law was practifed. In place of taking out the writ for a debt, it charged the defendant with a pretended breach of the peace, in breaking through the inclofures of the plaintiff, *vi et armis.* This charge being of a criminal nature, juftified the *capias* againft the perfon of the defendant ; and being thus fecured and forced to give bail, the Court, confcious of the purpofe of the device, allowed the real action intended, to be infifted in. In fhort, the whole Englifh procefs, in a cafe of this kind, is a train of fic- tions,

* Vide Blackftone and Sullivan, as to the procefs and the effect of the Englifh outlawry.

tions, merely to get the better of the principle of the ancient common law, which denied perfonal execution at the inftance of one
fubjeft againft another, for a debt merely civil.   Judge Blackftone
apologifes for them by faying, ' That they are beneficial to all par-
' ties readily acquiefced in, being illuftrations of that maxim of
' law, that *in fictione juris confiftata equitas*.'   Thus, during the dependence of a civil debt in England, the defendant muft either be
actually a prifoner, or a prifoner out upon bail.   If he never made
appearance of any kind, he is rendered an outlaw, by the procefs
formerly defcribed, and his effects forfeited to the King.

   The compulfitors hitherto mentioned, are all intended to bring
the defender into Court, in order that the fuit may be proceeded in
and determined, and to enfure obedience to the decree there given.
We are now to take notice of the execution, which iffues upon the
decree when given in order to enforce obedience.   By the old
maxim of the common law, no other execution could go out after
the decree had been awarded, than had formerly iffued to enforce
the appearance of the debtor in the procefs itfelf.   At that period,
lands were not open to attachment for debt, and the debtor's perfon
was fafe by the law; nothing, therefore, remained to be taken in execution but the moveables; fo that, if thefe were infufficient, the creditor had no benefit by gaining his plea.   When damages, however,
were given for crimes or injuries, thefe were confidered as a punifhment which it behoved the debtor to fuffer.   And fo when debtors
came by the fiction of the law to be charged with a pretended injury or breach of the peace, in the cafe of actions for debt, or in the
cafes where perfonal execution was awarded by particular ftatutes,
then execution was iffued by attachment of the perfon, as well as
the property of the debtor, againft whom a judgment of Court had
been given.   Sir William Blackftone informs us: ' That the firft of
' thefe fpecies of executions is by writ of *capias ad fatisfaciendum* ;
                                                         ' which

* Vol. iii. p. 283.

' which diftinguifhes it from the former *capias ad refpondendum,*
' which lies to compel an appearance at the beginning of a fuit.
' And, properly fpeaking, this cannot be fued out againft any, but
' fuch as were liable to be taken upon the former *capias.* The in-
' tent of it is, to imprifon the body of the debtor, till fatisfaction be
' made for the debt, cofts, and damages*.' The writ of *capias ad
fatisfaciendum,* is an execution of the higheft nature, in as much as
it deprives a man of his liberty, till he makes the fatisfaction awarded; and, therefore, when a man is once taken in execution upon
this writ, no other procefs can be fued out againft his lands or
goods.

Such is the hiftory of execution againft the perfons of debtors in
England. Our ancient law agrees with it almoft in every particular; to be fatisfied of this, no more is neceffary than to read the
firft chapter of our ancient book, termed *Quoniam attachiamenta,* or
the Baron's laws. This chapter refpects the procefs itfelf, and the
writs neceffary to force the appearance upon the part of the defender. The attachment upon the goods and gear there mentioned,
anfwers to the Englifh *diftringas,* which was competent in pleas of
debt, convention, or moveable goods. Arreftment, we find, could
not be made upon the body of a man, but in pleas of tranfgreffion
or crimes. This laft writ then, is the fame as the Englifh *capias ad
refpondendum.* ' Attachment (fays Skene) in his notes upon the
' Latin copy, is a Gallic word for a kind of perfonal citation, for
' *attacher* is to bind, to tie; and, therefore, attachment is a tie by
' which we are cited to juftice; obliged, or as it were bound to ap-
' pear in judgment.—*Wrong* is an injury; an *unlaw* means fome-
' thing without or againft the law; thefe are purfued by *ficker
' burgh, i. e.* by fecure pledges or cautioners.' With regard to the
execution, our old law is equally confonant to that of England†.

In.

* Blackftone, Vol. iii. p. 414.
† Vide Quoniam Attachiamenta, chap. vii.

In thefe laws, we find no trace of the fictions which were afterwards devifed in England, to deceive the common law; by ftretch-
ing the execution competent only in real injuries, or criminal matters, to cafes of civil debt. On the contrary, from the 39. cap.
of the Quon. Attach. we learn, That a freeman fhould not be imprifoned upon a complaint of another, ' fwa that he find fufficient
' pledges to anfwer as law will to the party complaining upon him,
' excepting in the crimes therein mentioned, in which bail cannot
' be received.' By the laws too of Robert, William, and Alexander,
we find a fpecification of public crimes, for which the perfons guilty
were fubject to incarceration ; but none of them refpects civil debts,
excepting one of Robert I. which will afterwards be noticed.

It is here neceffary to ftop, and to introduce to your acquaintance
another jurifdiction, from which an execution arofe againft the perfons of debtors, more univerfal, and more fevere than any thing yet
mentioned. In a former treatife, we had occafion to take fome notice of it, but it will now be neceffary to be more particular ; becaufe, without a more fpecial information than has hitherto been
given, it is impoffible to underftand our own acts of Parliament ; or
to connect the hiftory of perfonal execution with the letters of
horning and other writs, which continue in daily practice. The
jurifdiction we mean is that of the Ecclefiaftics, which is founded
upon the words of our Saviour : ' If your brother has offended
' you, reprove him by himfelf ; if he will not hear you, call two
' or three witneffes ; if he will not hear them, complain to the
' church ; and if he will not hear the church, let him be as a finner
' and as a heathen.' The Apoftles difcharged Chriftians to carry
their differences before the Magiftrates of the Gentiles ; and ordered
them to chufe arbitrators among themfelves. Chriftian Emperors
extended this power, and the church herfelf was peculiarly attentive
to lofe none of the privileges beftowed upon her. In procefs of
time, the clergy withdrew their own members entirely from the
power of the civil courts ; and under multiplied pretences, they for-

med

med to themselves an exclusive jurisdiction over the greatest part of the national business in Europe. As the notaries who formed the writs of private parties were all clergymen, one of the most successful devices fallen upon, was, to insert in private contracts and obligations, a solemn oath, binding the performance. This oath became a fixed clause of style, and carried every question respecting the performance to the ecclesiastical courts. If the person who had bound himself, and made the oath to performance, failed in doing so, the other party immediately made his complaint to the bishop, and their officials, who issued consecutive orders against them to the number of three, requiring them specifically to perform their obligations; whether such performance consisted in *facta praestanda*, or in payment of liquid debts. If after all the party refused or delayed, the ecclesiastics, without considering the circumstances of the case, issued out the terrible sentence of excommunication; excluding the unhappy debtor from the sacraments of the church,—cutting him off from Christian society,—discharging every body from selling him the necessaries of life, or from holding intercourse with him of any kind. The churchmen had not the power of inflicting bodily punishment upon the disobedient, but they reached that end in the most effectual manner, by forcing the secular judges to exert the civil power against the persons excommunicated, until they procured absolution from the ecclesiastical sentence. The frequency of these sentences, in course of time, diminished that respect due to oaths, and to excommunication itself. Various methods were put in practice to uphold their efficacy. In order to this, the canonists invented a clause, once celebrated all over Europe, and now sunk in oblivion; it was termed the clause *de nisi*. The purpose was, that in place of delaying the excommunication until an actual breach of faith took place, it was consented to by the contract; and fulminated immediately after executing the deeds against such of the parties, as might thereafter happen to fail in performance. The bishop declared that he did ' *ex nunc, prout ex tunc, et ex tunc prout ex nunc,*

' now as then, and then as now, publicly excommunicate and ana-
' thematife the party who fhould fail in good faith and perform-
' ance to each other.' The claufe *de nifi* came to be inferted in
deeds as common ftyle, and the terms of it were, ' obligamus nos
' fub poenis camerae apoftolicae et per obligationem *de nifi.*'

We have faid that the ecclefiaftical jurifdiction eftablifhed itfelf in
France, in England, and in Scotland. During the Anglo-Saxon government, as formerly mentioned, the bifhop and the fheriff acted
jointly, and aided one another; but upon the Norman Conqueft,
William feparated the two courts, and affigned them refpective
jurifdictions. From that time the ecclefiaftics bent their whole
power, influence, and attention, to draw to themfelves the civil
bufinefs of the nation. The great engine made ufe of for this purpofe, was a method which they termed the proroguing of their
jurifdiction by making parties to fuits confent to accept of their determination. From being arbiters in particular cafes, their notaries
inferted claufes of confent in all private deeds which they were called upon to make out; fo that in Scotland and in France, they may
be faid, at a certain period, to have made their point good. The
Englifh oppofed them with more fpirit than any other people. It
does not appear, that in England, the bifhops were ever allowed to
iffue writs by their own authority, for imprifoning the perfons of
thofe who lay under excommunication; they were obliged to require the aid of the civil power to fupport their fentences. Though
the ecclefiaftical jurifdiction has been long confined to what they
term its proper bounds; yet ftill, the fentence of excommunication
may be inflicted upon various occafions; and ftill a man may be
imprifoned in England, for difobedience of the order of the church.
The church of England receded to a lefs diftance from that of
Rome than any other of the reformed religion. To us who got
quit of its fetters altogether, it muft appear to be paffing ftrange,
that a people fo enamoured of political liberty fhould fuffer a power
of this kind to fubfift in thefe times; and that Sir William Black-

ftone

ftone fhould call the interpofition of the civil power ; ' the kindly
' lending a fupporting hand to-a tottering authority.' This can
only be accounted for, by the gentle ufe, which it-feems, is made of
this formidable power by the Englifh clergy, by the natural effect
of long eftablifhed cuftom. We would term the hand that enforced the excommunications of our ecclefiaftic courts, officious and
tyrannical ; and we would perhaps confider it to be the moft dangerous encroachment upon the liberties of this part of the United
Kingdom. This liberty, unknown to the fouth part of the ifland,
we owe to the famous ftatute 10th Anne cap. 6. § 10. which enacts,
' That no civil forfeiture or difability fhall be incurred by reafon of
' any excommunication or profecution, in order to excommunica-
' tion by the church judicatures in Scotland ; and all civil magi-
' ftrates are prohibited to compel any perfons to appear when fum-
' moned.; or to give obedience to fuch fentence when pronounced.'
Thus fell to the ground the ecclefiaftical power of the Church of
Scotland over the perfons of the fubject.

After the hiftory of clerical imprifonment in England, it will be
proper to attend to the progrefs it once made in our own country.
Amongft the laws of Fordun, Boethius, and other writers of the
Scot's Chronicles, we find the following, and a number of fimilar inftitutions, which according to them, are of the higheft
antiquity.—' *Item*, That all bifhops of this realm fall have
' powar to decide before them, all actions pertaining to faith
' of body, with powar to caufe the pepell keep their faith, promit-
' tit to their neighbours, and to punifh them for violation thereof.'
We have, however, more pofitive authority for our direction in
this matter; by chap. 6. of the ftatutes of Robert III. it was ordained, ' That all jufticiars, fheriffs, and others, the King's minifters,
' fall await upon, and anfwer to all letters of caption to be direct
' to them, be all bifhops and their officials ; and fall caufe mak law-
' ful execution of the famin, conform to the old form, notwith-
' ftanding any appellations or reafons alledged or preponed to the

' contrarie.'

' contrarie*.' From this, it appears, that in the days of Robert III. letters of caption for impriſoning the perſon of the ſubject, were directly granted by the biſhops and their officials themſelves ; and that the civil judges acted under them as miniſterial officers. Theſe letters are here ſaid to be ' *conform to the auld form ;*' ſo that this branch of the eccleſiaſtical juriſdiction muſt have been eſtabliſhed at a period too remote to be aſcertained by any hiſtory or record we are now poſſeſſed of. At the period when this ſtatute was enacted, excommunication in the other countries of Europe had been extended to perſonal debts, and to the purpoſe of enforcing all manner of private contracts ; ſo that we cannot entertain a doubt, that the caption here mentioned proceeded for perſonal debts, the payment whereof was enjoined by eccleſiaſtical cenſures. By another article of the ſame ſtatute, ſuch as conſidered themſelves wronged in the matter of excommunication, are allowed an appeal to the conſervator of the clergy at any time within forty days. This was an officer elected within the kingdom, for determining all clerical diſputes, upon account of the great ſchiſm which at that time ſubſiſted in the church, in conſequence of the conteſted election of the two Popes, Urban and Clement. At this time, people apprehended for leſſer crimes, and for contumacy in civil actions, were liberated upon finding pledges and caution, as they continue to be at this moment. The 14th ſtatute of Robert III. points out thoſe high criminals for whom no caution could be received ; ſuch as murderers, notorious thieves, wilful fire raiſers, and amongſt theſe we find perſons excommunicated, taken by the command of the biſhop. No further light is thrown upon this matter by our more ancient written laws ; but the ſubject is immediately taken up by our Statute Book, which begins with James I.

Lord Kaimes favoured the public with a very ingenious tract upon perſonal execution for payment of debt, to which the preſent

ſubject

---

* Balfour, p. 682.

fubject will oblige us frequently to refer. ' The firft ftatute (fays this
' refpectable author) in this ifland, introducing perfonal execution, is
' the 11th of Edward I. which, as appears from the preamble, was
' to fecure merchants and encourage trade*.' His Lordfhip has
here been led into a miftake, the firft ftatute that introduced perfonal execution, is that of Marlebridge, in the 52d year of Henry III.
the father of Edward I. The act provides, ' That if bailiffs, who
' ought to make account to their Lords, do withdraw themfelves,
' and have no lands or tenements, whereby they may be diftrained,
' then they fhall be attached by their bodies ; fo that the fheriff, in
' whofe bailywick they may be found, fhall make them to come to
' make their account.' This act was afterwards almoft literally a-
dopted in Scotland. This appears by the act of Robert III. chap.
14. already mentioned ; for among thofe prifoners who could not be
admitted to bail, particular mention is made of baillies, ' wha
' maks not juft count to their mafters, but at foot of the account
' refts owing to them arrearages or certain fums.' Edward I. was
the next Prince who introduced perfonal execution by exprefs ftatute. The great body of the people, neglected and oppreffed, came
at that time, from certain political caufes, to be held in more eftimation. The advantages of commerce began to be felt, and the
good policy of Edward gave it every encouragement. Without an
alteration of the law, the progrefs of mercantile people muft have
ftopt, becaufe it afforded them no method fufficiently effectual for
the recovery of their debts. Edward, therefore, in the 11th year of
his reign, obtained the famous act, called *Statute Merchant.* It
narrates that many merchants had fallen into poverty, for want of a
fpeedy remedy for recovering their debts ; and, therefore, after fubjecting the moveable goods for payment, it provides, ' That failing
' goods, the body of the debtor is to be taken and kept in prifon till
' he agrees with his creditor.' This act was extended, and in many
                                                            refpects

* Law Tracts, p. 345.

refpeɛts improved, by another ftatute paffed in the 13th year of the fame Prince. Whatever enmity fubfifted at this period, between the nations of England and Scotland, fuch was the fimilarity of their laws and ufages, that Robert Bruce, fuperior to national prejudices, did not hefitate to borrow good laws from Edward, the determined enemy of his family. By him the Statute Merchant was tranfplanted, almoft verbatim, into Scotland *.

The ftatute of Edward eftablifhes a record of recognifance, *i. e.* it fuppofes, that the debtor acknowledges the debt, which therefore renders the common trial by jury quite unneceffary. The recognifance is held as a judgment; and the imprifonment was a direɛt execution of that judgment. The Scottifh aɛt does not appoint a recognifance, it fuppofes, that the debt is owing by judgment of affize, or by any other manner, fo that the imprifonment awarded is alfo an execution of the decree. This is the firft ftatute which in this kingdom introduced the direɛt imprifonment of the perfon of the debtor for a civil debt; but the effeɛt of it with us, was, as in England, limited to debts due to merchants. In all other cafes, the ancient law of the realm fubfifted. Lord Kaimes fuppofes, that the ftatute of Robert I. is the real foundation of the *aɛt of warding* peculiar to our royal boroughs. This conjeɛture of his Lordfhip, is equally ingenious, as it is in the higheft degree probable. *From a variety of laws in our old capitulary, we find that the difficulty of recovering debts from ftrangers and country people, due to the trafficking inhabitants of our towns, introduced a number of fhort proceffes, both in the matter of poinding and moveables, and attachment of land within borough. The ftatutes of Edward and of Robert, are both direɛted to the magiftrates of towns, calculated for fupporting their commerce, and expediting their payments. It is, therefore, moft reafonable to fuppofe, that our boroughs gladly accepted the benefit of this law.

Excepting

* Vide, 2d Stat. of Robert I. cap. 19.

Excepting the caption iffued by the ecclefiaftics againft perfons excommunicated, the act of warding is not only the earlieft, but what is ftill more worthy of obfervation, it continues at this moment, to be the only direct and reafonable execution for payment of debt in this kingdom; all the reft are indirect, or properly fpeaking, fictions of the law. The common execution of a burgal decree, is by poinding and imprifonment. It correfponds to the ftatute of Robert I. with this variation, that the ftatute appoints the body of the debtor firft to be feized, and then his goods comprifed and delivered for payment; whereas the practice in the act of warding, agreed with the original law of the ifland, which directs the moveable goods of the party to be applied to payment of the debt, before the perfon could be touched. According to the prefent practice, the town-officers in Edinburgh, at leaft, never give themfelves the trouble of fearching for moveables; but they fcruple not to certify with great folemnity, that they have done fo. The act of warding, therefore, is a direct execution againft perfons within borough, fimple in its principles, and prompt in execution. It is to be remembered, however, that by thefe principles, and by the form of the warrant, it can, or at leaft, ought to be iffued only for liquid debts; and not *ad facta praeftanda;* becaufe no poinding or apprifement of moveables can proceed, but upon a clear and fpecial debt, as merchants, debts for the recovery of which the execution was originally intended. Warrants of this kind can only be iffued againft inhabitants of boroughs fubject to the jurifdiction of the magiftrates, which all perfons are, who have refided forty days within the royalty.

The act of warding iffues upon all writs regiftered in the books of Royal boroughs, becaufe thefe regiftrations are decrees of their magiftrates. It is here neceffary to mention, that the advantage and convenience of this mode of execution, brought on a very great abufe in the matter of regiftration within borough; bonds, bills, and other writings, were regiftered without the leaft regard, either to the refidence of the parties, or even to any confent in the claufes

of

of regiftration. This bad practice was corrected by an act of fede-
derunt 10th December 1713. ' The Lords of Council and Seffion,
' prohibit and difcharge all execution by charge, poinding, or ar-
' reftment, to pafs upon writs regiftered in the town court books of
' Edinburgh, or in any other town court books within Scotland,
' from the firft day of January next in all time thereafter; unlefs
' fuch extract or writ bear a fpecial warrant for that effect; and or-
' dain thefe prefents to be printed and publifhed, and a copy there-
' of to be given to the magiftrates of the good town of Edinburgh,
' that they, and all others concerned, may obferve the fame, as they
' fhall be anfwerable.' In all writs, therefore, which are to be regiftered in the books of royal boroughs, the claufe of regiftration
ought to bear a fpecial confent for the purpofe.

We now return to the ftatute of Robert I. from which this
branch of our perfonal execution originated. Lord Kaimes fpeaking
of the ftatute merchant of Edward III. proceeds in the following
words : ' As this was found a fuccefsful expedient for obtaining
' payment of debt, it was afterwards extended to all creditors, by
' the 25th Edward III. cap. 17. And thus in England, the creditor
' may begin with attaching the perfon of his debtor, by a writ
' named *capias ad fatisfaciendum* ; the fame with an act of warding
' in Scotland, againft inhabitants of royal boroughs. But as this act
' of Edward III. was not adopted by our Legiflature, there is to
' this day with us no authority for a *capias ad fatisfaciendum*, ex-
' cept in the fingle cafe of an act of warding *.'

The vivacity of his Lordfhip's genius, in reafoning too quickly
from flight analogies, has led him into a miftake. The act 25th of
Edward III. did not extend the arreftment of the perfon to all creditors. This did not happen till the 19th of Henry VII. cap. 9 †.
In England, the creditor at no period could, nor can now, begin
by attaching the perfon of the debtor, by a *capias ad fatisfaciendum*.

It

---

* Tracts, p. 346. † See Blackftone's Commentaries, vol. iii. p. 281.

It is the *capias ad reſpondendum*, with which all ſuits begin ; and no act of Parliament of this iſland, nor no uſage ever allowed any action to be begun by a *capias ad ſatisfaciendum*. This laſt writ has no doubt the ſame effect with an act of warding in Scotland ; but an act of warding is not the beginning of the action, it is a writ for executing a ſentence already given by the magiſtrates of a borough, juſt as an ordinary caption proceeds on a decree of the Court of Seſſion ; for no act of warding is ever iſſued, without a previous charge upon fifteen days ; or ſuch a number of days as are mentioned in the clauſe of regiſtration.

Having thus developed the more remote manners, and poſitive laws of both parts of the iſland, in the matter of perſonal execution, from the earlieſt periods, down to the commencement of our own regular Parliaments ; we are prepared for the remainder of our journey, through the reigns of the five Jameſes ; and for diſcovering the fundamental principles of the real progreſs of our perſonal execution, and the writs authorſing it, preſently in practice.

The weak irregular government of the Duke of Albany, and the factions of the Nobles, during the long abſence of James I. had filled the country with enormities, and heightened the barbarity of the inhabitants to a degree altogether incompatible with any idea of civil government. The power of the law was very little felt even in the centre of the kingdom ; but the Highlanders and Borderers were in a ſtate of abſolute ferocity, divided among themſelves, and ſubſiſting entirely upon depredations on the middle counties. Upon the return of James, who by long reſidence at the Court of England, had been the ſpectator of (comparatively ſpeaking) a regular and advanced government ; he bent his whole power and attention to correct the barbarous manners of his people, and to reduce them under law and order. For this purpoſe, he was obliged, contrary to his nature, to make large ſacrifices to juſtice ; and we find the greateſt part of the ſtatutes of that reign made and directed to that great end. The 86th chap. of his 6th Parliament, determines the

VOL. I.   K k   form

form of proceſs in the Spiritual Court. It is extremely curious, and throws light upon our ſubject. This is one of the few acts of our Statute Book, which were drawn up in Latin; and is a certain mark, that the churchmen predominated in the Parliament, framed the laws and expreſſed them in their own manners. It is a ſtatute of the utmoſt importance in the hiſtory of our law. It affords us perfect evidence, that in the reign of James I. the ſentences of the church courts both in civil and profane cauſes, were enforced by excommunication; nay, we learn, that the defenders were obliged to anſwer under the ſame pain, and to pay the money decreed within fifteen days after the date of the decree, or ſubmit to be excommunicated. We have already ſeen, that in conſequence of each of theſe ſentences, a writ of caption went out againſt the debtor, which the ſheriff of the county was obliged to execute. From the ſame act we have undeniable evidence of another very curious circumſtance, viz. that the procedure in the courts of common law, and in the church courts, were preciſely the ſame. The excommunication for non-appearance, anſwers to the *capias ad reſpondendum;* and the excommunication for non-payment, to the *capias ad ſatisfaciendum.* There cannot remain a doubt then, that the forms of the common law have been originally copied from thoſe of the church courts. Several other acts of James I. are employed in directing the method of purſuing murderers, felons, and other criminals. The act 89th of the ſame Parliament, directs the ſheriff to uſe *the King's horn* on the ſlayers; and to raiſe the country in his ſupport; and ſo to take them or fugitate them forth of the realm. The 99th act of the ſame Parliament orders the King's officers to be diſtinguiſhed by particular marks, which are retained to this day : ' It is ordained that ilk officiar of the Kingis, ' as *Mair* or Kingis *ſerjeand,* and Baronne ſerjeand, ſall not paſs in ' the countrie, nor Baronne ſerjeand in the baronnie, but ane *horne* ' and his *wand.*' At this period, the kingdom was divided into three civil juriſdictions. The ſheriffdoms under the King, the regalities under

under the ſeveral lords thereof, and the boroughs under their magiſtrates. *Mair* is a title of high antiquity.—In France, it was an
office of importance, and always meant a judge. The *Mair du Palais*
was the firſt officer of ſtate; and the *Mair de la Ville* or *Prevot,*
is the firſt magiſtrate of a city, as the Lord Mayor ſtill is. In the
capitulary of our elder Princes, we find the word *mair* or *marus,*
was an officer of court, who executed the citations, and other orders
of the judge; and it is probable, that he had a command over the
reſt of the officers*. Our macers of Seſſion and Juſticiary, are the
lineal deſcendants of theſe officers. The officers of the different
juriſdictions, are by this act ordered to be furniſhed with *wands* of
different colours to diſtinguiſh them. *Wands,* or rods, among the
northern nations, were held to be enſigns of authority; and in the
Engliſh ſtatutes, we find ſeveral officers appointed to attend the
King's courts with painted ſtaves, to take into cuſtody ſuch as were
committed by the court. One of the wardens of the Fleet priſon is
termed *baſtan,* the French word for a ſtaff, a term familiar in another part of our forms. The bearing of painted wands by the meſſengers, ordered by this act, is evidently one of the cuſtoms which
our James I. borrowed from the Engliſh courts, where he had been
accuſtomed to ſee them. The officers are alſo to be provided with
horns to alarm the country; and to proclaim the fugitives from
juſtice to be rebels or outlaws. Though the trumpet be one of the
moſt ancient inſtruments of martial muſic, it was only an improvement upon the horn, the undoubted original. Among the Saxons
and the Normans, the horn was an implement of the greateſt uſe and
conſequence. Even Caeſar takes notice that the Germans adorned
them, and uſed them in their feaſts †.

K k 2

We

---

* Vide Skene de Verb. Sig.

† Among the Saxons, the gift, and ſometimes the ſale of lands, were made by delivery of an inſtrument in that ſhape. The famous horn preſerved in the Cathedral
of York, is made of ivory. Ulphus the proprietor filled it with wine; and kneeling
before the altar, ' Deo et Sancto Petro, omnes terras et reditus propinavit.'

We now proceed to the hiſtory of the legal diligences. By the 10th act 5th Parliament James II. the ſheriffs are ordained, to arreſt the perſons of ſpoilers, and charge them to reſtore the goods taken away, under the pain of ' blawing them to the King's horn as ' rebels.' This act regards the criminal law. Diſobedience in this caſe was certainly a rebellion, and was a proper object for outlawry. The firſt act of the next Parliament is of a different nature,—it is intended to ſupport the eccleſiaſtical juriſdiction ; and in general, it may be obſerved, that in theſe days, our Parliaments opened with a ſtatute in favours of the powers and privileges of the church *. The old law referred to in this ſtatute, refers to chap. 6th of Robert III. already mentioned ; and the only difference is, that by this time, in imitation of the Engliſh, the direct power of iſſuing the caption, which in Robert's time belonged to the biſhop or his official, had now reverted to the Crown. The ſecond alteration is, that beſides the diligence by caption againſt the perſon, the lands and goods of the debtor are to be arreſted and appriſed to the party, *likeas for other debts* ; which clearly proves, that the ex-communication and caption authoriſed by this act, were meant of debts purely civil, which could be ſatisfied by lands and goods. But the goods are only to be attached, in caſe the debtor fly from the caption, ſo that the clerical, as well as the civil law, diſcharged the attachment both of body and eſtate at once ; if the one was taken, it behoved the other to be free. The next alteration is that, beſides being excommunicated by the church, debtors were, in the caſe of abſtracting their perſons and leaving no property behind them, to be made rebels to the King, by being proclaimed outlaws or put to the horn †.

This

* 6th Parliament James II. c. 12.

† The form of the caption iſſued by the King, againſt perſons excommunicated, in conſequence of the act of Parliament above mentioned, was diſcovered annexed to an
old

This executive writ is precifely in the ftyle of the Englifh writ *de excommunicato capiendo;* as may be found from the new *Natura Brevium,* and proves, that our ecclefiaftical forms over all Britain, carried the fame titles, and were attended with the fame effects. The rebellion declared by this act might have been avoided, either by the furrender of the debtor's perfon or moveable eftate; and, therefore, did not appear to be rigorous at the time.

By the 30th act of the 6th Parliament of the fame Prince, the method of forcing defenders to appear before the King and Council is fet down; the form is exactly the fame with the Englifh action at common law, already defcribed; there are three different diets of appearance, and three different fines leviable by diftrefs upon the goods of the defendant, precifely in terms of the Englifh writ of *Diftringas.* If after all the defender continues abfent, then the caufe is to be given againft him, and his lands and goods feized for the payment; ' and gif (continues the act) he has no lands nor ' goods, then fhall he be outlawed, and put to the King's horn.' Here is an outlawry provided in civil cafes by ftatute, which did no more than confirm the common law; it might alfo be avoided by furrender either of goods or perfon. No other act upon the fubject occurs in the reign of James II. who died in the 1457. From thefe ftatutes,

---

old manufcript copy of the Regiam Majeftatem. ' Jacobius, &c. Vicecomiti et balivis ' fuis de Aberdeen, nec non dilectis noftris A. B. C. ac eorum cuilibet conjunctim et ' divifim vicecomitibus noftris in hac parte falutem. Significavit nobis Reverendus in ' Chrifto Pater W. L. Epifcopus Aberdonenfis per fuas literas patentes in fubfidium ' Sanctae Matris Ecclefiae, noftrae Regiae Majeftatis, brachlium invocando. Quod G. F. ' et R. D. &c. (Here the debt and decreet have been recited) Quapropter dictus Reve. ' rendus Pater fuum proceffum excommunicationis et aggravationis contra eofdem ful- ' minavit et ipfos tanquam tales publicari et denunciari fecit. Quare vobis precipimus ' et mandamus quatenus dictos R. C. D. ubicunque poterint inveniri per captionem et ' incarcerationem corporum eorundem ad fatisfaciendum Deo et Sanctae Matri Eccle- ' fiae, ita celeriter compellatis quod pro veftro defectu amplius inde juftam queremo- ' niam non audiamus. Ad quod faciendum vobis,' &c.

ftatutes, we begin to fee the foundation of the extraordinary circumftance, which afterwards eftablifhed itfelf in the law of Scotland; I mean that of making rebellion to the Prince the univerfal
confequence of difobedience of his commands in the matter of civil
debts as well as crimes. A more unreafonable and cruel ufage never
took place in the jurifprudence of any country. This barbarity did
not fuddenly contaminate our law, but crept in by infenfible degrees,
grew familiar, and kept its footing even to our own times.

No other act appears, relative to this fubject, during the reigns
of James III. and James IV. excepting that the procefs of outlawry and horning continued to be awarded by fundry ftatutes
againft criminals of various denominations. The opinions of the
reformers began to fpread in the reign of James V. the clergy imagined that rigorous meafures were the moft proper for fupporting
an authority which began to fhake to the center. Thefe fentiments
produced the 9th act of the 4th Parliament of James V. It fhews
the degree of paffion and terror, which the clergy of the old church
allowed themfelves to be betrayed into by the times. To this ftatute, however, we fhall be obliged for certain information, in the
hiftory of execution of all kinds for debt, and particularly in our
prefent fubject, the execution againft the perfon. Many people,
it feems, held the horrible fentence of curfing in contempt, fo
much fo, that even the caption granted by the old law, did not
force them into obedience. Thefe captions were indifcriminately
granted, both for payment of liquid debts, and for performance of
facts and deeds. Before this time, the execution of the church decrees were limited to the imprifonment of the body, except in the cafe
where the party fled, and had no lands and goods; in which cafe
alone, by the act of James II. he could be denounced rebel; but by
this ftatute of his fucceffor James V. letters were to iffue for poinding and apprifing their goods, moveable and immoveable; and if
the debt was not thereby paid, and that the perfons had been *curfed*
for not doing or fulfilling of any act or deed, letters were to be
directed

directed ' in the firſt, ſecond, third, and fourth forms, conform to the
' ordinary letters of curſing.' Beſides all this, if the creditor choſe,
he might have the old letters of caption. Formerly, by the act of
James II. if a man had property in moveables and land, his body
could not be impriſoned by the caption for liquid debts; and though
he wilfully abſented, he could not be put to the horn; but by this laſt
ſtatute, his body might at once have been impriſoned, and his property, moveable and immoveable, ſeized upon at the ſame time. If
the church decree ordained him to do or perform any act or deed,
letters of four forms were to iſſue againſt him, not in the common ſtyle, but in terms of the letters of curſing, ſo that it behoved
him either to obey the church ſentence *in terminis*, or be denounced
rebel to the King, and thereby forfeit his whole moveables in the
firſt place, and his land in the next. This vengeful ſtatute of the
headſtrong churchmen of James V. was the firſt which introduced
in Scotland the attachment both of body and goods for liquid debts
at the ſame time, and denounced rebellion for non-performance of
facts and deeds, without any inquiry whether the diſobedience proceeded from want of ability or want of will. This act is alſo the
firſt of our ſtatutes, which makes mention of letters of *four forms*;
we ſhall ſpeak to the ſtyle of them, after carrying down our ſtatute
law upon the ſubject, the length of the Reformation.

The adminiſtration in the minority of Mary, finding the reformers growing in ſtrength and number, applied the old remedy of in-
creaſing the penalties of the church cenſures. To this purpoſe, an
act paſſed in her 4th Parliament c. 7. anno 1541, ordaining that all
perſons lying under excommunication for a year and a day, ſhould
forfeit or eſcheat their whole moveables to the Queen, to be diſ-
poſed of at her Grace's pleaſure, after payment of the debt contained in the diligence. By this ſecond oppreſſive ſtatute, we find
that no diſtinction was made by the churchmen, between liquid
debts, or performance of facts and deeds. All were ſubjected alike to
the heavieſt cenſures the church could inflict; and the ſame conſequences

quences provided to follow rebellion to the church, as followed rebellion to the King, without any outlawry, denunciation, or other form, than the excommunication itself.

During all the reigns preceding this period, no provision appears for imprisoning the bodies of debtors for non-payment of civil debts, excepting thefe debts were conftituted by the ecclefiaftical judges. From this we may moft affuredly infer, that the greateft part of the civil bufinefs of the nation had been engroffed by the bifhops and their officials; and that very little was left to the other judges ordinary, but the cognifance of crimes and mifdemeanours. Accordingly, the whole tenor of our ftatutes points out, that they were principally fo employed.

We now arrive at an act of Parliament, which difcovers a third cafe, in which the penalty of rebellion was made the confequence of non-payment of money. It was formerly mentioned, that as early as the monarchy itfelf, the King affumed the power or prerogative of imprifoning his fubjects for debts due to the Crown. That the fame power was exercifed in Scotland, no doubt can remain. Accordingly, by the 55th act of the 6th Parliament of Queen Mary, we find, that taxes granted by Parliament, were levied by letters of horning iffued by the Privy Council, commanding the fubjects to make payment, under the pain of rebellion. The churchmen, it feems, did not relifh this method, when put in practice upon themfelves, and remonftrated to the Queen. They found immediate redrefs. The act declares, ' That nae procefs of horning pafs againft ' kirkmen, if the Lords of the Spirituality find fome other reafon- ' able method for the payment thereof.' Since, then, the public taxes were raifed, under the pain of rebellion, the exceffive feverity of involving the fubjects in the fame confequence, for not payment of fums of money, muft have before this period difappeared in the eyes of the people, merely by the effect of cuftom. Whether the horning mentioned in this ftatute, proceeded upon four forms, *i. e.* four charges, or upon one charge only, cannot with certainty be

known

known; the words of the ftatute feem to point out one charge only. At this remarkable aera, both of our hiftory, and our law, *i. e.* the reign of Mary, it appears, that the procefs of horning and outlawry had become the fole compulfitor, or writ of execution in all cafes civil and criminal without exception.

The courts in England were eftablifhed at an early period, and their executive writs fixed in the beginning of their jurifprudence, continued through ages, and ftill continue in their original form, alterable by the fupreme power of the King and Parliament alone. In this country, the Supreme Courts had no ftability, until the eftablifhment of the College of Juftice. During thefe changes, the King and Privy Council iffued executive writs upon all emergencies, in which exercifing the powers of government, apparently abfolute, they changed the ftyle, fhortened the legal days of appearance, and enforced their commands by fuch penalties, as to them feemed proper. In this our government exactly copied that of France, whofe orders are all executed by letters under the *Royal Cachet* or Signet, made out by the Secretaries of State and their clerks, anfwering to our Clerks to the Signet. Letters in the fame ftyle are alfo iffued by the Court of England, but they are entirely limited to matters of ftate, and to the exercife of the royal prerogative. By the Englifh procefs, to which our ancient form for ages correfponded, it behoved every defendant to appear in perfon, or to give fufficient bail for his appearance; and, thereafter, to find fecond bail for paying obedience to the decreet when given. The inattention of our inferior judges, the changes and irregularities in the procedure of our courts, brought about a total neglect of the preliminary forms. The ancient brieves, or fixed writs of our courts, upon which all actions commenced, were dropped; complaints and fummonfes fucceeded; and, confequently, no previous bail was demanded from the defendant, either for appearance, during the courfe of the action, or for obedience to the fentence to be given. The fheriffs and inferior judges, in all events, poffeffed only the ancient power of diftreffing the debtors or defendants into obedience, by poinding their moveables ; and there it behoved the matter to reft, if the debt happened to be liquid ; but if it confifted in the performance of facts, the party applied to the Supreme Court for their warrant to compel the defendant to obey, under the penalty of being denounced a rebel ; and in this manner the procefs of outlawry came to be applied with us as the fole executive writ againft the perfons of debtors.

'It is probable (fays Lord Kaimes) that the charge neceffary to be 'given upon decrees, did originally proceed upon four diftinct 'letters or warrants ; but it being found that one letter or warrant 'being a fufficient authority for the four charges, the form was 'changed according to the model of the letters of four forms lateft in 'ufe.' Lord Kaimes conjectures rightly. Our Scottifh letters of four forms are nothing elfe than the writs of *alias, pluries,* and *exegi facias,* of which the Englifh outlawry confifted, put together in one writ. Anciently the Scottifh outlawry was executed by the fheriff of the county, and differed in nothing from the Englifh *. The fheriff in England returns that he has fought the party four feveral times ; and that as he did not appear in court, therefore he had been outlawed, according to the law of the kingdom of England. The writs of outlawry, therefore, anfwer precifely to our old letters of four forms ; and the return of the fheriff agrees with the four executions of the meffenger, who in Scotland, is the fheriff *in that part.* Both of thefe forms are originally derived from the writ of excommunication ; which, anterior to the final fentence, contained four requifitions. Each of thefe was executed and publifhed, and returns made of the fact by priefts commiffioned for the purpofe ; fo that from the church forms, we had the direct practice of making of fheriffs in that part. This was the method when excommunication had been pronounced by the bifhops of the diocefe upon

the

* Vide the procefs c. 59. of the Quoniam Attachlaments.

the fpot. Rome was at a diftance, and, therefore, when the Pope
iffued an excommunication, the whole was contained in one bull,
which contained four different progreffive requifitions, rifing
in importance above one another*. Our Judges in Scotland,
who upon every occafion copied the forms of the Court of Rome,
modelled their letters of outlawry upon that of the Roman bull, and
inferted the four forms in one letter. Lord Kaimes fuppofes that
this change took place upon principle, after the progrefs of induftry
tended to fhorten the multiplicity of legal fteps. This circumftance,
however, had not the leaft influence upon the matter. The firft alteration was introduced from the practice of government, which
has been defcribed by the acts of Parliament preceeding this period
of our hiftory, in iffuing letters againft criminals, for furrendering
their perfons to trial upon fingle charges of ten and fix days. It
was formerly mentioned in what manner creditors in obligations for
civil debts, copying after thofe fhort forms, made their debtors confent, that letters of horning upon a fingle charge of fix days, fhould
pafs againft them for payment †. Creditors have always dictated,
and debtors obeyed. And it is not in the leaft furprifing, that the
latter fhould have firft confented to abridge the number of charges
from four to one, *i. e.* to agree that letters of horning fhould pafs
againft them, in place of four forms; and alfo to agree to a charge of
fix days, in place of the ordinary days of law, which were fifteen.

The next change is ftill more deferving of attention. ‘ In hand-
‘ ling this curious fubject (fays Lord Kaimes) we muft be fatisfied
‘ to grope our way in the dark paths of antiquity, almoft without
‘ a guide. And the firft thing we difcover, is, that letters of four
‘ forms were not the only warrant for execution *in facta praeftan-*
‘ *da* ‡.’ His Lordfhip’s earlieft proof of this is an act of Parlia-

ment

---

* Vide the celebrated bull of damnation and excommunication, fulminated by Pope
Paul III. againft Henry VIII. of England, in Bifhop Burnet’s Collection of Records,
No. 9.

† Vide Claufe of Regiftration. ‡ Elucid. p. 350.

ment in the 1572, pofterior to all the laws and hiftorical facts which we
have detailed. His general reafoning and conjectures, however, on
this point, are both ingenious and juft. And we have fupported
them by proving, that perfonal execution fubfifted in Scotland for
payment of debts, by means of the ecclefiaftics, beyond the period
of any written law or cuftom we are poffeffed of. We conclude
this period of our hiftory, with an authority from Balfour, which
has efcaped Lord Kaimes, who fuppofes that letters of four forms,
impofed no other hardfhip upon the debtor, than to oblige him to
furrender his perfon in ward, if he did not pay. In drawing this
conclufion, his Lordfhip trufted to the letter of the writ ; but the
law it feems, at that period, put a different conftruction upon it.
' Letters, (we are told by Balfour) of four forms, gevin conform to
' ane decreet, aganis ony perfon, and beand execute againft him in
' all the four charges, be reffoune of his difobedience or contu-
' macy, it is not leafum to him, after the ifche and end of the days
' whereupon he is charged, *purgare moram ;* and thereby to efchew
' the pane of the letters ; and mairover, albeit he after the fierd
' charge, had obeyit the letters, yet the King, be reffoune of his
' contumacy and contemption, may juftly caufe him to be denounced
' rebel, and confifcat of all his moveabell gudes; becaufe, in *deci-*
' *foriis judiciorum,* fic as execution of fentence, and in criminal tref-
' paffes, fic as contumacie, difobedience, and contemption of the
' King's authority ; or yet, quhair ane certain day is affixt, or ane
' fpecial pane enjoynit, as ufe is in letters of four forms. *Non ad-*
' *mittitur purgatio morae,* 18th February 1546. Lord Lindfay a-
' gainft Alexander Keyninmouth*.'

Here feveral of the diftinctions which we are apt to make at this
diftance of time, are all blended together. The difobedient debtor
is ranked with the criminal ; and though he obeyed at laft by furrendering his perfon, yet, when in prifon, he lay, it feems, at the King's
                                                                    mercy

* Balfour, p. 390.

mercy for contumacy, and not obeying upon the firſt requiſitions. In this ſituation, it is not to be wondered at, if the people did not much feel the change now ſoon to take place, of denouncing debtors rebels directly for not payment or performance, which Lord Kaimes terms a brutal practice, admitting of no excuſe.

We are now to trace the progreſs and changes of this branch of the law, from the Reformation down to the preſent times, guided by the unerring evidence of ſtatute law, marking the alterations and improvements of each period. In Auguſt 1560, the Reformers, by their own authority, held a meeting which they termed a Parliament, in which they ſet about reforming the ſtate, as well as the church. None of their acts are inſerted in the ſtatute book, becauſe their convention was not ſanctified by royal authority. No more than three of the acts made in that convention, are mentioned by hiſtorians ; but a great deal was done. Biſhop Keith recovered the heads of theſe other intended laws, and has publiſhed them in his hiſtory. The firſt of them is, ‘ That all acts made before for cen-‘ ſures of curſing, were annulled, and ordained to be delete furth ‘ of the book of the record of Parliament.’ As by cutting off the form of curſing, they alſo put an end to the perſonal execution for civil debts, which for ages had been accuſtomed to follow upon the ſentences of the church courts, it appeared neceſſary to ſupply it. Therefore, by another article, it was ordained: ‘ That letters ſhould be given on ‘ acts without curſing upon liquidate debt, and four forms for ful-‘ filling of a debt.’ The letters to be thus given, were to be letters of horning, and the four forms the ſame as thoſe awarded by the act of James V.

The church courts were totally aboliſhed, but the Revolution was too ſudden ; the people felt the want, and demanded the reſtoration of them. The Queen, therefore, granted a commiſſion for appointing commiſſaries for exerciſing of the old juriſdiction, for which purpoſe, our commiſſary court was appointed, anno 1563.

As

As the ancient compulfitor of their fentences could no more be ufed, it appears from their books of federunt, that, in order to fupply the defect, Queen Mary, the next year, wrote a letter to the Lords of Seffion, defiring them to award letters of horning upon the decrees of commiffaries, where the fentences confifted *in facto*, and of poinding where it was given for a civil debt. The Lords of Seffion, it feems complied with this requeft, and a recommendation of the fame kind was alfo inferted in the inftructions to the commiffaries. The application was made to them by way of a *bill* or petition, which was produced with the decree of the commiffaries, and the precept duly executed. This is the origin of our prefent *bills* for diligence. The commiffaries followed the practice of their own court, in which actions were brought in the ftyle of the civil law, *per modum querelae*, and not by brieves ; and from this time forward, the Court of Seffion were accuftomed to grant hornings *in facto*, and letters of poinding for liquid debts, upon bare production of the commiffaries decrees. Thus the commiffaries, the reprefentatives of the church courts, who had poffeffed and been fuddenly deprived of the moft complete and perfect modes of execution of their fentences, were by a kind of juftice preferred to all inferior courts, and indulged with an execution more expeditious, and lefs expenfive, than any other judges of the kingdom. To underftand this more perfectly, it is neceffary to recollect, that, when the decrees of fheriffs, magiftrates of boroughs, or other inferior judges, were to be executed out of their own jurifdiction, parties were under the neceffity of bringing a new action before the Court of Seffion, libelling upon the decree of the lower houfe, and concluding to have a judgment of the Court of Seffion, in the precife terms of the former. This, when obtained, was termed *a decreet conform* ; and warranted diligence in any part of the kingdom. The principle of the form, was, that the king was underftood to be prefent in the Supreme Court, and to execute its judgments ; but he was not underftood to be prefent in inferior courts, or of confequence to

execute

execute the decrees pronounced by them. This fecond decree was
an expenfive and dilatory form ; and it was firft difpenfed with in
favour of the commiffaries, the reprefentatives of the old ecclefiaftical judges. Thus the acts of the irregular convention 1560, came
to be carried into execution ; *inter alia*, it is there faid, ' That or-
' dinances are made in what manner fupplications *per modum que-*
' *relae* fhould be purfued before the temporal judge, and nae mair
' before the fpiritual judge.'

During the preceeding reigns, we have found no laws authorifing
the execution againft the perfons of debtors, but fuch as paffed in
aid of the church courts, or for non-payment of the public taxes,
and *ad facta praeftanda*. Thefe executions were held fufficient for
the purpofes of the kingdom ; and our writers are greatly miftaken,
when they fuppofe, that perfonal execution for payment of liquid
fums took place only after the Reformation. In the latter reigns
of James V. and Mary, we have feen the churchmen call into their
fupport, the whole civil compulfitors againft the goods and lands of
debtors for liquid debts, and even letters to make them rebels to
the king. All thefe dreadful powers fell at the Reformation ; the ecclefiaftical courts were new modelled, and entirely ftripped of the
terrible weapons wielded by their predeceffors. Since people could
no longer be excommunicated for not payment of their debts, and
fince the whole ecclefiaftical compulfitors were fallen to the ground,
it is natural to fuppofe that it behoved a fet of new diligences or
executorials to be entrufted in different hands ; and that rebellion to
the King would be quickly fubftituted, in place of the excommunication. While the ecclefiaftical courts had fuch weapons in their
hands to enforce the recovery of civil debts, the defect of execution
in the other judges ordinary were not much felt or regarded. The
acts of Parliament, which we are now to confider in their order, are
a clear proof of this. They reftore perfonal diligence in another
fhape ; which reftoration has been miftaken by our writers for the
original introduction of it. Whatever reformation religion under-
went

went at this period, it cannot be faid that the morals of the people were much mended. So frequent had denounciations of rebellion become for civil debts, that the efcheats and forfeitures following upon them, proved to be a conftant fubject of avarice and rapacity to the people in power, and their creatures. The practice was fhameful to government, and deftructive of national manners; yet to fuch a monftrous length was it carried, that gifts of the efcheats of individuals were applied for and obtained, to take place, when they might afterwards happen to be denounced rebels *. The hint of this infamous practice was evidently taken from the ecclefiaftics. They folicited the benefices of their brethren, when living and in good health, as we do offices now, and the claufe in the gift is verbatim copied from the claufe *de nifi*, formerly explained, which, by a forehand ceremony, excommunicated people, when they fhould happen to fail in their contracts. It is no wonder that this tranfaction fhould be difcharged by ftatute; for how many fnares muft have been laid in the way of innocent men, at the inftance of thofe who had fo much intereft in betraying them into rebellion?

The reformed clergy, in abolifhing the powers of the church courts, had been, as they were in every thing, rafh and precipitate. They made no diftinction between perfons curfed for civil debts, and thofe curfed for difobedience to the private dictates of the church, in matters of religion. The new clergy foon found out their miftake, and corrected it by procuring to themfelves the re-ftoration of the whole cenfures of the old church in its utmoft feve-rity. This was done by the 53d of the 3d Parliament of James VI. anno 1572.

By this ftatute, the whole ancient power of the Roman Church was reftored to the Church of Scotland, in matters of their own difcipline, with this difference only, that the letters of caption, in place of proceeding upon the warrant of excommunication, as in

the

---

* Vide the 23d act of the 1ft. Parliament of James VI. anno 1567.

the days of James **V.** *i. e.* for imprifoning the body of the debtor as a rebel to God Almighty, proceeded upon the letters of four forms for imprifoning him as a rebel to the King; and ever fince the Reformation, rebellion againft the King, has been the fole foundation in this country for execution againft the perfon in all cafes civil and ecclefiaftical. It has the fame effect in criminal matters, where parties fly from juftice.

The next ftatute enacted in behalf of this branch of the law, is the 75th of the 6th Parliament of James VI. This ftatute is of very great importance, and remains partly in force at prefent. The difobedience which the ftatute complains of, was a natural and unavoidable confequence of debafing the Sovereign's authority, rendering it the fole ground of common and mean execution of the recovery of petty debts between the fubjects. When punifhment is totally difproportionate to the crime, the common fenfe of mankind will bring them to a level, and muft, in the end, get the better of pofitive inftitutions. This act makes no diftinction between rebels for crimes, and rebels for not payment of debts; but the people foon faw and acknowledged the folid and true diftinction. The real crime came to be termed *rebellion*, and the other only *civil rebellion*. The laft was often innocent and unavoidable; for by this time, people were denounced principally by means of regiftrations of confent for not payment of liquid debts, without any alternative of faving themfelves by furrender of their perfons to prifon. Inftead of altering the mode of the perfonal execution, for which they had a direct model in the acts of warding of royal boroughs, government were pleafed to increafe the very caufe of the evil, and involve innocent debtors, criminals, and rebels in the very fame punifhment. The Lords of Seffion, it feems, in order to heighten their own authority, had been the firft authors of this cruel and impolitic meafure; * and government were weak enough to adopt it from them. This act explains the claufe in the letters of four forms, which was

* Vide the Act.

immediately inſerted in conſequence of the ſtatute, viz. ' and im-
' mediately after your ſaid denunciation, that ye make intimation
' to the ſheriff of our ſhire, where our ſaid rebel is, and ſicklike to
' theſaury and his clerk, conform to our act of Parliament made
' thereanent.' To make the matter perfectly ſure, a regiſter
of hornings is appointed. From this we ſee the cruel and impolitic origin of this regiſter. It was merely to ſupply the defect of private information given to the Crown, which had been ordered by the Lords of Seſſion, and by the tenor of the diligence.
This record, unlike the reſt of our regiſters, was founded to in-
creaſe the miſery, and not to be ſubſervient to the utility of the people ; nor has it, from the date of this act to the preſent moment,
been of any material ſervice to the national buſineſs. It is a dead
form, ſupported only by the fees annexed to it. The next clauſe of
the act eſtabliſhes the mode of relaxation, which is likewiſe appointed to be regiſtered, in order to relax the debtors ; ſo that this
record formed a charge and diſcharge of rebellion between the King
and his ſubjects. The act next proceeds to direct the mode of levying the eſcheats. This extraordinary ſtatute concludes with making
proviſion for a caſe, which, conſidering the nature of the enactment,
might well be expected to have happened, viz. reſiſtance upon the
part of the ſubject. From the lamentable weakneſs of the Scotch
monarchy, aroſe the barbarous letters of fire and ſword, which we
ſee authoriſed by this ſtatute. The king was to pillage one part of
his ſubjects for pretended rebellion, and for not paying their debts ;
and the execution of this robbery was to be committed to others of
the ſubjects, armed with letters of fire and ſword. The traffic of
theſe eſcheats, and the mode of their execution, tended greatly to
kindle and ſpread thoſe deadly feuds, which embittered the after
days of this Prince ; and which his better notions of government, and
the real power to which he ſucceeded, was never able to extinguiſh.

We obſerved, that, after the Reformation, the want of the perſonal execution, which the church courts afforded for liquid debts,
was

was very foon felt; becaufe no other diligence now proceeded upon them in common, but letters of poinding againft their lands and moveables. In this fituation, creditors were eafily difappointed by the debtors concealing their property, and holding it under borrowed names. The firft remedy attempted to be applied, was by the Lords of Seffion in the 1582, who appointed, ' That letters of horn-' ing, as well as of poinding fhall be directed upon decreets for li-' quid fums, in the fame manner as formerly given upon decreets, ' *ad facta praeftanda* ;' and this act of federunt is ratified by the act 139. Parliament 1584.

It is here to be particularly obferved, that the horning and poinding contained in the ftatute, are declared to be ' the ane not preju-' dicial to the other.' Thefe are words that well deferve elucidation,—they introduced into our law, what was till then unknown, execution againft the body, lands, and goods of debtors for liquid debts, all at once and by one writ. We have heard, that by the ancient law, the body could not be imprifoned for civil debt. We have heard, that if a man be taken upon the writ of *capias ad fatisfaciendum* in England, it is held to be an execution of the higheft nature, and nothing farther can proceed againft his eftate or effects. Even by the act of James V. 1535, a man excommunicated for debt could only be taken by virtue of a caption ; and, if that was done, no poinding could proceed. The civil courts never had any fuch powers, and the effect even of the act of James V. as to poinding and arreftment, vanifhed with the religion to which it belonged. Letters of four forms and decrees of confent, afterwards proceeded for liquid debts ; but if the debtor furrendered himfelf to ward in obedience to the letters, there the procefs muft have refted. A man taken by the *capias ad fatisfaciendum* in England, might have continued in prifon, and retained his property, as is often done at this moment. A debtor in Scotland might have done the fame thing. At laft the Court of Seffion found, that his property might, notwithftanding, be poinded ; but, before this could be done, it be-

hoved

hoved the creditor to relieve the perſon of his debtor out of priſon. The following clear and plain authority from Balfour, at once proves and explains this very material point in our law : ' Decrete ' beand given before ane judge againis ony perſon for payment of ' ony liquidate ſum or debt, with letters executorials thereupon ; ' under the pane of warding of his perſone, gif he beand denounced ' rebel, and put to the horn, enters his perſon in ward, conform to ' the ſaid letters, intending thereby to evacuate and eſchew farder ' execution of the ſaid decrete aganis him, ſic as poinding or com- ' priſing : the Lords at the inſtance of the party in quhais favours ' decrete is given, may direct their letters to poind and diſtrenzie ' the ſaid perſons movabell gudes and gear, againis whom the de- ' creet is given ; and failzeing thereof, to appriſe his lands and heri- ' tage ; providing always that the ſaid perſon be relievit out of ward, ' and put to liberty. November 1558, Gillraith againſt Edingtown *.'

There is an evident inconſiſtency in the ſtyle of the letters of four forms, which is explained by the act of Parliament. I mean, that an inventory ſhould be made of the effects of the debtor, as the proper- ty of the King, in conſequence of the rebellion, and ordered to be ſeized upon, and inbrought to his uſe ; and yet that the meſ- ſenger ſhould be the next moment authoriſed to poind and appriſe them for the debt due to the complainer in the letters. The Writers to the Signet did not attempt to reconcile this ; but retained the old ſtyle of the four forms, and obeyed the act of Parliament, by ad- ding the poinding, the contradiction between which, affords the moſt complete evidence, that the poinding was inconſiſtent with the warrant againſt the perſon ; or, in other words, that execution both againſt the perſon and effects of the debtor in one writ, was con- trary to the common law of the realm, and came to be joined only by the force of the act of Parliament laſt mentioned ; and we ſhall afterwards ſee, that our preſent letters of horning have continued to

this

* Balfour, p. 392.

this moment the fame very curious mark of the ancient law of the kingdom.

The next alteration in this part of our law was introduced by the 181ft act of the 13th Parliament of James 6th 1593. Here the letters of four forms are ordered to be reduced to one charge of ten days upon the decrees of magiftrates. At this period, therefore, the commiffaries and the bailies were put upon the fame footing ; both were entitled to have letters of horning, by bills to the Lords, upon one form in place of four. So matters continued till the 10th act of the 18th Parliament, and the 15th act of the 20th Parliament of the fame Prince ; when fheriffs, ftewarts, bailies of regality, and the judge of the admiralty, were put upon the like footing, *i. e.* in place of obtaining decrees conform, the lieges were entitled to have letters of horning, for the execution of the decrees of thefe judges, by bills to the Lords.

Epifcopacy being eftablifhed in Scotland, at the Union of the Crowns, in the perfon of James VI. the then Bifhops chofe to have the ancient power of the church in fome degree reftored ; and, particularly, the power of naming their own officials, and commiffariot, which was accordingly beftowed upon them, by the 6th act of the 20th Parliament of James VI. anno 1609. The Court named in Mary's time, gave place to this new erection. Letters of horning are ordained by the ftatute 1609, to pafs upon their decrees as formerly ; but another act was judged neceffary to regulate this point, and put the Court upon the fame footing with the other judicatories of the kingdom. This was done by act 7th of the 21ft Parliament of James VI. 1612.

While the Court of Seffion were thus diftributing their authority, for the execution of the decrees of inferior judges by the fhort and effectual method of horning upon one charge, the old letters of four forms continued to be the only diligence iffuable upon their own fentences. It was certainly a circumftance replete with abfurdity, that the Superior Court fhould poffefs a flower and lefs effectual

mode

mode of putting their judgments into execution than their infe-
riors ; and, therefore, upon the 23d of November 1613, the
Lords adopted the letters of horning, and entirely laid afide the old
letters of four forms. From this time the univerfal writ, iffued by the
Court of Seffion for the execution of their own fentences, and of the
decrees of the other inferior judges, came to be letters of horning upon
a fingle charge of fifteen days, which are the ancient *induciae* of all
ordinary decrees , or upon fix days, in terms of the confent of parties in decrees of regiftration.   All the orders of government, and
all the civil bufinefs of this nation, were alfo enforced by letters of
horning on fingle charges.   By force of thefe alone, public taxa-
tions were collected, fines were levied, and in fhort, the whole laws
of the police of the kingdom were executed.   We do not mean in
this place, to enter into the legal confequences of the civil outlawry
òr rebellion fo eftablifhed.   Every circumftance of that matter may
be found in the decifions of the Court, during the laft century, and
in our writers upon the inftitutions of the law.   It is enough to obferve, that thefe confequences were equally penal, equally terrible, as
in the outlawry or fugitation for the higheft crimes, nor do our ancient ftatutes mark any diftinction between thefe cafes.   We wifh
only to give the great outlines of the progrefs of our forms, to
fhow their connection with the national manners, and to defcend
into thofe particulars only, from which the ftyles and the cuftoms,
which are the proper objects of practice, have originated.

   In the days of Mr Dallas of St Martin, the paffing of the gifts of
efcheats conftituted a great part of the bufinefs of a writer, and accordingly, he has made it the fubject of the fecond part of his ftyles;
an unqueftionable proof of the height to which this corrupt branch of
bufinefs had arrived in the reign of Charles II.   Even in the beginning of the prefent century, it continued to be made, as Lord Kaimes
fays, a handle of oppreffion, and as then underftood, even the
fingle efcheat was a terrible prerogative of the law of Scotland.
The liferent efcheat belonging to fubject fuperiors was no lefs fo.
                                                          Nay,

Nay, fo great was the influence which this laft was fuppofed to beftow, that the then adminiftration from timidity, not from virtue, were happily induced to abrogate the whole confequences of civil rebellion by the jurifdiction act 1746, 20th George II. c. 50. §. 11. Thus our Scots procefs of horning and outlawry was, notwithftanding the ftyle, reduced to a warrant for perfonal execution—to an act of warding univerfal over the kingdom,—or to the fimple executive writ of *capias ad fatisfaciendum.* After deviating in form and principle for feveral hundred years, the law of both England and Scotland have in fubftance entirely coincided. By the ancient and original common law of both kingdoms, the body of no fubject could be imprifoned for a debt merely civil. The Englifh, to get the better of this maxim, feigned a crime, a breach of peace to have been committed by the debtor, and hence arofe the writ of *capias ad fatisfaciendum.* We, in Scotland, in order to get over the fame original principle, feigned a very ferious crime, viz. that non-payment of debt was rebellion againft the King, and hence our prefent letters of caption.

Style

Style of the Letters of Horning.

THE laws of the Romans were promulgated and executed by means of letters iffued in the name of the Emperors. Thefe letters were fometimes directed to the people in general, at other times to particular cities and provinces, and often to the great officers of the empire. They began with a falute to the perfon or perfons to whom they were addreffed ; then the reafons were given which induced the law or regulation, and they concluded with the command itfelf, which is the natural form of all writs of this kind.

The Princes of modern Europe, inclined to govern upon the fame principles, received the Roman law into their refpective dominions, and ftruggled to eftablifh it as the univerfal rule, even in preference to their own ancient cuftoms. In the Emperors they found models for every fituation which they themfelves wifhed to arrive at, and nothing could be more enviable or flattering, than the power of making what laws they pleafed, and executing them by the imperial method of iffuing *letters*. Thefe forms were eftablifhed at the earlieft periods of our monarchies. In France the civil and criminal bufinefs, the police of the kingdom, and the affairs of ftate, have been, and ftill continue to be, managed and executed by *letters*, the general ftyle or form of which are the fame, though each of them has obtained a different title taken from the particular fubject upon which it is directed. The general title is *Lettres Royaux*, and thefe are feparated into three kinds, the *Lettres d'Etat*, which carry the

orders

orders of state and government ; *Lettres de Grace*, such as pardons, dispensations, &c. flowing from the grace, or liberality of the Sovereign ; and *Lettres de Justice* founded upon the law of the kingdom, and which carry the orders of the supreme power for the execution of the municipal law, at the instance of the subjects against each other. In the early periods of the English monarchy, when one individual was injured by another in a matter of property, he was obliged to apply to the Chancellor of the realm. The Chancellor heard the circumstances of the case ; and if the complainer was entitled to a remedy in the law, that officer formed a writ in the King's name, directed to the proper judge, requiring him to do justice in that behalf. These forms were collected into a register under the title of *brieves*, and the *registrum brevium* is the most ancient book of the law of England. As the brieves for bringing parties into courts were thus early established, the writs for the execution of their decrees when given, were also fixed to a precise style, alterable only by the King and the Parliament. Each court has its own peculiar writs of execution for rendering sentences given in it effectual, which are all issued in the King's name, and formed upon the precise words of the judgment of court. These answer to the French letters of justice. In matters of state, or in the execution of those things immediately under the royal prerogative, the Kings of England in ancient times did, and continue still to issue letters in a style and form exactly coinciding with the *Lettres d'Etat*, the absolute mandates of the French. Such are proclamations, warrants for executing criminals, holding courts-martial, &c.

In this country the ancient brieves fell by degrees into disuse, leaving a few behind which have continued in practice. Our Supreme Courts at these times had very little stability,—changes of judges, of their judicative powers, and consequently of their mode of procedure, were frequent and sudden. In this situation, the executive writs suffered proportionable variations, till at last the form of the French letters were adopted by the government, and issued upon all occasions civil and criminal. With regard to execution againſt the perſon, we have heard that it came to proceed upon diſobedience to one of theſe royal mandates, and that a debtor is not impriſoned for refuſing to pay his debt, but for rebellion to the King. The horning, therefore, was conſidered in a light perfectly different from the ancient writs of execution, it is a direct order from the Sovereign to pay the debt or be denounced rebel to the ſtate, and be put out of the protection of the law. It differs very little from a *lettre de cachet* of France, which is a particular letter or command of ſtate, directed againſt an individual ſubject. On a former occaſion we pointed out the model, from which our letters of four forms were copied, and we demonſtrated that our preſent horning is exactly the letters of four forms abridged, and reduced to one charge of payment, without the old alternative of ſurrendering the perſon. After the brieves and executive writs of our original law went out of practice, the other mandates of government will all be found to be modelled in the ſame ſtyle, made out by the ſame officers, and iſſued by the ſame authority, viz. by the Clerk or Secretary of the Privy Council of Scotland, and his aſſiſtants, who came to be termed *Clerks to the Signet.*

From the cauſes juſt mentioned, has ariſen the capital difference between the executive writs of Scotland and England, and the co-incidence of ours with the forms and practice of France. We know very little difference in the ſtyle or form of letters of ſtate iſſued in exerciſe of the royal prerogative, and letters iſſued in execution of civil juſtice, or of the ſentences of the courts; and hence, as in France, we have a great variety of letters under the general name of ſignet letters, diſtinguiſhed by the ſubjects of their reſpective direction ; but in ſtyle and form, there is no difference between proclamations and other mandates of the ſtate, iſſued in exerciſe of the royal prerogative. Our Scottiſh Princes of the latter ages, ſo far from being poſſeſſed of real power, were themſelves governed by the violence of the faction accidentally predominant at the time ; yet

they

they iffued out letters upon every emergency framed *pro re nata*, without the leaft regard to law, cuftom, or to the liberty of the people.

Prefident Montefquieu obferving, when in England, the form of the Britifh executive writs, and that all of them proceeded in the name, and by the authority of the King alone, who he well knew did not poffefs the power which feemed to be thereby indicated, makes a reflection worthy of the difcernment of fo great a man. ' It may be that this nation, (fays he) having been once fubject to ' arbitrary power, has upon feveral occafions preferved the ftyle of ' it, in fo much that, upon the foundation of a free government, the ' the forms are preferved of a government that has been abfolute *.'

We now proceed to confider the ftyle of the horning, and in fo doing, the commentary we are to make will in a great meafure be applicable to the whole of our *fignet letters.*

' *Charles by the grace of God, King of Great Britain, France and* ' *Ireland,* &c.—Our Kings originally judged in perfon, and have ever been fuppofed to be prefent, and to fupport the exercife of juf- tice, by means of their royal prerogative; the nobleft part of which, the executive power of the realm, is lodged in the Crown for that purpofe. Some of the Princes of Europe affected long pompous titles in their letters and writs, lengthened by a catalogue of their dominions. To thefe they were particularly proud of adding their conquefts. In this they were imitated by their nobility, who in their writs vied with each other, in a vain difplay of their offices, dig- nities, and names of their lands. The tafte for this inflated ftyle, is juftly fuppofed to have been communicated to the Europeans, by the Princes of the Eaft, during the croifades. The title of our Kings from the earlieft ages to the union of the kingdoms, un- der James VI. was fimply *King of Scots.* We find, however, that James VI. upon returning from England, borrowed the addition of the *grace of God.*

N n 2

The

---

* Spirit of the Laws, 19. c. 27.

The Kings of England varied their ftyle, as they happened to be fuccefsful in their wars, fometimes adding, and at other times omitting the conquefts they or their anceftors had made. The reafon of the addition of *Defender of the Faith*, adopted by Henry VIII. is well known. It is an excellent fpecimen of words remaining in deeds, when the caufes for which they were inferted are no more. The firft and warmeft wifh of our James VI. upon afcending the throne of England, was to bring about an union with the two kingdoms of England and Scotland, and to extinguifh for ever the differences which had fubfifted fo long between them. With this view, he iffued a proclamation in the year 1604, giving his reafons at large, and particularly infifting on the coincidence of the ancient laws of both countries, and the remaining marks which proved them to have been the fame people: ' Wherefore, (fays James) we have ' thought good to difcontinue the divided names of England and ' Scotland, out of our legal ftyle; accordingly, we do by thefe pre- ' fents, by force of our kingly power and prerogative, affume to ' ourfelf, by the clearnefs of our right, the name and ftyle of King ' of Great Britain, France and Ireland, Defender of the Faith, and ' do hereby publicly promulgate and declare the fame *.'

' *To our lovites.*'—The Pope addreffed his letters to princes and great men, *dilectis filiis fuis*, or *dilecto filio fuo.* The Bifhops did the fame in their diocefan letters. The Kings of Europe adopted the fame ftyle in letters or mandates to their fubjects, when commiffion- ed to execute any thing by royal authority. The King of England fays *to our beloved*, or *well beloved.* The King of France, *à nos amés*, or *à nos bien amés.* And the King of Scotland *to our lovites;* but when vaffals or officers are addreffed, the King of France fays, *à nos amés et feaux,* and the Kings of Scotland *to our right trufty and well beloved.* In France the word *amés* is general to the whole fub- jects, but *feaux,* or trufty, is only ufed to the vaffals of the Crown.

The

* Rhymer's Foed. vol. vii. part. ii.

The old Englifh brieves directed to the fheriffs, did not give them any epithet, it was ' Rex vicecomiti fuo de A.' The ftyle of our old brieves was the fame. The words *dilecto fuo* were only ufed in government letters, or extraordinary mandates addreffed to individual fubjects. Thus the precepts directed to fuperiors to enter their vaffals, bear, ' dilecto noftro A. B. fuperiori terrarum infra fcript.' The reafon was, that the fuperior, being an immediate vaffal of the Crown, is, as fuch, entitled to the diftinction here made.

When the brieves went out of practice, and were fupplied by letters under the fignet, in the form of letters of ftate, the fheriffs for the firft time were termed *lovites*, and the meffengers who fucceeded them, as *fheriffs in that part*, had the title continued to them. It will be obferved, that in the horning of our text book, it is the meffengers who are the *lovites*, and fuch was the ftyle of all the diligences of thefe days. The reafon cannot be given, why for forty or fifty years paft, the Writers have transferred the expreffion of royal kindnefs from the meffengers to their own clients. When this happens to be a nobleman, the old letters made the King term him *our well beloved coufin and counfellor*, all of that high rank being prefumed to be related to the Sovereign, befides being by birth his hereditary counfellors. But thefe fwelling titles are now often omitted, in fignet letters at leaft, and a nobleman is defcribed by his ufual titles of honour.

' *Meffengers, our fheriffs in that part conjunctly and feverally, fpe-*
' *cially conftitute.*'—The ftyle and practice of appointing judges and commiffaries in that part, were borrowed from the ecclefiaftics, the greateft part of whofe bufinefs was done by thefe deputations. They were termed *judices in partibus.* At the precife period that we dropped the old forms of our brieves, we began to fupply them by the forms of France, where much bufinefs was in ufe to be done by judges and commiffioners in that part. This alteration in the form, brought on feveral moft material changes and corruptions in our law. It was principally occafioned by the office of the fheriff
being

being in the greateſt part of Scotland hereditary in families, who, content with the honour, negleɛted the duty ; nay, from our ſtatutes, we ſee that they often refuſed even to hold courts, or to diſtribute juſtice to the lieges, far leſs was the miniſterial execution of it to be depended on. After the brieves fell, the regular conneɛtion between the ſheriff, and the chancery, or the ſuperior courts of the kingdom, alſo ceaſed. In England, on the other hand, this connection gained ſtrength with time, and became the great engine upon which the civil government of the kingdom depended. Hence their forms have continued through ages to be the ſame, nor do they know any thing of ſheriffs in that part. The ſheriff of the county, by himſelf or his officers, muſt execute all the writs of the ſuperior courts, and anſwer to the public and party for his conduɛt. The incurable negligence and partialities of the ſheriffs in Scotland, forced our debile government to have recourſe to the French method of conſtituting ſheriffs in that part. Theſe at firſt were not meſſengers or public officers, but any perſons who could be got to undertake the buſineſs. At firſt, the writs were direɛted to the ſheriff of the county, *nominatim*, and failing him, to the other perſons who undertook to be ſheriffs in that part, in order that the buſineſs might be done by them, if the other delayed or refuſed. Where ſummonſes were on one diet even in St Martin's time, they could be executed by any perſon whatever *. But as the meſſengers increaſed in number, they were employed in excluſion of others. It came, however, to be early eſtabliſhed, that none but meſſengers could execute hornings, becauſe none but the King's officer could denounce any man a rebel. Upon this Balfour has preſerved a deciſion, ' gif ony perſon be chargit be our Sovereign Lords letters to ' find ſovertie to underlay the law before the juſtice and his de-
' putes, for ſlauchter, or ony other crime, the executor of the let-
' ters aucht and ſould be the ſheriffs officiars, or officiar of the
' King's

* Page 290.

' King's Grace, utherways gif the faid perfon be denouncit rebel,
' and put to the horn be ony other officiar or fheriff in that part,
' the famen denunciation is of nane avail, and aucht and fould be
' reduced.—25th Junii 1535, William Lord Semple againft John
' Lord Leyle *.'

' *Conjunctly and feverally, fpecially conftituted.*'—For a long period
the name of the fheriffs in that part, or the meffengers, were always
filled up, and if the letters gave a warrant for poinding, or executing any thing where refiftance was to be apprehended upon the part
of the debtor, three or four meffengers and fheriffs in that part
were inferted *nominatim.* Therefore it was, that thefe perfons are
conjunctly and feverally empowered, in order that one or all of them
might act as neceffity required. They were alfo *fpecially conftituted.*
To underftand this, it will be recollected, that it was a principle in
the ancient law of this ifland, that no judges fupreme or inferior,
had any jurifdiction, but what was committed by the particular
brieve directed to them for the purpofe, far lefs had meffengers or
fheriffs in that part, who were mere minifterial officers, any power
or authority, without being as they are in the ftyle *fpecially conftituted.*

' *Greeting.*'—The form of letters from all antiquity, as mentioned on another occafion, bore a falute or wifh for the fafety of the
perfon to whom it was directed. The Popes added the apoftolic
benediction : ' Salutem et apoftolicam benedictionem.' The word
greeting is from the Latin verb *grator,* and has been ufed ever fince
our public writs were iffued in Englifh.

' *Forafmeikleas A. B. as principal, and C. D. as cautioner, by their
' bond, dated,' &c.*—In this cafe, the bond is fuppofed to be regiftered in the books of Seffion, and a decree of the Lords of confequence interponed to it. The King, as mentioned before, is prefumed to prefide in his Supreme Court, and confequently, to know
what

* Balfour, p. 558.

what has been done, he therefore recites the bond from his own knowledge. Anciently it was prefumed that obedience would immediately be given to the decree of the Supreme Court; and, therefore, after obtaining it, parties were obliged to inform the Lords by a bill or petition, that obedience had been *de facto* refufed. The old letters of four forms accordingly appear to be always granted upon bills. But after the Court of Seffion was by act of Parliament authorifed to iffue both horning and poinding upon their decrees, an exprefs warrant for that purpofe was adjected, and from that time, *i. e.* anno 1613, the form of prefenting bills upon decrees of the Supreme Court, entirely ceafed. Such decrees were held to be warrants fufficient for the Writers to the Signet to expede, and the Keeper of the Signet to put the King's feal to letters of horning, and other executive writs. This can only be done when the letters proceed in the name of the perfon obtainer of the decree; for, when another having right to it by affignation or by a fervice as heir, choofes to have the letters in his name, he muft apply in the old manner, and produce that title with his bill, that it may be feen and confidered by the Lords, in which cafe the ftyle of the letters alters to ' *Whereas it is humbly meant and fhown to us by our lovite.*' If the decree has been pronounced, or, which is the fame thing, the bond regiftered in an inferior court, then, in terms of one or other of the acts of Parliament we have confidered, a bill muft be prefented requefting the interpofition of the Supreme Court, and therefore, the ftyle is the fame as already mentioned. The King recites the decree from the bill, and the raifer of the horning is termed the complainer. This, however, cannot be done until the fifteen days, which are the ancient days of law, be expired, and, according to our genuine form, no horning fhould be given by the Court of Seffion, unlefs the precept of the inferior judge be actually executed, and the charge expired. The reafon is fuggefted by the preambles of the act of Parliament formerly under our view. The interpofition of the Supreme Court is awarded, in order to fupply the defect of

the

the execution of inferior courts, arising from their limited jurifdiction, and to reach the effects of debtors who withdrew them, in order to elude the execution of the inferior fentence ; but, if this has not been done, and the precept of the inferior court has not been difobeyed, there is no neceffity for the interpofition of a higher authority, and confequently letters of horning ought not to be granted. Therefore it is, that all our bills and letters bear the production of the bailie's or sheriff's precept duly executed, and confequently difobeyed. Practice has difpenfed with the actual execution, providing fifteen days be expired from the date of the decree. The reafon was, that when debtors retired out of the jurifdiction, and left no houfe or effects behind them, the precept of the sheriff could not poffibly be executed ; fo that a horning was the only remedy. The clerks to the bills could not know the fact in thefe cafes ; they were obliged to truft the affertion of the writer ; and, therefore, to shorten matters, they required only the expiration of the fifteen days.

' *By their bond dated the   day of   for the caufes* ' *therein fpecified.*'—In executive writs, the obligatory part alone is to be taken notice of, not the reafons inductive of the obligation ; becaufe decree being now given, the obligement is, *res judicata,* fufficient to conftitute the debt. The original caufes of granting, therefore, would be quite impertinent in hornings, or other writs of execution ; whereas, in fummonfes or libels, they are a neceffary and important part of the facts fet forth. Writers always ufe this expreffion, '*for the caufes therein fpecified,*' merely to hint that fufficient caufes exifted ; but the phrafe is unneceffary. Next follows the recital of the bond, viz. the date, the fum, the term of payment of the principal, annualrents, and penalty, which always concludes with a general reference to the obligement or decree themfelves. The purpofe of this is to correct any miftake that may happen in the recital of the diligence, and to show that nothing is meant to be commanded in the letters, but what is authorifed by the original ground of the debt itfelf. Next comes the efficient part of the

O o   letters,

letters, the command of the Prince given in confequence of the reafons affigned in the preamble.

' *Our will is berefore, and we charge you ftriftly, and command,*'
&c.—Thefe are the words which differenced the *letters of ftate* from
the *writs of juftice.* We have already feen in what manner our
writs of juftice in Scotland were confounded with letters of ftate,
and confequently the ftyle of the latter applied to both, and the reafon of the diftinction being preferved in England. From the executive writs of Scotland and France, as adopted in the latter periods
of either monarchy, a perfon would be led to think that juftice was
done only in both kingdoms becaufe it is the King's pleafure it
fhould be fo; for *tel eft notre plaifir,* fays the one; *our will is
berefore,* fays the other.

' *That incontinent thefe our letters feen, ye pafs.*'—*Incontinent* is an
old formal word once ufed by the Englifh writers for *immediately.*
In this fenfe it is obfolete in the South, and is only ufed by us in the
forms of writs. To *pafs,* is alfo obfolete in the fenfe in which it is
here put. It is one of the many Gallicifms adopted in Scotland
from the ftyle of the French writs, where the verb *paffar* is ufed in
this and a variety of other fignifications.

' *Command and charge the faid A. B. and the faid C. D, his cau-*
' *tioner, conjunftly and feverally, perfonally or at their refpective*
' *dwelling-places, to make payment to the faid G. D. of the forefaid*
' *fum of   of principal, of   of expences, and annuals*
' *of the faid principal for all years bygone refting owing and unpaid.*'
—This claufe, in practice, is called the command of the letters. It
is the meffenger's fixed rule for making out his charges, and therefore principally deferves the attention of the writer who expedes the
letters. He is to take care that the command contains nothing but
what is precifely due by the warrant or ground of debt, and that no
part of the debt be there omitted. He is alfo to attend to the manner in which the debtors are bound, whether by equal parts or conjunctly and feverally, as in the cafe before us. When any part of
the

the debt, principal or intereft, has been paid, the command of the letters is the place for the mention of it. This is ufually done by the general words, '*deducing all partial payments, conform to the 'receipts or difcharges thereof*,' in order to throw the proof of their extent upon the debtor poffeffed of them. When there is but one known payment, it is fpecially deducted.

'*And ficklike yearly and termly, during the not payment thereof, 'the terms of payment of the fame being firft come and bygone.*'—This claufe was intended to fave the charges of raifing new hornings for payment of fums becoming due *in futuro*, fuch as in leafes, bonds of annuity, &c. Of old, the words '*the terms of payment being 'firft come and bygone*, were alfo neceffary in the cafe of bonded debts, when annualrents were confidered to be only due from term to term ; but, ever fince intereft has been held by law to be due *de die in diem*, the words are not neceffary. This claufe has had the effect of fupporting a horning raifed before the term of payment of a bond. A decifion upon that point is thus reported by Durie : '*In an action, the Earl of Galloway *contra* Vauns, the Lords fu- '*ftained a charge of horning executed by virtue of letters raifed be- '*fore the term of payment contained in the bond whereupon the '*faid letters were raifed, feeing the letters bore to charge the party '*obliged to make payment, when the term of payment was bypaft, '*and that no charge was execute upon the faid letters until the term '*was bypaft, albeit the letters were raifed before the term ; and '*therefore they repelled the alledgeance, whereby the horning and '*letters were impugned for that reafon *.'*

'*After the form and tenor of the faid bond and decreet forefaid in- 'terponed thereto in all points.*'—Thefe words are added for the fame purpofe as the general words in the preamble, viz. to correct any errors in the letters for or againft the parties, by expreffing that the charge is intended to be reftricted to the precife terms of the original ground of debt.

'*Within*

---

* December 17. 1623 ;—Durie, p. 92.

' *Within fix days next after the charge.*'—The ancient days of law were fifteen. The letters of four forms generally required the fame fpace, though we find them varying confiderably. Thefe diligences, for a long time, were not granted of courfe by the judges. The debtor's refidence, in relation to the diftance from Edinburgh, or the caftle in which he was ordered to furrender his perfon, was taken into confideration. For this reafon it was, that the act 139th of the 8th Parliament of James VI. authorifing letters of horning and poinding to be granted upon the decrees of the Lords contains the following provifo : ' Providing always that confideration be had ' upon the fpace and days of the charges, and that according to the ' diftance of the defender's dwelling-places, and the quantity of the ' fums contained in the faid decreets.'

This laft part of the act, which directs the Lords to take into confideration the *quantum* of the fum in fixing the days of the charge in their letters, was an idea dictated by humanity. That circumftance has been entirely forgot in practice. However, fo far the Lords paid obedience to this act, that, when they abolifhed the four forms, by their act of Sederunt 1613, they ordered that letters of horning fhould be directed, upon fifteen days, againft fuch as dwelt upon the fouth fide of the river Dee, and upon twenty-one days againft all inhabitants upon the north fide thereof. By a former act, *anno* 1600, *c.* 25. it had been enacted, that no letters fhould be directed againft inhabitants north of the fame river, under a fhorter charge than fifteen days. The act of Sederunt, with refpect to the charge of twenty-one days, may be faid to have gone into defuetude, that circumftance being feldom attended to at prefent, fo far as can be learned. The regulation ought to be renewed ; for it is certainly a diftreffing circumftance upon the inhabitants of diftant counties to be unable to obtain fufpenfions of the charges given them. It is true, that caption cannot go out till the horning returns to Edinburgh ; but, where the diligence proceeds upon decrees of confent, and charges of fix days, they may and are daily poinded,

before

before it be poffible to procure a fift upon a fufpenfion. The Lords
have varied in their decifions upon this point. In the 1625, they
found a charge of horning, given upon fix days to a perfon living
upon the north fide of the Dee, to be null, although it proceeded
upon a bond, confenting that letters fhould pafs upon fix days *.
By an after decifion in the 1664, they found, that the act of Parliament, ordaining all hornings beyond Dee to be on fifteen days,
reaches not to hornings in which, by the agreement of parties, they
are reftricted to a lefs number †. The firft decifion was right; but
the Court are not to be blamed for paying fuch regard to the argument of parties, when we find our legiflature, at a much later date,
acting upon the fame principle.

It is the method of extorting the confent of debtors to unreafonable conditions, which has defeated almoft every regulation of the
legiflature in their favour. This circumftance rendered ineffectual a
very proper act made in favours of the inhabitants of Orkney and
Shetland, June 16. 1685, ordaining forty days to be the legal time
of charge in hornings againft them, except where, in claufes of
deeds, the parties may have confented to a fhorter fpace. The act
of Parliament ought not to have made this exception; the former
act of King James VI. fhould have been remembered, made againft
unlawful and impoffible conditions, whereby the taking a debtor's
confent to have himfelf charged at the market crofs of Edinburgh,
although living in a diftant county, was prohibited. There is, in
this point, an aftonifhing inconfiftency in both our law and practice.
If a debtor be abroad, he muft be charged at the market crofs of
Edinburgh, pier and fhore of Leith, upon fixty days warning, without the leaft regard to the *induciae* ftipulated in the claufe of regiftration. Now, this edictal citation, as it is termed, was not introduced by any fpecial law. It crept into our practice by degrees, and
yet it is allowed to have an effect fuperior to our ftatute law; at leaft,

it

---

* Durie, 4th February 1625, Stewart *contra* Bruce.
† Stair, December 16. 1664, Laird of Phirloh *contra* Forbes.

it has done what the legiflature has not attempted; it has contradicted the unreafonable ftipulation of parties. It is here neceffary to obferve, that writers have not authority to infert warrants out of the kingdom, as they are termed. Bills muft, or at leaft ought to be prefented, requefting that liberty from the Court.

   ' *Wherein if they faillie, the faids   days being firft come and* ' *bygone, that incontinent thereafter ye denounce them our rebels, put* ' *them to the horn, and efcheat and inbring all their moveable goods* ' *and gear to our ufe for their contempt.*'—A forfeiture of the moveables of the rebel took place immediately after the denunciation, which was termed the fingle efcheat, from the French *echoir*, to fall. When the debtor continued a year and a day in this fituation, his liferent efcheat fell to the fuperior, *i. e.* the rents of his lands, or the produce of his heritable property. The order to the meffenger to bring in the produce of the moveables to the King's ufe, is in confequence of an ordinance of the Lords of Seffion, mentioned in the act, *c.* 75. 1579, formerly explained; whereby it was provided, that the officer and the fheriff, immediately after denunciation of any perfon to the horn, fhould make a juft inventory of his goods, to the effect that the fame might be inbrought to his Heinefs ufe for that contempt. The writers have, with great propriety, borrowed the very words of the act.

   ' *And alfo, that ye ufe the bail remanent order againft them pre-* ' *fcribed by act of Parliament made thereanent.*'—The act of Parliament here alluded to is the fame *c.* 75. 1579; and the remanent order is to regiftrate the horning, publifh the name of the rebel at the market crofs of the head fheriffdom, and give notice to the King's treafurer to inventory and feize upon his effects. Of this order, the only part now happily remaining is the regiftration of the horning. All the reft of the barbarous procedure is at an end. Here the *horning* properly terminates. The next claufe,

   ' *And ficklike, that ye, in our name and authority forefaid, fence,* ' *arreft, apprife, compell, poind,*' &c.—is the warrant for poinding
                                  and

and arreftment, which being quite diftinct from the horning, we referve for explanation in its proper place.

In the laft difcourfe, we pointed out the ftatute by which the
poinding and arreftment came to be iffued in the fame letters with
the horning, or, in other words, when, for the firft time, execution was awarded both againft the body and eftate of the debtor, and
we remarked the inconfiftency thereby introduced into our diligence,
which was retained even in our prefent letters of horning. This is
the place in which that contradiction appears. The meffenger to
whom the letters are directed, is ordered to efcheat and inbring the
moveables of the rebel to his Majefty's ufe ; and yet, in the very
next claufe, he is ordered to poind and arreft them for the fole behoof of the complainer or creditor. This is diametrically oppofite
to the order prefcribed by the act of Parliament, but, at the fame
time, points out the ancient law of this country, which abfolutely
refufed execution both againft the perfon and effects of the debtor
at the fame time, for the fame debt.

The diligence againft the body of the debtor was, as we have
heard, limited to the cafe where he was bound to perform fomething in his power, which is explained by the following decifion
preferved by Balfour. ' A decreet being given againft ony perfon,
' and it be not in his power to obey the fame; execution fhould ceafe
' againft him upon finding caution for damage and intereft ; bot gif
' he againft whom decreet is given, may onyways fulfill the famen,
' or gif the famen may be eafily done by him, he fould not be re-
' leivit fra the execution thereof albeit he offer the intereft in man-
' ner forefaid *.' Accordingly, the horning or diligence againft the
perfon is the only execution that can, at this moment, proceed in
fimilar cafes : I mean, where parties are decreed *ad facta praeftanda;*
and, therefore, in writing hornings upon fuch decrees, we are always to ftop at this place, and conclude with ' *according to juftice.*'

The

---

* February 1543, Reid againft Abbot of Melros.—Balfour, p. 390.

The reason given by our syftematic writers for this, is, that poinding cannot proceed for performance of facts, because it is impossible to value the moveable goods of the debtor, or to proportion them to the particular fact he stands charged to perform. This is true; but it is but one of the reasons, and that a consequential one, arising from the nature of the thing, and not from the history of the law, which shows us that hornings, or personal execution, were, for near two centuries, awarded *ad facta praestanda* before they were issued upon liquid debts. The reason was, first, because the original common law of the island absolutely denied execution for personal debts; and, secondly, because a subject was obliged to obey the King's order, when it was evidently in his power to obey; reasons very different from those our lawyers have assigned, which did not at all enter into the original idea of the thing.

' And, *failing of the moveable goods and gear poindable, that ye*
' *apprise all and sundry their lands and heritages, conform to act of*
' *Parliament, to the avail and quantity of the foresaid sums, and make*
' *the said G. completely paid thereof.*'—The act of Parliament here mentioned is the 36th chapter of the 5th Parliament of James III. *anno* 1469, which did not introduce, as our syftematic writers tell us, but only renewed and regulated the mode of apprising (or poinding, as it is termed) the lands of debtors for payment of their debts. Poinding was, of old, a term equally applicable to lands and to moveables. The act of James III. authorised letters both of poinding and apprising moveables and land in a new form; and, when a warrant for poinding was, by the statute of James VI. appointed to be conjoined with horning in the same letters, the Writers to the Signet, accustomed to make no distinction in these things, added them both to the four forms. When the letters of four charges came to be abridged to one, this addition continued, whereby the expence of separate letters of apprising were saved, as we see from this paragraph in St Martin's Horning; so that the creditor,

ditor, in virtue of this fingle warrant, might attack the perfon, the moveables, or the land-property of his debtor at pleafure.

' *After the form and tenor of the faid obligation or decreet inter-* ' *poned thereto in all points.*'—As reference is made to the grounds of debt for the direction of diligence againft the perfon, fo it is here again repeated as the rule of execution againft the effects. It will be remarked, that St Martin's Horning is, in fact, a compound of three different diligences, viz. letters of four forms, letters of poinding and arreftment, and letters of apprifing upon the act of James III. The apprifings gave place to adjudications in the 1672; and therefore, fince that period, the warrant for apprifing laft mentioned has been laid afide.

' *According to juftice.*'—Thefe are the only words of ftyle which diftinguifh our writs of execution from royal mandates. The generality of the old brieves concluded with the words *fecundum legem et confuetudinem regni*, which, when fignet letters came in place of brieves, were changed into *according to juftice.* The royal letters, in matters of government, never have thefe words; the only and curious difference is in the ftyle.

' *As you will anfwer to us thereupon. The which to do we com-* ' *mit to you, conjunctly and feverally, our full power by thefe our* ' *letters.*'—This claufe is common both to the old brieves and the King's letters. ' As ye will anfwer to us thereupon,' is a tranflation of the phrafe in the mandates of moft of the Princes of Europe. ' Ac prout nobis fubinde refpondere volueritis nullatenus omitta-' tis.' Though the command of the Prince fupplies the power to execute; yet, as it was imagined that warrants to the fubject to act in the King's name, could not exceed in folemnity and precifion; therefore all writs, precepts, and letters, contain a fpecial delegation of authority for the execution of the thing demanded.

' *Delivering them by you duly executed and indorfed again to the* ' *bearer.*'—By the bearer is meant the creditor, raifer of the letters, who delivers them to the meffenger; and the meffenger, after do-.

ing his duty, is by thefe words enjoined to deliver them back duly indorfed, *i. e.* properly executed. Executions, according to the cuftoms of thefe times, were written on the back, which feems to import, that the back of the letters is the only proper place for writing the execution.

' *Per decretum Dominorum Concilii.*'—All letters from the King bear the particular authority upon which they are iffued, *i. e.* the authority of the court or officer to whom that department is committed. Therefore the letters which paffed the fignet, by the authority of the Court of Seffion, were marked ' *Ex deliberatione Do-* ' *minorum Concilii,*' as the Lords were for fome time termed, the word *Seffion* being a pofterior addition. When the letters pafs upon a bill, the old ftyle is ufed, ' *ex deliberatione;*' alluding to the confideration which the Court is fuppofed to take of the bill or petition when prefented, before granting the defire of it, by the ' *fiat ut pe-* ' *titur*.*' Befides bearing the authority under which they were iffued, the letters were figned by the Secretary of State, the Keeper of the Signet, and fometimes by the Prefident of the Council, or other great officers, when the letters concerned the affairs of the public. Letters for expediting private juftice were written by the clerks of the Secretary,

---

* Before, and even after the inftitution of the College of Juftice, the Clerks to the Signet, it feems, fometimes wrote the *fiat ut petitur* upon the bill, to the prejudice of the officers of Court. The Gentlemen of the Signet, at the fame period, feem likewife to have ufed a little liberty with one another, by carrying off bills which did not belong to them, and making out the letters for the clients of their brethren. Thefe wrongs were both redreffed by the following curious act, being part of the inftitution of the College of Juftice : ' *Item,* that na Clerk of the Signet ' enter in the Council-houfe for delivering of any bills, bot that the deliverance ' be written by *an writer of the Council;* and, to provide that nane fruftrate another ' of his labours and profit, that every Clerk of the Signet that writes ony bills mark ' the famen with his *awin name* in the bill written within, and the famen fall be de- ' livered to him again or the party, quhilk of them cummis to afk the faid bill, they ' payand to the writer of the deliverance four pennies.'—5th Parliament of 'James V. c. 61.

Secretary, or Keeper of the Signet, who were the immediate predeceffors of our Writers to the fignet ; but the letters were not always fubfcribed by them. Before the 1582, the King's feal, affixed with wax, was the fole mark both of authority and authenticity. In imitation of the French, bufinefs of every kind, civil and criminal, public and private, came to be done by *letters.* Of this government paved the way, as formerly mentioned, by ordering their arbitrary and capricious refolutions to be executed by *letters under the fignet.* The *Writers,* in civil bufinefs, following the example, deferted the ftyles in their hands, introduced new ones of their own, and gave out letters fuited to the particular bufinefs and intereft of their employers. A ftop was endeavoured to be put to thefe very great evils by act c. 13. of the 10th Parliament of James VI. By this ftatute, we fee a proper diftinction eftablifhed between the fignet letters iffued by prerogative and by juftice. For the form of the latter the *Writers to the Signet* are to be anfwerable ; and we learn from the act, that the original reafon of figning the letters was not to add authority to the King's fignet, but to make each *Writer to the Signet* anfwerable for his own works. In place of figning the ordinary letters upon the back, as is mentioned in the act, the Writers continued the practice, already begun, of figning at the foot immediately below ' *Per decretum Dominorum Concilii.*' The fignatures in Exchequer ftill continue to be fubfcribed on the back, in terms of the ftatute. As the original intention of figning the letters was not to add to their authority, but merely to afford a check upon the Writers, and to oblige them to pay attention to the ftyle, they were not, like deeds or extracts of the Court of Seffion, fubfcribed at the junctures of the fheets. The Lords of Seffion were of opinion, that letters fhould be fo fubfcribed ; and therefore, upon the 8th of July 1691, they iffued an order for that purpofe, without affigning any reafon.

The fignet was originally the private cachet of the King, impreffed upon white wax, containing the lion and the crown, furround-

P p 2   ed

ed with a ring of paper to keep it on. When we began to copy
from the French, red wax was ufed. A particular feal was afterwards appropriated for letters paffing under the fignet, having nearly the fame impreffion. The bufinefs at this office always growing
greater, and the number of diligences increafing in proportion to
the internal commerce of the country, the fealing, dating, and fubfcribing of fo many letters grew an intolerable burden upon the
Keeper of the Signet, and created inconvenient delays and attendance upon the part of the Writers and their clerks. In order to be
delivered from thefe grievances, the Keepers and the Writers joined
in a petition to the Lords upon the 18th of February 1718; and,
from the date of the act made in confequence of this application,
the prefent expeditious method of ftamping the letters has been continued.

In executing the horning, the meffenger, the fheriff in that part
originally acted as the fheriff of the county would have done, or
ftill does, in the execution of the King's writs. The fheriff reports
what he does in obedience to the writs directed to him, and this is
termed the *fheriff's return;* but, when thofe good old forms gave
way to the royal letters, meffengers and others were employed inftead of the fheriffs; and the returns made by them came to be called *executions,* a term of the French practice. The act of the officer
in charging the party, or obeying the command of his warrant, is
by them, with propriety, termed the execution; and the recital of
the fact fo done, attefted by the officer, is termed the *proces verbal.*
Anciently we alfo diftinguifhed thefe things in fome degree, by
terming the act of the meffenger the execution, and the certificate
of it the indorfation. We have now improperly confounded both
in the word *execution.*

The ancient mode of execution was thus: The meffenger, having
his letters of four forms with him, went to the perfonal prefence of
the parties, or to their dwelling-houfes, and commanded them to make
payment, in terms of the will of his letters; but, from the old executions,

ecutions, it does not appear that any copy or schedule was left for the party at his dwelling-house. Written copies in these days were not an easy ceremony ; and, as it behoved four charges to be given before denunciation, it could scarcely happen that the parties would not get notice. However, as the penalty in denunciation was terrible, it behoved to be natural for the debtor to excuse himself, if possible, from disobedience by ignorance of the charge. To remove these excuses, real or pretended, personal intimation, and written copies, were rendered absolutely necessary, as appears from a decision in Balfour *. When the letters of four forms were changed to letters of horning by the act of Sederunt 23d November 1613, the charge was appointed to be given to the party at his dwelling-house, and also at the parish kirk upon a Sunday forenoon, in time of preaching or prayer, and a copy left upon the most patent door of the church. This double solemnity was intended to supply the four charges formerly given upon the letters of four forms. The execution at the church was never properly obeyed, principally owing to the stupidity of the messengers, who, in general, could not write, or even subscribe their names. At this period, executions were not signed by witnesses, and had no other authority than the messenger's stamp ; and thus the business continued till the act 26th May 1686, when the subscription of witnesses was made a necessary solemnity, and the sealing or stamping the executions was taken away.

We shall now proceed to analise the execution of the horning ; and, in doing this, we shall have recourse to the well known Tract of the Office of a Messenger, where the form may be found. The copy or schedule mentioned in the form to be delivered to the party, which came in place of the former solemnities, was found necessary in all cases, whether the party was personally found or not. Accordingly, a horning was found null which bore delivery of a ticket to the debtor, containing the tenor and substance of the letters,

because

* 12th January 1565; Douglas against Prior of Caterhouse.—Balfour, p. 560.

becaufe it bore not the word *copy* [*]. It is this copy which is termed a charge of horning, but moft improperly. It is only a charge to pay the debt, under the pain of being put to the horn. This has arifen from the impropriety of the term *horning* being given to the letters themfelves, which is, however, a ftatutary epithet, and will, no doubt, be continued.

' *In his Majefty's name and authority, command and charge you M.*
' *B. to make payment to the faid C. D. of the fum of* &c.
—The word *charge* is directly from the French *charger* ; and the effential requifite of it is to be in precife terms with the will and letters, from which the meffenger has not power to deviate in a fingle iota. The narrative of the horning in the copy muft alfo be taken *verbatim* from the letters ; and, if there be any tranfmiffions by affignation, or other right, which carries the debt to the raifer of the horning, thefe muft be recited in the fame manner as in the letters. In fhort, the terms of the letters is the rule to which the meffenger muft adhere in his copy ; for, fuppofing an error to be in the warrant, he is not entitled to rectify it. The will of the letters muft alfo be the rule for the precife days of the charge ; and the certification in the copy is properly referred to the letters. The copy bears alfo, ' *Per decretum Dominorum Concilii ;*' becaufe the authority under which the letters of horning had been granted, have always been confidered as an effential part of it ; for which reafon, the words of authority are inferted in the copy. The date and the figneting are alfo effential, becaufe it puts it in the power of the party charged to know with certainty whether fuch letters have been iffued againft him or not, and, confequently, deprives the meffenger of the poffibility of acting upon a falfe warrant.

When a meffenger executes a diligence, he ought to be poffeffed of the warrant, in order to exhibit it if required. A queftion of this kind came before the Court 11th July 1699, Lermont againft Lermont.

* Hope, 20th July 1627, Monteith againft Kirkwood.

mont. In a procefs of ranking and fale, it was objected to the execution of a meffenger, that he wanted the fummons, the warrant thereof; and, being required by the defender's advocate to fhow it, he refufed. The Lords found the meffenger not obliged to fhow his warrant to third parties, not defenders, and that law prefumed he had it on him, unlefs the contrary were proved. If, then, a meffenger be obliged to fhow even a fummons to the party defender who demands it, there can be no doubt that he muft exhibit the principal letters of horning, otherwife the debtor cannot be obliged to receive a copy; nor will the charge be good for any thing. Of this no queftion can be made, if the debtor has fufficient prefence of mind to take a notorial inftrument upon the fact. Where hornings proceed upon decrees againft many debtors in different parts of the country, it is the practice to raife two or three letters, fo as each meffenger may be furnifhed with his own warrant. Formerly, the copies delivered contained the date in figures, and did not mention the witneffes prefent; fo that the meffengers might have got an execution made up *ex poft facto* at pleafure. Abufes were accordingly difcovered; and, at the time when efcheats and other confequences followed upon denunciation to the horn, thefe abufes called out for correction. Accordingly, by act 12. 1ft. Parl. W. M. 1693, it was exprefsly provided, ‘ That all copies of fummonfes, charges,
‘ inhibitions, arreftments, or other letters whatfoever given to the
‘ party, fhall bear at length, and not in figures, the day and date of
‘ the delivery thereof; as alfo, the names and defignations of the
‘ witneffes infert as the execution or indorfation did and doth bear
‘ the fame; certifying the meffenger who fhall omit to infert the
‘ faid day, and date, and witneffes in his copy, that he fhall incur
‘ deprivation and tinfel of his office.’
‘ *A juft copy whereof I have delivered to the faid A. perfonally*
‘ *apprehended in E. upon the faid   day of   and year fore-*
‘ *faid, before thefe witneffes.*’—Of all modes of execution, that which is made againft the debtor perfonally is the moft certain and unexceptionable.

unexceptionable. It leaves no objection to be made, provided only a copy of the execution be delivered.

' *The like copy of charge I left for the said A. within his dwel-*
' *ling house in E. with his servant, to be given to him, because I*
' *could not apprehend him personally, upon the said   day of*
' *before these witnesses.*'—The fix-d rule, in our executions, is, that if the party be in the kingdom, they must be made to him either personally, or at his dwelling house. An execution, therefore, which mentioned the delivery of a copy to the party's wife was found to be insufficient, because it did not say it was delivered to her in her husband's dwelling-house *. This was a very proper decision; because, had the Court sustained the execution, they would, in fact, have found an execution against the wife to be the same thing as against her husband.

Hornings ought always to be executed at the principal dwelling-houses of the party, as required by act 75. of the Parliament 1540; and therefore executions at lodgings or town-houses, after the family was removed to the country, have repeatedly been found insufficient. It is also requisite to describe the dwelling by its local situation. The reason is, that if the word *dwelling house* was to be held sufficient, the messenger would be judge of that matter; and, tho' false, it behoved his assertion to be received without the possibility of contradiction. The Lords carried this matter so far, that, in a case where an execution bore a charge to be given to a party designed burgess of a town at his dwelling-place, they found it null for want of the word *there*, or in *the said town*, which was certainly attention sufficient to the letter of the law †.

' *The like copy of charge I have affixed and left for the said A. up-*
' *on the most patent gate or door of his dwelling-house, after my*
' *knocking six several audible knocks upon the said gate or door, be-*
' *cause*

---

* Stair, 11th December 1679, Countess of Cassillis against E. Roxburgh.
† 14th July 1624, Adams against Bailies of Air.

' *caufe I neither could get accefs to the faid houfe, nor apprehend the*
' *faid A. perfonally.*'

No part of our forms has been fo carefully preferved as the
knocks. Diligences have feveral times been fet afide for want of the
precife fix. Others have been rejected, becaufe the meffenger did
not affix the copy upon the door, but certified that he left it, without telling with whom *. Meffengers and concurrents, as they call
them, have a common trick of carrying away the copies, after af-
fixing them on the door or crofs. This is a dangerous practice; for,
if it could be proved, it would annull the diligence †.

' *And the like copy I affixed and left for the faid D. at prefent*
' *furth of Scotland, at each of the market crofs of Edinburgh, pier*
' *and fhore of Leith.*'—It is unneceffary, at prefent, to go into the
edictal execution of the horning, becaufe we fhould afterwards be
under the neceffity of repeating it in the cafe of inhibition, where
every part of the form, and the niceties of practice, continue to be
of as much, if not of more importance. Hornings fhould always be
executed at lawful hours; but, as they are only commands or notices, the Court refufed to find a charge null which was given in the
night-time, though they did not approve of the practice ‡. If the
money be not paid within the time of the charge, which muft be
fix, fifteen, or other days complete, *i. e.* the day of the charge not
counted, then the denunciation follows. The folemnity is thus defcribed in the Treatife on the Office of a Meffenger. The officer goes,
with the letters in his hand, in prefence of two witneffes, to the market crofs of Edinburgh, as *communis patria*, or to the market crofs of
the head burgh of the fhire or ftewartry where the party charged
dwells, and there he cries three feveral oyeffes with an audible voice,
and reads publicly the letters and execution of the charge, and thereafter denounces him rebel, and puts him to the horn by three blafts

* Fount. 8th July 1698, Blair againft Creditors of Main.
† Stair, 11th February 1674, Mackulloch againft Gordon.
‡ Ibid.

thereof, *i. e.* the messenger blows his horn three times. *Oyes* is a gross corruption of the imperative of the French verb *oyé, hear!* Denunciation is evidently from the Latin *denunciare,* to foretel, warn, or declare before hand. Craig uses it, in all cases, for to warn in removings. The word in the legal sense used by us, is a direct Gallicism from the French practice. The English term, and the proper one, is *proclamation of rebellion;* a form analogous to our denunciation, and proceeding exactly upon the same original cause, viz. disobedience to the Sovereign's authority.

' *Therefore I B. messenger, passed to the market cross of Edinburgh,* ' *(or to the market cross of A. head burgh of the sheriffdom thereof,* ' *within which the said C. resides.'*)—Of old, it seems, denunciations were not regularly made at the market cross of the county where the party dwelt, but generally at Edinburgh. This was chiefly owing to the necessity and bad government of the times; for there were several county towns in the kingdom to which safe access could not be had for business of that kind. The act 75. Parl. 1579, clearly appoints the denunciation to be made at the market cross of the shire where the party dwells; and, in a case marked in the Dictionary [*], the Lords found, that a party put to the horn must be denounced, conform to the act 1579, notwithstanding one hundred years uninterrupted custom to the contrary [†]. In the 1666, the Lords found a denunciation at the market cross of Edinburgh, as *communis patria,* sufficient against a party out of the country [‡]. The same causes which rendered the denunciations irregular before the act of Parliament, were again attended with the same effects, and brought a number of denunciations to the market cross of Edinburgh. This was attended with one very happy consequence. The absurd custom of single escheats, and other consequences of denunciation, received the first effectual check from this fortunate irregularity. One
of

[*] Vol. 1. p. 261.   [†] Colvil, 1583, E. Angus against the donator of his escheat.   [‡] Newbeath, 1st February 1666, Cunningham against Cunningham.—Dict. vol. 1. p. 261.

of thefe confequences was, that the party could not defend himfelf in any law fuit. But the Lords found, ' That the denunciation at ' the crofs of Edinburgh could not hinder the party denounced to ' have *perfonam ftandi in judicio* *.' From this decifion we learn, that captions upon denunciations at the market crofs of Edinburgh came in by a practical abufe, and that the efcheat confequent upon the rebellion was confidered to be a much heavier punifhment than the imprifonment of the perfon. The Judges, therefore, feem to have paffed over every objection which ftood in the way of the debtor's imprifonment. They looked upon it as a matter of little moment, and laid hold of every circumftance to prevent the confequences of the efcheat. Meantime, creditors who had no intereft but to recover their debts, continued to denounce their debtors at the market crofs of Edinburgh ; and thus a great number of hornings were reduced to be nothing more than fteps towards obtaining captions.

' There, after my crying of three feveral oyeffes, making open pro-
' clamation and public reading of the within written letters and ex-
' ecution.'—So much were the ideas of our Judges improved towards the end of the laft century, and fo hateful did the procefs of efcheats appear to them, that they annulled a horning becaufe the denunciation bore only *thee oyeffes*, in place of three oyeffes; fo that there was nothing wanting but the letter *r* *. The decifions varied upon this point in the cafe of other diligences. The number of the oyeffes were not entirely fixed. Fountainhall tells us, that, in a cafe, 7th December 1698, the Lord Regifter was ordained to try the cuftom as to the oyeffes ; and, though an act of Sederunt was intended to regulate them for the future, it was not made ; and fo the cuftom remained unfixed. Practice has certainly, fince that time, fixed them to the number of three. Befides crying the oyeffes, the meffenger

adds,

---

* 24th January 1674, Blair againft Blair.
† Fount. 20th February 1680, Gordon againft Gray.

adds, *making open proclamation.* It is not known what the officer
confiders the oyeffes to be ; for they are certainly open proclamation. Another part of it, is the public reading of the letters, and
execution. In a cafe in Fountainhall, it was objected to a denunciation, that it did not bear the reading of the execution, as it did
the horning itfelf, as was conftantly in ufe to be done, conform to a
teftificate under the hand of the keeper of the regifter of hornings.
The Lords found, that there was no exprefs law or act of Parliament requiring that folemnity ; and that cuftom was not come to
be fo fixed as to be obligatory, there being denunciations both ways;
and, though fome cautious meffengers adjected that formality, this
was not enough to make it grow up to an univerfal uniform practice ; therefore they repelled the nullity, and fuftained the denunciation *.

 ‘ *I duly and lawfully denounced the faid A. his Majefty's rebel,*
‘ *and put him to the horn, by three feveral blafts, for his difobedience.*
—The three blafts, like the three oyeffes, were not, at firft, points
of form. Hornings, in the beginning of the feventeenth century,
before the injuftice of efcheats had made a proper impreffion upon
the Judges, were often fuftained, though deficient in that article †.

 Since the abolition of efcheats by the jurifdiction act, the ceremonies of this bufinefs are, in moft cafes, of very little confequence,
being only preparatory fteps to the caption, or warrant of imprifonment. Accordingly, few or no queftions have incurred upon their
import, except in the particular cafe we are foon to mention. If no
denunciation is made within year and day of the date of the execution, the charge falls, and the horning muft be executed again.
This is not only a point of eftablifhed practice, but is a part of the
ancient law common to the whole ifland of Great Britain. The
Englifh carry it farther than we do. If, after judgment obtained,
no

---

* 28th July 1702, Bogle againft Axmore.
† 4th March 1624, Dryfdale againft Soornbegg.

no execution be taken out upon it for a year and a day, the law presumes that the sentence of Court has been obeyed; and no execution can issue until the defendant be again called into Court, to show reason why it should not issue. This directly coincides with our summons of wakening, and, in some degree, with our process of horning; for, if no denunciation follows within the same space, our law also presumes that obedience has been paid to the charge, until a new one is given to the debtor.

The next step is to register the horning, in terms of the often mentioned act, c. 75. anno 1579. The practice, in these points, is to make a copy of the horning and of the executions almost *verbatim*. This copy is carried to the register of hornings, with the principal letters: There they are compared by the clerk, and the copy retained, in order to be laid up and booked. The clerk next day returns the principal, with two certificates of the registration, and its dates;—one in the foot of the principal letters, and the other below the executions. This, in terms of the act 1579, must be done within fifteen days of the date of the denunciation. The original purpose of which, was no other than to give information to the Crown of the single escheat having fallen upon the denunciation, that the party might be punished, in terms of that barbarous act. If the registration be omitted within the fifteen days of the denunciation, the practice is to denounce again, and to register the second execution.

As the country was divided into regalities, baillieries, and stewartries, belonging to the great vassals of the Crown, who were not taken notice of in the act 1579, they found themselves hurt by registrations going entirely to the King's sheriffs. They complained, and obtained redress by the 268th act of the 15th Parliament of James VI. which appointed the denunciations to be at the market crosses of the several jurisdictions, and the registration to begin their books. Registrations were at that period judicial acts, a great deal more solemn than any thing we now are accustomed to; and therefore

fore they could only be done while the Judges were fitting. These Judges from negligence, and oftener from partiality, threw many bars in the way of this form. To remedy these things, another act was made immediately subsequent to the former one, c. 269. of the same Parliament. This act is the original authority of the general register of hornings at Edinburgh. We reserve what we have further to say upon it until we come to treat of the inhibition.

The distinction between a denunciation upon which escheat followed, and that which, by practice, warranted the ordinary caption, was, at an early period, so great, that the latter were granted upon hornings without registration. This was corrected by an act of Sederunt 19th of November 1679. Government, so far back as the 1592, became sensible of the extreme absurdity of denouncing a man rebel for a civil debt, by no greater solemnity than they proclaimed him a rebel or traitor to the state. By an act of that Parliament, therefore, it was ordained, that letters of treason should thenceforth be executed by heralds or pursuivants, bearing their coats of arms, and not by blasts of a horn, but by sound of trumpet.

The only remainder that we now have of the effect of denunciation regards the currency of annualrent. This was first established by the 20th act of the 20th James VI. anno 1621. The penal effect of this statute was for some time allowed, just as captions were, without either regular denunciation or registration, and that upon the absurd idea of adding to the penalties of civil rebellion. But, by the decisions in the beginning of this century, more liberal Judges so far banished these ideas, disgraceful to our jurisprudence, that, without offending the letter of the law, they found, that unless hornings were denounced and registered in the precise terms of the acts of Parliament, though they might be warrants for captions, they did not entitle the creditor to interest upon the sum total of his diligence. The decisions will be found in the different collections, particularly in Lord Kaimes's remarkable decisions. If, therefore, you

intend

intend to accumulate principal and intereſt into one ſum, due by a debt upon which horning has followed, you muſt be careful to have it denounced at the market croſs of the head burgh of the county where the debtor reſides, and to have it recorded in the books of the ſheriff of the ſame ſhire ; for the regalities and other ſubaltern juriſdictions were totally aboliſhed by the juriſdiction act 1746.

Caption.

Caption.

WHEN a debtor furrendered his perfon, in terms of the letters of four forms, he became a prifoner, not to the creditor, but to the King; and, of confequence, he was confined in a royal caftle, fuch as Edinburgh, Stirling, Blacknefs, &c. where, as a prifoner of ftate, he enjoyed the free air, confined alone to the precincts of garrifons. For this purpofe, the debtor himfelf was, by the four forms, directed to apply to the Keeper of the Signet for letters from the King to the Governour of the Caftle, commanding him to receive the bearer, and to detain him in ward, until his Majefty's pleafure fhould be further known. From the tenor of thefe warrants, it would appear, that the prifoner might have been liberated at the King's pleafure; and upon principles, we may infer, that this originally was in the King's power, efpecially fince he could have granted a protection to the party againft the diligence of his creditor, and all its confequences. The words of the letters of four forms are: ' To enter his perfon in ward within our Caftle of ' Dunbarton, therein to remain upon his own expences, ay and ' while he hath fulfilled the command of thir our letters, and be ' freed by us therefrae.' A debtor who had thus obediently delivered himfelf to confinement, was undoubtedly under the King's mercy, and, by our old law, was entitled to feveral advantages. ' Gif any perfon (fays Balfour) be in the King's ward or captivity, ' all actions intentit againft him or contrare any other perfon, ' qubilk

' quhilk may be prejudicial to his heritage, aucht and fould ceafe,
' untill he be freed and relievit of the faid ward, and may compear
' to mak his defence as principal party, or zit for his interes *.'

As, for a long period, nobody was imprifoned but for refufing to
do or perform fomething which was prefumed to be in his power ;
fo, upon the voluntary furrender of a man's perfon to ward, the
nature of the charge was taken into confideration, and the party
liberated, upon finding caution to pay damage and intereft, in cafe
it was found that performance could not be made *in terminis*. If,
on the other hand, the party did not obey the third charge, but allowed himfelf to be denounced rebel, his obedience came too late ;
and, though he did deliver up his perfon, yet he was confidered as
a rebel, and his efcheat took place ; but, if he ftill difobeyed, a
warrant was, in the next place, iffued out by the Court of Seffion,
under the Signet, to feize him wherever he could be found. ' Eaque
' denunciatione facta (fays Craig) literae ad quofcunque magiftratus·
' in quorum territoriis debitor apprehendi poteft, a Senatu dirigun-
' tur ut debitoris corpus cuftodiae mandent.' A caption or warrant
of this kind being iffued, the fituation of the debtor altered greatly
to the worfe ; he was now made guilty of contumacy, difobedience,
and rebellion. He had forfeited his rights as a fubject ; and, therefore, in place of being received under the King's ward in a caftle,
he was to be feized upon in whatever place, and by whatever magiftrate he could be found, and detained in a burgal tolbooth, a dungeon, or any place of confinement neareft to the fpot where he
happened to be taken. Although our Barons and great proprietors
had prifons in their caftles, yet thefe were kept for the punifhment
of delinquents within their own jurifdictions. They were not obliged to receive debtors, or the prifoners of the King. Our counties
never feem to have had prifons appropriated to them as feparate jurifdictions ; and therefore the royal boroughs came, of neceffity, to

R r   have

* 24th April 1505, Kennedy againft Sheriff of Lanark.—Balfour, p. 269.

have the cuftody of all debtors apprehended for civil debts. In this manner the place of confinement of debtors in Scotland came to be changed from the refpectable and wholefome ward of our caftles, to the dirty and unhealthful dungeons of our burghs.

The Privy Council of Scotland, and very often the Lords of Seffion, were in ufe to iffue letters, appointing people accufed of crimes, and fometimes merely *fuper inquirendis*, to appear before them at a day certain, under the pain of rebellion. Lord Stair, in mentioning this kind of procedure, terms thefe letters *extraordinary executorials;* and moft extraordinary they were upon many occafions. ‘ Upon thefe, (fays he), not only denunciation may pafs upon which ‘ efcheat and liferent fall; but likewife, in fome cafes, the certifica- ‘ tion of thefe letters is under the pain of treafon, in cafes where it ‘ is fo appointed by ftatute or cuftom; and likewife letters of fire ‘ and fword, in cafe of deforcement or refiftance of the ordinary ex- ‘ ecutions by continued open force in arms. But the charges againft ‘ fuch perfons to enter their perfons in fuch prifons, under the pain ‘ of treafon, are competent for making captions effectual, and fhould ‘ be firft ufed before letters of fire and fword, which are the laft le- ‘ gal executions warranting all manner of force of arms that is com- ‘ petent in war *.’ Of the captions here mentioned by Lord Stair, we have an inftructive inftance in the warrant granted by the Privy Council upon the 8th June 1566, againft the perfons accufed of the murder of David Rizzio †. From this act of the Privy Council, we fee that the fixed ftyle of the caption is of great antiquity, little or no alteration having been made upon it fince the reign of Mary. The principles are alfo entirely the fame; and there was little or no difference between the warrant for feizing a traitor, a murderer, or a debtor. All of them were to be taken not as criminal murderers or debtors, but as rebels to their Sovereign ; the one for non-appearance in court, and the other for non-payment of their debt.— We fhall now proceed to confider the ftyle of this diligence.

The

---

* P. 755.   † Vide Keith’s Appendix, p. 132.

The horning being properly executed, denounced, and regiftered, is given in to the Bill Chamber, with a bill, ftating that the debtor had been duly denounced rebel, and put to the horn, for not ma- king payment of fuch a fum, contained in fuch a bond, &c. and therewith produced ; therefore praying for letters of caption, in common form. The clerk to the bills examines the horning ; and, finding the formalities duly obferved, he writes upon the bill, ' *Fiat* ' *ut petitur*, becaufe the Lords have feen the regiftered horning ' within mentioned.' This bill is the warrant for expeding the let- ters of caption. It would be fuperfluous to enter into the minutiae of the ftyle of the firft part of this diligence, as every thing that can be faid upon it will be found in the preceeding treatife upon letters of horning. It will be obferved, however, that it is not the refufal to pay the debt which, in the preamble or narrative of the caption, the King takes fo much amifs ; it is the denunciation to the horn, and the debtor's continuing in rebellion, in contempt of the laws, which calls forth the refentment of the Sovereign, and feems to juf- tify the ftern and peremptory order for imprifonment.

In the courfe of the hiftory which preceded this difcourfe, it was mentioned, that the execution of all decrees and fentences of fupe- rior courts belonged to fheriffs, ftewarts, and magiftrates of burghs, within their refpective jurifdictions, and that this execution pro- ceeded upon writs iffued from the fuperior courts to the inferior judges, who executed them accordingly, and returned a certificate of what they had done in confequence thereof. We likewife re- marked, that the extreme negligence of our heritable fheriffs, in do- ing their duty, introduced the neceffity of making *fheriffs in that part* to do the common bufinefs of the nation, all of which, to this moment, continues to be performed in England by the municipal officers themfelves. In James V.'s time, the heralds, purfuivants, and macers, came to be fpecially conjoined, as we find from the 58th act of the Inftitution of the College of Juftice, anno 1537. Our ancient ftatute-book is full of complaints againft fheriffs and judges, who were fometimes fined, deprived, and condemned in payment of the party's debt, which was, no doubt, the proper and natural punifhment; but, owing to the unceafing calamities of the times, no fteady methods were practifed. Balfour reports three deeifions in which the fheriffs and magiftrates of towns were fubjected by the fupreme court, for refufing and delaying to execute deerees, in confequence of letters directed to them, in payment of the debts, and their goods ordered to be poinded to the amount.

The extreme weaknefs of the Scottifh government arofe chiefly from the Crown being not only entirely ftripped of its proper landed patrimony, but even of its political government, by the infatiable nobility, who held their jurifdictions by the fame title as that of their eftates; fo that the King had little or no authority over the judges, fheriffs, or other officers of his kingdom. We formerly had occafion to obferve, that the whole diforders of the kingdom were attributed to the difobedience of authority, and the opportunities of eluding the law, which brought upon the body of the fubjects the horning and outlawry for civil rebellion. The fame caufes involved the inferior judges in the fame confequences with a great deal more juftice; for what obedience could be expected from the people, when the civil officers were often themfelves the greateft contemners of authority? Among the many acts compelling inferior judges to their duty, there is a particular one in the 12th Parliament of James VI. c. 126. anno 1587, ' anent the duties of fhe-
' riffs and judges ordinar, their deputes and clerks.' They are thereby ordered to put the laws of the realm to due execution, ' Specially in the fearching, feeking, following, perfuing, appre-
' hending, committing to waird, and prefenting to juftice of decla-
' red traitors and rebels contemmandly remaining at the horn, and
' ftanding regiftrate in their awin bukes unrelaxed, or in doing juf-
' tice upon them, gif they have commiffion to that effect; and, gif
' they cannot apprehend the faids traitors and rebels within the
' bounds of their awin jurifdiction, to make denunciation to the fhe-
' riffs

' riffs and judges ordinar of the four halfs about, that fik perfons are
' fled within their bounds, requiring them to ufe the like diligence
' in fearching and apprehenfion of them, as they will anfwer to his
' Majefty at their peril, and under the fame pain that the traitors
' or rebels has incurred.' Notwithftanding this act has met with
the approbation of Sir George M'Kenzie, who perhaps found it
fuitable to the temper of the times, yet, to the prefent age, it appears
fraught with wanton feverity. Indeed, nothing can place the miferable impotence of the civil government of Scotland in a ftronger
light than the form now under examination. In the reign of
James VI. the government of Scotland appears to have been at regular war with the nation. It inflicted its heavieft punifhment, the
punifhment of rebellion, equally upon the innocent debtor who
could not pay, and the judge who delayed to be the inftrument of
his misfortune. Both were to be involved in rebellion, and to fuffer the punifhment of traitors. Upon thefe extraordinary principles our caption is modelled ; and, without knowing them, the ftyle
would be totally unintelligible.

' *We charge you, that incontinent thir our letters feen, ye pafs, and*
' *in our name and authority command and charge the fheriffs of the*
' *fheriffdoms,*' &c.—This is not, in fact, a caption, or plain warrant
to incarcerate the party ; it is, in reality, a norning, authorifing a
meffenger, or fheriff in that part, to charge the real fheriffs of the
county, and other inferior judges, to exert their diligence in fearching for the debtor. To the lift of the inferior judges are added
' meffengers at arms,' who, by the act of James V. formerly quoted,
were bound to execute the decrees of the fupreme judges in con-
junction with the fheriffs. Even the other meffengers, whofe concurrence might be neceffary in this bufinefs, were not to be required
as fervants of the King, and executors of the law, but to be charged
by the brother meffenger to whom the letters of caption are directed,
under the fame penalty with the other judges.

' *To*

' *To pass, search, seek, take, and apprehend the said A. B. and C.*
' *D. rebels forefaid, wherever they may or can be apprehended within*
' *the bounds of their offices and jurisdictions.*'—The letters of horning
are only directed to meffengers, or fheriffs in that part, becaufe they
had nothing to do but to charge and denounce the debtor, in which
no affiftance was neceffary. But the caption is directed in a very
different manner. The *apprehending* of a man was an act of too
great moment to be affected by a fingle officer, or even by feveral of
them, without the affiftance of the judge of the jurifdiction, and
his *poffe comitatus*, or officers of the burgh. No attempt of that
kind could be made with fuccefs, or even with fafety. Thefe judges,
however, efpecially thofe of the regalities, and other heritable jurifdictions, looked upon the interference of the King's meffengers, and
other fheriffs commiffioned for the purpofe, with a jealous eye.
They confidered their attempts as incroachments upon the rights and
privileges of their offices, and therefore were naturally inclined to
affift rebels of all kinds, and to protect, inftead of feizing them.
By addreffing the letters of caption then directly to the fheriffs,
ftewards, and magiftrates, their privileges were, in appearance, preferved entire; but they paid dearly in the fequel for this diftinction.

' *And being apprehended therein, to keep, detain, and withold them*
' *in fure ward, firmance, and captivity, within their refpective toll-*
' *booths, and others their warding places.*'—From the letters of four
forms, we learned that the King's caftles were the only places for
confining the fubjects of the kingdom for civil debt. There were
no prifons for that purpofe, becaufe the law acknowledged no execution againft the body of the debtor for non-payment of money,
or non-performance of contracts. That the dignified churchmen
had prifons for punifhment of their own irregular or criminal members, is a certain fact. No bifhop's palace wanted a place of that
kind; and feveral of their palaces, fuch as St Andrews, were caftles
equal in ftrength to any in the nation. Our hiftory is full of im-
prifonments of people in thefe places; and it may juftly be prefumed,

med, that the prisons of the bishops, and their officials, received the debtor taken upon caption for disobedience to the church. The burghs, we see, had places of confinement so early as Robert I. by whom acts of warding within burgh were originally authorised. The word *tollbooth* plainly shows what sort of prisons our burghs, as well as those of England, were first possessed of; for *tollbooth* is an old English word used by several of their authors. The *tollbooth* was no other, than a temporary hut of boards or planks erected in fairs and markets, in which the customs or duties were collected, and where such as did not pay were of consequence confined.

'*Therein to remain, upon their proper charges and expences, until*' '*they have fulfilled and obeyed the command and charge of our letters*' '*of horning, and be orderly relaxed from the process of horning there-*' '*in contained.*'—As civil rebellion was held to be such a grievous crime against the sovereign authority, so the debtor being once denounced and imprisoned, payment of the debt did not liberate him. He had been proclaimed a rebel by the King's letters, and therefore it behoved him to receive a pardon in form by other letters, termed, '*letters of relaxation,*' which also contained a warrant or charge against the keepers to give him his liberty. For being incarcerated as the King's prisoner, by virtue of a royal mandate, another order was necessary for his discharge. At the same time, it came in time to be understood, that this could not be done without the consent of the creditor. It behoved, therefore, both the King and the private party to concur in the liberation, as we find by a decision reported by Balfour *.

'*And, for that effect, that you make striked and locked fast houses,*' '*gates, and doors, open and patent, and use our keys thereto.*'—This part of the warrant is authorised by the barbarous statutes formerly noticed, provided for the pursuing, taking, and apprehending of rebels, and particularly of the 33d of the 2d Parliament of James VI. anno

---

* 29th July 1566, Montgomery against Semple.—Balfour, p. 561.

anno 1575, which provides, ' That it fall be leifume to ony man to
' follow and purfue common thieves and rebels to take them ; and,
' gif they enter in houfes, it fall be lawful to invade, break, or de-
' ftroy the faid houfes by fire or other ways, to the intent of taking
' or flaying the faid thieves or rebels.' Force and violence authe-
rifed by the government are, by an old and vulgar proverb, termed
King's keys, meaning the hammers, axes, and other inftruments
ufed in force.

' *Within three days next after they be charged by you thereto, un-*
' *der the pain of rebellion, and putting them to our born ; with certi-*
' *fication to them, if they faillie, our other letters will be directed,*
' *charging them thereto* fimpliciter.'—The preceding command was
thus to be performed in three days. The caption then, as before
obferved, is, in reality, nothing more than letters of horning iffued
againft the fheriffs and magiftrates, who, by that means, had three
days to confider whether they were to do a piece of duty, which could
not, perhaps, admit of a moment's delay. After the expiration of this
fpace, they were to be charged by other letters upon three days more,
to do the fame thing, and then a new fet of officers were to be charged
to denounce them rebels. It may well be afked, What the principal
debtor was doing all the time ? for, in following out fuch a round-
about procefs, the party creditor muft very foon have loft fight of
him altogether. The whole of this ridiculous bufinefs had truly
been an innovation in our law, occafioned by a great abufe of the
procefs of outlawry, which was only fitted for a very few particular
cafes, to which it always was, and continues ftill to be applied in
England. We cannot be better convinced of this, than by comparing the unnatural, conftrained terms of our prefent caption, with
the plain, fimple precept of the ancient writ, which went under the
fame title, directed to the fheriff, for apprehending debtors excommunicated by the church. ' Quare vobis praecipimus et manda-
' mus quatenus dictos B. C. D. ubicunque poterint inveniri per cap-
' tionem et incarcerationem corporum eorundem ad fatisfaciendum
					' Deo

' Deo et sanctae Matri Ecclesiae ita celeriter compellatis quod pro
' vestro defectu amplius inde justam quaeremoniam non audiamus.
' Ad quod faciendum vobis,' &c.

' *And, if thir our letters be put to execution within our burgh of*
.' *Edinburgh, that the concurrence of the magistrates thereof be had*
' *and obtained thereto.*' This is generally supposed to have been a
compliment inserted in the caption by royal order. This opinion
is very probable; but there was a more substantial reason for it.
That it is an addition made, long after the style of the caption had
been fixed, is evident from its inconsistency with the other parts of
the will of the letters, which is a warrant to charge the magistrates
themselves to seize the debtor, and consequently by no means agrees
with the order to ask their concurrence previous to the execution.
It is also evident, that, at the period of the insertion of this order,
messengers had been in practice of apprehending debtors without
troubling the magistrates, or even giving them any notice. The
city of Edinburgh was too often the scene of tumult, insurrection,
and disorder, occasioned by the concourse of people from all quarters of the kingdom attending upon the King and the courts of justice. To strengthen the hands of the magistrates, an act was made,
c. 187. of the 13th Parl. of James VI. intituled, ' Anent tumults
' within the city of Edinburgh, and obedience to be given to the
' magistrates thereof.' The statute sets forth the inconveniencies of
these tumults, and enacts, that no person disobey or contraveen the
command or charge of the provost or bailies of Edinburgh in the
execution of their offices, under the severe penalties specified in the
act. And, for enforcing their authority, the magistrates are authorised to convocate themselves in armour, to raise men of war, and
to carry arms of all kinds. If they killed any person, they were
not to be liable for the consequences. This statute points out the
origin of this clause in the caption, which we find was inserted immediately after the date of this act. No piece of business created
more sudden frays and tumults than that of putting captions into

execution; and therefore meffengers were exprefsly ordered to give the magiftrates of Edinburgh previous notice, in order that they might take meafures for preventing difturbances upon that occafion. By requiring the concurrence of the magiftrates, it is not meant that they could refufe to give it, or that it was requifite to the legality of the execution; it is no more than an order of expedience and compliment. In practice, however, this compliment continued to be paid until within thefe ten or fifteen years paft. The method was this: The meffenger delivered in the caption to the Council Chamber, and got it returned with a written concurrence to its execution, figned by one of the bailies. This very often created delay; and, what was of worfe confequence, the people about the office, feeing the captions lying publicly upon the table, gave notice to the debtors, who by that means efcaped to fanctuary. The meffengers, upon repeated inftances of this inconvenience, at firft complained, and afterwards ventured to omit the ceremony of concurrence, which may now be faid to be in entire defuetude.

Having thus analifed the ftyle of the caption, we fhall turn to the amalagous writ in the law of England, viz. the *commiffion of rebellion* iffued againft parties who refufe to make appearance to the *fubpoena* of the Chancellor of England. It proceeds upon the very fame principles of outlawry with our horning and caption; and from the form, it will occur, that it is, in fubftance, precifely the fame with the caption, and that there is not much difference even in words *.

The

* ' George, &c. to, A. B, C. D, E. F. and G. H., greeting: Whereas by public ' proclamation made on our behalf, by the fherff of Middlefex in diverfe places of ' that county, by virtue of our writ to him directed, A. B., hath been commanded, ' upon his alledgeance, perfonally to appear before us, in our Court of Chancery, at ' a certain day now paft, yet he hath manifeftly contemned our faid command ' Therefore we command you, jointly and feverally, to attach, or caufe the faid A. ' B. to be attached wherefoever he fhall be found within our kingdom of *Great Bri-* ' *tain*, as a rebel and contemner of our laws, fo as you have him, or caufe him to ' be before us in our faid Court on,   wherefoever it fhall then be, to anfwer

' us,

The close resemblance must afford the clearest evidence, that the original process of outlawry was the very same in England as in Scotland, and that the difference of the executive writs of the two nations, at this moment, has entirely arisen from the contamination of French customs admitted into our practice during the fifteenth and sixteenth centuries, and to the very great abuse of the process of outlawry itself. The law of both countries has in this, as in many other things, rejoined in the same channel, after ages of deviation. It will be observed, that the Chancellor has been pleased to extend his commission too far ; for, by the words, it should have effect over the whole kingdom of *Great Britain.* The reason is, that the King is always supposed to be actually present in Chancery ; but the writs of that Court have no authority in Scotland, and, it is to be hoped, they never will. Our caption is now a warrant as simple in its nature as the *capias ad satisfaciendum;* though, in style and form, it is really a commission of rebellion. We now acknowledge no outlawry in civil matters, as it is entirely confined to crimes ; and therefore the only writ which substantially agrees with the English commission is our process of fugitation against criminals who fly from justice.

The next thing we are to consider is the mode of executing this writ, which, though now looked upon as a warrant to seize the body of the debtor, is, as before observed, no more than a letter to charge the sheriffs, magistrates, and other inferior judges, to seize

S s 2 . the

‘ us, as well touching the said contempt, as also such matters as shall be then and
‘ there objected against him, and farther to perform and abide such order as our said
‘ Court shall make in this behalf, and hereof fail not. We also hereby strictly
‘ command all and singular mayors, bailiffs, constables, and other our officers and
‘ loyal servants and subjects whatsoever, as well within liberties as without, that
‘ they, by all proper means, diligently aid and assist you, and every one of you, in
‘ all things in the execution of the premisses. In testimony whereof, we have caused
‘ these our letters to be made patent   Witness ourself at Westminster, this
   day of   in the   year of our reign.

the debtor as a rebel. Before we come to the prefent practice in
this bufinefs, let us inquire how it was originally done; and, that
being well underftood, the other will create very little difficulty.
Anciently, by which word we are here to underftand the three preceeding centuries, the form we have examined was literally underftood and followed out. Meffengers, in thefe times, were not able
to feize or detain debtors in the places of their refidence. The officer could bring no power equal to what the debtor poffeffed in his
friends and neighbours. The voice of the law was very weak. Too
little refpect was paid to the perfons of judges themfelves, far lefs to
men in the fubaltern ftation of meffengers. Accordingly, we find,
that, though they encountered the debtor, or knew, with certainty,
where he was to be found, they feldom or never attempted to lay
hands upon him; but, on the contrary, charged the fheriffs of the
county, or the magiftrates of towns, to feize him, in terms of their
warrant. If the magiftrates did not obey, the next ftep was to take
out the letters threatened againft them in the certification inferted in
the caption, in the following words, viz. ' With certification to them,
' if they fail, our other letters will be directed, charging them thereto
' *fimpliciter.*' Accordingly, our formalift, in a practical note, tells us,
' That a magiftrate being charged, by virtue of the letters of caption,
' to apprehend the rebels, and refufing or delaying to give obedience,
' upon production of the caption and meffenger's execution, the
' Lords will grant fimple horning, or, as fome term them, letters of
' Second Caption.' We have the ftyle of this writ in the fame page *.
It proceeds upon a narrative of the former horning and caption,
with the meffenger's charge, againft the magiftrates, and fubfumes
in thefe terms : ' Neverthelefs the faid A. B. wrongfully refufes,
' poftpones, and defers to give obedience to the faid charge, without
' he and the remanent magiftrates of the faid burgh be further com-
' pelled; wherefore neceffary it is to the faid complainer to have
' thefe our letters direct, at his inftance, againft them, in manner
                                                        ' and

* Vide Dallas's Styles.

' and to the effect after specified.' The will of the letters, it will be observed, is no more than a second caption, but so far differing from the first, that it contains a warrant for denouncing the magistrates rebels, in case of disobedience. Mr Dallas's next direction is in these terms: ' The magistrates, or any of them, (which is sufficient for ' the haill, being one corporation), being charged, by virtue of the ' foresaid letters, and not giving obedience, may, after the days of ' the charge are elapsed, be denounced, regiftrate at horn, and cap- ' tion raised against them.' Then he gives the form of this caption, which differs in nothing from a common one but in the recital of the case. These writs are retained in our chamber style-books, and may be issued at this moment, if the creditor chooses to take that method.

All our writers upon the law are agreed that letters of four forms were totally abolished, and that there is no remainder of them in our practice. These writs against the magistrates, however, form an exception to this rule; for they are, in fact, exactly letters of four forms, aukwardly termed Letters of First and Second Caption. The warrant, in every ordinary caption, to charge the magistrates, is the *first form*; the charge, under pain of denunciation, is the *second form*; the denunciation itself is the *third form*; and what has been termed the Second Caption, or warrant for imprisonment, is the *fourth*. The nature of the charge, like the original four forms, is *ad factum praestandum*; and the space is exactly the same as these were, viz. three days each; and hence letters of four forms may pass the Signet at any time, if magistrates shall refuse to do their duty of incarcerating a debtor, after being regularly charged to that effect.

From our old decisions, it appears, that this business of seizing and incarcerating debtors, was one of the most burdensome, and at the same time most dangerous parts of the duty of inferior judges. When the mode of their obedience did not please the creditors, the consequence always was a personal action against the magistrates.

The

The sheriffs of the counties were also, for a considerable time, in the same predicament; but, as there were no public prisons belonging to the counties, all that the sheriff could do, was to carry the rebel to the prison of the head burgh of his shire, after which he had no further concern. Thus, in a case collected by Durie, the Lords assoilzied a sheriff from paying a rebel's debt, whom he had taken and committed to the tollbooth of the head burgh of the shire, though the prisoner had thereafter escaped; because, after imprisonment, the sheriff *functus erat officio* *. If the sheriff, however, had received a charge, and did not apprehend the party, he was made liable. Spottiswood has noted the case of the sheriff of Berwick, who, being pursued for a debt, because he disobeyed a charge of this kind, alledged that he had received it when he was sitting in judgment at Eymouth upon some *witches*, and he was not obliged to leave the court and obey the charge. Replied, That the rebel was sitting in court, and discoursing with him at the time. This would have subjected the sheriff, had he not offered to prove that the debtor had actually left the court before the charge was given. Durie gives us another case, where a sheriff was pursued to pay a debt for not taking a rebel, after being charged to do so, because he kept company with him diverse times thereafter. The Lords found, that the charge given should make him, the sheriff, liable for a year and day after its date, and no longer †. This year and day is a remainder of our most ancient law, founded upon a just presumption that the debtors have satisfied the debt. The distance of the sheriff's residence, and the want of prisons proper to his own jurisdiction, threw this business entirely upon the magistrates of the burghs, who, we accordingly find, were for a long period most unreasonably distressed by processes at the instance of creditors; and the more desperate the debt was, the more ready were creditors to take advantage of any circumstance in the conduct of magistrates, who were better

marks

---

* 2d March 1627, Brown against Sheriff of Wigton.
† Durie, 14th July 1630, Hay against Earl Marshall.

marks for their money. The court of justice seems, for a considerable time, to have favoured these claims, and to have subjected these public officers to very rigorous diligence in this branch of their duty. The principle was the very same which induced severity against the debtors themselves, viz. a strong desire to strengthen the hands of government, by producing strict obedience to its mandates. Thus it was found, that the magistrates of towns, charged to seize debtors under caption, are liable to pay the debts if they do not obey the first charge, and may be pursued directly, even after the debtor's death, without any previous process constituting the debt against the debtor's heirs, which was not only hard, but materially unjust [*]. Nay, we find several instances where the moveables of magistrates fell under escheat in consequence of these charges ; and Durie mentions an instance where a gift of that kind was found null, because the process of horning wanted the charges which we have lately described [†]. Lord Stair thus describes the manner of this business as it subsisted in his Lordship's own time, and would still be the rule where the interposition of magistrates might be necessary : ' Magi-
' strates use to offer to go with messengers foot by foot, if he can
' show where the person taken is, of which he doth show any pro-
' bable evidence ; but otherwise it were unreasonable that a sheriff,
' or his depute, should follow a messenger, at uncertainty, to any
' place of his shire. Magistrates of burghs are liable to more dili-
' gence for executing captions, because of their town or jurisdiction
' is narrow ; and therefore ordinarily the messengers do, of consent,
' take their officers and other assistance to search for and apprehend
' the party [‡].'

In proportion as the people of this country grew more populous, polished, and tractable, the voice of the law came to be better heard and obeyed. Messengers, of consequence, came to stand less in need of these extraordinary assistances in the execution of these warrants ; and

* Durie, 26th March 1634, Dunbar against Provost of Elgin.
† 16th January 1632, Drumlaindrig against Cashogil.   ‡ P. 748.

and very few cafes have occurred in which a fingle officer, with one or two affiftants, are not equal to the bufinefs. The difputes, therefore, between private parties and our fheriffs and magiftrates are, in a great meafure, vanifhed out of practice; and, even in Dallas's time, the method of charging the magiftrates, and taking out firft and fecond captions, had given way to action of damages. ' If the ' party pleafes, (fays Mr Dallas), he needs not be at the pains of ' horning and caption againft magiftrates, in cafe the prifoner was ' offered to them; for he may purfue them for the debt; and the ' rebels being offered, and they refufing or accepting, and not incar- ' cerating, the magiftrates will be liable.'

The next thing to be confidered is the time in which captions may be executed. All our lawyers are agreed, that captions may be executed at any hour in the day or night, although a poinding muft be done between fun and fun. The reafon is, that the caption is more likely to take effect in the night than in the day, and no third party has an intereft in its execution. This is not the cafe in poindings; becaufe the goods attached may belong to ftrangers; and becaufe, fuppofing them to be the property of the debtor in the warrant, the diligence of other creditors may be ready, to entitle them to a fhare. In the fame manner, it has been repeatedly decided in the Englifh courts, that arrefting in the night is lawful. Before the Reformation, we had, like all other Roman Catholic nations, a great number of holidays; and, although Sunday was, or ought to have been, the principal day of that kind, yet we find, that, fo far from being fet apart as it has been fince the Reformation, it was the principal day for the execution and citation of a moft the whole writs of the law. As captions were iffued againft men not as debtors to their fellow fubjects, Sunday, fo far as we are able to learn, does not feem to have protected them from imprifonment. The firft captions in this country, we have learned, we e iffued by authority of the churchmen then felves, who, of confequence, never would throw any impediment in the way of their own authority. Thence
the

the cuftom had eftablifhed itfelf. That this was the cafe, is proved
by the Prefbyterian act, c. 14 1644 *, which they were pleafed to
term the third Parliament of Charles I. The keeping of Sunday in
the ftrict letter of the Jewifh law, was the banner of the Calvinifts,
and particularly of the Church of Scotland. The words of this act
are : ' For the better obfervation of the Lord's day, and of other
' days fet apart for his folemn worfhip, difcharges all execution of
' letters of caption, raifed for civil debts, in any time of the Lord's
' day, or upon ordinary week days appointed for folemn faft or
' thankfgiving, during the time of divine fervice.' A fimilar ftatute
paffed in England on the 29th of Charles II. c. 7. enacting, ' That
' no perfon, upon the Lord's day, fhould ferve or execute any writ,
' procefs, judgment, warrant, or decree, excepting in the cafes there-
' in mentioned; but the fervice of every fuch writ fhall be void, and
' the perfon executing the fame liable for damages, as if he had
' done the fame without a warrant.' Though our Sunday act was
refcinded with the other laws of the fame Parliament, it has continued, in practice, to be ftrictly obferved ; for upon that day, and
upon the general fafts appointed by government, no warrants of
imprifonment can be legally executed. Even fuch debtors as have
abfconded or fled to fanctuary, vifit their friends upon thefe days,
and enjoy an interval of liberty.

We now come to ftate the different legal impediments to the execution of the caption. The firft obftruction is a *protection.*—Perfonal execution being awarded, in Scotland, for the crime of rebellion againft the King, it fcarcely feemed a ftretch to pardon the
fault, or, by a fpecial warrant, to protect the rebel from the confequences. Writs of this kind were familiar to the Princes of both
nations, from a very ancient cuftom of the King taking particular
focieties under his fpecial protection, in confequence of a royal warrant in their favour. To this kind the ftatute of the 11th Parl. of

VOL. I. T t James

* Refcinded acts.

James I. c. 134. relates ; and the writ itſelf may be found in Balfour * Theſe royal protections came to be inverted to private and hurtful purpoſes, under the title of *licences* and *ſupercederes.* The abuſe, ariſen to a great height, was endeavoured to be corrected by the 47th act of the 11th Parl. of James VI. This act was not obeyed ; and, what appears a great deal worſe, not only the Privy Council, but the other courts of law, ventured, contrary to the conſtitution of the kingdom, to aſſume the power of diſpenſing with law itſelf, by granting illegal protections. This appears from c. 13. of the 23d Parl. of the ſame Prince, which mentions; that ſundry protections were ſought by bankrupts, and others, to the prejudice of juſtice : ' Therefore diſcharging the Lords of Seſſion to grant them, ' under the pain of being liable for the debt.' By poſterior acts, in the reign of Charles II. the ſame prohibition was extended to the Privy Council, Exchequer, and Juſticiary ; ' Under the exception ' of protecting witneſſes and others neceſſarily appearing before ' them ; and that, if ſuch protections ſhould be granted, execution ' might notwithſtanding legally take place.' We are informed by Sir George M'Kenzie, ' That albeit the act diſcharged the granting ' of protections, and makes the granters liable, yet the contemners ' of the protection are puniſhed ; and that, accordingly, a Writer to ' the Signet was ſuſpended in November 1678 for cauſing appre- ' hend a perſon notwithſtanding of the protection of the Lords.' This Writer to the Signet certainly did honour to his profeſſion ; yet Sir George M'Kenzie, as he always does, ſeems inclined to defend this ſhameful act of power. At the ſame time he informs us, ' That the Council, to prevent the granting of protections, whereby ' the private intereſt of the ſubject was ſo much deſtroyed, and the ' execution of the law eluded, made an act againſt the practice ; ' and then to elide (as he terms it) that act, they changed the name ' into licences and ſupercederes to perſons to ſtay in the country, ' free of all execution, and that the King diſcharged this act by a ' letter

* P. 651.

' letter to the Council.' All would not do: It was too fweet a mor-,
fel of power to be parted with ; and therefore protections continued
to be awarded, under different modes and titles, down to the Revolution. To fuch a height was the abufe of thefe arbitrary writs
arrived at that period, that the nation, with one voice, required
them to be abolifhed. Accordingly, the claim of rights exprefsly
declares, ' That the granting of perfonal protections is contrary to
' law.' From the Revolution downwards to the act for regulating
bankruptcies, the very name of *protection* was unheard of. By the
laft mentioned act it is revived in a legal and expedient form ; and
power is committed to the Court of Seffion to grant protections in
certain circumftances to the bankrupt, upon the application, and for
the benefit of his creditors.

The next circumftance is, in what places captions cannot be executed. By thefe we mean places of fanctuary. Afylums, fanctua-
ries, or places of refuge, were known and allowed among the
Greeks, Jews, and Romans. The temples, the altars, the cities of
refuge, and (when the Empire became Chriftian) the churches, afforded protection to criminals and debtors infolvent. The clergy,
who fet no bounds to their ufurpations upon the civil authority,
turned churches at laft into a receptacle for the moft atrocious murderers. Several of our Scottifh laws regard the privilege of fanctuary, which was called *girth*, an old original word for an inclofure
or defence. In the reign of James III. it required an act of Parliament * to bring an intentional murderer out of a church to punifhment ; and even this could not be done until the intention, or forethought felony, was fixed upon him by a jury. The churchmen
would not yield to this moft reafonable ftatute, but defended all forts
of villains who put their truft in them. The mifchiefs thereby
brought upon the country occafioned the making another act, fo late
as the 4th Parl. of James V. which exprefsly declares, That fpirit-

T t 2 ual

---

* Viz. c. 35. of the 5th Parl. anno 1469.

ual men, masters of girths, would not deliver forethought felons to
the King's officers : and therefore these spiritual men were ordered
to appoint masters of girths under them, who should be personally
answerable for their proper conduct. It appears by two decisions
preserved by Balfour in the end of the fifteenth century, that the
churchmen were in practice of excommunicating the sheriff and his
officers in the execution of their offices, such as in poinding even
for the King's debts ; and therefore it is declared, that the bishops,
or other ecclesiastical persons, who shall do so in time coming, may
be punished and corrected by the King.

The same privileges existed in England even to a higher degree.
There, every church and church-yard afforded a sanctuary against
legal warrants of every kind, excepting sacrilege and treason. All
these overgrown abuses vanished with the religion which gave them
birth, leaving no other asylum or sanctuary, either in England or
Scotland, for the persons of debtors against warrants of imprisonment, but that species of protection arising from the reverence due
to the presence of our Princes, which came to be extended to the
places of their residence. This privilege belonged, from the highest
antiquity, to the palaces of our Princes, and, in particular, to
those of the Kings of England and Scotland. The word *palais*
is, in France, the established term for a court of justice ; and we
say the *King's palace*, the *King's court*, much in the same sense.
The reason was, that the courts of justice anciently followed the
King's person, and were held in his house or palace. The respect
for the person of Majesty, together with the obedience and solemnity necessary in the administration of justice, concur in laying a
restraint upon the behaviour of all persons attending in these places.
Besides, in order to encourage the approach of the feudal vassals to
do homage to the person of their Sovereign, it appears to have been
a sacred rule, that their persons, upon these occasions, were under
the King's special protection.

This

This neceſſary and proper reſpect for the perſon of the Prince, and the decorum of juſtice, grew naturally into a privilege, the benefit of which accrued to offenders and to civil debtors. Palaces and courts became an aſylum for the time, and even continued when the courts of juſtice were ſeparated from the King's reſidence. The difference was, that, in the former, it ſubſiſted only during the ſittings of the court; whereas, in the latter, the effect was conſtant. It is therefore an axiom in the law of England coeval with the power of execution itſelf, that no arreſt can be made in the King's preſence, nor within the verge of his royal palace, nor in any place where the King's juſtices actually ſit, or where his royal perſon reſides. In Henry VIII.'s time, the confines of his palace included a great part of the city of London; but, by a ſtatute in the 28th year of his reign, it was limited in point of extent. So ſtrongly was this idea of the privilege annexed to the King's reſidence impreſſed upon the minds of the people, that a number of lanes and alleys in and around the metropolis were in a manner taken poſſeſſion of by a ſet of deſperate people, who, under pretence of the privilege of theſe places, as being formerly the ſites of royal houſes, joined in a kind of defenſive covenant to protect themſelves againſt arreſts, and the proceſs of courts. The ordinary police was unable to root them out, becauſe the people looked upon it as an attack upon their privileges; and therefore it required no leſs than three or four acts of Parliament, in the reigns of William, Anne, and George I. to clear the metropolis of theſe ſeminaries of idleneſs, diſorder, and miſchief. A few years ago, upon a motion of the Judges, ſaid to have come from Lord Mansfield, the privilege of the verge of court was aboliſhed; ſo that debtors have no aſylum in England, though ſtill arreſtments cannot be executed within the palaces, and the courts of juſtice, whereby the original purpoſe of preſerving peace and reſpect in theſe places is anſwered, and the abuſe completely reſtrained.

In Scotland, all the cauſes above mentioned concurred in beſtowing the privilege of an aſylum upon the Palace of Holyroodhouſe.

It

It was originally an abbey, erected by a charter from David I. in
the year 1128 James V. erected a houfe near the Abbey to live
in. as a change from the Caftle. Mary, his dau·hter, and James VI.
rcfided principally at Holyroodhoufe ; fo that it had a double title
to the privilege of affording an afylum to debtors and to leffer criminals ; but, as it poffeffed that quality as an abbey, in the firft place,
fo it continues, to this day, to be termed the *fanctuary*, which, like
the old word *girth*, is proper to denote the protection afforded by a
church. Upon the acceffion of James VI. to the throne of England, fo fond were we of the leaft memorial of royalty, that Holyroodhoufe continued. by confent of the nation, in full poffeffion
of its privilege as a fanctuary for civil debts. The Duke of Hamilton, hereditary keeper, or, in the language of the former times,
mafter of the girth, the only one now in Britain, appoints a bailie
under him. This officer has a jurifdiction within the limits of the
place, which extends from the Abbey Strand, and comprehends
Arthur's Seat, with the whole grounds and houfes within the wall.
A record is kept by the deputy, in which debtors who intend to take
the benefit of the protection, are immediately entered by name and
defignation ; and therefore the firft thing the debtor does, is to have
himfelf *booked*, as it is termed. The Lords lately found, that no
perfon is entitled to the benefit of this fanctuary, after twenty-four
hours refidence in it, unlefs his name be fo recorded ; and this decifion is founded upon common fenfe and expediency ; for, in many
cafes, the fact, of debtors flying to the Abbey, is of the utmoft confequence in determining queftions ; and an extract from this regifter
is the ready and diftinct evidence of the fact. It is therefore unreafonable that any man fhould pretend to take the benefit of fanctuary, without affording to his creditors the legal evidence of his being there, or that the creditors fhould be loaded with the truth of fo
material a fact. The Abbey, however, will afford no afylum to obftinate or fraudulent debtors ; and, where this is known or fufpected,
the Court of Seffion, upon application of the creditors, will grant a

                                                          warrant

warrant to bring the debtor before them, and commit him to prifon, or reftore him to the privilege, as his conduct may deferve.

The fame prejudices exifted among the people of this country as among thofe of England; they were inclined to hold the privileges of fanctuary to be annexed to all the ancient refidences of our Princes, and particularly to the Caftle of Edinburgh, and to the Mint. The laft had never been a royal dwelling; but, as the general notions of the vulgar are feldom or never without fome foundation, it is, with great probability, fuppofed that the King's fervants in that place were anciently protected during the time of their employment in the fervice of the public. The privilege of fanctuary, however, has long been denied to the Mint. With regard to the Caftle, the point was determined in the cafe of Belfches *contra* Kinloch, 4th July 1751, when the Lords, with great propriety, found that the Governour of the Caftle was bound to grant accefs to meffengers at arms, or other officers having the King's letters, in order to their putting the fame into execution.

If our neighbouring country has abolifhed the privileges of fanctuary, it has preferved an afylum of a different kind, common to every fubject in the nation, where he may be fafe, if he pleafes, againft all arrefts, and that is his *own dwelling houfe*. This was the law of Rome, and it was the ancient law of the whole ifland: ‘ Domus fua cuique tutiffimum refugium eft et receptaculum.’ The Englifh writers feem to be proud of borrowing the very expreffions of the civilians upon this point. A man's houfe is, with them, his caftle of defence, an afylum wherein he fhould fuffer no violence. In England, many cafes have occurred, where bailiffs have loft their lives in endeavouring to force open the houfe of debtors to make arrefts; and the general opinion given and adhered to by the judges was, ‘ That the bailiff was flain in doing an unlawful act, as he ‘ ought not to have broke open the houfe; for, under pretence of ‘ fuch authority, any one might enter; and every one is to defend ‘ his

' his own houfe *.' At the fame time it has been decreed, ' That,
' if a window be open, and a bailiff touches a perfon's hand, either
' as he puts it out of the window, or the bailiff puts in his hand and
' touches him, he having a warrant to take him, he is then his
' prifoner, and he may juftly break open the houfe to take him
' away.' From the hiftory of the execution againft the perfons of
debtors in Scotland, the reafon of the very remarkable difference in
our law and practice will be perceived. Here a man's houfe is no
afylum. Meffengers may enter it in confequence of their warrant,
and break every door and every keeping capable of concealing the
mafter. We have heard the barbarous acts of Parliament which
authorifed this violence. The debtor and his houfes are thus treated
not becaufe he is a debtor, but becaufe he is a rebel and a criminal.
That our ancient law knew no fuch violation of the rights of mankind, could be proved by undeniable arguments drawn from a variety of our primitive cuftoms. Let one fuffice. The houfes of
debtors in this country cannot, at this moment, be entered by an
officer to execute a poinding. Before letters of horning came to be
granted for liquid debts, letters of poinding and apprifing were the
only warrants of execution ; but, if the debtor fhut his doors, the
officer had no authority to enter his houfe. After hornings became
the general and eftablifhed writs of execution, officers, knowing how
the law ftood, were careful to be provided with a caption ; and then,
under-pretence of fearching for the rebel, they forced the doors
open, and poinded the houfes. *Letters of open doors* were next invented ; but, like many other letters contrived about the fame time,
were contrary to law. A man's houfe ought to be the caftle of a
North, as well as of a South Briton. The law of our country has
been defeated, firft by the monftrous abufe which arofe in the beginning of the feventeenth century, of applying the procefs of outlawry to the cafe of civil debts, and by a trick of practice, where
                                                          the

* Law of arrefts, p. 72.

the goods within the houfe, and not the man himfelf, were intended to be taken in execution. But no houfe ought to protect a fubject who, by the commiffion of a crime, has forfeited the right of a citizen; and therefore it is laid down in the laws of England, that the breaking open the doors of a houfe where an offender is fheltered, may be juftifid in feveral inftances. ' Firft, On a *capias*, grounded upon an indictment for any crime whatfoever. Secondly, Upon a *capias* from the King's Bench or Chancery, to compel a man to find fureties for the peace or good behaviour, or upon a warrant from a juftice of the peace for that purpofe, Thirdly, Upon a *capias utlagatum*, or *capias pro fine*, in any action.' Thus, though we hold a debtor to be guilty of no crime, and though our caption is, at prefent, no more than a fimple warrant, yet have the houfes of the people of Scotland loft the facred privilege of protecting the mafters of them; becaufe, by the force of a word, and antiquated form, debtors, it feems, are ftill outlaws, and a caption is a *capias utlagatum*. Thus one abufe is grown out of another; and, though the original error is no more, the confequences of it continue to be a reproach upon the law and practice of this country.

In England, nine-tenths of common debts and claims are made up, and the ruin of many families prevented, by the protection which is afforded to their perfons in their own houfes; and hundreds have retired to our fanctuary and fettled their affairs, which otherwife could never have been done. Till fuch time, then, as our law returns to its ancient channel, it is right that there fhould be a public fanctuary in the kingdom.

The next ftep to be confidered is the ceremony of *apprehending* and *incarcerating*, which we fhall take from a book called the *Office of a Meffenger* *, every word of which, the forms excepted, is copied from Lord Stair, with a very few practical alterations: ' Firft,

VOL. I. U u ' then,

---

* P. 231.

' then, the meffenger muft fix and difplay his blazon on his breaft,
' fo as the impreffion of the arms may be feen, that thereby his au-
' thority and warrant may appear. If any affront be done him in
' the exercife of any part of his office, when he wants his blazon it
' will not import a deforcement, unlefs the actor knew him to be a
' meffenger.' When the rebel is found, the officer touches him
with his rod or wand, reads to him the letters of caption, and gives
him a figned copy; ' yet, if he have witneffes and affiftants fuffi-
' cient to make him go to prifon, if he were unwilling, the not
' reading of the letters, or the not giving a copy, figned by the
' meffenger, would not annul the caption. If the party taken fhould
' efcape, the reading of the letters, and giving a copy, would not
' have the fame effects as if the blazon were feen, and the party
' touched with the rod, thefe being evidences of the meffenger's au-
' thority which the party cannot deny, but that he knew him to be
' a meffenger at arms, and thereby might not only be liable to the
' penalty of deforcement, but to the other penalties of his contempt
' and violence.'

This *blazon* the meffenger is obliged to difplay upon his breaft, in
order that the party may not pretend ignorance of his office and authority. If he omits to do this, the debtor, it is faid in our law-
books, may refift, and refufe to be taken. The private perfonal
knowledge, however, of the debtor, has been held equivalent, which
does not appear to have been well decided; becaufe, where enfigns
of office are given, it is to thefe that refpect is due, and not to
the perfon of the officer. Meffengers found by experience, that
the wand (which anciently was three quarters of a yard long)
was too confpicuous for the convenient execution of their office;
and therefore they converted it into an ebony baton fix inches
long, tipt with filver. The rod and the blazon are delivered to
them by the Lyon at their admiffion. Formerly, as a fignal of
deforcement, they broke their long rod in two pieces; but, as
it was not convenient to break the modern elegant machine, they
contrived

contrived an emblem of an emblem. They put a ring upon their little baton, and now mark a deforcement by fliding this ring from the one end to the other. It is the touch of this wand which deprives the debtor of his liberty, and conftitutes him a prifoner. Various are the effects of this touch. The meffenger tells the debtor, at the fame time, in the King's name, that he is a prifoner; after which, though he fhould get off either by force or ftratagem, the officer may follow and bring him back, even out of the fanctuary of Holyroodhoufe. Formerly, it was fuppofed that the execution of the caption was not complete until the debtor was actually committed to prifon; and it followed of confequence, that a fift upon a fufpenfion delivered him out of the hands of the officer. By feveral decifions, however, within thefe twenty years, founded apparently upon Englifh ideas, the debtor is held to be in prifon from the moment he is in the cuftody of the meffenger; and, therefore, though a fift be prefented, that officer is not obliged to take any notice of it. Thefe decifions have gone upon a right principle; for a debtor in the cuftody of a meffenger is completely deprived of liberty; and confequently the diligence has received full execution before the fift arrives.

The effential part of the form, both in England and Scotland, is the corporal touch of the body of the debtor; for, after this is done, it is time enough for the officer to fhow and read his warrant, if required. This point is completely eftablifhed in England. In a cafe where the bailiff had not laid his hands on the defendant, but only fhowed his warrant, and pronounced the word ' *arreft,*' it was found that there had been no feizure, or, as they term it, no *legal arreft*. But it was agreed, that, if he had but touched the defendant even with the end of his finger, it would have been an arreft; and he might have broke the houfe to feize upon him had he efcaped into one, in the fame manner as a bailiff who has a warrant againft a perfon who is in a houfe, and lays his hand upon him through the window, may break the houfe to come to him.

U u 2 A

A fimilar queftion occurred, a very few years ago, in a political
difpute in this country. When the Town-Council of Edinburgh
were met for the purpofe of electing a member to reprefent them in
Parliament, and were proceeding to bufinefs, a meffenger appeared,
and demanded liberty to feize the perfon of one of the members, in
confequence of a caption he had againft him. The meffenger, however, was in the outfide of the bar of the Council Chamber, and orders were privately given to keep it clofe. The officer did not attempt to get over the bar, but made a noife, fhowed his baton, his blazon, and his caption, and declared that the perfon named in the diligence was his prifoner. In the mean time a fift on a fufpenfion was
procured againft the proper creditor, and intimated to the meffenger.
The point afterwards came before two Judges of the Court of Seffion, to whom it was ftated, that the meffenger never had touched
the perfon of the individual in queftion, nor had obeyed the will of
the caption, by forcing open gates and doors, and ufing the King's
keys thereto, but had merely contented himfelf with looking at
him, which never could amount to an actual arreft or feizure. The
Judges accordingly found fo, and fufpended the diligence.

The bailiffs in England carry no blazons, or other infignia of office. Their whole art lies in concealing, difguifing themfelves,
and executing their writs with addrefs. For this purpofe they
generally go in mafques, ftudy to perfonate all characters; and he
who is the beft actor is the beft officer. The bailiff is obliged to
detain perfons arrefted twenty-four hours in a private houfe before lodging them in prifon, on purpofe that they may find bail,
or agree with their adverfaries. Several acts have been made for
preventing the extortion of officers upon thefe occafions; and they
are difcharged from carrying them to any public-houfe but by their
own confent. The ftatutes, however, have not proved of very great
ufe; the bailiffs keep public-houfes; and, as the benevolent Mr
Howard obferves, when the bailiff himfelf keeps a public-houfe, it

                                                            feems

feems to preclude the debtor's choice; he muſt either go to that houſe, or directly to priſon, after the twenty-four hours. From the noted extortion of theſe places, they are termed *ſpunging-houſes;* and there debtors are allowed to live as long as they have money. But, although the expence be great, it cannot be denied, that this delay of going to priſon is often a matter of convenience to debtors; for many matters are, by that opportunity, often made up without being made known to the world; whereas, when a man goes to priſon, his affairs are made deſperate at once. In this country, the practice formerly was to carry the debtor directly to goal; and it is the caſe in all places where the magiſtrates are charged, or their aſſiſtance demanded. The perſonal danger, from the repeated deciſions of the courts, has taught them not to give a moment's delay. But in this and other large towns, where meſſengers act by themſelves, their method is to carry the debtor to a public-houſe; and, from an idea of the Engliſh practice which has got among them, they ſometimes venture to keep the debtor in their cuſtody twenty-four hours; but, in general, if the caption be executed any time in the day, the delay is no longer than ten or eleven o'clock at night. It were to be wiſhed that our meſſengers could contrive ſomething to have the good effects of the Engliſh ſpunging-houſes; ſome purgatory or middle ſtate, to laſt for a few days, in place of carrying their priſoners at once to a dungeon.

The bailiffs in England are not allowed to take any thing from debtors for the arreſt, but what they freely give, or what ſhall be determined by a juſtice of peace; but, in reality, very large fees are extorted upon theſe occaſions, according to the circumſtances and ſituation of the debtor.

Upon a complaint againſt one of our meſſengers for malverſation in the year 1738, the Lords found, ' That all meſſengers ought to be ' paid of their fees and expences for executing letters of horning and ' caption by the creditor-employer, and not by exaction from the
' debtor;

‘ debtor ; and that any meſſenger claiming, exacting, or taking from
‘ any perſon or perſons under diligence, by horning or caption, any
‘ ſum or ſums of money, or ſecurity for the ſame, under colour of
‘ fees, or expence of going or coming to or from any place or places
‘ towards, or in order to the execution of ſuch diligences, is un-
‘ warrantable, illegal, and oppreſſive, and opens a door to high and
‘ grievous exactions from ignorant, diſtreſſed, and indulgent per-
‘ ſons.’　The Lord Lyon iſſued injunctions to the meſſengers,
after adviſing with the Lords.　The 14th article ordains, ‘ That
‘ no meſſenger, in executing diligence of any kind, ſhall exact,
‘ take, or receive, on his own account, from the perſon againſt
‘ whom ſuch diligence is executed, or meant to be executed, any
‘ ſum whatſoever, under any name or pretence whatſoever, as he
‘ ſhall be anſwerable in any court competent.’

In London, the bailiff muſt carry his priſoner to the priſon of
that court from whence the writ iſſues.　With us, the meſſenger has,
by practice, the choice of the priſon, if there be two at any equal
diſtance ; but he will be puniſhed for oppreſſion if he forces the
debtor to go further off.　The eſtabliſhed rule is, that the debtor is
to be carried to the priſon of the juriſdiction where he is apprehended, unleſs he deſires to be carried to another.　Thus people of any
ſtation, taken in Edinburgh, generally requeſt to go to the Canongate, becauſe the accommodation is greatly better than that of Edinburgh priſon, which is an abominable dungeon, dark, cold, and un-
wholeſome.　There is no public improvement ſo much wanted as a
public priſon, where the unfortunate might ſuffer the loſs of liberty
without endangering their lives by that ſlow, and therefore cruel
torture, which the law-books of Scotland term *ſqualor carceris.*

When the meſſenger brings his priſoner to the goal, he produces
the caption to the clerk as the warrant for receiving him ; and
the clerk enters upon his regiſter the name of the priſoner, the
ground of debt, and the amount of the ſum for which he is committed.

mitted. The booking-money is then paid, which, by act of Council in July 1728, is a halfpenny Sterling for each pound Scots, or sixpence per pound Sterling, which goes to the keeper of the prison. The captain is answerable to the magistrates for every damage suffered by his neglect; and, as the magistrates are liable in the first place, it was absolutely necessary that they should know the extent of their obligation. Hence arose the necessity of prison registers, and the exaction of booking-money, as a perquisite to the keeper. It is a custom universal in our burghs, and it is reasonable, that the gealers should have some certain advantage for their risk and trouble. From our decisions, however, it appears that very few towns in Scotland kept goal records before the beginning of the present century; but now, unless the booking-money be paid, and the debtor entered, the magistrates and keepers are not obliged to receive the prisoner. At the same time, the Lords found, that it was not the business of the messenger, but of the keeper, to see it done. The effect of booking is, that the magistrates, in case of an escape, are liable for no more than the debt specified, although it be far below the sum mentioned in the caption; and, for this good reason, that, by such entry, the imprisonment is restricted to that sum. This has, in several instances, been serviceable to magistrates in actions for escape; because, purposely to diminish the goal fees, creditors booked their prisoners for very small sums; and they were, at that time, safe to do so, because the debtor could not be liberated without obtaining letters, and giving the magistrates a charge to set him at liberty. These letters, by the form, could not be obtained without intimation to the creditor, who instantly arrested the debtor for the remainder of the debt. When we come to the more agreeable business of liberation of the debtor, we shall give the reasons how this device came to be rendered of no avail. At present, it is sufficient to mention, that the Lords found, that arrestment was only a continuation of imprisonment: Therefore the booking-money must be paid upon arresting, as well as incarcerating; and the magistrates

are

are at liberty to difcharge the party, upon payment of the booking-money. In in this moft difagreeable part of practice, it is now a fixed rule that a debtor muft be booked for a fum no lefs than that for which the creditor is content to liberate him ; becaufe, upon confignation of that fum, he may gain his liberty at any time.

When a man is in prifon, it is common for his other creditors to arreft him in it. The form is this : The meffenger goes to the keeper of the goal, produces the new caption, and charges him, in virtue thereof, to detain the prifoner until the debt be paid. Formerly, the officer touched the prifoner with his rod, and charged him to remain in prifon till the debt upon which the caption proceeded fhould be paid. At prefent, he only leaves the principal caption with the goaler, and returns a certificate of the *res gefta*, or execution, fubfcribed by himfelf and two witneffes. This method of arreftment is the only one in which a fecond caption can be executed againft the debtor, already in prifon ; and it has the effect of affording action againft the town, in cafe of an efcape ; becaufe the goal keeper is the deputy of the magiftrates. When captions are granted againft more debtors than one, who live in different places, if the meffenger be not provided with captions againft each of them, he muft, at leaft, produce the principal letters to the goaler, and leave a full copy of them in his hands, with an atteftation of its being a true copy, duly fubfcribed. It is a capital part of the liberty of the fubject in this kingdom, that no man can be incarcerated without a legal warrant ; and that the keeper of the prifon where he is confined fhall be poffeffed of that warrant, or a double of it, properly authenticated, otherwife the party cannot be detained in prifon ; and therefore every debtor is entitled to call for a copy from the keeper, in order to know the caufe of his confinement, and to take meafures for his liberation.

When a creditor or a meffenger has further ufe for the principal letters of caption lodged with the goaler, one or other of them muft

grant

grant a receipt, containing an obligation to make them forthcoming when demanded. This is done in order to protect the keeper of the prison, and his conftituents the magiftrates of the town, from any future action that may be brought for wrongous imprifonment.

In the laft century, when a debtor was incarcerated at the inftance of one creditor, and another, whofe diligence was not ready, had reafon to fufpect that he would fettle with the creditor incarcerator, he applied for a remedy, now utterly and juftly out of practice. It was termed *letters of fummar arreftment*, and is certainly to be claffed among thofe letters which the Writers to the Signet, without regard to the law of the country, thought proper to fhape to the particular exigencies of the cafe of the employer. Thefe deduced the ground of debt, and narrated, that the debtor, as the complainer was informed, being incarcerated at the inftance of the other creditors, intended privately to obtain himfelf liberated, and to depart the kingdom, before fuch time as the complainer could, by courfe of law, obtain other letters of caption againft him; and therefore bears warrant to meffengers to fence and arreft him in prifon, therein to remain until payment of the debt, or finding fufficient fecurity. It is true, that thefe letters have now vanifhed out of practice; but it will, no doubt, occur, that they left behind them a progeny as mifchievous as themfelves, we mean, our prefent warrant upon alledgeance *de meditatione fugae*; though, no doubt, a warrant of that kind may be applied for even againft a man in prifon; and, in that cafe, it anfwers the very fame purpofe as thefe antiquated letters of fummar arreftment. The difference is, that the one paffed of courfe, and the other requires an oath of credulity upon the part of the creditor.

Liberation.

THE will of the caption bears, that the debtor was to remain in prison ' ay and while he fulfil and obey the command and ' charge of our other letters of horning, and be orderly relaxed ' from the procefs therein contained.' We formerly noticed, that it was not fufficient that the debt fhould be paid, and a difcharge granted by the creditor. It behoved the party alfo to be *difcharged* by the King. The form was, to obtain letters of relaxation and liberation, upon a bill to the Lords, with which the Writer produced the difcharge of the debt, and a receipt for the compofition of the fingle efcheat ; and hence the claufe in all the old difcharges, which we find in our formalift, ' Confenting that the principal and ' cautioner be relaxed from the horn, whereunto they are denoun- ' ced, by way of fufpenfion or otherwife, as accords, and that with- ' out caution or configuation.' Thefe letters were exceedingly ex- penfive, and bore very hard upon poor people, who being unable to procure them, were fometimes oblig d to remain in prifon upon that account, after their debts were paid. The keepers of the pri- fons, in general, ventured to difpenfe with this form. The keeper of the Edinburgh tollbooth, however, flood more upon punctilio, which produced an act of Sederunt *, allowing debtors to get out of prifon, without a charge to fet at liberty, if the debt did not ex- ceed 200 merks, whereby a very mean and partial relief was afforded. In order to fave the booking-money, and at the fame time, to avoid the confequences of this act, creditors entered the prifoners for ten or

twelve

* February 5. 1675.

twelve merks more than the two hundred, and then arrested for the
remainder of the debt ; but the magistrates of Edinburgh having
humanely ventured to liberate the prisoner in these cases, *without a
charge* to set at liberty, the Lords, by a solemn decision *, found
them only liable for the restricted sum entered in the prison-books ;
and, as they could, in no event, be subjected for any more, letters
of liberation went entirely *into disuse.* What contributed to this alteration of practice, was the odium under which escheats upon civil
rebellion fell, after the Revolution. . The general sentiments of the
nation altered in consequence of the claim of right ;—civil liberty,
and gentler manners, taught men to hold that scandalous forfeiture
in just detestation ;—the Exchequer no more demanded compositions
for escheats ;—and the Keeper of the Signet made no complaint
against the magistrates for dispensing with the letters of liberation.
Another circumstance had paved the way to this improvement :
Creditors sometimes consented to the temporary liberation of prisoners, without discharging the debt ; and magistrates had been accustomed to set people at liberty upon these consents. Nothing is more
instructive in the history of our business than the progressive forms
themselves. This deed recites, That whereas D. is incarcerate, at
my instance, in such a prison, for not payment making of such sums,
conform to a caption ; and I being willing to allow him *some liberty*
to go about his affairs, that he may be the better enabled to pay his
debts ; therefore consents that he be forthwith liberated, in so far
as concerns any execution, at my instance, against him, and that
without necessity of *any suspension, relaxation, or charge to set at liberty,* whereanent this shall be a sufficient warrant to the magistrates and keepers of the tollbooth ; and, in case suspension, relaxation, and charge to set at liberty, be found necessar, in that case I
consent to the passing thereof without *caution* or *consignation ;* providing that he crave no suspension of the debt, but only of the let-

X x 2   ters,

---

* 11th November 1704, Blair against the Town of Edinburgh..

ters of caption ; or, at leaft, that he ufe the fame no farther, but for
his prefent liberty, and but prejudice to me to put the letters in execution againft him whenever I fhall think fit, notwithftanding of
the faid confent or fufpenfion, &c. upon which conditions only the
confent is granted and accepted, and no otherways."

This form points out the nature of this bufinefs in the end
of laft century. At prefent, the ceremony is wonderfully leffen-
ed. Upon lodging a difcharge or extraƈt with the clerk of the
prifon, the debtor is immediately fet at liberty. To fave, however,
either the expence of an extraƈt, or the inconvenience of leaving
the difcharge, the creditor writes a confent to the *liberation* in the
prifon books, oppofite to the entry ; and, for the moft part, the
keeper is contented with a holograph letter, confenting to the liberation of the debtor ; but this letter muft be fent by a meffenger, or
other perfon known to the clerk of the prifon, who makes that perfon give an atteftation on the foot, that the letter is genuine, and of
the hand-writing of the creditor ; and this he confiders as a fufficient warrant.

ACT of GRACE.

The will of the caption alfo bears, that the debtor is to remain in
prifon upon his own proper charges and expences. This claufe was
inferted at that period of our law when caption proceeded upon letters of *four forms* ; when, after imprifonment of his body, no further execution could go out againft his effeƈts ; and therefore he is
ordered to remain upon *his own expences*. Thus the letters of four
forms themfelves bear, that, if the debtor furrendered himfelf to-
ward within the King's caftle therein mentioned, he was to remain
there *upon his own proper charges and expences* ; otherwife, as a prifoner of ftate, he would have been entitled to fupport.

Here

Here is a circumstance worthy of observation. Our old law did not allow execution against both the debtor and the goods at once; it presumed the debtor to be in possession of effects, and therefore made no provision for his subsistence in prison *. The creditor might seize his property; but, if he did, it behoved his person to be set at liberty. When the law and the principles of incarceration altered, no provision was made for the unhappy individual, nor no inquiry set on foot, whether he had any fund of subsistence or not; so that, from the humane principle of our ancient law, arose the bitterest circumstance in the situation of debtors. To the very close of the sixteenth century, we find not a hint given of the least relief afforded to the most innocent inhabitants of a goal, the prisoners for civil debt, though the justices of peace, in the reigns of James VI. and Charles II. were entitled to tax the counties for the support of indigent criminals. Debtors, it seems, were all this time entirely thrown upon the charity of the burghs, a circumstance which does no honour either to the manners or police of the nation.

At last, this unfortunate set of men grew so numerous, that the burghs were unable to keep them in life. They complained in a body to Parliament, which produced the famous act 1696, ' anent ' the aliment of poor prisoners.' This act proceeds not upon consideration of the sufferings of the wretched people described in it, but was intended merely to alleviate the expences of the burghs charged with their maintenance. Besides answering that little purpose, it has served the more noble end of relieving thousands from misery; of removing, in a great degree, the evils of imprisonment of the inferior and useful class of people for small debts, and thence justly deserved the title of the ACT OF GRACE.

The first question which occurred upon this act was, Whether intimation to a factor for an English merchant should be held to be

equal

* Except in the case of debtors to merchants, by the act of Robert Bruce, if the party had no goods, the merchant was obliged to find him in bread and water until the debt should be paid out of his lands.—Stat. 2. Robert I. c. 19.

equal to intimation to the creditor himfelf. The Lords, with great propriety, thought the factor, who had power to put him in, had likewife power to take him out ; and therefore fuftained the intimation as fufficient. This was extremely right ; but, in the fame cafe, they were pleafed to find, that, as the act had been intended as a favour to the royal burghs, and not to the debtor, magiftrates had a difcretionary power to detain the prifoner, if they thought proper. They further found, that the act was correctory, unfavourable, and nowife to be extended ; and, therefore, that, in cafe magiftrates modified too large an aliment, it might be reftricted by the Lords themfelves. ' All knew (fays Fountainhall) ' that there was a miftake in the act, which fhould have fixed a ' *maximum*, beyond which magiftrates fhould not go, as well as it ' had made threepence the *minimum* ; and it was obferved, that, ' fince this act, bankrupts fought no more the benefit of *ceffio bona-* ' *rum*, by perfuading magiftrates to modify a greater fum than cre- ' ditors could comply with.' Another queftion occurred, Whether the debtor fhould be obliged to grant a difpofition *omnium bonorum*. As the act was filent upon that article, the Lords left it to the magiftrates to require it if they thought fit ; only, it is to be obferved, that in Edinburgh they always exact fuch a difpofition before liberating the prifoner [*]. In a few years afterwards, however, the fentiments of the Court altered. They found, that the magiftrates had not a difcretionary power to liberate or detain a prifoner as they thought proper, and that it behoved them either to aliment the prifoner themfelves, or let him go free [†].

If a creditor be able to condefcend upon any fund poffeffed by the prifoner, the benefit of this act will be refufed. Thus a debtor, who ftood upon the charity of the Exchequer for fifteen pounds *per annum*, was found not to be entitled to any other aliment [‡]. The only

* December 28. 1710, Durham againft Glafwell.
† February 20. 1713, Grierfon againft Magiftrates of Dumfries.—Forbes.
‡ July 24. 1734, M'Kenzie againft Blair.

only other queſtion of importance is, Whether a priſoner ſet at liberty upon this *act of grace*, can be again incarcerated upon the
ſame diligence. The Lords have varied in their determination of
this point. A debtor liberated from Edinburgh tollbooth was again
incarcerated upon the ſame caption in the Canongate goal. The
debtor complained to the Lords ; and they moſt juſtly found, that
the impriſonment was unwarrantable ; that the debtor could not
again be incarcerated by virtue of the ſame caption, but *cauſa cog-
nita*, by warrant of the Lords, who conſidered the liberation equivalent to a ſuſpenſion and relaxation *. In the ſame ſpirit, the
Lords again found, that a debtor being once incarcerated for a debt,
and liberated upon the act of grace, the magiſtrates of a burgh may
refuſe to incarcerate him again for the ſame debt, although the creditor offered to aliment him †. In a later caſe, the Lords were pleaſed to reverſe theſe deciſions of their predeceſſors, and to find a creditor at liberty to execute his caption a ſecond time. On this occaſion, it was obſerved, ' That, although a liberation on the act 1696
' does not legally diſcharge the diligence, or reſtrain the creditor
' from again putting it in execution ; yet, if he commit a moral
' wrong, by uſing that diligence in an oppreſſive manner, he is cen-
' ſurable in equity, and the debtor may obtain relief by ſuſpen-
' ſion ‡.' This deciſion is quoted by Mr Erſkine as an authority
for a ſecond impriſonment, and as the preſent rule in this buſineſs.
The juſtice of the deciſion may, however, be queſtioned. The act
of Parliament gives no authority for a ſecond impriſonment ; and,
though it may be true that the debt and diligence is not diſcharged, yet the Lords themſelves, according to the deciſion 1709,
ought to be judges of the change of circumſtances. It is their
warrant alone which ought to authoriſe a ſecond impriſonment.
Were

* Forbes, December 10. 1709, Law againſt White.
† July 8 1724, Boyle againſt the Magiſtrates of Forres.
‡ June 19. 1759, Abercromby againſt Brodie.

Were the point to be again tried, the Court would, no doubt, return to the solid opinion of their predecessors.

It is not our intention to enter into the form of procedure used in applying for the benefit of the act of grace. The whole may be found in Boyd's Judicial Proceedings, to which we here beg leave to refer. The observations we have to add are, that the intimation made to all the creditors is meant to have the same effect as against the creditor-incarcerator, founded upon a special decision of the Court, where they, with great propriety, found, that if, after intimation to the creditor incarcerator, the debtor be arrested by another creditor during the running of the ten days, or after elapse thereof, there is no necessity for a new intimation to him; but, in terms of the penult clause of the act, he must find instant security to aliment, otherwise the prisoner may be set at liberty *.

It is certain, that poor prisoners in England were entirely thrown upon the county allowance, which differs in every place, and upon the charity of the public, till the 32d year of George II. when a statute was made for regulating and improving prisons; whereby it is enacted, that, upon the debtor's making oath that he has no funds for immediate subsistence, the creditor should be obliged to pay him *a groat* a day, or two and sixpence a week. Had this act of Parliament copied the simplicity of our act of grace, it would have proved a happy relief to hundreds of miserable people; but the difficulty of obtaining it is so great, that Mr Howard tells us, that, in Middlesex and Surry, he had not found twelve debtors who had been able to make it effectual. This is a strange contrast. Our act 1696 was not intended for the relief of debtors, and yet it proved the most gracious law which they have received in any country of Europe. The act of George II. was expressly intended for the relief of prisoners, and yet it has done them little or no good. It may be said, that, in England, there is no act of grace,

and

* 27th January 1736, Dowie against Crocket.

and the law never admitted the Roman *ceſſio bonorum.* In ſuch a populous and commercial kingdom, imprisonment muſt be attended with terror and uncertainty. Inſolvent acts, therefore, paſs at different periods for liberating all debtors under the deſcriptions there given, and who have ſuffered confinement for any length of time. This relief is uncertain ; but, when it arrives, it is more complete than our *ceſſio.* The debtor makes a ſurrender of the ſame kind, upon oath, in favour of his creditors, and comes out a free man.

BOND of PRESENTATION.

It is now propoſed to treat of thoſe practical caſes which are frequently conſequent upon perſonal diligence, viz. the *bond of preſentation,*—the *bill of ſuſpenſion,*—and the *ſuſpenſion and liberation.*—The two firſt are the modes of preventing the actual imprisonment of the debtor, and the ſuſpenſion and liberation ſets him at liberty after the incarceration has taken place.

When a debtor is in the hands of a meſſenger, he ſometimes applies to be allowed a time certain to raiſe money, and regulate his affairs. The creditor, and often the meſſenger himſelf, agrees to this, conditionally that the debtor find ſufficient bail to preſent himſelf, in order to the complete execution of the diligence, upon the day, hour, and place agreed upon. Bail of this kind is eaſily found by debtors of any character and credit, becauſe it is in their power to perform. They may afterwards, indeed, not be able to pay, but they have it in their power to preſent their perſons, agreeably to the agreement, for the cautioner's relief; and the failure of a debtor, in ſuch a caſe, is reckoned one of the moſt diſhonourable acts that can be committed in the buſineſs of civil life. The deed executed upon this occaſion is termed *a bond of preſentation.* We ſhall take the common form of it from Spottiſwood. After the preamble, it proceeds thus:
‘ Therefore wit ye me to be bound and obliged to preſent the per-

‘ ſon

' fon of the faid B. to the faid C. or to any having his commiffion,
' at Edinburgh, in the houfe of   upon the 15th day of Sep-
' tember next to come, between the hours of ten and eleven fore-
' noon, without any longer delay, fraud, or guile.'

There is here a neceffity for precifion in *time* and *place*. The creditor, or his meffenger, commonly gives punctual attendance ; but,
though they fhould not, the cautioner and the debtor muft be punctual ; and, in order to prove it, an inftrument muft be taken after
the fame manner as is done in ufing an order of redemption *. There
was a claufe in the old bonds of this kind, that, in place of appearing at a private houfe, or making any appointment upon the head,
he the debtor fhould, againft a day certain, enter his body in a prifon
fpecified, and book himfelf in common form. In cafes of this kind,
the cautioner borrows the caption from the creditor, or, at leaft,
provides himfelf with an extract of it from the Signet, otherwife
the keeper of the prifon will not receive the debtor. In fome cafes
reported by Lord Stair, and mentioned in the Dictionary, the Lords
allowed the cautioner a new day to prefent, where the delay had
been moderate, and the excufe plaufible ; but thefe decifions are not
to be depended upon.

' Then and there to be perfonally apprehended and difpofed of at
' the will or pleafure of the faid C. or any having his commiffion,
' conform to the faid letters of caption in all points, without any
' fufpenfion, protection, *ceffio bonorum*, or other ground or warrant
' whatfoever, that may ftop, hinder, or impede the faid B. appre-
' hending the faid C. and incarcerating of him, and putting the faid
' letters of caption to their full and final execution in all points.'

By the word *protection*, we fee at once that this ftyle is not the
production of the prefent century. As the word *protection*, however, is a general term, and underftood in a different fenfe from what
it formerly was, it may not be improper to retain it in the ftyle of
the

* 22d November 1695, Pitlado againft Main.

the prefentation. It is from this laft claufe that the danger of the cautioner in a bond of this kind arifes. The intermediate execution of another caption, the imprifonment for a crime, or any other accident which may arife from the fault of the debtor or cautioner, or their neglect, will forfeit the bond. Thus a cautioner prefented his party at the day and place appointed; but, when the meffenger attempted to do his duty, the debtor produced an atteft of his being inlifted as a dragoon, which, by act of Parliament, fecured him againft the diligence. The Lords, therefore, found the cautioner liable *. In the fame manner, a cautioner was fubjected where the principal had, *medio tempore,* been taken upon another caption; and in vain he pled that the prefentment had thereby become *factum impreſtabile.* In this laft cafe, it was admitted, that ficknefs, or any accident not occurring by the prifoner's fault, might have been relevant, if the party had been offered fo foon as that accident ceafed; but it cannot be extended to any impediment by the prifoner, or his cautioner's fault or fact, fuch as to be under the hazard of other captions; for, if that had been expreffed, as it is pretended to be implied, no man of fenfe would have difmiffed a prifoner in thefe terms, that he fhould be produced fuch a day, if he were not taken by other captions for his own debt. ' The Lords repelled the reafon ' fimply, albeit the prifoner had been offered immediately after he ' was free of the other caption †.'

' And that under the penalty of   Scots money, befides ' performance.'—This is by much too general, and throws the import of the obligement entirely into the power of the Court, who may afcertain the damages or penalty in any manner they pleafe. The proper penalty, in this cafe, is the payment of the debt; and it fhould be conceived not as a penalty, but as an alternative, which, of confequence, will receive a ftricter interpretation in favour of the creditor. For the creditor's benefit, therefore, the alternative fhould

Y y 2   be,

* 27th July 1710, Henderfon againft Graham.
† Stair, 7th July 1681, Polftead againft Scot.

be, and is now generally expreſſed in this manner : ' Or other-
' wiſe, in caſe I happen to fail in performance of the premiſſes,
' or any part thereof, or that it ſhall be my pleaſure not to preſent
' the ſaid C. D. as above mentioned ; then, and in either of theſe
' caſes, I bind and oblige me, my heirs, executors, and ſucceſſors, to
' make payment to the ſaid   of the foreſaid ſum of.
' of principal, of   of annualrents, making together the ſum
' of,   and that at the term of Whitſunday next, with a fifth
' part more of penalty in caſe of failure,' &c. &c.—Here we ob-
ſerve a further term is given to the cautioner to pay the debt ; and
it remains a matter of indifference to the creditor whether the bond
is forfeited from neceſſity or from choice.

In order to make the bond of preſentation a ground for a ſummary charge, it ſometimes concludes with the following clauſe :
' Laſtly, I hereby conſent that an inſtrument taken in the hands of
' a notary public, before two witneſſes, upon my failure to preſent
' the ſaid C. D. in terms of the preceeding engagement, together
' with theſe preſents regiſtered in manner after mentioned, ſhall be
' ſufficient to found a ſummary charge againſt me for payment of
' the ſaid debt, reſerving all other objections againſt the ſaid inſtru-
' ment, or the facts therein ſet forth.'—Without a clauſe of this
kind, a bond of preſentation is certainly not a ſufficient warrant for
ſummary diligence, and that any ſuch charge, if given, ought to be
ſuſpended without caution or conſignation.

From the deciſions upon this ſubject, it was obſerved, that the
ſickneſs of the debtor is ſuſtained in law as a ſufficient excuſe to the
cautioner for not preſenting him in terms of the bond. With this
view, Spottiſwood tells us, ' That it is moſt expedient to make pro-
' viſion againſt all unforeſeen accidents, ſuch as ſickneſs ; and, in
' that caſe, the clauſe muſt run thus : " Likeas it is hereby ſpecial-
" ly provided and declared, That in caſe the ſaid B. ſhould be ſo
" indiſpoſed by *ſickneſs*, that he cannot go to the foreſaid place at
" the ſaid time without danger to his health ; then, and in that caſe,
" it

" it shall be a sufficient exoneration to me to take the said messenger,
" or any other the said C. shall appoint, to the house where the said
" B. shall be lodged for the time, and there present him to the said
" messenger, the house being always within the town of Edin-
" burgh *."—Something of this kind may be done; but, to the
honour of the country, no instances have happened which prove the
necessity of it. Creditors among us have not hitherto betrayed that
cruelty of temper which requires any particular law to protect the
sick or diseased debtor from their vengeance; neither have we any
ordinance to protect the aged and infirm from the ordinary diligence. The later Imperial law gives an example worthy the imitation of mankind. It did not allow the creditor to disturb his debtor
by any kind of process or legal execution when *in sickness*. If he
ventured to do so, and the debtor died in his custody, the law condemned him in a sum equal to the debt to the heir of the debtor,
and a third part of his whole estate to the public; and, besides, he
thereby stood convicted of notorious infamy. ' There is no doubt,'
' says Lord Bankton, ' that if such cruel usage were followed with
' us, it would be redressed; but how far a creditor or executor of
' such diligence would be liable to such punishment and damages to
' the party or his heirs, may be doubted.'

Having thus explained the principles and style of the bond of
presentation, we conclude the subject by mentioning, that, when
parties attend at the time and place of presentment, each of them
ought to carry a notary public in their company; the one to take
an instrument upon the performance of the obligement, and the
other to take an instrument upon the forfeiture of the bond, in case
it be not performed. It is unnecessary to go into the forms of these
instruments. The one taken by the cautioner, recites the bond and
the appearance of the debtor, in the precise terms thereof; he then
protests that his obligement is performed *in terminis*; and, therefore,

* P. 118.

fore, that he is thenceforth totally free and difcharged thereof, and of all penalty, claim, or demand, either for prefenting the perfon of the debtor, or for payment of the debt in time coming. The inftrument, upon the part of the creditor, mentions the punctual attendance of the party and the meffenger, having the caption to receive the debtor as a prifoner, and that for one full hour at leaft, (better for two hours). The creditor then protefts, that, in refpect of the non-appearance of the debtor and cautioner, that the penalty in the bond is incurred; that he fhall not be obliged to receive the debtor thereafter; and that the cautioner has thereby become liable to him in payment of the debt, principal, intereft, and expences, in terms of the alternative in his bond; and alfo in payment of the liquidate penalty therein contained. It is alfo neceffary to know, that cautioners in thefe bonds of prefentation have no relief againft the other cautioners in the principal bond. In this refpect, they are in the fame fituation as magiftrates who have fuffered debtors to efcape out of their prifons *.

Cautioners in bonds of prefentations are not bound for liquid fums, but *ad factum praeftandum*; and therefore they are not entitled to the feptennial limitation introduced by the act 1695. This point is illuftrated by a fingular cafe, Monro *contra* Bain, 22d July 1741, reported by Kilkerran, under the title *Prefcription.* A cautioner became bound in a bond of prefentation, that the principal fhould, upon a day certain, compear perfonally at Invernefs, in the meffenger's houfe, and then and there pay the whole fums, principal, annualrent, and penalty, mentioned in the letters of caption, with all other expences of diligence. The Lords found, ‘ That this obligation upon the cautioner fell under the act of Par- ‘ liament anent the prefcription of cautioners.’ Kilkerran obferves, ‘ That a fimple bond of prefentation, that the debtor fhould prefent ‘ himfelf, would not have fallen under the act of Parliament; but ‘ the

‘ the cautioners being here bound that the debtor fhould alfo pay,
‘ was found to diftinguifh the cafe : Notwithftanding it was plead-
‘ ed, that, by the words, the cautioner was not bound to pay, but
‘ only that the principal fhould pay ; and fo the cautioner being
‘ only liable confequentially upon the principal’s failure, he was no
‘ more bound for a fum of money, than he is in a fimple bond of
‘ prefentation, whereby he becomes alfo confequentially liable upon
‘ the principal’s failure to prefent *.’

In practice, obligations of this kind are more frequently granted
by letters in a hurried manner in public-houfes. Whether the Court
would make any diftinction between thefe and the effect of formal
bonds, is not known ; but there can be no doubt that a formal deed
is in every cafe to be preferred. One thing we venture to recommend, that, when we are laid under the difagreeable neceffity of ordering captions to be executed, it is for the intereft of our employers to defire the meffenger to accept a good bond of prefentation.
The chance for the recovery of the debt becomes thereby much
greater. There is the neglect of the cautioner and the party, on
the one hand ; and, on the other, the debtor will exert himfelf to
the utmoft to fettle the debt, and to fave himfelf.

We have now left no circumftance behind us in the execution
againft the body of the debtor. We judge it the more requifite,
that, fince the late infolvent acts, the execution againft the moveables has been very feldom ufed, becaufe little or nothing was to be
got by it but expence and trouble ; and therefore more debts have
been recovered by caption fince that period, than by any other diligence of the law. In doing this, creditors wifely avoid the actual
incarceration of their party ; but, by holding him in conftant dread
of it, are fure to get hold of every fecurity in the debtor’s power to
give.

Sufpenfion.

* P. 420.

Suspension.

BY the constitution of the kingdoms of England and Scotland, the King is the sole fountain of jurisdiction. This jurisdiction, too heavy to be exercised in person, is committed to judges of his own appointment, by special writs or brieves issued from his Chancery. As the Roman Emperors acted by the ministry of a great officer or secretary, who had a general superintendance over the executive writs issued for the government of the empire; so the several kingdoms of Europe, formed out of the members of that vast body, had in each of them a great officer who filled a similar department. In France, and in this island, this great man got the title of *Chancellor*. To his province it fell to devise and make out all writs, brieves, and letters patent; and, in order to give them authority, he had the custody of the King's seals, that he might seal them, or, as it is termed, *order the seal to be appended to them*. When, therefore, any grants were improperly obtained from the Crown, to the prejudice either of the Prince or his subjects, it was the Chancellor's business to inquire into the matter, to *stop* or *suspend* the execution of the writ, and to recal it if improper. When the courts of law, proceeding upon the strict terms of the King's original brieves, were unable to give the redress to a party which his case required; or when, by a rigorous application of the common law, the subject suffered real injustice, no other method was left to the injured party but an humble application to the King for relief.

Upon

Upon thefe occafions, the Chancellor, who was prefumed to unite‘ in his perfon both piety and learning, was called upon to advife in what manner juftice was to be reconciled with ftri&t law. This was an appeal to the King's confcience ; and, as the Chancellor directed it, that dignified officer got the title of *the keeper of the King's confcience.* From thefe beginnings, and by flow degrees, arofe the power of the Chancellor of England, and the grand diftin&tion between the courts of common law, and the great court of equity in which that officer prefides. Upon due confideration of the circumftances of the cafe, he mitigates the feverity, and fupplies the defe&ts of the judgments pronounced in the courts of law. The form in which an application is, at this moment made, is by *a bill* or complaint, ftating the circumftances of the cafe, the reafons drawn from it, and concluding with a humble prayer for relief. The Chancellor, if neceffary, grants upon *this bill, an injunction,* commanding all execution to ceafe until the matter fet forth in the bill be inquired into and determined. This injunction prote&ts the party complainer; but, to bring the perfon complained upon into court, a writ of fummons is iffued, under the name of a *fubpoena,* fo called from the confequences of non-appearance, which are the fame with our certification. In the courts of law, all proceffes or a&tions commence upon brieves iffuing from the Chancery, commanding the judge to do juftice, which is a form extremely different from a humble fupplication to the Chancellor for redrefs.

We had formerly occafion to obferve, that, of old, all a&tions and fuits proceeded by brieves iffuing from the Chancery of Scotland, which, as in the South, was the *officinum juftitiae,* under the direction of the Chancellor of the kingdom. Redrefs in equity was applied for to the King, who granted it by the affiftance of his Chancellor and Council. The ancient brieves, upon the univerfal prevalence of the Roman law, and the continental fyftem of feudalifm, went by degrees into difufe. Our inferior judges affumed the jurifdi&tion of caufes upon complaints *per modum quereleae,* and fum-

monfes by their own authority. At the eftablifhment of the College
of Juftice, the power formerly exercifed by the King and his Council,
fo far as regarded the civil bufinefs of the nation, was entirely devolved upon that body. The College of Juftice became thenceforth
the King's Court ; the powers of the Chancellor were united to it ;
and the 40th article of the Inftitution provides, ' That the Lord
' Chancellor being prefent in the town of Edinburgh, or any other
' place, he fhall have a vote, and be Prefident of the faid Council.'
Being thus invefted with the powers of the judges of common law,
and the Pretorian or fupreme jurifdiction of the King or his Chancellor, they iffued writs of procefs by their own authority ; fummonfes in the King's name, and under his fignet, took place of the
ancient brieves iffued by the Chancery ; and the equitable powers
which formerly refided in the King, his Chancellor, and Council,
refted entirely in the new Court.

This equitable, pretorian, or correctory jurifdiction, came to be
exercifed by applications to the Lords, and the writs for that purpofe, from the Latin word, and ecclefiaftical practice well known
in France, were termed *fufpenfions*. The injunction they called a
fift, and the *fubpoena* was granted in the fame writ, in the form of a
fummons ; which accordingly makes a remarkable part of the will
of our fufpenfions at this moment. The fufpenfion then is the writ
by which the equitable powers of our Court are exercifed ; and by
which every error in the decrees of inferior judges, or in the decrees of the Supreme Court itfelf, is ultimately corrected. The form
retains a coincidence with that of the Chancery of England, which
proves the deduction we have given, and the analogy we have
pointed out : ' Sir Edward Coke fays, That the Chancellor, or *Can-*
' *cellarius*, has his name *a cancellando*, from cancelling the King's
' letters patent, when granted contrary to law, which is the higheft
' point of his jurifdiction.'—' Gif the King (fays Balfour) give any
' privy writing whilk is direct contrare to the adminiftration of
' juftice, or hinders and poftpones it, the Lords of Council may
' difcharge or fufpend the fame.'

In

In this narrow country, the same firm and broad distinction could not be made as in England. The civil business of the nation was often too much blended with the political government ; and, therefore, though the King had united his Chancellor with the College of Justice, yet he retained a personal jurisdiction for himself and his Privy Council, which clashed with that of the civil judges, and continued from the days of James V. down to the union of the kingdoms in the reign of Queen Anne, to distract and confound the business of this country So long as the Privy Council of Scotland and their powers lasted, a constant collision in point of jurisdiction took place between them and the Court of Session, which deprived the subjects of real security for their persons or their property ; and from this divided power, may fairly be deduced the greatest part of the evils under which the people of this country groaned, during that long and unhappy period.

Balfour tells us, ' That the Lords of Session were not judges ' competent in causes of suspension of any letters of horning, direct ' by the Lords of Secret Council, because the Lords of Secret Coun- ' cil, wha were the givers of the decrete, are judges to all letters and ' other contraversies, whilk flows and arises from the said decrete, ' 13th June 1545, Marion Tours against the Laird of Weems.'— ' But gif the party fulfils and obeys this said decreet, the Lords of ' Council may suspend the letters of horning given by the Lords of ' Secret Council*.' The meaning of this last decision is, that the Lords might retain the party from the consequences of rebellion. and escheat, following upon the horning issued by the other jurisdiction. This was a disagreeable situation for the subject. Two courts, whose views and interests were often entirely different, had it in their power to oppres the subject by the very same mode of execution. Both of them were Royal Courts, the King was supposed to be present in each ; and, therefore, both assumed the same

Z z 2   mode

* Page 267.

mode of explicating their jurifdiction, which formerly belonged to the King alone, viz. the terrible procefs of outlawry : Whereas no judge in England poffeffed it, but the Chancellor, to whom alone it is to this day confined.

Let us now examine the particular part of bufinefs, which in this country created the neceffity and multiplied the number of thefe applications in equity. Officers and meffengers were not formerly under good regulations ; and it was not uncommon to obtain decrees upon falfe executions in abfence of the defender. In fuch circumftances, it would have been the height of injuftice not to hear the parties. Decrees in abfence, or as they were then termed, for *null defence*, were often pronounced ; and the then ftate of the country afforded a variety of plaufible excufes for the non appearance of defenders. Many other cafes occurred but particularly that one of decrees of confent upon regiftered writs. If the parties were not heard by fome fuch device, they could not be heard at all. Even in caufes where the parties had been heard, and decree given, as the civilians fay, *in foro contradiftorio*, evidence often emerged after fentence, and before execution ; which, had it been known before, would have prevented the decree.

The form of the Englifh bill in equity, and the Scottifh fufpenfion, was exceedingly natural and fimple. An action lies to every fubject who has fuffered, or is fuffering a wrong trom another. A party who obtains a falfe decree, or a decree upon unjuft grounds, is guilty of a wrong ; and, confequently, may be called by the party fuffering before a Court, to have the wrong prevented. This is the principle of a fufpenfion, and confequently the ftyle, which, as we noticed before, joins both the bill and the *fubpoena*, is nearly that of a fummons, in which the fituation of the parties is inverted. He who was formerly purfuer, is the defender, and the defender in the fufpenfion becomes the purfuer. But a fummons would not have met the circumftances of this cafe. Summonfes were granted eafily ; and of courfe, as they import no more than a demand to be made

good

good in judgment, but here one of the parties had already obtained a decree. We have heard that the interruption or stopping of execution is not a favourite measure, either of the law or police; but if a simple summons had that effect, execution must always have been stopt, and the creditor would in no respect have been benefited by his decree. On the other hand, a common summons would not have availed the debtor, because it did not stop execution, and he might have been poinded, denounced, or imprisoned. These purposes were answered on both sides, by the form of presenting a petition to the Court; upon which an immediate stop was given to further execution, and the judges had an opportunity of determining at leizure, whether a summons of suspension should be granted. Accordingly, we are told in the old form of process left us by Sir John Skene, who wrote in the reign of James VI. ' that na suspen-
' sions of decreets are granted, but be an special supplication of the
' partie soyter thereof, given to the Lords in weit, and subscribed
' be them, at least be twa of them, in the name of the rest of the
' Lords.'

The idea of a suspension is by some writer found in the *induciae moratoriae* of the Roman law. However that may be, it is evident, that the rule of exacting caution was thence taken. The Emperors seldom interposed in delaying the execution of decrees, ' nisi idonea
' fidei-jussio super debiti solutione praebeatur.' And nothing can be more just; for, if an execution is stopt, the creditor, who might at that time have recovered his money, is at least entitled to have caution, that he shall certainly recover it in the end, in case his diligence has been unjustly suspended. This was first introduced into our practice by an act of Sederunt, dated 25th October 1577. The bail thus given, however, proved in many cases no better than the principal; as few laws subsisted, at that time, to check the frauds of private parties. When a decree came to be executed, every thing was covered by collusive deeds, assignments, and sales. Of this we are informed by the act of Parliament 1584, c. 139. which mentions,

tions, ' That the malice of persons had daily so increased, that the
' execution of decreets obtained by maist langsome process, was al-
' together frustrate.' The act, therefore, provides, ' That na sus-
' pension be granted of the same decreets, but upon payment or
' consignation.' This was with great propriety intended to distinguish decrees obtained by *langsome process*, that is in *foro contentiosissi-*
mo, from all others ; but the purposes of this act were lost by inattention in practice.

Reasons of suspension were originally intended to be more speed-
ily judged of, than any other action ; and, therefore, it was held to
be a rule, that they must have been instantly verified, otherwise the
bill could not pass ; and, when it did pass, the Lords, in their deliverance or warrant, always fixed the day to which the other party behoved to be summoned, because experience proved, that this was
not to be trusted to the raiser of the suspension, who had nothing to
gain by the issue of the question. Another rule prevailed, that,
when a party gave in a bill of suspension, he behoved to state in it
all his reasons or exceptions against the debt ; and, when the matter
came before the Court, he was heard upon nothing but what his
own summons contained. This strictness as Lor ' Stair informs us)
arose from an abuse upon the part of the debtors, who formerly
used to give in one suspension after another, and drew out the matter to an unsufferable length. Pretences, however, were soon found
for getting the better of this rule. Skene says, ' That the Lords used to
' grant special licence to widows, pupils, poor folks, &c. to eke and
' reform their reasons of suspension ; and, by degrees, this method
' of eking became general, and continues to this moment ; so that, if
' reasons are stated in the bill sufficient to pass it, the suspender may
' afterwards insist upon as much new matter as he pleases ; and it is
' not uncommon to hear a cause pled, without mentioning any one
' of the reasons stated in the libel.'

In presenting bills of suspension, parties frequently gave very partial and unjust accounts of the grounds of debt which they craved to
be

be fufpended, whereby the Lords were much impofed upon. They
were further mifled by falfe difcharges, and other writs produced
with the bill, and afterwards withdrawn ; and, therefore, by an act
of Sederunt, 27th July 1599, it was ordained, ' That all decreets,
' regiftered contracts, and obligations, whereupon fufpenfion is
' craved, be extracted and given in with the bill of fufpenfion ; and
' that all difcharges produced fhould be fubfcribed by the procurator
' for the party, and retained at the Bill Chamber.'

The practice of debtors very foon fhewed the purpofe of their applying for fufpenfions. After bills were paffed, and the day of appearance filled up, they allowed them to lie in the hands of the
clerk ; and, when that day came, prefented a new bill. This was
corrected by an act of Sederunt, 24th May 1599, difcharging the
clerk of the bills to annex the date to any bill till caution be found,
or confignation made, and then to be marked of that date.

Sufpenfions, it feems, became very frequent, and numbers of
them, upon trial, turned out to be frivolous. Cautioners, as then
taken, were only liable for the contents of the decree ; and, therefore, for the better indemnification of the creditor, the Lords, by an
act of Sederunt. 23d November 1613, ' appointed caution to be ta-
' ken not only for obedience to the charge, but alfo for payment of
' fuch expences as the Court fhould modify ; and alfo for payment
' of damages, in cafe of wrongful fufpending.'

Cautioners being bound only for the performance of the party
fufpender, difputed their obligements when the fufpender died during the dependence, and fucceeded. Forged receipts and vouchers
continued to be produced, in order to pafs the bills ; but, when the
fufpenfion came to be difcuffed, thefe receipts did not make their
appearance. Cautioners had been offered and received under falfe
defignations. Thefe were egregious abufes committed by the parties, and reflect little honour on their doers. The Court itfelf was
not blamelefs. Each Judge, it feems, paffed bills as he thought proper ; and, what muft now appear ftrange, the Lords indulged themfelves

felves in a practice of granting warrants and injunctions against the paffing of particular bills. Single Judges carelefsly allowed bills against decrees *in foro*, contrary to the act of Parliament, and the juftice of the cafe. To clear away thefe numerous abufes, a long act of Sederunt was paffed upon the 29th June 1650, which, among a variety of other regulations, ordains the clerks to detain all the papers produced with the fufpenfion ; or, if they happened to be taken away by the practitioners, they were to be liable for the fame. They were alfo obliged to give a certificate that the cautioners were truly defigned in the bonds of caution. Several other practical evils had received a check about the fame period. Reference had been made to the oaths of parties ; and, at the difcuffing, thefe references were deferted, and new reafons infifted upon. Bills were alfo paffed by all the Judges without diftinction. To prevent thefe practices in time coming, an act was made on the 16th January 1650. By thefe acts, to which, as they are very long and particular, reference is here made, the procefs upon bills of fufpenfion is brought into tolerable maturity, and every article of it remains in force. The former regulation appointed bills to be paffed only by the Lord Ordinary on the bills ; but it did not difcharge other Lords to grant fifts and ftops. Hence the old irregularity once more took place. At twenty five years diftance, another act of Sederunt became neceffary to reftore order in this branch of practice. This act is dated 9th February 1675 ; and, *inter alia*, difcharges all the Judges except the Lord Ordinary upon the bills to read bills of fufpenfion. or to grant fifts or ftops upon them. It then gives particular directions to the Ordinary on the bills how to act, which to this day remain in full obfervance.

It behoved fufpenfions prefented by people in prifon to contain a charge to liberate the prifoner, which therefore are termed SUSPENSION AND LIBERATION. Imprifonment being the laft and full effect of the diligence intended to compel obedience, payment ought to be the only method of immediate liberation. If fufpenfion, however, is demanded, that ought only to be granted upon confignation ; for

it

it is palpable injustice to make the creditor enter into the trouble and expence of a new plea, without absolute security for his debt. Liberations, however, were frequently obtained without consignation, and even upon very indifferent caution, whereby the diligence of the law came often to be defeated. A remedy for this evil was introduced by an act of Sederunt, 21st July 1675, which ordains the party to give intimation to the charger, before a notary and witnesses, of his intention of applying for suspension and liberation, and orders the instrument of intimation to be produced with the suspension. This was a necessary and beneficial regulation, and, as such, remains in full force.

All these acts are in favour of the creditor; the poor debtor had nothing to oppose against the rigour of his party, thus seconded by Judges armed even with legislative authority. Yet necessity, fertile in resources, appears to have been an overmatch for both. The Judges, when over-reached and provoked, made sometimes angry resolutions; and, when cool, softened the practice, which reduced matters to the old level. Thus juratory caution was introduced, not by any special statute, but by practical indulgence. There behoved to be poor men who had good exceptions to the claims made against them; but these exceptions could not be heard, because they were unable to find sufficient caution. Every evil has its remedy, and the Roman law suggested an easy one in this case. Therefore, where the suspender made oath that he could find no caution, or no better caution, any person was accepted of. This humanity was soon abused; and people possessed of sufficient property pretended that they could find no caution. Bills were passed in that manner unknown to the charger, whose diligence was thereby defeated. The practitioners ingeniously presented bills of suspension, containing offers of sufficient caution, in order to procure a favourable reception for the reasons; and, so soon as the bill passed, they added new reasons, and offered juratory caution. These abuses called loudly for amendment; and, for that purpose, an act of Sederunt was made upon the

8th of November 1682, which enacts, that all persons wishing to get suspensions on juratory caution, must mention that circumstance in their bills; and they must make intimation to the creditor of their intention, and produce the instrument with their suspension.

Even after suspensions were passed, the obtainers produced or intimated them to the party, or the messenger, but did not *expede them* at the Signet; and, as the effect of this was uncertain at the time, it fully answered the purpose of delay. The creditor was thus left at a loss what to do, because, not being summoned, he could not bring his party into Court; nor was the cautioner bound to him in that situation. This practical abuse was remedied by an act, 3d July 1677, ordaining the sist only to last for fourteen days, where suspensions had been passed but not expede at the Signet. A method was in a few years discovered, of eluding this salutary regulation. When the fourteen days were expired, a new bill was presented to a different Ordinary, and a new sist obtained. This practice, however, was discharged by act of Sederunt, 9th November 1680.

The former appointments, however strict, were, it seems, insufficient to repress the abominable practice of producing forged writs, which appears to have been the great engine of obtaining suspensions. The Lords were obliged to renew the act 1650, which certainly would not have been necessary, had the clerks to the bills done their duty; however an act passed, 11th November 1691, which inflicted severe additional penalties. The root of this inveterate evil lay in the rule of receiving no reasons of suspension, but such as were instantly verified. Many suspensions were rejected upon this account; and, to make sure, forgeries were committed, and known to be forgeries. For it is observable, that the users of false writs are not prosecuted as forgers; heavy damages and expences were the only penalties against the suspenders detected in that practice.

Where cautioners were unknown or dubious, suspenders offered to get them attested by people of better credit. These attestations
imported

imported no more than the opinion of the atteſtors; and, when the cautioners proved inſufficient, the chargers were landed in a proof of the condition of the cautioner at the time of the atteſt. Decrees charged upon were often found to be informal, or entirely in abſence, which the Court, therefore, turned into libels, *i. e.* they held the parties to be in Court, in the ſame manner as if the ſuſpender had been ſued upon a ſimple ſummons; and, when that happened, the cautioners inſiſted upon being free from their bond. To regulate theſe matters, an act of Sederunt was paſſed, 27th December 1709, which tied down both cautioners and atteſtors in all the caſes we have mentioned. The laſt part of this act, reſpecting cautioners, appears to be extremely hard and unreaſonable. They are bound only in the event of the charge's being right and formal; but the turning them into libels, ſhews that they are not ſo, and that the chargers were not entitled to obtain judgments in their favour; and, conſequently, that the cautioner ought to be free. The reaſon aſſigned in the act is far from being a good one; for, though it be true, that creditors allow many bills to paſs, on purpoſe to get additional ſecurity for their debt, yet it is plain, that a charger upon an informal decree could not have prevented a ſuſpenſion from taking place; and therefore he had no title to the ſecurity of the bond.

Anterior to this period, bills of ſuſpenſion muſt either have been refuſed or paſſed *in totum*; a circumſtance attended with much inconvenience, and the cauſe of a great deal of unneceſſary litigation, which, with other abuſes, was corrected by act of Sederunt, dated 20th November 1711. No other act became neceſſary, in the matter of ſuſpenſions, till of late, when the expence of diſputing the admiſſion of bills aroſe to a degree deſerving notice. Many of them were refuſed; and, where no penalty happened to be charged for, this expence could not readily be recovered. The Lords, therefore, by act, 19th December 1778, ordained that the Lord Ordinary on

ther

the bills should be allowed to award expences against parties suspending on frivolous grounds.

Our present forms, then, in bills of suspension, are the result of two hundred years experience; and, from the several regulations made in that period, we easily discover the reason and necessity of all the steps now in practice.

The first thing is to draw or prepare the bill. For this purpose, we must be possessed of the charge given by the messenger, and of the decree, bond, contract, or other ground of debt demanded. These we are, in the first place, carefully to read over. If it be a decree, we may analize it, and consider whether the demand or conclusion of the libel be fairly authorised by the narrative. We next attend to the production, and how far the libel is thereby proved by writing. If all or part of it be made out or founded upon parole testimony, we consider whether such evidence was competent in the question; and examine the interlocutors of the judge allowing the proof. When this is done, we peruse attentively the depositions of witnesses, and the final interlocutor. Hence we form our opinion whether the judgment is right or wrong, in point of fact; or whether it goes further than the written or parole evidence imports. Being thus masters of facts in the case, we are able to form a judgment of the story told by our employer; and what facts it may be proper to add, or what further evidence it may be safe to offer. The next thing is the law, and the reasoning. With these we are furnished in the papers of debate, which the extract contains in the order given in the process. We reduce them into short points; then consult the Institutes for the general principles; next the course of decisions upon the subject, correcting what was wrong in the argument of the decree, and supplying what seems to have been there omitted. Last of all, we search for exceptions in point of form; and, from our notes taken upon the whole, we compose the bill of suspension. If the charge is grounded upon deeds of any kind, we should not be satisfied with particular parts of clauses, but

ought

ought to read them *verbatim* from beginning to end, and be particularly attentive to the testing clause ; for, in that place, material additions or conditions are frequently inserted ; and particular notice should be taken whether there be any defect in the statutary solemnities.

A bill of suspension consists of three parts. First, It specifies the demand made, and the authority for that demand ; whether decree, registered bond, or bill, &c. For doing this, the charge given must be the rule. It is the duty of the clerk to compare this part of the bill with the charge, and to refuse to present it if there is a discrepancy. The reason is, that the terms of the charge are the rule for the terms of the bond of caution. The next part of the bill is a narrative of the transaction between the parties. Here the suspender accounts for the manner in which he became bound, granted the deed charged upon, or stands subjected to the demand made. In composing this narration lie the chief art and address of the practitioner : It ought to be perspicuous, probable, and adapted to persuasion, by pointing out, in easy and forcible language, but in a general manner, the errors in law, in fact, or in reasoning, which have brought the suspender into that situation. If this is properly done, the particular objection will arise during the perusal. The mind of the Judge is thereby toned and prepared to receive the reasons favourably, because they coincide with his own preconceived opinion. These reasons compose the third part, and ought to be so many plain and natural inferences from the recital. In point of order, the established rule in reasoning should be followed, *i. e.* part of the strongest reasons should be placed first, in order to strike the judgment of the reader ; the weakest should be ranged in the middle ; and the remainder of the best reasons in the end ; because, what is last heard, leaves, in general, the strongest impression.

When the bill of suspension is presented, the clerk writes the date upon the back, towards the top of the sheet. He then reads it to the Lord Ordinary on the bills, who, if dissatisfied with the reasons, refuses

refuses it *instanter*; upon which the clerk writes the refusal upon the bill. Sometimes the Lord Ordinary adds the reason of refusal; and formerly, by the act of Sederunt 1675, was obliged to do so. This refused bill is detained by the clerk, in terms of that act, in order to produce when a new one is presented.

If the reasons appear good or plausible, the Lord Ordinary orders execution to be sisted, and the bill to be answered; and, for that purpose, generally intimated to the charger. This is written in a detached place towards the foot of the bill, as directed by the act of Sederunt 1675; because, if the bill afterwards passes, the sist, being a matter of expedience, is not connected with, or mentioned in the interlocutor of passing. The order to see and answer is also directed by the act 1695, with this difference, that it was formerly only done upon application of the party; whereas it is now done of course in every case. The Lord Ordinary is not obliged to appoint intimation in all cases, because it is presumed the suspender will take that method for his own safety. Public intimation is also presumed to be given by a sist-roll hung up in the Bill Chamber, of all suspensions presented, in terms of the act 1711, to which every new bill is instantly added. In most cases, the Ordinary appoints bills to be intimated, especially where they contain any pointed allegations which appear to admit of an immediate answer. Formerly, it was the practice, that, when the suspender got back his bill, he was obliged to leave a copy of it for the charger in the Chamber. These copies came afterwards to be made by the assistant clerk in the office, and make one of their chief perquisites. The Ordinary may, if he pleases, sist for a month; but ten days is the usual time; and the act of Sederunt 1680 declares, that fourteen days is the full time for seeing and expeding the bill, that is, for doing the whole business.

The sist thus granted is delivered to the presenter, who intimates it to the charger, or his doer, by a notary public, or by his own clerk, or any other person, though formerly it always was done in presence

:presence of a notary public and witnesses, in order that a contempt might evidently be proved.

On the other hand, the agent for the charger, who suspects the suspender's intention of presenting a bill, if he either determines to oppose, or to procure proper caution for his employer, does not trust to these intimations. He gives in a note to the clerk of the bills of the names of the parties, and requires him to give notice so soon as such a bill is presented. He is, besides, attentive to the public and daily rolls, and Minute-Book kept in the Bill Chamber. If by any of these means he is properly apprised, he either prepares and lodges answers, or consents to the bill being passed, upon sufficient caution.

In answering bills, we are obliged to follow the order of the reasons, that is, we give a state of the facts or procedure from the information of our employer, contrasting it strongly with the recital in the bill, and thence deducing the answer to each reason in a close, pointed style, carrying an air of conviction in the writer. This answer is followed by a reply from the suspender; so that the passing of a bill becomes a hot dispute, or preliminary process, which draws time, and occasions considerable expence.

Written debates upon bills of suspension carried on in this manner, were early found to be distressing both to the Judges and the parties; insomuch that, by a clause in an act of Sederunt, not yet mentioned, June 2. 1675, ' The Lords discharged any written dis-
' pute upon bills of suspension or advocation; but, where the Or-
' dinary upon the bills shall think fit to allow a bill to be seen, that
' he call the parties the next day, and hear what they have to say
' *viva voce,* without taking in written answers.' This prohibition was not observed; only, it has ever since been held, that an answer cannot be received without an order from the Judge. It must, upon the whole, be confessed, that this part of the business is attended with a great deal of trouble to the practitioners.

Suspenders kept up their principal bills, and would not return them to the Chamber to be answered or advised. The timidity of

chargers

chargers suffered this practice to become a real nuisance; whereas nothing prevented them from executing their diligence after
the days are elapsed; for it will be remembered, that the acts of
Sederunt allowed but fourteen days in common; and the Lord Ordinary himself has no power to continue it above a month. The
Court, however, having punished some real contempts of their authority in matters of suspension, messengers grew timid, and were
often terrified from their duty by suspenders assuring them that their
bills remained in dependence, though, in fact, refused. To remove
these scruples, parties obtained certificates from the clerks, that such
a bill was refused; and this certificate was given to the messenger
with the caption. Hence a notion has prevailed, that, after a suspension is once intimated, nothing can be done till a certificate be
taken out; but for this there is no foundation; nor is the certificate, in these cases, of any real use.

When the written debate is ended, the Lord Ordinary peruses the
whole, and either refuses or passes the bill. If the charger desires
it, the bill is passed, and the consent marked in the interlocutor,
which is in these words, generally written below the principal deliverance ' *Pass of consent*,' or the ' *Lord Ordinary passes this bill of*
' *consent.*' Nothing more is written on the bill till caution be
found; and, by act of Sederunt 1677, this lasts just fourteen days;
these days being given to find caution, and expede the letters, unless
a further delay is given for that purpose by special deliverance; but
this day must not exceed a month, in terms of the act 1677. If
further time be wanted, a new bill must be given in; and, by act
1680, presented to three Lords, in time of vacation, or to the whole,
in time of session; but this act is nugatory; for that proviso only
delays the matter longer, as, bills once passed, the same reasons are
seldom refused in a second, if a good apology be made for the delay.

A bond of caution is next made out and executed by the cautioner to be proposed, the form of which may be found in Dallas
                                                              and

and Spottifwood. Almoft every word of this bond is dictated by the acts of Sederunt which we have heard. After the narrative, it proceeds thus :

'*Bind and oblige me, my heirs, executors, and fucceffors whatfo-*'*ever, as cautioners, fureties, and full debtors with and for C. D.*'
—This is obvioufly in obedience to the act 1650; it is to bind the cautioner, after the death either of the charger or fufpender, by making him equally debtor as the fufpender himfelf.

'*Acted in the books of Council and Seffion,*'—*i. e.* enacted in the books of Seffion, the bonds being originally written in a book, by way of a judicial act, in the fame manner as the enactments of cautionry are, at this moment, in the books of inferior courts. Afterwards, for the convenience of people at a diftance, they were taken feparately, but ftill confidered as an enactment of Court.

'*That he fhall make payment to the faid C. D. or any other perfon*'*who fhall be found to have right thereto.*'—This alternative is the addition appointed by the act 1717, in order to meet the cafe of third parties appearing for their intereft in the courfe of the fufpenfion, and claiming the proceeds ; and which entitles the party found to have the right, to give a direct and fummary charge. Spottifwood fays, that this claufe is proper to fufpenfions upon double poindings ; but he is miftaken, the act and the purpofe being equally general.

'*As alfo, of what further fums may be decerned for by our faid*'*Lords, in name of expences of plea, and damage, in cafe of wrongful*'*fufpending.*'—This is in obedience to the act of Sederunt 1613. Spottifwood omits this altogether in the ftyle he gives in his collection, which is a great error ; but it is fupplied in the form given in the fupplement to his book.

When this bond is executed, it is offered to the clerk of the bills, who either accepts it from his own knowledge, or demands an atteftor, in cafe of doubt. If the fufpender agrees, an atteftation is executed, which is worded in terms of the act 1709, and renders the atteftor equally liable as the cautioner, after the latter is difcuffed.

If the suspender is of opinion, that the cautioner he offers is sufficient, and an attestation inconvenient, he must protest against the clerk of the bills for his damages, in terms of an act of Sederunt made in this behalf, 18th February 1686 *, which puts the clerk to the bills in a very perilous situation ; but the danger equals not the appearance : It is only the reputation of the party at the time, which the clerk has to answer for. So far not only is the depute clerk liable, but also the principal, and even the Lord Register. If the clerk to the bills persist in the refusal, there is no remedy but an application to the Lords. Lord Stair says, though the Lords be judges of the clerk's reasons of refusal, yet they seldom enter into that debate, but allow the clerk to do as he judges best. In practice, this point is generally settled between the agents for the parties ; and, where the cautioner is unknown to the clerk, some person of credit must inform him as to that person. This dispute about the cautioner often draws more time than the fourteen days ; but, until he is positively refused, the sist is understood to remain in force.

If no cautioner be offered, or if the person offered be refused, and the fourteen days expired, without any new sist or prolongation, the charger may proceed in his diligence ; but, for security, he generally takes a certificate of that fact from the clerk. In case a bond had been actually lodged and objected to, and the objection sustained, the clerk adds a note, expressive of the case, to the certificate. When the bond is received or accepted by the clerk, then, and not till then, he, in terms of the act of Sederunt 1599, fills up the days of compearance in the blank of the bill, together with the name of
the

* ' The Lords of Council and Session considering that parties may be prejudged, ' not only by the clerk to the bills his receiving of insolvent cautioners, but also by ' refusing of cautioners who are sufficient ; therefore they declare, That the clerk of ' the bills shall be liable for the party's damage, as well where he refuses a caution- ' er who is sufficient, or is holden and repute to be sufficient, as where he receives ' an insufficient cautioner.'

the cautioner; and, upon the margin, he marks caution received, and figns his initials. The bill then becomes a proper warrant for authorifing the letter of fufpenfion to pafs the Signet.

If a fecond bill be prefented, it muft be to three Lords, in time of vacation, or reported to the whole Lords, in time of Seffion, in terms of the act, 9th November 1680, as before obferved. If a bill be refufed in the vacation, another may be prefented to the Lords in courfe, who, by the act 1675, muft not pafs the fame without advifing with three Lords. By the fame act, the clerk muft produce to him the refufed bill; but, in order to avoid this, it is ufual to annex new matter, or new reafons, to the fecond bill, which juftifies the Ordinary in confidering and paffing the fame by himfelf. In thefe cafes, the execution is held to be fifted till three Lords meet, who muft pafs the fame *unico contextu.*

If the decree was pronounced by the Court of Seffion *in foro contradictorio,* that is, when compearance had once been made by the defender, and defences proposed, though fuch appearance fhould afterwards be withdrawn, the bill cannot be paffed but by the whole Lords, or by three Ordinaries; and, that this circumftance might be known to the clerk of the bills, a lift of all decrees *in foro* is appointed to be fent him by the Keeper of the Minute-Book, by the regulations 1672; but this is now omitted in practice. Neither ought a bill of this kind to be paffed but upon confignation, though, in practice, caution is every day received.

If a bill be refufed in time of feffion, it is not the practice to prefent a fecond; in place of that, a petition is given in to the Court, ftating the reafons, complaining of the judgment of the Ordinary, and praying the Lords to pafs the bill. This petition is either refufed fimply, or appointed to be anfwered againft a day certain. When the anfwer comes in, the matter is at once put into the fhort roll, and advifed. If the Lords pafs it, it is termed a bill paffed *in praefentia.* Parties, in fome cafes, willing to get clear of the diet of compearance, consent to discuss the reasons upon the bill. This belongs to the form of process, and so cannot at present be entered into.

The bill being passed, it is carried to the Signet, with the letters as the warrant for signeting, and left with the Keeper, who carefully lays it up as a matter of record, and gives extracts of it upon occasions, which will afterwards be explained.

It is now time to consider the letters of suspension, which we shall take from St Martin; for, if we thoroughly understand the old forms, we can never be at a loss for the new ones. This form, it will be observed, is exactly that of a summons, or *fiat summonitio*, the charge is libelled; the reasons which render it unjust and illegal, and the caution found; and then it concludes, that the same should be suspended by the Lords.

'*Wrongously and unjustly.*'—*Wrongous* is an old Scotticism, now obsolete. There is no such English word; it should be *wrongfully*. The reasons of suspension being, in general, grounded upon equity, and pointed against the letter and rigour of the law, the writ uses the language of complaint, applied to the equitable powers of the Court.

'*Suspended upon the complainers*,'—*i. e.* hung up over them, so as not to fall or take effect; for a suspension does not extinguish the ground of debt. To do this, an action of reduction is requisite.

'*Relaxed from the horn,*' &c.—This conclusion, at that time, was most necessary, for reasons already explained.

'*And others to be proponed at discussing.*'—This was added to insure to the party the power of eiking or adding his further reasons at discussing, which was anciently disallowed. The day to which the charger is appointed by the will to be summoned, is fixed by the deliverance on the bill; and the diligence is only suspended till the next day mentioned in the will, *that the verity be known;* by which it was originally meant, that the intervening space between the day of compearance, and the day of suspension, was sufficient

for

'for difcuffing reafons, which, by law, muft or ought to have been either inftantly verified or repelled. As that bufinefs, however, was found to draw longer time, it was early underftood, that the effect of the fufpenfion continued during the dependence of the queftion; at the fame time, if the fufpender did not execute his fufpenfion, by fummoning the charger to the day fixed by the letters, the effect of it ceafed at the expiration of the fecond day, according to the literal terms of the will, and the charger was at liberty to proceed. In order to underftand this perfectly, it muft be noticed, that, according to the ancient form, a party defender had no method of forcing his adverfary into Court, unlefs he was poffeffed of an execution of fummons; and, in common actions, it is the cafe at this moment; confequently, at that time, a charger who ftood defender in the fufpenfion, in cafe it was not executed againft him, had no other remedy but the expiration of the days. After cautioners, however, were introduced, and looked to as the fecurity, this method did not fuit the charger's intereft; he did not choofe that the fufpenfion fhould drop; and hence the remedy of proteftation came to be allowed him, whether the fufpenfion was executed or not. Since that time, few fufpenfions have been executed. This may, however, be done at any time, and is, without doubt, the moft regular method of procedure.

' *Becaufe J. B. has become cautioner for the complainer.*'—When cautioners were introduced, the Keeper of the Signet, as a further check, was ordered not to fix the feal to any fufpenfions in which caution was not found, and mentioned to be fo in the letters; in the fame manner as he was afterwards difcharged to receive any letters but fuch as had annexed to them the name of the Judge who paffed the bill. Thence it came to be a general rule, to infert, in every cafe, the whole words of the deliverance in all letters paffing the Signet, immediately after the words *according to juftice;* from the firft word, this claufe came to be termed the *becaufe*, which always makes a parenthefis. This is the place which the Keeper of the
Signet

Signet compares with the bill ; and, if any of the words are omitted, he rejects the letters.

The date of the suspension is always the date of presentment of the bill, because the intermediate procedure is then held to be of no consequence, and the bill is presumed to have passed, like others, upon the day of being presented.

If we act for the charger, it is our duty to inquire whether or not the suspension be truly expeded at the Signet within fourteen days after the caution is received, and the bill passed ; for, if that is not done, we are at liberty to proceed, in terms of the act, 9th November 1680. If we neglect this, and trust to the putting up of a protestation when the session sits, we may lose the benefit of the caution ; for, unless the letters have been signeted, the cautioner is not bound.

In case the debtor be in prison before the suspension be applied for, we must give notice to the creditor or his agent, under form of instrument, by a notary and witnesses, of the time when the bill is to be presented, and produce an instrument to that purpose. In this case, it will be remembered, that juratory caution cannot be received. If the bill passes, the letters contain a warrant to charge the magistrates of the burgh where the debtor is confined, to give him immediate liberty. The compulsitor, in case of non-compliance with the charge, is the old one, of denouncing the magistrates to the horn ; so that it is in their power to detain the prisoner in jail for a considerable time ; and this, we are told, was frequently practised previous to the Revolution ; but, since that time, instant obedience is given to the letters of liberation.

Thus we have gone through the whole law and practice relating to bills of suspension. At present, we proceed no further than the *expeding of the letters*, because the after steps are properly judicial, and make a part of the forms of process before the Court. This subject, therefore, will be properly concluded with two or three specialities.

cialities which belong to it, but which would have interrupted the course of our inquiry.

When bills are passed upon consignation, the clerk is entitled to one shilling in the pound, or five *per cent.*; one half of which is paid by the consigner, and the other by the receiver; although, when sums are large, a composition is always accepted of. A bond of caution must, notwithstanding, be given for the expence of process, and for damages.

Though suspension be truly a summons, and is granted by a *fiat summonitio*, yet it is termed *letters of suspension.* All writs passing the Signet are divided into *summonses* and *letters. Letters* are said to respect immediate execution, or something to take instantaneous effect in behalf of the party who obtains them; but *summonses* have no effect but that of bringing a defender into Court; and, as a suspension has the effect of stopping diligence without bringing the party into Court, it is ranked among the letters.

As bail-bonds are excepted from the stamp-act, and a bond in a suspension is properly an act of Court, it is not written upon stamped-paper. When bills of suspension pass on juratory caution, the debtor ought to appear in person before the Lord Ordinary, and make an oath that he can find no other caution. He should also, like a pursuer in a *cessio bonorum*, lodge a disposition *omnium bonorum* with the clerk. The Lord Ordinary generally grants a commission to the clerk to take the oath, which he writes on the back of the disposition. This disposition lies in the records of Court; and, if the charger prevail, he extracts it at the same time with his decree, and claims the property to the extent of his debt, which generally brings on a second action, where little can be got but trouble and expence. The Court have established, that cautioners in suspensions are not liberated, though no diligence be done in seven years from the date, but that they continue bound so long as the charge lasts, which therefore runs the long prescription of forty years.

years. This circumstance renders cautionry in suspensions more dangerous than in any other transaction; and, what adds to the hazard, is the uncertainty of the amount; for the expence of procefs often exceeds the original debt; yet there is no obligation which people, in general, fo eafily go into; and, therefore, when we act for cautioners, it is our duty to explain to them the extent of their undertaking.

Binding.

Poinding.

IN treating the curious and very interesting subject of Poinding, it is necessary to distinguish the several kinds of it established in our law. That done, we shall single out the species which is to be particularly considered, borrowing only from the others what may be necessary for illustration. The first kind of poinding is that by land-proprietors and superiors for the rents and duties owing by their vassals and tenants. We term this the *first*, because it is the most ancient, and evidently appears to have given birth to the whole practice. The next species, in the order of time, is the poinding of moveables, at the instance of creditors, for payment of their debts. The third is the poinding of tenants by heritable creditors, which we denominate *poinding the ground*, but which, in reality, differs not from the first kind, except in form, the principle being the same; and, lastly, there is the poinding of the land itself, the true poinding of the ground before the introduction of adjudication, and which was commonly termed *apprising*.

It is the poinding or execution against moveables, for payment of common debt, which we are at present particularly to treat of; but all the rest mentioned are intimately connected, frequently meet in the course of their progress, and reflect a mutual light upon each other. While the military or feudal system remained in what is termed its purity, land was the only object of property; moveables stood in no consideration; the land was held by the vassal by a variety of conditions; and a breach of any of them forfeited the fief, and entitled the lord to re-enter to the possession of it. Traffic being unknown amongst a people fitted for, and employed in war alone, the only debts or claims then existing were feudal, arising from the rents or services due for land; so that, for a long period, land alone may be said to have been taken in execution, in the first instance. Afterwards, this rigour declined; feus were granted upon other considerations; and the people, by enjoying long possession of the same spot, acquired a stock of goods and cattle. It appeared, in this situation, evidently unnecessary and unjust in the lords to seize upon the land, when the moveables upon it were more than sufficient to answer the amount of his demands; and hence arose the practice of the lord seizing the goods of his vassal, instead of the land itself. It will here be observed, that the superior's true claim lay against the lands themselves, and not against the goods which were not held of him; and, therefore, though he seized the goods, he did not apply them in payment, but was obliged to detain them as a pledge, in order to force or distress the tenant into payment, or performance of what he was due for the lands. Hence the thing seized was termed *a distress*; and the action of the superior in seizing it, was called *distressing*. The goods seized not being made the property of the lord, he was obliged to have a place for keeping them, which was termed a *park* or *pound*; and it continues in England to be so termed at this moment. The putting the goods or cattle seized into this place, always was, and is yet termed *pounding them*; and hence, by a small variation in our orthography, we have our common word *poind*, which does not seem to have been applied in the manner in which it now is, until about the middle of the fifteenth century. This mode of distressing vassals was done by the proper authority of the lords themselves, *i. e.* they seized and poinded the goods; but the King's officers or judge of the place had power to redeliver them to the vassal or tenant, upon his finding security for his lord's satisfaction. This

was.

was termed *repledging*; and the interference of the King's judge was held to be a *juftification*. A plain remainder of thefe manners we have in the poinding by our heritors or barons for their rents.

One of the capital difputes between Henry III. of England, and his barons, refpected the powers which thefe barons affumed, of doing every thing at their own hand. They feized the goods by themfelves and their officers, and they refufed to allow them to be repledged. They drove the cattle into other counties, and committed the moft grievous oppreffion in every poffible fhape. Even thefe men who had obtained Magna Charta, who had eftablifhed liberty fword in hand, meant that liberty for none but themfelves; nay, they included in their idea of it, the power of oppreffing every creature under them. An old chronicle, mentioning this circumftance, fays, that the barons, after they carried their point, *evaferunt totidem ty-ranni*; and, as the commons could not refift their oppreffion, the only altar of refuge was in the Crown. The barons infifted upon determining their own acts of oppreffion in their own courts, and protecting their officers, the tools of their cruelty, under their own jurifdiction. ' Thofe powers (fays the Honourable Daines Bar- ' rington) which they could not obtain from the King, they exer- ' cifed during the enfuing troubles; and it was high time to put a ' ftop to thefe enormities and violations of juftice, which was effec- ' ted by removing the complaint from the court of the great baron ' to thofe of the King, where the judges were indifferent between ' the oppreffed peafant and the tyrannical lord *.'

In the very ancient ftatute to which Barrington here refers †, the diftinction is clearly marked between the poinding of vaffals, and the poinding of debtors. Landlords were entitled to make their diftrefs *brevi manu*, and they are fo at this moment by their own officer. The ufurpation corrected was, that thefe barons or great men refufed to be juftified by the King's courts, *i. e.* they refufed to do juftice

to

---

* Barrington on the Statutes, p. 58. † 52d Henry III. c. 1.

to the party by allowing the legality of the diſtreſs, or claim, to be tried by the law. Following the example of the great men, private people ventured to diſtreſs one another for debts. In theſe, it was illegal to make the diſtreſs itſelf without the award of court; and the practice is accordingly diſcharged.

The ſame practice had taken place in Scotland, but not to ſuch a high degree, though our national troubles had been greater and longer than in England. With regard to great men, a ſtatute of Robert I. remains equally explicit with that of Henry III. Lord Kaimes mentions ſeveral of the ſtatutes by which ſuch licences were reſtrained. The firſt is c. 7. of the firſt ſtatute of the ſame Prince, Robert I. ſtatuting, ' That, in time coming, na man ſall take ane poynd for ' anie debt auchtand to himſelf within ane other man's land or he-' ritage, bot gif the King's baillie, or the baillie of the ground, be ' preſent.'

That theſe acts, like that of Henry III. were correctory of an il-legal practice, is evident from ſection fourth of the laſt act. ' Na ' man ſall take ane diſtreſs or poind, without his awn fee or heri-' tage, for ſervice aucht to him furth of lands halden of him, nor ' ſall not take any ſuperfluous diſtreſs.' Here, it will be obſerved, the ſame diſtinction is made as in the Engliſh ſtatute. A landlord might legally take a diſtreſs, at his own hand, within his own fee and heritage ; but it never could be legal that he ſhould do ſo in any place without that juriſdiction. Creditors in ordinary debts were, in no ſhape, entitled to make the diſtreſs *brevi manu,* without the authority of an officer of the law. The ſame law is diſtinctly renewed by c. 12. of the ſtatutes of Robert III. ' *Item,* It is ſtatute ' generally by the King, that na man ſall take ane poynd without ' the King's officears, or the lord's officears of the land, bot within ' his awn dominions, for his fermis or proper debts.' ' And gif ' anie man take ane poynd without officears of the King, or of the ' lord of the ground, troubles any man's lands, or takes or carries ' away any thing furth of them ; that poinding before the lieute-
' nant

' nant or the jufticiar fall be efteemed and halden as rief be dittay
' or be pledge, *i. e.* (Skene adds) be borgh or caution to be found
' by the poynder at a certain day.'

The repetitions of the fame laws at different periods, fhow that the
practice was always illegal ; for, fuppofing we had loft all the ftatutes prior to Robert III. it would be a miftaken inference thence to
fuppofe that the practice had been legal prior to the date of that act.
The taking of thefe diftreffes was not an execution, but merely to
force the party to appear before the judge, and to find caution for
performance of the decree. Thus, by the 22d chapter of the 4th
book of Regiam Majeftatem, which exprefsly treats of this fubject,
it is provided, ' That pledges being found, the poind fall be fent
' back again to the place wherein they were firft taken ; and he
' qua took the poind, if he pleafe, fall come to that place, and crave
' his debt.'

A remainder of *brevi manu* poinding ftill exifts, viz. the poinding
of cattle trefpaffing upon fields that belong to other men, which,
from the neceffity of the thing, exifts in every country of Europe.
A poinding of this kind is not an execution, i. e. the cattle are not
feized with an intention to alter the property, but to force payment
of the damage done by them. Our writers generally confound thefe
circumftances of ancient poindings.

By a proper explanation of the doctrine of diftreffes, the vail is
in a manner drawn from before the ancient forms and principles of
the law both in England and Scotland. All jurifdiction, from the
baron to the King, was founded upon feudal ideas. Attendance at
the lords courts, or fuit fervice, was a part of the duty due by the
vaffal for the land ; and, as the whole fubjects were feudatories of
the Sovereign, they all owed attendance at his courts. The payment of rents, or the non-performance of duties, we have heard,
were, after the eftablifhment of the vaffal's property in the land, enforced by feizure or diftrefs of his moveables. If the lord's claim
confifted in performance of fomething upon the part of the vaffal to
which

which a diftrefs could not be commenfurated ; or, in the language
of our law, if the demand was not liquid, fo as a poinding could be
executed to the exact amount, then one diftrefs followed another,
till the vaffal was conftrained to performance ; which practice is yet
well known, under the title of *diftrefs infinite.* Now, the fuit in
fervice, or the attendance at the court of the lord, in obedience to
his decrees, was evidently a feudal duty incumbent upon the vaffal,
in confequence of the property held by him. If he failed in rendering this fervice, he was liable to a fine ; and the payment of this
fine was inforced by diftrefs. If he did not pay or perform the fecond time, he was again diftreffed, and fo *ad infinitum,* till he rendered due obedience. From this fource arofe the profits, unlaws,
fines, and amerciaments of the feudal courts, from thofe of the Sovereign down to the baron ; and thus the fyftem of diftreffes came
to be completely eftablifhed over the whole kingdom. Obedience
to the decrees of the courts became, in this view, a part of the duty
of the lieges or fubjects, independent of all other confiderations,
upon which politicians and moralifts build the fabric of fociety. If
the parties did not appear in court, they were compelled by a diftrefs of their effects ; and, if they did not obey the judgment given,
the decree was alfo made good by diftrefs, which was the general
fyftem eftablifhed in the country. Let us next inquire into the progrefs of the fame bufinefs in our burghs.

By charter 47th chapter of the Leges Burgorum, it is provided,
' That nae burgefs may tak a poynd frae another burgefs, but he fhall
' pafs to his houfe with ane officear or fergeant, and fall affign him
' ane day to compear at the next court. Gif he refufes to pay the
' debt, and gif he pleafe to pay it, he fall pay it. And gif he com-
' pears not at the day affigned to him, he fall be unlawed, and fall
' be fummoned again to compear at the next courts following.'
The poind here mentioned was not meant to be taken in execution,
but as a pledge for appearance in court, and obedience to the decree. The fuit being determined, execution could not take place but
by

by authority. So we find by c. 4. of thefe laws, ‘ That ane
‘ burgefs may not poynd ane other burgefs dwelland within the
‘ famen burgh, without licence of his provoft.’ But, with refpeƈ
to ftrangers, the cafe altered widely. The 3d chapter of the fame
laws declares, ‘ That a burgefs may poynd ane uplandfman, (fo
‘ Skene tranflates *foris babitantes*), or the burgefs of another burgh,
‘ without the time of mercat within or without the houfe.’ By
chapter 37. it is provided, ‘ That uplandfmen may repledge their
‘ poynds three times, frae ane ouke to another ouke; and thereaf-
‘ ter by thrie days, and na longer.’

‘ And gif they will not, be reafon of frowartnefs, loufe their
‘ poynds, be finding of pledges therefore, and they die for hunger;
‘ gif it be ane horfe, or other beaft, the burgefs fall caufe it be drawn
‘ forth of the houfe and gar flea it, and fall keep the forehead and
‘ the taill, and thereafter fall take ane other poynd for his debt.’

Here is evidently the continued diftrefs of the Englifh law; for
the poinder could not fell the horfe or other animal poinded; it was
no more than a diftrefs to force him to find a pledge or bail for the
debt within the jurifdiƈtion of the burgh.

Lord Kaimes falls into a miftake in treating of this fubjeƈt. He
conftantly fuppofes the diftrefs for appearance, and the execution
for payment, to be the fame thing. ‘ While the practice (fays his
‘ Lordfhip) fubfifted of poinding *brevi manu* for payment of debt,
‘ there was no neceffity for the interpofition of a judge to force pay-
‘ ment. When courts, therefore, were inftituted, a procefs of debt
‘ was not known. The rough practice of forcing payment by pri-
‘ vate power being prohibited, an aƈtion became neceffary; and the
‘ King interpofed by a brieve, direƈting one or other judge to try
‘ the caufe *.’

The purpofe of the *brevi manu* poinding in the burghs, which his
Lordfhip had juft mentioned, had no other intention than to force
the:

* Traƈts, p. 303.

the stranger before a court; and such was the sole purpose of this species of poinding both by landlords and creditors. The execution for payment of the debt was, from the earliest notices of history or record, by public authority alone. Were we to admit hasty conjecture, it would be to allow, that there was no law in the kingdom anterior to the statutes of the Scottish Princes quoted by his Lordship; and that the first jurisdiction known was established by brieves from the King, which became necessary after the prohibition of the rough practices he alludes to. This would be wide, indeed, of historical truth. The Saxon polity, which existed before the conquest, is the boast of English lawyers and politicians. The business of the nation was, at that period, executed in the county courts in a manner envied by after ages. The Conqueror ruined that masterpiece, as it is termed, of judicial polity, and erected upon its ruins the Aula Regis; and thence issued the Norman brieves, purposely (as Judge Gilbert observes) to give the nation to know, that not a motion was to be made, or a suit to be determined, without a special command from the Prince. The same forms were introduced into Scotland at the earliest periods we are acquainted with; and it is clear, that a complete set of brieves, suited to the business of the nation, had been long and perfectly established prior to the laws by which Lord Kaimes tells us the *brevi manu* poinding was discharged, and the brieves rendered necessary.

We will now proceed to the writs which authorised the execution of poind or distress in both kingdoms; and here we are sorry to be obliged to correct another error of that eminent lawyer. ' The brieve ' of distress (says he) corresponding to the English brieve *justities*, ' must be examined more deliberately, because it makes a figure in ' our law.' After mentioning the effect of the Scots brieve of distress, he says, ' This brieve explains a maxim of the common law ' of England, Quod placita de catallis, debitis, &c. quae summam ' quadragintorum

* P. 303.

' quadragintorum folidorum attingunt vel excedunt, fecundum le-
' gem et confuetudinem Angliae fine brevi regis placitari non de-
' bent *.' The original jurifdi&ion of the fheriff of England extended to all civil caufes whatever. The reftri&ion of it to forty
fhillings without a brieve, did not arife from an indulgence; it arofe
from the revolution in the government of the kingdom introduced
after the Norman conqueft. If the fheriff happened to be an Eng-
lifhman, he was ignorant of the new fyftem of Norman laws; and
if a Norman, which was generally the cafe, his jury or affize were
Saxons, and would not find in the cafe as he directed; which at laft
brought the county courts into difrepute, and carried every thing to
the Aula Regis, the court of the King. This was a part of the
plan laid by the Conqueror, and purfued by his fons, to fubdue the
kingdom, and they completely effected it. The fupreme courts refufed to receive trifling caufes, and reftri&ed the value to forty fhillings; and therefore it was that fuitors were afterwards obliged, before being entitled to bring an action in the King's courts, to make
affidavit that the value of the thing claimed exceeded forty fhillings.
The limitation of the jurifdi&ion of the fheriff, therefore, to this
fmall extent, did not, as Lord Kaimes fuppofes, proceed from an
indulgence granted by the Crown; it was a remainder of an original jurifdi&ion vefted in him by the old common law of England;
and therefore the writ or fummons proceeded, and ftill proceeds, by
his own authority. It is termed a *diftringas*, or county warrant,
and is in this form: ' Preceptum eft ballivo ibidem quod diftrin-
' gat F. D. per omnia bona et catalla fua quod fit ad proximum co-
' mitatum meum ad refpondendum A. B. de placito debito, tefte
' meipfo.' &c. The fheriff derived his right from the ancient *comes*
or *earl* of the county. His power was confidered to be ftri&ly ter-
ritorial or feudal; and, therefore, as lord of the county, he could
only inforce that jurifdi&ion by diftrefs infinite, juft iike a proprie-

VOL. I. 3 D tor

---

* This rule he quotes from Bacon's abridgement.

tor of land ; and, for every default of appearance, the defendant, like a tenant or vaſſal, is, at the moment, diſtrainable till he come into court, and give common bail. The King, however, in ſome caſes, in order to ſave expence to parties, returned to the ſheriff his ancient juriſdiction in a particular caſe. This he did, or ſtill may do, by a brieve, termed *juſtities,* which is the writ mentioned by Lord Kaimes as analogous to our brieve of diſtreſs.

‘ In the county courts, (ſays Dalton), pleas are ſometimes holden ‘ by the King’s writ out of Chancery, which is called *a juſtities,* or ‘ vicecomitial writ, for that it doth give ſpecial power to the ſheriff ‘ to hold plea in his county court ; and this writ is for the diſpatch ‘ of juſtice in ſpecial cauſes, wherewith the ſheriff, of his own au- ‘ thority, cannot deal in his county court, and is, in effect, but a ‘ commiſſion, and giveth this authority to the ſheriff in theſe words * : “ Praecipimus tibi quod juſtities A. quod juſte et ſine dilatione red- “ dat B. viginti ſolidos quos ei debet, ut dicit, ſicut rationabiliter “ monſtrare poteſt, quod ei reddere debet, ne amplius inde clamo- “ rem audiamus pro defectu juſtitiae,” &c.

The very ſame brieve we find to have been an eſtabliſhed form in the law of Scotland, as early as any knowledge we have of that law. It was termed *breve de debitis,* the brieve of diſtreſs for debts ; and, by c. 5. of the Regiam Majeſtatem, c. 4. we find, ‘ That it was to ‘ be determined before the juſticear, ſheriff, or baillies of burghs, as ‘ it ſhould pleaſe the King by his letter to command them particu- ‘ larly, within his juriſdiction †.’ The difference between our brieve of diſtreſs, and the Engliſh *juſtities,* lay only in this circumſtance, that the execution upon the *juſtities* proceeded by diſtreſs in the ſame manner as in a common caſe. The compulſitor, therefore, was limited to mere diſtreſs, as in a cauſe of forty ſhillings value. The Scots brieve of diſtreſs gave the ſheriff not only a power to ſell, but, upon defect of the ſale, to compriſe and deliver them to the creditor

in

* P. 420.   † Vide Quon. Attach. c. 49.

in payment of his debt, which was a plain and a complete remedy. Lord Kaimes juftly obferves, that this method was preferable to that prefently in ufe, which enjoins not a fale of the goods, but that they be delivered to the creditor at apprifed values. ' This fays his ' Lordfhip' is unjuft ; becaufe, inftead of money, which the credi- ' tor is entitled to claim, goods are impofed upon him to which he ' has no claim *.' Our prefent form does contain a kind of fale previous to the adjudication of the goods to the creditor. We fhall afterwards point out in what manner our old form came to be cor- rupted into the barbarous and unjuft execution againft the move- ables, which has long fubfifted, and continues to fubfift in Scotland. Another remarkable difference between the *juftities* and our brieve of diftrefs was, that the former appears only to have been granted to a particular fheriff, authorifing him to judge in a particular debt ; whereas the latter is granted to all fheriffs to whom the brieve is prefented, and authorifes them to judge in every queftion of debt due to the bearer ; in all which circumftances, our brieve of diftrefs coincides with the French *lettres de debitis.* Accordingly, in the or- der of our Chancery preferved in Balfour's Collection, the writ is termed *letters compulforial.*

· This brieve paffed of courfe from the Chancery of Scotland, and was not granted upon any particular confideration, like the Englifh *juftities ;* and hence we are entitled to conclude, that, to the ufe of this writ is entirely to be attributed the jurifdiction of our fheriffs in matters of debt. In this part of the ifland, we have not, like Eng- land, any certain knowledge of the powers or jurifdiction of the fheriff anterior to the Norman conqueft ; but it was after the con- queft only, that the jurifdiction appears wholly vefted in the Crown, and emanating, by means of brieves, directed to any judge to whom it pleafed the King to delegate his authority. The old Saxon jurif- diction of the Englifh fheriffs had been deftroyed, at leaft reftrained to a mere trifle by force, after the conqueft of the kingdom. A hatred to

3 D 2   the

* P. 332.

the laws of the conquerors long exifted among the people; and
a natural jealoufy arofe both in the King and his courts, of the
lower or county courts, where the native Englifh were affizers.
From this circumftance arofe the difference between the power of
the Scots and Englifh fheriffs, which we fhall find growing more
and more remarkable in the courfe of our hiftory. Scotland bowed
under no conqueror, and had admitted no mixture of foreign oppreffion. The King, therefore, had not the fame jealoufy of his
fubjects. When he beftows a jurifdiction upon the fheriff, he gives
it completely. The brieve of diftrefs was not only a writ of courfe,
but it was granted to fheriffs and all other judges, and extended to
debts in general. The fheriff was not only empowered to determine
pleas between the parties, but alfo to enforce obedience to his decree, by complete execution both of the moveables and of the land
of the debtor. The Englifh fheriffs, on the contrary, when they
happened to be authorifed by a writ of *juftities*, had no other execution than what originally belonged to them, the power of diftrefs.
In order to make fale of that diftrefs, they needed new authorities
from the fuperior court, which are extant in the law-books, under a
variety of titles, fuch as *Venditioni exponas, Fieri facias exeutio-
nem*, &c. This material circumftance kept in view, lays open the
true original caufe of the pofterior differences between the law and
form of both countries, which we fhall have occafion afterwards
particularly to remark.

Lord Stair entertained a very erroneous idea of the writ we are
talking of. ' The third executorial (fays he) is by letters of poind-
' ing, which, of old, was called the *brieve of diftrefs*, paffing out of
' the Chancery of courfe, by which the goods not only of tenants,
' but of poffeffors of their lands, were poinded for debts, much like
' the fubjects of one ftate againft another, by letters of mart ' In
another place he tells us, that ' of old there was no execution for
' debt, but only againft moveables, by the brieve of diftrefs or
                                                          ' poinding.'

* P. 750.

' poinding *.' The brieve of diftrefs, in place of being a letter of
mart, was a mode of juftice common to both France and England.
It was not a writ of execution ; it was a commiffion of juftice, authorifing a judge to hear the parties, to give judgment, and to execute that judgment. To borrow an Englifh term, it was a commiffion of oyer and terminer, which has not the moft diftant relation
to the barbarous idea of a letter of mart, imputed by Lord Stair to
the ancient law of his country.

Before going further, we muft remark the following circumftances
in the brieve of diftrefs. Firft, A diftrefs is made by the fheriff according to the quantity of the debt, in order to force the defender to
appear and to anfwer, as a fecurity for the obedience to the decree.
This afforded caution *judicio fifti.* Forty days are then allowed as
the *induciae* for the defender to anfwer ; and he is permitted to repledge the diftrefs, *i. e.* to take it back again upon finding caution,
according to the directions of the firft chapter of the Quon. Attach.
When the caufe is concluded, the debtor is condemned to pay the
debt within fifteen days ; after which, execution, or the fecond diftrefs, proceeds againft the effects of the debtor and his cautioner,
or againft the effects firft poinded as a pledge, in cafe no cautioner be found. In France, thefe fifteen days were termed the *quin-
fieme.* In England, though diftreffes taken by fubjects for rents
were mere pledges, which could only be retained, but not fold or
applied in payment of the debt ; yet, in the cafe of the King, they
could be fold, but not till after fifteen days from the date of the feizure. In Scotland, fo early as the reign of Alexander II. we find,
that, when a decree was given by the fheriff, the debtor's moveables were firft to be taken ; and then, by the ftatutes of that
Prince, the fheriff is ordered to advertife the debtor that he was
bound to fell his lands within fifteen days ; and, by the brieve of
diftrefs, no execution could take place againft the moveables till fifteen days after the date of the decree. Here is the original of what
we

* P. 405.

we term *our days of law ;* for, to this moment, no horning can proceed upon the decree of a sheriff, till either a charge of fifteen days be given upon the decree, or at least till after expiration of fifteen days from the date thereof.

To the procefs following on the brieve we find feveral advantages annexed, which are thus expreffed in chapter 49. of the Quon. Attach. The firft is, ' That nae effoinzies has place in ' this brieve, becaufe command is given that the debt be paid and ' given without delay to him who proves the fame.' *Effoinziei* is the Scottifh tranflation of *excufationes,* delays, or dilators, which, it feems, by this mode of procefs were entirely excluded. The next is, ' That it took from the baron liberty to had court upon his man, ' wha is called for payment of his own debt.' This was a great advantage ; for it behoved to be a very difficult matter to recover a debt from the vaffal of a baron, who could only be judged by his own mafter. The next is, ' That the creditor could fimply, with- ' out any challenge, conform to the folemn words of the law, afk ' and crave his debt, otherwife than ufe is, in pleas of wrong and ' unlaw ;' *i. e.* the creditor was not obliged to accufe his party of any injury which might give him the chance of determining the matter by combat, he was only bound fimply to demand the debt due to him. Laft of all, ' the debt might be afked without amer- ' ciament of either of the parties.' By the ancient conftitution of the kingdom, the Sovereign was not obliged, either in England or Scotland, to admit the differences of his fubjects into his own courts, or to take the trouble of determining them. When he did fo, a fine was exacted from either party. Every perfon liable in a fine was faid to be *in mifericordia regis,* of which the word *amerciament* is a corruption. In this cafe, as one of the parties had purchafed the King's brieve to the inferior judge, neither the purfuer nor defender were held to be *in mifericordia.* Thefe advantages difcover the reafon why the brieve of diftrefs became the moft general mode of recovery of debts in Scotland, while the analogous writ of *jufti-*

ties,

ties, in England, feems to have been but rarely applied for or granted. Another reafon was, that the *juftities* is iffued to the fheriff alone; whereas (as the text expreffes it) the brieve of diftrefs might be purfued before the juftitiar, the provoft, or bailies of burghs, as might pleafe the King to command by his letters.

The writ of *juftities* appears to have become lefs frequent in England, becaufe the King's courts being eftablifhed and fettled at Weftminfter at an early period, drew to themfelves the whole civil bufinefs of the nation; and, in proportion as their power and reputation increafed, all other inferior courts, and that of the fheriff in particular, naturally funk. In Scotland, on the contrary, the brieve of diftrefs became more and more common; the reafons were, that the King's courts, long in a very unfettled ftate, followed the court of the Prince; and fometimes they held ayres, circuits, or affizes, but at long and uncertain intervals. Parties, therefore, were under an abfolute neceffity of applying to the fheriff and other inferior judges, in order to obtain juftice. Though, from the whole laws in our old code, we find that the fixed method of ordinary procefs of our fheriffs, and other judges, was by attachment of the effects of the defender, to compel him to find fecurity to anfwer to the fuit, and by diftrefs or poinding of the effects both of principal and cautioner for the debt; yet, as the Crown had improvidently parted with its own jurifdiction, in granting baronies, regalities, &c. to the feudal lords, it was extremely difficult to bring any confiderable proprietors, their vaffals and tenants, to juftice in the ordinary way; becaufe no fooner were they attacked, than their fuperiors repledged them to their own courts, *i. e.* claimed the cognifance of the caufe in prejudice of the fheriff, who was then acting in his common capacity; but, when the fheriff acted by fpecial command from the King, no defender could be fo repledged; it behoved him to anfwer to the brieve of diftrefs.

We have confidered the feveral advantages annexed to the purchafe of this brieve, the principal of which was that expreffed in

the

the Quon. Attach. c. 40. ' It took from the baron the .liberty of
' halding court upon his man who was called for payment of his
' own debt.' In all cafes, therefore, where the debt was confiderable, where vaffals were the debtors, and refided under various jurifdictions, the brieve of diftrefs was the moft eligible and effectual
method of procedure ; but it does not thence follow, as Lord Stair
fays, and as all the authors of our Inftitutes have repeated after him,
that there was of old no execution againft the moveables, except in
virtue of the brieve of diftrefs. When the fheriff poinded in confequence of the brieve of diftrefs, he acted upon a fpecial commiffion or delegation from the Crown. When he executed decrees
pronounced by himfelf, in ordinary cafes, without any brieve, he
acted in his proper original judicative capacity. There was another
branch of the office of a fheriff, both in England and in Scotland,
which our writers, when they talk of ancient poinding, feem to
have forgot ; we mean, the duty of the fheriff, as a minifterial officer under the King and his proper courts. In England, they were
fometimes termed *the King's bailiffs* ; and, after the Norman conqueft, when their original jurifdiction was limited to forty fhillings,
they found themfelves, in lieu of it, reduced to officers, in place of
judges. The fentence was tranfmitted them by their fuperiors, in
order to be by them fimply executed. In Scotland, we find the fheriff in the full exercife of this minifterial branch of bufinefs. He
was the King's great officer, bound to execute all the precepts and
orders of the King and his fuperior judges. Nay, by a ftatute of
Robert II. we find that the fheriff was ordered not to give implicit
obedience to the writs under the feals, until he had confidered their
legality ; and, if they appeared to be contrary to law, he is directed
refpectfully to indorfe his opinion upon the back, and to return it
back unexecuted.

The difference between the Englifh and the Scottifh fheriffs ftood
demonftrably thus. The Englifh fheriff had as much of his original
jurifdiction preferved to him, as amounted to pleas of forty fhillings
value.

value. In all other civil cafes, he was a mere miniſterial officer, bound to execute the precepts and commands of the ſuperior courts. Few or no brieves were directed to him even by the Crown, excepting ſometimes the writ of *juſtities*. Accordingly, Glanvile, in his firſt chapter, which treats of the pleas belonging to the ſeveral courts, mentions only the brieve of right, and of bond men, as belonging to the juriſdiction of the ſheriff; whereas, in the correſponding chapter of our Regiam Majeſtatem *, a variety of brieves are enumerated, all competent before the ſheriff, and particularly the brieve of diſtreſs.

From the difference in the juriſdictions and powers thus veſted in the judge ordinary, aroſe all the differences of the laws and cuſtoms of the two kingdoms, in the matter of execution againſt moveables.

By the brieve of diſtreſs, the Scots ſheriff was directed to drive the goods or cattle to the market croſs, and there they are to be ſold by the creditor. If they are not ſold, the King's officers, at the cloſe of the market, are to comprize and deliver them to the creditor in payment of his debt. The brieve of diſtreſs was not a returnable brieve; the cauſe was judged of, and the execution completed by the ſheriff himſelf; whereas the Engliſh ſheriff, acting in virtue of a *juſtities*, needed an additional writ to authoriſe the ſale of the goods. Now, let us inquire in what manner this buſineſs was executed.

‘ In England, (ſays Lord Kaimes), attachment of moveables for ‘ payment of debt, is warranted by the King's letter directed to the ‘ ſheriff, commonly called a *Fieri facias*; and this practice is derived from common law, without a ſtatute. The ſheriff is commanded to ſell as many of the debtor's moveables as will ſatisfy ‘ the debt, and to return the money with the writ into the court at ‘ Weſtminſter †.' The method is the ſame at this day, without any remedy where a purchaſer is not found. To underſtand the

Vol. I. 3 E Engliſh

* Book 1. c. 5. † Tracts, p. 328.

Englifh execution, it is neceffary to know, that the writ of *Fieri fa-cias* iffues from the King's courts to the fheriff, in confequence of the judgments given in thefe courts. It is directed to the fheriff, as our letters of poinding formerly ufed to be. There is this difference, however, that the *Fieri facias* is a part of the procefs. The fheriff is here a minifterial officer, in the ftricteft fenfe of the word; he cannot pay the creditor, after making money of the goods; he does not give an execution indorfed to the bearer of the letters; but he makes a return or certificate of what is done in confequence of the writ, to the court from which it iffued. With the return, he tranf-mits the money which has been levied in obedience to the writ it-felf, or otherwife the return contains the reafons why the money is not fent. With the money thus returned, the creditor is publicly paid in court, and the debtor confequently acquitted by the record. From this neceffity of the fheriff acting under the authority of the fuperior court, and returning the writ, with the execution of it, arofe another capital difference which afterwards followed in the matter of poinding, as practifed in the two kingdoms. There is an analogous remainder in the forms of our brieves fufficient to make the idea familiar. Some of our brieves are ftill returnable, or, as we fay, retourable; *i. e.* the fheriff, after executing a brieve of mortanceftry, for example, returns the fervice to Chancery; but, when he executes a brieve of divifion or tierce, no return is made. The fheriff's own execution completes the right. We may, there-fore, confider the Englifh *Fieri facias* as a retourable brieve, and the Scots letters of poinding as an unretourable one.

Before going further, we fhall give as diftinctly as we are able the progrefs of the Englifh writs againft moveables, in which we fhall clearly difcern the origin and principles of every circumftance in the Scottifh diligence. We have heard, that the execution in the county courts could only be by diftrefs; and therefore the writ was by *levari facias, i. e.* the goods and chattels were only to be feized upon, and detained as a pain to diftrefs the party into payment. The fame

fame mode of procefs iffued from the King's court; and, according to Chief Baron Gilbert *, it is the moft ancient judicial procefs of the law. The words are, ' Praecipimus tibi quod diftringas B. per ' terras et Catalla, ita quod nec ipfe, nec aliquis pro eo nec per ipfum, ' manum apponat terris, tenementis bladis nec aliis catallis.' This writ, it will be obferved, reaches to the rents of lands, as well as to the goods and cattle; and it goes no farther than a mere feizure for diftrefs. In the King's courts, however, they foon found it necef-fary to introduce an improvement. ' The King's courts (fays Baron ' Gilbert) at laft came to give more effectual remedy than was given ' in any other; *adjudicare querenti debitum petitum;* and hence, in ' executions, they went one ftep further, *i. e.* to command the fhe-' riff to levy a certain fum mentioned in the judgment, by which ' the fheriff had authority not only to feize, which he could do at ' common law, but likewife to fell the goods fo levied †.' Some-times the *ipfa corpora* of the goods feized were returned to the court of the King, who publicly ordered them to be fold; and, if not fold, they affigned them over to the party : ' Yet, (continues Judge ' Gilbert), they had not ufed the way of apprifement, (*i. e.* they ' delivered them without apprifement) ; but the ftatute of Acton 'Burnal was the firft that put this in practice, which fays, that the ' goods fhould be apprifed and delivered over to the party according ' to the apprifement ‡.' This fucceeded fo well, that, by the ftatute of Weftminfter II. they ufed, in all cafes, either to fell the goods by the *Fieri facias*, or to deliver them at a price upon *the elegit*.

The ftatute of Acton Burnal is the firft part of the famous law made by Edward I. for the fecurity of payment of merchants debts. The other ftatute, which is generally called Weftminfter II. is no-thing more than the fequel or improvement of that act; the one made in the 11th, and the other in the 13th year of the fame reign, but at different places, Acton Burnal and Weftminfter. By thefe

3 E 2 ftatutes,

---

ftatutes, authority is given to the mayors of towns, and fheriffs of counties, to feize upon and fell the moveables of the debtor for payment of the merchant's debt ; or, if they cannot be fold, to deliver them over in payment, as alfo the rents and profits of the debtor's lands ; or otherwife, in the option of the merchant, to deliver him the poffeffion of the one half of the lands themfelves.

Though, before thefe ftatutes, fays Gilbert, the execution at common law was fometimes awarded by the words *Habeas denarios,* —*Fieri facias denarios,*—*Levari facias denarios,*—being words tantamount to the fame thing ; yet, from the date of thefe ftatutes, the execution was broke into two diftinct forms of *Fieri facias* and *elegit.* The *Fieri facias* continued to be the execution upon judgments ; and both the *Fieri facias* and the *elegit* were the executions proper to merchants debts, or to debts by recognifance, which, with us, is the fame thing as heritable debts. If the creditor choofed to have his money for the goods, the fheriff fold them by the *Fieri facias ;* or he delivered them together with the lands upon the *elegit.* The fheriff might alfo have levied the rents and profits of the lands in confequence of the word *levari* in the writ ; but this was not equal to the delivery of the poffeffion ; therefore the *levari* went entirely out of common practiee, though it remains in Chancery upon fome particular occafions. From what has been faid, we have a pretty complete view of the Englifh executions. The *levari* and the *Fieri facias* were the old writs of the common law. The latter went to the goods alone, and the former both to the goods and profits of the land. It anfwered the purpofe of our prefent arreftment and forthcoming againft tenants ; but the ftatute of Weftminfter introduced a more complete remedy, the poffeffion of the goods by and apprifement, or of the lands themfelves. ‘ By the common law, ‘ (fays Blackftone), a man could only have fatisfaction of goods, ‘ chattels, and the prefent profits of lands by the writs of *Fieri fa-* ‘ *cias* or *levari facias,* but not the poffeffion of the lands themfelves ; ‘ a natural confequence of the feudal principles, which prohibited

‘ the

' the alienation, and, of courfe, the incumbering of a fief with the
' debts of the owner.'—' The ftatute, therefore, (meaning the Weft-
' minfter), granted a writ called an *elegit*, (becaufe it is in the choice
' or election of the plaintiff, whether he will fue out this writ, or
' one of the former), by which the defendant's goods and chattels
' are not fold, but only apprifed ; and all of them are delivered to
' the plaintiff at a reafonable apprifement and price, in fatisfaction
' of his debt *.' If a creditor, by a judgment or decree of the fuperior court, choofes only to proceed by execution of the moveables of
his debtor alone ; or, as we would fay, by poinding alone, he gets
a *Fieri facias*, directed to the fheriff, who feizes and fells the goods ;
but, though there be no purchafers, he cannot affign them by apprifement, becaufe the *Fieri facias* was a writ at common law, in
the procefs of which no apprifement was known. That method was
introduced by the ftatute of Acton Burnal ; and, therefore, if the
creditor choofes to have the goods themfelves by apprifement, he
muft fue out an *elegit* upon that ftatute. In this manner the fale
and the apprifement of the goods joined together in our brieve of
diftrefs, and only pretended to be joined in our prefent mode of
poinding, were feparated from each other in the law of England.

Suppofing there were no purchafers, the fheriffs cannot deliver
the defendant's goods to the plaintiff in fatisfaction of the debt, but
muft return the execution in court. Inftead of doing fo, he muft
return, that the goods remain in his own hand for want of buyers.
Upon this a writ is directed of *venditioni exponas*, authorifing him
to fell at fuch price as can be had ; and, without this, he is not obliged to fell below the firft upfet price, which is generally fixed by a
jury called by the fheriff's own authority. Thus no inconvenience
is ever felt in the execution of the *Fieri facias* from the want of
purchafers, which Lord Kaimes fuppofes to be a capital defect remaining in that fpecies of execution.

Wilth

With refpect to the *elegit*, the ftatute of Acton Burnal affigns feveral fatisfactory reafons for intioducing the method of delivery by apprifement. The debtor, when he grants the recognifance, knows the confequences of that writ; and, therefore, as the act fays, ' has himfelf to blame if he does not fell his goods with his own ' hands,' and fo fave his eftate from coming under the *elegit*. In order, however, to do the debtor all the juftice which the nature of the thing will admit, the goods are to be delivered *per rationabilem appretiationem*, and the lands *per rationabile extentum*; and fuch price and extent muft be fixed by an inqueft, called for the purpofe by the fheriff *. This inqueft proportions the value to the quantity of the debt. If the value of the goods be fufficient, they proceed no further; if not, *they extend the land*, as it is termed, to the value of the remaining debt. A return is made by the fheriff to the Court of Chancery, from which the writ proceeded; and there the objections from the debtor are heard againft the procedure, if he has any. If there be no lands to fuffer extent, the apprifement and delivery of the goods are confidered as done upon a *fieri*, or *levari facias*; in which, if any of the debt be found due, *a capias ad fatisfaciendum*, may proceed againft the body of the debtor, which cannot be done if there were lands; becaufe, by the ftatute, though the creditor may take goods and body, he cannot take goods, body, and lands.

Thus we have endeavoured to explain in what manner both the intereft of the creditor and debtor is preferved in the execution, or, as we fay, the poinding of moveables, in the law of England. We may thence perceive by what means the injuftice and abfurdity of our diligence has been avoided in the practice of that law. With them, the bufinefs was anciently trufted to, and continues at this moment to be executed by officers of character and refponfibility; and yet they are, in that department, mere minifters of juftice, under the immediate infpection and controul of the King's courts, to whom they are anfwerable for neglect and malverfation in every

particular

* Com. Sheriff, p. 274.

particular act of this kind. It was formerly mentioned, that the whole differences in the practice arose from the different powers. of the sheriffs of the two kingdoms; that the English sheriffs, by the jealousy of the Norman Princes and their courts, were reduced to mere ministers of justice; while the Scottish sheriffs, on the contrary, were endowed by their native Princes with an extensive jurisdiction, and, in their ministerial capacity, entirely trusted with the execution both of their own and their superior's decrees. Hence our process of poinding declined in its propriety and justice, in proportion to the abuses of these powers, and to the neglects and misconducts of these judges; and, at last, the whole business, by a total desertion of their duty, fell into the hands of a different race of men who were chosen to supply their place, *i. e.* the King's messengers, or sheriffs in that part, by whom the execution against moveables has been rendered disgraceful to the jurisprudence of Scotland.

We now go back to trace the particulars of this progress, and to compare the conduct of the English sheriff, in the different parts of the practice of this business, with that of our own sheriff, and our own practice. The first observation we have to make is, that the Scottish brieve of distress contains the substance of all the English writs we have mentioned, and may fairly be said to be a compound of the whole. A commission of justice from the King to the sheriff, for determining an action of debt, is the same as the English *justicies.* The sheriff is thereby authorised to seize upon the goods both of the debtor and his husbandman, and to sell them for payment of the debt. This was the essential powers both of the *levari* and the *Fieri facias*; for, by taking the goods of the husbandmen and tenants, it clearly reached the profits or produce of the lands, as well as the moveable goods of the debtor. The apprising and delivery upon defect of sale, gave it, in the next place, the effect of the *elegit,* so far as regarded the moveable goods. The appretiation, too, was to be made by *liel, i. e.* honest men of different baronies; and, as their valuation:

valuation was supposed to be just, the goods are to be delivered to the creditor immediately after the market was over; so that they were to be exposed but for one market day at such upset price as the sheriff thought proper, and then apprised by a jury, and delivered to the creditor. For the legality of the process the sheriff was not immediately answerable;—all these things he was empowered to do by the King's brieve itself. That brieve was a pleadable one, but not returnable to any court of the King; and therefore the debtor, if injured, could only be heard by way of complaint. To complete the resemblance to the English writs, let us see in what manner execution extended to the land itself; and this will clearly show in what further particulars the practice of the two kingdoms was analogous, and in what it differed.

By the 24th chapter of the statutes of Alexander II. it is provided, in the precise terms of the brieve of distress, that ' Gif the debtor ' or his tenants has moveable goods, first of all, they fall be distren- ' zed for payment of the debt to the creditor. And, gif they have ' na strenzeable gudes, the sheriff and the King's servants, before ' the court rise, fall advertise the debtor, that, for inlaik of moveable ' goods, they are bound be the law to sell his lands and possessions, ' to satisfy the creditor within fifteene days. The debtor not doing ' this within fifteen days, the sheriff and the King's servants fall ' sell the lands and possessions perteining to the debtor.' By this statute, the brieve of distress is made to reach the lands of the debtor in a manner more effectual than the statute merchant of Edward, or any statute yet made in England. The sheriff is authorised to sell the lands of the debtor for payment of the debt; and he appears to have been totally trusted with this important process, being no more liable to any immediate controul, than he was in the case of moveables. Alexander began his reign in the year 1214, and Edward I. of England in the 1272; so that the execution against land was both earlier and more complete in Scotland than in England.

At

At this period, the execution against moveables in England stood entirely upon the *levari* and *Fieri facias.*

Edward introduced the statute merchant in the 13th year of his reign, and consequently the apprisement and the delivery of the moveable goods for payment of debts by the *elegit.* This merchant law, introduced by the two statutes of Edward, was adopted without much alteration by Robert I.*. His motive, no doubt, was the same, the encouragement of merchants, by a proper provision for payment of their debts, the good effects of which had become visible in England. This act authorised execution against the body, the moveables, and the lands, for payment of the debts due to merch ts. The debtor is to be a quarter of a year in prison, on purpose that he may sell his own moveables; after which, upon a certificate to the Chancellor, it is provided, that the moveable goods and lands pertaining to the debtor, should be taken, comprised, and given in payment of the debt. From the statute, it is clear, this was to be done by a writ from the Chancellor to the sheriff. Accordingly, by section 8. it is provided, ' That gif the sheriff declares ' to the King that the debtor cannot be apprehended, the merchant ' shall have the King's brieve, directed to all sheriffs within whas ' sheriffdoms the debtor has any lands, to deliver all his cattle and ' lands, under ane reasonable extent, to the creditor.'

Thus we see, in the time of Robert I. the brieve of distress in Scotland became equivalent to, and comprehended the powers of the whole English executive writs both against moveables and land. From the last statute, we perceive in what manner the brieves of distress were directed to sheriff's in general; and we have the reason why the words *poinding* and *apprising* are equally applicable, in our law, both to moveables and land. They were both attachable by force of the brieve of distress directed to the sheriff; and the property of them was made to pass from the debtor to the creditor by

* 2d Stat. Robert I. c. 19.

the fame form, viz. apprifement to the extent of the debt. We are not, at prefent, to go farther into the execution againft land, which is only mentioned becaufe of its infeparable connection with the prefent fubject.

We have now viewed the execution of the Englifh fheriff againft the moveable property of debtors, as it proceeded in confequence of his own original judicative capacity, without the authority of a brieve; likewife as it proceeded upon the commiffion of juftities; and, laftly, as it proceeded, in his minifterial capacity, as an officer of the fuperior courts. We have only confidered the Scottifh fheriff as acting under the authority of the brieve of diftrefs, becaufe it appears extremely difficult to difcover the particular cafes in which he acted without a brieve. The broken materials of our old law-books and ftatutes do not afford fufficient guides for that purpofe; tho', even from them, a variety of inftances might be collected, in which he feems to have proceeded independent of any fpecial command either from the King or his courts. Neither is it an eafy matter to define the exact particulars of his minifterial duty. Let it fuffice to fay, that, from a great variety of the laws in our old code, and in the capitularies of our Princes anterior to the reign of James I. it is clear, that the fheriffs of Scotland were immediately fubject to the directions not only of the King, but of the Chancellor and Jufticiary; whofe precepts, in the adminiftration of juftice, and civil government of the kingdom, were executed by that officer. But in what particulars his execution of thefe fuperior precepts, in the matter of diftrefs and feizure of moveables for debts, differed from the procefs of the brieve of diftrefs, it is impoffible to determine with certainty.

None of the acts of James I. relate to the fubject of the prefent difcourfe. The earlieft notice relating to it which we meet with, is in the firft act of the 6th Parliament of James II. entitled, 'Letters of caption to be executed againft curfed or excommunicated perfons.' This act provides, ' That gif thefe perfons be fugitive,

' and

'¹ and may not be overtain by the sheriff and his officers, the lands
'¹ fall be, and their gudes arrested and apprifed to the party likeas
'¹ for other debts, at certain mercat days as effeirs.' All that can be
inferred from this act is, that the goods and lands of debtors were
expofed to fale by the sheriff upon fo many market days; and, if
no purchafers appeared, they were apprifed and delivered to the creditor at that valuation. The particulars of the procefs, however, it
is impoffible to afcertain.

In March 1457, Lords of Seffion were appointed by the 61ft act
of the 14th Parliament of this fame Prince; and a jurifdiction is
given them to determine upon obligations, contracts, and all manner of debts in civil actions. Thefe Judges were a kind of affize or
judices in itinere, who travelled over the kingdom. The sheriffs
were to proclaim the particular time of the holding their feffion in
particular counties, which it appears they were to vifit only once in
feven years. It behoved the decrees of thefe Judges to be executed
by the sheriffs; but, as to the mode of execution, we are ftill left
entirely in the dark. Sir George M'Kenzie's obfervations regard
only the competency of appeals from that Court, as the immediate
precurfors of the College of Juftice. With regard to every other
circumftance relating to thefe Lords of Seffion, he either was entirely ignorant of them, or he has not condefcended to leave his obfervations to pofterity.

The next act we meet with is the 36th of the 5th Parliament of
James III. bearing for a title, ' That the poor tenants fhall pay nae
' farther than their term's mail, for their lord's debt, by the brieve
' of diftrefs.' From this remarkable ftatute we learn the mode of
execution which had principally taken place in Scotland during the
long period preceding. When debts were due to proprietors of land,
the practical and effectual writ of recovery had been the brieve
of diftrefs. And one of the numerous advantages attending this
kind of execution was, that it proceeded againft all the tenants and
poffeffors of the debtor's ground; their moveables, as well as his

own,

own, were feized upon by force of the writ. This practice, first authorifed by the ftatute of Alexander II. c. 24. had, it feems, in the time of James III. been carried to a very great height ;. and, as the act emphatically expreffes it, occafioned the ' heirfhip and de-' ftruction of the King's common mailers and tenants of lord's ' lands.' The debts for which the poor tenants were thus diftreffed, were not the debts of the land, or, as we now would fay, heritable debts, but merely the perfonal debt of the lord. It becomes a matter of curiofity, how a practice fo unjuft and unnatural got footing in the kingdom. Lord Kaimes derives it from the fuppofed original flavery of the whole tenants in Scotland to their mafters: He fuppofes them to have been totally incapable of property; and, therefore, that their goods and cattle were fuppofed to be their mafter's. This pofition of his Lordfhip's we are afterwards minutely to confider when we come to the hiftory of leafes. We have only, at prefent, to mention, that it is evident from the feveral old laws formerly noticed, made to prevent poinding *brevi manu*, that creditors in common debts, after the example of proprietors of land, treated their debtors in the fame manner, and made no diftinction between the proprietors, their tenants, and their vaffals ; thus confounding, in the execution, two things perfectly diftinct in their nature. Another circumftance appearing from the hiftory we have given, contributed to eftablifh that right in Scotland. The ancient execution in England was by the *levari* or *Fieri facias* only. Thefe writs reached the whole moveables of the debtor, including the rents and profits of his land. In virtue of them, the fheriff not only feized the goods and cattle of the debtor, but he levied his rents and duties. For this purpofe, the writ put him in place of the party ; and therefore the demand was limited to the rents and duties due by the tenants to the debtor in the writ ; and this was confidered as diftreffing the debtor *per terras et catalla.* Our Scottifh brieve intended the fame kind of diftrefs, *per terras et catalla*, when it ordered the fheriff to take and apprehend the cattle of the debtor's

hufbandmen,

Husbandmen, which, it seems, came to be executed literally and strictly. Our sheriff's seized the whole cattle they could find upon the land, after the example of the proprietor himself; nay, by the terms of the brieve, he seems to have been obliged to do this, even in preference to the seizure of the proprietor's proper and unquestionable effects. This barbarous practice totally excluded the original idea of the *levari facias ;* it was levying the rents and profits of the land at one stroke, by confounding the property of the tenant with the master. Such was the monstrous abuse which the statute of James III. intended to remedy. In the manner of doing it, we evidently see, that the legislature considered the practice as a mere corruption, which had crept in, in executing the brieve of distress. ' The cattle of puir men (says the act) are taken and distrenzied for ' the lord's debts, where the maills extends not to the avail of the ' debt ;' which is just saying in as many words, that the brieve of distress was intended only as an authority to levy upon their tenants the rents truly due to their master. It ought to have gone no further in Scotland than the *levari facias* did in England. The act therefore provides, ' That the puir tenants shall not be distrenzied ' for their lord's debt further than their term's maill extends to.' The purpose effected by this act is nothing more than the restoration of the brieve of distress to its ancient principles and effect of execution. So far as the tenants stood indebted to their master, the sheriffs were ordained to levy upon their goods, in the first place, to the amount of the debt in the brieve. This statutary limitation converted one clause of the brieve of distress exactly into the ancient English *levari facias.* If the debt be not thereby paid, the sheriff is next authorised to discharge the remainder out of the proper goods of the debtor, ' if he has sae meikle within the shire.' This is the *Fieri facias,* which is the term of the writ for execution against moveables in the possession of the debtor himself. In the next place, if the debtor has nothing within the shire, the creditor is directed to come to the King, and bring certification from the sheriff of how much he

the wants; and the King fhall direct his letters ' to ony other fhe-
' riffs where the debtor has any other gudes or maills within the
' realme, and gar them be prized, and pay the faid creditour within
' fifteen days, after the form of law.' This act of Parliament regulates execution alone. The decree has been recovered upon the
procefs of the brieve before the firft fheriff; but, as execution could
proceed upon it only within that judge's territory, the King
engages, by the ftatute, to grant letters of diftrefs, directed to all
other fheriffs. In obeying thefe letters, the fheriffs acted as mere
minifterial officers; they executed the decree of another by command of the King, their fuperior, in the fame manner as the Englifh fheriffs did upon a *Fieri facias* from the fupreme court. Here
we find the firft letters of poinding, properly fo termed; and the
only difference between them and the Englifh *Fieri facias* is, that
the latter was returnable to the court from whence it iffued; whereas the Scottifh fheriff, by the former, was appointed to make payment of the debt to the creditor himfelf from the proceeds of his
poinding. As thefe letters were incidental, they, in all probability,
iffued under the King's feal or fignet, and not from Chancery, for
they are termed *letters*; and we cannot difcover one circumftance
to fhow that any additional brieve was devifed in Chancery, from
the reign of James III. In his time it was that the language and the
forms of the French law began to mix with, and corrupt our ancient
native jurifprudence. The days of the brieve of diftrefs, however,
were to run in each fheriffdom; the fheriff was only to pay the creditor in fifteen days, after the form of law. If the judge before
whom the brieve of diftrefs was purfued, had made a fufficient diftrefs or attachment in the beginning of the fuit, and that fuch diftrefs remained unrepledged, *i. e.* that the debtor had not found caution, or got back his goods, then the fifteen days were, according
to their ancient intendment, given for repledging the goods by payment of the debt. But, in the cafe, where the letters of poinding
proceeded merely for the purpofe of execution, the fifteen days were
given

given that the debtor might pay the debt, and prevent the execution altogether ; and, in this fenfe, thefe days of law continue at this moment. No poinding upon a fheriff's decree can proceed until after fifteen days, a remainder of our moft ancient law ftill in complete prefervation.

The act proceeds, ' And where the debtor has nae moveable ' goods but his lands, the fheriff before whom the faid fum is reco- ' vered by the brieve of diftrefs, fhall gar fell the land to the avail ' of the debt, and gar pay the creditor.' This was extending the brieve of diftrefs to the lands of the debtor. It was a renovation of the merchant law of Robert I. borrowed from the ftatutes of Edward of England. Next follows what we call a reverfion in favour of the debtor, *i. e.* a power to redeem the lands fo poinded and apprifed from him within feven years, by payment of the debt and all cofts. The Scottish legiflature did what had been done in England by a variety of acts of Parliament. In England, they extended the ftatute of Weftminfter to feveral other fpecies of debts, and the courts formed feveral executive writs upon the model of it. The act of James III. in the fame manner extends the brieve of diftrefs to lands, upon the model of the act of Robert Bruce, but it holds a middle courfe. Our ancient execution againft lands lay upon the ftatute of Alexander II. whereby the fheriff was authorifed to fell them for payment of the debt. The act of Robert Bruce refpected only merchants debts ; and, like the *elegit* of the Englifh ftatute, it gave the poffeffion, not the property of the lands in payment. The act of James III. had chiefly in view the relief of the tenants from the monftrous abufe of the brieve of diftrefs ; and, therefore, to leave no cafe in which that abufe could be renewed, it extended the new law to debts of every kind without exception. In terms of the ftatute of Alexander, it ordered the lands to be apprifed by inqueft, and conveyed to the creditor ; and it ordered the fuperior to infeft him. At the fame time, in terms of the ftatutes of Edward and Robert, it put it in the power of the creditor (or to ufe the Englifh expreffion, it gave him an *elegit*) to redeem his lands by payment in feven years.

From the analifis of this laft ftatute, we have the moft fatisfactory reafon for the words of the execution, *poinding* and *apprifing* being equally applicable to land and to moveables. They were both anciently feized upon by the fheriff; they were both apprifed and valued at a certain rate by neutral perfons, and delivered to the creditor in payment of his debt, in the fame manner as moveables are at this moment; and hence the execution againft the land itfelf, was the fubftantial, the capital fpecies of poinding in the law of Scotland. The fame analifis has demonftrated, that the law of Scotland and England, in the time of James III. differed only in a very few circumftances.

Lord Stair, M'Kenzie, and other authors, have greatly mifapprehended this ftatute of James III. They have confounded the poinding upon the brieve of diftrefs, which was merely perfonal, with the other fpecies of that diligence, we mean, the poinding of landlords for their rents and duties, and the poinding of the ground by real creditors. Thefe authors ftand corrected by Lord Kaimes as to this particular. Neither the brieve of diftrefs, or acts of Parliament, had any concern with thefe kinds of poindings. Our judges, however, from the principle of the act, humanity to tenants, were pleafed to correct the rigours of the other poindings upon the model of this ftatute; the particulars we will afterwards learn in their proper place.

From the after courfe of our ftatutes, it appears, that the fheriffs of Scotland continued, in their judicial capacity, to poffefs a complete cumulative jurifdiction with the other judges in the fame rank in the kingdom; and, in place of being limited, the fubjects were ordered by ftatute to bring all their actions before the judges ordinary, in the firft place, referving to the King and his council the power of controuling their decrees, and correcting fuch as were erroneous either in law or in equity. With regard to their minifterial powers, they

they were alfo further confirmed to them. By the 30th act of the 3d Parliament of James IV. anno 1491, the fheriffs and other judges are ordered to execute all decrees; and, for that purpofe, letters are appointed to be written to them. By the execution mentioned in this act, is meant poinding of goods and lands alone; and therefore the fheriff is thereby ordered to have for his office and fees ' 12 ' pennies of ilk pound fwa recovered, to be taken of the party that ' the faid decreet is given againft;' and, in cafe the fheriff does not make the parties pay, after the form of the King's letters, within twenty days, he is to be punifhed by the lofs of his office, and condemned in payment of the debt himfelf. This is the origin of the fheriff fees in poinding; it took place both in moveables and heritage, which came to be diftinguifhed by the words *poinding* and *apprifing*. No other rule is yet eftablifhed in execution againft moveables. It is ftrange that M'Kenzie fhould declare this act to be in defuetude. We maintain that it is in force at this moment. The King's letters are, indeed, executed by fheriffs in that part; but no man can doubt, that any fheriff is entitled to exercife that office. Practice has difpenfed with his execution of the poinding; but he may certainly do it if he pleafes; and, of confequence, he would be entitled to demand the fee which the fheriff in that part now receives. The twenty days allowed by this act to the fheriff, are the fifteen upon which it behoved the debtor to be charged, and five more allowed to the fheriff himfelf to execute the bufinefs. Thus, in the fame manner, the fhe.iff in the Englifh writ of *Fieri facias* is ordered to return the money to court in three weeks. This circumftance of the twenty days, which Sir George M'Kenzie fo quickly paffes over, explains another material point of our prefent practice. The brieve of diftrefs, and the ftatute of James III. perfectly explained the fifteen days of the charge neceffary upon the decrees of fheriffs; and here we have the origin of the fame *induciae* upon the decrees of the fupreme court. This act relates to the decrees given at juftice airies, or circuit courts, as they are now termed; and the

King's letters for that purpose were directed to the sheriff upon twenty days, which was the old *induciae* of fifteen to the party, and five to the sheriff himself. The capital difference between the execution of the Scottish and English writs still continued; we mean, that of the latter returning the writ, or immediately accounting to the superior court for the execution of his duty; whereas the former paid the debt, or applied the proceeds of the execution himself. In this and the preceding reigns, remedies are introduced for the correction of this and other inferior judges. By the 103d act of the 14th Parliament of James III. the justiciar is ordered to hold an assize upon the sheriff in the last day of the aire or circuit, in order to try complaints against him in the execution of his duty, and to punish him if the complaint be proved. By the last mentioned act, the sheriff, in default of the execution of a decree, is rendered answerable to the party for the debt, which was a very effectual remedy.

About this period, it appears, that they began to use freedom with the brieves of the Chancery, and to devise letters suited to particular occasions, in their place, which was endeavoured to be corrected by c. 24. of the 3d Parliament of James IV. anno 1491. In place of the Lords of Session, a court of daily council was appointed to sit constantly at Edinburgh, by the 58th act of the 6th Parliament of the same Prince. By this time sheriffs, from the increase of business, had become tired of that part of their duty, which consisted in executing decrees by poinding. They appointed deputes to officiate for them in that department; and creditors, dissatisfied with their conduct, obtained letters directed to people of their own nomination, under the title of *vicecomitibus in hac parte*, a title borrowed from the practice of the churchmen. The fees of these new ministerial officers were disputed; and, therefore, to put the matter out of doubt, they were fixed to twelve pennies in the pound of the sum recovered, by an act in the 6th Parliament of James IV. c. 66.

This

This is the firft ftatute in which we meet with thofe refpectable characters *the fheriffs in that part*; and, to this relaxation of the law, in difpenfing with the minifterial duty of the real fheriffs, in accepting in their place the partial fervices of hirelings, is to be attributed the total corruption which enfued in the execution of the law of Scotland both againft moveables and land. The law of England retained, and at this moment retains over us a determined fuperiority in thefe particulars, by a firm adherence to their ancient regulations. This great barrier being entirely broke down, we fhall find the difference in our practice of the execution againft moveables grow wider at every ftep.

The next act of Parliament to be found upon this fubject is c. 98. of the 7th Parliament of James IV. anno 1509. It is in thefe words: *Item,* ' It is ftatuted and ordained, that, in time to come, na manner ' of fcheriff nor officear poind nor diftrenzie the oxen, horfe, nor ' other gudes pertaining to the pleuch, and that labouris the ground ' the time of labouring the famin, quhair ony other gudes or land ' are to be apprifed or poinded, according to the common law.' This act is extremely curious, and requires explanation. By the common law of England, no landlord or proprietor could take the plough, or the cattle employed in the plough, as a diftrefs for his rents and duties, becaufe it prevented the vaffal or tenant from payment or performance of the very rents and duties for which the compulfitor by diftrefs was intended. But, as common debts had no connection with the lands, the *Fieri facias* paid no refpect to thefe articles. The fheriff was to make money of every moveable belonging to the debtor, his body clothes excepted. The writ of *elegit*, however, proceeding upon the ftatute of Weftminfter, in appointing the goods and land of the debtor to be delivered to the creditor, excepted the oxen and horfes of the plough. ' Praeterea boves et affros de car- ' ruca,' are the words of the writ; and the reafon was, that the feizure of thefe cattle would have prevented the debtor from the cultivation of the remainder of his lands, one half of which only could, by that execution, be delivered to the sheriff. Hence, in the Scottish brieve of distress, while it extended only to moveables, no exception was made of the beasts of the plough; it was no other than the English *Fieri facias;* and therefore the seizure was thereby authorised of the whole cattle belonging to the husbandmen. The act of James III. which extended our brieve of distress to lands, omitted the exception in the English writ; and this omission was supplied by the statute of his son James IV. now under consideration. In doing this, however, our legislature seems to have totally forgot the the ancient distinction of the common law, although it seems only declaratory of it. This shows us that our old practice, or common law, had been the same as in England, in the matter of distress by landlords. The act indeed provides, that the ploughs were to be excepted in the time of labouring only, whereas the law of England contains no such speciality. By this time the French laws were pouring in upon us; and, from our act losing sight of the distinction of the English common law, it is pretty plain that the idea of the statute was taken from the French. By the ancient law of France, it is provided, ' That no inhabitant shall be aggrieved in his arms, ' horses, oxen, or other beasts used for the plough, by their being ' distrained, except they have no other goods.' This peculiarity, *except they have no other goods,* is not to be found in the English statutes, but makes a part of our act of Parliament, and therefore gives another certain indication of the source from which we derived it. The custom of France is the same at this moment, as are the laws of several other nations on the continent.

This act ordains, ' That na manner of sheriff-officear poind the ' oxen, horse, or plough.' This shows, that, by this time, there were different kinds of sheriffs, by appointment of other officers in their place. These new ministerial officers could not be appointed by the judges ordinary themselves, and therefore must, without doubt, have been constituted by letters from the King or the superior courts, for the particular and limited purpose of executing their decrees.

decrees. From various circumstances appearing from our statutes, it is certain, that these letters or brieves were not at first granted of course. Particular reasons were assigned for obtaining them, generally founded upon relationship, feuds, delays, or other suspicions against the judge ordinary ; and the names of the sheriff or sheriffs in that part were always filled up in the letters. Other reasons, however, brought these delegations to be granted of course, viz. the neglect of the sheriffs themselves, and the uncertainty of the debtor's residence, the common method of eluding justice by flying, and removing their effects from place to place. Upon this account it was, that the brieve of distress was directed to all sheriffs and judges ordinary. Now, as the business must have been a novelty in each jurisdiction, it was pretended to be more effectually done by sheriffs in that part, who understood the nature of the affair, set it on foot, and followed it to a conclusion. Upon this account it is, that, in the writs of outlawry in England, certain commissioners are added *nominatim* to the sheriffs, who may, without interruption, continue the pursuit of the rebel and his effects. In this manner it was, that the ministerial part of the office of the Scottish sheriffs came to be divided from their other duties ; nay, we may say, in a manner wholly transferred to people of little credit or consequence, suggested by creditors themselves, and named in the King's brieves and letters.

The same period of time is likewise remarkable for another very great change in the ancient law of Scotland, whereby it was made to deviate still more from the ancient practice, we mean, the change of our original brieves for letters under the Signet, and for precepts of the inferior judges. This remarkable and important alteration, by which a new face and a new language came to be given to the business of our northern part of the island, took place in this manner. The unsettled situation of our supreme courts, and the varieties which they had undergone for some preceding reigns, unavoidably threw the greatest part of the civil business, and particularly the complaints of the malversation of several judges ordinary, upon the

King

King himfelf, his Chancellor, and Council, who exercifed the fupreme judicative powers of the nation, and determined either by
law or equity, as to them feemed proper. The other courts inftituted in the courfe of this and the preceding reigns, fuch as the
Lords of Council, the Lords of Seffion, the Juftices of Aire, or Affize, &c. all acted by the authority of brieves iffued from the Scottifh Chancery, in the fame manner as the Judges of the King's
Bench and Common Pleas then did, and ftill do in England. But
the Chancery is the King's Court, where he is fuppofed to be perfonally prefent : Therefore no fuit is brought in Chancery by a
brieve ; becaufe it would be abfurd for his Majefty to command
himfelf, or his Chancellor, the fame as himfelf. From the Chancery,
therefore, writs iffue in the King's name, and by authority of the
Chancellor. In the fame manner, no brieve could iffue from our
Chancery to the King and Council ; he therefore iffued his commands by letters under his own fignet, in the management of the
Chancellor. This mode of government, fo eafy and expeditious,
was imported from France ; and, accordingly, in the reign of
James IV. and V. we find the King's letters to be a remedy at hand,
always ready to be directed upon every occafion. By the 9th act
of the 4th Parliament of James V. anno 1535, made againft people
excommunicated by the church, it is provided, ' That the party at
' whaes inftance the perfons are curfed, fall have our Sovereign
' Lord's letters to poind, apprife, and diftrenzie their gudes, move-
' able and unmoveable, for payment of the fums for which they lay
' under the faid fentence.' Here, for the firft time, we find warrants of poinding and apprifing given by letters from the King, in
execution of an ecclefiaftical fentence, quite different from the brieve
of diftrefs, and different from the act of James III. though the letters muft have been executed in terms of that ftatute.

By this time we fee clearly in what manner letters of poinding
multiplied. When a decree was obtained before an inferior judge,
the party, in order to reach the debtor in every jurifdiction, applied

to the superior court for *letters conform ;* a title directly borrowed
from the French practice, and, in several cases, preferred by Balfour.
In the 1532, we find, that, notwithstanding the new practice of
naming sheriffs in that part, parties were entitled to have their letters addressed to the real sheriff, stewart, or bailie, if they pleased.
' And (says Balfour) if the said sheriff, judge, or bailie, being requi-
' red to that effect, refusis or neglects to do the samin, he aught and
' fould make payment of the debt himself *.'

In a little time after, a model of an entire new court, the College
of Justice, was brought to James V. and by him established, taken
from that of the Parliament of Paris. In this Court were reunited
the whole jurisdiction and powers belonging to the King's former
courts of law, and also the supreme power, in civil cases, executed
by the King and his Council. For that purpose, the Chancellor was
made President ; and the Clerks of the King's Signet, who formerly acted under the Chancellor alone, were made members of the
Court. After this, brieves could no more be directed to this supreme Court, than they could formerly have been to the King, his
Chancellor, and his Council. The Chancellor of both kingdoms
had the government of the Chancery, and its writs particularly committed to him ; but, being now President of the College of Justice,
he could not order a brieve to be directed to himself. Every thing
thenceforth fell from the old Chancery into the department of the
Clerks to the Signet, and passed under the King's seal, in the same
form as was observed in the Chancery of France and of England.
For this reason, there is at the present moment very little difference
between the form of our signet letters, and the form of the writs
issued by the English Court of Chancery, in exercise of its equitable
powers. The College of Justice was instituted by statute in May
1537. The principal part of the old business of the Chancery directly ceased, and summonses came in place of brieves. These
brieves contained a long *induciae* of forty days, and were attended
with

* P. 392. c. 27.

with several dilatory circumstances in point of form. For this reason, James V. in the 1540, three years after the institution of the
College of Justice, in order to extend the reform to the sheriff and
other inferior courts, procured the act 72. of his 6th Parliament, ordaining all their precepts to be directed upon fifteen days. The tenor of this act is clear and express, perfectly accounting for this
change in the constitution of our inferior courts. Thus the old
brieves to the sheriff were dispensed with by special statute, as those
directed to the superior courts fell by the coalition of the whole judicative power in the College of Justice. The Chancery dues, by
this last act, were saved to the parties; the long *induciae* of forty
days were limited to fifteen; and the sheriff's precept or summons
was substituted in place of the former brieve, notwithstanding (as
the act expresses it) ' of the old laws and constitutions made of
' before.' At the same time it is declared, that this reform respects
personal actions only, and that all other matters and actions are to
continue to have ' sic process as they have had in times bygane.'
This last clause is of the utmost importance, and accounts for the
subsistence of the remaining brieves which still continue to be issued
from the Chancery to the sheriff, and executed by him after the ancient form.

There was, at this period, no diligence competent for payment
of liquid debts but letters of poinding and apprising against moveables and land, founded upon the act 1649, which did nothing more
than new model or improve the ancient brieve of distress, by limit-
ing its effects against tenants, and extending it against the land of
the debtor. When we say, that there was no executorial but poinding, we except the captions upon the decrees of the church, and the
letters of four forms or horning *ad facta praestanda*. By this time,
decrees of registration upon consent had become a part of our practice; but, by consenting that letters should pass, letters of poinding
were only intended. These words, however, included the poinding
both of moveables and land; for these two things very often went
together

together in the fame warrant. ' Letters of poinding (fays Balfour)
' allanarly fhould be direct for execution of ane contract made be-
' twixt twa parties, contenand liquidat foumis, beand regiftrat in the
' buikes of ony judge, with provifion thereuntill, that letters pafs
' thereon in form as effeiris.' For this he quotes a decifion, 14th
December 1570.

The brieve of diftrefs, and the mode of applying for letters directed to the particular fheriffs, in terms of the act of James III.
being now entirely out of ufe, thefe ufages were fupplied by citing
the party againft whom an inferior decree had been obtained, before
the College of Juftice, according to the practice of France and its Parliaments, and obtaining a new decree, conform to, or in the terms
of that pronounced by the fheriff; after which, letters were iffued
under the Signet, in the fame manner as if the judgment had been
originally pronounced by the fupreme Court.

The goods and lands of debtors, were poinded either in virtue of
letters proceeding from the fupreme court; in virtue of precepts of
fheriffs, and other inferior judges within their own jurifdictions; or
in virtue of decrees conform, granted in the manner juft mentioned.
Thefe decrees conform were very tedious and expenfive; and,
therefore, by a variety of pofterior ftatutes, which we formerly confidered, they were in a manner difcharged, and letters of horning
appointed to be directed by the Lords, upon production of the decree or precept of fheriffs, commiffaries, &c. duly executed. A palpable omiffion in thefe acts gave rife to a fingularity in practice now
almoft forgotten, but neceffary in the hiftory of our forms. In all
the ftatutes, horning was ordained to be granted upon the inferior
decrees, but nothing was faid of poinding; while, at the fame time,
the decrees conform, formerly in ufe, were in a manner difcharged.
The confequence was, that poinding could only proceed upon the
precept of the inferior judge; fo that, if the debtor removed his effects out of the jurifdiction, the law afforded no diligence to reach
them. This defect was allowed to continue till the 12th of June

1649, one of those termed *rebellious* Parliaments, when, by act 7. of that year, letters of poinding were ordered to be direct by deliverance to the Lords, in the same manner as letters of horning. This act received immediate obedience; it was rescinded at the Restotation, but re-enacted by c. 29. of the first Parliament of Charles II. anno 1661. By these statutes, letters of poinding and apprising, formerly granted in separate warrants, came to be joined together in one letter, called *horning* and *poinding*. Another defect in poinding, as it then stood, arose from this circumstance, that no previous charge was necessary to be given. The creditor only waited till fifteen days after the date of his decree, or registered bond; and then he executed his poinding, without giving the least notice of his intention. This was an evident remainder of the old brieve of distress. The sheriff, neither by that brieve, nor by the act of James III. was appointed to charge the debtor upon fifteen days, before poinding his property. He was to do no more, than to delay for fifteen days after the date of his decree; the purpose of which was, to give the debtor (who, by the then practice, must have been personally in court) time to repledge the goods attached, for securing obedience to the judgment, which was the first step of a common action; or to give him an opportunity of preventing further execution, by payment of the debt in that time. The same rule continued in the inferior courts, in all cases of civil debt.

When letters of horning and poinding were awarded in the same warrant, by the act 1661, the warrant for poinding was inserted after the charge of horning, and consequently, by the plain tenor of the letters, could not be executed till after the expiration of the charge; but still the poinding without a charge continued upon registered bonds and decrees of inferior courts; ' Whereby (says Sir ' George M'Kenzie) noblemen and persons of quality were oftimes ' poinded and affronted, and merchants surprised and ruined, before ' they knew that a decreet was recovered against them, or their ' bonds registered.'

.According

According to the alteration of our law and practice, this was a very great evil; and therefore an act was made to remove it in the 2d Parliament of Charles II. anno 1669. This act does not dispense with the fifteen days, the ancient days of law; for, before the date of the statute, it behoved these days to expire; and it behoves them still to do so, before a horning can be applied for from the Court of Seffion; and, when that horning is obtained, a new charge must be given upon fifteen days more, in the fame manner as was formerly done upon decrees conform, or as it is yet done upon decrees of the Court of Seffion itself. The alteration made upon the decrees of the inferior courts, is, that a poinding cannot proceed upon their decrees, or upon regiftrations in their books, without a charge. At the fame time, this charge may be given upon their precepts immediately after pronouncing the decree; fo that the fifteen days of law will, by that means, make a part of the charge; we fay, a part of the charge; becaufe the decree, if it is of any length, cannot be inftantly extracted. The practice is therefore to take out a precept, which, without engroffing the procedure, fhortly mentions that fuch a decree has been pronounced, and contains a warrant of poinding.

From the hiftory we have given of inferior courts, the reafon will be perceived why they never had the power of awarding diligence againft the perfons of debtors. The merchant law of Robert Bruce extended only to burghs. Burghs therefore alone, of all other inferior judges, remain in poffeffion of the power of granting acts of warding againft perfons of debtors. At the inftitution of sheriffs, no other diligence fubfifted but poinding againft moveables. The statutes of Alexander II. and James III. extended the brieve of diftrefs to lands. The captions which proceeded upon the decrees of the church, were given under the feal of the King and Council; and the sheriff, in the execution, was only a minifterial officer. When the old ecclefiaftical polity fell at the Reformation, the acts of Parliament provided, that letters of horning, *i. e.* execution againft the perfon, could only be given by deliverance of the Court of Seffion upon the decrees of inferior courts ; and, confequently, to this moment the jurifdiction of fheriffs, ftewarts, &c. does not, in any civil matter, extend to the perfon of the fubject.

We come now to confider the ftyle of the warrant which makes a part of our letters, called *horning* and *poinding*. ' And ficlike, that ' ye, in our name and authority forefaid, fence, arreft, apprife, com- ' pell, poind, and diftrenzie, all and fundry the faid A. B. his readieft ' moveable goods, gear, corns, cattle, infight plenifhing, horfe, nolt, ' fheep, debts, fums of money, and others whatfoever pertaining and ' belonging to him, wherever, and in whofe hand the fame may or ' can be apprehended ; and, failing of moveable goods and gear ' poindable, that ye apprife all and fundry his lands and heritages, ' conform to act of Parliament, to the avail and quantity of the ' forefaid fums, and make the faid C. D. compleatly paid thereof.'

' *Compell, poind, and diftrenzie.*'—*Poind* comes, as formerly mentioned, from the old *pound*, or inclofure, into which cattle feized upon by landlords were put, to compel payment of their rents and duties. That kind of poinding was the original of the whole procefs ; and the language of it was made to ferve for all the other fpecies. The word *compell* is only applicable to that kind of feizure which was meant not as an execution, but as a pain to force or compell performance.—' *Diftrenzie*' is an old Scottifh Gallicifm, from the ancient Latin term *diftringere*, to diftrefs ; a word alfo belonging to the diligence againft tenants and vaffals.

' *Sums of money, and others.*'—Thefe words belong to arreftment, and not to poinding ; though we cannot help here obferving, that what we call *arreftment* is only a modern writ ; for every thing was of old reached by the *levari facias*, and which is the reafon why we find the terms here blended, in the fame manner as the *Fieri* and *levari facias* were in England, which are juft the Latin words for poinding and arreftment, reaching the money or effects of the debtor, wherever the fame could be found.

' *And,*

' *And, failing their moveable goods, that ye apprise all and sundry*
' *their lands and heritages, conform to act of Parliament.'*—The act
of Parliament is that of James III. which we have so minutely explained, and which authorised the poinding of land by the same
form as that of moveables. The apprisings continued in consequence of this warrant, or of separate letters of apprising, till the
1672, when they were changed for adjudications, competent only by
action before the Court of Seffion ; and thus the diligence of the law
of Scotland against lands, was completely feparated from that against
moveables. It was entirely changed from the old footing of the
brieve of diftrefs, or the Englifh *elegit*, to a novel form borrowed
from the laws of France. Nothing remained to the fheriff, or other
inferior judges, but the execution of the letters of poinding. The
warrant of apprifing, after the 1672, was dropped out of the ftyle
of our horning ; and, in place of it, the following words were added to the warrant of poinding :   ' *Make penny thereof, to the avail*
' *and quantity forefaid, and cause the faid complainer be compleatly*
' *fatisfied and paid of the fame.'*

Let us now confider the ceremony and mode of execution. The
meflenger engages two witnefles to go along with him, two apprifers, and a notary public. The attendance of the notary is a remainder of the old form, in which meflengers, as acting in the place
of fheriffs, were confidered in the light of judges. The clerks of all
the fheriffs, and other inferior courts, were notaries public ; and
therefore the fheriffs in that part, in poindings of any moment, chofe
always to have a notary, as clerk to the procedure. As a judge may
act without a clerk, fo a notary is not neceffary in a poinding ; we
mean, his affiftance is not effential to the validity of the procefs ;
but it is always prudent and advifeable that a notary fhould attend :
He is an officer to whofe inftruments the law gives credit ; and therefore it is proper that the procedure of the meflenger fhould be fupported by a regular inftrument under his hands. When thefe un-
welcome guefts arrive at the dwelling of the unhappy debtor, they
feize his cattle, goods, and effects of every kind, and drive and tum-
ble.

ble them together into one place. In this fituation they are *poinded* and *diftrenzied;* and, as an authority, the letters are publicly read with the execution of charge, to fhow that the act of Parliament, in that particular, has been complied with. This is particularly re-quifite to be done by the meffenger, who not being an ordinary judge, derives all his powers from the letters in his hand. This done, he proceeds to value or apprife the goods upon the fpot, which ought to be done by the appretiators of the bounds, but they feldom officiate. No fuch ceremony was requifite in the old poindings : Nothing was done till the goods were carried to the market crofs; and there they were fairly expofed to fale, and apprifed if not fold. The apprifers upon the ground are always two people in the conftant employ of the meffenger, and entirely at his devotion. If, however, there be common appretiators by office in the place, the meffenger, at the debtor's requeft, would be obliged to admit them in preference to his own followers, or any other ftranger ; and their apprifement would be received, in cafe of refufal. The apprifers, whoever they are, being *defigned*, (as the officers call it), the meffenger mutters an oath to them about the faithful adminiftration of their office ; and then they proceed in a loofe and partial manner to put what they call *fair values* upon the goods. The notary and meffenger take notes of fuch valuation, and extend the whole into one fum.

In the next place, the meffenger makes proclamation, by three oyeffes, in order to convocate the people ; declares the price at which the goods are apprifed ; and thereafter offers them to the debtor three feveral times, or to any other perfon in his name, con-ditionally that they pay the price to which they are apprifed ; with certification, that, if this is not done, the goods will be delivered at the apprifed value to the creditor. No offer upon the part of the debtor being made, the goods are immediately carried to the market crofs of the head burgh of the county, or other neareft jurifdiction ; and there the very fame ceremonies and offers are repeated, with this difference, that two other apprifers are added to the former ; and, as

these

these are likewise generally in the messenger's employ, there is a perfect agreement about the value.

Lord Kaimes expresses himself with feeling and propriety upon the above procedure. ' In letters of poinding, (says he), a blank ' being left for the name of the messenger, the creditor is empower- ' ed to choose what messenger he pleases, and, of consequence, to ' choose also the appretiators, by which means he is, in effect, both ' judge and party. In a practice so irregular, what can be expected ' but an unfair appretiation, always below the value of the goods ' poinded ? and, for grasping at this undue advantage, the creditor's ' pretext is but too plausible, that, contrary to the nature of his ' claim, he is forced to accept goods in lieu of money. Thus our ' execution against moveables, in its present form, is irregular and ' unjust in all views. Wonderful, that, contrary to the tendency of ' all public regulations toward perfection, this should have gradual- ' ly declined from good to bad, and from bad to worse * !'

These reflections of his Lordship are no less eloquent than true. Evils of the same kind followed in the apprising of land, which were remedied by the introduction of the adjudications in the 1672 ; but, in moveables, the abuse still continues a disgrace to the jurispru- dence of Scotland. A form thus inconsistent, and teeming with ab- surdity, could not be the produce of law. It is the corruption of forms originally good, generated by the avarice of creditors, and the ignorance of messengers, upon whom the ministerial duty of our in- ferior judges totally devolved.

By the brieve of distress, the goods were to be carried by the she- riff to the market cross, and exposed to a fair sale. The only mean- ing of carrying them to that place, was upon account of the public market held there ; and it is clear they could only be carried in a market day ; for the words of the brieve bear, that they are not to be apprised but in default of sale ; and that in the end of the mar- ket, before which, that circumstance could not be known. In this respect,

* Tracts, p. 332.

respect, our brieve was exactly the *Fieri facias* of England. Our sheriff was to make money of the goods if he could; if not, he was to deliver them to the creditor by apprisement of ' liel men of diffe- ' rent baronies.' The English writ of *elegit*, which extended the execution for debt to lands, directed the sheriff to apprise both the land and the goods by an inquest, and to deliver them both, at an apprised value, to the creditor. This circumstance, of the goods being sold for money, or delivered by apprisement, then made, and still makes the difference between the *Fieri facias* and the *elegit*. The act of James III. in the same manner as that of Westminster, extended the brieve of distress, which was our *Fieri facias*, to lands; and hence the reason of our apprising answering to the *elegit*. The sheriff is, by the act 1469, ordered to make the goods be apprised and delivered; but that act says nothing of the sale of them. After the brieve of distress upon this act went out of use, letters of poinding and apprising were issued in their place; for, without a previous poinding, or attempt to poind, no apprising could go on. The words were, ' That ye apprise, compell, poind, and distrenzie their goods ' and lands; and, failing their moveable goods, that ye apprise their ' lands,' &c. Accordingly, it behoved the execution of this diligence to bear, that the messenger had searched for the moveable goods, in order to apprise them, before he could take a single step against the land.

When moveable effects were seized by a person who meant only to take the lands, the officers judged it safe and proper to proceed in their execution against these moveables, in the same forms that were observed in the process against the land. They dropt entirely the idea of selling the goods, but proceeded to apprise and deliver them at the apprised value, exactly as they did in England upon the *elegit*. Now, let us see in what manner the land was poinded. We find, by the form preserved by Dallas, that the first thing the officer did, was to go to the ground of the land; and there he made open proclamation by three several oyesses; after which he denounced the lands

to

to be apprifed againft fuch a day. In the fame manner, in the poinding of moveables, the meffenger goes to the fpot, collects the goods, makes proclamation, reads the letters, and declares that he has poinded thefe effects. From the ground, the meffenger, in ap-prifing of land, went to the market crofs, and there he repeated the fame ceremony. He denounced and warned the parties, that, un-lefs they paid the debt, the lands would be apprifed againft fuch a day. In the poinding of moveables, the very fame thing is done; the meffenger declares, that, if the money be not paid, he will de-liver the goods to the creditor. When the day for apprifing comes, the inqueft is called; and the value being by them fixed, the judge (fays St Martin *) ' caufes offer the land thrice at the door to the ' parties, or any in their name who will come and buy them, for ' payment of the fums for which they are apprifed; with certifica-' tion, that the lands will be adjudged to pertain to the creditor; ' and none appearing, the judge affigns the land to the procurator ' for the purfuer, in terms of the act of Parliament.' It behoved this ceremony to proceed within the tolbooth of the head burgh of the fhire, if that circumftance did not happen to be fpecially dif-penfed with.

The procefs in moveables is thus. The meffenger goes to the market crofs, calls his apprifers, values the goods, and makes offer of them to the debtor, or any in his name, at the prices put upon them; and, if nobody appears, they are, as the lands were, affign-ed to the creditor. In thefe procefles, there are only two circum-ftances of difference which we are able clearly to account for. The firft is, the appretiation upon the ground of the lands, before going to the market crofs; which is an abfurdity, occafioned by the following occurrences. In fmall poindings, and in the cafe of particular per-fons, the carriage to market crofs was found inconvenient and ex-penfive, particularly in poindings for minifter's ftipends; and there-

VOL. I.   3 I   fore

* P. 29.

fore an act was made in the refcinded Parliament 1649, and afterwards re enacted by c. 21. 1663. The words are: ' Therefore
' his Majefty, with advice and confent of the eftates of Parliament,
' declares, that it fhall be fufficient to the minifters forefaid, in
' poinding, apprifing, and diftrenzieing of goods of perfons deficient
' in payment of their rents and ftipends, to comprife the faid goods
' by honeft fworn men, upon the ground of the lands and place
' where the goods are, which fhall be as fufficient as the fame were
' done at the faid market crofs.' The fame privilege was afterwards
extended to a great variety of different kinds of poindings, fuch as
for the excife, King's rents, annuity, &c. &c. So that this method
of apprifing upon the ground, from its frequent repetition, came, by
the ignorance of meffengers, to be thought neceffary in all poindings.
However thefe ftatutes fhortened the particular fpecies mentioned,
they doubled the ceremony in other common poindings. This would
have been lucky, had the defects of the diligence been in any circumftance corrected ; but doubling the ceremony ferved only to
double the abfurdity and expence.

In this manner was our execution againft moveables confounded
with that againft land. Every ftep in the procefs of apprifing of
land had an obvious and fenfible intendment. The denunciations upon the ground, and at the market crofs, were indifpenfibly neceffary, to warn the debtor of the apprifing of his lands,
which was the mode prefcribed by the act of Parliament. No fale
took place ; and therefore they could only be offered to the debtor
himfelf, upon payment of the debt ; for no third party was entitled
to interpofe. Now, when this is applied to moveables, the diligence becomes abfurd, and attended with confequences the moft unjuft and inconfiftent imaginable. We fhall now notice the other
circumftance in which the form differed. The meffenger in the
poinding offers back the goods to the party, not for payment of the
debt, but for payment of the prices at which they are valued ; and
lawyers were not long of difcovering, that if the debtor, or any
                                                        body

body for him, paid the money, in cafe fuch payment was not
equal to the debt, the meffenger had nothing to do but to poind
them over again. No offer of this kind is ever made; and therefore the whole ceremony of poinding is perfectly devoid of meaning. It refolves juft into this, that a creditor, in confequence of a
warrant of poinding, can put any value he pleafes upon the goods
of his debtor, and appropriate them to himfelf by a piece of fenfe-
lefs form, managed by the dregs of the people.

Lord Bankton fays, ' That he apprehends that the terms of the
' offer to the debtor ought to be, that he fhall have the goods upon
' his relieving them by payment of the debt; for otherwife, if he
' fhould take the goods at the apprifed value, and the debt not be
' thereby fatisfied, the meffenger might prefently anew diftrain them
' for what is owing; and it is plain, the intent of the offer to the
' debtor is, that he may relieve the goods, which, by the meffenger's
' feizing and apprifing, becomes a *pignus praetorium*, or judicial
' pledge *.' His Lordfhip, in this place, confounds the execution
againft land with that againft moveables. The lands by the apprifing, no doubt, do become a *pignus praetorium*; but the property of
the moveables is inftantly altered. The meffenger, by the very next
word he pronounces, affigns them to the creditor; to whom, by the
law, they from that moment belong, without redemption. The
wrong in the procedure arifes from the very circumftance of applying the form proper to land, to moveables, which are abfolutely taken in execution; and, fo much did the avarice of creditors induce
them to take advantage of this error, that, in a cafe reported by
Durie, a creditor infifted upon taking goods at his own apprifement,
although the debtor offered higher values upon the fpot. This is
the only inftance of fuch an offer in the records of Court; but the
Lords moft juftly found, that the offer of the debtor ought to have
been accepted †. This offer by the meffenger has always been not

3 I 2   for

---

* Vol. 3. p. 27.   † 23d Feb. 1628, Gagie againft Guthrie.

for payment of the debt, but for the prices fixed by the appretiators; and we shall now show in what manner this palpable inconsistency established itself in the form of poinding. When the creditor's object was to apprise lands for his debt, he took out letters of
poinding or apprising, in the style of which the moveable goods
were slightly mentioned. But, when the object was the moveables,
the creditor took out letters of poinding *per se*, the style of which
was much more particular, viz. ' All and sundry the said A. B. his
' readiest goods, gear, corns, cattle, insight plenishing, horse, nolt,
' sheep, and others whatsoever pertaining or belonging to him,
' make penny thereof, and cause the said complainer be completely
' satisfied and paid.' When letters of poinding were warranted to
be issued at the same time with the horning, the Writers, taking
advantage of that expression, added a warrant for apprising of the
lands also *. They left out the words ' *make penny thereof*;' but,
after the act 1672, when apprisings were abolished, the clause respecting the land was omitted, and these old essential words of the
poinding restored; and so the style continues at this moment. It
made, however, no alteration in the practice; the messengers per-
sisted in their old way to apprise moveables, in the form of the act
of James III. in the same manner as they did the land; and so the
absurdity has been continued to our own time.

If we look back to the English process in the same business, it
will at once point out in what manner they have avoided the unpardonable errors into which we have fallen. The act 1672, abo-
lishing adjudications, returned to our warrant of poinding the effect
of the *Fieri facias*. The Writers to the Signet altered the style,
and yet it had no effect in correcting the practice. From that time,
i. e. the 1672, the goods poinded ought to have been fairly exposed to sale, in terms of the old brieve of distress, at a public market; and they ought to have been delivered to any person who offered

* Vide Dallas's Styles, p. 8. & 9.

fered the higheft price. In default of buyers only, they ought to have been delivered to the creditor at the apprifed values, after being offered to the debtor upon payment of the debt, which is the procefs of the *Fieri facias* in England, and was the procefs of our ancient execution againft moveables. By holding firmly, therefore, to their original writ of *Fieri facias* againft moveables, to the *elegit* on land, and to the minifterial office of the fheriff of the county, and his fair inqueft, in place of our miftaken executions by meffengers, fheriffs in that part; they have preferved this branch of jurifprudence from the injuftice and abfurdity in which ours at prefent is confeffedly involved.

When the poinding is completed, the meffenger leaves a fchedule for the debtor, of the particulars of the effects taken by the diligence, together with a copy of the letters and executions figned by himfelf and the witneffes; and this ferves for a difcharge of the debt, as far as the goods poinded go. This is neceffary, becaufe by our practice, as formerly obferved, the whole of the bufinefs is trufted to the meffenger; whereas the Englifh fheriff muft return the money to the fuperior court from whence the *Fieri facias* iffues; and there the debtor's objections to the procedure are heard before payment. If he has none, the creditor is publicly paid, the fact entered upon the record, and the debtor thereby completely difcharged; the purpofe of which is, to inftruct the regularity of the procefs, in cafe of any after quarrel at the debtor's inftance. After delivering the fchedule, our officers make out a full execution of the whole procedure, which is figned by themfelves, the witneffes, and the notary public.

When the heritable jurifdictions of barony, regality, &c. were abolifhed in the year 1748, it was declared lawful, by a claufe in the act, to carry the poinded goods to the market croffes of thefe jurifdictions. This was to fave the expence of the diftant carriage to the head burghs of the fhire. It was certainly a pity that the legiflature, upon this occafion, was not directed to a higher object, viz.

viz. a fair fale of the goods at the market crofs, which would have reftored fenfe and meaning to the diligence : For what is the purpofe of removing the goods from the fpot, if they are only to be offered to the debtor, and poinded again upon his acceptance of that offer ? What is the ufe of the proclamation, or the words of the warrant requiring the effects to be converted into money? All thefe circumftances concur in proving, that the prefent form is nothing more than an ignorant corruption of our original execution.

Struck by the imperfection of the diligence of poinding, the Court of Seffion, in the 1754, made an act of Sederunt, ordaining all officers, executors of poindings, to report their execution within forty-eight hours to the fheriff of the county, that he may give directions for a fair and public fale of the goods. That act of Sederunt unluckily embraced too great a variety of objects ; it contained regulations for reducing the diligence of creditors to an equal, or *pari paffu*, divifion of the debtor's effects ; and, as the confequences of fuch a confiderable alteration in the common law could not be forefeen, it was cautioufly made a temporary act, to continue no longer in force than the 20th of Auguft 1758. The variety of its objects did not anfwer, in practice, what they promifed in theory ; and therefore it was allowed to expire. Had it related to poinding of land, the regulations introduced would, in all probability, have anfwered the purpofes intended by our judges.

The Englifh diftrefs by landlords for their rents, befides ploughgoods and the cattle, admits a great variety of exceptions. The reafon was, that fuch diftrefs is not an execution, but a mode of compelling payment of their rent. The *Fieri facias,* on the other hand, for perfonal debts, reaches to every thing belonging to the debtor, his body clothes excepted. In the fame manner, our poinding is without any other limitation but that of the plough-goods and cattle, in terms of the act 1503, formerly mentione 1. This act, however, protects thefe articles only in the time of labour, and fixes no certain part of the year. Our judges, therefore, have defined

fined it to be ' the time in which the tenant is actually employed in
' ploughing.' If the tenant's work is done, againft whom the diligence is directed, it matters not that his neighbours are ftill at labour ; and, though the neighbours have given over, if the debtor's
work be not finifhed, the law will continue to protect him. This
ploughing, however, is reftricted to the year's crop without fallow-
ing, otherwife the diligence might be excluded for the greateft part
of the feafon. The ftatute is, in fact, of very little ufe, becaufe it
protects the labourer only, who has other goods to poind, preventing the meffenger from the arbitrary feizure of the plough goods
and cattle, becaufe the want of them would occafion the heavy con-
fequential lofs of his year's crop. But, if there be no moveables, or
if they be not fufficient to fatisfy the debt, it has been found that
the meffenger may lawfully proceed *.

In this matter the laws of France are much more humane than
thofe either of England or Scotland. They protect the plough-
goods, cattle, and labouring inftruments, even againft the King's
duties, except for the rent of the farm, and for the price of thefe
articles themfelves. They alfo difcharge the feizure of the debtor's
clothes, and the bed he lies on, together with the arms, horfes, and
warlike equipage of officers and foldiers. Nay, what is truly benevolent, creditors in rural poindings are obliged to leave a cow, three
fheep, and two goats, for the fuftenance of the debtor's family, unlefs the debt be for the price of thefe very articles.

The property of moveables is prefumed from being found in the
debtor's poffeffion ; and therefore the meffenger may, by our practice, feize the whole. If a third party appears, and offers to make
oath that the goods, or any part of them, belong to him, the officer,
in confequence of his judicative authority, is bound to receive the
oath ; but, before doing this, he is allowed to put fpecial interro-
gatories to the claimant, in order to a difcovery of the fact. If, in
confequence

* Home, March 168t, Goodfire.

confequence of this inveftigation, the claim appears to be falfe or collufive, the meffenger may reject it, and proceed. The claimant protefts for damages, and brings an ordinary action both againft the meffenger and his employer, for recovery; but, if the party produces a written title to the goods, and offers to fortify that title by an oath of verity, the officer muft ftop, and yield up the articles claimed; it being hitherto underftood, that his judicial power does not reach to the cognifance of written conveyances; and, upon thefe occafions, it is his duty to proteft againft the claimant for payment of the debt, and damages. We fhould alfo think it prudent, upon fuch an occafion, to make the notary to the poinding take a proper copy of the conveyance produced, or to infift upon the confignation of it in the hands of the neareft judge, to prevent pofterior alterations. If it be a writing obvioufly defective in the ftatutory folemnities, it is imagined that the meffenger would be entitled to proceed; at any rate, it is his bufinefs to report the *res gefta* in his execution. It is prudent in the claimant to allow the goods to be fully apprifed before he makes his demand, otherwife the value remains uncertain; and, if the obftruction be afterwards found improper, the claimant will be fubjected in the fame manner as if he had deforced the meffenger, there being no difference to the poinder between force and fraud *. But, if the poinding be fuffered to be completed before the claim be made, the goods muft be recovered by an ordinary action. Formerly, the oaths of the debtor's wife and children were admitted in the abfence of the proprietor of the goods, but they are now refufed. A common action is the only remedy. The oaths given by the claimants, upon thefe occafions, have no effect upon the point of right; they are no more than oaths of credulity, which may be redargued by every habile mode of proof, in a pofterior action for that purpofe. The Englifh fheriff, when claims of this kind are made upon him, calls an inqueft, which is termed *de bene effe*, and regulates himfelf by their verdict.

                                                    The

* Edgar, June 10. 1724, Gordon.

The laft regulation in the affair, is that of the 12th of his prefent Majefty, c. 47. intended, like the former act of Sederunt, to remedy the evils attending upon infolvency, which obliged the creditor poinding to deliver the goods to a factor appointed by the Court of Seffion, in cafe the effects of the debtor be fequeftrated in thirty days from the date of the poinding. This ftatute put an end to three fourths of that kind of diligence in this country, and altered the compulfitors of the law from execution againft the moveables, to that againft the perfon. Like the former act, it has fallen entirely fhort of its purpofe. Even with refpect to poinding, the laft act committed a very great overfight; it provided that the creditor fhould only be bound to deliver the goods; or, if fold, to account for the apprifed values; whereas it ought to have adhered to the old remedy of appointing the goods to be fairly fold at the fight of the fheriff; for many creditors have availed themfelves of unjuft appretiations, and, by fudden pretended fales, gained great advantages over other perfons concerned.

Growing corns, or other goods not tranfportable, are poinded by famples. The property is thereby transferred, and the quantity and price remain to be fixed before feparation from the ground. The creditor is bound to do this regularly before intromitting, otherwife he is liable in the confequence of a *fpuilzie*; and he muft be careful to complete the bufinefs, by afcertaining the extent in proper time. If he neglects this, a fecond poinding will put him out. At the fame time, a creditor, who either does poind by famples, or is ready to do fo, is in fafety to make a purchafe from the debtor, and will thereby exclude pofterior creditors whofe diligences were not ready. The fafeft way in fuch a cafe, is to proceed in the poinding as far as it can be done; and then to make the purchafe by written agreement, expreffing every circumftance of the facts. The quantities and prices, when the execution proceeds in the common manner, muft be fixed by threfhers, cafters, and meafurers; all of whom muft be fworn to a faithful execution of the work, and the execution ought diftinctly to narrate the procedure.

· If the debtor appears at any period of the execution, and offers to pay the debt, the poinding muft ftop, and a proper time be allowed for making out a difcharge. If the creditor is not prefent to grant fuch difcharge, the debtor, if he pleafes, may pay the money to the meffenger, upon his receipt and delivery of the diligence. But, as the meffenger has no fpecial authority to receive it, the payment to him is no more than a confignation upon the peril of the eonfigner; and therefore the proper and fafe method is, to confign the money in the hands of the neareft judge ordinary, or his clerk; upon which the goods muft be redelivered to the debtor, and the *res gesta* narrated in the meffenger's execution, the debtor, at the fame time, taking inftruments in the hands of the notary to the poinding. Lord Stair fays, that the execution of the meffenger, in this cafe, together with a proper difcharge produced to the Lord Ordinary on the bills, will be fufficient ground for a fummary charge againft the configner to pay the money to the creditor.

An illegal poinding is, in law, held to be a *fpuilzie*, the form of procedure in which belongs to a title diftinct from this fubject. ·

Letters

Letters of Open Doors.

IN the difcourfe upon the execution againft the perfon of the debtor, we had occafion to fhow the high degree of refpect which the Roman code, and the ancient law of this ifland, paid to the dwelling-houfes of individuals. We mentioned, that our neighbours in England have maintained this privilege, fo confonant to the manners of a free people; and we pointed out in what manner it was loft to the inhabitants of this country, by the abufe of the procefs of outlawry, in making rebellion to the Prince the eftablifhed penalty of non-payment of civil debts.

If the houfe of a fubject, by the ancient law, could not be violated by the forcible execution of any procefs againft the perfon, far lefs could an attack by force be made upon it in the lower execution againft moveables. The fheriff, by the Englifh poinding, or *Fieri facias*, is indemnified as far as he acts neceffarily, in order to the taking of the goods: ' And, therefore, (fays Baron Gilbert), if he
' break open a cheft, in which goods are locked up, or a barn not
' adjoining to a dwelling-houfe, which is made for the confervation
' of goods only, he is indemnified by the writ; but he is not by the
' writ authorifed to break the dwelling-houfe, which is built for the
' protection of the man and his family *.'—' This protecting a man
' in his own houfe, (continues the Baron), was very agreeable to
' the ancient law; becaufe, in perfonal contracts, they did only

3 K 2   ' fubject

* Law of Executions, p. 18.

' fubject their chattels, and not their perfons, nor their freeholds;
' and though afterwards, by fubfequent laws, the freehold and per-
' fon were made liable to execution, yet they have not taken away
' the privilege a man had by common law to defend his own houfe,
' which ftill continues.'

The principles and practice of our own ancient law were the very fame. There is not a veftige in our old ftatutes which indicates the exiftence of any authority in the fheriff, or any officer, to enter a man's houfe upon any pretence, but that of a crime committed by the owner, and of the fictitious crime, which afterwards became fo prevalent, of civil rebellion. Of this we have a certain proof, from the neceffity which exifts at this moment of obtaining what we call *Letters of Open Doors*, in all cafes where accefs is denied, and where the meffenger is not poffeffed of a caption againft the party. The nature of this arbitrary warrant betrays, of itfelf, the unlucky quarter from whence we unhappily derived it, and many other cuftoms contrary to the genius of our own law, and to the manners of a free people. We formerly obferved, that, after the inftitution of the College of Juftice, a fwarm of new letters and new warrants appeared under the Signet, altogether unknown to our anceftors; till at laft this practice defcended fo low, that the Writers framed letters fuited almoft to every incident of their employers bufinefs. In Balfour's fyftem of the law, there is no indication of letters of open doors; but, in the 1541, which was immediately after the Inftitution of the College of Juftice, we find letters directed, charging the threfhers of the adjacent country to pafs and threfh out poinded corns, at the requeft of the officer executor of the poinding, upon the debtor's expences [*]. If the meffengers were thus eafily accommodated with incidental warrants, it might be fafely conjectured, that they would very foon come to apply for letters to break open doors, and enter houfes by force; and our judges, whofe forms were now modelled

upon

[*] Balfour, p. 389. c. 19.

upon thofe of France, had a plain authority for their direction. In that kingdom, the warrant of poinding is totally committed to an officer, *huiffier*, or door-keeper of court, much in the fame ftation and degree of knowledge or refpect as our meffengers. ' When the ' doors of a houfe are fhut, and accefs denied, the officer (fay the ' French lawyers) ought to make his verbal procefs upon the fact, ' and to apply to the neareft judge of the jurifdiction, who, upon ' examining the verbal procefs, will authorife him by a warrant to ' break open the doors, in prefence of two witneffes, whom the ' judge at the fame time names *.' In Paris, there is an officer appointed for this fpecial purpofe, called *the commiffary of open doors.*

After the whole executive bufinefs of this nation fell from the hands of the real fheriffs into thofe of meffengers, or fheriffs in that part, it became a neceffary axiom in the law, that thefe officers were limited to the ftrict words of the warrant upon which they acted. When, therefore, a meffenger acted upon letters of poinding *per fe,* he could not enter any houfe, if the doors were fhut againft him, and ought never to have done fo. According to the French method, he returned an execution of the fact, which being produced with the letters of poinding, the Lords, upon a bill, granted new letters of poinding, with an addition of a warrant for breaking open the doors of the debtor's houfe by force, in order to carry off the whole furniture, or other effects found in it. The ftyle of thefe letters will be found in our formalift Mr Dallas †. There is nothing material to be remarked relative to the ftyle of this diligence, as it is merely compofed of the letters of poinding, and the warrant of open doors commonly inferted in letters of caption, which have both been already analifed. In the preamble, indeed, the debt and the letters of horning are recited ; and it concludes with a fhort narrative of the meffenger's having found the doors fhut, or repofitories locked, whereby he was prevented from putting his letters of poinding

into

* Encyclopedie ;—vide Saifie.   † P. 70.

into complete execution. The Writers of the laſt century, when they gave a warrant for poinding moveables, always added to it a warrant for appriſing the land, both of them being founded upon the act of James III. 1649. Theſe letters were almoſt neceſſary in every caſe, before the horning and poinding were joined together in one warrant; but, after that time, a trick of practice rendered the letters of open doors ſeldom requiſite. The meſſengers took care to be poſſeſſed of captions before attempting to execute the poinding; and, if the doors were cloſed, they forced them open, under the pretence of ſearching for the debtor or rebel, upon the authority of the warrant in the caption. Having, under this pretence, got admiſſion, they poinded the effects. Nay, from ſeveral ſtyle-books in the laſt century, we find, that diligence againſt any other perſon was made uſe of for this purpoſe, the meſſenger pretending that the man againſt whom he had the caption was in ſuch a houſe. All mean devices of this kind ought to be diſcouraged; they corrupt the officers, and tend to debaſe the people. We do not know if this trick be ever put in practice; but, we apprehend, no meſſenger is entitled to enter a houſe in virtue of a caption againſt a third party, unleſs he can ſhow a ſpecial information to that purpoſe; and, if he refuſes to give ſatisfaction upon this head, he may be reſiſted, and ought to be puniſhed. Where the caption applies to the debtor whoſe effects are to be poinded, there is no remedy; the device always has, and will continue to take effect. The only caſes now in which letters of open doors are neceſſary, are where a poinding is attempted upon the warrant in a horning, without having raiſed a caption; and the other and moſt frequent is, in fortification of the decrees of ſheriffs and other inferior judges. When doors were cloſed againſt their precepts, the old practice was always to apply to the Court of Seſſion for a warrant of open doors; becauſe it was long and juſtly doubted, whether ſheriffs or other inferior judges poſſeſſed ſuch a degree of power as to authoriſe the commiſſion of violence upon the houſe of any ſubject. In our formaliſt's time, it

was

was thought they could not do it. ' The meffenger or officer comes
' to poind, (fays he), and yet cannot, there being no patent doors,
' or warrant to make any ; and fo they must return *re infecta* ; nor
' is it in the power of an inferior judge to grant fuch warrants.'
Therefore the ftyle given by Mr Dallas is in fupplement of a fheriff's precept. His idea is certainly confonant to our ancient law,
which trufted no inferior judge with fuch formidable powers. Durie, however, has reported a decifion *, in which it feems to be a-
greed on all hands, that magiftrates had authority to grant a warrant
for open doors, in fupporting the execution of their own precepts of
poinding ; and, fince the beginning of this century, it is certain
that fheriffs, ftewarts, and bailies, have been in the daily practice of
granting warrants of open doors, upon returns of their own officers ;
which we, with great fubmiffion, take to be a very culpable incroach-
ment of thefe judges upon the law of the country, and the rights of
the people. In June 1748, a Writer to the Signet, with great propriety, refufed to fubfcribe letters of open doors, upon the decree of
a baron in the execution of his office. Upon report of the cafe, the
Lords directed the Ordinary to refufe the bill ; for this reafon, becaufe they could not interpofe where there had been no interpofition of the fheriff's authority to the baron's decree. The reafon of
this was, that the fheriff of old, as the King's judge, had the immediate controul of the baron's court ; and the decree of the latter
could not be noticed by the fuperior court till it was approved by
the fheriff. Lord Kilkerran, in whofe collection this decifion is reported, obferves, ' That the Prefident gave it as his opinion, that the
' baron himfelf might execute his own decree, and give the warrant
' for open doors.' A baron has now no jurifdiction but for recovery of his own rents. Even under the dominion of the feudal
principles, an Englifh baron was never poffeffed of fuch a degree of
power ; nor have we any precedent in this country to fhow that a
Scottifh.

---

* Dick againft Lawds, 7th December 1630.

Scottish one had any pretensions to it. The opinion, therefore, given by the Lord President in the 1748, when the powers of our baron courts were reduced to shadows, was extraordinary indeed. However, several barons, and particularly the magistrates of the city of Edinburgh, as such, relying upon this decision, have assumed the power of giving warrants for forcing the doors of debtor's open, in order to poind their moveables.

Arrestment.

Arreſtment.

THE firſt ſtep in every action of old, was attachment of the perſon's goods, to force his appearance in court, and ſecure obedience to the judgment. ‘ Attachment (ſays the Quoniam At- ‘ tachiamenta) is a lawful band, by the whilk the party defender is ‘ conſtrained to ſtand to the law, and to anſwer judicially to the ‘ party complaining upon, in form of law.' Attachment was not only applied, in our old law, to the ſeizure of the perſons of crimi- nals, but was alſo the proper term for the diligence which we now call *arreſtment upon a depending action.*

There is another ſpecies of arreſtment which is now an eſtabliſhed diligence againſt moveables, diſtinct from poinding, and which aroſe at a later period, and from cauſes quite different from our arreſt- ment upon a depending action. Although we are accuſtomed to conſider this execution as different from the poinding, it is, in fact, merely a branch of it, which has degenerated by time into the pre- ſent form of arreſtment. When a defender in a law-ſuit produced his pledges or his cautioners, execution by poinding went againſt them both, for payment of the ſums awarded by the decree. Or, if the goods attached remained with the judge, they were ſold, and the price applied; ſo that poinding was the only diligence againſt move- ables known in Scotland. This leads us to explain ſome circum- ſtances in the nature of old poindings which, at firſt ſight, ſeem to belong to the former diſcourſe, but, for obvious reaſons, have been reſerved for the preſent one.

As foon as a writ of *Fieri facias* is delivered to the Englifh fheriff, the whole effects belonging to the debtor are held to be invefted in him, in the fame manner as if they had been fpecially transferred ; and, confequently, all fales or conveyances made to elude the effect of this judicial transfer, are void and null. In this fituation, there could be no ufe for any thing like our prefent arreftment. The fheriff can fell the moveables, feize upon them in whofe hands foever they are within his jurifdiction, and recover the debts due by third parties to the debtor, in the fame manner as he could have done himfelf.

In Scotland, although our old code, and the ftatutes anterior to James I. are, like thofe of England, full of rules for attachment of the effects of debtors to anfwer in actions, there is not one word to be met with, of arreftments confidered as an execution. We entertained no idea of a diligence fo imperfect, after having a decree in our poffeffion. The *Fieri* and *levari facias* in England, and the brieve of diftrefs in Scotland, made no diftinction between the goods in the debtor's real poffeffion, and the rents due to him for his land. The fheriff fold the one, and levied the other, in the right of the debtor, which was equal, in effect, both to our prefent arreftment and our forthcoming. This effect does not appear to have been determined with fuch precifion as in England ; becaufe, from the reign of James III. downwards, our law and practice was in a ftate of declination from the ancient fyftem common to the whole ifland ; and we were imbibing the cuftoms of France, and the principles of the Roman jurifprudence, in oppofition to the common law of the land. The property feems only to have been transferred, not from the date or delivery of the writ, but from the date of the actual feizure by the fheriff. When we fay this, we muft be underftood to fpeak of third parties, purchafers, and not of other creditors of the fame debtors ; for we fhall foon fee, that, *quoad* them, a different rule fubfifted.

Although

Although the term *arreftment* occurs frequently in the acts of the five Jameses, yet it always refpects the arreftment of criminals by the King's officers, and has no kind of relation to the prohibitory diligence which at prefent goes under that name. Nay, though a variety of acts are to be found, difcharging the whole artillery of the law upon debtors, under the cenfures of the church, there is no mention of arreftment of their effects; but the letters, by thefe ftatutes, are always for poinding, apprifing, and diftrenzieing the moveables of the parties. Poinding anfwered every purpofe, and there was no neceffity for doing the half of the bufinefs by arreftment. Thus we find it determined by a decifion preferved by Balfour in the year 1569, that ' a decreet being obtained againft any ' man, the farms being in his tenant's hands, and auchtand to him, ' may be poinded and diftrenzied for execution of the faid decreet, ' albeit he againft whom the decreet is given, has goods and gear ' ftrinzieable therefore *.' By feveral other decifions of the fame period, it is clear, that the then practice was to poind the effects of debtors in the hands of third parties, and not to arreft them †.

About the time of the inftitution of the College of Juftice, the old method of attaching moveables ceafed, becaufe the precept or fummons did not, like the brieve of diftrefs, contain any warrant for that purpofe. To fupply this, letters of arreftment were iffued, which did not bear an order to feize upon the debtor's goods, but only to arreft them, *i. e.* to prohibit the debtor, in the King's name, to touch them, until he fhould find caution to pay the debt in the event of a decree being given againft him. When the property of goods was claimed by different perfons, letters were obtained by one of them to arreft the goods in difpute, to remain untouched by any of the parties, until the point of right fhould be determined by the proper judge. This fpecies of arreftment ftill continues, under the title of *fequeftration*, and belongs to a different branch of our practice.

3 L 2   As

As the principal moveables of thefe days confifted in corn, either growing or cut, cattle, and rural implements, the arreftment for fecurity of debts was always ufed upon them; and this, it feems, was fometimes done without giving notice to the owner, which we find firft corrected by a decifion in Balfour *. All arreftments of this kind were loofeable upon caution; and therefore, if the party arrefter refufed to accept of fecurity, the judge, upon application, obliged him to receive it; and the nature of the bail was, that the fame goods, or their value, fhould be forthcoming to any party having intereft. The crime of breach of arreftment was not laid upon the injury done in difappointing the creditor of his fecurity; but, like civil rebellion, it turned upon the difobedience of the command of the King's letters, or thofe of the fuperior by whom the order was granted. It therefore impofed a heavy punifhment. The particulars of it appear from the following decifion collected by Balfour †.
' Arreftment by the King's letters being lawfully made upon any
' debaitable corais, gudes, or gear, gif ony perfon or perfons breaks
' the fame, and beis convict thereof, all their moveable gudes may
' be confifcat, applyit, and inbrocht to the King's ufe; and alfwa,
' they may be chargit to enter their perfons in ward, at the King's
' will, there to remain for zeir and day; and farder, at the King's
' will, upon their awin expences, for their contemption done to his
' Hienefs in breaking of the faid arreftment,'

Thefe were the firft arreftments; and, it is evident, they were all of the nature of what we now underftand by fequeftrations, prohibiting the parties to touch their own goods in their own poffeffion. In fact, this was the firft deviation from our ancient law. Our fheriffs, of old, poinded, i. e. feized the real poffeffion of the goods of debtors until caution was found. But, when the executive bufinefs of the nation devolved upon meffengers, fheriffs in that part, a power of this kind was inconfiftent with their character, or with the fafety of

of the people ; and therefore they were truſted with no more than
the execution of a probitory order, arreſting the goods upon the
ſpot, and impoſing a penalty upon the breakers of it. This idea of
arreſtment in a man's own hands, remained long in the law, after its
principles and origin ſeem to have been entirely forgot. A creditor
of a lady arreſted a quantity of wool in her own hands, and purſued
a third party, who had purchaſed from the lady. The Lords
' found, that this arreſtment, albeit it was only made in the lady's
' own hands, and nowiſe known to the buyer, nor intimate to him,
' yet did ſo affect the wool really, at the inſtance and to the behoof ·
' of the arreſter, that, after the laying on of the ſame, none could
' profitably bargain, or do any deed which might fruſtrate the effect
' of the arreſtment, and prejudge him of execution thereupon ; and
' therefore ſuſtained the action *.' This was a deciſion replete with
injuſtice. If this arreſtment was uſed in the lady's hands upon a
dependence, ſhe alone could be attacked for breach of arreſtment ;
but, if it was uſed upon a decree by way of execution, the arreſtment was an ineffectual diligence, as the goods ought to have been
poinded †.

We now go back to bring up the other, and ſtill ſubſiſting kind,
intended to reach debts due to the debtor, which, according to our
practice, cannot be come at by poinding. The Engliſh ſheriffs were
veſted, by delivery of the writ, not only with the moveables in poſſeſſion of the debtor, but with all the debts due to him; ſo that they
could ſue for, or order the recovery of any debt, in the ſame manner as could be done by the party himſelf. But a truſt of this kind
was incompatible with the character of our ſheriffs in that part ; and
therefore debts due to the debtor were arreſted and ſtopped in the
hands of third parties, in the ſame manner as they were in the
hands of the debtor himſelf, which was all that the diligence authoriſed the officer to do.

About

---

* 10th January 1624, Innerweek againſt Wilkie.
† Vide Lord Stair, p. 388.

About the time of the inſtitution of the College of Juſtice, neither an arreſtment in the debtor's own hands, nor in the hands of the debtors to him, gave (as they now do) the arreſter any preference. All the effeɛ̃t of ſuch writs, was to detain the goods in the hands of the parties for the behoof of all having intereſt. It was the decree of the Court which created a preference, or formed any lien upon the property. ' Divers and ſundry decreets (ſays Balfour) ' being obtained, by divers and ſundry perſons, aganis ony man, ' gif the obtainaires thereof cauſe arreſt his maillis, ferms, and du ' ties, in his tenants hands, for payment to be made to them there ' of, the tenants aucht and ſould pay firſt to him wha obtained the ' firſt decrete ; and he being fully and compleatly paid, they ſould ' make payment to him wha obtained the ſecond decrete ; and he ' being compleatly paid, they ſould conſequently pay the reſt of the ' creditors wha obtained decreets, and cauſet arreſtments to be made ' after the order and priority of time in obtaining of their decreets *.' From this deciſion, and ſeveral others to be found in the ſame col leɛ̃tion, it is poved, that the arreſtment at that period had no effeɛ̃t in preferring the creditor-arreſter, even where it was executed after the decree had been obtained. Such being our law, it is plain, that we had no more uſe in our praɛ̃tice for an arreſtment in execution, than the Engliſh had. The delivery of their writs carried the debts of the party to the ſheriff, and our decrees carried it to the creditor himſelf.

The ſame deciſions further inform us, that the method of poind ing the tenants for the rents due to their maſters, had given place to the ſimple arreſtment in their hands ; and upon this footing it has ever ſince continued. It is now an eſtabliſhed rule, that the rents due by tenants are affeɛ̃table only by arreſtment, which is a very great relief to that uſeful claſs of men. We wiſh here to be under ſtood as ſpeaking of perſonal debts of land proprietors. The powers of ſuperiors and landlords, in recovery of their rents and duties,

come

* Balfour, p. 391.

come under a different title, and are ſet apart for particular examination.

The next queſtion is, In what manner our law came to alter from
the rule of the deciſion quoted by Balfour ; and, in place of regarding the date of the judgment and decree obtained by creditors,
ſhould prefer them according to the date of the arreſtment uſed by
the meſſenger in virtue of his letters ? There is a large blank in the
deciſions of our Court ; for, from the collection made by Balfour in
the reign of Queen Mary, we have little or nothing to be depended
on, till Sir Alexander Gibſon of Durie began his work in the
1621. In this dark period, however, a number of conſiderable
changes in our law took place, all occaſioned by a fond and faſhion-
able imitation of the cuſtoms of France. In Durie's time, we find
this point completely eſtabliſhed ; and the very firſt reflection upon
the laws of France muſt convince every perſon, that the whole ſyſtem of our modern arreſtments has been, in the period we have
mentioned, implicitly borrowed from that quarter.

‘ According to the cuſtoms of France, (ſays the commentator of
‘ that of Normandy), the firſt arreſter of moveables, though poſte-
‘ rior in date, is preferred upon the axiom of the Roman law, *vigi-*
‘ *lantibus jura ſubveniunt.*’—‘ Seizure and arreſt (ſay the modern
‘ French lawyers) is that which the creditor makes againſt his debt-
‘ or in the hands of a third party, who owes money to the ſame
‘ debtor ; and the effect is, that this third party, in whoſe hands ar-
‘ reſtments are made, cannot quit with any thing in his hands to the
‘ prejudice of the arreſter. This ſeizing and arreſtment may be
‘ made anterior to a decree, in virtue of an ordinance of a judge.’
‘ The writ uſually contains a ſummons againſt a third party, to aſ-
‘ certain what he owes, and to be decreed to empty his hands into
‘ thoſe of the arreſter *.’ Theſe rules of the laws of France are ſo
preciſely conſonant to thoſe of this country, that we cannot entertain

* Grand Ency. voyez Saiſie et Arret.

tain a doubt from whence we borrowed the whole rules of our modern arreftment. Accordingly, at the time when Sir Alexander Gibfon began to collect his decifions, we find thefe rules eftablifhed in practice. We find, that the execution of an arreftment, even upon a pofterior decree, is preferred to a fecond execution upon the firft decree, in direct oppofition to our ancient law.

We now proceed to the pofitive laws made in behalf of this branch of practice. By c. 118. of the 7th Parliament of James VI. it is ftatuted, ' That the perfons convicted of breach of arreftment ' fhall be punifhed by efcheat of moveables, and that the creditor- ' arrefter fhall be preferable to the efcheat for his debt, damages, and ' expences.' This ftatute did no more than revive the law which fubfifted in the fame cafe fifty years before, as we have learned from Balfour. Part of it ftill remains againft people who difobey the order of our courts by breach of fequeftration. That of arreftment is generally attended with no other penalty than payment of the debt.

A very curious remainder of the ancient power of our fheriffs remained for a long period with the meffengers. All the ancient attachments were loofeable by the debtor's finding pledges or cautioners, the fufficiency of which was judged of by the fheriff. This power, it feems, remained with the meffengers who came in their place; and, by a moft extraordinary and flovenly practice, the whole body of meffengers were fuppofed to be poffeffed of it. Owing to this circumftance, if an arreftment was laid on by one meffenger in virtue of letters under the Signet, it behoved to be loofed by another meffenger, by letters of loofing arreftment, to whom the debtor was obliged to deliver a bond of caution. Even this truft, fmall as it was, was abufed by thefe officers; and they were accordingly deprived of it by the act, c. 17. of the 22d Parliament of James VI. By this ftatute, the ancient powers of our fheriffs remaining with their reprefentatives the meffengers, were entirely and moft properly cut off; and, from that date, commenced the regular
method

method of finding caution in the books of Seſſion, which has ever ſince ſubſiſted.

Letters of arreſtment, when given out by themſelves, were, in fact, nothing more than inhibitions of moveables intended to effect them in the hands of the proprietor, as well as in the cuſtody of third parties. After the French rule of the *premier arreſſant* took place, we find the letters iſſued by themſelves in the ſame form as the inhibition ; and ſuch continues to be the ſtyle at this moment, viz. that the debtor, ' In defraud, hurt, and prejudice of the complainer, ' intends to ſell, diſpone, dilapidate, and put away, all and ſun- ' dry goods, gear, corns, cattle, horſe, nolt, ſheep, debts, ſums of ' money, inſight pleniſhing, maills, farms, and duties of lands, and ' all other moveable goods and gear belonging to him.' The will of the letters is, that ' ye fence and arreſt all and ſundrie the goods, ' gear, corns, &c. pertaining and belonging to the ſaid C. D. where- ' ever or in whoſe hands the ſame may or can be apprehended, to ' remain in their hands, under ſure fence and arreſtment, ay and ' while caution and ſoverty be found acted in our books of Council ' and Seſſion, that the ſame ſhall be made furthcoming as accords.' The firſt reflection upon this ſtyle, demonſtrates that theſe letters were intended to have effect in the hands of the debtor himſelf ; and, to prevent him from touching his moveables, with as much certainty as in inhibition ties up the hands of a land proprietor. If this had not been the caſe, how is an arreſtment to affect a man's corns, cattle, horſe, and even the furniture of his houſe, none of which articles could be in the poſſeſſion of any other perſon but himſelf? Such was the ſpecies of arreſtment which we borrowed from the French, and which came in place of our own ancient form, of forcing the defender to find caution for the event of an action. At firſt, theſe letters were always joined with inhibition ; and, according, in the act of Council dated the 3d of June 1597, aſcertaining the prices of ſignet letters, we find the inhibition and arreſtment joined together. Afterwards, when horning and poinding were allowed to be iffued in one warrant, the addition of the two words, *fence* and *arreft*, gave that compound diligence the additional power of an arreftment.

Letters of arreftment *per fe* are always taken upon depending actions, or upon grounds of debt upon which no other diligence can proceed; and the arreftments, in that cafe, are to fubfift only till caution be found   Letters of horning contain no fuch condition, becaufe the arreftments upon that warrant are not for fecurity, but for execution.   It is intended to reach every thing in the hands of third parties which cannot be got at by poinding; and therefore fuch an arreftment cannot be loofed by caution, or any other method than that of payment of the debt.

We do not intend to enter into the practical part of this diligence, as it belongs more properly to the proceffes of multiple-poinding and forthcoming.

Inhibition.

Inhibition.

THE precife period when letters of inhibition came into legal
practice has not been hitherto afcertained. It is probable, however, that, anterior to the 1469, when the ancient form of apprifing
was new modelled, the inhibition muft have been little known;
becaufe the firft ftep of the old procedure was a feizure of the land
itfelf; confequently there could be little occafion for a writ of that
kind, except to prevent the debtor from difpofing of his moveables.
The inhibition, from the period of its introduction, had, and continues to have the ftrongeft, the moft fudden and determinate effect
of any writ known in our law; and therefore its hiftory and its
principles are equally deferving of our curiofity, and neceffary to
our inftruction.

The provinces of France, termed *Les pays de droit ecrite*, notwithftanding the conquefts of the barbarians, retained a great part of the
jurifprudence of the Romans, their firft mafters; and, upon the revival
of the ftudy of the civil law, they added to their former ftock. The
cuftomary provinces alfo received the civil code, as law in every cafe
not determined by the feudal ufage; and thus, among the reft, the
whole doctrine of the Roman hypothecs became prevalent in France.
The notaries and churchmen, the only clerks in thefe days, very
foon took the advantage of thefe newly revived titles, in fecurity of
their own acquifitions, and alfo introduced them into the deeds and
tranfactions of private people. Not fatisfied with the tacit hypothec

competent

competent to masters upon the fruits of the land, and with the power of distress which the common law afforded to proprietors for the recovery of their rents, these ecclesiastical masters borrowed from the civil law the conventional hypothec, and extended it over the whole property, heritable and moveable, present and to come, belonging to their tenants. This they joined with the usage of distress, and stipulated, that they should be at liberty to seize upon the property of the tenant wherever it could be found ; nay more, to sell and dispose of it, without being accountable in any other shape but by a simple oath ; and, in order to make sure by every method human and divine, the tenants are made to consent to their being excommunicated by the granter's of the lease upon the failure of every term's rent.

The same laws were adopted, and the same style was practised in Scotland, of which there is evidence sufficient to be had in our charter chests, from the deeds executed in the middle of the fourteenth century, and downwards ; and, indeed, the noble collection of ancient records published by Mr Rymer, enables us to establish this fact in the history of our law by undoubted authority. Thus, by the bond granted by James I. to the King of England for his ransom, dated 28th March 1424, he was obliged not only to hypothecate his whole property, present and future, but also to submit himself to the jurisdiction of the Pope, or any other ecclesiastical court; and the bonds granted by the magistrates of the several royal boroughs for the same purpose, are all in a similar form. As further evidence that the same mode of obligation by hypothec continued in Scotland during the reign of the five Jameses, the following direct authority from Balfour will be attended to : ' It is leisom to ' any man to bind and oblige his goods and gear, present or to ' come, or the fruits of the ground pertaining to him, and yet beand ' thereupon : *Item,* guids or gear corporal, as horse, or incorporal, ' as debts, weddis, or liferentis *.'

When

* Balfour, p 150.

When a temporal judge admitted any caufe which the ecclefiaftics deemed to be within clerical jurifdiction, they iffued a writ, *inhibiting* and *difcharging* him to proceed. Hence we find the following inftruction to the commiffaries of Edinburgh fo late as the 1610. ' Gif ony temporal judge within this realm will proceed in caufes ' belonging to your jurifdiction, ye fhall direct precepts to *inhibit* ' them from all proceeding thereuntill *.'—' Inhibitions (we are told ' by Sir George M'Kenzie) have their origin from the canon law, ' whereby, if the fecular judge did interpofe in any thing that was ' ecclefiaftic, the ecclefiaftic judge did inhibit him to proceed. With ' us they were firft ufed in the matter of teinds in the fame fenfe, ' but now the word is extended to letters, whereby the judge inhi- ' bits debtors to fell in prejudice of creditors †.' This is one of the very few hints which our writers on the law have left us regarding the origin of our writs, and it is a juft, though fuperficial one. The bifhop's courts anciently iffued thefe inhibitions of teinds in Scotland ; and, confequently, it is an article of the inftructions given to the commiffaries, ' Ye fhall give forth inhibitions upon teinds great ' and fmall, as ye are defired upon the fight of the parties title al- ' lenarly ‡.' The purpofe of thefe letters or precepts was to difcharge the proprietors from carrying off the corn, until the churchmen who had right to the teinds, drew them out, or, as they termed, *tythed* the crop. They proceeded, therefore, upon a right to the corn, which affected the whole of it as it ftood upon the ground, *i. e* every tenth ftook, good or bad. Now, when any man granted either a general or a fpecial hypothec upon his whole property, heritable or moveable, in favour of a creditor, that creditor had, according to the idea of the Roman law, a right extending over the eftate of this debtor preferable to all other creditors. Thefe hypothecs were corroborated by the oath of the party, and by a prorogation or fubjection of the matter to the ecclefiaftical jurifdiction ; and,

---

* Balfour, p. 665.   † Obf. on Stat. p. 257.   ‡ Balfour, p. 665.

and, therefore, when the creditor had reason to suspect that the debtor was destroying the subject of his hypothec, he applied to the ecclesiastical court to interpose by their writ of inhibition, which appears to be the origin of that diligence in our law. If, when the debt became payable, and the demand was made, the debtor did not comply, the process of cursing or excommunication went out against him by the church, proceeding upon his consent in the deed, and letters of poinding and apprising were issued against his property, moveable and immoveable. These terrible effects were often defeated by appellations from the sentence of cursing ; and several statutes in the reign of James III. and IV. are directed to shorten the delays occasioned by these appellations, particularly the act 36. of the 5th Parliament of James V. anno 1537, declares, that they are to last no longer than a year. Before that time they lasted for several years; and, upon these occasions, it is reasonable to suppose that the letters of inhibition were introduced in order to preserve the property *in medio*, and to discharge the lieges from having any dealings or intercourse with debtors in that situation. Every common creditor who had pactioned for it, was entitled to letters of cursing, which were a kind of interpellation against the lieges from having any communication with the person accursed, so far as concerned spirituals ; but, when creditors had the whole of their debtor's property hypothecated for their debt, they were entitled to the inhibition, to preserve their conventional right, and to notify it to the lieges. These letters, as well as interdictions, and many others, were current in Scotland long before they came to be noticed by any public act or statute, and appear to have been introduced by custom alone.

Our next inquiry must be for the causes which produced this singular writ in Scotland, while it remained unknown to our neighbours. We did not derive the idea of the inhibition from the Roman law, but we derived the form of the hypothec itself; and, from the whole deeds yet remaining from the fourteenth century downwards, it is certain that there is no contract or obligation, the

importance

importance of which made it be executed in authentic form; but in it we find a conventional hypothec ftipulated. This method came fo much into common ufe, that the notaries and churchmen expreffed only the firft words of the claufe, *i. e.* they wrote *binding and obliging*, &c. by which it was underftood that the granter bound and obliged his whole effects, prefent and to come, for the implement of that deed. As they were accuftomed to inhibitions and prohibitions of every kind, the extending of them to the fupport of contracts and deeds of hypothecation was obvious and natural. The inhibition of teinds was no other than a kind of monitor publifhed in the parifh churches, to prevent the intromiffion of proprietors with the victual, until it was tythed by the churchmen. The eafy and natural analogy of this form produced that of our prefent inhibition. This is proved by the perfect coincidence not only of the title, but of the ftyle of thefe writs. The granter of the hypothec had, in moft cafes, made an oath not to difappoint it; and therefore the authority of the church was called upon to terrify him into compliance. This method was found to have a double effect; it put it at once out of the debtor's power to counteract his obligations, by warning the people not to deal with him; and it did juftice to the people, by notifying the fituation of the individual. When prohibitory forms are introduced in civil matters, it is a certain confequence, that, where thefe forms are not ufed, people do not think themfelves prohibited. Thus, unlefs an inhibition of teinds was executed, the intromitter was not held to be guilty of a fpuilzie; and, if an inhibition againft a debtor was not ufed, every perfon thought himfelf at liberty to contract with a debtor, without inquiry whether his effects ftood hypothecated or not; and, confequently, the creditor had no right to recover from third parties purchafers. No fuch form happened to take place among the Romans or the French, and therefore the creditor hypothecator had, and ftill has right to actions againft third parties. This, in Scotland, muft unavoidably have made the right of fuch creditors depend entirely upon the writ

of

of inhibition itfelf, and confequently eftablifhed it as an effential branch in the practice in our law. How it became the right of creditors in general, we fhall afterwards endeavour to explain. Meantime, let us fee how this writ loft its effect upon moveables; or, in other words, how the ftyle of the inhibition came to alter into its prefent form. A prohibition fo extraordinary muft have been abfolutely incompatible with any degree of commerce in a country; and, accordingly, we find, that the cuftoms of Paris ran counter to it; and the example of that great city was foon followed by all the other provinces. By article 170. of the *Coutumieres de Paris*, it is declared, that moveables are not fubject to hypothecation without poffeffion. The fame change took place even in the provinces of the written or Roman laws, with this exception, that, fo long as the moveables remain in the poffeffion of the debtor, the creditor poffeffed of the conventional hypothec is preferred.

Our law, as it was originally the fame, changed with that of France. Craig informs us, that, though letters of inhibition extended to moveables, the utility of the public prevailed in that particular againft the intereft of creditors. As it is clear, that conventional hypothecs had once been adopted into our law, it is equally certain that they went entirely out of practice, even with refpect to landed property. In Rome, the conventional hypothecs were attended with great inconvenience to third parties purchafing *bona fide*; and therefore they adopted the Grecian method of putting marks or notices upon the fubject hypothecated, in order to make their fituation known to ftrangers. The French adopted thefe marks, to point out property that was actually in the hands of juftice; but, in the matter of hypothecs, they never were ufed. In order, however, to fupply the want, and to create notoriety of their hypothecs, they invented a kind of fictitious delivery of the heritage, from the analogy of the feudal feifine *.

In

* Encyclop. Hypoth.

In Scotland, on the contrary, the Roman mode of hypothec, it feems, did not prove fufficiently effectual. In the conveyance of the property itfelf, we adhered ftrictly to the feudal form of feifine, and to the ideas of fuperior and vaffal. When wadfets and rights of annualrent became frequent, they were all conftituted in the fame manner, and, no doubt, excluded the creditors by conventional hypothecs, which muft, upon that account, have vanifhed out of our law, leaving no trace behind them except the writ of inhibition, which, ftill retains ftrong features of its origin. This deduction is fupported by the nature of the thing; for, fo foon as the idea of real rights came to be annexed to the charter and feifine, the hypothecs, of confequence, muft have been undermined and excluded from practice. At the fame time the inhibitions continued, and came to be granted upon grounds of debt of every kind, providing they were clear and liquid; for it is certain, that to fuch debts alone they continued for a long time to be reftricted. Even Sir George M'Kenzie tells us, that they proceeded either on a decree or regiftered bond; ' which (fays Mr Erfkine) carries a ftrong infinuation ' as if inhibitions could not be grounded upon any unregiftered ' deed *.' The introduction of the inhibition, as already mentioned, rendered the hypothec ineffectual of itfelf: It behoved to be fupported by the prohibition; and therefore people naturally looked to that diligence for the whole effect, forgetting entirely upon what it had been originally founded. It is in this manner that we prefume inhibition continued in our law, and that its effects upon heritable property were preferved.

The French, on the contrary, have preferved the ancient hypothec upon their lands; and therefore the inhibition is, at this day, equally unknown to them as it was to the Romans. They have different methods of making thefe rights known to their people. The poftponed creditors are obliged to pay the debts privileged by hypo-

Vol. I.   3 N   thecs,

* P. 370.

thecs, and to take conveyances to them, as we do in the cafe of
prior inhibitions. The Englifh have a remainder of the fame nature,
which they have doubtlefs derived from the laws of Normandy. 'In
' the new abridgement of the Englifh law, (fays Lord Kaimes), we
' find the following paffage. " As to lands, they are bound from the
" time of the judgment ; fo that execution may be of this, though
" the party aliens *bona fide*, before execution fued out. So of fta-
" tute merchant, ftaple, and recognifances, which alfo bind the
" lands from the time of entering into them." ' From this paffage
' it cannot juftly be inferred, that a judgment in a procefs, or any
' of the covenants above mentioned, are real rights, or make a real
' *alien*, as termed in England. They have only the effect of an in-
' hibition to bar voluntary alienations. Hence the reafon why let-
' ters of inhibition are unknown in England *.'

When the conventional hypothecs went out of ufe with us, and
infeftments were found to anfwer all their purpofes, in a manner
more fecure for the party, and fafer for the public, the ideas of our
lawyers were wholly bent to the effects of that form ; fo that it left
us no private contracts, judgments, decrees, or other writs which
had effect upon land in any other fhape ; and, as the Latin language afforded no term for our wadfets, annualrent rights, or heritable bonds, which are no other than fpecial hypothecs by infeftment, Sir Thomas Craig, Dirleton, and our old conveyancers, exprefs all thefe by the general term *hypothecae*. Thus, without any
fpecial act of Parliament or exprefs law, this fingular writ came to
be eftablifhed in the practice of Scotland ; and, although the inhibition was originally an ecclefiaftical execution, it foon came into
the hands of our civil courts. After the inftitution of the College of
Juftice, that tribunal foon eclipfed all others in the nation, whether
ecclefiaftical or civil. Its Judges continued to be compofed chiefly
of churchmen ; and therefore it was natural for the lieges to apply

to.

* Elucid. p. 120.

to the Lords of Seffion for letters of inhibition, by whom they were iffued in the name of the King.

When the origin of the inhibition came to be totally forgot in the manner we have ftated, creditors continued to apply for it upon all occafions ; but, being at a lofs for grounds or principles to go upon, they ftumbled upon the pretence that their debtors intended to defraud them. From feveral old decifions, however, it appears, that the Lords of Seffion viewed this matter in a proper light, and refufed to grant inhibitions without a fufficient ground alledged and proved by the creditor, of actual fraud, bankruptcy, or bad defign, upon the part of the debtor. ‘ Letteris of inhibition (fays Balfour) ‘ may not be given againis ony Erle, Lord, or Baron, be the Lords, ‘ without an juft and fufficient caufe, becaufe the famin is hurtful to ‘ ’men’s fame and honour ; and moreover, no perfon fould be ftoppit ‘ in the adminiftration of his goods and gear without ane lauchful ‘ and fufficient caufe *.’ Nay, it appears, that the Judges removed thefe inhibitions with very little ceremony, upon the application of the party injured, when they judged them to be too lightly granted. This, in fome degree, being irregular, was corrected by the following decifion : ‘ Interdiction beand lauchfully made at the inftance ‘ of divers and foundrie creditours upon ane perfoun, the famin ‘ may not be loufit or refcindit be ane judge without their fpecial ‘ confent, at leaft quhile they be callit to that effect †.’ The principle of this decifion fhould have influenced every fubfequent one upon the fubject of inhibitions, and ought to have remained in full force. Where a creditor ftands poffeffed of liquid grounds of debt exigible *de praefenti*, the inhibition does not appear to be an unreafonable or exceptionable ftep, becaufe fuch a creditor may inftantly proceed to affect the lands by the real diligence of adjudication ; and therefore a prohibition to alienate or contract debt upon the land, is the mildeft ftep that he can take ; but the great

3 N 2   abufe

* 11th July 1543, John Maxwell againft Laird of Telling.—Balfour, p. 476.
† 15th February 1537.

abuse of this diligence arose from this, that, by frequency, it passed unnoticed, and came, at last, to be granted to all creditors, real and pretended, for illiquid debts, depending actions, and, in short, for every claim that one man could muster up against another. In this view, it is the most cruel and impolitic diligence that was ever introduced into the law of any country. Because one man pretends or imagines that another is indebted to him, and the experience of every day shows us upon what slight grounds these claims are reared up ; is it reasonable that another of landed property should, by a judicial writ taken out in the common routin of court, receive a blow upon his credit, be recorded not only as an actual, but a kind of insolvent debtor, and, in effect, have the amount of that pretended claim made *pro tempore* a debt upon his lands ? For, although an inhibition upon a depending action is nothing more than a simple and conditional interdict ; yet so it is, that, until the effect is discharged, the claim upon which it proceeds is considered as an incumbrance upon the estate. So long, indeed, as the old brieve of distress remained in practice, the citation for payment, the poinding of the moveables, and the apprising of the land, were no other than as many acts of the same process following one another in a determined order ; and, therefore, in case of danger, inhibition might perhaps have been issued in the course of such diligence, more especially as the ancient method of all law-suits was to begin by taking security or a pledge for the consequences. An inhibition upon a depending action, to people impressed with such ideas of procedure, might appear a just and expedient point of practice. As the letters of inhibition were introduced into Scotland by custom, without any express law ; so there is no public regulation to be found for ages, for directing the mode of their execution or publication. The forms in this business were borrowed from the French, with whom, as formerly noticed, letters of inhibition were unknown ; but interdictions of persons incapable to manage their

own

own affairs, both judicial and voluntary, were in universal practice, and the method of their publication distinctly prescribed. From the French we adopted the forms in the execution or publication of the interdiction, and we applied them to the inhibition. Accordingly, we find the method to have been established, and quite familiar, in the 1554. ' The Lords letters of publication passed upon an inter-
' diction against any man; and executed at the mercat cross of Edin-
' burgh allenarlie, the samin execution and indorsation is null, and
' of nane avail; gif he wha was interdicted dwelt at the same time
' within an uther jurisdiction and sherriffdom, because all publica-
' tions and interdictions aught and should be made at the mercat
' cross of the head burgh or town of the sherriffdom where the per-
' sons interdicted dwells in the mean time *.' This execution at the market cross of the head burgh of the jurisdiction where the party resided, was, in the early part of our law, as Lord Kaimes ob-serves, found to produce notoriety sufficient ; and therefore the in-terdiction and inhibition needed no other mode of publication. Be-fore inhibition, then, came to be noticed in any public act of the legislature, it appears, that not only the style, but also the mode of execution and publication of this writ were completely established. In this situation the diligence stood in the 1581, when the act of Par-liament was made relative to the register of inhibitions †. By this time several of our registers had been established for notifying dili-gences to the lieges ; and, from the preamble to the act, it is pro-ved, that, as Lord Stair observes, ' inhibitions had been long in use
' before the statutes ordaining them to be registered ; and therefore
' the lieges could not be put *in mala fide*, to buy from or bargain
' with the person inhibited, unless the inhibition were published at
' the mercat cross of the jurisdiction where he lived, and at the mer-
' cat cross of the several jurisdictions where his lands lay ; but these
' publications easily passing observation and remembrance, great in-
                                                    ' convenience

---

* Balfour, p. 86.   † 7th Parl. James VI. c. 119.

" convenience arose to creditors and purchasers *." In this statute no directions are given about the execution of the diligence; reference is simply made to the practice which the act presumes to be known and familiar. Two material points are, however, established by it; 1st, That the inhibition must be registered in the books of the sheriffdom where the party makes his residence, and also in the shire where his lands lie; and, 2d, That this must be done within forty days from the date of the last execution. Sir George Mackenzie tells us, that it was first doubted whether the day whereupon the letters are executed or registered is to be numbered among the forty days; but it was afterwards found sufficient that either of these days be free. The omission of the registration voids the diligence *in totum ;* but, in whatever county it was registered, the lands lying there were affected by it; and, notwithstanding the vague, uncertain terms of the statute, it was held to be a rule, that the diligence was null, or of no effect, as to lands lying in any other county where it was not registered.

As no jurisdiction was in this act mentioned but that of sheriffs, the stewarts of stewartries, and bailies of regalities, complained, and with reason, because not only inhibitions but hornings stood in the same situation. This produced an act of Parliament in favour of the latter jurisdictions in the 1597 †. This was the first act in which the publication of the inhibition at the market cross is expressly mentioned or appointed; but the solemnity is thereby proved to have been long, and so completely established by practice as not to require a statute. This act is not to introduce, but to extend the usage to the jurisdiction omitted by the preceding statute.

Irregularities, it seems, had been committed in the registration of the ordinary diligence in inferior courts; and it appears, that certain sheriffs and their clerks, owing to partialities, or connection with the debtors, refused to register these letters. To remedy these disorders, another act immediately followed the former one ‡, by which the

several

---

feveral letters are appointed to be regiftered judicially, or before a notary and four witneffes. If the party appeared when the Judge was fitting, and produced his letters judicially for regiftration, he was entitled to an act of the Court upon the fact, and to an extract for the probation of it ; but perhaps the Court might not fit within the forty days prefcribed by the ftatute, and therefore regiftration is appointed to be made before a notary and four witneffes. But, if the inferior judge refufed to record the letters, the party is to take inftruments, and prefent them to the next inferior judge, or to the Clerk Regifter at Edinburgh, or his deputes, which is the origin of the General Regifter of Inhibitions at Edinburgh.

The importance of the Regifter of Inhibitions appeared in proportion to the increafe of thefe diligences ; and, notwithftanding the folemnity of the former act in the matter of regiftration, many negligences appeared upon the part of the fheriff-clerks, which proved fatal to the parties concerned. To correct thefe wrongs, a ftatute was made in the 15th Parliament of James VI. anno 1597 *, by which the fheriff-clerks and their regifters were put under the fame controul as the protocols of the notaries public ; which, it feems, had fo good an effect as to render the judicial forms of regiftration unneceffary, at leaft it was expected to do fo, as appeared from what followed. As thefe folemnities attending the regiftration of the inhibition were found by experience to be troublefome and expenfive to the lieges, the practice was totally abolifhed, about three years afterwards, by an act of the 16th Parliament of James VI. anno 1600. From this time downwards, the regiftration became a private act between the perfon who produces the letters and the clerk of court. The publication is entirely trufted to the regifter itfelf, and to the neceffity which individuals know they are under of fearching them for their own fafety. Another act paffed in the fame feffion of Parliament, which eftablifhed that proper and neceffary regulation ftill obferved, of referring to the particular page in the regifter, in the certificate of the regiftration written upon the back of
the

the letters. But the omiffion of it is no nullity. The clerks alone
incur a penalty, which is certainly proper, becaufe the regulation is
only a matter of expediency, not effential to the diligence. No
other law was enacted in behalf of this matter until the general regulation of judicatures in the reign of Charles II. anno 1672, when
the keepers of our feveral regifters were appointed to make minute-
books of the writs recorded, for the benefit of the lieges. Thus
matters continued till the year 1680, when the Lords of Seffion, by
an act of Sederunt, of date 10th of February that year, were pleafed
to point out a method for extending the effect of this diligence further than practice had been able to carry it. The granters of wadfets and of annualrent rights, where eftates were their own property, burdened only with thefe debts, did not think themfelves obliged
to pay attention to inhibitions againft the wadfetters, or heritable
creditors; they obferved the terms of the reverfion, and paid the
money *bona fide.* They confidered themfelves not as taking alienations of the lands of other people, but only as removing the burdens
from their own lands; in which bufinefs they were not obliged to
take notice of inhibitions againft their creditors; and, by this means,
a confiderable part of heritable property efcaped the power of this
diligence. The Lords, therefore, interpofed by an act of Sederunt *,
ordaining the inhibiter to intimate this diligence to the perfon in the
right of the reverfion, and declaring, that, in fuch cafe, any after
renunciations or redemptions will not be fuftained, unlefs the fame
proceed by way of action, to which the inhibiter muft be cited.
This act is clearly within the power of the Court. It is a declaration of the rules which the Lords are to follow in time coming,
and appears to be exceedingly well devifed for the purpofe. It
throws the trouble and expence of fearching into the records
upon the ufer of the inhibition; and it gives him the effect of
his diligence only upon condition of complying with the directions of this act. Hence we fhould remember, that it is not
enough to raife, execute, and regifter an inhibition. All that is
thereby

* 19th February 1680.

thereby done is to prevent the direct alienation of lands or heritable debts by the debtor; but if we mean to prevent him from receiving payment from the proper debtors, we must be careful to make the search and intimations prescribed by this act.

Inhibitions, it seems, were formerly defeated by the feudal forfeiture of recognition, arising from deeds done by the person inhibited, after the execution of the diligence. These deeds, no doubt, were often purposely done, and the forfeiture brought about by collusion between the vassal inhibited, and the superior. This became so common as to require an act of Parliament to correct it, by ordering that lands falling under recognition, should be burdened with prior inhibitions *.

It appears that the appointment of the act anno 1672, had not been duly obeyed, and that our keepers had relapsed into their old confusion and neglect, in so much that it roused the attention of Parliament, who renewed the old regulations with additions†. The appointment in this act of the presentee signing the minute-book, is nothing but a revival of a part of the old method. It was the addition of a solemnity, and presence of another person as a check upon the Clerk of Register, ' whereby (as Lord Stair says) there could be ' no debate concerning the times of presenting, nor durst the keep- ' er adventure to neglect the registration within the days, having so ' good a proof against him‡.'

The copies delivered to the parties in executions of inhibitions, and other diligences, bore the date of the execution only in figures; and did not mention the designations of the witnesses present, which no doubt occasioned many mistakes; and put it in the power of messengers to injure private parties. This slovenly practice was corrected by the act 12th of William and Mary, 1st Parliament May 30. 1693. In the 1748 the heritable stewartries and regalities were abo-

VOL. I.   3 O   lished,

lished, and the records transmitted to the respective sheriff courts. Yet people continued to execute hornings and inhibitions at the head boroughs of the abolished jurisdictions. The Lords, therefore, by their act 29th February 1752, discharged these registrations as erroneous; and appointed diligences of every kind to be published at the market-cross of the head boroughs of the counties, and registered in the books of the respective sheriffs.

Thus we have endeavoured to give the origin and principles of this business; together with an historical account of the statute law regarding it, in the order of time. Before proceeding to the practical application of these laws, we shall consider the form of the writ, and its executions; because that form being early established, has remained unaltered ever since, and will be necessary to our understanding the practice. It may be observed, that this extraordinary writ proceeds entirely upon a train of suppositions*; the creditor, after stating his ground of debt, alledges, that the debtors are conscious, that execution of all kinds is to issue out against them for payment.—This is one supposition. It is next said, ' That they ' upon that account intend, in manifest defraud and hurt of him the ' creditor thereanent, to dispose of their effects.'—This is another supposition, and a very injurious one to the debtors; the evidence, or rather the apology, is, that he is ' informed it is to be so.' The complaint is, that the debtors intend only to defeat the diligence of the law, for the plain meaning of this language is, that if the debtors did not know or dread execution being taken out against them, the alienation of their property would not be a wrong. The creditor, therefore, by this means prays the interposition of the law, not in support of his private right as a creditor, but in support of its own authority. This most ingenious stretch in common creditors to make a title to inhibitions, is convincing evidence that these letters were originally founded upon a right in the person of the creditor;

* *Vide* the Style in Dallas, p. 18.

creditor ; and that that right could be no other than the ancient hy-. pothec, which we have explained.

It is ftrange information, that the creditor pretends to have got upon this occafion. ' He is told (he fays) that the debtor means to ' fell, annalzie, wadfet, difpone, renounce, delapidate, and put ' away, all and fundry his lands, rooms, poffeffions, and others.' After the word ' poffeffions' in the ancient ftyle, were added ' corns, ' cattle, goods, and gear, or any part thereof,' as we find in the form given by Lord Stair*. Before St Martin's time, the effect of the inhibition upon moveables was at an end ; and therefore, in his ftyle, and ever fince, the fpecification of the moveables is omitted, and the following expreffion fubftituted in its place ; ' And others ' whatfoever.' Confidering that this writ has confeffedly no other foundation than fuppofitions, the executive part of it gives them confequences, as folid, ftrong, and general, as could iffue upon a pofitive right in the eftate of the debtor. The firft thing to be done is to inhibit the party himfelf from doing what the creditor alledges he intended to do; and he is difcharged even to contract more debts, or to give any kind of fecurity therefor. The debtor may notwithftanding grant bonds and take on debts, as thefe only fall under the effect of the inhibition, when they are ufed as foundations for attacking the land; and accordingly, the ftyle is fo qualified, for it is only fuch bonds and debts that are difcharged, ' whereby the right to the ' lands may be evicted and apprifed from the creditor inhibiter.' Notwithftanding this ftrict prohibition laid upon the debtor, the difobedience of it was never attended with any penalty or confequence, fo far as can be learned from our law or practice ; nay, there is not the leaft veftige of its being taken notice of as a contempt of authority. The reafons are obvious ; when inhibitions came to be granted as matters of courfe, upon the mere alledgeance of the creditor, the eafe of the injunction created the fame eafe in

3 O 2

the

* P. 762.

the difobedience. The diligence was looked upon to be a ftretch of the law, which it ought not have allowed. The execution, therefore, againft the party, ferves only to put him in *mala fide* from contracting with ftrangers. It is to them that the injury is truly done, and not to the creditor at whofe inftance the letters proceed.

In the next claufe of the ftyle, which, as it contains the public prohibition, is the fubftantial part of the writ, open proclamation is ordered to be made ' at the market crofs of   and other places needful.' Before the act of Parliament 1581, inhibitions were only executed or publifhed at the market crofs of the jurifdiction where the debtor lived ; and that act makes no difference upon the mode of execution then in ufe ; but only appoints them to be recorded in the regifter of thofe jurifdictions in which the debtor had lands. As the effence of the bufinefs, however, lay in proper publication, meffengers, in order to anfwer the words of ftyle, ' and ' other places needful,' got into a practice of executing inhibitions, not only at the market crofs where the party dwelt, but alfo, from the analogy of warnings they executed them at the kirk-doors, and at the market croffes of all the jurifdictions where the acts of Parliament required the regiftration. Lord Stair fays, ' That this practice ' arofe from the advantage of meffengers, in order to the making of ' more work, and larger allowance ; but he concludes, that there is ' no neceffity to publifh at the mercat croffes where the debtor's ' other lands lie ; yet it is certain, that the inhibition will not be ' effectual againft any lands, but where it is either regiftrated in the ' particular regifter of the jurifdictions where the lands lie, or in the ' general regifter which fupplies all thefe regifters ; whence it is evi- ' dent, that inhibitions may be effectual where they are regiftrate, ' though they be not there' publifhed *.'

It muft here be obferved, in fupport of the act of Sederunt which rendered intimation neceffary to cover heritable debts, that, though the debtor is inhibited from renouncing his reverfions, his heritable creditors

* P. 763.

creditors are not (with the other lieges) inhibited, by the ftyle, from receiving difcharges and renunciations ; and, to the reafons already given, it is neceffary to add a general rule, that inhibitions do not ftrike againft fuch deeds as the debtor is under the neceffity of granting by obligations prior to the inhibitions. Now, all heritable creditors ftand bound, by the terms of the reverfions, to renounce upon payment; a circumftance which farther demonftrates the neceffity of a particular intimation in thefe cafes, as directed by the act of Sederunt.

' *Certifying them that do on the contrary, that the fame fhall* ' *make no faith in judgment.*'—By this part of the ftyle, a perfon would be led to think, that deeds done *fpreta inhibitione*, are null in themfelves, or, as the lawyers fay, they become fo *fimpliciter*, upon making the exception ; but fo it is, that the Court, at no period, allowed this to be done. To give an inhibition effect, a procefs of reduction muft actually be brought upon it. The letters import no more than a perfonal prohibition againft the party, which requires a declarator and refciffory action, in which it may be found that the prohibition of the law has been contemned, and that the certification may be applied. There is no exception to this rule but in the competition and ranking of creditors, where, to fave time and expence, the Lords are accuftomed to give effect to this diligence by way of exception.

' *And that ye caufe regiftrate thir our letters, with the execution* ' *thereof, within forty days, conform to act of Parliament.*'—As the publication to the lieges is trufted to the meffenger, the executor of the letters, he is alfo trufted with the regiftration of them, which is the circumftance the moft effectual for putting the public upon their guard. In practice, it is always done by the creditor himfelf, or his doers, who have principally intereft in complying with it. It is neceffary to remark, that, in all cafes where a perfon is out of the kingdom, letters of inhibition ought to have a fpecial warrant for inhibiting the party at the market crofs of Edinburgh, pier and fhore

of

of Leith, becaufe this is a moft unfavourable diligence, often hurtful to the party, and ftill more detrimental to other debts; therefore the meffenger is limited to the exprefs terms of the letters; and, unlefs they contain a warrant for execution furth of the kingdom, the execution will be null, as done without authority. We conclude what we have to fay upon this form with a general obfervation, that, in regard to the ftrict interpretation of the letters of inhibition, and the unequitable confequences that often flow from them upon pofterior creditors, judges are naturally inclined to defeat their effects upon flight objections. The dread of this has induced the Writers to preferve the ftyle entire, without venturing to add a fingle word fince the days of St Martin; and, for the fame reafon, the letters ought to be carefully written, the execution fhould be attentively performed, and the regiftration of the whole duly attended to. As the ftyle of the fchedule to be left for the party is always uniform, meffengers have them printed with blanks, for fpecifying the date of the delivery, the ground of debt, and the witneffes names and defignations prefent, which muft be done at length, and not in figures, by the act 1693; this copy muft be figned by the meffenger, but need not be figned by the witneffes, delivered to the party perfonally; or, if he cannot be found, it muft be delivered to his wife or fervants, within his dwelling-houfe; but not till after inquiring for the debtor himfelf, and being told that he is abfent, or accefs pointedly refufed him. If the door is kept fhut, the copy may be left in the lock-hole, or upon the moft patent door or gate. After fix audible knocks are given to obtain admittance, if the party is actually known to be refident in another county at the time, the letters ought to be executed againft him both perfonally and at his ordinary dwelling-place; at leaft, it is the fafeft method fo to do, though not abfolutely neceffary.

This perfonal execution being made, the meffenger goes to the head burgh of the fheriffdom in which the debtor is inhibited; and there, at a proper time of the day, he ought to make open proclamation,

mation, read the letters aloud, and verbally inhibit the lieges, by reading the copy ; which having done, he affixes it upon the crofs in the form of a placard, for the information of the public. Thefe ceremonies were all anciently appointed for the proper *certioration*, as it was called, of the lieges, who, for a long period, had no other chance of being put upon their guard ; but the carelefs performance of them, and particularly a practice which we fee daily done, of tearing away the copy from the crofs the moment it is fixed, added to the other reafons before mentioned, obliged the legiflature, for the public fafety, to appoint a record of thefe material executions. This was done about two years after the regiftration of hornings, in the 1579 ; but it was done upon much better principles. The regifter of hornings was intended to furnifh materials for the oppreffion of the public ; whereas the record of inhibitions had no other purpofe than to guard the people againft an infidious diligence, which the law of their country had unwarily admitted. We retain fo much of the ancient cautions fpoken of by Lord Stair, that, if an inhibition be executed at the dwelling-place of the party, and againft himfelf perfonally at another place, it is alfo executed at the market crofles of both jurifdictions ; but the fixed and indifpenfible rule is, always to make fure of having the letters executed at the market crofs where the party is perfonally ferved. The actual ceremony being over, the meffenger returns a certificate, which is termed an *execution*, of all he faid, and all he did.

The folemnities of the inhibition ferve a purpofe diametrically oppofite to that of their firft inftitution. The public is feldom obliged to them for any knowledge of the matter. They are preferved, therefore, as impediments upon this unfavourable diligence, that, from the errors and omiffions attending them, the Judges may have it in their power to defeat the effects of it, when fet up in contradiction to found equity and juftice.

When the party to be inhibited is out of the kingdom, the letters muft be executed at the market crofs of Edinburgh, pier and fhore of of Leith, if they contain a warrant for that purpose. The extending of the diligence to people in this situation, was undoubtedly a stretch made from the analogy of summonses, which is an alteration, or rather addition to the style of the ancient inhibition. Indeed, our practitioners seem to have adopted it as a general rule, that, whatever can be done against a man in person, may also be done against him at the market cross, pier and shore. In the case of inhibition, this shews, that the party is not presumed to incur any penalty or consequence from disobedience of the order; for nothing can be more absurd than a penal prohibition fictitiously laid on. When a man is personally inhibited, third parties have at least the chance of his honesty in their favour, that he will not sell them a property, when under an inhibition, without giving them to know his situation; but a man of the best character, when absent from the country, may innocently ensnare others who have confidence in him; nor can he be certain of his own situation, until he search the registers to know what has been done in his absence. On the other hand, if the edictal prohibition was not allowed, people would leave their country on purpose to have the power of alienating at pleasure. In short, this diligence has a radical inconsistency in itself, which unavoidably draws many more after it; and, though not a favourite of the courts of justice, it has always been a favourite of creditors who have struggled for it in every case, and who have procured the extention of it even to persons out of the kingdom.

When the letters are duly executed, and executions returned by the messenger, the whole must be registered within the forty days, in terms of the several acts of Parliament. The forty days run from the date of the last execution made by virtue of the letters; and, although the act 1581 prescribed the registration of this diligence only in the jurisdiction where the greatest part of the debtor's lands lay, yet it has always been the practice to explain this indistinct appointment into registration in the books of each jurisdiction where
the

the debtor has lands, or in the general regifter at Edinburgh; and the law has limited the effect of the inhibition accordingly.

Having given the hiftory of this diligence, examined its fteps and formalities, we now come to inquire into the real import of thefe formalities, and into the effect which our Judges have actually given to the inhibition itfelf. Too much pains cannot be taken to acquire a familiar and perfect underftanding of a writ which makes fuch a capital figure in our law and practice.

Craig is thought to have written about the year 1600; the regiftration of inhibitions was only ordered in the 1581; yet, from his account of the matter, it is evident, that, notwithftanding that act, which appointed publication only at one market crofs, practice had very foon after made publication neceffary, wherever regiftration was fo, and the regiftration, at that period, took place in every county where the debtor had lands.

Although inhibitions had ceafed to effect the commerce of moveables long before the end of the 16th century, yet, as the ftyle remained untouched, creditors ftill endeavoured to give it effect. Growing corns, we have often heard, were confidered as *partes foli.* A perfon inhibited conveyed his corns in that fituation, and the inhibiter brought a reduction of the affignment. The Lords, however, affoilzied, becaufe they found, that an inhibition only affects heritable rights, and not moveables; fo that growing corns were no more confidered as *partes foli* *. A party who had inhibited upon a fimple moveable bond, brought a reduction of an heritable right. The defender objected, that, unlefs real diligence had followed upon this perfonal debt, it could not be a ground for reducing a real right. This gave the inhibition an immediate and terrible effect; and it has ever fince been fuftained as a title for reducing all the heritable rights againft which it ftrikes, but ftill it gives the inhibiter no hold of the lands. His reduction only prevents them from being touched

VOL. I. 3 P to

---

* Lord Braco againft Ogilvy, March 22. 1623.—Durie, p. 69

to his prejudice by other people, untill he shall be pleased to effect them by real diligence at his own instance. The warrant in the inhibition was always strictly interpreted; so that if the party did not act precisely in terms thereof, he, of consequence, had no authority to plead it in his own behalf. This point of practice is well illustrated by the next decision *. A party took out letters of inhibition, containing a warrant for execution at the maket cross, pier and shore, upon 60 days; but it contained no warrant for execution against the party himself, either personally, or at his dwelling place. Nothing, it seems, was done upon these letters till the party returned to Scotland, when they were executed personally against him, and at the market cross where the lands lay. An objection was made, that this personal execution wanted a warrant; which the Lords sustained, in regard that he ought to have craved a warrant to do the same. A case of the same kind happened soon after. An inhibition, containing only a warrant out of the kingdom, was executed at the party's dwelling house, and the same objection made. The inhibiter endeavoured to defend himself by the words of stile, 'and other places ' needful.' He also pled, that the debtor being abroad, was comprehended under the general inhibition of the lieges at the market cross, pier and shore; but neither of these evasions would do. To the last one the answer was obvious: The lieges were inhibited not to contract with the debtor, but the debtor was not discharged to contract with them †. The next determination finally established the point already mentioned, that an inhibition upon a personal debt strikes against posterior debts, though heritable, so soon as the second debt is made the ground of real diligence for affecting the lands of the debtor ‡.

When parties lie under prior obligations to grant deeds, the implement of these obligations cannot be said to be in defraud of any

person;

---

* Erskin against Erskin, 24th January 1627.—Durie, page 262.
† March 19. 1628, Lamb against Blackburn.
‡ Douglas against Johnston, July 2. 1630.

perfon; and, confequently, ought not to be cut down by intervening inhibitions. This rule is early laid down by Spottifwood; and cafes foon happened in which the meaning of it was afcertained. A debtor difponed his lands to another perfon, who held his obligation long before the inhibition: The obligation bore alfo, that the debtor fhould infeft the creditor in an annualrent of his money out of any of his lands; yet the Lords found, 'that the alienation could not be thereby fupported *.' The practical inference from thefe cafes is, that prior obligations, when inhibitions are known to intervene, ought to be implemented in *terminis;* for, had the creditor, in the cafe of Scott againft Turnbull, taken an annualrent right in place of a difpofition, that right would have been fuftained. The beft method, therefore, is to take feparate deeds; one of them in terms of the obligement; and the other puts it in the power of the creditor either to pay the debt, or to take whatever advantage may lie againft the inhibiter's diligence.

Inhibitions, it feems, had all along preferved their original effect upon lands; and were held not only to debar the debtor from alienation of the property he ftood actually poffeffed of at the date of the execution of the diligence, but alfo to prevent him from difpofing of the heritable property he might acquire or fucceed to, from that time forward. This is certainly a wonderful effect of a writ, given upon flight, and even fictitious reafons. A creditor, furely, in every cafe trufts his money to the eftate that the debtor is poffeffed of at the time, and not to what he may afterwards fucceed to or acquire. Neither can it be faid that a debtor intends to difpofe of his property in defraud of any perfon, which he neither poffeffes, nor is perhaps in expectation of; and yet fo it is, that inhibitions have affected, and continue to affect, thofe future acquifitions, in the fame manner as it does the prefent eftate. Were there no other circumftance than this, to point out the antient fource from which the in-

hibition

---

* January 21. 1629, Scott againft Turnbull.

hibition has arisen, we should humbly think it sufficient for the purpose. When the doctrine of hypothecs made a part of the law, and
a man expressly hypothecated his whole effects, heritable and moveable, which he was then possessed of, or which he might thereafter
succeed to, *any manner of way*, (for these were the words of the
style), he gave a solid ground for the effect of the inhibition; but,
when the creditor had no right of any kind to pretend in the property of his party, the simple existence of his own debt excepted, to
allow him to lay such an extravagant injunction upon the debtor,
in virtue of a single writ obtained upon a fictitious pretence, seems
to be devoid of every principle either in law, equity, or reason. So
it is however; our forefathers have admitted it, and we must continue to do so.

From the 1642, where Durie's collection of decisions stops, we
have no journal of the proceedings of our supreme Court, until Lord
Stair recommenced that necessary work in June 1661. The first
decision he notices upon the subject, is the 18th of July 1662,
Swinton. A woman falling heir to a person inhibited, instantly sold
the lands, which had become the property of the deceased after the
inhibition. It was objected, that the inhibition was not registered
in the books of the county where the lands sold lay. ' The Lords
' found the defence relevant, that the inhibition could not extend to
' the lands in other shires falling to the person inhibited, *quocunque*
' *titulo*; but that the pursuer ought to have inhibited *de novo*, or
' published and registrate in that shire; seeing all parties count them
' selves secure if no inhibitions be registrate in the shire where the
' lands lie, without inquiring farther.' This decision points out a
material circumstance in the nature of inhibitions, notwithstanding
their prodigious effects. These effects are only personal, drawn from
a prohibition against the individual: They expire with his life, and
the heir stands free from all impediments.

A few years afterwards, this material point came more directly
under the cognisance of the Court; in which we find it denied that

it

it was ever exprefsly decided that inhibitions did reach lands acquired after the execution. The anfwer affords the beft apology to be
had for the extraordinary effect attributed to this diligence. ' It is
' faid, that the prohibition refpects the perfon inhibited directly, and
' the lands but indirectly, as they belong to him; fo that there is no-
' difference whether they belonged to him before or after; for *hoc*
' *ipfo* that they are his, they fall under the reftraint, and the aliena-
' tion thereof is to the prejudice of the ufer of the inhibition.' The
nature of the inhibition is here pointed out with a happy precifion,
illuftrative of the true principles of this writ. So far as regards the
debtor's property, it can go no further than to what he is actually
poffeffed of at the time; *quoad futura*, the prohibition is fimply perfonal. In the fame manner, the obligement binding or hypothecating a man's future acquifitions, muft have been fimply perfonal; and
there is no other principle upon which this effect of the diligence of
inhibition can be founded with any degree of probability; for almoft every word of the prefent ftyle contradicts the idea of its ex-
tenfion *ad acquirenda*. The lieges are only prohibited from purchafing the lands pertaining or belonging to the debtor in defraud of
the creditor. A purchafer, therefore, of lands acquired after the
date of the inhibition is not in defraud of the ufer of it, who is in
the fame fituation he ftood in at the date of its publication. The
Lords exprefsly found, that inhibition did reach to lands acquired
after their publication *.

The next decifion goes to a point, which in our prefent fyftem of
bufinefs occurs every day. A depending action, or alledgeance of
debt, was early found to entitle the purfuer to an inhibition. A
party having executed an inhibition upon the dependence, fubmitted his caufe. The arbiters pronounced a decree upon the fubmiffion in favour of the claimant, formerly the purfuer, who therefore
infifted that his inhibition remained effectual, but the Lords had no
refpect.

* Feb. 22. 1667, Ellis againft Wifhart.

respect to the diligence, in regard no decree of Court had followed upon it, so that the decree-arbitral was considered in no other light than a private deed*. When a defender stands inhibited, a clause ought to be inserted in the submission, preserving the effect of the diligence, but how far that would effect third parties, is a question not yet decided. A surer method would be to reserve power to obtain a decree in the depending action, notwithstanding the decree-arbitral, and to take a judgment in terms thereof accordingly; but even to this several objections would occur.

An execution appeared, which did not mention a copy to be left at the market-cross according to the accustomed form. The objection was made and sustained †. At this period it was a frequent device, to grant deeds and obligations blank in the names of the creditor and disponee; and when an inhibition was executed, they attempted to defeat it, by filling up additional names or sums in the blanks of the deeds; but as often as such cases occurred, the Court found that all these operations were struck at by the inhibition. A messenger in executing an inhibition, either omitted to give a copy to the party, or to mention that fact in his execution. The execution was delivered in these terms, and the messenger attempted to supply the omission by a marginal note. The Lords with great propriety found the inhibition null, and that the delivering a copy was a necessary solemnity, which not being contained in the register, they would not admit the same to be supplied by probation ‡.

By the act of Parliament, the inhibition must be registered within forty days after the date of the last execution; but it is proper to know whether the effect of the execution takes place from the execution against the lieges, or from the day of the registration. The first determination of this point is found in a case preserved by Dirleton, where the Lords found : ' That a disposition being made

' after

---

* Kae against Stewart Gilmour.—16th December 1668, Fraser against Keith.— Stair, vol. 1. page 571.   † Napier against Gordon, Feb. 12. 1670.

‡ Keith against Johnston, July 28. 1671.

' after inhibition, but before the registration of the fame, may be
' reduced *ex capite inhibitions*; feeing the execution of the inhibi-
' tion doth put the lieges in *mala fide*. And after the fame is com-
'' plete, and thereby the debtor and lieges are inhibit to give and
' take rights, the inhibition *ipfo momento* thereafter is valid and per-
' fect; but *refolvitur fub conditione*, if it be not regiftered in due
' time *. Mr Erſkine informs us that the rule laid down by this
decifion, is in force at this moment; but if the cafe were again to
occur, we fhould be much inclined to try the validity of this doctrine; for it is now an undeniable fact, that notice of an inhibition is feldom or never to be had by publication; and we are
entirely at a lofs to find private juftice or public expediency in
allowing one man who has voluntarily brought his money into
danger, by trufting it to the perfonal fecurity of a debtor, to
throw his misfortune upon an innocent purchafer, who means to
acquire the property itfelf, and is taught by the law to depend upon
the public records for his fafety. The following decifion holds up
a cafe, which muft fince that time have frequently occurred. A creditor apprifed an eftate for feveral debts in his perfon. Upon one
of thefe debts an inhibition had been executed; and upon that title
he brought a reduction of a difpofition granted by his debtor. The
purchafer offered to pay the debt, upon the ordinary condition of
obtaining an affignment. Now, the inhibiter's other debts were pofterior to this inhibition; fo that, had he fimply affigned, the affignee
might have immediately got back his money by reducing thefe other
debts in the perfon of the cedent. He therefore very fenfibly objected, that he could only be bound to difcharge in a cafe of that
kind, and not to affign to his own prejudice. The Lords ordained
the affignation to be granted, with a provifo that it fhould not be
made ufe of againft the other right in the perfon of the cedent †.

An

* Cruickfhanks againft Watt, Feb. 12. 1675.—Noticed alfo by Stair of the fame
date.
† Bruce againft Mitchell, Feb. 11. 1676.

An execution of an inhibition appeared, in which the meffenger
faid, that he had lawfully inhibited the lieges. ' It was objected,
that this execution did not bear the public reading of the letters at
the crofs, and crying three feveral oyeffes; and that the omiffion
could not be fupplied by witneffes.' The Lords found the execution of the inhibition null *. This was a very proper judgment.
The diligence of inhibition is merely a creature of the law: It is entirely compofed of forms; and if any part of thefe be omitted, the
creditor has no title to any benefit from the law. Before the ftatutory order for regiftration, the whole force of the diligence lay upon the proclamation. The lieges had no other chance of being apprifed of their danger; and even fince that time the fame prefumption holds good for forty days after the execution.

When lawyers fay that a debt or deed is reduced *ex capite inhibi-*
tionis, it is not meant that the deed is really void; for, *quoad* every
other perfon but the inhibitor, it remains perfectly fufficient; becaufe reductions, *ex capite inhibitionis,* are, properly fpeaking, de-
clarators; importing no more than that notwithftanding the alienation quarrelled, the inhibitor fhould have accefs to effect the lands
inhibited for his debt †. And for the fame reafon, it has no effect
but from the date of the fentence; becaufe the deed of alienation
by the perfon inhibited is not fimply void, but only voidable; and
therefore, in bygone rents, before the date of the fentence, even
thofe *in medio,* and uplifted were found to belong to the difponee,
and effectable by his creditors ‡. Two or three years afterwards, another inhibition was produced in Court, bearing to be executed at the
dwelling houfe after feveral knocks; but did not fpecify the number of *fix* knocks; upon which the Lords found the inhibition *ipfo*
jure null §. We have heard, that in executions at the market crofs,
pier

---

* Stevenfon againft Innes, July 11. 1676.   † January 7. 1680. Hay againft
Lady Balgerno.   ‡ February 1. 1684. Crichton againft Anderfon.
§ July 29. 1680, Hay againft Laird of Purey.

pier and shore, a copy must be affixed at each of these places: A party produced an execution, bearing a copy to be affixed on the cross, without mentioning any copy being affixed on the pier. The defect was objected to, and the inhibition found null *. As this diligence has extraordinary consequences, every circumstance of its execution has received a judicial determination. A messenger had omitted to mention that he had made three oyesses: The Lords sustained the objection, and annulled the diligence †. Execution at the market cross, pier and shore, is only intended to reach those persons actually out of Scotland at the time. Whenever there is any uncertainty about a fact of this kind, our business is to execute the inhibition at the common dwelling place of the party, at the market cross of the sheriffdom at which that house is situated, and at the market cross, pier and shore ‡.

Formerly inhibitions were sustained upon blank summonses, duly executed, which were held to make a dependence. One of these inhibitions coming into Court, the pursuer, conscious of the absurdity, inserted his libel, and produced it to support the inhibition. The Lords reduced the diligence, as wanting a sufficient warrant; but, in order to advertise the lieges of their hazard, they resolved to make an act of federunt, ' That inhibitions served upon dependencies should ' engross the tenor of the summons, otherwise should not be sus- ' tained §;' but, as all summonses must now be libelled before execution, no such point can again occur.

Although inhibitions are generally allowed of course, it is the right of the party against whom they are raised without a sufficient cause, to complain to the Court to have these malicious diligences recalled, as abuses of the law, and order of justice. The Judges always paid due attention to these applications. A liferentrix absolutely

---

* February 22. 1681, Ewen against Burnet.   † February 1683, London against Trotter.   ‡ February 22. 1687, Muschet against Lord Mar.
§ Fountainhall, December 27. 1698, Mill against Cockburn.

lately fecured in her lands inhibited the proprietor; he immediately complained, and the Lords difcharged the regiftration of the inhibition till it fhould be tried what foundation there was for it *.

In the beginning of this century, inhibitions and other diligences came to be obtained in a very eafy manner. Not fatisfied with having them upon actual dependencies, they were not at the pains even of executing the fummons, but produced it figneted with the bill of inhibition. This fhameful practice foon received a proper check. An objection was made to one of them, that it proceeded upon a falfe narrative, as no fummons had been executed, and confequently no depending procefs exifted at the time of raifing the inhibition.; and the Lords found the inhibition null †.

By the 119th act of the 7th parliament of James VI. the clerk to the regifter of inhibitions is ordered to fubfcribe an atteft of the letters and executions being regiftered: This, in practice, is done both upon the letters and upon the executions. One of the executions at the market crofs was objected to, as not marked or fubfcribed by the clerk, and the Lords fuftained the objection ‡: But, upon the matter being again brought before their Lordfhips, they altered their opinion, ' In refpect there is no certification of nullity adjected in ' the act; and therefore, though the neglect of the clerk's fubfcrip-' tion might fubject him to cenfure, the diligence ftands good, being ' duly recorded, which anfwers all the end of the clerk's fubfcrip-' tion ‖.' This decifion ought not to be trufted to; and it is our bufinefs to take care that the clerk fhall always fubfcribe the atteft of regiftration. Lord Bankton adds upon this head, that, if the inhibition be not duly recorded, the fame is void, even though the regifter book for the year, whereon it was marked on the back to be recorded, was wanting; and cites for this a decifion, January 25. 1745,—Kennedy §.

There

There are fome actions where the libel is general ; fuch as count-
and reckoning, and others, in which no fpecial fum or balance is
libelled againft the defender.   The hardfhip and impropriety of admitting the diligence of inhibition, upon account of a claim without
fpecification, was reprefented ; and the defender contended, that actions of that kind could not be a ground for the diligence.   The
anfwer given was, That practice admitted that mode of libelling, and
the law admitted inhibitions upon every depending action.   The
Lords fuftained the inhibition ; which, indeed, for any thing appearing, ought not to have been done.   If a purfuer cannot fpecify the
exact amount of his debt, he has no right to tie up his parties hands
by an extraordinary remedy, which fhould only belong to a certain
debt :   However, 'fo it is to this day; whether a man is unjuftly or
generally inhibited, he muft be at the expence of an application to
do himfelf a common piece of juftice *.

An eftate was fold in confequence of a voluntary right from a
bankrupt, and the price about to be divided among the creditors :
An inhibiter attempted to reduce the fale; but the Lords, with perfect propriety, refufed to allow it, ' In refpect that he could not al-
' ledge the fale was at an under value, and that the price remained
' *in medio* †.'

It is clear, from the nature and ftyle of this diligence, that it can
extend no further than to the exact debt upon which the inhibition
is raifed.   The debtor is to do no deed which may prejudge the complainer ' *anent the fulfilling to him of the obligation, decree, or procefs,*
' *produced to the Lords.*'   From this it follows, that an inhibition,
ufed upon a bond, can go no further than the debt and annualrents
therein contained :   Confequently, the effects of a bond of corroboration, fo far as regards the accumulation of the debt, will be cut off
by a fecond inhibition intervening, at the inftance of another credi-

3 Q 2   tor.

---

* November 1722, Competition of Creditors of Tofts.
† February 1. 1739, Carlyle againft the Truftees of Mathiefon's Creditors.

tor *. This point is eftablifhed by repeated decifions. Where, therefore, a debt is fecured by an inhibition, and afterwards corroborated, if the fum be confiderable, the fecure method would be to execute a fecond inhibition upon the bond of corroboration, which would at leaft fecure the accumulations againft all pofterior creditors.

When an inhibition is executed againft a man refiding in a different part of the country from that in which his ordinary dwelling-houfe is fituated, it is to be confidered whether he has lived in that place forty days; for that fpace conftitutes a domicile in the fpot of his prefent refidence; and therefore the inhibition muft be publifhed at the market crofs of the head borough of the county where he lives at the time. This was the next point in the bufinefs determined by the Court. It was objected, ' That an inhibition record- ' ed in one jurifdiction was not effectual as to lands in another; but ' that publication muft neceffarily be at the head burgh of the jurif- ' diction where the party dwells for the time; and that in no cafe ' is it regular to execute an inhibition perfonally at a debtor's dwell- ' ing houfe within one jurifdiction, and againft the lieges at the mer- ' cat crofs of another.' The Lords fuftained the objection to the inhibition, that the fame was not publifhed within the jurifdiction where the debtor lived at the time of executing †.

A debtor poffeffed of a good eftate, thought himfelf entitled to complain of an inhibition being execute againft him, as his circumftances were unqueftionably good. But ' the Lords refufed to recal ' the inhibition, being of opinion, that, let a man's circumftances be ' what they will, an inhibition againft him could not be ftopped, ' when ufed for *a liquid debt*. The more folvent the debtor is, the ' lefs excufable is the deferring payment; by procuring which, in- ' hibition, imprifonment, and other legal compulfitors, have been ' contrived.'

* June 27. 1745, Rutherford againft Stewart.
† July 27. 1745, Dunbar againft the Creditors of Grangehill.

'contrived.' The purfuer had been encouraged to this point by a determination of the Judges, given in the cafe of the Royal Bank in July 1728; but, though the debt claimed againft the Bank was a juft one, the inhibition appeared to be malicious, as the credit of the Company was fully and completely known and eftablifhed.

The next decifion, which regards the matter of execution, feems flatly to contradict the cafe of Dunbar, determined in July 1745. An inhibition had been perfonally executed againft a debtor at Edinburgh, who commonly refided at Banff; and the letters were publifhed at the market crofs of Banff. This inhibition was objected to, becaufe it had not been executed at the market crofs of Edinburgh, where the debtor refided at the time. The Lords repelled the objection. In the cafe of Dunbar, the Judges found, that the inhibition muft be publifhed at the market crofs of the debtor's *refidence for the time*, in preference to that of his ordinary domicile; and, on the very next occafion, they find, that the ordinary domicile was preferable to the occafional refidence: Nay, Lord Kilkerran hints, that it was not thought clear that publication at the laft place would not have been liable to objection; which is juft telling us that either way will do, and yet both are doubtful. How is a practitioner to conduct himfelf upon a matter of this kind, between the abfolute and occafional refidence of his party? If his information be not very explicit, his only method is to publifh at both market croffes, and regifter letters in both counties, or in the general regifter. In the fame procefs another point occurred, which it is material to attend to. An inhibitor, forty days after the firft publication of his inhibition, difcovered that his debtor was poffeffed of lands in Sutherland and Murray; he therefore publifhed it again at the market croffes of Sutherland and Murray. This was objected to, and the objection fuftained; 'In refpect of the exprefs directions of the act 119th, 'parliament 1581, which requires no publication at any other crofs 'than that of the head burgh of the fhire where the party dwells, 'and regiftration within forty days thereof; and enacts, that, where
'he

'he has lands in another shire, the inhibition be registered, within
' the same forty days, in the books of the said shire *. The same
questions came soon after under the cognisance of the Court in another shape. When a debtor happened to be out of the kingdom,
the practice was to execute the inhibition against the lieges at the
market cross of Edinburgh, pier and shore of Leith, as well as against
himself; but this practice was not uniform; for sometimes, when the
party had a known residence in the country, inhibitions were executed at the market cross of the jurisdiction in which his dwelling
house was situated. In this manner an inhibition happened to be
executed against Sir Alexander Murray of Stenhope; and, in the
ranking of his creditors, the diligence met with the objection, that,
by the practice, all edictal executions for publication were made
against the lieges at the market cross of Edinburgh, pier and shore
of Leith, when the party is out of the kingdom. ' The Lords re-
' pelled the objection †.' To this decision Lord Kilkerran has been
pleased to add some observations: But his opinion is in direct contradiction to the decision of Dunbar, and, indeed, it is not easily understood. His Lordship says, ' That though a man reside at Edin-
' burgh or Glasgow a sufficient time to constitute a domicile, yet the
' execution of the lieges must be at Orkney, or wherever his ordi-
' nary residence is.' In fact, we all know that these executions answered very little purpose any where; and therefore, all reasoning
upon their supposed effects lead to error; for the law has bound the
lieges in general to the form of the publication; and therefore, no
one part of the people have a better right to hear it than another:
But what are we to make of the distinction between an ordinary
and extraordinary place of residence; for the only idea which the
law gives us of the constitution of a domicile, is an actual change of
the former residence to the latter; and in this confusion we know

no

* Dec. 1748, Creditors of Kinminnity against Innes.
† Feb. 2. 1750, Creditors of Sir A. Murray against the Earl of March.

no remedy but that already mentioned, the publication in both ; and that where the party is out of the kingdom, as well as when he is in it. This decision only gives birth to a number of new difficulties : For example, what is to be done where a man has no known or ordinary dwelling house, and yet is out of the kingdom ? Surely the market cross of Edinburgh is the only place where such an inhibition can be published ; although it would certainly be more safe to publish it both at the market cross of Edinburgh, and at the market cross of the county where his lands lay. It is true that the style does not bear an express warrant for inhibiting the lieges at the market cross, pier and shore. It will follow as a direct consequence, that the lieges out of the kingdom cannot be inhibited ; and, consequently, that any of them may safely contract with their own countrymen abroad, and plead the above decision in their favour. On the other hand, it is to be considered, that practice alone introduced the inhibiting of the debtor at the market cross, pier and shore ; and the same custom has also introduced the publication against the lieges at these places ; consequently, both customs should be held equally good.

As this singular diligence did not affect moveables, it followed that it did not reach to the bygone annualrents upon heritable subjects, because these are moveables falling to executors ; but the effect of the inhibition is not regulated by the simple distinction of heritable and moveable. There are several things heritable in a strict sense which are not reached by inhibition ; such as heritable bonds upon which no infeftment has followed, and bonds secluding executors, &c. Charters, dispositions, and other rights to land, are reached by this diligence, though no infeftment followed upon them ; and even heritable bonds upon which infeftment has followed, though rendered moveable by requisition or change, are still in the same predicament. It is material, therefore, for us to know the exact criterion which established this distinction. A case came before the Court relative to inhibition, which in a great measure determined

termined this material point. A creditor, in virtue of an heritable
bond upon the eftate of Langton, by a deed in the 1732, conveyed
the annualrents of an heritable debt due from the 1723. This conveyance was fought to be reduced upon an inhibition executed in
the 1730; and the Lords upon a hearing unanimoufly found, 'That
'the conveyance was not affected by the inhibition.' Another objection occurred againft the fame inhibition; the bill, it feems, was
paffed upon production of letters of horning, without the grounds
of debt; and the letters bore, '*becaufe the Lords had feen the letters*
'*of horning.*' Lord Kilkerran tells us, 'That the Court was inclined
'to have fuftained the objection, as there is no other legal ground
'for an inhibition, but either a decree, a liquid inftruction of the
'debt, or a fummons executed; but a horning is neither: A creditor
'may have got payment of his debt, and not delivered up the horn-
'ing; and, by the fame rule, an inhibition might proceed upon a
'caption; but no interlocutor was pronounced upon it, as unnecef-
'fary, after having found the inhibition ineffectual, even if it had
'been formal *.' This point came again before the Court in the 1751.
Falconer reports, that it was pled in fupport of the inhibition, 'That
'a horning, which could not have been got without a bond, is evi-
'dence of the debt. Inhibitions pafs on decreets without their
'grounds on fummonfes; and againft heirs on general charges. Up-
'on this,' continues he, 'it was obferved by the Court, that practice
'only determined on what foundation this diligence might proceed,
'as it was difficult to know on what principles this was fettled at
'firft †.' This practice was a very bad one. The decifion is not
to be trufted to, for the very good reafon mentioned by Lord Kilkerran; and it is not fuppofed that an inhibition of this kind would
now, as it was then, be fupported.

The

---

* June 15. 1750, Scott againft Coutes and others.
† July 3. 1751, Scott againft Creditors of Langton.

The ftyle of the letters, among other alienations, particularly pro-
hibits that of tacks; but by this it is not to be underftood that a
landholder is incapacitated from granting leafes of his eftate; for
thefe are not fales, but acts of adminiftration. The meaning of the
letters is, that a tackfman fhall not alienate his leafes to the prejudice of his creditor; for leafes, with us, are ranked amongft abfolute
immoveables; and therefore their alienation is exprefsly ftruck at by
the diligence of inhibition.

After this prohibitory writ came to be currently iffued upon
depending actions and undetermined claims, it came alfo to be
granted upon bills, and other grounds of debt, without putting
them even upon record. This, indeed, generally happens when
the inhibition is applied for before the term of payment of thefe
debts, and, confequently, before the creditor be entitled to a decree
of regiftration. Such inhibitions may be either ftopped or recalled,
unlefs the creditor can point out a change of circumftances in the
debtor, entitling him to fuch a preventative remedy. The change,
in law language, is exprefled by the phrafe *vergens ad inopiam.*

We have heard that the inhibition, being only perfonal to the
debtor, falls at his deceafe; and that the heir is at liberty to fell, unlefs the diligence be renewed againft him. It is neceffary therefore
to know how this is to be moft effectually done. Every heir may
either accept or renounce the fucceffion falling to him by the death
of any of his predeceffors, as he finds it moft fuitable to his intereft.
For this purpofe, the law allows him a year for deliberation; within
which no procefs can proceed, or execution pafs againft him. As
the heir is not debtor in the obligation, he cannot be inhibited upon
a deed with which he has no apparent connection: The debt muft
be connected with him by a fummons; which, being duly executed,
gives ground for inhibiting upon the dependence. Anciently, it was
not allowable to execute a fummons within the year of deliberation;
but it may now be done, provided the day of appearance falls without the year. But it may be uncertain whether the perfon inhibited

be legal heir or not, or whether or not he may renounce. If he does fo, no perfonal decree can go out againſt him; and, as the effect of all inhibitions upon depending actions reſts upon the decree, if none be recovered, the inhibition falls to the ground. The firſt ſtep againſt an heir, in the recovery of a debt, is to charge him to enter within forty days, in virtue of letters of general charge. The charge to enter upon theſe letters was admitted not to be a purſuit or execution, but a ſtep preparatory to it; and therefore the heir was allowed to be charged to enter, within the year of deliberation. As a ſummons could not be executed in that time, creditors thought of inhibiting apparent heirs upon the general charge, holding that to be a dependence againſt them. This was contrary to the principle of allowing the general charge itſelf; but the Lords, influenced by the idea of expediency, inclined to ſuſtain theſe inhibitions, becauſe the heir might otherwiſe diſappoint or defraud the predeceſſor's creditors; which was a ſtretch made againſt the intendment of the general charge, and in contradiction to its form. Theſe letters never ſpecified the debt: They only ſtated, in general, that the complainer had ſundry claims and actions to purſue againſt the eſtate of the deceaſed, from which he ſtood prevented by the heir lying out unentered. This fixed ſtyle proved that the general charge, the creature of a particular ſtatute, was never meant to found any diligence, or ſerve any other purpoſe than what that ſtatute directed; and it was leaſt of all fitted to the inhibition: When, therefore, the objection came to be made, the Lords annulled the inhibition, proceeding upon a common general charge; nor would they admit the anſwer, that the debt ſtood particulariſed by the conſequent ſummons *. Our lawyers ſoon underſtood, and profited by this diſtinction. A general charge, in which the debt was ſpecially libelled, came to be tried, which was accordingly ſuſtained †. When, therefore, we

                                                    intend

---

* June 25. 1706, Davidſon againſt Randal.
† Feb. 17. 1713, Livingſton againſt Forreſt.

intend to inhibit an heir upon a general charge, we muft be careful to recite the debt, or debts, in the fame manner as they are done in any other diligence; and we may add the general words, that the complainer has fundry other actions and claims. An inhibition upon a general charge, againft an apparent heir, is thought to be preferable to that upon a common fummons; becaufe the heir cannot be inhibited properly within the year of deliberation upon a common fummons; and therefore the inhibition upon the general charge fecures againft his deeds in the mean time; and, if the fummons be not called in Court within a year, the inftance falls, and the inhibition with it, whereas the other remains good, and takes full effect both on the eftate of the anceftor in the mean time, and the proper eftate of the heir himfelf, fo foon as he enters to his predeceffor's.

We have now endeavoured to give a detail of the practice in the matter of inhibition. It will no doubt be obferved that we have faid nothing upon a very material point, the effect which this diligence has in the ranking of creditors. To enter upon that diftinct branch of bufinefs would at prefent lead us greatly too far : It is referved for the procefs of ranking and fale, which well deferves a title for itfelf. In the mean time, we take leave of the prefent fubject with a few words relating to the difcharging, or, as it is termed, *purging* the inhibition. This is done by a fimple difcharge of the debt and diligence, containing the ufual claufe of regiftration. The inhibition and regiftration is always fpecially recited in the difcharge, which is generally regiftered in the books of Seffion, in order that it may be pointed out at any time, to balance the record of the diligence. It is certainly a very great defect that the fame regifter does not take in both the inhibition and the difcharge, whereby a kind of charge and difcharge might eafily be kept with refpect to the inhibitions againft the landed intereft of Scotland.

END OF THE FIRST VOLUME.